Practical Skills in Chemistry

PEARSON

We work with leading authors to develop the
strongest educational materials in chemistry,
bringing cutting-edge thinking and best
learning practice to a global market.

Under a range of well-known imprints, including
Prentice Hall, we craft high quality print and
electronic publications which help readers to understand
and apply their content, whether studying or at work.

To find out more about the complete range of our
publishing, please visit us on the World Wide Web at:
www.pearsoned.co.uk

Practical Skills in Chemistry

Second Edition

John R. Dean
Alan M. Jones
David Holmes
Rob Reed
Jonathan Weyers
Allan Jones

Prentice Hall
is an imprint of

Harlow, England • London • New York • Boston • San Francisco • Toronto • Sydney • Singapore • Hong Kong
Tokyo • Seoul • Taipei • New Delhi • Cape Town • Madrid • Mexico City • Amsterdam • Munich • Paris • Milan

Pearson Education Limited
Edinburgh Gate
Harlow
Essex CM20 2JE
England

and Associated Companies throughout the world

Visit us on the World Wide Web at:
www.pearsoned.co.uk

First published 2002
Second edition published 2011

© Pearson Education Limited 2011

ISBN: 978-0-273-73118-4

British Library Cataloguing-in-Publication Data
A catalogue record for this book is available from the British Library

Library of Congress Cataloging-in-Publication Data
Practical skills in chemistry / John Dean ... [et al.]. -- 2nd ed.
        p. cm.
Includes bibliographical references and index.
ISBN 978-0-273-73118-4 (pbk.)
I. Dean, John A. (John Aurie), 1921-2001.
QD33.2.P73 2011
542--dc22
                                        2010044158

10 9 8 7 6 5 4 3 2 1
15 14 13 12 11

Typeset in 10/12 pt Times Roman by 73

Printed and bound in Malaysia,CTP-PJB

Contents

Contents

List of boxes

List of boxes

Preface to the second edition

Practical skills form the cornerstone of chemistry. However, the diversity of skills required in the laboratory means that a student's experience may be limited. While some techniques do require specific skills, many of them are transferable generic skills that are required throughout the subject area.

Limited time constraints of the modern curriculum often preclude or minimise laboratory time. It is the aim of this book to provide a general guidance for use in and out of practical sessions and also to cover a range of techniques from the basic to the more advanced.

In creating the second edition of *Practical Skills in Chemistry*, we have maintained the approach of the previous edition, with the aim of providing support to students taking chemistry-based courses in a concise and user-friendly manner. Key points, definitions, illustrations, 'how to' boxes, checklists worked examples, tips and hints are included where appropriate. However, we have also used this opportunity of the new edition to restructure the layout, to add to the content and to emphasise some of the broader aspects of transferable skills. As a result, this edition contains a new section at the front of the book dealing with study and examination skills, with additional chapters on transferable skills, time management, working with others, note-taking and revising, as well as assessments and exams. A chapter has been added on CV preparation, since we feel that this provides a focus on the outcome of undergraduate study from the outset. In creating these new chapters, we have been mindful of the Quality Assurance Agency UK Subject Benchmarking statements for Chemistry, published in 2007, and have attempted to cover all of the generic skills, along with the practical aspects of the subject-specific topics in chemistry. Perhaps the most important skill required of a modern science degree student is the ability to evaluate information, and we have added a new chapter on this key aspect, within an expanded section dealing with information technology and library resources.

We have also taken the opportunity to revise the subject-specific content of the text in response to feedback from students and staff. Thus we have added new chapters on X-ray fluorescence and combinatorial chemistry. We have updated significantly and added further material to many chapters, especially in fast-moving subjects such as the use of the Internet/World Wide Web, chemometrics and computational chemistry. Every chapter is now supported by a section giving key sources for further study – these include conventional printed texts as well as Web-based material. Furthermore most chapters have study exercises to reinforce the learning process and advance expertise in problem solving. Some of the numerical examples and answers appear to be 'long winded' but we make no apology for this, since the purpose is to demonstrate the cognitive processes required for problem solving rather than the application of formulae without thought.

To students who buy this book, we hope you will find it useful in the laboratory during your practical classes and in your project work – this is not a book to be left on the bookshelf.

We would like to acknowledge the support of our families and the help provided by colleagues who have been involved in the preparation of both editions of this book: Gary Askwith, Dave Bannister, Jon Bookham, Susan Carlile, Jim Creighton, Sarah Cresswell, Martin Davies, Mike Deary, Les Dix, Marcus Durrant, Jackie Eager, Gordon Forrest, Derek Holmes, Ed Ludkin, Dave Osborne, Justin Perry, Jane Shaw, Tony Simpson, Dave Wealleans and Ian Winship.

Despite this help, the responsibility for any errors rests with us and we would be grateful if readers could alert us to any errors so that we can make amends as soon as possible.

JOHN R. DEAN (john.dean@northumbria.ac.uk)

ALAN M. JONES (alanjones559@btinternet.com)

DAVE HOLMES (david.holmes@northumbria.ac.uk)

ROB REED (r.reed@cqu.edu.au)

ALLAN M. JONES (a.m.jones@dundee.ac.uk)

JONATHON WEYERS (j.d.b.weyers@dundee.ac.uk)

Definitions of key terms and concepts are highlighted in the text margin.

Tips and Hints provide useful hints and practical advice, and are highlighted in the text margin.

Key Points highlight critical features of methodology.

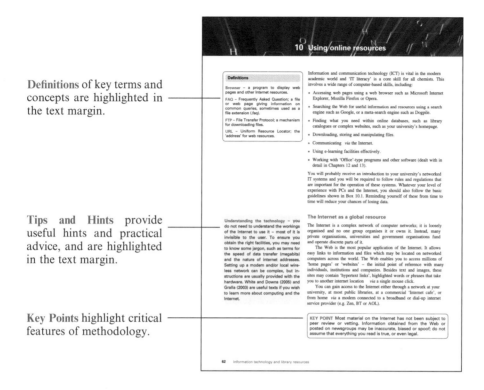

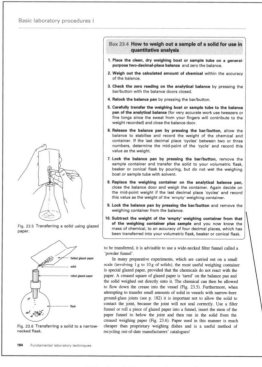

Examples are included in the margin to illustrate important points without interrupting the flow of the main text.

Worked Examples and 'How to' boxes set out the essential procedures in a step-by-step manner.

Figures are used to illustrate key points, techniques and equipment.

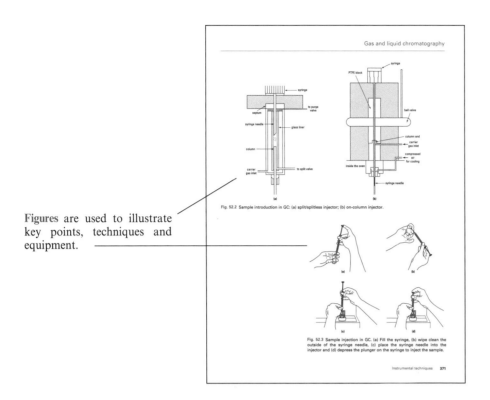

Gas and liquid chromatography

Fig. 52.2 Sample introduction in GC: (a) split/splitless injector; (b) on-column injector.

Fig. 52.3 Sample injection in GC. (a) Fill the syringe, (b) wipe clean the outside of the syringe needle, (c) place the syringe needle into the injector and (d) depress the plunger on the syringe to inject the sample.

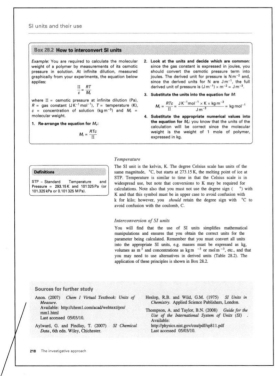

Sources for further study – every chapter is supported by a section giving printed and electronic sources for further study.

Study exercises are included in every chapter to reinforce learning with problems and practical exercises.

This book aims to provide guidance and support over the broad range of your undergraduate course, including laboratory classes, project work, lectures, tutorials, seminars and examinations, as outlined below.

Chapters 1–7 cover general skills

These include a number of transferable skills that you will develop during your course, for example: self-evaluation; time management; teamwork; preparing for exams; creating a CV.

Chapters 8–19 deal with IT, library resources and communication

These chapters will help you to get the most out of the information and resources available in your library and on the World Wide Web, as well as providing helpful guidance on the use of software packages for data analysis, preparing assignments, essays and laboratory reports, alongside support in relation to oral, visual and written forms of communication. The ability to evaluate information is an increasingly important skill in contemporary society and practical guidance is provided, as well as more specific detailed advice, such as Internet resources for chemistry.

Chapters 20–59 cover a wide range of specific practical skills required in chemistry

These techniques, relating to synthesis, separation and analysis, are based on the authors' experience of the questions students often ask in practical classes and the support that is needed to get the most out of particular exercises. The text includes tips, hints, definitions, key points, worked examples and 'how to' boxes which set out the procedures in a step-by-step manner, with appropriate comments on safe working practices. The material ranges from basic laboratory procedures, such as preparing solutions, through purification, separation and wet analysis, to advanced instrumental analytical methods and the more complex operations that you might use during a final year project, e.g. inert atmosphere reactions and hyphenated analytical techniques such as LC-MS.

Chapters 60–67 explain data analysis and presentation

This will be an important component of your course and you will find that these chapters guide you through the techniques and skills required, from the presentation of results in graphical or tabular formats through to the application of statistical tests: worked examples are used to reinforce the numerical aspects wherever possible. Finally, a glimpse of the future is provided in a section on computational chemistry.

Study exercises

We have added these as a new feature in the second edition, following comments from students and staff at UK universities, who felt that this would provide a useful opportunity to practise some of the skills covered in the book and a check on the understanding of the material. We hope that the exercises will be useful both to learners and to their tutors: some of the exercises are based on the material contained within the corresponding chapter, while others provide opportunities to further develop understanding in a particular topic area. Where numerical calculations are involved in both the text and study exercises we have deliberately used a formal step-wise procedure which develops the thought process for solving the problem: facility for 'short circuiting' the problem comes with experience!

Most of the problems assume that students are working on their own, using the information provided; however, tutors might wish to provide alternative starting material (e.g. a set of data from a practical class). We have assumed that students will have access to a library, a scientific calculator and, sometimes, to a networked PC with typical 'office' programs (especially word processor and spreadsheet plus the Internet.

Answers are given at the back of the book for all exercises. For numerical problems, the working out is also shown along with the final answer, while the non-numerical exercises also have 'answers' in the form of tips, general guidance or illustrative examples, etc. We recommend that students work together for some exercises – this is a valuable means of learning and, where there is no single correct answer to a problem, teamwork provides a mechanism for checking and discussing your answer.

We hope that you find this book a helpful guide throughout your course, and beyond.

Acknowledgements

We are grateful to the following for permission to reproduce copyright material.

Text abstracts from the following databases: *Analytical Abstracts, Catalysts & Catalysed Reactions, Methods in Organic Synthesis, Natural Product Updates, Chemical Hazards in Industry, Laboratory Hazards Bulletin, Mass Spectrometry Bulletin, Chromatography Abstracts* and *The Dictionary of Substances and their Effects* in Chapter 11, 'Internet Resources for Chemistry', reproduced by kind permission of The Royal Society of Chemistry.

Tables

Table 11.4 from Analytical Abstracts, http://www.rsc.org/aa, Royal Society of Chemistry 2010; Table 11.5 from Catalysts and Catalysed Reactions http://www.rsc.org/catalysts, Royal Society of Chemistry 2010; Table 11.6 from Methods in Organic Synthesis http://www.rsc.org/mos, Royal Society of Chemistry 2010; Table 11.7 from Natural Product Updates http://www.rsc.org/npu, Royal Society of Chemistry 2010; Table 11.8 from Chemical Hazards in Industry http://www.rsc.org/chi, Royal Society of Chemistry 2010; Table 11.9 from Laboratory Hazards Bulletin http://www.rsc.org/lhb, Royal Society of Chemistry 2010; Table 11.10 from Mass Spectrometry Bulletin http://www.rsc.org/msb, Royal Society of Chemistry 2010; Table 11.11 from Chromatography Abstracts http://www.rsc.org/chromabs, Royal Society of Chemistry 2010; Table 11.12 from The Dictionary of Substances and their Effects http://www.rsc.org/dose, Royal Society of Chemistry 2010.

While every effort has been made to trace the owners of copyright material, in a few cases this has proved impossible and we take this opportunity to offer our apologies to any copyright holders whose rights we may have unwittingly infringed.

A	absorbance
AAS	atomic absorption spectroscopy
AC	affinity chromatography
ACN	acetonitrile
ACS	American Chemical Society
AES	atomic emission spectroscopy
ANOVA	analysis of variance
AO	atomic orbital
APCI	atmospheric pressure chemical ionisation
A_r	relative atomic mass
ASE	accelerated solvent extraction
ATP	adenosine triphosphate
b.pt.	boiling point
BIDS	Bath Information and Data Services
CCD	central composite design
CCP	cubic close packed
CE	capillary electrophoresis
CEC	capillary electrochromatography
CGE	capillary gel electrophoresis
CI	chemical ionisation
COSHH	control of substances hazardous to health
CoV	coefficient of variation
CRM	certified reference material
CW	continuous wave
CZE	capillary zone electrophoresis
dp	decimal point
DAD	diode array detection
DCM	dichloromethane
DNA	deoxyribonucleic acid
dpm	disintegrations per minute
DSC	differential scanning colorimetry
DTA	differential thermal analysis
DVB	divinylbenzene
ECD	electron capture detector
EDTA	ethylenediaminetetraacetic acid
EI	electron impact (ionisation)
EIE	easily ionisable element
EMR	electromagnetic radiation
en	ethylenediamine
EOF	electroosmotic flow
ESI	electrospray ionisation
F	Faraday constant
FAAS	flame atomic absorption spectroscopy

FID	flame ionisation detector
FT	Fourier transform
FT–IR	Fourier transform–infrared spectroscopy
GC	gas chromatography
GC–MS	gas chromatography–mass spectrometry
GFC	gel filtration chromatography
GPC	gel permeation chromatography
h	Planck constant
HASAW	hazards at work
HCB	hexachloro-1,3-butadiene
HCL	hollow cathode lamp
HCP	hexagonal close packed
HEPES	N-(2-hydroxyethyl)-N'-piperazine ethane sulphonic acid
HIC	hydrophobic interaction chromatography
HPLC	high performance liquid chromatography
HS	headspace
HTML	hypertext markup language
ICP	inductively coupled plasma
ICP–MS	inductively coupled plasma–mass spectrometry
IEC	ion exchange chromatography
IEF	isoelectric focusing
IR	infrared (radiation)
ISE	ion selective electrode
IUPAC	International Union of Pure and Applied Chemistry
K_a	acid dissociation constant
kg	kilogram
K_{ow}	octanol–water partition coefficient
K_s	solubility product
K_w	ion product of water
LC–MS	liquid chromatography–mass spectrometry
LGC	Laboratory of the Government Chemist
LOD	limit of detection
LOQ	limit of quantitation
m.pt.	melting point
MAE	microwave assisted extraction
MDL	minimum detectable level
MEKC	micellar electrokinetic chromatography
MEL	maximum exposure limit
MO	molecular orbital
M_r	relative molecular mass
MS	mass spectrometry

NH	null hypothesis
NIST	National Institute of Standards and Technology
NMR	nuclear magnetic resonance
NP–HPLC	normal phase high performance liquid chromatography
ODS	octadecylsilane
OEL	occupational exposure standard
PAGE	polyacrylamide gel electrophoresis
PCA	principal component analysis
pdf	portable document format
PDMS	polydimethylsiloxane
PEEK	poly(etheretherketone)
PFA	perfluoroalkoxyvinylether
PFA	perfluoroalkoxy fluorocarbon
PFE	pressurised fluid extraction
pH	$\log_{10}$ proton concentration (activity)
PLOT	porous layer open tubular (column)
PMT	photomultiplier tube
ppb	parts per billion (10^9)
PPE	personal protection equipment
ppm	parts per million (10^6)
PTFE	polytetrafluoroethylene
QA	quality assurance
R	universal gas constant
RA	relative abundance
R_f	relative frontal mobility
RNA	ribonucleic acid
RP–HPLC	reversed phase high performance liquid chromatography
rpm	revolutions per minute

RSC	Royal Society of Chemistry
RSD	relative standard deviation
SAX	strong anion exchange
SCOT	support coated open tubular (column)
SCX	strong cation exchange
SDS	sodium dodecyl sulphate
SE	standard error (of the sample mean)
SEM	scanning electron microscopy
SFE	supercritical fluid extraction
SI	Système Internationale D'Unités
SPE	solid phase extraction
SPME	solid phase microextraction
STP	standard temperature and pressure
TCA	trichloroacetic acid
TCD	thermal conductivity detector
TG	thermogravimetry
TLC	thin layer chromatography
TMS	tetramethylsilane
TOF-MS	time-of-flight mass spectrometry
TRIS	tris(hydroxymethyl)aminomethane or 2-amino-2-hydroxymethyl-1,3-propanediol
UKAS	United Kingdom Accreditation Services
URL	uniform resource locator
USEPA	United States Environmental Protection Agency
UV	ultraviolet
WCOT	wall-coated open tubular (column)
WWW	World Wide Web
z	net charge on an ion

Study and examination skills

1 The importance of transferable skills

Skills terminology – different phrases may be used to describe transferable skills, depending on place or context. These include: 'personal transferable skills' (PTS), 'key skills', 'core skills' and 'competences'.

This chapter outlines the range of transferable skills and their significance to chemists. It also indicates where practical skills fit into this scheme. Having a good understanding of this topic will help you place your work at university in a wider context. You will also gain an insight into the qualities that employers expect you to have developed by the time you graduate. Awareness of these matters will be useful when carrying out personal development planning (PDP) as part of your studies.

The range of transferable skills

Table 1.1 provides a comprehensive listing of university-level transferable skills under three skill categories. There are many possible classifications – and a different one may be used in your institution or field of study. Note particularly that 'study skills', while important, and rightly emphasised at the start of many courses, constitute only a subset of the skills acquired by most university students.

Using course materials – study your course handbook and the schedules for each practical session to find out what skills you are expected to develop at each point in the curriculum. Usually the learning objectives/outcomes (p. 26) will describe the skills involved.

The phrase '*Practical Skills*' in the title of this book indicates that there is a special subset of transferable skills related to work in the laboratory. However, although this text deals primarily with skills and techniques required for laboratory practicals and associated studies, a broader range of material is included. This is because the skills concerned are important, not only in chemistry but also in the wider world. Examples include time management, evaluating information and communicating effectively.

> **KEY POINT** Chemistry is essentially a practical subject, and therefore involves highly developed laboratory skills. The importance that your lecturers place on practical skills will probably be evident from the large proportion of curriculum time you will spend on practical work in your course.

Example The skills involved in teamwork cannot be developed without a deeper understanding of the interrelationships involved in successful groups. The context will be different for every group and a flexible approach will always be required, according to the individuals involved and the nature of the task.

The word 'skill' implies much more than the robotic learning of, for example, a laboratory routine. Of course, some of the tasks you will be asked to carry out in practical classes *will* be repetitive. Certain techniques require manual dexterity and attention to detail if accuracy and precision are to be attained, and the necessary competence often requires practice to make perfect. However, a deeper understanding of the context of a technique is important if the skill is to be appreciated fully and then transferred to a new situation. That is why this text is not simply a 'recipe book' of methods and protocols and why it includes background information, tips and worked examples, as well as study exercises to test your understanding.

Transferability of skills

Transferable skills are those which allow someone with knowledge, understanding or ability gained in one situation to adapt or extend this for application in a different context. In some cases, the transfer of a skill is immediately obvious. Take, for example, the ability to use a spreadsheet to summarise chemical data and create a graph to illustrate

Table 1.1 Transferable skills identified as important in chemistry. The list has been compiled from the UK Quality Assurance Agency for Higher Education Subject Benchmark Statement for Bachelors Honours Degree Programmes in Chemistry (2007). Particularly relevant chapters are shown for the skills covered by this book.

Skill category	Examples of skills and competences	Relevant chapters in this textbook
Chemistry-related cognitive abilities and skills	Ability to demonstrate knowledge and understanding of essential facts, concepts, principles and theories.	22, 23, 24, 25, 26
	Ability to apply such knowledge and understanding to the solution of qualitative and quantitative problems of a familiar and unfamiliar nature.	31–59
	Ability to recognise and analyse novel problems and plan strategies for their solution.	
	Skills in the evaluation, interpretation and synthesis of chemical information and data.	8, 9, 10, 11, 27, 29, 30
	Ability to recognise and implement good measurement science and practice.	27, 29, 30
	Skills in presenting scientific material and arguments clearly and correctly, in writing and orally, to a range of audiences.	14, 15, 16, 17, 18, 19
	Computational and data-processing skills, relating to chemical information and data.	11, 61, 65, 66, 67
Chemistry-related practical skills	Skills in the safe handling of chemical materials, taking into account their physical and chemical properties, including any specific hazards associated with their use.	20, 21, 22
	Skills required for the conduct of standard laboratory procedures involved in synthetic and analytical work, in relation to both inorganic and organic systems.	22, 23, 24, 25, 26
	Skills in the monitoring, by observation and measurement, of chemical properties, events or changes, and the systematic and reliable recording and documentation thereof.	18, 27, 28, 29, 30
	Competence in the planning, design and execution of practical investigations, from the problem-recognition stage through to the evaluation and appraisal to results and findings; this to include the ability to select appropriate techniques and procedures.	27, 29, 30, 46
	Skills in the operation of standard chemical instrumentation such as that used for structural investigations and separation.	31–59
	Ability to interpret data derived from laboratory observations and measurements in terms of their significance and the theory underlying them.	31–59, 63, 64, 66, 67
	Ability to conduct risk assessments concerning the use of chemical substances and laboratory procedures.	20, 21
Transferable skills	Communication skills, covering both written and oral communication.	14, 15, 16, 17, 18, 19
	Problem-solving skills, relating to qualitative and quantitative information, extending to situations where evaluations have to be made on the basis of limited information.	31–59, 67
	Numeracy and computational skills, including such aspects as error analysis, order-of-magnitude estimations, correct use of units and modes of data presentation.	27, 28, 60, 61, 62, 63, 64
	Information-retrieval skills, in relation to primary and secondary information sources, including information retrieval through online computer searches.	8, 9, 10, 11
	Information-technology skills such as word-processing and spreadsheet use, data-logging and storage, Internet communication, etc.	12, 13, 60, 61
	Interpersonal skills, relating to the ability to interact with other people and to engage in teamworking.	3
	Time-management and organisational skills, as evidenced by the ability to plan and implement efficient and effective modes of working.	2, 3, 4, 5, 6
	Study skills needed for continuing professional development.	1

results. Once the key concepts and commands are learned (Chapter 12), they can be applied to many instances outside chemistry where this type of output is used. This is not only true for similar data sets, but also in unrelated situations, such as making up a financial balance sheet and creating a pie chart to show sources of expenditure. Similarly, knowing the requirements for good graph drawing and tabulation (Chapters 60 and 61), perhaps practised by hand in earlier work, might help you use spreadsheet commands to make the output suit your needs.

Other cases may be less clear but equally valid. For example, towards the end of your undergraduate studies you may be involved in designing experiments as part of your project work. This task will draw on several skills gained at earlier stages in your course, such as preparing solutions (Chapter 22), deciding about numbers of replicates and experimental layout (Chapters 27 and 29) and perhaps carrying out some particular method of synthesis, observation, measurement or analysis (Chapters 31–59). How and when might you transfer this complex set of skills? In the workplace, it is unlikely that you would be asked to repeat the same process, but in critically evaluating a problem or in planning a complex project for a new employer, you will need to use many of the time management, organisational and analytical skills developed when designing and carrying out experiments. The same applies to information retrieval and evaluation and writing essays and dissertations, when transferred to the task of analysing or writing a business report.

Personal development planning

Many universities have schemes for personal development planning (PDP), which may go under slightly different names such as progress file or professional development plan. You will usually be expected to create a portfolio of evidence on your progress, then reflect on this, and subsequently set yourself plans for the future, including targets and action points. Analysis of your transferable skills profile will probably form part of your PDP. Other aspects commonly included are:

- your aspirations, goals, interests and motivations;
- your learning style or preference (see p. 22);
- your assessment transcript or academic profile information (e.g. record of grades in your modules);
- your developing CV (see p. 40).

Taking part in PDP can help focus your thoughts about your university studies and future career. This is important, as chemistry degrees do not lead only to a single, specific occupation. The PDP process will introduce you to some new terms and will help you to describe your personality and abilities. This will be useful when constructing your CV and when applying for jobs.

What your future employer will be looking for

At the end of your course, which may seem some time away, you will aim to get a job and start on your chosen career path. You will need to sell yourself to your future employer, firstly in your application form and

---

Opportunities to develop and practise skills in your private or social life – you could, for example, practise spreadsheet skills by organising personal or club finances using Microsoft Excel, or team-work skills within any university clubs or societies you may join (see Chapter 7).

Types of PDP portfolio and their benefits – some PDP schemes are centred on academic and learning skills, while others are more focused on career planning. Some are carried out independently and others in tandem with a personal tutor or advisory system. Some PDP schemes involve creating an online portfolio, while others are primarily paper-based. Each method has specific goals and advantages, but whichever way your scheme operates, maximum benefit will be gained from being fully involved with the process.

Definition

Employability – 'the possession by an individual of the qualities and competences required to meet the changing needs of employers, and thereby help realise his or her aspirations and potential in work.' (The Confederation of British Industry (CBI) definition of employability)

curriculum vitae (Chapter 7), and perhaps later at interview. Companies rarely employ chemistry graduates simply because they know how to carry out a particular lab routine or because they can remember specific facts about their chosen degree subject. Instead, employers tend to look for a range of qualities and transferable skills that together define an attribute known as 'graduateness'. This encompasses, for example, the ability to work in a team, to speak effectively and write clearly about your work, to understand complex data and to manage a project to completion. All of these skills can be developed at different stages during your university studies.

> **KEY POINT** Factual knowledge is important in degrees with a strong vocational element, but understanding how to find and evaluate information is usually rated more highly by employers than the ability to memorise facts.

Most likely, your future employer(s) will seek someone with a organised yet flexible mind, capable of demonstrating a logical approach to problems – someone who has a range of skills and who can transfer these skills to new situations. Many competing applicants will probably have similar qualifications. If you want the job, you will have to show that your additional skills place you above the other candidates.

Identifying your skills

The Higher Education Academy, Physical Sciences Centre has identified the range of skills employers expect you to develop. Your chemistry degree course, however, will provide you with the sorts of skills a graduate can expect to have learned and developed (Table 1.2).

In addition, employers have also identified the attributes they seek in recruiting chemistry graduates and these are shown in Table 1.3.

Table 1.2 Chemistry transferable skills: chemistry course view.

Employability skills	Evidence
Problem solving	Conduct experiments and apply knowledge and understanding to solve problems of an unfamiliar and familiar nature
The ability to work with others in a team	Group laboratory projects, voluntary work
Communication skills, both oral and written	Listening, conveying complex information, presenting scientific material and arguments clearly and correctly, in writing, and orally during tutorials and seminars
Planning and organising skills	Planning, design and execution of practical investigations, from problem recognition to evaluation stages, organising workload
Decision making skills	Practical assignments, ability to select appropriate techniques and procedures
Initiative	Practical investigations, recognition of novel problems
Independent learning skills	Time-management and organisational skills demonstrated through independent research

Table 1.3 Chemistry transferable skills: employer view.

Employer skills	Evidence
Cognitive skills/Brainpower	The ability to identify and solve problems; work with information and handle a mass of diverse data, assess risk and draw conclusions
Generic competencies	High-level and transferable key skills such as the ability to work with others in a team, communicate, persuade and have interpersonal sensitivity
Personal capabilities	The ability and desire to learn for oneself and improve one's self awareness and performance. To be a self starter (creativity, decisiveness, initiative) and to finish the job (flexibility, adaptability, tolerance to stress)
Technical ability	For example, having the knowledge and experience of working with relevant modern laboratory equipment
Business and/or organisation awareness	An appreciation of how businesses operate through having had (preferably relevant) work experience
Practical elements – vocational courses	Critical evaluation of the outcomes of professional practice; reflect and review own practice; participate in and review quality control processes and risk management

Sources for further study

Drew, S. and Bingham, R. (2004) *The Student Skills Guide,* 2nd edn. Gower Publishing Ltd, Aldershot.

McMillan, K. and Weyers, J.D.B. (2006) *The Smarter Student: Skills and Strategies for Success at University*. Pearson Education, Harlow.

Race, P. (1999) *How to Get a Good Degree: Making the Most of Your Time at University*. Open University Press, Buckingham.

Study exercises

1.1 Evaluate your skills. Examine the list of skill topics shown in Table 1.1 (p. 4). Now create a new table with two columns, like the one on page 8. The first half of this table should indicate *five* skills you feel confident about and show where you demonstrated this skill (for example, 'working in a team' and 'in a first year group project in chemistry'). The second half of the table should show *five* skills you do not feel confident about, or you recognise need development (e.g. 'communicating in verbal form'). List these and then list ways in which you think the course material for your current modules will provide opportunities to develop these skills, or what activities you might take to improve them (e.g. 'forming a study group with colleagues').

1.2 Employability skills. Using the information in Table 1.2, identify examples of how you have developed your employability skills and map them against the attributes and qualities desired by employers (Table 1.3).

1.3 Find skills resources. For at least one of the skills in the second half of Table 1.1, check your university's library database to see if there are any texts on that subject. Alternatively, carry out a search for relevant websites (there are many); decide which are useful and 'bookmark' them for future use (Chapter 10).

1.4 Analyse your goals and aspirations. Spend a little time thinking what you hope to gain from university. See if your friends have the same aspirations. Think about and/or discuss how these goals can be achieved, while keeping the necessary balance between university work, paid employment and your social life.

Skills I feel confident about	Where demonstrated
1.	
2.	
3.	
4.	
5.	
Skills that I could develop	**Opportunities for development**
6.	
7.	
8.	
9.	
10.	

2 Managing your time

Definition

Time management – a system for controlling and using time as efficiently and as effectively as possible.

Advantages of time management – these include:

- a feeling of much greater control over your activities;
- avoidance of stress;
- improved productivity – achieve more in a shorter period;
- improved performance – work to higher standards because you are in charge;
- increase in time available for non-work matters – work hard, but play hard too.

Example The objective 'to spend an extra hour each week on directed study in physical chemistry next term' fulfils the SMART criteria, in contrast to a general intention 'to study more'.

One of the most important activities that you can do is to organise your personal and working time effectively. There is a lot to do at university and a common complaint is that there isn't enough time to accomplish everything. In fact, research shows that most people use up a lot of their time without realising it through ineffective study or activities such as extended coffee breaks. Developing your time management skills will help you achieve more in work, rest and play, but it is important to remember that putting time management techniques into practice is an individual matter, requiring a level of self-discipline not unlike that required for dieting. A new system won't always work perfectly straight away, but through time you can develop a system that is effective for you. An inability to organise your time effectively, of course, results in feelings of failure, frustration, guilt and being out of control in your life.

Setting your goals

The first step is to identify clearly what you want to achieve, both in work and in your personal life. We all have a general idea of what we are aiming for, but to be effective, your goals must be clearly identified and priorities allocated. Clear, concise objectives can provide you with a framework in which to make these choices. Try using the 'SMART' approach, in which objectives should be:

- **S**pecific – clear and unambiguous, including what, when, where, how and why.
- **M**easurable – having quantified targets and benefits to provide an understanding of progress.
- **A**chievable – being attainable within your resources.
- **R**ealistic – being within your abilities and expectations.
- **T**imed – stating the time period for completion.

Having identified your goals, you can now move on to answer four very important questions:

1. Where does your time go?
2. Where should your time go?
3. What are your time-wasting activities?
4. What strategies can help you?

Analysing your current activities

The key to successful development of time management is a realistic knowledge of how you currently spend your time. Start by keeping a detailed time log for a typical week (Fig. 2.1), but you will need to be truthful in this process. Once you have completed the log, consider the following questions:

- How many hours do I work in total and how many hours do I use for relaxation?
- What range of activities do I do?

Time slots	Activity								Notes
7.00–7.15									
7.15–7.30									
7.30–7.45									
7.45–8.00									
8.00–8.15									
8.15–8.30									
8.30–8.45									
8.45–9.00									
9.00–9.15									

Fig. 2.1 Example of how to lay out a time log. Write activities along the top of the page, and divide the day into 15-minute segments as shown. Think beforehand how you will categorise the different things you do, from the mundane (laundry, having a shower, drinking coffee, etc.) to the well-timetabled (tutorial meeting, sports club meeting) and add supplementary notes if required. At the end of each day, place a dot in the relevant column for each activity and sum the dots to give a total at the bottom of the page. You will need to keep a diary like this for at least a week before you see patterns emerging.

- How long do I spend on each activity?
- What do I spend most of my time doing?
- What do I spend the least amount of my time doing?
- Are my allocations of time in proportion to the importance of my activities?
- How much of my time is ineffectively used, e.g. for uncontrolled socialising or interruptions?

If you wish, you could use a spreadsheet (Chapter 12) to produce graphical summaries of time allocations in different categories as an aid to analysis and management. Divide your time into:

- Committed time – timetabled activities involving your main objectives/goals.
- Maintenance time – time spent supporting your general life activities (shopping, cleaning, laundry, etc.).
- Discretionary time – time for you to use as you wish, e.g. recreation, sport, hobbies, socialising.

Avoiding time-wasting activities

Look carefully at those tasks that could be identified as time-wasting activities. They include gossiping, over-long breaks, uninvited interruptions and even ineffective study periods. Try to reduce these to a minimum, but do not count on eliminating them entirely. Remember also that some relaxation *should* be programmed into your daily schedule.

Organising your tasks

Having analysed your time usage, you can now use this information, together with your objectives and prioritised goals, to organise your activities, both on a short-term and a long-term basis. Consider using a diary-based system (such as those produced by Filofax, TMI and Day-Timer) that will help you to plan ahead and analyse your progress.

Quality in time management – avoid spending a lot of time doing unproductive studying, e.g. reading a textbook without specific objectives for that reading. Make sure you test your recall of the material, if you are working towards an examination (p. 31).

Being assertive – if friends and colleagues continually interrupt you, find a way of controlling them, before they control you. Indicate clearly on your door that you do not wish to be disturbed and explain why. Otherwise, try to work away from disturbance.

WEEKLY DIARY				Week beginning:			
	Sunday	Monday	Tuesday	Wednesday	Thursday	Friday	Saturday
DATE							

	Sunday	Monday	Tuesday	Wednesday	Thursday	Friday	Saturday
7–8 am		Breakfast	Breakfast	Breakfast	Breakfast	Breakfast	
8–9		Preparation	Preparation	Preparation	Preparation	Preparation	Breakfast
9–10	Breakfast	PE112(L)	PE112(L)	PE112(L)	PE112(L)	BIOL(P)	Travel
10–11	FREE	CHEM(L)	CHEM(L)	CHEM(L)	CHEM(L)	BIOL(P)	WORK
11–12	STUDY	STUDY	STUDY	STUDY	STUDY	BIOL(P)	WORK
12–1 pm	STUDY	BIOL(L)	BIOL(L)	BIOL(L)	BIOL(L)	TUTORIAL	WORK
1–2	Lunch	Lunch	Lunch	Lunch	Lunch	Lunch	Lunch
2–3	(VOLLEY-	CHEM(P)	STUDY	SPORT	PE112(P)	STUDY	WORK
3–4	BALL	CHEM(P)	STUDY	(VOLLEY-	PE112(P)	STUDY	WORK
4–5	MATCH)	CHEM(P)	STUDY	BALL	PE112(P)	SHOPPING	WORK
5–6	FREE	STUDY	STUDY	CLUB)	STUDY	TEA ROTA	WORK
6–7	Tea	Tea	Tea	Tea	Tea	Tea	Tea
7–8	FREE*	STUDY	STUDY	FREE*	STUDY	FREE*	FREE
8–9	FREE*	STUDY	STUDY	FREE*	STUDY	FREE*	FREE
9–10	FREE*	FREE*	STUDY	FREE*	STUDY	FREE*	FREE

	Sunday	Monday	Tuesday	Wednesday	Thursday	Friday	Saturday
Study (h)	2	10	11	4	11	6	0
Other (h)	13	5	4	11	4	9	15

Total study time = 44 h

Fig. 2.2 A weekly diary with example of entries for a first year science student with a Saturday job and active membership of a volleyball club. Note that 'free time' changes to 'study time', e.g. for periods when assessed work is to be produced or during revision for exams. Study time (including attendance at lectures, practicals and tutorials) thus represents between 42% and 50% of the total time.

Divide your tasks into several categories, such as:

- **Urgent** – must be done as a top priority and at short notice (e.g. doctor's appointment).

- **Routine** – predictable and regular and therefore easily scheduled (e.g. attending lectures or playing sport).

- **One-off activities** – usually with rather shorter deadlines and which may be of high priority (e.g. a tutorial assignment or seeking advice on a specific issue).

- **Long-term tasks** – sometimes referred to as 'elephant tasks' that are too large to 'eat' in one go (e.g. learning a language). These are best managed by scheduling frequent small 'bites' to achieve the task over a longer timescale.

You should make a weekly plan (Fig. 2.2) for the routine activities, with gaps for less predictable tasks. This should be supplemented by individual daily checklists, preferably written at the end of the previous working day. Such plans and checklists should be flexible, forming the basis for most of your activities except when exceptional circumstances intervene. The planning must be kept brief, however, and should be scheduled into your activities. Box 2.1 provides tips for effective time management during your studies.

Use checklists as often as possible – post your lists in places where they are easily and frequently visible, such as in front of your desk. Ticking things off as they are completed gives you a feeling of accomplishment and progress, increasing motivation.

Matching your work to your body's rhythm – everyone has times of day when they feel more alert and able to work. Decide when these times are for you and programme your work accordingly. Plan relaxation events for periods when you tend to be less alert.

KEY POINT Review each day's plan at the end of the previous day, making such modifications as are required by circumstances, e.g. adding an uncompleted task from the previous day or a new and urgent task.

Box 2.1 Tips for effective planning and working

- Set guidelines and review expectations regularly.
- Don't procrastinate: don't keep putting off doing things you know are important – they will not go away but they will increase to crisis point.
- Don't be a perfectionist – perfection is paralysing.
- Learn from past experience – review your management system regularly.
- Don't set yourself unrealistic goals and objectives – this will lead to procrastination and feelings of failure.
- Avoid recurring crises – they are telling you that something is not working properly and needs to be changed.
- Learn to concentrate effectively and don't let yourself be distracted by casual interruptions.
- Learn to say 'no' firmly but graciously when appropriate.
- Know your own body rhythms: e.g. are you a morning person or an evening person?
- Learn to recognise the benefits of rest and relaxation at appropriate times.
- Take short but complete breaks from your tasks – come back feeling refreshed in mind and body.
- Work in suitable study areas and keep your own workspace organised.
- Avoid clutter (physical and mental).
- Learn to access and use information effectively (Chapter 9).
- Learn to read and write accurately and quickly (Chapters 4 and 16).

Sources for further study

Anon. *Day-Timer*. Available: http://www.daytimer.co.uk Last accessed: 12/07/09.
[Website for products of Day-Timers Europe Ltd., Chene Court, Poundwell Street, Modbury, Devon PL21 0QJ]

Anon. *Filofax*. Available: http://www.filofax.co.uk Last accessed: 12/07/09.
[Website for products of Filofax UK, Unit 3, Victoria Gardens, Burgess Hill, West Sussex RH15 9NB]

Anon. *TMI Website*. Available: http://www.tmi.co.uk Last accessed: 12/07/09.
[Website for products of TMI (Time Manager International A/S), 50 High Street, Henley-in-Arden, Solihull, West Midlands B95 5AN]

Mayer, J.L. (1999) *Time Management for Dummies*, 2nd edn. IDG Books Worldwide, Inc., Foster City.

Study exercises

2.1 **Evaluate your time usage.** Compile a spreadsheet to keep a record of your daily activities in 15-minute segments for a week. Analyse this graphically and identify areas for improvement.

2.2 **List your short-, medium- and long-term tasks and allocate priorities.** Produce several lists, one for each of the three timescales, and prioritise each item. Use this list to plan your time management, by scheduling high priority tasks and leave low priority activities to 'fill in' the spare time that you may identify. This task should be done on a regular (monthly) basis to allow for changing situations.

2.3 **Plan an 'elephant' task.** Spend some time planning how to carry out a large or difficult task (learning a language or learning to use a complex computer program) by breaking it down into achievable segments ('bites').

3 Working with others

Definitions

Team – a team is not a bunch of people with job titles, but a congregation of individuals, each of whom has a role which is understood by other members. Members of a team seek out certain roles and they perform most effectively in the ones that are most natural to them.

Team role – a tendency to behave, contribute and interrelate with others in a particular way.

(both after Belbin, 1993)

Peer assessment – this term applies to marking schemes in which all or a proportion of the marks for a teamwork exercise are allocated by the team members themselves. Read the instructions carefully before embarking on the exercise, so you know which aspects of your work your fellow team members will be assessing. When deciding what marks to allocate yourself, try to be as fair as possible with your marking.

Gaining confidence through experience – the more you take part in teamwork, the more you know how teams operate and how to make teamwork effective for you.

It is highly likely that you will be expected to work with fellow students during practicals and study exercises. This might take the form of sharing tasks or casual collaboration through discussion, or it might be formally directed teamwork such as problem-based learning (Box 6.1) or preparing a poster (Chapter 14). Interacting with others can be extremely rewarding and realistically represents the professional world, where teamworking is common. The advantages of working with others include:

- Teamworking is usually synergistic in effect – it often results in better ideas, produced by the interchange of views, and better output, due to the complementary skills of team members.

- Working in teams can provide support for individuals within the team.

- Levels of personal commitment can be enhanced through concern about letting the team down.

- Responsibilities for tasks can be shared.

However, you can also feel both threatened and exposed if teamwork is not managed properly. Some of the main reasons for negative feelings towards working in groups include:

- Reservations about working with strangers – not knowing whether you will be able to form a friendly and productive relationship.

- Worries over rejection – a perception of being unpopular or being chosen last by the group.

- Concerns over levels of personal commitment – these can be enhanced through a desire to perform well, so the team as a whole achieves its target.

- Fear of being held back by others – especially for those who have been successful in individual work already.

- Lack of previous experience – worries about the kinds of personal interactions likely to occur and the team role likely to suit you best.

- Concerns about the outcomes of peer assessment – in particular, whether others will give you a fair mark for your efforts.

Teamwork skills

Some of the key skills you will need to develop to maximise the success of your teamworking activities include:

- Interpersonal skills. How do you react to new people? Are you able to both listen and communicate easily with them? How do you deal with conflicts and disagreements?

- Delegation/sharing of tasks. The primary advantage of teamwork is the sharing of effort and responsibility. Are you willing/able to do this? It involves trusting your team members. How will you deal with those group members who don't contribute fully?

- Effective listening. Successful listening is a skill that usually needs developing, e.g. during the exchange of ideas within a group.

- Speaking clearly and concisely. Effective communication is a vital part of teamwork, both between team members and when presenting team outcomes to others. Try to develop your communication skills through learning and practice (see Chapter 15).

- Providing constructive criticism. It is all too easy to be negative but only constructive criticism will have a positive effect on interactions with others.

Collaboration for learning

Much collaboration is informal and consists of pairs or groups of individuals getting together to exchange materials and ideas while studying. It may consist of a 'brainstorming' session for a topic or piece of work, or sharing efforts to research a topic. This has much to commend it and is generally encouraged. However, it is vital that this collaborative learning is distinguished from the collaborative writing of assessed documents: the latter is not usually acceptable and, in its most extreme form, is plagiarism, usually with a heavy potential punishment in university assessment systems. Make sure you know what plagiarism is, what unacceptable collaboration is, and how they are treated within your institution.

Studying with others – teaming up with someone else on your course for revision (a 'study buddy') is a potentially valuable activity and may especially suit some types of learners (p. 22). It can help keep your morale high when things get tough. You might consider:

- sharing notes, textbooks and other information;
- going through past papers together, dissecting the questions and planning answers;
- talking to each other about a topic (good for aural learners, p. 23);
- giving tutorials to each other about parts of the course that have not been fully grasped.

> **KEY POINT** Collaboration is inappropriate during the final phase of an assessed piece of work unless you have been directed to produce a group report. Collaboration is encouraged during research and learning activities but the final write-up must normally be your own work. The extreme of producing copycat write-ups is regarded as plagiarism (p. 54) and will be punished accordingly.

Web-based resources and support for brainstorming – websites such as http://www.brainstorming.co.uk give further information and practical advice for teamworking.

The dynamics of teamworking

It is important that team activities are properly structured so that each member knows what is expected of them. Allocation of responsibilities usually requires the clear identification of a leader. Several studies of groups have identified different team roles that derive from differences in personality. You should be aware of such categorisations, both in terms of your own predispositions and those of your fellow team members, as it will help the group to interact more productively. Belbin (1993) identified eight such roles, recently extended to nine, as shown in Table 3.1. Several of the categories shown in Table 3.1 are suitable for a leader, including 'co-ordinator' and 'shaper'.

In formal team situations, your course organiser may deal with these issues; even if they do not, it is important that you are aware of these roles and their potential impact on the success or failure of teamwork. You should try to identify your own 'natural' role: if asked to form a team, bear these different roles in mind during your selection of colleagues and your interactions with them. The ideal team should contain members capable of adopting most of these roles. However, you should also note the following points:

- People will probably best fit one of these roles naturally as a function of their personality and skills.

- Group members may be suited to more than one role.

Table 3.1 A summary of the team roles described by Belbin (1993). A good team requires members who are able to undertake appropriate roles at different times. Each role provides important strengths to a team, and its compensatory weaknesses should be accepted within the group framework

Team role	Personality characteristics	Typical function in a team	Strengths	Allowable weaknesses
Co-ordinator	Self-confident, calm and controlled	Leading: causing others to work towards shared goals	Good at spotting others' talents and delegating activities	Often less creative or intellectual than others in the group
Shaper	Strong need for achievement; outgoing; dynamic; highly strung	Leading: generating action within team; imposing shape and pattern to work	Providing drive and realism to group activities	Can be headstrong, emotional and less patient than others
Innovator	Individualistic, serious-minded; often unorthodox	Generating action; imposing shape and pattern to work activities	Creative, innovative and knowledgeable	Tendency to work in isolation; ideas may not always be practical
Monitor–evaluator	Sober, unemotional and prudent	Analysing problems and evaluating ideas	Shrewd judgement	May work slowly; not usually a good motivator
Implementer	Well-organised and self-disciplined, with practical common sense	Doing what needs to be done	Organising abilities and common sense	Lack of flexibility and tendency to resist new ideas
Teamworker	Sociable, mild and sensitive	Being supportive, perceptive and diplomatic; keeping the team going	Good listener; reliable and flexible; promotes team spirit	Not comfortable when leading; may be indecisive
Resource investigator	Extrovert, enthusiastic, curious and communicative	Exploiting opportunities; finding resources; external relations	Quick thinking; good at developing others' ideas	May lose interest rapidly
Completer–finisher	Introvert and anxious; painstaking, orderly and conscientious	Ensuring completion of activity to high standard	Good focus on fulfilling objectives and goals	Obsessive about details; may wish to do all the work to control quality
Specialist	Professional, self-motivated and dedicated	Providing essential skills	Commitment and technical knowledge	Contribute on a narrow aspect of project; tend to be single-minded

> **Recording group discussions** – make sure you structure meetings (including writing agendas) and note their outcomes (taking minutes and noting action points).

- In some circumstances, team members may be required to adapt and take a different role from the one that they feel suits them.

- No one role is 'better' than any other. For good teamwork, the group should have a balance of personality types present.

- People may have to adopt multiple roles, especially if the team size is small.

> **KEY POINT** In formal teamwork situations, be clear as to how individual contributions are to be identified and recognised. This might require discussion with the course organiser. Make sure that recognition, including assessment, is truly reflective of effort. Failure to ensure that this is the case can lead to disputes and feelings of unfairness.

Your lab partner(s)

Many laboratory sessions in chemistry involve working in pairs or small groups. In some cases, you may work with the same partner(s) for a series of practicals or for a complete module. The relationship you develop as a team is important to your progress, and can enhance your understanding of the material and the grades you obtain. Tips for building a constructive partnership include:

- Introduce yourselves at the first session and take a continuing interest in each other's interests and progress at university.

- At appropriate points, discuss the practical (both theory and tasks) and your understanding of what is expected of you.

- Work jointly to complete the practical effectively, avoiding the situation where either partner dominates the activities and gains most from the practical experience.

- Share tasks according to your strengths, but do this in such a way that one partner can learn new skills and knowledge from the other.

- Make sure you ask questions of each other and communicate any doubts about what you have to do.

- Discuss other aspects of your course, e.g. by comparing notes from lectures or ideas about in-course assessments.

- Consider meeting up outside the practical sessions to study, revise and discuss exams.

Text reference

Belbin, R.M. (1993) *Team Roles at Work*. Butterworth-Heinemann, Oxford.

Source for further study

Belbin, R.M. *The Belbin Website*. Available: http://www.belbin.com/
Last accessed: 12/07/09.

Study exercises

3.1 Evaluate your 'natural' team role(s). Using Table 3.1 as a source, decide which team role best fits your personality.

3.2 Keep a journal during a group activity. Record your feelings and observations about experiences of working with other students. After the event, review the journal, then draw up a strategy for developing aspects where you feel you might have done better.

3.3 Reflect upon your teamwork abilities. Draw up a list of your reactions to previous efforts at collaboration or teamwork and analyse your strengths and weaknesses. How could these interactions have been improved or supported more effectively?

Choose note-taking methods appropriately – the method you choose to take notes might depend on the subject; the lecturer and their style of delivery; and your own preference.

Compare lecture notes with a colleague – looking at different sets of notes for the same lecture may reveal interesting differences in approach, depth and detail.

Adjusting to the styles of your lecturers – recognise that different approaches to lecture delivery demand different approaches to note-taking. For example, if a lecturer seems to tell lots of anecdotes or spend much of the time on examples during a lecture, do not switch off – you still need to be listening carefully to recognise the key take-home messages. Similarly, if a lecture includes a section consisting mainly of images, you should still try to take notes – chemical structures, apparatus set-up, MO theory and Lewis diagrams. These will help prompt your memory when revising. Do not be deterred by lecturers' idiosyncrasies; in every case you still need to focus and take useful notes.

Note-taking is an essential skill that you will require in many different situations, such as:

- listening to lectures and seminars;
- attending meetings and tutorials;
- reading texts and research papers;
- finding information on the World Wide Web.

> **KEY POINT** Good performance in assessments and exams is built on effective learning and revision (Chapters 5 and 6). However, both ultimately depend on the quality of your notes.

Taking notes from lectures

Taking legible and meaningful lecture notes is essential if you are to make sense of them later, but many students find it difficult when starting their university studies. Begin by noting the date, course, topic and lecturer on the first page of each day's notes. Number every page in case they get mixed up later. The most popular way of taking notes is to write in a linear sequence down the page, emphasising the underlying structure via headings, as in Fig. 16.2. However, the 'pattern' and 'Mind Map' methods (Figs 4.1 and 4.2) have their advocates: experiment, to see which method you prefer.

Whatever technique you use, don't try to take down all of the lecturer's words, except when an important definition or example is being given, or when the lecturer has made it clear that he/she is dictating. Listen first, then write. Your goal should be to take down the structure and reasoning behind the lecturer's approach in as few words and phrases as possible. At this stage, follow the lecturer's sequence of delivery. Use headings and leave plenty of space, but don't worry too much about being tidy – it is more important that you get down the appropriate information in a readable form. Use abbreviations to save

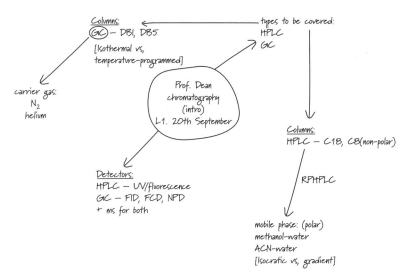

Fig. 4.1 An example of 'pattern' notes, an alternative to the more commonly used 'linear' format. Note the similarity to the 'spider diagram' method of brainstorming ideas (Fig. 16.2).

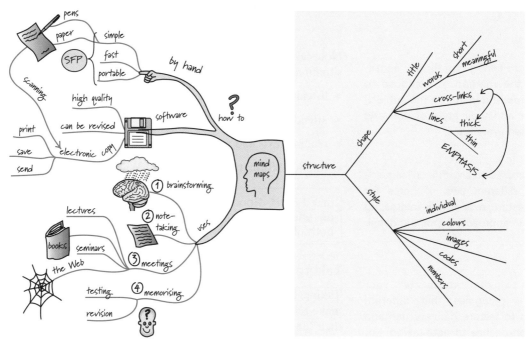

Fig. 4.2 Example of the 'Mind Map' approach to note-taking and 'brainstorming'. Start at the centre with the overall topic title, adding branches and sub-branches for themes and subsidiary topics. 'Basic' maps consist of a branched hierarchy overwritten with key words (e.g. shaded portion). Connections should be indicated with arrows; numbering and abbreviations are encouraged. To aid recall and creativity, Buzan (2006) recommends use of colour, different fonts, 3-dimensional doodles and other forms of emphasis (e.g. non-shaded portion).

Example Commonly used abbreviations include:

$\exists$	there are, there exist(s)
$\therefore$	therefore
$\because$	because
$\propto$	is proportional to
$\rightarrow$	leads to, into
$\leftarrow$	comes from, from
$\rightarrowtail$	involves several processes in a sequence
$1°, 2°$	primary, secondary (etc.)
$\approx, \cong$	approximately, roughly equal to
$=, \neq$	equals, not equal to
$\equiv, \not\equiv$	equivalent, not equivalent to
$<, >$	smaller than, bigger than
$\gg$	much bigger than
$[X]$	concentration of X
$\sum$	sum
Δ	change
f	function
$\#$	number
∞	infinity, infinite

You should also make up your own abbreviations relevant to the context, e.g. if a lecturer is talking about gas chromatography, you could write 'GC' instead, etc.

time. Recognise that you may need to alter your note-taking technique to suit different lecturers' styles.

Make sure you note down references to texts and take special care to ensure accuracy of definitions and numerical examples. If the lecturer repeats or otherwise emphasises a point, highlight (e.g. by underlining) or make a margin note of this – it could come in useful when revising. If there is something you don't understand, ask at the end of the lecture, or make an appointment to discuss the matter if there isn't time to deal with it then. Tutorials may provide an additional forum for discussing course topics.

Lectures delivered by PowerPoint or similar presentation programs

Some students make the mistake of thinking that lectures delivered as computer-based presentations with an accompanying handout or Web-resource require little or no effort by way of note-taking. While it is true that you may be freed from the need to copy out large diagrams and the basic text may provide structure, you will still need to adapt and add to the lecturer's points. Much of the important detail and crucial emphasis will still be delivered verbally. Furthermore, if you simply listen passively to the lecture, or worse, try to work from the handout alone, it will be far more difficult to understand and remember the content.

If you are not supplied with handouts, you may be given access to the electronic file, so that you can print out the presentation beforehand, perhaps in the '3 slides per page' format that allows space for notes alongside each slide (Fig. 4.3). Scan through this before the lecture if you can; then, during the presentation, focus on listening to what the lecturer

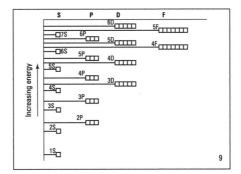

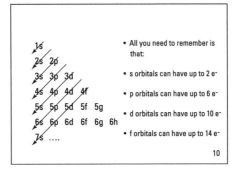

Fig. 4.3 An example of a printout from PowerPoint in 'Handouts (3 slides per page)' format.

has to say. Note down any extra details, points of emphasis and examples. After lectures, you could also add notes from supplementary reading. The text in presentations can be converted to word processor format if you have access to the electronic file. In PowerPoint, this can be achieved from the *Outline View* option on the *View* menu. You can copy and paste text between programs in the normal fashion, then modify font size and colour as appropriate.

'Making up' your notes

As soon as possible after each lecture, work through your notes, tidying them up and adding detail where necessary. Add emphasis to any headings you have made, so that the structure is clearer. If you feel it would be more logical for your purposes, change the order. Compare your notes with material in a textbook and correct any inconsistencies. Make notes from, or copy, any useful material you see in textbooks, ready for revision.

Taking notes from books and journal papers

Scanning and skimming are useful techniques.

Scanning

This involves searching for relevant content. Useful techniques are to:

- decide on key words relevant to your search;
- check that the book or journal title indicates relevance;
- look through the contents page (either paper titles in a journal volume, or chapter titles in a textbook);
- look at the index, if present.

Skimming

This is a valuable way to gain the maximum amount of information in the minimum amount of time, by reading as little of a text as is required. Essentially, the technique (also termed 'surveying') requires you to look at the structure of the text, rather than the detail. In a sense, you are trying to see the writer's original plan and the purpose behind each part of the text. Look through the whole of the piece first, to gain an overview of its scope and structure. Headings provide an obvious clue to structure, if present. Next, look for the 'topic sentence' in each paragraph (p. 117), which is often the first. You might then decide that the paragraph contains a definition that is important to note, or it may contain examples, so may not be worth reading for your purpose.

When you have found relevant material, note-taking fulfils the vital purpose of helping you understand and remember the information. If you simply read it, either directly or from a photocopy, you risk accomplishing neither. The act of paraphrasing (using different words to give the same meaning) makes you think about the meaning and forces you to express this for yourself. It is an important active learning technique. A popular method of skimming and note-taking is called the SQ3R technique (Box 4.1).

> **KEY POINT** Obtaining information and then understanding it are distinct, sequential parts of the process of learning. As discussed in Chapter 5 (Table 5.1), you must be able to do more than recall facts to succeed.

Methods for finding and evaluating texts and articles are discussed further in Chapters 8 and 9.

Printing PowerPoint slides – use the 'Black and White' option on the Print menu to avoid wasting ink on printing of coloured backgrounds. If you wish to use colour, remember that slides can be difficult to read if printed in small format. Always print a sample page before printing the whole lecture.

Scanning effectively – you need to stay focused on your key words, otherwise you may be distracted by apparently interesting but peripheral material.

Spotting sequences – writers often number their points (firstly, secondly, thirdly, etc.) and looking for these words in the text can help you skim it quickly.

Making sure you have all the details of a source – when taking notes from a text or journal paper: (a) always take full details (Chapter 8); (b) if copying word-for-word make sure you indicate this using quotes and take special care to ensure you do not alter the original wording.

Box 4.1 The SQ3R technique for skimming texts

Survey   Get a quick overview of the contents of the book or chapter, perhaps by rapidly reading the contents page or headings.

Question   Ask yourself what the material covers and how precisely it relates to your study objectives.

Read   Now read the text, paying attention to the ways it addresses your key questions.

Recall   Recite to yourself what has been stated every few paragraphs. Write notes of this if appropriate, paraphrasing the text rather than copying it.

Review   Think about what you have read and/or review your notes as a whole. Consider where it all fits in.

Sources for further study

Anon. *Mind Map*. Available: http://en.wikipedia.org/wiki/Mind_map. Last accessed: 12/07/09. [An independent review of mind-mapping and its history]

Anon. *FreeMind – Free Mind Mapping Software*. Available: http://freemind.sourceforge.net/wiki/index.php/Main_Page. Last accessed: 12/07/09. [An alternative to pen-and-paper mind mapping]

Anon. *How to make a Mind Map*®. Available: http://www.mind-mapping.co.uk/make-mind-map.htm.

Last accessed: 12/07/09. [Details of how to construct a mind map]

Buzan, A. (2006) *The Ultimate Book of Mind Maps*. Harper Thorsons, New York.

Smith, J. and Morris, S. (2002) *Mind Maps in a Week*. 2nd edn. [Foreword by Buzan, A.] Hodder and Stoughton, London.

Study exercises

4.1 Experiment with a new note-taking technique. If you haven't tried the pattern or mind-mapping methods (Figs 4.1 and 4.2), carry out a trial to see how they work for you. Research the methods first by consulting appropriate books or websites.

4.2 Carry out a 'spring clean' of your desk area and notes. Make a concerted effort to organise your notes and handouts, investing if necessary in files and folders. This will be especially valuable at the start of a revision period.

4.3 Try out the SQ3R technique. The next time you need to obtain information from a text, compare this method (Box 4.1) with others you may have adopted in the past. Is it faster, and does it aid your ability to recall the information?

There are many different ways of learning and at university you have the freedom to choose which approach to study suits you best. You should tackle this responsibility with an open mind, and be prepared to consider new options. Understanding how you learn best and how you are expected to think about your discipline will help you to improve your approach to study and to understand chemistry at a deeper level. Adopting active methods of studying and revision that are suited to your personality can make a significant difference to your performance. Your department will publish material that can help too. Taking account of learning outcomes and marking/assessment criteria, for example, can help you focus your revision.

> **KEY POINT** At university, you are expected to set your own agenda for learning. There will be timetabled activities, assessments and exam deadlines, but it is your responsibility to decide how you will study and learn, how you will manage your time, and, ultimately, what you will gain from the experience. You should be willing to challenge yourself academically to discover your full potential.

Learning styles

We don't all learn in the same way. Your preferred learning style is simply the one that suits you best for receiving, communicating and understanding information. It therefore involves approaches that will help you learn and perform most effectively. There are many different ways of describing learning styles, and you may be introduced to specific schemes during your studies. While methods and terminology may differ among these approaches, it is important to realise that the important thing is the *process* of analysing your learning style, together with the way you use the information to modify your approach to studying, rather than the specific type of learner that you may identify yourself to be.

A useful scheme for describing learning styles is the VARK system devised by Fleming (2001). By answering a short online questionnaire, you can 'diagnose' yourself as one of the types shown in Box 5.1, which also summarises important outcomes relating to how information and concepts can be assimilated, learned and expressed. People show different degrees of alignment with these categories; and research indicates that the majority of students are multi-modal learners – that is, falling into more than one category – rather than being only in one grouping. By carrying out an analysis like this, you can become more aware of your personal characteristics and think about whether the methods of studying you currently use are those that are best suited to your needs.

> **KEY POINT** Having a particular learning preference or style does not mean that you are automatically skilled in using methods generally suited to that type of learner. You must work at developing your ability to take in information, study and cope with assessment.

Significance of learning styles – no one learning style is 'better' than the others; each has its own strengths and weaknesses. However, since many university exams are conducted using 'reading and writing' modes of communication, you may need to find ways of expressing yourself appropriately using the written word (see Box 5.1).

Learning styles and teaching styles – there may be a mismatch between your preferred learning style and the corresponding 'teaching style' used by your lecturers, in which case you will need to adapt appropriately (see Box 5.1).

Box 5.1 How to diagnose your learning preferences using the VARK learning styles scheme

Visit www.vark-learn.com to carry out the online diagnostic test, reflect on whether it is a fair description of your preferences, and think about whether you might change the way you study to improve your performance. None of the outcomes should be regarded as prescriptive – you should mix techniques as you see fit and only use methods that you feel comfortable adopting. Adapted with permission from material produced by Fleming (2001).

Learning style *Description of learning preferences*	Outcomes for your learning, studying and exam technique		
	Advice for taking in information and understanding it	**Best methods of studying for effective learning**	**Ways to cope with exams so you perform better**
Visual: *You are interested in colour, layout and design. You probably prefer to learn from visual media or books with diagrams and charts. You tend to add doodles and use highlighters on lecture and revision notes and express ideas and concepts as images.*	Use media incorporating images, diagrams, flowcharts etc. When constructing notes, employ underlining, different colours and highlighters. Use symbols as much as you can, rather than words. Leave plenty of white space in your notes. Experiment with the 'mind map' style of note-taking (p. 18).	Use similar methods to those described in column two. Reduce lecture notes to pictures. Try to construct your own images to aid understanding, then test your learning by redrawing these from memory.	Plan answers diagrammatically. Recall the images and doodles you used in your notes. Use diagrams in your answers (making sure they are numbered and fully labelled). As part of your revision, turn images into words.
Aural: *You prefer discussing subjects and probably like to attend tutorials and listen to lecturers, rather than read textbooks. Your lecture notes may be poor because you would rather listen than take notes.*	Make sure you attend classes, discussions and tutorials. Note and remember the interesting examples, stories, jokes. Leave spaces in your notes for later recall and 'filling'. Discuss topics with a 'study buddy'. Record lectures (with lecturer's permission).	Expand your notes by talking with others and making additional notes from the textbook. Ask others to 'hear' you talk about topics. Read your summarised notes aloud to yourself. Record your vocalised notes and listen to them later.	When writing answers, imagine you are talking to an unseen examiner. Speak your answers inside your head. Listen to your voices and write them down. Practise writing answers to old exam questions.
Read–Write: *You prefer using text in all formats. Your lecture notes are probably good. You tend to like lecturers who use words well and have lots of information in sentences and notes. In note-taking, you may convert diagrams to text and text to bullet points.*	Focus on note-taking. You may prefer the 'linear' style of note-taking (p. 115). Use the following in your notes: lists; headings; glossaries and lists of definitions. Expand your notes by adding further information from handouts, textbooks and library readings.	Reduce your notes to lists or headings. Write out and read the lists again and again (silently). Turn actions, diagrams, charts and flowcharts into words. Rewrite the ideas and principles into other words. Organise diagrams and graphs into statements, e.g. 'The trend is . . .'.	Plan and write out exam answers using remembered lists. Arrange your words into hierarchies and points.

(continued)

Box 5.1 (continued)

Kinesthetic: *You tend to recall by remembering real events and lecturers' 'stories'. You probably prefer lab work to theory and like lecturers who give real-life examples. Your lecture notes may be weak because the topics did not seem 'concrete' or 'relevant'.*	Focus on examples that illustrate principles. Concentrate on applied aspects and hands-on approaches, but try to understand the theoretical principles that underpin them. When taking in information, use all your senses – sight, touch, taste, smell, hearing.	Put plenty of examples, pictures and photographs into your notes. Use case studies and applications to help with principles and concepts. Talk through your notes with others. Recall your experience of lectures, tutorials or experiments.	Write practice answers and paragraphs. Recall examples and things you did in the lab. Role-play the exam situation in your own room.
Multi-modal: *Your preferences fall into two or more of the above categories. You are able to use these different modes as appropriate.*	If you are diagnosed as having two dominant preferences or several equally dominant preferences, read the study strategies above that apply to each of these. You may find it necessary to use more than one strategy for learning and communicating, feeling less secure with only one.		

Example A set of learning objectives taken from an introductory lecture on inorganic chemistry.

- ☐ Define the following terms:
  - ✓ Periodic Table
  - ✓ period
  - ✓ group
  - ✓ electronic configuration
  - ✓ Aufbau Principle
  - ✓ Hund's Rules
- ☐ Identify selected groups of elements in the Periodic Table, e.g. noble gases, halogens, alkali metals, alkaline earth metals.
- ☐ Determine the electronic configuration of elements B to Ne.
- ☐ Using the mnemonic for the Aufbau Principle, write down the electronic configuration for the following elements: Pb, Mn, Hg, Sn, Cs, Ti, La, Au, Pt and Bi.

Thinking about thinking

The thinking processes that students are expected to carry out can be presented in a sequence, starting with shallower thought processes and ending with deeper processes, each of which builds on the previous level (see Table 5.1). The first two categories in this ladder apply to gaining basic knowledge and understanding, important when you first encounter a topic. Processes three to six are those additionally carried out by high-performing university students, with the latter two being especially relevant to final-year students, researchers and professionals. Naturally, the tutors assessing you will want to reward the deepest thinking appropriate for your level of study. This is often signified by the words they use in assessment tasks and marking criteria (column four, Table 5.1, and p. 123), and while this is not an exact process, being more aware of this agenda can help you to gain more from your studies and appreciate what is being demanded of you.

KEY POINT When considering assessment questions, look carefully at words used in the instructions. These cues can help you identify what depth is expected in your answer. Take special care in multi-part questions, because the first part may require lower-level thinking, while in later parts, marks may be awarded for evidence of deeper thinking.

The role of assessment and feedback in your learning

Your starting point for assessment should be the learning outcomes or objectives for each module, topic or learning activity. You will usually find them in your module handbook. They state in clear terms what your tutors expect you to be able to accomplish after participating in each part

Table 5.1 A ladder of thinking processes, moving from shallower thought processes (top of table) to deeper levels of thinking (bottom of table). This table is derived from research by Benjamin Bloom *et al.* (1956). When considering the cue words in typical question instructions, bear in mind that the precise meaning will always depend on the context. For example, while 'describe' is often associated with relatively simple processes of recall, an instruction like 'describe how the human brain works' demands higher-level understanding. Note also that while a 'cue word' is often given at the start of a question/instruction, this is not universally so.

Thinking processes and description (in approximate order of increasing 'depth')	Example in chemistry	Example of typical question structure, with *cue* word highlighted	Other cue words used in question instructions
1. **Knowledge (knowing facts).** If you know information, you can *remember* or *recognise* it. This does not always mean you understand it at a higher level.	You might know that the elements are organised in a format known as the Periodic Table.	*Describe* the general arrangement of elements in the Periodic Table.	• define • list • state • identify
2. **Comprehension.** If you comprehend a fact, you *understand* what it means.	You might know that the elements in the Periodic Table are organised into columns, known as Groups, and rows, known as Periods.	*Distinguish* between metals and non-metals in the Periodic Table.	• contrast • compare • distinguish • interpret
3. **Application.** To apply a fact means that you can *put it to use* in a particular context.	You might be able to take Period 2, within the Periodic Table, and look at changes in first ionisation energy as the element increases in atomic number.	*Illustrate* the trend in first ionisation energy by plotting the values against atomic number for elements in Period 2.	• calculate • illustrate • solve • show
4. **Analysis.** To analyse information means that you are able to *break it down into parts* and show how these components *fit together*.	You might be able to determine why the trend in first ionisation energy does not change in a linear manner.	*Consider* how the electron configuration changes across Period 2.	• compare • explain • consider • infer
5. **Synthesis.** To synthesise, you need to be able to *extract relevant facts* from a body of knowledge and use these to *address an issue in a novel way* or *create something new*.	You might be able to determine how 's' and 'p' orbits fill with electrons across Period 2.	*Test* the hypothesis that 'dips' in first ionisation energy are due to electron–electron repulsion as the orbits are filled.	• design • integrate • test • create
6. **Evaluation.** If you evaluate information, you *arrive at a judgement* based on its importance relative to the topic being addressed.	You might be able to comment on trends in other Periods within the Periodic Table.	*Evaluate* how the trend in first ionisation energy changes in Period 3.	• review • assess • consider • justify

and reading around the topic. Also of value will be marking/assessment criteria or grade descriptors, which state in general terms what level of attainment is required for your work to reach specific grades. These are more likely to be defined at faculty/college/school/department level and consequently published in appropriate handbooks or websites. Reading learning outcomes and grade descriptors will give you a good idea of what to expect and the level of performance required to reach your personal goals. Relate them to both the material covered (e.g. in lectures and practicals, or online) and past exam papers. Doing this as you study and revise will indicate whether further reading and independent studying is required, and of what type. You will also have a much clearer picture of how you are likely to be assessed.

Definitions

Learning objectives/outcomes – statements of the knowledge, understanding or skills that a learner will be able to demonstrate on successful completion of a module, topic or learning activity.

Formative assessments – these may be mid-term or mid-semester tests and are often in the same format as later exams. They are intended to give you feedback on your performance. You should use the results to measure your performance against the work you put in, and to find out, either from grades or tutor's comments, how you could do better in future. If you don't understand the reason for your grade, talk to your tutor.

Summative assessments – these include end-of-year or end-of-module exams. They inform others about the standard of your work. In continuous or 'in-course' assessment, the summative elements are spread out over the course. Sometimes these exams may involve a formative aspect, if feedback is given.

KEY POINT Use the learning objectives for your course (normally published in the handbook) as a fundamental part of your revision planning. These indicate what you will be expected to be able to do after taking part in the course, so exam questions are often based on them. Check this by reference to past papers.

There are essentially two types of assessment – formative and summative, although the distinction may not always be clear-cut (see margin). The first way you can learn from formative assessment is to consider the grade you obtained in relation to the work you put in. If this is a disappointment to you, then there must be a mismatch between your understanding of the topic and the marking scheme and that of the marker, or a problem in the writing or presentation of your assignment. This element of feedback is also present in summative assessment.

The second way to learn from formative assessment is through the written feedback and notes on your work. These comments may be cryptic, or scribbled hastily, so if you don't understand or can't read them, ask the tutor who marked the work. Most tutors will be pleased to explain how you could have improved your mark. If you find that the same comments appear frequently, it may be a good idea to seek help from your university's academic support unit. Take along examples of your work and feedback comments, so they can give you the best possible advice. Another suggestion is to ask to see the work of another student who obtained a good mark, and compare it with your own. This will help you judge the standard you should be aiming for.

Preparing for revision and examinations

Before you start revising, find out as much as you can about each exam, including:

- format and duration;
- date and location;
- types of question;
- whether any questions/sections are compulsory;
- whether the questions are internally or externally set or assessed;
- whether the exam is 'open book', and if so, which texts or notes are allowed.

Your course tutor is likely to give you details of exam structure and timing well beforehand, so that you can plan your revision; the course handbook and past papers (if available) can provide further useful details. Always check that the nature of the exam has not changed before you consult past papers.

Organising and using lecture notes, assignments and practical reports

Given their importance as a source of material for revision, you should have sorted out any deficiencies or omissions in your lecture notes and practical reports at an early stage. For example, you may have missed a lecture or practical due to illness, etc., but the exam is likely to assume attendance

Time management when revising – this is vital to success and is best achieved by creating a revision timetable (Box 5.2).

Filing lecture notes – make sure your notes are kept neatly and in sequence by using a ring binder system. File the notes in lecture or practical sequence, adding any supplementary notes or photocopies alongside.

Box 5.2 How to prepare and use a revision timetable

1. **Make up a grid showing the number of days until your exams are finished.** Divide each day into several sections. If you like revising in large blocks of time, use am, pm and evening slots, but if you prefer shorter periods, divide each of these in two, or use hourly divisions (see also the table in study exercise 5.1).

2. **Write in your non-revision commitments,** including any time off you plan to allocate and physical activity at frequent intervals. Try to have about one-third or a quarter of the time off in any one day. Plan this in relation to your best times for useful work – for example, some people work best in the mornings, while others prefer evenings. If you wish, use a system where your relaxation time is a bonus to be worked for; this may help you motivate yourself.

3. **Decide on how you wish to subdivide your subjects** for revision purposes. This might be among subjects, according to difficulty (with the hardest getting the most time), or within subjects, according to topics. Make sure there is an adequate balance of time among topics and especially that you do not avoid working on the subject(s) you find least interesting or most difficult.

4. **Allocate the work to the different slots available on your timetable.** You should work backwards from the exams, making sure that you cover every exam topic adequately in the period just before each exam. You may wish to colour-code the subjects.

5. **As you revise, mark off the slots completed** – this has a positive psychological effect and will boost your self-confidence.

6. **After the exams, revisit your timetable** and decide whether you would do anything differently next time.

Using feedback from tutors – it is always worth reading any comments on your work as soon as it is returned. If you don't understand the comments, or are unsure about why you might have lost marks in an assignment, ask for an explanation.

throughout the year. Make sure you attend classes whenever possible and keep your notes up to date. Your practical reports and any assignment work will contain specific comments from the teaching staff, indicating where marks were lost, corrections, mistakes, inadequacies, etc. Most lecturers are quite happy to discuss such details with students on a one-to-one basis and this information may provide you with clues to the expectations of individual lecturers that may be useful in exams set by the same members of staff. However, you should never 'fish' for specific information on possible exam questions, as this is likely to be counter-productive.

Revision

Begin early, to avoid last-minute panic. Start in earnest several weeks beforehand, and plan your work carefully:

- Prepare a revision timetable – an 'action plan' that gives details of specific topics to be covered (Box 5.2). Plan your revision around when (and where) your examinations are to be held. Try to keep to your timetable. Time management during this period is as important as keeping to time during the exam itself.

- Study the learning objectives/outcomes for each topic (usually published in the course handbook) to get an idea of what lecturers expect from you.

Recognise when your concentration powers are dwindling – take a short break when this happens and return to work refreshed and ready to learn. Remember that 20 minutes is often quoted as a typical limit to full concentration effort.

- Use past papers as a guide to the form of exam and the type of question likely to be asked (Box 5.3).

- Remember to have several short (5 minute) breaks during each hour of revision and a longer break every few hours. In any day, try to work for a maximum of three-quarters of the time.

Box 5.3 How to use past exam papers in your revision

Past exam papers are a valuable resource for targeting your revision.

1. **Find out where the past exam papers are kept.** Copies may be lodged in your department or the library; or they may be accessible online.

2. **Locate and copy relevant papers for your module(s).** Check with your tutor or course handbook that the style of paper will not change for the next set of examinations.

3. **Analyse the design of the exam paper.** Taking into account the length in weeks of your module, and the different lecturers and/or topics for those weeks, note any patterns that emerge. For example, can you translate weeks of lectures/ practicals into numbers of questions or sections of the paper? Consider how this might affect your revision plans and exam tactics, taking into account (a) any choices or restrictions offered in the paper, and (b) the different types of questions asked (i.e. multiple choice, short-answer or essay).

4. **Examine carefully the style of questions.** Can you identify the expectations of your lecturers? Can you relate the questions to the learning objectives? How much extra reading do they seem to expect? Are the questions fact-based? Do they require a synthesis based on other

knowledge? Can you identify different styles for different lecturers? Consider how the answers to these questions might affect your revision effort and exam strategy.

5. **Practise answering questions.** Perhaps with friends, set up your own mock exam once you have done a fair amount of revision, but not too close to the exams. Use a relevant past exam paper and don't study it beforehand. You need not attempt all of the paper at one sitting. You'll need a quiet room in a place where you will not be interrupted (e.g. a library). Keep close track of time during the mock exam and try to do each question in the length of time you would normally assign to it (see p. 33) – this gives you a feel for the speed of thought and writing required and the scope of answer possible. Mark each other's papers and discuss how each of you interpreted the question and laid out your answers and your individual marking schemes.

6. **Practise writing answer plans and starting answers.** This can save time compared to the 'mock exam' approach. Practice in starting answers can help you get over stalling at the start and wasting valuable time. Writing essay plans gets you used to organising your thoughts quickly and putting your thoughts into a logical sequence.

- Include recreation within your schedule: there is little point in tiring yourself with too much revision, as this is unlikely to be profitable.

- Make your revision as active and interesting as possible (see below): the least productive approach is simply to read and reread your notes.

- Ease back on the revision near the exam: plan your revision to avoid last-minute cramming and overload fatigue.

Active revision

The following techniques may prove useful in devising an active revision strategy:

- 'Distil' your lecture notes to show the main headings and examples. Prepare revision sheets with details for a particular topic on a single sheet of paper, arranged as a numbered checklist. Wall posters are another useful revision aid.

- Confirm that you know the material by testing yourself – take a blank sheet of paper and write down all you know. Check your full notes to see if you missed anything out. If you did, go back immediately to a fresh blank sheet and redo the example. Repeat, as required.

Aiding recall through effective note-taking – the Mind Map technique (p. 18), when used to organise ideas, is claimed to enhance recall by connecting the material to visual images or linking it to the physical senses.

Question-spotting – avoid this risky strategy. Lecturers are aware that this approach may be taken and try to ask questions in an unpredictable manner. You may find that you are unable to answer on unexpected topics which you failed to revise. Moreover, if you have a preconceived idea about what will be asked, you may also fail to grasp the nuances of the exact question set, and thereby fail to provide a focused answer.

Revision checks – it is important to test yourself frequently during revision, to ensure that you have retained the information you are revising.

Final preparations – try to get a good night's sleep before an exam. Last-minute cramming will be counter-productive if you are too tired during the exam.

- Memorise definitions and key phrases: definitions can be a useful starting point for many exam answers. Make up lists of relevant facts or definitions associated with particular topics. Test yourself repeatedly on these, or get a friend to do this. Try to remember *how many* facts or definitions you need to know in each case – this will help you recall them all during the exam.

- Use mnemonics and acronyms to commit specific factual information to memory. Sometimes, the dafter they are, the better they seem to work.

- Use pattern diagrams or mind maps as a means of testing your powers of recall on a particular topic (p. 18).

- Draw diagrams from memory: make sure you can label them fully.

- Try recitation as an alternative to written recall. Talk about your topic to another person, preferably someone in your class. Talk to yourself if necessary. Explaining something out loud is an excellent test of your understanding.

- Associate facts with images or journeys if you find this method works.

- Use a wide variety of approaches to avoid boredom during revision (e.g. record information on audio tape, use cartoons, or any other method, as long as it's not just reading).

- Form a revision group to share ideas and discuss topics with other students.

- Prepare answers to past papers, e.g. write essays or, if time is limited, write essay plans (see Box 5.3).

- If your subject involves numerical calculations, work through representative problems.

- Make up your own questions: the act of putting yourself in the examiner's mind-set by inventing questions can help revision. However, you should not rely on 'question spotting': this is risky!

The evening before your exam should be spent in consolidating material, and checking through summary lists and plans. Avoid introducing new material at this late stage: your aim should be to boost your confidence, putting yourself in the right frame of mind for the exam itself.

Text references

Bloom, B., Englehart, M., Furst, E., Hill, W. and Krathwohl, D. (1956) *Taxonomy of Educational Objectives: The Classification of Educational Goals. Handbook I: Cognitive Domain.* New York, Toronto: Longmans, Green.

Fleming, N.D. (2001) *Teaching and Learning Styles: VARK Strategies.* Neil Fleming, Christchurch.

Fleming, N.D. *VARK: A Guide to Learning Styles.* Available: http://www.vark-learn.com/ Last Accessed 12/07/09.

Sources for further study

Burns, R. (1997) *The Student's Guide to Passing Exams*. Kogan Page, London.

Hamilton, D. (1999) *Passing Exams: A Guide for Maximum Stress and Minimum Stress*. Cassell, London.

Many universities host study skills websites; these can be found using 'study skills', 'revision' or 'exams' as key words in a search engine.

Study exercises

5.1 Draw up a revision timetable. Use the techniques discussed in Box 5.2 to create a revision timetable for your forthcoming exams. You may wish to use or adapt the following arrangement, either on paper or within a spreadsheet.

A revision timetable planner

Date	Morning		Lunch	Afternoon		Tea/Dinner	Evening	
	Session 1	Session 2		Session 1	Session 2		Session 1	Session 2

5.2 Make use of past exam papers. Use the techniques discussed in Box 5.2 to improve your revision strategy: assess their effectiveness in a particular exam, or series of exams.

5.3 Try out new active revision techniques. Try any or all of the methods mentioned on pages 27–29 when revising. Compare notes with a colleague – which seems to be the most successful technique for you and for the topic you are revising?

6 Curriculum options, assessments and exams

Definition

Transcript – this is your record of achievement at university. Normally it will consist of details of each module or course you have taken, and an indication of the grade or mark achieved. It will also show your final (honours) classification, that is: first class, upper second class (2.1), lower second class (2.2), third class or unclassified (note: some UK universities do not differentiate second class degrees).

Many universities operate a modular system for their chemistry degree courses. This allows greater flexibility in subject choice and accommodates students studying on different degree paths. Modules also break a subject into discrete, easily assimilated components. They have the advantage of spreading assessment over the academic year (or semester), but they can also tempt you to avoid certain difficult subjects or to feel that you can forget about a topic once the module is finished.

> **KEY POINT** You should select your modules with care, mindful of potential degree options and how your transcript and CV will appear to a prospective employer. If you feel you need advice, consult your personal guidance tutor or study adviser.

Aiming high – your goal should be to perform at your highest possible level and not simply to fulfil the minimum criteria for progression. This will lay sound foundations for your later studies. Remember too that a future employer might ask to see your academic transcript, which will detail all your module grades including any fails/resits, and will not just state your final degree classification.

As you move between levels of the university system, you will be expected to have passed a certain number of modules, as detailed in the progression criteria. These may be expressed using a credit point system. Students are normally allowed two attempts at each module exam and the resits often take place at the end of the summer vacation. If a student does not pass at the second attempt, they may be asked to 'carry' the subject in a subsequent year, and in severe cases of multiple failure, they may be asked to re-take the whole year or even leave the course. Consequently, it is worth finding out about these aspects of your degree. They are usually published in relevant handbooks.

You are unlikely to have reached this stage in your education without being exposed to the examination process. You may not enjoy being assessed, but you probably want to do well in your course. It is therefore important to understand why and how you are being tested. Identifying and improving the skills required for exam success will allow you to perform to the best of your ability.

Assessed coursework

Avoiding plagiarism – this is a key issue for assessed coursework - see p. 54 for a definition and Chapter 8 for appropriate methods of referring to the ideas and results of others using citation.

There is a component of assessed coursework in many modules. This often tests specific skills, and may require you to demonstrate thinking at deeper levels (Table 5.1). The common types of coursework assessment are covered at various points in this book:

- practical exercises (Chapters 20–59, 66, 67);
- essays (Chapters 16 and 17);
- numerical problems (Chapter 62);
- data analysis (Chapters 62–64);
- poster and spoken presentations (Chapters 14 and 15);
- literature surveys and reviews (Chapter 19);
- project work (Chapters 18 and 30);
- problem-based learning (Box 6.1).

At the start of each year or module, read the course handbook or module guide carefully to find out when any assessed work needs to be

Box 6.1 Problem-based learning (PBL)

In this relatively new teaching method, you are likely to be presented with a 'real world' problem or issue, often working within a team. As you tackle the problem, you will gain factual knowledge, develop skills and exercise critical thinking (Chapter 9). Because there is a direct and relevant context for your work, and because you have to employ active learning techniques, the knowledge and skills you gain are likely to be more readily assimilated and remembered. This approach also more closely mimics workplace practices. PBL usually proceeds as follows:

1. **You are presented with a problem** (e.g. a case study, a chemical synthesis, a topical issue).

2. **You consider what issues and topics you need to research,** by discussion with others if necessary. You may need to identify where relevant resources can be found (Chapters 8–11).

3. **You then need to rank the issues and topics in importance,** allocating tasks to group members, if appropriate. A structured approach is an important aspect of PBL.

4. **Having carried out the necessary research, you should review what information has been obtained.** As a result, new issues may need to be explored and, where appropriate, allocated to group members.

5. **You will be asked to produce an outcome, such as a report, diagnosis, seminar presentation or poster.** An outline structure will be required, and for groups, further allocation of tasks will be needed to accomplish this goal.

If asked to carry out PBL as part of your course, it is important to get off to a good start. At first, the problem may seem unfamiliar. However, once you become involved in the work, you will quickly gain confidence. If working as part of a group, make sure that your group meets as early as possible, that you attend all sessions and that you do the necessary background reading. When working in a team, a degree of self-awareness is necessary regarding your 'natural' role in group situations (Table 3.1). Various methods are used for assessing PBL, including written, oral and poster presentations, and the assessment may involve peer marking.

submitted. Note relevant dates in your diary, and use this information to plan your work. Take special note if deadlines for different modules clash, or if they coincide with social or sporting commitments.

> **KEY POINT** If, for some valid reason (e.g. illness), you will be late with an assessment, speak to your tutors as soon as possible. They may be able to take extenuating circumstances into account by not applying a marking penalty. They will let you know what paperwork you may be required to submit to support your claim.

Summative exams – general points

Summative exams (p. 26) normally involve you answering questions without being able to consult other students or your notes. Invigilators are present to ensure appropriate conduct, but departmental representatives may be present for some of the exam. Their role is to sort out any subject-related problems, so if you think something is wrong, ask at the earliest opportunity. It is not unknown for parts of questions to be omitted in error, or for double meanings to arise, for example.

Planning

When preparing for an exam, make a checklist of the items you'll need (see p. 37). On the day of the exam, give yourself sufficient time to arrive at the correct room, without the risk of being late. Double-check the times and places of your exams, both well before the exam, and also on arrival. If you arrive at the exam venue early, you can always rectify a mistake if you find you've gone to the wrong place.

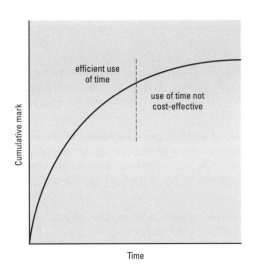

Fig. 6.1 Exam marks as a function of time. The marks awarded in a single answer will follow the law of diminishing returns – it will be far more difficult to achieve the final 25% of the available marks than the initial 25%. Do not spend too long on any one question.

Using the question paper – unless this is specifically forbidden, you should write on the question paper to plan your strategy, keep to time and organise answers.

Checking exam answers – look for:
- errors of fact;
- missing information;
- grammatical and spelling errors;
- errors of scale and units;
- errors in calculations.

Adopting different tactics according to the exam – you should adjust your exam strategy (and revision methods) to allow for the differences in question types used in each exam paper.

Tackling the paper

Begin by reading the instructions at the top of the exam paper carefully, so that you do not make any errors based on lack of understanding of the exam structure. Make sure that you know:

- how many questions are set;
- how many must be answered;
- whether the paper is divided into sections;
- whether any parts are compulsory;
- what each question/section is worth, as a proportion of the total mark;
- whether different questions should be answered in different books.

Do not be tempted to spend too long on any one question or section: the return in terms of marks will not justify the loss of time from other questions (see Fig. 6.1). Take the first 10 minutes or so to read the paper and plan your strategy, before you begin writing. Do not be put off by those who begin immediately; it is almost certain they are producing unplanned work of a poor standard.

Underline the key phrases in the instructions, to reinforce their message. Next, read through the set of questions. If there is a choice, decide on those questions to be answered and decide on the order in which you will tackle them. Prepare a timetable which takes into account the amount of time required to complete each section and which reflects the allocation of marks – there is little point in spending one-quarter of the exam period on a question worth only 5% of the total marks. Use the exam paper to mark the sequence in which the questions will be answered and write the finishing times alongside; refer to this timetable during the exam to keep yourself on course.

Reviewing your answers

At the end of the exam, you should allow at least 10 minutes to check through your script. Make sure your name and/or ID number is on each exam book as required and on all other sheets of paper, including graph paper, even if securely attached to your script, as it is in your interest to ensure that your work does not go astray.

> **KEY POINT** Never leave any exam early. Most exams assess work carried out over several months within a time period of 2–3 hours and there is always something constructive you can do with the remaining time to improve your script.

Special considerations for different types of exam question

Essay questions

Essay questions let examiners test the depth of your comprehension and understanding as well as your recall of facts. Essay questions give you plenty of scope to show what you know. They suit those with a good grasp of principles but who perhaps have less ability to recall individual details.

Before you tackle a particular question, you must be sure of what is required in your answer. Ask yourself 'What is the examiner looking for in this particular question?' and then set about providing a *relevant*

Box 6.2 **Writing under exam conditions**

Make sure you go into an exam with a strategy for managing the available time.

- **Allocate some time (say 5% of the total) to consider which questions to answer and in which order.**

- **Share the rest of the time among the questions, according to the marks available.** Aim to optimise the marks obtained. A potentially good answer should be allocated slightly more time than one you don't feel so happy about. However, don't concentrate on any one answer (see Fig. 6.1).

- **For each question divide the time into planning, writing and revision phases** (see p. 122).

Employ time-saving techniques as much as possible:

- **Use spider diagrams** (Fig. 16.2) **or mind maps** (Fig. 4.2) to organise and plan your answer.

- **Use diagrams and tables** to save time in making difficult and lengthy explanations, but make sure you refer to each one in the text.

- **Use standard abbreviations** to save time repeating text but always explain them at the first point of use (e.g. HPLC, high performance liquid chromatography).

- **Consider speed of writing and neatness** – especially when selecting the type of pen to use – ballpoint pens are fastest, but they can tend to smudge. You can only gain marks if the examiner can read your script.

- **Keep your answer simple and to the point**, with clear explanations of your reasoning.

Make sure your answer is relevant.

- **Don't include irrelevant facts** just because you memorised them during revision, as this may do you more harm than good. You must answer the specific question that has been set.

- **Time taken to write irrelevant material is time lost from another question.**

---

answer. Consider each word in the question and highlight, underline or circle the key words. Make sure you know the meaning of the terms given in Table 17.1 so that you can provide the appropriate information, where necessary. Spend some time planning your writing (see Chapter 16). Refer back to the question frequently as you write, to confirm that you are keeping to the subject matter. Box 6.2 gives advice on writing essays under exam conditions.

It is usually a good idea to begin with the question that you are most confident about. This will reassure you before tackling more difficult parts of the paper. If you run out of time, write in note form. Examiners are usually understanding, as long as the main components of the question have been addressed and the intended structure of the answer is clear. Common reasons for poor exam answers in essay-style questions are listed in Box 6.3.

Penalties for guessing – if there is a penalty for incorrect answers in a multiple choice test, the best strategy is not to answer questions when you know your answer is a complete guess. Depending on the penalty, it may be beneficial to guess if you can narrow the choice down to two options (but beware false or irrelevant alternatives). However, if there are no such penalties, then you should provide an answer to all questions.

Multiple-choice and short-answer questions

Multiple-choice questions (MCQs) and short-answer questions (SAQs) are generally used to test the breadth and detail of your knowledge. The various styles that can be encompassed within the SAQ format allow for more demanding questions than MCQs, which may emphasise memory work and specific factual information.

A good approach for MCQ papers is as follows:

1. First trawl: read through the questions fairly rapidly, noting the 'correct' answer in those you can attempt immediately, perhaps in pencil.

2. Second trawl: go through the paper again, checking your original answers and this time marking up the answer sheet properly.

Box 6.3 Reasons for poor exam answers to essay-style questions

The following are reasons that lecturers often cite when they give low marks for essay answers:

- **Not answering the exact question set.** Either failing to recognise the specialist terms used in the question, failing to demonstrate an understanding of the terms by not providing definitions, failing to carry out the precise instruction in a question, or failing to address all aspects of the question.

- **Running out of time.** Not matching the time allocated to the extent of the answer. Frequently, this results in spending too long on one question and not enough on the others, or even failing to complete the paper.

- **Not answering all parts** of a multiple part question, or not recognising that one part (perhaps involving more complex ideas) may carry more marks than another.

- **Failing to provide evidence** to support an answer. Forgetting to state the 'obvious' – either basic facts or definitions.

- **Failing to illustrate an answer appropriately**, either by not including a relevant diagram, or by providing a diagram that does not aid communication, or by not including examples.

- **Incomplete answer(s).** Failing to answer appropriately due to lack of knowledge.

- **Providing irrelevant evidence** to support an answer. 'Waffling' to fill space.

- **Illegible handwriting.**

- **Poor English**, such that facts and ideas are not expressed clearly.

- **Lack of logic** or structure to the answer.

- **Factual errors**, indicating poor note-taking, poor revision or poor recall.

- **Failing to correct obvious mistakes** by re-reading an answer before submitting the script.

At higher levels, the following aspects are especially important:

- **Not providing enough in-depth information.**

- **Providing a descriptive rather than an analytical answer** – focusing on facts, rather than deeper aspects of a topic.

- **Not setting a problem in context**, or not demonstrating a wider understanding of the topic. However, make sure you don't overdo this, or you may risk not answering the question set.

- **Not giving enough evidence of reading around the subject.** Wider reading can be demonstrated by quoting relevant papers and reviews and by giving author names and dates of publication.

- **Not considering both sides of a topic/debate, or not arriving at a conclusion.**

3. Third trawl: now tackle the difficult questions and those that require longer to answer (e.g. those based on numerical problems).

One reason for adopting this three-phase approach is that you may be prompted to recall facts relevant to questions looked at earlier. You can also spend more time per question on the difficult ones.

When unsure of an answer, the first stage is to rule out options that are clearly absurd or have obviously been placed there to distract you. Next, looking at the remaining options, can you judge between contrasting pairs with alternative answers? Logically, both cannot be correct, so you should see if you can rule one of the pair out. Watch out, however, in case *both* may be irrelevant to the answer. If the question involves a calculation, try to do this independently from the answers, so you are not influenced by them.

In SAQ papers, there may be a choice of questions. Choose your options carefully – it may be better to gain half marks for a correct answer to half a question, than to provide a largely irrelevant answer that apparently covers the whole question but lacks the necessary detail. For

Answer the question as requested – this is true for all questions, but especially important for SAQs. If the question asks for a diagram, make sure you provide one; if it asks for a specified number of aspects of a topic, try to list this number of points; if there are two or more parts, provide appropriate answers to all aspects. This may seem obvious, but many marks are lost for not following instructions.

the SAQ form of question, few if any marks are given for writing style. Think in 'bullet points' and list the crucial points only. The time for answering SAQ questions may be tight, so get down to work fast, starting with answers that demand remembered facts. Stick to your timetable by moving on to the next question as soon as possible. Strategically, it is probably better to get part-marks for the full number of questions than good marks for only a few.

Practical and information-processing exams

The prospect of a practical or information-processing exam may cause you more concern than a theory exam. This may be due to a limited experience of practical examinations, or to the fact that practical and observational skills are tested, as well as recall, description and analysis of factual information. Your first thoughts may be that it is not possible to prepare for such exams but, in fact, you can improve your performance by mastering the various practical techniques described in this book.

You may be allowed to take your laboratory reports and other texts into the practical exam. Don't assume that this is a soft option, or that revision is unnecessary: you will not have time to read large sections of your reports or to familiarise yourself with basic principles, etc. The main advantage of 'open book' exams is that you can check specific details of methodology, reducing your reliance on memory, provided you know your way around your practical manual and notes. In all other respects, your revision and preparation for such exams should be similar to theory exams. Make sure you are familiar with all of the practical exercises, including any work carried out in class by your partner (since exams are assessed on individual performance). If necessary, check with the teaching staff to see whether you can be given access to the laboratory, to complete any exercises that you have missed.

At the outset of the practical exam, determine or decide on the order in which you will tackle the questions. A question in the latter half of the paper may need to be started early on in the exam period (e.g. a chemical reflux requiring 2 hours in a 3-hour exam). Such questions are included to test your forward-planning and time-management skills. You may need to make additional decisions on the allocation of material; e.g. if you need to run a melting point, IR spectrum and a uv/visible spectrum determine how much compound may be required for each before starting, particularly if some of the compound is required to answer another question.

Make sure you explain your choice of apparatus and experimental design. Calculations should be set out in a stepwise manner, so that credit can be given, even if the final answer is incorrect (see p. 448). If there are any questions that rely on recall of factual information and you are unable to remember specific details, make sure that you describe the item fully, so that you gain credit for observational skills. Alternatively, leave a gap and return to the question at a later stage.

Oral exams and interviews

An oral interview is sometimes a part of final degree exams, representing a chance for the external examiner(s) to meet individual students and to test their abilities directly and interactively. In some departments, orals

---

Examples These are principal types of question you are likely to encounter in a practical or information-processing exam:

Manipulative exercises Often based on work carried out during your practical course. Tests dexterity, specific techniques (e.g. sample injection in gas chromatography).

'Spot' tests Short questions requiring an identification, or brief descriptive notes on a specific item (e.g. define the operation of a hollow cathode lamp). Tests knowledge of seen material or ability to transfer this to a new example.

Calculations May include the preparation of aqueous solutions at particular concentrations (Chapter 25) and statistical exercises (Chapter 64). Tests numeracy.

Data analyses May include the preparation and interpretation of graphs (Chapter 60) and numerical information, from data either obtained during the exam or provided by the examiner. Tests problem-solving skills.

Chemical synthesis May include details of starting reagents and require possible likely products to be suggested.

Chemical structure elucidation A series of spectra are provided (IR, nmr) which require interpretation and identification of the probable chemical compound.

Terminology – the oral exams are sometimes known simply as 'orals' or, borrowing Latin, as 'viva voce' (by the living voice) exams or 'vivas'.

are used to validate the exam standard, or to test students on the borderline between degree classifications. Sometimes an interview may form part of an assessment, as with project work or posters. This type of exam is often intimidating – many students say they don't know how to revise for an oral – and many candidates worry that they will be so nervous they won't be able to do themselves justice.

Preparation is just as important for oral exams as it is for written exams:

- Think about your earlier performances – if the oral follows written papers, it may be that you will be asked about questions you did not do so well on. These topics should be revised thoroughly. Be prepared to say how you would approach the questions if given a second chance.

- Read up a little about the examiner – he or she may focus their questions in their area of expertise.

- Get used to giving spoken answers – it is often difficult to transfer between written and spoken modes. Write down a few questions and get a friend to ask you them, possibly with unscripted follow-up queries.

- Research and think about topical issues in your subject area – some examiners will feel this reflects how interested you are in your subject.

Your conduct during the oral exam is important, too:

- Arrive promptly and wear reasonably smart clothing. Not to do either might be considered disrespectful by the examiner.

- Take your time before answering questions. Even if you think you know the answer immediately, take a little while to check mentally whether you have considered all angles. A considered, logical approach will be more impressive than a quick but ill-considered response.

- Start answers with the basics, then develop into deeper aspects. There may be both surface and deeper aspects to a topic and more credit will be given to a student who mentions the latter.

- When your answer is finished, stop speaking. A short, crisp answer is better than a rambling one.

- If you don't know the answer, say so. To waffle and talk about irrelevant material is more damaging than admitting that you don't know.

- Make sure your answer is balanced. Talk about the evidence and opinions on both sides of a contentious issue.

- Don't disagree violently with the examiner. Politely put your point of view, detailing the evidence behind it. Examiners will be impressed by students who know their own mind and subject area. However, they will expect you to support a position at odds with the conventional viewpoint.

- Finally, be positive and enthusiastic about your topic.

Allow yourself to relax in oral exams – external examiners are experienced at putting students at ease. They will start by asking 'simple-to-answer' questions, such as what modules you did, how your project research went, and what your career aspirations are. Look on the external as a friend rather than a foe.

Creating an exam action list – knowing that you have prepared well, checked everything on your list and gathered together all you need for an exam will improve your confidence and reduce anxiety. Your list might include:

- Verify time, date and place of the exam.
- Confirm travel arrangements to exam hall.
- Double-check module handbooks and past papers for exam structure.
- Think through use of time and exam strategy.
- Identify a quiet place near the exam hall to carry out a last-minute check on key knowledge (e.g. formulae, definitions, diagram labels).
- Ensure you have all the items you wish to take to the exam, e.g.
  - pens, pencils (with sharpener and eraser);
  - ruler;
  - correction fluid;
  - calculator (allowable type), if required;
  - sweets and drink, if allowed;
  - tissues
  - watch or clock;
  - ID card
  - texts and/or notes, if an open book exam;
  - lucky charm/mascot.
- Lay out clothes (if exam is early in the morning).
- Set alarm and/or ask a friend or family member to check you are awake on time.

Box 6.4 Strategies for combating the symptoms of exam anxiety

Sleeplessness – this is common and does little harm in the short term. Get up, have a snack, do some light reading or other activity, then return to bed. Avoid caffeine (e.g. tea, coffee and cola) for several hours before going to bed.

Lack of appetite – again commonplace. Eat what you can, and take sugary sweets into the exam to keep energy levels up in case you become tired.

Fear of the unknown – it can be a good idea to visit the exam room beforehand, so you can become familiar with the location. By working through the points given in the exam action list on p. 37, you will be confident that nothing has been left out.

Worries about timekeeping – get a *reliable* alarm clock or a new battery for an old one. Arrange for an alarm phone call; ask a friend or relative to make sure you are awake on time. Make reliable travel arrangements, to arrive on time. If your exam is early in the morning, it may be a good idea to get up early for a few days beforehand.

Blind panic during an exam – explain how you feel to an invigilator. Ask to go for a supervised walk outside. Do some relaxation exercises (see below), then return to your work. If you are having problems with a specific question, it may be appropriate to speak to the departmental representative at the exam, to check that you are not misinterpreting the question.

Feeling tense – shut your eyes, take several slow, deep breaths, do some stretching and relaxing muscle movements. During exams, it can be a good idea to do this between questions, and possibly to have a complete rest for a minute or so. Before exams, try some exercise activity or escape temporarily from your worries by watching TV or a movie.

Running out of time – don't panic when the invigilator says 'five minutes left'. It is surprising how much you can write in this time. Write note-style answers or state the areas you would have covered: you may get some credit.

Counteracting anxiety before and during exams

Adverse effects of anxiety need to be overcome by anticipation and preparation well in advance (Box 6.4). Exams, with their tight time limits, are especially stressful for perfectionists. To counteract this tendency, focus on the following points during the exam:

- Don't expect to produce a perfect essay – this won't be possible in the time available.

- Don't spend too long planning your answer – once you have an outline plan, get started.

- Don't spend too much time on the initial parts of an answer, at the expense of the main message.

- Concentrate on getting all of the basic points across – markers are looking for the main points first, before allocating extra marks for the detail.

- Don't be obsessed with neatness, either in handwriting, or in the diagrams you draw, but make sure your answers are legible.

- Don't worry if you forget something. You can't be expected to know everything. Most marking schemes give a first class grade to work that misses out on up to 30% of the marks available.

After the exam – try to avoid becoming involved in prolonged analyses with other students over the 'ideal' answers to the questions; after all, it is too late to change anything at this stage. Go for a walk, watch TV for a while, or do something else that helps you relax, so that you are ready to face the next exam with confidence.

> **KEY POINT** Everyone worries about exams. Anxiety is a perfectly natural feeling. It works to your advantage, as it helps provide motivation and the adrenaline that can help you 'raise your game' on the day.

There is a lot to be said for treating exams as a game. After all, they are artificial situations contrived to ensure that large numbers of candidates can be assessed together, with little risk of cheating. They have conventions and rules, just like games. If you understand the rationale behind them and follow the rules, this will aid your performance.

Sources for further study

Acres, D. (1998) *Passing Exams Without Anxiety: How to Get Organised, be Prepared and Feel Confident of Success.* How to Books, London.

Burns, R. (1997) *The Student's Guide to Passing Exams.* Kogan Page, London.

Hamilton, D. (1999) *Passing Exams: A Guide for Maximum Success and Minimum Stress.* Cassell, London.

Many universities host study skills websites; these can be found using 'study skills', 'revision' or 'exams' as key words in a search engine.

Study exercises

6.1 **Analyse your past performances.** Think back to past exams and any feedback you received from them. How might you improve your performance? Consider ways in which you might approach the forthcoming exam differently. If you have kept past papers and answers to continuous assessment exercises, look at any specific comments your lecturers may have made.

6.2 **Share revision notes with other students.** Make a revision plan (see pp. 11 and 28) and then allocate some time to discussing your revision notes with a colleague. Try to learn from his or her approach. Discuss any issues you do not agree upon.

6.3 **Plan your exam tactics.** Find out from your module handbook or past papers what the format of each paper will be. Confirm this if necessary with staff. Decide how you will tackle each paper, allocating time to each section and to each question within the sections (see p. 122). Write a personal checklist of requirements for the exam (see p. 37).

> **Definition**
>
> Curriculum vitae (or CV for short) – a Latin phrase that means 'the course your life has taken'.

Personal development planning (PDP) and your CV – many PDP schemes (p. 5) also include an element of career planning that may involve creating a draft or generic CV. The PDP process can help you improve the structure and content of your CV, and the language you use within it.

Understanding skills and qualities – it may be helpful to think about how the skills and qualities in Tables 1.1 and 7.1 apply to particular activities during your studies, since this will give them a greater relevance.

Focusing on evidence – it is important to be able to provide specific information that will back up the claims you make under the 'skills and personal qualities' and other sections of your CV. A potential employer will be interested in your level of competence (what you can actually do) and in situations where you have used a skill or demonstrated a particular quality. These aspects can also be mentioned in your covering letter or at interview.

Seeing yourself as others see you – you may not recognise all of your personal qualities and you may need someone else to give you an honest appraisal. This could be anyone whose opinion you value: a friend, a member of your family, a tutor or a careers adviser.

Many students only think about their curriculum vitae immediately before applying for a job. Reflecting this, chapters on preparing a CV are usually placed near the end of texts of this type. Putting the chapter near the beginning of this book emphasises the importance of focusing your thoughts on your CV at an early stage in your studies. There are four main reasons why this can be valuable:

1. Considering your CV and how it will look to a future employer will help you think more deeply about the direction and value of your academic studies.

2. Creating a draft CV will prompt you to assess your skills and personal qualities and how these fit into your career aspirations.

3. Your CV can be used as a record of all the relevant things you have done at university and then, later, will help you communicate these to a potential employer.

4. Your developing CV can be used when you apply for vacation or part-time employment.

> **KEY POINT** Developing your skills and qualities needs to be treated as a long-term project. It makes sense to think early about your career aspirations so that you can make the most of opportunities to build up relevant experience. A good focus for such thoughts is your developing curriculum vitae, so it is useful to work on this from a very early stage.

Skills and personal qualities

Skills (sometimes called competences) are generally what you have learned to do and have improved with practice. Table 1.1 summarises some important skills for chemists. This list might seem quite daunting, but your tutors will have designed your courses to give you plenty of opportunities to develop your expertise. Personal qualities, on the other hand, are predominantly innate. Examples include honesty, determination and thoroughness (Table 7.1). These qualities need not remain static, however, and can be developed or changed according to your experiences. By consciously deciding to take on new challenges and responsibilities, not only can you develop your personal qualities, but you can also provide supporting evidence for your CV.

Personal qualities and skills are interrelated because your personal qualities can influence the skills you gain. For example, you may become highly proficient at a skill requiring manual dexterity if you are particularly adept with your hands. Being able to transfer your skills is highly important (Chapter 1) – many employers take a long-term view and look for evidence of the adaptability that will allow you to be a flexible employee and one who will continue to develop skills.

Developing your curriculum vitae

The initial stage involves making an audit of the skills and qualities you already have, and thinking about those you might need to

Table 7.1 Some positive personal qualities

Adaptability
Conscientiousness
Curiosity
Determination
Drive
Energy
Enthusiasm
Fitness and health
Flexible approach
Honesty
Innovation
Integrity
Leadership
Logical approach
Motivation
Patience
Performance under stress
Perseverance
Prudence
Quickness of thought
Seeing others' viewpoints
Self-confidence
Self-discipline
Sense of purpose
Shrewd judgement
Social skills (sociability)
Taking initiative
Tenacity
Tidiness
Thoroughness
Tolerance
Unemotional approach
Willingness to take on challenges

Setting your own agenda – you have the capability to widen your experience and to demonstrate relevant personal qualities through both curricular and extracurricular activities.

Paying attention to the quality of your CV – your potential employer will regard your CV as an example of your very best work and will not be impressed if it is full of mistakes or badly presented, especially if you claim 'good written communication' as a skill!

develop. Tables 7.1 and 1.1 could form a basis of this self-appraisal. Assessing your skills may be easier than critically analysing your personal characteristics. In judging your qualities, try to take a positive view and avoid being overly modest. It is important to think of your qualities in a specific context, e.g. 'I have shown that I am trustworthy, by acting as treasurer for the Chemical Society', as this evidence will form a vital part of your CV and job applications.

If you can identify gaps in your skills, or qualities that you would like to develop, especially in relation to the needs of your intended career, the next step is to think about ways of improving them. This will be reasonably easy in some cases, but may require some creative thinking in others. A relatively simple example would be if you decided to learn a new language or to keep up with one you learned at school. There are likely to be many local college and university courses dealing with foreign languages at many different levels, so it would be a straightforward matter to join one of these. A rather more difficult case might be if you wished to demonstrate 'responsibility', because there are no courses available on this. One route to demonstrate this quality might be to put yourself up for election as an officer in a student society or club; another could be to take a leading role in a relevant activity within your community (e.g. voluntary work such as hospital radio). If you already take part in activities like these, your CV should relate them to this context.

Basic CV structures and their presentation

Box 7.1 illustrates the typical parts of a CV and explains the purpose of each part. Employers are more likely to take notice of a well-organised and well-presented CV, in contrast to one that is difficult to read and assimilate. They will expect it to be concise, complete and accurate. There are many ways of presenting information in a CV, and you will be assessed partly on your choices.

- **Order**. There is some flexibility as to the order in which you can present the different parts (see Box 7.1). A chronological approach within sections helps employers gain a picture of your experience.

- **Personality and 'colour'**. Make your CV different by avoiding standard or dull phrasing. Try not to focus solely on academic aspects: you will probably work in a team, and the social aspects of teamwork will be enhanced by your outside interests. However, make sure that the reader does not get the impression that these interests dominate your life.

- **Style**. Your CV should reflect *your* personality, but not in such a way that it indicates too idiosyncratic an approach. It is probably better to be formal in both language and presentation, as flippant or chatty expressions will not be well received.

- **Neatness**. Producing a well-presented, word-processed CV is very important. Use a laser-quality printer and good-quality paper; avoid poor-quality photocopying at all costs.

- **Layout**. Use headings for different aspects, such as personal details, education, etc. Emphasise words (e.g. with capitals, bold, italics or underlining) sparingly and with the primary aim of making the structure clearer. Remember that careful use of white space is important in design.

There is no right or wrong way to write a CV, and no single format applies. It is probably best to avoid software templates and CV 'wizards' as they can create a bland, standardised result, rather than something that demonstrates your individuality.

You should include the following, with appropriate sub-headings, generally in the order given below:

1. **Personal details**. This section *must* include your full name and date of birth, your address (both home and semester-time, with dates, if appropriate) and a contact telephone number at each address (or your mobile telephone number). If you have an email account, you might also include this. You need only mention sex if your name could be either male or female.

2. **Education**. Choose either chronological order, or reverse chronological order and make sure you take the same approach in all other sections. Give educational institutions and dates (month, year) and provide more detail for your degree course than for your previous education. Remember to mention any prizes, scholarships or other academic achievements. Include your overall mark for the most recent year of your course, if it seems appropriate. Make sure you explain any gap years.

3. **Work experience**. Include all temporary, part-time, full-time or voluntary jobs. Details include dates, employer, job title and major duties involved.

4. **Skills and personal qualities**. Tables 1.1 and 7.1 give examples of the aspects you might include. Emphasise your strengths, and tailor this section to the specific requirements of the post (the 'job description'): for example, the practical skills you have gained during your degree studies if the post is a chemical one, but concentrate on generic transferable skills and personal qualities for other jobs. Provide supporting evidence for your statements in all cases.

5. **Interests and activities**. This is an opportunity to bring out the positive aspects of your personality, and explain their relevance to the post you are applying for. Aim to keep this section short, or it may seem that your social life is more important than your education and work experience. Include up to four separate items, and provide sufficient detail to highlight the *positive* aspects of your interests (e.g. positions of responsibility, working with others, communication, etc.). Use sections 4 and 5 to demonstrate that you have the necessary attributes to fulfil the major requirements of the post.

6. **Referees**. Include the names (and titles), job descriptions, full postal addresses, contact telephone numbers and email addresses of two referees (rarely, some employers may ask for three). It is usual to include your personal tutor or course leader at university (who among other things will verify your marks), plus another person – perhaps a current or former employer, or someone who runs a club or society and who knows your personal interests and activities. Unless you have kept in touch with a particular teacher since starting university, it is probably best to choose current contacts, rather than those from your previous education.

Some other points to consider:

●   Try to avoid jargon and over-complicated phrases in your CV: aim for direct, active words and phrases (see Box 16.1).

●   Most employers will expect your CV to be word-processed (and spell-checked). Errors in style, grammar and presentation will count against you, so be sure to check through your final version (and ask a reliable person to second-check it for you).

●   Aim for a *maximum* length of two pages, printed single-sided on A4 paper, using a 'formal' font (e.g. Times Roman or Arial) of no less than 12 point for the main text. Always print onto good quality white paper. Avoid fussy use of colour, borders or fonts.

●   Don't try to cram in too much detail. Use a clear and succinct approach with short sentences and lists to improve 'readability' and create structure. Remember that your aim is to catch the eye of your potential employer, who may have many applications to work through.

●   It is polite to check that people are willing to act as a referee for you and to provide them with an up-to-date copy of your CV.

Your single-page covering letter should have four major components:

1. **Letterhead**. Include your contact details, the recipient's name and title (if known) and address, plus any job reference number.

2. **Introductory paragraph**. Explain who you are and state the post you are applying for.

3. **Main message**. This is your opportunity to sell yourself to a potential employer, highlighting particular attributes and experience. Keep it to three or four sentences at the most and relate it to the particular skills and qualities demanded in the job or person specification.

4. **Concluding paragraph**. A brief statement that you look forward to hearing the outcome of your application is sufficient.

Finally, add either 'Yours sincerely' (where the recipient's name is known) or 'Yours faithfully' (in a letter beginning 'Dear Sir or Madam') and then end with your signature.

- **Grammar and proofreading**. Look at your CV carefully before you submit it, as sloppy errors give a very poor impression. Even if you use a spell-checker, some errors may creep in. Ask someone whom you regard as a reliable proofreader to comment on it (many tutors will do this, if asked in advance).

- **Relevance**. If you can, slant your CV towards the job description and the qualifications required (see below). Make sure you provide evidence to back up your assertions about skills, qualities and experience.

- **Accuracy and completeness**. Check that all your dates tally; otherwise, you will seem careless. It is better to be honest about your grades and (say) a period of unemployment, than to cover this up or omit details that an employer will want to know. They may be suspicious if you leave things out.

Creating a generic CV – as you may apply for several jobs, it is useful to construct a CV in electronic format (e.g. as a Word file) which includes all information of potential relevance. This can then be modified to fit each post. Having a prepared CV on file will reduce the work each time you apply, while modifying this will help you focus on relevant skills and attributes for the particular job.

Adjusting your CV

You should fine-tune your CV for each post. Employers frequently use a 'person specification' to define the skills and qualities demanded in a job, often under headings such as 'essential' and 'desirable'. This will help you decide whether to apply for a position and it assists the selection panel to filter the applicants. Highlight relevant qualifications as early in your CV as possible. Be selective – don't include every detail about yourself. Emphasise relevant parts and leave out irrelevant details, according to the job. Similarly, your letter of application is not merely a formal document but is also an opportunity for persuasion (Box 7.1). You can use it to state your ambitions and highlight particular qualifications and experience. However, don't go over the top – always keep the letter to a single page.

> **KEY POINT** A well-constructed and relevant CV won't necessarily guarantee you a job, but it may well get you onto the short list for interview. A poor-quality CV is a sure route to failure.

Sources for further study

Anon. (2000) *How to Write a Curriculum Vitae*. University of London Careers Service, London.

Anon. *Doctorjob.com Website*. Available: http://www.doctorjob.com.my/ Last accessed: 12/07/09.

Anon. *Graduate Prospects Website*. Available: http://www.prospects.ac.uk/cms/ShowPage/ Home_page/p!eLaXi

Last accessed: 12/07/09. [Higher Education Careers Services Unit, containing good examples of CVs]

Anon. *Applying for Jobs*. Available: http://admin.hero.ac.uk/sites/hero.uk/studying/careers_and_life long_learning/applying_for_ jobs285.cfm Last accessed: 12/07/09.

Study exercises

7.1 **Evaluate your personal attributes.** Using Table 7.1, list *five* qualities that you would use to best describe yourself, and cite the evidence you might give to a potential employer to convince them that this was the case. List *five* attributes you could develop, then indicate how you might do this.

7.2 **Create a generic CV.** Drawing on your school record of achievement, or any CV already prepared, e.g. for a part-time job, create a word-processed generic CV. Save the file in an appropriate (computer) folder and make a back-up copy. Print out a copy for filing. Periodically update the word-processed version. If appropriate, save different versions to be used in different contexts (e.g. when applying for a vacation job).

7.3 **Think about your future career and ask for advice.** Make an appointment with one of the advisers in your university's careers service. Ask about career options for graduates with your intended degree, or determine what qualifications or module options might be appropriate for occupations that interest you.

Information technology and library resources

Browsing in a library – this may turn up interesting material, but remember the books on the shelves are those not currently out on loan. Almost by definition, the latter may be more up-to-date and useful. To find out a library's full holding of books in any subject area, you need to search its catalogue (normally available as an online database).

Example The book *Inorganic Chemistry*, 3rd edn, by C. Housecroft and A. Sharpe (2007; Prentice Hall) is likely to be classified as follows:

Dewey Decimal system:

where 500	refers to natural sciences and mathematics
540	refers to chemistry
546	refers to inorganic chemistry

Library of Congress system:

where Q	refers to science
QD	refers to chemistry
QD 146–197	refer to inorganic chemistry

The ability to find scientific information is a skill required for many exercises in your degree programme. You will need to research facts and published findings as part of writing essays, literature reviews and project introductions, and when amplifying your lecture notes (p. 17) and revising for exams (p. 27). You must also learn how to follow scientific convention in citing source material as the authority for the statements you have made.

Sources of information

For essays and revision

You are unlikely to delve into the primary literature (p. 48) for these purposes – books and reviews are much more readable. If a lecturer or tutor specifies a particular book, then it should not be difficult to find out where it is shelved in your library, using the computerised index system. Library staff will generally be happy to assist with any queries. If you want to find out which books your library holds on a specified topic, use the system's subject index. You will also be able to search by author or by key words.

There are two main systems used by libraries to classify books: the Dewey Decimal system and the Library of Congress system. Libraries differ in the way they employ these systems, especially by adding further numbers and letters after the standard classification marks, e.g. to signify shelving position or edition number. Enquire at your library for a full explanation of local usage.

The World Wide Web is an ever-expanding resource for gathering both general and specific information (see Chapters 10 and 11). Sites fall into analogous categories to those in the printed literature: there are sites with original information, sites that review information and bibliographic sites. One considerable problem is that websites may be frequently updated, so information present when you first looked may be altered or even absent when the site is next consulted. Further, very little of the information on the web has been monitored or refereed. Another disadvantage is that the site information may not state the origin of the material, who wrote it or when it was written. This is considered in more detail in Box 10.5.

Examples of book classification

	Dewey	Library of Congress
Chemistry	540	QD1-999
Analytical Chemistry	543	QD71-145
Chromatography	543.544	QD117.C5; QD79.C4
Crystallography	548	QD901-999
Electrochemistry	541.13	QD551-571; QD261, TP250-261
Inorganic Chemistry	546	QD146-197
Organic Chemistry	547	QD241-449
Physical Chemistry	541.1	QD450-731
Radiochemistry	541.28	QD601-655
Spectroscopy	543.42	QD95-96; QC450-467; QD272.56
Surface Chemistry	541.18	QD506-508
Synthesis (organic)	547.07	QD262

Finding and citing published information

Web resources – your university library will provide you with access to a range of web-based databases and information systems. The library web pages will list these and provide links, which may be worth bookmarking on your web browser. Resources especially useful to chemists include:

- ISI Web of Knowledge, *including the Science Citation Index*
- IngentaConnect *(previously known as BIDS), including* Ingenta Medline
- CSA Illumina
- Dialog
- PubMed
- ScienceDirect
- Scopus
- Ovid, *including* Cinahl *and* Medline

Most of these electronic resources operate on a subscription basis and may require an 'Athens' username and password – for details of how to obtain these consult library staff or your library's website.

Definitions

Journal/periodical/serial – any publication issued at regular intervals. In chemistry, usually containing papers (articles) describing original research findings and reviews of literature.

eJournal – a journal published online, consisting of articles structured in the same way as a paper-based journal. A valid username and password may be required for access (arranged via your library, if it subscribes to the eJournal).

The primary literature – this comprises original research papers, published in specialist scientific periodicals. Certain prestigious general journals (e.g. *Nature*) contain important new advances from a wide subject area.

Monograph – a specialised book covering a single topic.

ebook – a book published online in downloadable form.

ebrary – a commercial service offering ebooks and other online resources.

For literature surveys and project work

You will probably need to consult the primary literature. If you are starting a new research project or writing a report from scratch, you can build up a core of relevant papers by using the following methods:

- Asking around: supervisors or their postgraduate students will almost certainly be able to supply you with a reference or two that will start you off.

- Searching an online database, either via the Internet (see Chapter 10) or on CD-ROM: these cover very wide areas and are a convenient way to start a reference collection, although a charge is often made for access and sending out a listing of the papers selected (your library may or may not pass this on to you).

- Consulting the bibliography of other papers in your collection – an important way of finding the key papers in your field. In effect, you are taking advantage of the fact that another researcher has already done all the hard work.

- Referring to 'current awareness' online databases: these are useful for keeping you up to date with current research; they usually provide a monthly listing of article details (title, authors, source, author address) arranged by subject and cross-referenced by subject and author. Current awareness databases cover a wider range of primary literature than could ever be available in any one library. Examples include: *Current Contents Connect* (ISI), the *Current Advances* series (Elsevier), *Chemical Abstracts* and *Analytical Abstracts* (Thompson Scientific). Some online databases also offer a service whereby they will email registered users with updates based on saved search criteria. Consult library staff or your library website to see which of these databases and services are available to you.

- Using the *Science Citation Index* (SCI): this is a valuable means of exploring the published literature in a given field, because it lets you see who has cited a given paper; in effect, SCI allows you to move forward through the literature from an existing reference. The Index is available online *via* ISI *Web of Science*.

For specialised information

You may need to consult reference works, such as encyclopaedias and books providing specialised information. Some of this is now available on the Web, or online (consult your library's information service web pages). Three sources worth noting are:

- The *Handbook of Chemistry and Physics* (Haynes, 2010; online via CHEMnetBASE): the Chemical Rubber Company's publication (affectionately known as the 'Rubber Bible') giving all manner of physical constants, radioisotope half-lives, etc.

- *The Merck Index* (O'Neil *et al.*, 2006), which gives useful information about organic chemicals, e.g. solubility, whether poisonous, etc., now also available online.

Alternative methods of receiving information – RSS (really simple syndication) feeds and email updates from publishers are increasingly used to provide automated information services to academic clients – for example, by supplying links to relevant contents of new editions of online journals.

Copyright law – In Europe, copyright regulations were harmonised in 1993 (Directive 93/98/EEC) to allow literary copyright for 70 years after the death of an author and typographical copyright for 25 years after publication. This was implemented in the UK in 1996, where, in addition, the Copyright, Designs and Patents Act (1988) allows the Copyright Licensing Agency to license institutions so that lecturers, students and researchers may take copies for teaching and personal research purposes – no more than a single article per journal issue, one chapter of a book, or extracts to a total of 5% of a book.

Obtaining and organising research papers

Obtaining a copy

It is usually more convenient to have personal copies of key research articles for direct consultation when working in a laboratory or writing. The simplest way of obtaining these is to photocopy the originals or download and/or print off copies online (e.g. as '.pdf' files). For academic purposes, this is normally acceptable within copyright law. If your library does not subscribe to the journal, it may be possible for them to borrow it from a nearby institute or obtain a copy via a national borrowing centre (an 'inter-library loan'). If the latter, you will have to fill in a form giving full bibliographic details of the paper and where it was cited, as well as signing a copyright clearance statement concerning your use of the copy. Alternatively, you might try emailing the communicating author and requesting an electronic copy ('.pdf' file) of the article.

Organising papers

Although the number of papers you accumulate may be small to start with, it is worth putting some thought into their storage and indexing before your collection becomes disorganised and unmanageable. Few things are more frustrating than not being able to lay your hands on a vital piece of information, and this can seriously disrupt your flow when writing or revising.

Indexing your references

Whether you have obtained a printed copy, have stored downloaded files electronically, or have simply noted the bibliographic details of a reference, you will need to index each resource. This is valuable for the following reasons:

- You will probably need the bibliographic information for creating a reference list for an assignment or report.

- If the index also has database features, this can be useful, allowing you to search for key words or authors.

- If you include an 'accession number' and if you then file printed material sequentially according to this number, then it will help you to find the hard copy.

- Depending on the indexing system used, you can add comments about the reference that may be useful at a later time, e.g. when writing an introduction or conclusion.

The simplest way to create an index system is to put the details on reference cards, but database software can be more convenient and faster to sort, once the bibliographic information has been entered. If you do not feel that commercial software is appropriate for your needs, consider using a word-processor or spreadsheet; their rudimentary database sorting functions (see Chapters 12 and 13) may be all that you require.

If you are likely to store lots of references and other electronic resources digitally, then you should consider carefully how this information is kept, for example by choosing file names that indicate what the file contains and that will facilitate sorting.

Making citations in text

There are two main ways of citing articles and creating a bibliography (also referred to as 'references' or 'literature cited').

The Harvard system

For each citation, the author name(s) and the date of publication are given at the relevant point in the text. The bibliography is organised alphabetically, and by date of publication for papers with the same authors. Formats normally adopted are, for example, 'Smith and Jones (1983) stated that …' or 'it has been shown that … (Smith and Jones, 1983)'. Lists of references within parentheses are separated by semi-colons, e.g. '(Smith and Jones, 1983; Jones and Smith, 1985)', normally in order of date of publication. To avoid repetition within the same paragraph, an approach such as 'the investigations of Smith and Jones indicated that' could be used following an initial citation of the paper. Where there are more than two authors it is usual to write 'et al.' (or *et al.* if an italic font is available); this stands for the Latin *et alia* meaning 'and others'. If citing more than one paper with the same authors, put, for example, 'Smith and Jones (1987; 1990)' and if papers by a given set of authors appeared in the same year, letter them (e.g. Smith and Jones, 1989a; 1989b).

The 'Katritzky' system

A third system has been popularized in publications involving Professor Roy Katritzky (University of Florida, USA) and uses the best features of both the Harvard and Vancouver systems. For each reference in the text a code is written comprising the year of publication, the journal and the page of the journal. In the reference section the coded references are cited, together with the full reference – authors, journal, year, volume and page – *in year order* and a list of journal codes in alphabetical order can be provided. For example:

in the text

    … Robinson and Watt (34JCS1536) found …

in the reference section

  34JCS1536 R. Robinson and S.J. Watt, *J. Chem. Soc.*, 1934, 1536.

The advantage of this system is that it is easy to insert missed references into the text, a great disadvantage of the otherwise neat Vancouver system. For details consult the reference section in *Comprehensive Heterocyclic Chemistry*, ed. A.R. Katritzky and C.W. Rees, Pergamon, Oxford, 1984.

The numerical or Vancouver system

Papers are cited via a superscript or bracketed reference number inserted at the appropriate point. Normal format would be, for example: 'computational chemistry[4,5] has shown that …' or 'Jones [55, 82] has claimed that …'. Repeated citations use the number from the first citation. In the true numerical method (e.g. as in *Nature, Science*), numbers are allocated by order of citation in the text. This is by far the most common approach in chemistry journals. Note that with this latter

Examples – Incorporating references in text – this sample shows how you might embed citations in text using the Vancouver approach:

'...Smith *et al.* reported the separation of PAHs using GC.[1] However, others used RPHPLC.[2–3] In addition, Black[3,4] concluded that a mobile phase of methanol : water (50:50, v/v) could separate PAHs effectively....'

Examples

Paper in journal:

Smith, A.B., Jones, C.D. and Professor, A. (2000). *Journal of New Results,* **11**, 19–25.

Book:

Smith, A.B. (2005). *Summary of my Life's Work.* Megadosh Publishing Corp., Bigcity. ISBN 0-123-45678-9.

Chapter in edited book:

Jones, C.D. and Smith, A.B. (2003). Earth-shattering research from our laboratory. In: *Research Compendium 1998* (ed. A. Professor), pp. 123–456. Bigbucks Press, Booktown.

Thesis:

Smith, A.B. (2006). *Investigations on my Favourite Topic.* PhD thesis, University of Life, Fulchester.

Note: if your references are handwritten, you should indicate italics by underlining text or numerals.

Finding dates on websites quickly – when visiting a particular page, you can find occurrences of year dates beginning '200' by pressing the *Control* and *F* keys together, entering 200 in the *Find* window that appears, then carrying out a search using the *Find next* command.

method, adding or removing references is tedious, so the numbering should be done only when the text has been finalised.

> **KEY POINT** The main advantages of the Harvard system are that the reader might recognise the paper being referred to and that it is easily expanded if extra references are added. The main advantages of the Vancouver system are that it aids text flow and reduces length.

How to list your citations in a bibliography

Whichever citation method is used in the text, comprehensive details are required for the bibliography so that the reader has enough information to find the reference easily. Citations should be listed in alphabetical order with the priority: first author, subsequent author(s), date. Unfortunately, in terms of punctuation and layout, there are almost as many ways of citing papers as there are journals. Your department may specify an exact format for project work; if not, decide on a style and be consistent – if you do not pay attention to the details of citation you may lose marks. Take special care with the following aspects:

- **Authors and editors:** give details of *all* authors and editors in your bibliography, even if given as *et al.* in the text.

- **Abbreviations for journals:** while there are standard abbreviations for the titles of journals (consult library staff), it is a good idea to give the whole title, if possible.

- **Books:** the edition should always be specified as contents may change between editions. Add, for example, '(5th edition)' after the title of the book. You may be asked to give the International Standard Book Number (ISBN), a unique reference number for each book published.

- **Unsigned articles:** e.g. unattributed newspaper articles and instruction manuals – refer to the author(s) in text and bibliography as 'Anon.'.

- **Websites:** there is no widely accepted format at present. You should follow departmental guidelines if these are provided, but if these are not available, we suggest providing author name(s) and date in the text when using the Harvard system (e.g. Hacker, 2006), while in the bibliography giving the URL details in the following format: Hacker, A. (2006) *University of Anytown Homepage on Aardvarks.* Available: http://www.myserver.ac.uk/homepage. Last accessed: 14/07/09. In this example, the webpage was constructed in 2006, but accessed in July, 2009. If no author is identifiable, cite the sponsoring body (e.g. University of Anytown, 2006), and if there is no author or sponsoring body, write 'Anon.' for 'anonymous', e.g. Anon. (2006), and use Anon. as the 'author' in the bibliography. If the web pages are undated, *either* use the 'last accessed' date for citation and put no date after the author name(s) in the reference list, *or* cite as 'no date' (e.g. Hacker, no date) and leave out a date after the author name(s) in the reference list – you should be consistent whichever option you choose.

Adding web references in other systems – if you are using a different referencing system than Harvard, consult Pears and Shields (2005) or McMillan and Weyers (2006) for further advice on how to cite websites in these systems.

- **Unread articles:** you may be forced to refer to a paper *via* another without having seen it. If possible, refer to another authority who has cited the paper, e.g. '... Jones (1980), cited in Smith (1990), claimed that ...'. Alternatively, you could denote such references in the bibliography by an asterisk and add a short note to explain at the start of the reference list.

- **Personal communications:** information received in a letter, seminar or conversation can be referred to in the text as, for example, '... (Smith, pers. comm.)'. These citations are not generally listed in the bibliography of papers, though in a thesis you could give a list of personal communicants and their addresses.

- **Online material:** some papers and articles are published solely online and others are available online ahead of publication in printed form. The item may be given a digital object identifier (DOI), allowing it to be cited and potentially tracked before and after it is allocated to a printed issue (see http://www.doi.org/). DOIs also allow for web page redirection by a central agency, and *CrossRef* (http://www.crossref.org/) is the official DOI registration organisation for scholarly and professional publications. DOIs can be used as 'live' hyperlinks in online articles, or cited in place of the volume and page numbers for the article, with the remainder of the details cited in the usual fashion, e.g. 'Smith, A. and Jones, B. (2009) Our latest important research in the form of a web-published article. *Online Chemistry* 8/2008 (p. 781). Published Online: 26 March 2009. DOI: 10.1083/mabi.200680019'.

Text references and sources for further study

Anon. *CHEMnetBASE*. Available:
http://www.chemnetbase.com
Last accessed: 12/07/09.
[Access to the *Handbook of Chemistry and Physics*]

Anon. *ISI Web of Knowledge*. Available:
http://wok.mimas.ac.uk
Last accessed: 12/07/09.
[Requires Athens password]

Haynes, W.M. (ed.) (2010) *CRC Handbook of Chemistry and Physics*, 91st edn. CRC Press, Boca Raton.

McMillan, K.M. and Weyers, J.D.B. (2006) *The Smarter Student: Skills and Strategies for Success at University*. Pearson Education, Harlow.

O'Neil, M.J., Heckelman, P.E., Koch, C.B. and Roman, K.J. (2006) *Merck Index: An Encyclopedia of Chemicals, Drugs, and Biologicals*, 14th edn. Merck & Co. Inc., Whitehouse Station.

Pears, R. and Shields, G. (2005) *Cite them Right: the Essential Guide to Referencing and Plagiarism*. Pear Tree Books, Newcastle upon Tyne.

Ridley, D.D. (2009) *Information Retrieval – Scifinder*, 2nd edn. Wiley, Chichester.

Study exercises

8.1 Test your library skills. This exercise relies on the fact that most university-level libraries serving science departments will take the scientific journal *Nature*. To help you answer these questions, it may be beneficial to attend a library induction session, if you haven't already. Alternatively, the library's help or enquiry desks may be able to assist you if you are having problems.

(a) First, find out and provide the name of the classification system that your University uses for cataloguing its books and periodicals.

(b) Using your library's cataloguing system (online, preferably) find out the appropriate local classification number for the journal *Nature*.

(c) Where is *Nature* shelved in your library? (Your answer need refer only to most recent issues if some have been archived.)

(d) What is the exact title of the landmark papers in the following two volumes? (i) *Nature* **171**, 737–738 (1953); (ii) *Nature* **318**, 162–163 (1985).

8.2 Explore different methods of citing references. Go to your library and seek out the journal area for chemistry. Choose *three* different journals in your subject area and from a recent edition write down how they would print a typical citation for a multi-author journal paper in the 'references' or 'literature cited' section. Where used, indicate italicised text with normal underline and bold text with wavy underline. Pay attention to punctuation.

Compare these methods with each other, with the methods recommended on p. 50 of this book and with the recommendations your department or your course handbook makes. Are they all the same?

8.3 Make website citations. Use a search engine (p. 67) to find an informative website that covers each of the following:

(a) The use of SI units.

(b) Description of a Diels–Alder reaction.

(c) Melting point determination.

Indicate how you would cite each website at the end of an essay (follow your department's guidelines or use those in this chapter).

8.4 Compare the Harvard and Vancouver methods of citation. Pair up with a partner in your class. Each person should then pick one of the two main methods of citation and consider its pros and cons independently. Meet together and compare your lists. Given the choice, which method would you choose for (a) a handwritten essay; (b) a word-processed review; (c) an article in an academic journal, and why?

Example A web search for the letters 'PAH' (e.g. using the search engine Google, p. 68), will reveal that this acronym appears in several million websites. Not all of these deal with polycyclic aromatic hydrocarbon – the listed websites include: The Princess Alexandra Hospital, an NHS hospital; The Princess Alice Hospice, in Esher, Surrey; and a healthcare professionals site for Pulmonary Arterial Hypertension. These examples are easy to identify as irrelevant to research on 'PAH, the group of molecules', but considering the many websites that do actually cover this topic, which might contain the exact information you seek? How valid is the information? Is it biased towards one viewpoint or hypothesis? Does it represent current mainstream thinking on the topic? These are some of the issues that an evaluation of the information sources might deal with.

Definition

Plagiarism – the unacknowledged use of another's work as if it were one's own. In this definition, the concept of 'work' includes ideas, writing, data or inventions and not simply words; and the notion of 'use' does not only mean copy 'word-for-word', but also 'in substance' (i.e. a copy of the ideas involved). Use of another's work is acceptable, if you acknowledge the source (Box 9.1).

Checking the reliability of information, assessing the relative value of different ideas and thinking critically are skills essential to the scientific approach (p. 220). You will need to develop your abilities to evaluate information in this way because:

- you will be faced with many sources of information, from which you will need to select the most appropriate material;
- you may come across conflicting sources of evidence and may have to decide which is the more reliable;
- the accuracy and validity of a specific fact may be vital to your work;
- you may doubt the quality of the information from a particular source;
- you may wish to check the original source because you are not sure whether someone else is quoting it correctly.

KEY POINT Evaluating information and thinking critically are regarded as higher order academic skills. The ability to think deeply in this way is greatly valued in chemistry and will consequently be assessed in coursework and exam questions (see Chapter 6).

The process of evaluating and using information can be broken down into four stages:

1. **Selecting and obtaining material.** How to find sources is covered in Chapter 8. Printed books and journals are important, but if you identify a source of this kind there may be delays in borrowing it or obtaining a photocopy. If the book or journal is available online, then downloading or printing sections or papers will be more convenient and faster. The Internet is often a first port of call if you wish to find something out quickly. However, for many websites, it can be difficult to verify the authenticity of the information given (see Box 10.5).

2. **Assessing the content.** You will need to understand fully what has been written, including any technical terms and jargon used. Establish the relevance of the information to your needs and assure yourself that the data or conclusions have been presented in an unbiased way.

3. **Modifying the information.** In order to use the information, you may need to alter it to suit your needs. This may require you to make comparisons, interpret or summarise. Some sources may require translation. Some data may require mathematical transformation before they are useful. There is a chance of error in any of these processes and also a risk of plagiarism (see Box 9.1).

4. **Analysis.** This may be your own interpretation of the information presented, or an examination of the way the original author has used the information.

Box 9.1   How to avoid plagiarism and copyright infringement

Plagiarism is defined on page 54. Examples of plagiarism include:

- Copying the work of a fellow student (past or present) and passing it off as your own.

- Using 'essay-writing services', such as those on offer on certain websites.

- Copying text or images from a source (book, journal article or website, for instance) and using this within your own work without acknowledgement.

- Quoting others' words without indicating who wrote or said them.

- Copying ideas and concepts from a source without acknowledgement, even if you paraphrase them.

Most students would accept that some of the above can only be described as cheating. However, many students, especially at the start of their studies, are unaware of the academic rule that they must *always* acknowledge the originators of information, ideas and concepts, and that not doing so is regarded as a form of academic dishonesty. If you adopt the appropriate conventions that avoid such accusations, you will achieve higher marks for your work as it will fulfil the marker's expectations for academic writing.

Universities have a range of mechanisms for identifying plagiarism, from employing experienced and vigilant coursework markers and external examiners to analysing students' work using sophisticated software programs. Plagiarism is always punished severely when detected. Penalties may include awarding a mark of zero to all involved – both the copier(s) and the person whose work has been copied (who is regarded as complicit in the crime). Further disciplinary measures may be taken in some instances. In severe cases, such as copying substantive parts of another's work within a thesis, a student may be dismissed from the university.

If you wish to avoid being accused of plagiarism, the remedies are relatively simple:

1. **Make sure the work you present is always your own.** If you have been studying alongside a colleague, or have been discussing how to tackle a particular problem with your peers, make sure you write on your own when working on your assignments.

2. **Never, ever be tempted to 'cut and paste'** from websites or online sources such as word-processed handouts. Read these carefully, decide what the important points are, express these *in your own words* and *provide literature citations to the original sources* (see Chapter 8). In some cases, further investigations may be required to find out details of the original sources. The lecturer's reading list or a book's references may help you here.

3. **Take care when note-taking.** If you decide to quote word for word, make sure you show this clearly in your notes with quotation marks. If you decide to make your own notes based on a source, make sure these are original and do not copy phrases from the text. In both cases, write down full details of the source at the appropriate point in your notes.

4. **Place appropriate citations throughout your text, where required.** If you are unsure about when to do this, study reviews and articles in your subject area (see also Chapter 8).

5. **Show clearly where you are quoting directly from a source.** For short quotes, this may involve using quotation marks and identifying the source afterwards, as in the example '... as Samuel Butler (1877) wrote: ''a hen is only an egg's way of making another egg'' '. For longer quotes (say 40 words or more), you should create a separate paragraph of quoted text, usually identified by inverted commas, indentation, italicisation or a combination of these. A citation must *always* be included, normally at the end. Your course handbook may specify a layout. Try not to rely too much on quotes in your work. If a large proportion of your work is made up from quotes, this will almost certainly be regarded as lacking in originality, scoring a poor mark.

Copyright issues are often associated with plagiarism, and refer to the right to publish (and hence copy) original material, such as text, images and music. Copyright material is indicated by a symbol © and a date (see, for example, page iv of this book). Literary copyright is the aspect most relevant to students in their academic studies. UK Copyright Law protects authors' rights for life and gives their estates rights for a further 70 years. Publishers have 'typographical copyright' that lasts for 25 years. This means that it is illegal to photocopy, scan or print out copyright material unless you have permission, or unless your copying is limited to an extent that could be considered 'fair dealing'. For educational purposes – private study or research – in a scientific context, this generally means:

- no more than 5% in total of a work;

- one chapter of a book;

- one article per volume of an academic journal;

- 20% of a short book;

- one separate illustration or map.

You may only take one copy within the above limits, may not copy for others, and may not exceed these amounts *even if you own a copy of the original*. These rules also apply to web-based materials, but sometimes you will find sites where the copyright is waived. Some copying may be licensed; you should consult your library's website or helpdesk to see whether it has access to licensed material. Up-to-date copyright information is generally posted close to library and departmental photocopiers.

KEY POINT Advances in communications and information technology mean that we can now access almost limitless knowledge. Consequently, the ability to *evaluate* information has become an extremely important skill.

Evaluating sources of information

One way of assessing the reliability of a piece of scientific information is to think about how it was obtained in the first place. Essentially, facts and ideas originate from someone's research or scholarship, whether they are numerical data, descriptions, concepts or interpretations. Sources are divided into two main types:

Distinguishing between primary and secondary sources – try the 'IMRaD test'. Many primary sources contain information in the order: Introduction, Materials and Methods, Results and Discussion. If you see this format, and particularly if data from an experiment, study or observation are presented, then you are probably reading a primary source.

1. **Primary sources** – those in which ideas and data are first communicated. The primary literature is generally published in the form of 'papers' (articles) in journals, whether printed or online. These are usually refereed by experts in the academic peer group of the author, and they will check the accuracy and originality of the work and report their opinions back to the editors of the journal. This peer review system helps to maintain reliability, but it is not perfect. Books and, more rarely, websites and articles in magazines and newspapers, can also be primary sources but this depends on the nature of the information published rather than the medium. These sources are not formally refereed, although they may be read by editors and lawyers, to check for errors and unsubstantiated or libellous allegations.

Example If a journalist wrote an article about a new 'cancer drug treatment' for the *New York Times* that was based on an article in the *British Medical Journal*, the *New York Times* article would be the secondary source, while the *British Medical Journal* article would be the primary source.

2. **Secondary sources** – those which quote, adapt, interpret, translate, develop or otherwise use information drawn from primary sources. It is the act of quoting or paraphrasing that makes the source secondary, rather than the medium. Reviews are examples of secondary scientific sources, and books and magazine articles are often of this type.

When information is modified for use in a secondary source, alterations are likely to occur, whether intentional or unintentional. Most authors do not deliberately set out to change the meaning of the primary source, but they may unwittingly do so, e.g. in changing text to avoid plagiarism or by oversimplification. Others may consciously or unconsciously exert bias in their reporting, for example, by quoting evidence that supports only one side of a debate. Therefore, the closer you can get to the primary source, the more reliable the information is likely to be. On the other hand, modification while creating a secondary source could involve correcting errors, or synthesising ideas and content from multiple sources.

Taking account of the changing nature of websites and wikis – by their very nature, these sources may change. This means that it is important to quote accurately from them and to give a 'last accessed' date when citing (see p. 51).

Authorship and provenance

Clearly, much depends on who is writing the source and on what basis (e.g. who paid them?). Consequently, an important way of assessing sources is to investigate the ownership and provenance of the work (who and where it originated from, and why).

Can you identify who wrote the information? If it is signed or there is a 'by-line' showing who wrote it, you might be able to make a judgement on the quality of what you are reading. This may be a simple

Finding out about authors and provenance – these pieces of information are easy to find in most printed sources and may even be presented just below the title, for convenience. In the case of the Web, it may not be so easy to find what you want. Relevant clues can be obtained from 'home page' links and the header, body and footer information. For example, the domain (p. 66) may be useful, while the use of the tilde symbol (~) in a URL usually indicates a personal, rather than an institutional, website.

Assessing substance over presentation – just because the information is presented well (e.g. in a glossy magazine or a particularly well-constructed website), this does not necessarily tell you much about its quality. Try to look below the surface, using the methods mentioned in this chapter.

decision, if you know or can assume that the writer is an authority in the area; otherwise a little research might help (for example, by putting the name into a web search engine). Of course, just because Professor X thinks something does not make it true. However, if you know that this opinion is backed up by years of research and experience, then you might take it a little more seriously than the thoughts of a school pupil. If an author is not cited, effectively nobody is taking responsibility for the content. Could there be a reason for this?

Is the author's place of work cited? This might tell you whether the facts or opinions given are based on an academic study. Is there a company with a vested interest behind the content? If the author works for a public body, there may be publication rules to follow and they may even have to submit their work to a publications committee before it is disseminated. They are certainly more likely to get into trouble if they include controversial material.

Evaluating facts and ideas

However reliable the source of a piece of information seems to be, it is probably a good idea to retain a slight degree of scepticism about the facts or ideas involved. Even information from impeccable primary sources may not be perfect – different approaches can give different outcomes, and interpretations can change with time and with further advances in knowledge. Table 9.1 provides a checklist for evaluating sources.

Table 9.1 Checklist for assessing information in science. How reliable is the information you have been reading? The more 'yes' answers you can give below, the more trustworthy you can assume it to be

Assessing sources

- ❏ Can you identify the author's name?
- ❏ Can you determine what relevant qualifications he/she holds?
- ❏ Can you say who employs the author?
- ❏ Do you know who paid for the work to be done?
- ❏ Is this a primary or secondary source?
- ❏ Is the content original or derived from another source?

Evaluating information

- ❏ Have you checked a range of sources?
- ❏ Is the information supported by relevant literature citation?
- ❏ Is the age of the source likely to be important regarding the accuracy of the information?
- ❏ Have you focused on the substance of the information presented rather than its packaging?
- ❏ Is the information fact or opinion?
- ❏ Have you checked for any logical fallacies in the arguments?
- ❏ Does the language used indicate anything about the status of the information?
- ❏ Have the errors associated with any numbers been taken into account?
- ❏ Have the data been analysed using appropriate statistics?
- ❏ Are any graphs constructed fairly?

Critically examining facts and ideas is a complex task depending on the particular issues involved, and a number of different general approaches can be applied. You will need to decide which of the following general tips are useful in your specific case:

- **Make cross-referencing checks** – look at more than one source and compare what is said in each. The cross-referenced sources should be as independent as possible (for example, do not compare a primary source together with a secondary review based on it). If you find that all the sources give a similar picture, then you can be more confident about the reliability of the information.

- **Look at the extent and quality of citations** (Chapter 8) – if references are quoted, these indicate that a certain amount of research has been carried out beforehand, and that the ideas or results are based on genuine scholarship. If you are doubtful about the quality of the work, these references might be worth looking at. How up to date are they? Do they cite independent work, or is the author exclusively quoting their own work, or solely the work of one person?

- **Consider the age of the source** – the fact that a source is old is not necessarily a barrier to truth, but ideas and facts may have altered since the date of publication, and methods may have improved. Can you trace changes through time in the sources available to you? What key events or publications have forced any changes in the conclusions?

- **Try to distinguish fact from opinion** – to what extent has the author supported a given viewpoint? Have relevant facts been quoted, *via* literature citations or the author's own researches? Are numerical data used to substantiate the points used? Are these reliable and can you verify the information, for example, by looking at the sources cited? Might the author have a reason for putting forward biased evidence to support a personal opinion?

- **Analyse the language used** – words and their use can be very revealing. Subjective wording might indicate a personal opinion rather than an objective conclusion. Propaganda and personal bias might be indicated by absolute terms, such as 'everyone knows . . .'; 'It can be guaranteed that ...' or, a seemingly one-sided consideration of the evidence. How carefully has the author considered the topic? A less studious approach might be indicated by exaggeration, ambiguity or the use of 'journalese' and slang. Always remember, however, that content should be judged above presentation.

- **Look closely at any numbers** – if the information you are looking at is numerical in form, have statistical errors been taken into consideration, and, where appropriate, quantified? If so, does this help you arrive at a conclusion about how genuine the differences are between important values?

- **Think carefully about any hypothesis-testing statistics used** – are the methods appropriate? Are the underlying hypotheses the right ones? Have the results of any tests been interpreted correctly in arriving at the conclusion? To deal with these matters, you will need at least a basic understanding of the 'statistical approach' and of commonly used techniques (see Chapters 63–64).

Learning from examples – as your lecturers introduce you to case studies, you will see how chemists have applied critical thinking to understand reaction mechanisms, molecules and elements. Some of your laboratory sessions may mimic the processes involved – observation, hypothesis, experimental design, data gathering, analysis and formulating a conclusion (see Chapter 29). These skills and approaches can be applied in your degree programme, e.g. when writing about a chemical issue or carrying out a research project.

'You can prove anything with statistics' – leaving aside the issue that statistical methods deal with probability, not certainty (Chapter 64), it is often possible to analyse and present data in such a way that they support one chosen argument or hypothesis rather than another. Detecting a bias of this kind can be difficult, but the critical thinking skills involved are essential for all chemists (see e.g. Box 60.3).

Critical thinking

Critical thinking involves the application of logic to a problem, or case study issue. It requires a wide range of skills. Key processes involved include: acquiring and processing information; creating appropriate hypotheses and formulating conclusions; and acting on the conclusions towards a specific objective.

> KEY POINT Critical thinking needs reliable knowledge, but it requires you to use this appropriately to analyse a problem. It can be contrasted with rote learning – where you might memorise facts without an explicit purpose other than building your knowledge base.

Critical thinking is particularly important in chemistry, because the subject deals with complex and dynamic systems. These can be difficult to understand for several reasons:

- they are often multi-faceted, involving many interactions;
- it can be difficult to alter one variable in an experiment without producing confounding variables (see p. 222);
- many variables may be unmeasured or unmeasurable;
- heterogeneity (variability) is encountered at all scales from the elemental scale to the whole molecule;
- perturbation of the system, e.g. chemical reaction, can lead to unexpected ('counter-intuitive') results.

As a result, conclusions in chemical research are sometimes not clear-cut. Critical thinking allows you to arrive at the most probable conclusion from the results at hand; however, it also involves acknowledging that other conclusions might be possible. It allows you to weigh up these possibilities and find a working hypothesis or explanation, but also to understand that your conclusions are essentially dynamic and might alter when new facts are known. Hypothesis-testing with statistics (Chapter 64) is an important adjunct to critical thinking because it demands the formulation of simple hypotheses and provides rational reasons for making conclusions.

Recognising fallacies in arguments is an important aspect of critical thinking. Philosophers and logicians recognise different forms of argument and many different fallacies in each form. Damer (2004) provides an overview of this wide-ranging and complex topic.

Interpreting data

Numerical data

Information presented in public, whether as a written publication or a spoken presentation, is rarely in the same form as it was when first obtained. Chapters 27, 46–47 deal with processes in which data are recorded and manipulated – take particular care over percentages and proportions (p. 492), while Chapter 63 describes the standard descriptive statistics used to 'encapsulate' large data sets. Chapter 62 covers some relevant mathematical techniques. Sampling (essentially, obtaining

Analysing a graph – this process can be split into six phases:

1. *Considering the context and purpose of the graph.*

2. *Recognising the type of presentation and examining the axes.*

3. *Looking closely at the scale on each axis.*

4. *Examining the data presented (e.g. data points, symbols, curves).*

5. *Considering errors and statistics associated with the graph.*

6. *Reaching conclusions based on the above.*

These processes are amplified in Chapter 60.

representative measurements) is at the heart of many observational and experimental approaches in chemistry (see Chapters 27 and 29), and analysis of samples is a key component of hypothesis-testing statistics (Chapter 64). Understanding these topics and carrying out the associated study exercises will help you improve your ability to interpret numerical data.

Graphs

Frequently, understanding and analysis in science depend on your ability to interpret data presented in graphical form. Sometimes, graphs may mislead. This may be unwitting, as in an unconscious effort to favour a 'pet' hypothesis of the author. Graphs may be used to 'sell' a product, e.g. in advertising, or to favour a viewpoint as, perhaps, in politics. Experience in drawing and interpreting graphs will help you spot these flawed presentations, and understanding how graphs can be erroneously presented (Box 60.3) will help you avoid the same pitfalls.

Tables

Tables, especially large ones, can appear as a mass of numbers and thus be more daunting at first sight than graphs. In essence, however, most tables are simpler than most graphs. The construction of tables is dealt with in Chapter 61.

Analysing a table – as with analysing a graph, this process can be split into six phases:

1. *Considering the context and purpose.*

2. *Examining the subheadings to see what information is contained in the rows and columns.*

3. *Considering the units used and checking any footnotes.*

4. *Comparing the data values across rows and/or down columns, looking for patterns, trends and unusual values.*

5. *Taking into account any statistics presented.*

6. *Reaching conclusions based on the above.*

Text reference

Damer, T.E. (2004) *Attacking Faulty Reasoning: A Practical Guide to Fallacy-Free Arguments*, 5th edn. Wadsworth, Belmont, CA.

Sources for further study

Anon. *Critical Thinking*. Available: http://en.wikipedia.org/wiki/Critical_thinking
Last accessed: 20/07/09.
[A frequently updated review of terminology and techniques, with additional links and references]

Ridley, D.D. (2009) *Information Retrieval – Scifinder*, 2nd edn. Wiley, Chichester.

Smith, A. *Evaluation of Information Sources*. Available: http://www.vuw.ac.nz/staff/alastair_smith/evaln/evaln.htm
Last accessed: 20/07/09.
[Part of the web-based Information Quality Virtual Library]

Turnitin® UK. Available: http://turnitin.com/static_jisc/ac_uk_index.html
Last accessed: 20/07/09.
[Originality checking software for detection of plagarism]

Van Gelder, T. *Critical Thinking on the Web*. Available: http://www.austhink.org/critical/
Last accessed: 20/07/09.
[Includes a useful directory of web resources]

Study exercises

9.1 Distinguish between primary and secondary literature. Based on their titles and any research you can do in your library, determine whether the following journals are primary or secondary sources:

(a) *Chemical Communications*
(b) *Analyst*
(c) *Organic & Biomolecular Chemistry*
(d) *Chemical Society Reviews*
(e) *Polymer Chemistry*
(f) *Natural Product Updates*
(g) *Dalton Transactions*
(h) *Faraday Discussions*
(i) *Analytical Abstracts*
(j) *Green Chemistry*

9.2 Consider a controversial issue from both sides. Select a current chemical topic being discussed in the newspapers or other media. Controversial issues such as 'nuclear energy' or 'global warming' would be good examples. Next, write out a statement that you might use for a motion in a debate, such as 'Is nuclear energy the solution to our energy problems?' or 'Is global warming really happening?' Then, write at least five points in support of either side of the argument, which you should organise in tabular form. If you can find more than five points, add these to your table, but for each point that you add to one side, you should add one to the other side.

9.3 Analyse graphic presentations in the media. Many newspapers provide graphic presentations related to current issues, and graphs are frequently used in television news reports. Practise critical thinking skills by determining whether the graphs presented are a fair representation of the facts.

Definitions

Browser – a program to display web pages and other Internet resources.

FAQ – Frequently Asked Question; a file or web page giving information on common queries, sometimes used as a file extension (.faq).

FTP – File Transfer Protocol; a mechanism for downloading files.

URL – Uniform Resource Locator; the 'address' for web resources.

Information and communication technology (ICT) is vital in the modern academic world and 'IT literacy' is a core skill for all chemists. This involves a wide range of computer-based skills, including:

- Accessing web pages using a web browser such as Microsoft Internet Explorer, Mozilla Firefox or Opera.
- Searching the Web for useful information and resources using a search engine such as Google, or a meta-search engine such as Dogpile.
- Finding what you need within online databases, such as library catalogues or complex websites, such as your university's homepage.
- Downloading, storing and manipulating files.
- Communicating *via* the Internet.
- Using e-learning facilities effectively.
- Working with 'Office'-type programs and other software (dealt with in detail in Chapters 12 and 13).

You will probably receive an introduction to your university's networked IT systems and you will be required to follow rules and regulations that are important for the operation of these systems. Whatever your level of experience with PCs and the Internet, you should also follow the basic guidelines shown in Box 10.1. Reminding yourself of these from time to time will reduce your chances of losing data.

Understanding the technology – you do not need to understand the workings of the Internet to use it – most of it is invisible to the user. To ensure you obtain the right facilities, you may need to know some jargon, such as terms for the speed of data transfer (megabits) and the nature of internet addresses. Setting up a modem and/or local wireless network can be complex, but instructions are usually provided with the hardware. White and Downs (2005) and Gralla (2003) are useful texts if you wish to learn more about computing and the Internet.

The Internet as a global resource

The Internet is a complex network of computer networks; it is loosely organised and no one group organises it or owns it. Instead, many private organisations, universities and government organisations fund and operate discrete parts of it.

The Web is the most popular application of the Internet. It allows easy links to information and files which may be located on networked computers across the world. The Web enables you to access millions of 'home pages' or 'websites' – the initial point of reference with many individuals, institutions and companies. Besides text and images, these sites may contain 'hypertext links', highlighted words or phrases that take you to another internet location *via* a single mouse click.

You can gain access to the Internet either through a network at your university, at most public libraries, at a commercial 'Internet cafe', or from home *via* a modem connected to a broadband or dial-up internet service provider (e.g. Zen, BT or AOL).

KEY POINT Most material on the Internet has not been subject to peer review or vetting. Information obtained from the Web or posted on newsgroups may be inaccurate, biased or spoof; do not assume that everything you read is true, or even legal.

Box 10.1 Important guidelines for using PCs and networks

Hardware

- Don't drink or smoke around the computer.
- Try not to turn the computer off more than is necessary.
- Never turn off the electricity supply to the machine while in use.
- Switch off the computer and monitor when not in use (saves energy and avoids dangers of 'hijacking').
- ⚠ Rest your eyes at frequent intervals if working for extended periods at a computer monitor. Consult Health and Safety Executive publications for up-to-date advice on working with display screens (http://www.hse.gov.uk/pubns/)
- Never try to reformat the hard disk without the help of an expert.

CDs and USB drives

- Protect CDs when not in use by keeping them in holders or boxes.
- Label USB (Universal Serial Bus) drives with your name and return details and consider adding these to a file stored on the drive.
- Try not to touch the surface of CDs, and if they need cleaning, do so carefully with a clean cloth, avoiding scratching.
- Keep disks and USB drives away from moisture, excess heat or cold.
- Don't use disks and USBs from others, unless you first check them for viruses.
- Don't insert or remove a disk or USB drive when it is operating (drive light on). Close all files before removing a USB drive and use the *Safely Remove Hardware* feature.
- Try not to leave a disk or USB drive in the computer when you switch off.

File management

- Organise your files in an appropriate set of folders.

- Always use virus-checking programs on copied or imported files before running them.
- Make backups of all important files at frequent intervals (say, every 10 minutes), e.g. when using a word processor or spreadsheet.
- Periodically clear out redundant files.

Network rules

- Never attempt to 'hack' into other people's files.
- Do not give out any of your passwords to others. Change your password from time to time. Make sure it is not a common word, is longer than 8 characters, and includes numerical characters and punctuation symbols, as well as upper and lower case letters.
- Never use network computers to access or provide financial or other personal information: spyware and Trojan programs may intercept your information.
- Never open email attachments without knowing where they came from; always virus-check attachments before opening.
- Remember to log out of the network when finished; others can access your files if you forget to log out.
- Be polite when sending email messages.
- Periodically reorganise your email folder(s). These rapidly become filled with acknowledgements and redundant messages that reduce server efficiency and take up your allocated filespace.
- Do not play games without approval – they can affect the operation of the system.
- If you are setting up your own network, e.g. in your flat, always install up-to-date firewall software, anti-spyware and anti-virus programs.

The Golden Rule – always make backup copies of important files and store them well away from your working copies. Ensure that the same accident cannot happen to both copies.

Online communication

You will be allocated an email account by your university and should use this routinely for communicating with staff and fellow students, rather than using a personal account. You may be asked to use email to submit work as an attachment, or you may be asked to use a 'digital drop-box'

Box 10.2 Getting to grips with e-learning

Some key aspects of tackling e-learning are outlined below.

1. **Develop your basic IT skills, if required.** E-learning requires only basic IT skills, such as: use of keyboard and mouse; word-processing; file management; browsing and searching. If you feel weak on any of these, seek out additional courses offered by the IT administration or your department.

2. **Visit your e-learning modules regularly.** You should try to get into a routine of doing this on a daily basis at a time that suits you. Staff will present up-to-date information (e.g. lecture room changes) via the 'announcements' section, may post information about assessments, or links to the assessments themselves, and you may wish to provide feedback or look at discussion boards and their threads.

3. **Participate.** E-learning requires an active approach.

   - At the start of each new course, spend some time getting to know what's been provided online to support your learning. As well as valuable resources, this may include crucial information such as learning objectives (p. 26), dates of submission for coursework and weighting of marks for different elements of the course.

   - If you are allowed to download lecture notes (e.g. in the form of PowerPoint presentations), do not think that simply reading through these will be an adequate substitute for attending lectures and making further notes (see p. 17).

   - Do not be tempted to 'lurk' on discussion boards: take part. Ask questions; start new threads; answer points raised by others if you can.

   - Try to gain as much as you can from formative online assessments (p. 26). If these include feedback on your answers, make sure you learn from this and if you do not understand it, consult your tutors.

   - Learn from the critical descriptions that your lecturers provide of linked websites. These pointers may help you to evaluate such resources for yourself in future.

   - Don't think that you will automatically assimilate information and concepts, just because you are viewing them online. The same principles apply as with printed media: you must apply active learning methods (p. 22).

   - Help your lecturers by providing constructive feedback when they ask for it. You may find this easier to do when using the computer interface, and it may be more convenient than hurriedly filling out a feedback sheet at the end of a session.

4. **Organise files and web links.** Take the time to create a meaningful folder and file naming system for downloaded material in tandem with your own coursework files and set up folders on your browser for bookmarked websites (*Favorites* in Internet Explorer).

5. **Take care when submitting coursework.** Make sure you keep a back-up of any file you email or submit online and check the version you are sending carefully. Follow instructions carefully, for example regarding file type, or how to use your system's 'digital drop-box'.

within the university's e-learning system (Box 10.2). When using email at university, follow conventions, including etiquette, carefully:

- Check your email account regularly (daily). Your tutors may wish to send urgent messages to you in this way.

- Respond promptly to emails. Even if you are just acknowledging receipt, it is polite to indicate that you have received and understood a message.

- Be polite. Email messages can seem to be abrupt and impersonal. Take care to read your messages through before sending and if you are at all in doubt, do not send your message right away: re-read at a later time and consider how others might view what you say.

- Consider content carefully. Only send what you would be happy to hear being read out loud to classmates or family.

Spam, junk mail and phishing – these should be relatively easy to identify, and should never be responded to or forwarded. Some may look 'official' and request personal or financial details (for example, they may pretend to come from your bank, and ask for account details). Never send these details by email or your identity may be used illegally.

Using newsgroups – these can be useful for getting answers to a specific problem: just post a query to the appropriate group and wait for someone to reply. Bear in mind that this may be the view of an individual person.

- When communicating with tutors, take care with language and names. Slang phrases and text message shorthand are unlikely to be understood. Over-familiarity does not go down well.

- Use email for academic purposes only – this includes discussing coursework with classmates, but not forwarding off-colour jokes, potentially offensive images, links to offensive websites, etc. In fact, doing so may break regulations and result in disciplinary action.

- Beware of spam, junk and 'phishing' *via* email.

Similar rules apply to discussion boards.

The Usernet Newsgroup service is an electronic discussion facility, and there are thousands of newsgroups representing different interests and topics. Any user can contribute to the discussion within a topic by posting their own message; it is like email, but without privacy, since your message becomes available to all other subscribers. To access a newsgroup, your system must be running, or have access to, a newsgroup server which has subscribed to the newsgroup of interest.

With mailing lists, messages sent to the list address are distributed automatically to all members of the mailing list, *via* their personal emailbox, keeping them up to date on the particular topic of the mailing list. To receive such messages, you will need to join the mailing list. Relevant mailing lists for chemistry can be found at http://www.jiscmail.ac.uk/. Take care not to join too many lists, as you will receive a large number of messages, and many are likely to be of only marginal interest. A number of mailing lists also have archived files, offering a more selective means of locating relevant material.

Internet tools

The specific programs you will use for accessing the Internet will depend on what has been installed locally, on the network you are using, and on your Internet service provider. The best way to learn the features of the programs is to try them out, making full use of whatever help services are available.

E-learning systems

Most university departments present their courses through a mixture of face-to-face sessions (e.g. lectures, tutorials, practicals) and online resources (e.g. lecture notes, websites, discussion boards, computerised tests and assessments). This constitutes 'blended learning' on your part, with the online component also being known as e-learning.

The e-learning element is usually delivered through an online module within a virtual learning environment (e.g. Blackboard, WebCT, Moodle). It is important not to neglect the e-learning aspects of your course just because it may not be as rigidly timetabled as your face-to-face sessions. This flexibility is to your advantage, as you can work when it suits you, but it requires discipline on your part. Box 10.2 provides tips for making the most of the e-learning components of your courses.

Internet browsers

These are software programs that interact with remote server computers around the world to carry out the tasks of requesting, retrieving and

Examples – Useful web portals

Organic chemistry – Internet resources for recent topics, reactions and chemicals at: http://www.organic-chemistry.org/

INTUTE – Internet resources for chemistry at: http://www.intute.ac.uk/sciences/chemistry/

Examples Common domains and sub-domains include:

.ac	academic
.com	commercial
.co	commercial
.edu	education (USA mainly)
.gov	government (USA and UK)
.mil	military (USA only)
.net	Internet-based companies
.org	organisation
.uk	United Kingdom

displaying the information you require. Many different browsers exist, but the most popular are Internet Explorer, Mozilla Firefox and Opera. These three browsers dominate the market and have plug-ins and add-on programs available that allow, for example, video sequences to be seen online. Many browsers incorporate email and newsgroup functions. The standard functions of browsers include:

- accessing web documents;
- following links to other documents;
- printing the current document;
- maintaining a history of visited URLs (including 'bookmarks' for key sites);
- searching for a term in a document;
- viewing images and image maps.

Browsers provide access to millions of websites. Certain sites specialise in providing catalogued links to other sites; these are known as portals and can be of enormous help when searching within a particular area of interest. Your university's library website will almost certainly provide a useful portal to catalogues and search services, often arranged by subject area, and this is often the first port of call for electronic resources; get to know your way around this part of the website as early as possible during your course.

When using a browser program to get to a particular page of information on the Web, all you require is the location of that page, i.e. the URL (Uniform Resource Locator). Most web page URLs take the form http://, or https://, followed by the various terms (domains and sub-domains) that direct the system to the appropriate site. If you don't have a specific URL in mind but wish to explore appropriate sites, you will need to use a search tool with the browser.

Search tools

With the proliferation of information on the Web, one of the main problems is finding the exact information you require. There are a variety of information services that you can use to filter the material on the network. These include:

- search engines (Boxes 10.3 and 10.4);
- meta-search engines;
- subject directories;
- subject gateways (portals).

Search engines such as Google (http://www.google.com), AltaVista (http://uk.altavista.com) and Lycos (http://www.lycos.com) are tools designed to search, gather, index and classify web-based information. Searching is usually by keyword(s), although specific phrases can be defined. Many search engines offer advanced searching tools such as the use of Boolean operators to specify combinations of keywords to more precisely filter the sites. Box 10.3 provides tips for refining keyword searches, while Box 10.4 provides tips for enhanced searching with Google.

Box 10.3 Useful tips for using search engines

- **Keywords should be chosen with care.** Try to make them as specific as possible, e.g. search for 'naphthalene', rather than 'PAHs' or 'polycyclic aromatic hydrocarbons'.

- **Most search engines are case-insensitive.** Thus 'Nobel Prize' will return the same number of hits as 'nobel prize'. If in doubt, use lower case throughout.

- **Putting keyword phrases in double quotes (e.g. "capillary electrophoresis") will result in a search for sites with the phrase as a whole** rather than sites with both (all) parts of the phrase as separate words (i.e. 'capillary' and 'electrophoresis' at different places within a site). This feature allows you to include common words normally excluded in the search, such as 'the'.

- **Use multiple words/phrases plus similar words to improve your search,** for example 'Harold Kroto buckminsterfullerene discovery'. If you can, use scientific terms, as you are likely to find more relevant sites, e.g. search for the name of a particular chemical such as pentachlorophenol.

- **Adding words preceded with + or − will add or exclude sites with that word present** (e.g. 'cancer treatment + cisplatin' will search for all cancer treatments that use cisplatin). This feature can also be used to include common words normally excluded by the search engine.

- **Check that your search terms have the correct spelling**, otherwise you may only find sites with the same misspelled word. In some cases, the search

engine may prompt you with an alternative (correct) spelling. Remember that US and UK spellings may differ (e.g. sulphur/sulfur) and a search will only find hits from sites that use the spelling you specify.

- **Boolean operators (AND, OR, NOT) can be used with some search engines to specify combinations of keywords** to more precisely filter the sites identified (e.g. 'PAH AND analysis' will find sites about methods to analyse PAHs).

- **Some search engines allow 'wildcards' to be introduced with the symbol** *. For example, this will allow you to specify the root of a word and include all possible endings, as with pentachloro*, which would find pentachlorophenol, pentachlorocyclohexene, etc. If the search engine does not allow wildcards (e.g. Google), then you will need to be especially careful with the keywords used, including all possible words of relevance.

- **Numbers can be surprisingly useful in search engines.** For example, typing in 1,1,2,2-tet will find sites concerned with organic compounds that might contain halogens, e.g. 1,1,2,2-tetrachloroethane. If you know the phone number for a person, institute or company or the ISBN of the book, this can often help you find relevant pages quickly.

- **If you arrive at a large site and cannot find the point at which your searched word or phrase appears, press** Control **and** F **together** and a 'local' search window will appear, allowing you to find the point(s) where it is mentioned.

It is important to realise that each search engine will cover at most about 40% of the available sites and if you want to carry out an exhaustive search it is necessary to use several to cover as much of the Web as possible. Meta-search engines make this easier. These operate by combining collections of search engines. Examples include Mamma (http://www.mamma.com/), Dogpile (http://www.dogpile.com/index.gsp/) and Metacrawler (http://www.metacrawler.com/index.html/).

Some useful approaches to searching include the following:

- For a comprehensive search, use a variety of tools including search engines, meta-search engines and portals or directories.

- For a complex, finely specified search, employ Boolean operators and other tools to refine your keywords as fully as possible (Box 10.2). Some search engines allow you to include and exclude terms or restrict by date.

'Dissecting' a Web address – you can often find out more about a particular site by progressively deleting sections of the URL from the right-hand side. This will often take you to the home page of the organisation or company involved.

Box 10.4 Getting the most from Google searches

Google (http://www.google.com) has become the search engine of choice for millions of people, due to its simplicity and effectiveness. However, you may be able to improve your searches by understanding its default settings and how they can be changed.

- **Download the Google toolbar to your browser.** This is available from the Google homepage and will give you quick access to the Google search facility.

- **Understand how standard operators are used.** For combinations of keywords Google uses the 'minus' operator '−' instead of NOT (exclude) and the 'plus' operator '+' instead of AND (include). Since Google usually ignores small words ('stop words' such as *in* or *the*), use '+' to include them in a search. Where no operator is specified, Google assumes that you are looking for both terms (i.e. '+' is default). If you want to search for alternative words, you can use 'OR' (e.g. *sulphur OR sulfur*). Google does not allow brackets and also ignores most punctuation marks.

- **While wildcard truncation of words using '*' is not allowed, you can use '*' to replace a whole word (or number).** For example, if you type the phrase "*a bond is approximately * nanometres*" your results will give you results for web pages where the wildcard is replaced by a number.

- **Search for exact wording.** By placing text in double inverted commas (" "), you can ensure that only websites with this exact phrasing will appear at the head of your search results.

- **Search within your results to improve the outcome.** If your first search has produced a large number of results, use the *Search within results* option near the bottom of each page to type in a further word or phrase.

- **Search for words within the title of a web page.** Use the command *intitle:* to find a web page, for example *intitle: "reaction mechanism"* returns web pages with this phrase in the title (note that phrases must always be in double speech marks, not single quotes).

- **Search within a website.** Use the *site:* command to locate words/phrases on a specific website, for example *site:iupac.org inorganic* returns only those results for inorganic chemistry on the IUPAC website (www.iupac.org). Pressing *Control* and *F* when visiting a web page will give you a pop-up search window.

- **Locate definitions, synonyms and spellings.** The operator *define:* enables you to find the meaning of a word. If you are unsure as to the spelling of a word, try each possibility. Google will usually return more results for the correct spelling and will often also prompt you with the correct spelling (*Did you mean …?*).

- **Find similar web pages.** Simply click the *Similar pages* option at the end of a Google search result to list other sites (note that these sites will not necessarily include the term(s) searched for).

- **If a web link is unavailable, try the cached (stored) page.** Clicking on *Cached* at the end of a particular result should take you to the stored page, with the additional useful feature that the search term(s) will be highlighted.

- **Use the calculator function.** Simply enter a calculation and press *Enter* to display the result, for example '$10+(2\times 4)$' returns 18. The calculator function can also carry out simple interconversion of units, e.g. '2 feet 6 inches in metres' returns 0.762 (see Box 28.1 for interconversion factors between SI and non-SI units).

- **Try out the advanced search features.** In addition to the standard operators these include the ability to specify the number of results per page (e.g. 50) to reduce the use of the *next* button, language (e.g. English), file format (e.g. for PDF files), recently updated web pages (e.g. past 3 months), usage (e.g. free to use/share).

- **Find non-text material.** These include images, video and maps – always check that any material you use is not subject to copyright limitations (p. 49).

- **Use Google alerts to keep up to date.** This function (http://www.google.co.uk/alerts) enables you to receive regular updated searches by email.

- **Use Google Scholar to find articles and papers.** Go to http://scholar.google.com/ and type in either the general topic or specific details for a particular article, e.g. author names or words from the title. Results show titles/authors of articles, with links to either the full article, abstract or citation. A useful feature is the *Cited by …* link, taking you to those papers that have cited the article in their bibliography and enabling you to carry out forward citation searching to locate more recent papers. Also try out the advanced scholar search features to limit your search to a particular author, journal, date or subject area. However, you should note that Google Scholar provides only a basic search facility to easily accessible articles and should not be viewed as a replacement for your library's electronic journal holdings and searching software. For example, if you find the title of a paper *via* Google Scholar you may then be able to locate the electronic version through your own library's databases, or request it *via* inter-library loan (p. 49). Another significant limitation is that older (more cited) references are typically listed first.

- **Use Google Earth to explore locations.** Download from http://earth.google.com/. This allows you to zoom in on satellite images to find locations.

Downloading files from the Internet and emails – read-only files are often available as 'pdf' files that can be viewed by Adobe reader software (available free from http://www.adobe.com), while other files may be presented as attachments to emails or as links from web pages that can be opened by suitable software (e.g. Microsoft Word or 'paint' programs like Paint Shop Pro). Take great care in the latter cases as the transfer of files can result in the transfer of associated viruses. Always check new files for viruses (especially .exe files) before running them, and make sure your virus-detecting software is kept up to date.

- Use 'cascading' searching when available – this is searching within the results of a previous search.

- Use advanced search facilities to limit your search, where possible, to the type of medium you are looking for (e.g. graphics, video), language, sites in a specific country (e.g. UK) or to a subject area (e.g. news only).

However well defined your search is, you will still need to evaluate the information obtained. Chapter 9 covers general aspects of this topic while Box 10.5 provides specific advice on assessing the quality of information provided on websites.

Directories

A directory is a list of web resources organised by subject. It can usually be browsed and may or may not have a search facility. Directories often contain better quality information than the lists produced by search engines, as they have been evaluated, often by subject specialists or librarians. The BUBL information service directory of links, at: http://bubl.ac.uk, is a good example.

Understanding the impermanence of the Web – the temporary nature of much of the material on the Web is a disadvantage for academic purposes because it may change or even disappear after you have cited it. You may also find it difficult or impossible to find out who authored the material. A case in point are wikis, such as Wikipedia (www.wikipedia.org). This online encyclopaedia has many potential authors and the content may change rapidly as a result of new submissions or edits; nevertheless, it can be a useful resource for up-to-date general information about a wide range of topics, though it is not necessarily regarded as the best approach for researching scientific assignments.

Using the Internet as a resource

A common way of finding information on the Web is by browsing or 'surfing'. However, this can be time-consuming; try to restrict yourself to sites known to be relevant to the topic of interest. Some of the most useful sites are those that provide hypertext links to other locations. Some other resources you can use on the Web are:

- Libraries, publishers and commercial organisations. Your university library is likely to subscribe to one or more databases providing access to scientific articles; these include ISI Web of Science (http://wos.mimas.ac.uk), and Science Direct (http://www.sciencedirect.com). A password is usually required, especially for off-campus use; consult your library staff for further details. Some scientific database sites give free access, without subscription or password; these include the PubMed website of the National Center for Biotechnology Information (http://www.ncbi.nlm.nih.gov) and the HighWire Press (http://highwire.stanford.edu). Others allow free searching, but require payment for certain articles, e.g. the Scientific World (http://www.thescientificworld.com/) and Infotrieve (http://www4.infotrieve.com). Publishers such as Pearson and booksellers such as Amazon.com provide online catalogues and e-commerce sites that can be useful sources of information (see http://vig.pearsoned.co.uk and http://www.amazon.com).

Box 10.5 How to evaluate information on the World Wide Web

It is often said that 'you can find anything on the Web'. The two main disadvantages of this are, firstly, that you may need to sift through many sources before you find what you are looking for and, secondly, that the sources you find will vary in their quality and validity. *It is important to realise that evaluating sources is a key aspect of using the Internet for academic purposes, and one that you will need to develop during the course of your studies* (see also Chapter 9). The ease with which you can 'point and click' to reach various sources should not make you complacent about evaluating their information content. The following questions can help you to assess the quality of a website – the more times you can answer 'yes', the more credible the source is likely to be, and *vice versa*:

Authority

- Is the author identified?
- Are the author's qualifications or credentials given?
- Is the owner, publisher or sponsoring organisation identified?
- Is an address given (postal and/or email)?

It is sometimes possible to get information on authority from the site's metadata (try the 'View' 'Source' option in Internet Explorer, or look at the URL to see if it gives any clues as to the organisation, e.g. whether the domain name ends in .ac, .edu, .gov or .org, rather than .co or .com).

Content

- Is there any evidence that the information has been peer-reviewed (p. 131), edited or otherwise validated, or is it based on such sources?
- Is the information factual or based on personal opinion?
- Is the factual data original (primary) or derived from other sources (secondary)?

- Are the sources of specific factual information detailed in full (Chapter 8)?
- Is there any indication that the information is up to date, or that the site has been recently updated?
- What is the purpose of the site and who is it aimed at?
- Is the content relevant to the question you are trying to answer?
- Is there any evidence of a potential conflict of interest, or bias? (Is the information comprehensive and balanced, or narrowly focused?)
- Did you find the information *via* a subject-specific website (e.g. a chemistry gateway such as Intute), or through a more general source, such as a search engine (e.g. Google)?

The above questions are similar to those that you would use in assessing the value of a printed resource (p. 57), and similar criteria should be applied to web-based information. You should be especially wary of sites containing unattributed factual information or data whose primary source is not given.

Presentation

- What is your overall impression of how well the site has been put together?
- Are there any grammatical or spelling mistakes?
- Are there links to other websites, to support statements and factual information?

The care with which a site has been constructed can give you an indication of the credibility of the author/organisation. However, while a poorly-presented site may cause you to question the credibility of the information, the reverse is not always necessarily true: don't be taken in by a slick, well-presented website – authority and content are *always* more important than presentation.

Using traditional sources – remember that using the Internet to find information is not a substitute for visiting your university library. Internet resources complement rather than replace more traditional printed sources.

- Online journals and e-books. A number of traditional journals have websites. You can keep up to date by visiting the websites of *Nature* (http://www.nature.com), *New Scientist* (http://www.newscientist.com) and *Scientific American* (http://www.sciam.com), or ScienceDirect journals (at http://www.sciencedirect.com/science/journals). Some scientific societies make their journals and other publications available *via* their websites, e.g. the Royal Society of Chemistry at http://www.rsc.org. Journals solely published in electronic format are also available (e.g. *Cryst.Eng.Comm*, http://www.rsc.org/Publishing/

Remembering useful websites – create a 'bookmark' (= add a 'favorite') for the ones you find of value, to make revisiting easy. This can be done from the menu of your browser program. Make a copy of your bookmark file occasionally, to avoid loss of this information.

Note that URLs may change – make a keyword search using a search engine to find a particular site if the URL information you have does not lead you to an active page.

Examples – Selected websites of chemical interest:

Royal Society of Chemistry: http://www.rsc.org/

American Chemical Society: http://www.acs.org/

The WWW Virtual Library – Natural Sciences and Mathematics: http://vlib.org/science

Journals/ce/) but some require a subscription password for access; check whether your institute is a subscriber.

- Data and images. Archives of text material, video clips and photographs can be accessed, and much of the material is readily available. The HEA Physical Sciences Centre (http://heacademy.ac.uk/physsci/) is a good example. When downloading such material, you should check that you are not breaching copyright and avoid potential plagiarism by giving a full citation of the source, if you use such images in an assignment (see p. 54).

- Chemistry institutions. Many scientific societies and other chemistry institutions around the world are now online. Use their sites to obtain specific information about journals, resources, etc. They frequently provide lists of other relevant sites or topics, e.g. the Royal Society of Chemistry (http://www.rsc.org).

- Databases. In addition to those covering the scientific literature (e.g. ISI Web of Science, or the PubMed service of the US National Library of Medicine), others focus on specific topics (e.g. academic employment, http://www.jobs.ac.uk). Chapter 11 provides further guidance on using online chemistry databases.

Text references

Gralla, P. (2003) *How the Internet Works*, 7th edn. Pearson, Harlow.

White, R. and Downs, T. (2005) *How Computers Work*, 8th edn. Pearson, Harlow.

Sources for further study

Anon. *The Essentials of Google Search*. Available: http://www.google.co.uk/intl/en/help/basics.html Last accessed: 20/07/09. [Advice on using the Google search engine]

Brandt, D.S. *Why We Need to Evaluate What We Find on the Internet*. Available: http://www.lib.purdue.edu/research/techman/eval.html Last accessed: 20/07/09.

Grassian, E. *Thinking Critically about World Wide Web Resources*. Available: http://www2.library.ucla.edu/libraries/college/11605_12337.cfm Last accessed: 20/07/09.

Ridley, D.D. (2009). *Information Retrieval – Scifinder*, 2nd edn. Wiley, Chichester.

Study exercises

10.1 Explore the resources of the Web using a search engine. Using a search engine, find the answers to the following questions:

(a) Who is Linus C. Pauling, and what is he famous for? What prize did he win and when?

(b) What is the alternative name for *dichloromethane*?

(c) What is the postal address of the Royal Society of Chemistry's London headquarters?

10.2 Compare results from a variety of search engines. First, think of an appropriate chemistry keyword or phrase (e.g. a compound name) and enter this into several search engines. Make sure that you include meta-search engines such as Dogpile. Compare the outcomes to reveal the strengths and weaknesses of the individual search engines. Work with a colleague to compare different searches on a quantitative (i.e. number of hits) and qualitative (quality of hits) basis.

10.3 Organise your bookmarks. Enter the *'Organize favorites'* menu for your preferred browser and create folders with appropriate headings. Move existing bookmarks to these folders and save any new ones appropriately. Doing this will help you find bookmarks more easily, rather than searching through long lists.

11 Internet resources for chemistry

Definitions

RSS – Really Simple Syndication

Blog – a contraction of the words 'web log'; it is essentially a type of website, maintained by an individual, who can update commentary, videos or graphics on to the site.

Table 11.1 Example of electronic (e-) chemistry journals

E-Journal of Chemistry (http://ejchem.org/)

Crystallographic journals online (http://journals.iucr.org/index.html)

Internet Electronic Journal of Molecular Design (http://www.biochempress.com/index.html)

Beilstein Journal of Organic Chemistry (BJOC) (http://www.beilstein-journals.org/bjoc/home/home.htm)

Orbital – The Electronic Journal of Chemistry (http://www.orbital.ufms.br/index.php/dqi)

Table 11.2 Selected examples of useful institution websites

American Chemical Society
http://www.acs.org

The Royal Society of Chemistry
http://www.rsc.org

International Union of Pure and Applied Chemistry (IUPAC)
http://www.iupac.org/

The last decade has seen extensive development in the availability of chemical resources on the Internet. One way to find such material on the Internet is by browsing ('surfing') the World Wide Web (WWW). However, as this can be time-consuming and wasteful, browsing should be focused on relevant and appropriate sites. Many of the most useful websites are those providing detailed lists and hypertext links to other locations. A useful place to find out what the Internet offers the chemist can be found at the URL http://www.chemdex.org.

> **KEY POINT** Remember that the Internet should not be viewed as a substitute for your own University library and other local resources, but should complement, rather than replace, more traditional printed texts and other electronic material.

General information

Some of the principal resources you can utilise via the web are:

- **Libraries, publishers and companies.** These organisations recognise the significance of the Internet as a means of communication; for example, the Pearson higher education website at http://vig.pearsoned.co.uk/ allows information on specific catalogues and books to be requested online. A large number of scientific journals are also available in electronic format *via* ingenta.com (http://www.ingentaconnect.com). Ingenta journals offers a single point of access to over 11000 academic and professional journals. Access to browse and search the database of articles is free, as is the ability to display tables of contents, bibliographic information and abstracts. Full-text articles require a fee for access – check whether your institution subscribes. A broad range of scientific journals are also published by Elsevier and are available *via* the site http://www.elsevierdirect.com/index.jsp. You can keep up to date using *New Scientist* pages (at http://www.newscientist.com/), *Scientific American* (at http://www.scientificamerican.com/) or *Nature* (at http://www.nature.com/). A significant development is the publication of chemistry journals in electronic format only (Table 11.1).

- **Institutions.** Many research organisations, societies and educational institutions around the world are now online, with their own web pages. There is a detailed list of scholarly chemical societies at http://www.chemdex.org/. You can use the websites of these organisations to obtain specific information. They frequently provide hypertext links to other relevant sites for particular groups or topics: for example, the Royal Society of Chemistry web page (http://www.rsc.org) has links to various sites of interest to chemists. Use the web to obtain details of the activities of research organisations (e.g. GlaxoSmithKline, at http://www.gsk.com/) or individual laboratories and researchers at specific universities. Some other relevant websites are given in Table 11.2.

- **Data and pictures.** Archives of text material, photographs and video clips can be accessed and easily downloaded. However, downloading

Table 11.3 Other examples of chemical databases

CrossFire Database Suite
http://www.info.crossfiredatabases.com/

Chemical Abstracts Service
http://www.cas.org/

National Institute of Standards and Technology (NIST) WebBook
http://webbook.nist.gov

ChemExper Chemical Directory
http://www.chemexper.be/main.shtml

Cambridge Crystallographic Data Centre
http://www.ccdc.cam.ac.uk/

The Chemical Database Service
http://cds.dl.ac.uk/

The Wired Chemist
http://www.wiredchemist.com/index.html

Spectral Database for Organic Compounds
http://riodb01.ibase.aist.go.jp/sdbs/cgi-bin/cre_index.cgi?lang=eng

NMRshiftDB
http://www.ebi.ac.uk/nmrshiftdb/

ACDLabs
http://www.acdlabs.com/products/spec_lab/exp_spectra/spec_libraries/aldrich.html

eMolecules
http://www.emolecules.com/

Chemical Synthesis Database
http://www.chemsynthesis.com/

Organic Chemistry Portal
http://www.organic-chemistry.org/

Organic Syntheses
http://www.orgsyn.org/

ChemPortal
http://webnet3.oecd.org/echemportal/

graphical images may take quite a while, especially for remote links or at busy times.

- **Newsgroups (Usernet).** News articles on a wide range of topics are 'posted' at appropriate sites, where they are placed into subject groups (newsgroups). Any user can contribute to the discussion by posting his/her own message, to be read by other users via appropriate news software. An example of a usernet group is The Higher Education Academy (in the UK) that supports the Physical Sciences Centre which supports staff and students in Higher Education by promoting the enhancement of the student learning experience in chemistry, physics, astronomy and forensic science. Individuals can sign up to receive the email mailing list, RSS feeds to receive regular updates on news, blogs and periodical publications and twitter.

> **KEY POINT** Remember that the information from Internet newsgroups and similar websites may be unedited and may represent the personal opinion of the author of the article.

Chemical databases

A wide range of chemical databases are available on the Internet. The website Web of Knowledge (http://isiwebofknowledge.com/) provides access to databases covering subjects from science, engineering and medicine to economics, politics, education and the arts. The site is username and password protected so you will need access via your Department, School, Faculty or library. Some other selected examples of chemical databases are shown in Table 11.3. Specific examples of some of these databases are now discussed.

The Periodic Table

A good place to start for a chemistry student is finding information about the elements in the Periodic Table. One such resource is WebElements (http://www.webelements.com/) which provides key information on all elements in the Periodic Table. This database is searchable in terms of a range of properties of the elements including:

- The essentials (includes names, symbol, atomic number and atomic weight; block, period and group in Periodic Table; description; standard state; registry number; and isolation).

- History (meaning of name; discovery; and history of the element).

- Uses.

- Geology (abundance of elements in the universe; the Sun; meteorites; Earth's crust; oceans; and streams).

- Biology (abundance in humans; biological role; and health hazards).

- Compounds (halides, oxides, sulfides, hydrides and complexes; lattice energies; and reduction potentials).

- Electronegativity (Pauling, Sanderson, Allred Rochow, Mulliken-Jaffe and Allen).

- Bond enthalpies (of diatomic species).

- Lattice energies.

- Physical properties (includes boiling point; melting point; density; molar volume; thermal conductivity; electrical resistivity; bulk modulus; critical temperature; superconductivity temperature; hardness (mineralogical, Brinell and Vickers); linear expansion coefficient; Poisson's ratio; reflectivity; refractive index; rigidity modulus; Young's modulus; velocity of sound).

- Images (i.e. photographs of the elements).

- Reactions (reactions of element with air, water, halogens, acids and bases)

- Crystal structure.

- Thermochemistry (enthalpies of atomisation, fusion and vaporisation; thermodynamic properties).

- Electron shell properties: electronic configuration; term symbol; electron affinity; ionisation energies; and atomic spectra.

- Atom sizes (atomic radius, Shannon and Pauling ionic radii, covalent radius, metallic radius, element bond length and Van der Waals radius).

- Atomic orbital properties (effective nuclear charge; electron binding energies; and valence orbital radii maxima).

- Isotopes (isotope abundances; radioactive isotopes; isotope masses; nuclear spins; and nuclear magnetic moment).

- NMR properties (frequencies; isotopes; magnetogyric ratios; quadrupole moments; receptivities; and relative sensitivities).

In addition, another dedicated website provides details on atomic and molecular orbitals. Orbitron (http://winter.group.shef.ac.uk/orbitron/) provides information on atomic orbitals from energy level 1 to 7, i.e. 1s (energy level 1) through to 7s, 7p, 7d, 7f, 7g (energy level 7). In addition, hybrid orbitals are shown for 2s + 2p orbitals, i.e. sp, sp^2 and sp^3, as well as 3s + 3p + 3d hybrid orbitals, i.e. dsp^3, d^2sp^3. Finally, molecular orbitals are shown for dihydrogen (H_2) and dinitrogen (N_2).

Royal Society of Chemistry (RSC) databases

The RSC provides username/password protected access to four bibliographic databases and a further two databases (Chemical Safety Data Sheets and the UK nutrient Databank via the World Wide Web) are supported by The Royal Society of Chemistry (URL: http://www.bids.ac.uk/Tfedocs/rsc.html). The databases are:

- *Analytical Abstracts*

- *Catalysts & Catalysed Reactions*

- *Methods in Organic Synthesis*

- *Natural Product Updates*

- *Chemical Hazards in Industry*

- *Laboratory Hazards Bulletin*
- *Mass Spectrometry Bulletin*
- *Chromatography Abstracts*
- *Chemical Safety NewsBase/Environmental Chemistry Health & Safety*
- *The Dictionary of Substances and their Effects*

Analytical Abstracts (also known as *Analytical WebBase*) (http://www.rsc.org/Publishing/CurrentAwareness/AA/index.asp).

This is specifically aimed at analytical chemistry. In particular, the following areas are covered: general analytical chemistry; chromatography and electrophoresis; spectrometry and radiochemical methods; inorganic, organic and organometallic analysis; applied and industrial analysis; clinical and biochemical analysis; pharmaceutical analysis, including drugs in biological fluids; environmental analysis; agricultural analysis; and food analysis. The database is regularly updated and covers the period from 1980 onwards. A typical sample record is shown in Table 11.4.

Table 11.4 Sample record from *Analytical Abstracts*

Title: Addressing analytical uncertainties in the determination of tricholoroacetic acid in soil.

Author: Dickey, C. A.; Heal, K. V.; Cape, J. N.; Stidson, R. T.; Reeves, N. M.; Heal, M. R.[*]

Author Address: m.heal@ed.ac.uk, School Chem. Univ. Edinburgh, Edinburgh EH9 3JJ, UK

Source: Journal of Environmental Monitoring, 3 Feb 2005, **7** (2), 137–144

ISSN: 1464-0325

Publication Year: 2005

Language: English

Publication Type: Journal

Analyte: acetic acid, trichloro- [76-03-9] - detmn. of, in soil, by headspace analysis-GC-ECD, extraction in, chemometrics in

Matrix soil – detmn. of trichloroacetic acid in agricultural and forest, by headspace analysis-GC-ECD, extraction in, chemometrics in

Technique chemometrics – error analysis, in detmn. of trichloroacetic acid, in soil, by headspace analysis-GC-ECD, extraction in
chromatography, gas (GC)
electron capture detection (ECD)
extraction – of trichloroacetic acid, from soil, for detmn. by headspace analysis-GC-ECD, chemometrics in headspace analysis

Abstract Soil is important compartment in the environmental cycling of trichloroacetic acid (TCA), but soil TCA concentration is a methodologically defined quantity; analytical methods either quantify TCA in an aqueous extract of the soil, or thermally decarboxylate TCA to chloroform in the whole soil sample. The former may underestimate the total soil TCA, whereas the latter may overestimate TCA if other soil components (e.g. humic material) liberate chloroform under the decarboxylation conditions. The aim of this work was to show that extraction and decarboxylation methods yield different TCA concentration because the decarboxylation method can also determine 'bound' TCA. Experiments with commercial humic acid solutions showed there was no additional chloroform formation under decarboxylation conditions, and that all TCA in a TCA-humic acid mixture could be quantitatively determined ($108 \pm 13\%$). Anion exchange resin was used as a provider of solid-phase TCA binding; only $5 \pm 1\%$ of a TCA solution mixed with the resin was present in the aqueous extract subsequently separated from the resin, yet the decarboxylation method yielded mass balance ($123 \pm 22\%$) with TCA remaining in the resin. In aqueous extraction of a range of soil samples (with or without added TCA spike), the decarboxylation method was able to satisfactorily account for TCA in the extractant + residue post-extraction, compared with whole-soil TCA (+ spike) pre-extraction: e.g. mass balances for unspiked soil from Sikta spruce and larch forest were $99 \pm 8\%$ and $93 \pm 6\%$, respectively, and for TCA-spiked forest and agricultural soils were $114 \pm 13\%$ and $102 \pm 2\%$. In each case recovery of TCA in the extractant was substantially less than 100% (<20% for unspiked soils, <55% for spiked soils). Extraction efficiencies were generally lower in more organic soils. The results suggest that analytical methods which utilise aqueous extraction may underestimate whole-soil TCA concentrations. Application of both methodologies together may enhance insight into TCA behaviour in soil.

Table 11.5 Sample record from *Catalysts and Catalysed Reactions*

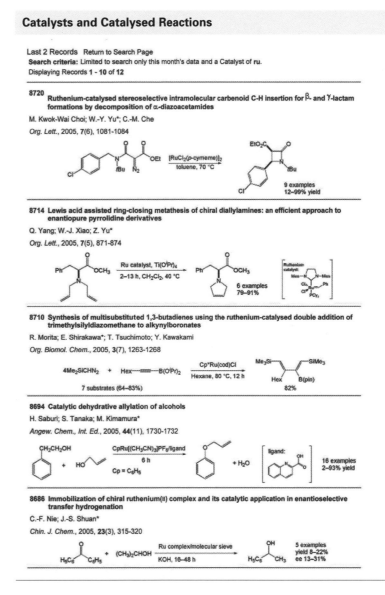

Catalysts and Catalysed Reactions

Last 2 Records   Return to Search Page
Search criteria: Limited to search only this month's data and a Catalyst of **ru**.
Displaying Records **1 - 10** of **12**

8720 Ruthenium-catalysed stereoselective intramolecular carbenoid C-H insertion for β- and γ-lactam formations by decomposition of α-diazoacetamides

M. Kwok-Wai Choi; W.-Y. Yu*; C.-M. Che

Org. Lett., 2005, **7**(6), 1081-1084

8714 Lewis acid assisted ring-closing metathesis of chiral diallylamines: an efficient approach to enantiopure pyrrolidine derivatives

Q. Yang; W.-J. Xiao; Z. Yu*

Org. Lett., 2005, **7**(5), 871-874

8710 Synthesis of multisubstituted 1,3-butadienes using the ruthenium-catalysed double addition of trimethylsilyldiazomethane to alkynylboronates

R. Morita; E. Shirakawa*; T. Tsuchimoto; Y. Kawakami

Org. Biomol. Chem., 2005, **3**(7), 1263-1268

8694 Catalytic dehydrative allylation of alcohols

H. Saburi; S. Tanaka; M. Kimamura*

Angew. Chem., Int. Ed., 2005, **44**(11), 1730-1732

8686 Immobilization of chiral ruthenium(II) complex and its catalytic application in enantioselective transfer hydrogenation

C.-F. Nie; J.-S. Shuan*

Chin. J. Chem., 2005, **23**(3), 315-320

Catalysts & Catalysed Reactions
(http://www.rsc.org/Publishing/CurrentAwareness/CCR/About.asp)

This is available in print and online. It contains a current awareness service as well as graphical abstracts of new developments in catalysis. The database covers all areas of catalysis research, including homogeneous, heterogeneous and biocatalysis with emphasis on current growth areas such as chiral catalysts, polymerisation catalysts, enzymatic catalysts and clean catalytic methods. A typical sample record is shown in Table 11.5.

Methods in Organic Synthesis (MOS)
(http://www.rsc.org/Publishing/CurrentAwareness/MOS/index.asp)

This is an alerting service that covers important current developments in organic synthesis. It covers the following areas: new

Table 11.6   Sample record from *Methods in Organic Synthesis*

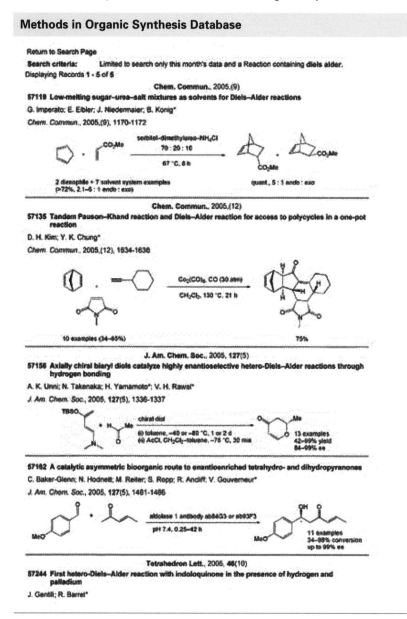

reactions and reagents; functional group changes; introduction of chiral centres; and enzyme and biological transformations. A typical sample record is shown in Table 11.6.

Natural Product Updates (NPU)
(http://www.rsc.org/Publishing/CurrentAwareness/npu/index.asp)

This provides graphical abstracts of new developments in natural product chemistry. It covers the following aspects: isolation studies; biosynthesis; new natural products; known compounds from new sources; structure determinations; and new properties and biological activities. A typical sample record is shown in Table 11.7.

Table 11.7 Sample record from *Natural Product Updates*

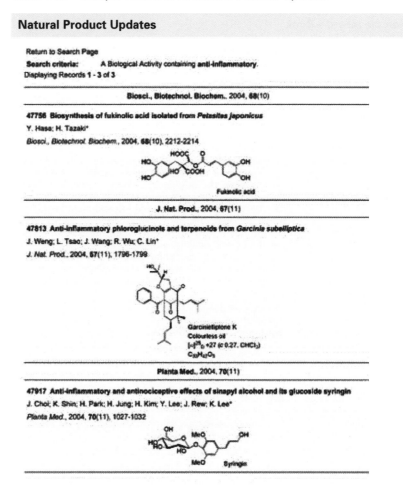

Natural Product Updates

Return to Search Page

Search criteria: A Biological Activity containing anti-inflammatory.
Displaying Records 1 - 3 of 3

Biosci., Biotechnol. Biochem., 2004, 68(10)

47756 Biosynthesis of fukinolic acid isolated from *Petasites japonicus*
Y. Hasa; H. Tazaki*
Biosci., Biotechnol. Biochem., 2004, 68(10), 2212-2214

Fukinolic acid

J. Nat. Prod., 2004, 67(11)

47813 Anti-inflammatory phloroglucinols and terpenoids from *Garcinia subelliptica*
J. Weng; L. Tsao; J. Wang; R. Wu; C. Lin*
J. Nat. Prod., 2004, 67(11), 1796-1799

Garcinielliptone K
Colourless oil
$[\alpha]_D^{25}$ +27 (c 0.27, CHCl₃)
$C_{30}H_{42}O_5$

Planta Med., 2004, 70(11)

47917 Anti-inflammatory and antinociceptive effects of sinapyl alcohol and its glucoside syringin
J. Choi; K. Shin; H. Park; H. Jung; H. Kim; Y. Lee; J. Rew; K. Lee*
Planta Med., 2004, 70(11), 1027-1032

Syringin

Chemical Hazards in Industry
(http://www.rsc.org/Publishing/CurrentAwareness/CHI/index.asp)

This covers the following: health and safety; chemical and biological hazards; disposal, storage and transportation; industrial hazards; waste management; plant safety and best practice; legislation; emergency planning; and protective equipment. A typical sample record is shown in Table 11.8.

Laboratory Hazards Bulletin
(http://www.rsc.org/Publishing/CurrentAwareness/LHB/index.asp)

This bulletin covers the following: chemical and biological hazards; leaks, spills and unplanned releases; hazardous waste management; fires and explosions; safety legislation; precautions and safe practices; occupational health and hygiene monitoring; and protective equipment. A typical sample record is shown in Table 11.9.

Mass Spectrometry Bulletin
(http://www.rsc.org/Publishing/CurrentAwareness/msb/index.asp)

This bulletin covers the following: instrument design and techniques; isotopic analysis, precision mass measurement, isotope separation, age

Table 11.8 Sample record from *Chemical Hazards in Industry*

Sample record – Book	
Book Title	Assessment and reclamation of contaminated land.
Author	Harrison, R.M. (Ed.); Hester, R. E. (Ed.)
ISBN	0 85404 275 X
Availability	Royal Society of Chemistry, Thomas Graham House, Science Park, Milton Road, Cambridge CB4 0WF, UK
Publication Year	2001
Language	English
Publication Type	Book
Abstract	Contaminated land and the methods and legal controls governing its reclamation for subsequent development and use are of great current interest and concern. This volume covers aspects of this subject, ranging from the origins and extent of contaminated land problems, including effects on human health, through investigative measures, to specific techniques of remediation. It is written in the context of the new UK contaminated land regime and includes human and ecological risk assessment methodology, and the legal liabilities and insurance aspects of contaminated land. Contents include: the extent of contaminated land problems and the scientific response; the new UK contaminated land regime; identifying and dealing with contaminated land; contaminated land and the link with health; human health risk assessment: guideline values and magic numbers; ecological risk assessment under the new contaminated land regime; remediation methods for contaminated sites; and legal liablilities and insurance aspects of contaminated land. Price £32.50.
Descriptors	book contaminated land remediation legislation & regulations UK

Table 11.9 Sample record from *Laboratory Hazards Bulletin*

Journal Title	Strategy to assess exposure of laboratory personnel to select OSHA-regulated chemicals at Massachusetts Institute of Technology.
Author	Julien, R.; DiBerardinis, L; Herrick, R.; Edwards, R.
Source	*Chemical Health and Safety*, Jul–Aug 2001, **8** (4), 25–29
Publication Year	2001
Language	English
Publication Type	Journal
Abstract	A study was made on exposure levels to five chemicals for laboratory personnel working at the Massachusetts Institute of Technology. The OSHA regulated substances were benzene, formaldehyde, chloroform, methylene chloride and arsenic compounds. Eight laboratories were selected for monitoring on the basis of detailed information collected from 88 laboratories. Data came from hazardous waste manifests. Personal and area sampling was carried out with standard National Institute of Occupational Safety and Health air sampling and analytical methods being used. Exposure levels were well below the OSHA permissible level and TLV levels recommended by the American Conference of Governmental Industrial Hygienists in all but one laboratory. In typical laboratory activitites, exposure levels can be kept below TLVs if engineering controls are working correctly.
Chemical Names	benzene; formaldehyde; chloroform; methylene chloride; arsenic compounds
[CAS Reg. No.]	71-43-2; 50-00-0; 67-66-3; 75-09-2
Descriptors	threshold limit value monitoring laboratory engineering control

determination, etc.; chemical analysis; organic chemistry; atomic and molecular processes; surface phenomena and solid state studies; and thermodynamics and reaction kinetics. A typical sample record is shown in Table 11.10.

Table 11.10 Sample record from *Mass Spectrometry Bulletin*

Example items from *Mass Spectrometry Bulletin* are given below:

- This item appeared in the **Organic Mass Spectrometry** section of *Mass Spectrometry Bulletin*.
  Formation and decomposition of the m/z 75 fragment ions from the molecular ion of ethyl lactate, $CH_3CH(OH)COOCH_2CH_3(A1)$
  Tajima, S., Watanbabe, D., Nakajima, S., Sekiguchi, O., Nibberomg, N.M.M.
  Int. J. Mass Spec., 2001, 207(3), 217–222
  Fragmentation mechanism, Molecular ions, Ethyl lactate
- This item appeared in the **Reactive Ion Processes** section of *Mass Spectrometry Bulletin*.
  Measurement of the autodetachment lifetime of SF_6^* as a function of electron energy in a free jet expansion(C3)
  Le Garrec, J-L., Steinhurst, D.A., Smith, M.A.
  J. Chem. Phys., 2001, 114(20), 8831–8835
  Detachment, Lifetimes, Negative ions, Rate constant, Structure confirmation, SF_6.

Table 11.11 Sample record from *Chromatography Abstracts*

2299 Capillary liquid chromatographic determination of neutral phenolic compounds in apple juices.
Blanco Gomis, D., Fraga Palomino, N., Mangas Alonso, J. J., *Anal. Chim. Acta*, 1 Jan 2001, **426**(1), 111–117

Capillary liquid chromatography (CLC) is evaluated as an alternative to conventional HPLC to analyse complex phenolics. Several neutral phenolic compounds were separated on a packed-reversed phase fused-silica capillary column, and determined with UV detection. Conventional liquid chromatographic equipment was adapted for such purposes. Application of the proposed method to the quantification of neutral phenols in apple juices is reported. Phenolics are extracted and fractionated into neutral and acidic compounds by means of a C_{18} solid-phase cartridge. Typical recoveries ranging from 90 to 105% are obtained and reproducibility between extractions is <7% in all cases. Mass detection limits are at the sub-nanogram level.

Chromatography Abstracts
(http://www.rsc.org/Publishing/CurrentAwareness/CHRA/index.asp)
This covers the following: general and miscellaneous techniques; gas chromatography; liquid chromatography; electrophoresis; and thin-layer chromatography. A typical sample record is shown in Table 11.11.

Chemical Safety NewsBase/Environmental Chemistry Health & Safety
(http://www.rsc.org/Publishing/CurrentAwareness/ECHS/index.asp)
This is a current awareness online database which provides up-to-date information on the relevant issues affecting the chemical and allied industries, plus the health and safety aspects relevant to laboratories.

The Dictionary of Substances and their Effects (DOSE)
(http://www.rsc.org/Publishing/CurrentAwareness/DOSE/index.asp)
This is a single source of all relevant data for the accurate assessment of the risks associated with the use of chemicals of environmental concern. A typical sample record is shown in Table 11.12.

Free access online databases

A range of free online chemical databases exist on the Internet that allow searching via chemical structure. These include: PubChem (http://pubchem.ncbi.nlm.nih.gov/); Drugbank (http://www.drugbank.ca/); ChEBI (http://www.ebi.ac.uk/chebi/); ChemSpider (http://www.chemspider.com/).

- PubChem: provides information on the biological activities of small molecules.

- DrugBank: This database is a bioinformatics and cheminformatics resource that combines detailed drug (i.e. chemical, pharmacological and pharmaceutical) data with comprehensive drug target (i.e. sequence, structure and pathway) information.

- ChEBI (Chemical Entities of Biological Interest): a dictionary of molecular entities focused on 'small' chemical compounds.

- ChemSpider: Perhaps the latest addition to the chemical database online resources is ChemSpider. This database allows searching of over 21 million chemical structures.

Table 11.12 Sample record from *Dictionary of Substances and their Effects*

B47 Benzene

C_6H_6 **Mol. Wt.** 78.11   **CAS Registry No.** 71-43-2

Synonyms benzol; benzole; coal naphtha; mineral naphtha; phenylhydride; pyrobenzol; pyrobenzole

EINECS No. 200-753-7   **RTECS No.** CY 1400000

Uses Solvent for fats, inks, oils, paints, plastics and rubber. Starting material in chemical manufacture of resins, plastics, nylon-66, polyamides and styrene. Used in the manufacture of detergents, explosives and pharmaceuticals (1).

Physical properties

M.Pt. 5.5°C   **B.Pt.** 80.1°C   **Flash point** –11°C   **Specific gravity** 0.8786 at 20°C with respect to water at 4°C

Partition coefficient log P_{ow} 2.15   **Volatility** v.p. 76 mmHg at 20°C; v.den. 2.77

Solubility Water: 1780 mg L^{-1} at 20°C. Organic solvents: miscible acetone, ethanol, diethyl ether

Occupational exposure

FR-VME 5 ppm (16 mg m^{-3})

JP-OEL 10 ppm (32 mg m^{-3})

SE-LEVL 0.5 ppm (1.5 mg m^{-3})   **SE-STEL** 3 ppm (9 mg m^{-3})

UK-LTEL MEL 5 ppm (16 mg m^{-3})

US-TWA 0.5 ppm (1.6 mg m^{-3})   **US-STEL** 2.5 ppm (8 mg m^{-3})

UN No. 1114   **HAZCHEM Code** 3WE   **Conveyance classification** flammable liquid

Supply classification Highly flammable, toxic

Risk phrases May cause cancer – Highly flammable – Toxic: danger of serious damage to health by prolonged exposure through inhalation, in contact with skin and if swallowed (R45, R11, R48/23/24/25)

Safety phrases Restricted to professional users – Avoid exposure – obtain special instruction before use - In case of accident or if you feel unwell, seek medical advice immediately (show label where possible) (S53, S45)

Ecotoxicity

Fish toxicity

LC_{50} (24-96 hr) fathead minnow, bluegill sunfish, goldfish 36-22 mg L^{-1} (1).

LC_{50} (96 hr) bass 6-11 ppm (1).

Invertebrate toxicity

LC_{50} (96 hr) grass shrimp 20-27 ppm (1,2).

Cell multiplication inhibition test, *Pseudomonas putida* 92 mg L^{-1}, *Microcystis aeruginosa* >1400 mg L^{-1}, *Entosiphon sulcatum* >700 mg L^{-1} (1).

LC_{50} *Brachionus calyciflorus* and *Brachionus plicatilis* >1000 mg L^{-1} (3).

EC_{50} (8 day) *Selenastrum capricornutum* 41 mg L^{-1} (4).

Bioaccumulation

Bioconcentration factor in Pacific herring larvae, eel 3.5-3.9 (1).

Table 11.12 (continued)

B47 Benzene

Environmental fate

Nitrification inhibition

Not inhibited at 500 mg L^{-1} (5).

Benzene inhibited ammonia oxidation, by ammonia monooxygenase, in *Nitrosomonas europaea* (concentration unspecified) (6).

Degradation studies

ThOD 3.07 g g^{-1}, COD 0.927 g^{-1} (7).

BOD$_{10}$ 67% reduction of dissolved oxygen in acclimatised sludge (1).

Benzene is subject to rapid volatilisation in water and from soil surfaces, and is very mobile is soil.

Biodegradation may occur in shallow aerobic ground water, but not under anaerobic conditions (8).

Confirmed biodegradable (9).

Mammalian and avian toxicity

Acute date

LD$_{50}$ oral rat, mouse 3400, 4700 mg kg^{-1} respectively (10, 11).

Short-term acute exposure in humans may cause initial exhilaration, followed by dizziness, headache, nausea, drowsiness and pulmonary irritation. 7500 ppm and above for approximately 30 min may produce narcosis and death (12).

Sub-acute and sub-chronic data

Exposure of rats to 50 ppm benzene vapour for several wk, led to a reduction in red and white blood cells and platelets; exposure to concentrations <100 ppm produced leucopenia and aplasia (12).

♂ mice were fed 0–790 mg l^{-1} in drinking water for 28 days. Stimulation of the hypothalamic-pituitary-adrenocortical axis and increased circulatory levels of corticosterone were observed at high dose levels (13).

Oral mouse (3 day) 660 mg kg^{-1} once day^{-1} in feed. Increase in the number of mature activated macrophages in the bone marrow, and enhanced production of hydrogen peroxide by bone marrow granulocytes and mononuclear phagocytes (14).

Carcinogenicity and chronic effects

Sufficient evidence for carcinogenicity to humans and animals, IARC classification group 1 (15). Chronic exposure to benzene, in humans, at concentrations that produce changes in the blood may result in leukaemia, especially acute myelogenous leukaemia (12).

There is clear evidence of carcinogenicity in mice and rats treated by gavage (103 wk) 100 and 200 mg L^{-1}.

Tumours have been reported in various tissues including adrenals, lung, liver, ovary, oral cavity, stomach and skin (16).

Benzene administered by gavage produced ovarian atrophy, cysts, hyperplasia and neoplasia in mice (17).

National Toxicology Program tested ♂ and ♀ rats and mice via gavage. Clear evidence of carcinogenicity in ♂ and ♀ rats and mice (18).

Rat Zymbal glands, nasal and oral cavities, mammary gland and bone marrow all have higher peroxidase activity than non-target tissue for benzene carcinogenicity. This ability to oxidise benzene to phenolic metabolites could explain the greater susceptibility of these tissues to benzene induced tumourigenesis (19).

Target organs of carcinogenicity: mouse and rat Zymbal's gland, mouse Harderian gland, mouse lung, mouse mammary gland, rat oral cavity, rat skin, rat stomach, and rat vascular system (20).

Teratogenicity and reproductive effects

Teratogenicity has been reported at high concentrations in rats, but there is no evidence of foetal malformations at concentrations which produce no maternal toxicity. Women are considered hypersusceptible to benzene, particularly during pregnancy and breast feeding, however, there are no reports of teratogenic effects or any incease in spontaneous abortion in women occupationally exposed to benzene (17, 21).

Benzene shows concentration-dependent embryotoxicity in rats. Lowest embryotoxic concentration is 1.5 μ mol ml^{-1} (22).

Metabolism and toxicokinetics

Benzene is partly eliminated unchanged in the breath and urine of humans. Oxidation occurs producing benzene epoxide, phenols and diphenols, including catechol, hydroquinone, benzoquinone and 1,2,4-benzenetriol, which are in turn conjugated in the liver and excreted in the urine (12,23).

Toxic amounts of benzene can readily be absorbed through the skin (12).

Cytochrome P450 (CYP) 2E1 activity in human liver microsomes metabolises benzene to hydroquinone and catechol (24).

EC$_{50}$ mitochondrial respiration 525 ppm (species unspecified) (25).

(continued)

Table 11.12 Sample record from *Dictionary of Substances and their Effects* (continued)

B47   Benzene

Cynomolgus monkeys were given 5, 50 or 500 mg of radiolabelled benzene intraperitoneally. Uring was collected for up to 24 hr. The proportion of excreted radiolabel decreased from 50 to 15% with increasing dose. The proportion of hydroquinone derivatives and muconic acid in the urine also decreased with increasing dose.

Catechol conjugates were not detected (26).

The *in vitro* penetration of ^{14}C-benzene was studied using freshly prepared human skin. The permeability coefficient under standard conditions (26°C) was 0.14 cm hr^{-1}. This increased to 0.26 cm hr^{-1} at 50°C. Application of baby oil, moisturiser or insect repellent had no effect, however, pretreatment with sunscreen caused an increase to 0.24 cm hr^{-1} (27).

Benzene oxide has been shown to be a product of hepatic benzene metabolism in man, rats and mice *in vitro*.

After 18 minutes of incubation of mouse liver microsomes with 1 mM benzene, 7% of the toal benzene metabolites were benzene oxide (28).

Irritancy

Dermal rabbit (24 hr) 15 mg caused mild irritation, and 2 mg instilled into rabbit eye caused severe irritation (29,30).

Genotoxicity

Salmonella typhimurium TA97, TA98, TA100, TA1535, TA1537 with and without metabolic activation negative (16,31).

Salmonella typhimurium TA102 with metabolic activation negative (32).

Escherichia coli K-12 *uvrB/recA* DNA repair host-mediated assay with and without metabolic activation negative (33).

In vitro human lymphoblastoid MCL-5 cells induced micronucleus formation (34).

In vitro rat bone marrow cells, induced micronucleated polychromatic erythrocytes and sister-chromatid exchange (35).

In vitro rat spleen lymphocytes, induced micronucleated polychromatic erythrocytes and sister-chromatid exchange (35).

In vivo rodent bone marrow autogenetic test positive induction of micronuclei and chromosomal aberrations (31).

Chromosomal aberrations in white blood cells and bone marrow in humans which could initiate leukaemia have been reported, but there is no evidence of aberrations at exposure levels of 25 ppm or less (12).

Inhalation ♂ mice 1 ppm induced chromosomal aberrations is spermatocytes and sister chromatid exchange in spermatogonia (36,37).

Other effects

Other adverse effects (human)

Thirteen published population-based and hospital-based case-control studies of multiple myeloma up to 1995 were examined for any relationship between this cancer and exposure to benzene or to surrogates for benzene exposure. No increased association was found between multiple myeloma and benzene or groups of chemicals that included benzene. Exposure to petroleum products, employment in petroleum-related occupations and cigarette smoking were not risk factors for multiple myeloma. However, there was a significant association with exposure to combustion products in engine exhaust (38).

Haematological and immunochemical investigation of 270 workers with chronic exposure to benzene evidenced changes to lymphocyte nuclei and disorders of the humoral immune response (39).

A cohort of 74,828 benzene-exposed and 35,805 non-exposed workers employed during 1972–1987 in 12 cities in China was studied to determine mortality from all causes. Demographic and occupational data were examined. Mortality was slightly increased in workers with greater cumulative exposure to benzene, the excess being largely due to cancer deaths. Mortality from lymphatic and haematopoietic malignancies, lung cancer and occupational injuries in direct relation to cumulative benzene exposure. Suggestive associations were also noted for nasopharyngeal and oesophageal cancer (40).

Other comments

Originally produced by coal carbonisation, but now largely derived from petroleum or by cyclisation and aromatisation of paraffinic hydrocarbons. LC$_{50}$ (48 hr) Mexican axolotl (3–4 wk after hatching) 370 mg L^{-1} (41).

Benzene exposure, experimental toxicology, epidemiology studies, human health and environmental effects have been extensively reviewed (42–67).

Epidemiological evidence on benzene and lymphatic and haematopoietic cancers reviewed (68).

World Health Organisation guidelines on drinking water, provisional limit 10 μg L^{-1}.

Table 11.12 (continued)

References

1. Verschueren, K. *Handbook of Environmental Data on Organic Chemicals* 2nd edn, 1983, Van Nostrand Reinhold.
2. Bringman, G. et al. *Nat. Res.* 1980, **14**, 231.
3. Herman, D. C. et al. *Bull. Environ. Contam. Toxicol.* 1991, 47(6), 874–881.
4. Herman, D. C. et al. *Aquat. Toxicol.* 1990, **18**(2), 87–100.
5. Richardson, M. *Nitrification Treatment of Sewage* 1985, RSC, London.
6. Keener, W. K. et al. *Appl. Environ. Microbiol.* 1994, **60**(6), 1914–1920.
7. Urano, K. *J. Haz. Mat.* 1986, **13**, 147.
8. Howard, P. H. (Ed.); *Fate and Exposure Data for Organic Chemicals* 1990, **2**, 29–39.
9. *MITI Report* 1984, Ministry of International Trade and Industry, Tokyo.
10. *Raw Materials Handbook* 1974, **1**, 5.
11. *Hyg. Sanit.* 1967, **32**, 349.
12. *Chemical Data Safety Sheets* 1988, **1**, 14–18, RSC, London.
13. Hsieh, G. C. et al. *Immunopharmacology* 1991, **21**(1), 23–31.
14. MacEachern, L. et al. *Toxicol. Appl. Pharmacol.* 1992, 117(2), 147–154.
15. *IARC Monograph* 1987, **Suppl. 7**, 120.
16. Ashby, J. *Mutat. Res.* 1988, 204, 17–115.
17. Maronpot, R. R. *Environ. Health Perspect.* 1987, 73, 125–130.
18. *National Toxicology Program Research and Testing Division* 1995, Report No. TR-289, NIEHS, Research Triangle Park, NC 27709.
19. Low, L. K. et al. *J. Am. Coll. Toxicol.* 1995, **14**(1), 40–60.
20. Gold, L. S. et al. *Mutat. Res.* 1993, **268**(1), 75–100.
21. Fishbein, L. et al. *IARC Environ. Carcinog.* 1988, 10.
22. Brown-Woodman, P. D. C. et al. *Reprod. Toxicol.* 1994, **8**(2), 121–135.
23. Lewis, J. G. et al. *Toxicol. Appl. Pharmacol.* 1988, **92**(2), 246–254.
24. Seaton, M. J. et al. *Carcinogenesis* 1994, **15**(9), 1799–1806.
25. Beach, A. C. et al. *J. Biochem. Toxicol.* 1992, **7**(3), 155–161.
26. Sabourin, P. J. et al. *Toxicol. Appl. Pharmacol.* 1992.
27. Nakai, J. S. et al. *J. Toxicol. Environ. Health* 1997, **51**(5), 447–462.
28. Lovern, M. R. et al. *Carcinogenesis* 1997, **18**(9), 1695–1700.
29. *Am. Ind. Hyg. Assoc. J.* 1962, **95**, 23.
30. Marhold, J. V. *Sbornik Vysledku Toxixologickeho Vysetreni Latek A Pripravku* 1972, 23, Prague.
31. Shelby, M. D. *Mutat. Res.* 1988, **204**, 3–15.
32. Mueller, W. et al. *Environ. Health Perspect.* 1993, **101**(Suppl. 3), 33–36.
33. Hellmer, L. et al. *Mutat. Res.* 1992, **272**(2), 145–160.
34. Crofton-Sleigh, C. et al. *Mutagenesis* 1993, **8**(4), 363–372.
35. Shi, X. C. et al. *J. Occup. Med. Toxicol.* 1993, **2**(1), 53–63.
36. Au, W. W. et al. *Teratog. Carcinog. Mutagen.* 1990, **10**(2), 125–134.
37. Zhu, Yufen. et al. *Weisheng Dulixue Zazhi* 1989, **3**(4), 228–230, (Ch.) (*Chem. Abstr.*, **113**, 72845d).
38. Bezabeh, S. et al. *Environ. Health Perspect.* 1996, **104**(Suppl. 6), 1393–1398.
39. Chirco, V. et al. *Rev. Roum. Med. Int.* 1981, **19**(4), 373–378.
40. Hayes, R. B. et al. *Environ. Health Perspect.* 1996, **104**(Suppl. 6), 1349–1352.
41. Slooff, W. et al. *Bull. Environ. Contam. Toxicol.* 1980, **24**, 439.
42. Jin, C. et al. *Br. J. Ind. Med.* 1987, **44**(2), 124–128.
43. Sandlar, D. P. et al. *Am. J. Epidemiol.* 1987, **126**(6), 1017–1032.
44. Schwartz, E. *Am. J. Ind. Med.* 1987, **12**(1), 91–99.
45. Damrau, J. Z. *Klin. Med.* 1990, **45**(23), 2063–2064, (Ger.) (*Chem. Abstr.*, **114**, 87806m).
46. Kipen, H. M. et al. *Adv. Mod. Environ. Toxicol.* 1989, **16**, 67–86.
47. Aksoy, M. *Adv. Med. Environ. Toxicol.* 1989, **16**, 87–98.
48. Lamm, S. H. *Environ. Health Perspect.* 1989, **82**, 289–297.
49. Sabourn, P. J. et al. *Adv. Mod. Environ. Toxicol.* 1989, **16**, 153–176.
50. Spitzer, H. L. *Adv. Mod. Environ. Toxicol.* 1989, **16**, 141–152.
51. Moszczynski, P. et al. *Med. Pr.* 1985, **36**(5), 316–324.
52. Kalt, G. T. *CRC Crit. Rev. Toxicol.* 1987, **18**(2), 141–159.
53. King, A. G. et al. *Mol. Pharmacol.* 1987, **32**(6), 807–812.
54. *ECETOC Technical Report No. 71* 1996, European Centre for Ecotoxicology and Toxicology of Chemicals, 4 Avenue E. Van Nieuwenhuyse (Bte 6), B-1160 Brussels, Belgium.
55. Goldstein, B. D. *Adv. Mod. Environ. Toxicol.* 1989, **16**, 55–65.
56. *Gov. Rep. Announce Index US* 1989, **16**, 131–139.
57. Bailer, A. J. et al. *Adv. Mod. Environ. Toxicol.* 1989, **16**, 131–139.
58. Wallace, L. A. *Adv. Mod. Environ. Toxicol.* 1989, **16**, 113–130.
59. Izmerov, N. F. *Scientific Reviews of Soviet Literature on Toxicity & Hazards of Chemicals* 1992–1993, **90**, Eng. Trans, Richardson, M. L. (Ed.), UNEP/IRPTC, Geneva.
60. Ghittori, S. et al. *J. Toxicol Environ. Health* 1993, **38**(3), 233–243.
61. Infante, P. F. et al. *Appl. Occup. Environ. Hyg.* 1992, **7**(4), 253–262.
62. Medinsky, M. A. et al. *Toxicology* 1995, **105**(2,3), 225–233.
63. Hallenbeck, W. H. et al. *Bull. Environ. Contam. Toxicol.* 1992, **48**(3), 327–333.
64. Medinsky, M. A. et al. *Environ. Health Perspect. Suppl.* 1994, **102**(Suppl. 9), 119–124.
65. Paustenbach, D. J. et al. *Environ. Health Perspect.* 1993, **101**(Suppl. 6), 177–200.
66. Tompa, A. et al. *Mutat. Res.* 1994, **304**(2), 159–165.
67. Huff, J. *J. Occup. Med. Toxicol.* 1992, **1**(2), 109–141.
68. Savitz, D. A. et al. *Am. J. Ind. Med.* 1997, **31**(3), 287–295.

Sources for further study

DrugBank: a knowledge base for drugs, drug actions and drug targets. Wishart, D.S., Knox, C., Guo, A.C., Cheng, D., Shrivastava, S., Tzur, D., Gautam, B. and Hassanali, M. (2008) *Nucleic Acids Res*. 36 (database issue): D901–D906.

de Matos, P., Alcántara, R., Dekker, A., Ennis, M., Hastings, J., Haug, K., Spiteri, I., Turner, S. and Steinbeck, C. (2010) Chemical entities of biological interest: An update. *Nucleic Acids Res*. 38 (database issue): D249–D254.

Study exercises

11.1 Visit WebElements (http://www.webelements .com/) and look up the following properties of chromium:

(a) melting point (in K and °C)
(b) electronegativity (Pauling)
(c) atomic weight
(d) ground state electron configuration
(e) atomic number

11.2 Tips:

(a) Visit the electronic journal websites listed in Table 11.1 and view the latest articles.

(b) Identify the role of each of the three organisations listed in Table 11.2.

(c) View the websites listed in Table 11.3 and identify which of these websites may be useful for you with your next assignment, laboratory practical or project work.

11.3 As a registered student at a University you will have access to a vast range of scientific journal information via your Institutions subscription to major publishing houses. Your task is to become familiar with these systems so that you can gain maximum benefit from their use.

12 Using spreadsheets

The spreadsheet is one of the most powerful and flexible computer applications. It can be described as the electronic equivalent of a paper-based longhand calculation, where the sums are carried out automatically. Spreadsheets provide a dynamic method of storing, manipulating and analysing data sets. Advantages of spreadsheets include:

- **Ease and convenience** – especially when complex calculations are repeated on different sets of data.

- **Accuracy** – providing the entry data and cell formulae are correct, the result will be free of calculation errors.

- **Improved presentation** – data can be produced in graphical or tabular form to a very high quality.

- **Integration with other programs** – graphs and tables can be exported to other compatible programs, such as a word processor in the same office suite.

- **Useful tools** – advanced features include hypothesis-testing statistics, database features and macros.

Spreadsheets can be used to:

- store and manipulate raw data by removing the drudgery of repeated calculations, allowing easy transformation of data and calculation of statistics;

- graph out your data rapidly to get an instant evaluation of results. Printouts can be used in practical and project reports;

- carry out statistical analysis by built-in procedures or by allowing construction of formulae for specific tasks;

- model 'what if' situations where the consequences of changes in data can be seen and evaluated.

- The spreadsheet (Fig. 12.1) is divided into rows (identified by numbers) and columns (identified by alphabetic characters). Each individual combination of column and row forms a cell which can contain either a data item, a formula or a piece of text. Formulae can include scientific and/or statistical functions and/or a reference to other cells or groups of cells (often called a range). Complex systems of data input and analysis can be constructed. The analysis, in part or complete, can be printed out. New data can be added at any time and the sheet will recalculate automatically. The power a spreadsheet offers is directly related to your ability to create arrays of formulae (models) that are accurate and templates that are easy to use.

Data entry

Spreadsheets have built-in commands which allow you to control the layout of data in the cells (see Fig. 12.2). These include number format, the number of decimal places to be shown (the spreadsheet always calculates using eight or more places), the cell width and the location of the entry within the cell (left, right or centre). An auto-entry facility assists

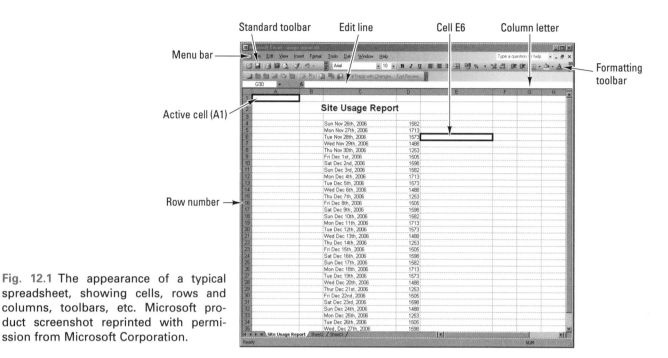

Standard toolbar   Edit line   Cell E6   Column letter

Menu bar

Formatting toolbar

Active cell (A1)

Row number

Fig. 12.1 The appearance of a typical spreadsheet, showing cells, rows and columns, toolbars, etc. Microsoft product screenshot reprinted with permission from Microsoft Corporation.

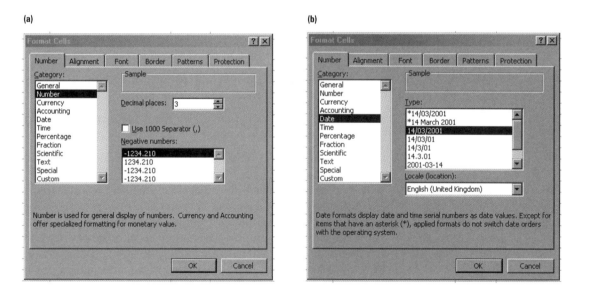

Fig. 12.2 Example of cell formatting options within a Microsoft Excel spreadsheet. These menus are accessed via the *Format > Cell* option and would apply to all of a range of selected cells. (a) Use of the number formatting option to specify that data will be presented to three decimal places (the underlying data will be held to greater accuracy). (b) Use of the date formatting option to specify that dates will be presented in day/month/year format (spreadsheet dates are stored numerically and converted to appropriate formats. This allows a period between two dates to be calculated more easily). Microsoft Product screenshots reprinted with permission from Microsoft Corporation.

greatly in entering large amounts of data by moving the entry cursor either vertically or horizontally as data are entered. Recalculation default is usually automatic so that when a new data value is entered the entire sheet is recalculated immediately.

Using hidden (or zero-width) columns – these are useful for storing intermediate calculations which you do not wish to be displayed on the screen or printout.

Operators and brackets in spreadsheets – the standard mathematical operators ÷ and × are usually replaced by / and * respectively, while ^ signifies 'to the power' (e.g. 10 ^ 4 = 10^4). In complex formulae, brackets should be used to separate the elements, otherwise the results may not be what you expect. For example, Excel will calculate =A1*B1/C1–D1 differently from (A1*B1)/(C1–D1).

Definition

Function – a pre-programmed code for the transformation of values (mathematical or statistical functions) or selection of text characters (string functions).

Example =sin(A5) is an example of a function in Excel. If you write this in a cell, the spreadsheet will calculate the sine of the number in cell A5 (assuming it to be an angle in radians) and write it in the cell. Different programs may use a slightly different syntax.

Working with empty cells – note that these may be given the value 0 by the spreadsheet for certain functions. This may cause errors, e.g. by rendering a minimum value inappropriate. Also, an 'error return' may result for certain functions if the cell content is zero.

The parts of a spreadsheet

Labels

These should be used to identify parts of the spreadsheet, for example, stating what data are contained in a particular column or indicating that a cell's contents represent the end point of a calculation. It may be useful to use the *Format > Cells > Border* and *Format > Cells > Patterns* functions to delimit numerical sections of your spreadsheet. Note that spreadsheet programs have been designed to make assumptions about the nature of data entry being made. If the first character is a number, then the entry is treated as numerical data; if it is a letter, then it is treated as a text entry; and if it is a specific symbol ('=' in Microsoft Excel), then what follows is a formula. If you wish to enter text that starts with a number, then you must type a designated character to show this (a single quote mark in Microsoft Excel).

Numbers

You can also enter numbers (values) in cells for use in calculations. Many programs let you enter numbers in more than one way and you must decide which method you prefer. The way you enter the number does not affect the way it is displayed on the screen as this is controlled by the cell format at the point of entry. There are usually special ways to enter data for percentages, currency and scientific notation for very large and small numbers.

Formulae

These are the 'power tools' of the spreadsheet because they do the calculations. A cell can be referred to by its alphanumeric code, e.g. A5 (column A, row 5) and the value contained in that cell manipulated within a formula, e.g. =(A5+10) or =(A5+B22) in another cell. Formulae can include various pre-programmed functions which can refer to a cell, so that if the value of that cell is changed, so is the result of the formula calculation. They may also include branching options through the use of logical operators (IF, TRUE, FALSE, OR, etc.).

Functions

A variety of functions is usually offered, but only mathematical and statistical functions will be considered here.

Mathematical functions

Spreadsheets offer a range of functions, including trigonometrical functions, angle functions, logarithms and random number functions. Functions are invaluable for transforming sets of data rapidly and can be used in formulae required for more complex analyses. Spreadsheets work with an order of preference of the mathematical operators in much the same way as a standard calculator and this must always be taken into account when operators are used in formulae. They also require a very precise syntax – the program should warn you if you break this.

Statistical functions

Modern spreadsheets incorporate many sophisticated statistical functions, and if these are not appropriate the spreadsheet can be used to carry out the calculations required for most of the statistical tests found in textbooks. The descriptive statistics normally available include:

- the sum of all data present in a column, row or block;
- the minimum and maximum of a defined range of cells;
- counts of cells – a useful operation if you have an unknown or variable number of data values;
- averages and other statistics describing location;
- standard deviations and other statistics describing dispersion.

A useful function where you have large numbers of data allows you to create frequency distributions using pre-defined class intervals.

The hypothesis-testing statistical functions are usually reasonably powerful (e.g. t-test, ANOVA, regression) and they often return the *probability* (P) of obtaining the test statistic when the null hypothesis (p. 510) is true (where $0 < P < 1$), so there may be no need to refer to statistical tables. Again, check on the effects of including empty cells within the statistical calculations.

Database functions

Many spreadsheets can be used as simple databases and offer a range of functions to support this, including filtering and sorting options. The rows and columns of the spreadsheet are used as the fields and records of the database (see Chapter 12). For many chemical purposes, this form of database is perfectly adequate and should be seriously considered before using a full-feature database product.

Copying

All programs provide a means of copying (replicating) formulae or cell contents when required and this is a very useful feature. This is usually accomplished by 'dragging' a cell's contents to a new range using the mouse. When copying, references to cells may be either relative, changing with the row/column as they are copied, or absolute, remaining a fixed cell reference and not changing as the formulae are copied (Fig. 12.3).

> **KEY POINT** The distinction between relative and absolute cell references is very important and must be understood; it provides one of the most common forms of error when copying formulae.

In Excel, copying is normally *relative* and if you wish a cell reference to be *absolute* when copied, this is done by putting a dollar ($) sign before and after the column reference letter, e.g. $C$56.

Naming blocks

When a group of cells (a block) is carrying out a particular function, it is often easier to give the block a name which can then be used in all formulae referring to that block. This powerful feature also allows the spreadsheet to be more readable.

Statistical calculations – make sure you understand whether the functions you employ apply to populations or samples (see p. 504).

Using text functions – these allow you to manipulate text within your spreadsheet and include functions such as 'find and replace' and alphabetical or numerical 'sort'.

(a)

	Cell	Formula	
Original → cell	A1	=B1+C1	← Original formula
Copied cells	A2	=B2+C2	Copied formulae (relative)
	A3	=B3+C3	
	A4	=B4+C4	

(b)

	Cell	Formula	
Original → cell	A1	=B1/$C$1	← Original formula
Copied cells	A2	=B2/$C$1	Copied formulae (mixed relative and absolute)
	A3	=B3/$C$1	
	A4	=B4/$C$1	

Fig. 12.3 Illustration of relative (a) and absolute (b) copying. In Excel, the $ sign before and after the column letter makes the cell reference absolute, as shown in (b).

Spreadsheet templates

A template is a pre-constructed spreadsheet containing the formulae required for repeated data analysis. Data are added when they become available, and results are available as soon as the last item is entered. To create a template, the sequence of operations is:

1. Determine what information/statistics you want to produce.

2. Identify the variables you will need to use, both for original data that will be entered and for any intermediate calculations that might be required.

3. Set up areas of the spreadsheet for data entry, calculation of intermediate values (statistical values such as sums of squares, etc.), calculation of final statistics and, if necessary, a summary area.

4. Establish the format of the numeric data if this is different from the default values. This can be done globally (affecting the entire spreadsheet) or locally (affecting only a specified part of the spreadsheet).

5. Establish the column widths required for the various activities.

6. Add text (labels) to identify input, intermediate formulae and output cells. This is valuable in error-tracking and when carrying out further development work. Text can be entered in designated cells, or cells can be annotated using the 'comments' feature (*Insert > Comment*).

7. Enter a test set of values to use during formula entry: use a fully worked example to check that formulae are working correctly.

8. Enter the formulae required to make all the calculations, both intermediate and final. Check that results are correct using the test data.

The spreadsheet is then ready for use. Delete all of the test data values and you have created your template. Save the template to a disk and it is then available for repeated operations.

Graphics display

Most spreadsheets now offer a wide range of graphics facilities which are easy to use, and this represents an ideal way to examine your data sets rapidly and comprehensively. The quality of the final graphics output (to a printer) is variable but is usually perfectly sufficient for data exploration and analysis. Many of the options are business graphics styles but there are usually histogram, bar chart, X–Y plotting, line and area graphics options available. Note that some spreadsheet graphics may not come up to the standards expected for the formal presentation of scientific data, unless you manipulate the initial output appropriately (see Box 60.2).

Printing spreadsheets

This is usually a straightforward, menu-controlled procedure, made difficult only by the fact that your spreadsheet may be too big to fit on one piece of paper. Try to develop an area of the sheet which contains only the data that you will be printing, i.e. perhaps a summary area. Remember that columns can usually be hidden for printing purposes and you can control whether the printout is in portrait or landscape mode, and for continuous paper or single sheets (depending on printer capabilities). Use a screen preview option, if available, to check your layout before printing. A 'print to fit' option is also available in some programs, making the output fit the page dimensions.

Sources for further study

Hart-Davies, G. (2003) *How to do Everything with Microsoft Office Excel 2003*. McGraw-Hill, Berkeley.

Harvey, G. (2003) *Excel 2003 for Dummies*. Wiley, New York.

(And similar texts for other release versions.)

Study exercises

The instructions and tips for these problems assume that you have Excel (2003 or later) available. If not, they should be readily modified for most advanced spreadsheet programs. If you have problems with any of the tasks, consult Box 60.2 or try using the program's *Help* facility.

12.1 Create a spreadsheet and graph (introductory).

(i) Copy the information in the table below into a spreadsheet. Name and save the spreadsheet file appropriately.

(ii) From the copied information, create a pie chart using the *Chart Wizard function.*

(iii) Adjust the colours selected so the chart will print out in black and white. Save the final version of your spreadsheet. Print the chart out directly from Excel.

Relative percentage composition of elements in the Earth's crust.

Element	Percentage
oxygen	46.2
silicon	28.2
aluminium	8.2
iron	5.6
calcium	4.2
sodium	2.4
magnesium	2.3
potassium	2.1
titanium	0.6
hydrogen	0.2
Total	100

12.2 Create a spreadsheet and graph (advanced).

(i) Copy the data in the table below into a spreadsheet. Name and save the file appropriately.

Decomposition of N_2O_5

Time (s)	[N_2O_5]
0	1.000
40	0.762
80	0.580
120	0.442
160	0.336
200	0.256
400	0.066
600	0.017

(ii) Use the spreadsheet and chart-making facilities to explore by eye which of the following transformations would result in the best linear fit for these data: reciprocal, square root, cube root or log.

(iii) Add a linear trend-line to the chart for the most appropriate transformation.

(iv) Copy the graph to a file in Word and print out.

12.3 Use a spreadsheet as a simple database. Copy the data in the table on p. 93 into cells within a spreadsheet. Modify the column widths so you can see all of the text on a single screen. Now sort the data in the following ways:

(a) by subject, in alphabetical order;
(b) by date and then by time of day;
(c) by topic, in reverse alphabetical order.

Use the *Column Hide* function (*Format* menu in Microsoft Excel) so that the information in columns 4 and 6 is not displayed. Find out how to undo this operation.

My exam timetable

Subject	Date	Time	Paper	Location	Question style
Physical Chemistry	3 Jun	Morning	1	Great Hall	Multiple choice
Physical Chemistry	17 Jun	Morning	2	Exam Hall 5	Written paper
Organic Chemistry	3 Jun	Afternoon	1	Small Hall	Short answer questions
Organic Chemistry	14 Jun	Afternoon	2	Exam Hall 5	Written paper
Inorganic Chemistry	4 Jun	Morning	1	Small Hall	Short answer questions
Inorganic Chemistry	1 Jul	Afternoon	2	Exam Hall 3	Written paper
Analytical Chemistry	13 Jun	Afternoon	1	Exam Hall 5	Written paper
Analytical Chemistry	2 Jun	Morning	2	Main Laboratory	Practical exam

Word processors

Word processing is a transferable skill valuable beyond the immediate requirements of your course. The word processor has improved the process of writing because of the ease of revising text. Using a word processor should enhance your writing skills and speed because you can create, check and change your text on the screen before printing it as 'hard copy' on paper. Once entered and saved, multiple uses can be made of a piece of text with little effort.

When using a word processor you can:

- refine material many times before submission;

- insert material easily, allowing writing to take place in any sequence;

- use a spellchecker to check your text;

- use a thesaurus when composing your text;

- carry out ongoing checks of the word count;

- produce high quality final copies;

- reuse part or all of the text in other documents.

The potential disadvantages of using a word processor include:

- lack of ready access to a computer, software and/or a printer;

- time taken to learn the operational details of the program;

- the temptation to make 'trivial' revisions;

- loss of files due to computer breakdown, or disk loss, or failure.

The computerised office – many word processors are sold as part of an integrated office suite, e.g. Corel Word-Perfect Office and Microsoft Office, with the advantage that they share a common interface in the different components (word processor, spread-sheet, database, etc.) and allow ready exchange of information (e.g. text, graphics) between component programs.

Word processors come as 'packages' comprising the program and a manual, often with a tutorial program. Examples are Microsoft Word and WordPerfect. Most word processors have similar general features but differ in operational detail; it is best to pick one and stick to it as far as possible so that you become familiar with it. Learning to use the package is like learning to drive a car – you need only to know how to drive the computer and its program, not to understand how the engine (program) and transmission (data transfer) work, although a little background knowledge is often helpful and will allow you to get the most from the program.

In most word processors, the appearance of the screen realistically represents what the printout on paper will look like. Because of variation in operational details, only general and strategic information is provided in this chapter: you must learn the details of your word processor through use of the appropriate manual and 'help' facilities.

Before starting you will need:

- the program (usually installed on a hard disk or available *via* a network);

Using textbooks, manuals and tutorials – most programs no longer come with paper-based manuals and support information is usually provided in one or more of the following ways: as a help facility within the program; as a help file on the program CD; or as an online help support site. It is still often worthwhile investing in one of the commercial textbooks that support specific programs.

- a medium for storage, retrieval and back-up of your own files when created;

- a draft page layout design: in particular you should have decided on page size, page margins, typeface (font) and size, type of text justification, and format of page numbering;

- an outline of the text content;

- access to a suitable printer: this need not be attached to the computer you are using since your file can be taken or sent to an office where a printer is available, providing it has the same word processing program.

Using a word processor – take full advantage of the differences between word processing and 'normal' writing (which necessarily follows a linear sequence and requires more planning):

- Simply jot down your initial ideas for a plan, preferably at paragraph topic level. The order can be altered easily and if a paragraph grows too much it can easily be split.

- Start writing wherever you wish and fill in the rest later.

- Just put down your ideas as you think, confident in the knowledge that it is the concepts that are important to note; their order and the way you express them can be adjusted later.

- Don't worry about spelling and use of synonyms – these can (and should) be checked during a separate revision run through your text, using the spell checker first to correct obvious mistakes, then the thesaurus to change words for style or to find the *mot juste*.

- Don't forget that a draft printout may be required to check (a) for pace and spacing – difficult to correct for on-screen; and (b) to ensure that words checked for spelling fit the required sense.

Deleting and restoring text – because deletion can sometimes be made in error, there is usually an 'undelete' or 'restore' feature which allows the last deletion to be recovered, usually available through the program's *'Edit'* menu or as an icon in the toolbar.

Laying out (formatting) your document

Although you can format your text at any time, it is good practice to enter the basic commands at the start of your document: entering them later can lead to considerable problems due to reorganisation of the text layout. If you use a particular set of layout criteria regularly, e.g. an A4 page with space for a letterhead, then make a template containing the appropriate codes that can be called up whenever you start a new document. Note that various printers may respond differently to particular codes, resulting in a different spacing and layout.

Typing the text

If new to word-processing, think of the screen as a piece of typing paper. The cursor marks the position where your text/data will be entered and can be moved around the screen by use of the cursor-control keys. When you type, don't worry about running out of space on the line because the text will wrap around to the next line automatically. Do not use a carriage return (usually the $\boxed{\text{ENTER}}$ or $\boxed{\leftarrow}$ key) unless you wish to force a new line, e.g. when a new paragraph is wanted. If you make a mistake when typing, correction is easy. You can usually delete characters or words or lines and the space is closed automatically. You can also insert new text in the middle of a line or word. You can insert special codes to carry out a variety of tasks, including changing text appearance such as underlining, **emboldening** and *italics*. Paragraph indentations can be automated using $\boxed{\text{TAB}}$ or $\boxed{\leftrightarrows}$ as on a typewriter but you can also indent or bullet whole blocks of text using special menu options. The function keys are usually pre-programmed to assist in many of these operations.

Editing features

Word processors usually have an array of features designed to make editing documents easy. In addition to the simple editing procedures described above, the program usually offers facilities to allow blocks of text to be moved ('cut and paste'), copied or deleted.

An extremely valuable editing facility is the find or search procedure: this can rapidly scan through a document looking for a specified word, phrase or punctuation. This is particularly valuable when combined with a replace facility so that, for example, you could find the word 'test' and replace it with 'trial' throughout your document simply and rapidly.

Most word processors have a command which reveals the normally hidden codes controlling the layout and appearance of the printed text. When editing, this can be a very useful feature, since some changes to your text will cause difficulties if these hidden codes are not taken into account; in particular, make sure that the cursor is at the correct point before making changes to text containing hidden code, otherwise your text will sometimes change in apparently mystifying ways.

Fonts and line spacing

Most word processors offer a variety of fonts depending upon the printer being used. Fonts come in a wide variety of types and sizes, but they are defined in particular ways as follows:

Presenting your documents – it is good practice not to mix typefaces too much in a formal document; also the font size should not differ greatly for different headings, subheadings and the text.

- **Typeface:** the term for a family of characters of a particular design, each of which is given a particular name. The most commonly used for normal text is Times Roman (as used here for the main text) but many others are widely available, particularly for the better quality printers. They fall into three broad groups: serif fonts with curves and flourishes at the ends of the characters (e.g. Times Roman); sans serif fonts without such flourishes, providing a clean, modern appearance (e.g. Helvetica or Arial); and decorative fonts used for special purposes only, such as the production of newsletters and notices.

- **Size:** measured in points. A point is the smallest typographical unit of measurement, there being 72 points to the inch (about 28 points per cm). The standard sizes for text are 10, 11 and 12 point, but typefaces are often available up to 72 point or more.

Preparing draft documents – use double line spacing to allow room for your editing comments on the printed page.

- **Appearance:** many typefaces are available in a variety of styles and weights. Many of these are not designed for use in scientific literature but for desktop publishing.

- **Spacing:** can be either fixed, where every character is the same width, or proportional, where the width of every character, including spaces, is varied. Typewriter fonts such as Elite and Prestige use fixed spacing and are useful for filling in forms or tables, but proportional fonts make the overall appearance of text more pleasing and readable.

- **Pitch:** specifies the number of characters per horizontal inch of text. Typewriter fonts are usually 10 or 12 pitch, but proportional fonts are never given a pitch value since it is inherently variable.

- **Justification:** the term describing the way in which text is aligned vertically. Left justification is normal, but for some documents both left and right justification may be used (as here).

Preparing final documents – for most work, use a 12 point proportional serif typeface with spacing dependent upon the specifications for the work.

You should also consider the vertical spacing of lines in your document. Drafts and manuscripts are frequently double-spaced. If your document has unusual font sizes, this may well affect line spacing, although most word processors will cope with this automatically.

Table construction

Tables can be produced by a variety of methods:

- Using the tab key ⬚ as on a typewriter: this moves the cursor to predetermined positions on the page, equivalent to the start of each tabular column. You can define the positions of these tabs as required at the start of each table.

- Using special table-constructing procedures (see Box 61.2). Here the table construction is largely done for you and it is much easier than using tabs, providing you enter the correct information when you set up the table.

- Using a spreadsheet to construct the table and then copying it to the word processor (see Box 61.2). This procedure requires considerably more manipulation than using the word processor directly and is best reserved for special circumstances, such as the presentation of a very large or complex table of data, especially if the data are already stored as a spreadsheet.

Graphics and special characters

Many word processors can incorporate graphics from other programs into the text of a document. Files must be compatible (see your manual) but if this is so, it is a relatively straightforward procedure. For professional documents this is a valuable facility, but for most undergraduate work it is probably better to produce and use graphics as a separate operation, e.g. using a spreadsheet (see Box 60.2).

You can draw lines and other graphical features directly within most word processors and special characters (e.g. Greek characters) may be available, dependent upon your printer's capabilities.

Inserting special characters – Greek letters and other characters are available using the 'Insert' and 'Symbol' features in Word.

Tools

Many word processors also offer you special tools, the most important of which are:

- **Macros:** special sets of files you can create when you have a frequently repeated set of keystrokes to make. You can record these keystrokes as a 'macro' so that it can provide a short-cut for repeated operations.

- **Thesaurus:** used to look up alternative words of similar or opposite meaning while composing text at the keyboard.

- **Spellchecker:** a very useful facility which will check your spellings against a dictionary provided by the program. This dictionary is often expandable to include specialist words which you use in your work. The danger lies in becoming too dependent upon such facilities as they all have limitations: in particular, they will not pick up incorrect words which happen to be correct in a different context (i.e. 'was' typed as 'saw' or 'see' rather than 'sea'). Be aware of American spellings in programs from the USA, e.g. 'color' instead of 'colour'. The rule, therefore, is to use the spellcheck first and then carefully read the text for errors which have slipped through.

- **Word count:** useful when you are writing to a prescribed limit.

Using a spellcheck facility – do not rely on this to spot all errors. Remember that spellcheck programs do not correct grammatical errors.

Printing from your program

If more than one printer is attached to your PC or network, you will need to specify which one to use from the word processor's print menu. Most printers offer choices as to text and graphics quality, so choose draft (low) quality for all but your final copy since this will save both time and materials.

Use a print preview option to show the page layout, if this is available. Assuming that you have entered appropriate layout and font commands, printing is a straightforward operation carried out by the word processor at your command. Problems usually arise because of some incompatibility between the criteria you have entered and the printer's own capabilities. Make sure that you know what your printer offers before starting to type: although specified details are modifiable

Using the print preview mode – this can reveal errors of several kinds, e.g. spacing between pages, that can prevent you wasting paper and printer ink unnecessarily.

at any time, changing the page size, margin size, font size, etc. all cause your text to be rearranged, and this can be frustrating if you have spent time carefully laying out the pages.

> **KEY POINT** It is vital to save your work frequently to a memory stick, hard drive or network drive. This should be done every 10 minutes or so. If you do not save regularly, you may lose hours or days of work. You should also save back-up copies on a regular basis. Many programs can be set to 'autosave' every few minutes.

Databases

Choosing between a database and a spreadsheet – use a database only after careful consideration. Can the task be done better within a spreadsheet? A database program can be complex to set up and usually needs to be updated regularly.

A database is an electronic filing system whose structure is similar to a manual record card collection. Its collection of records is termed a file. The individual items of information on each record are termed fields. Once the database is constructed, search criteria can be used to view files through various filters according to your requirements. The computerised catalogues in your library are just such a system; you enter the filter requirements in the form of author or subject keywords.

You can use a database to catalogue, search, sort and relate collections of information. The benefits of a computerised database over a manual card-file system are:

- The information content is easily amended/updated.

- Printout of relevant items can be obtained.

- It is quick and easy to organise through sorting and searching/ selection criteria, to produce subgroups of relevant records.

- Record displays can easily be redesigned, allowing flexible methods of presenting records according to interest.

- Relational databases can be combined, giving the whole system immense flexibility. The older 'flat-file' databases store information in files which can be searched and sorted, but cannot be linked to other databases.

Using databases in chemistry – this is covered in Chapter 11.

Relatively simple database files can be constructed within spreadsheets using the columns and rows as fields and records respectively. These are capable of reasonably advanced sorting and searching operations and are probably sufficient for most types of databases you are likely to require as an undergraduate. You may also make use of a bibliographic database specially constructed for that purpose (p. 50).

Statistical analysis packages

Using spreadsheet statistics functions – before using a specific statistics package, check whether your spreadsheet is capable of carrying out the form of analysis you require (see Boxes 63.3 and 64.3), as this can often be the simpler option.

Statistical packages vary from small programs designed to carry out very specific statistical tasks to larger packages (SYSTAT SigmaStat, Minitab, etc.) intended to provide statistical assistance, from experimental design to the analysis of results. Consider the following features when selecting a package:

- The data entry and editing section should be user-friendly, with options for transforming data.

- Data exploration options should include descriptive statistics and exploratory data analysis techniques.

- Hypothesis-testing techniques should include ANOVA, regression analysis, multivariate techniques, parametric and non-parametric statistics (see Chapter 64).

- The program may provide assistance with experimental design.

- Output facilities should be suitable for graphical and tabular formats.

Some programs have very complex data entry systems, limiting the ease of using data in different tests. The data entry and storage system should be based on a spreadsheet system, so that subsequent editing and transformation operations are straightforward.

> **KEY POINT** Make sure that you understand the statistical basis for your test and the computational techniques involved before using a particular program.

Presentation using computer packages – while many computer programs enhance presentational aspects of your work, there are occasions when they can make your presentation worse. Take care to avoid the following common pitfalls:

- Default or 'chart wizard' settings for graphs may result in output that is non-standard for the sciences (see Box 60.3).
- Fonts in labels and legends may not be consistent with other parts of your presentation.
- Some programs cannot produce Greek symbols (e.g. μ); do not use 'u' as a substitute. The same applies to scientific notation and superscripts: do not use 14C for ^{14}C, and replace e.g. $1.4E+09$ with 1.4×10^9. First try cutting and pasting symbols from Word, or if this fails draw correct symbols by hand.

Graphics/presentation packages

Microsoft Office programs can be used to achieve most coursework tasks, e.g. PowerPoint is useful for creating posters (Box 14.1) and for oral presentations (Box 15.1). Should you need more advanced features, additional software may be available on your network, for example:

- SigmaPlot can produce graphs with floating axes;

- Macromedia Freehand is useful for designing complex graphics;

- DreamWeaver enables you to produce high-quality web pages;

- MindGenius can be used to produce mind maps.

Important points regarding the use of such packages are:

- the learning time required for some of the more complex operations can be considerable;

- the quality of your printer will limit the quality of your output;

- not all files will readily import into a word processor such as Microsoft Word – you may need to save your work in a particular format. The different types of file are distinguished by the three-character filename extension, e.g. .jpg and .bmp refer to specific image file formats.

> **KEY POINT** Computer graphics are not always satisfactory for scientific presentation. You should not accept the default versions produced – make appropriate changes to suit scientific standards and style. Box 60.1 gives a checklist for graph drawing and Box 60.2 provides guidelines for adapting Microsoft Excel output.

Image storage and manipulation

With the widespread use of digital images, programs that facilitate the storage and manipulation of electronic image files have become increasingly important. These programs create a library of your stored images and provide a variety of methods for organising and selecting images.

The industry-standard program, Adobe Photoshop, is one of many programs for image manipulation that vary widely in capability, cost and associated learning time. Many are highly sophisticated programs intended for graphic artists. However, for most scientific purposes, relatively limited functions are required.

Sources for further study

Gookin, D. (2003) *Word 2003 for Dummies*. Wiley, New York.

Kaufield, J. (2003) *Access 2003 for Dummies*. Wiley, New York.

Wang, W. (2003) *Microsoft Office 2003 for Dummies*. Wiley, New York.

(And similar texts for other packages and release versions.)

Study exercises

13.1 Investigate intermediate/advanced Word features. The tasks in the following list are likely to be useful in preparing assignments and report writing within chemistry. Can you carry out all of the tasks? If not, use either a manual or the online *Help* feature to find out how to accomplish them. Tips are given in the answer section.

(a) Sort information in a list into alphabetical order.
(b) Replace a text string word or phrase with a new text string throughout your document.
(c) Replace a text string in normal font with the same text string in italics throughout your document.
(d) Add a 'header' and 'footer' to your document, the former showing the document's title and the latter containing page numbers in the bottom centre of the page.
(e) Adjust the margins of the page to give a 5 cm margin on the left and a 2 cm margin on the right.
(f) Change the type of bullets used in a list from standard (• or ■) to a different form (e.g. –, ◆ or ☑).
(g) Use the 'thesaurus' option to find a different or more suitable word to express your meaning. Try, for example, to find alternatives to the word 'alternative'.
(h) Carry out a spellcheck on your document.
(i) Carry out a word count on your document and on a selected part of it.
(j) Open two documents and switch between them.

13.2 Make precise copies of tables. Copy the following tables using a word processor such as Word.

Chemical	Results of analysis (units)		
	August	September	October
X			
Y			
Z			

Chemical	Results of analysis (units)		
	August	September	October
X			
Y			
Z			

13.3 Investigate what programs and packages are available to you as a student. Test each program with appropriate data, images, etc.

Communicating information

A scientific poster is a visual display of the results of an investigation, usually mounted on a rectangular board. Posters are used in undergraduate courses to display project results or assignment work, and at scientific meetings to communicate research findings.

In a written report you can include a reasonable amount of specific detail and the reader can go back and reread difficult passages. However, if a poster is long-winded or contains too much detail, your reader is likely to lose interest.

Learning from others – look at the various types of posters around your university and elsewhere; the best examples will be visual, not textual, with a clear structure that helps get the key messages across.

> **KEY POINT** A poster session is like a competition – you are competing for the attention of people in a room. Because you need to attract and hold the attention of your audience, make your poster as interesting as possible. Think of it as an advertisement for your work and you will not go far wrong.

Preliminaries

Before considering the content of your poster, you should find out:

- the linear dimensions of your poster area, typically up to 1.5 m wide by 1.0 m high;

- the composition of the poster board and the method of attachment, whether drawing pins, Velcro tape, or some other form of adhesive; and whether these will be provided – in any case, it is safer to bring your own;

- the time(s) when the poster should be set up and when you should attend;

- the room where the poster session will be held.

Design

Plan your poster with your audience in mind, as this will dictate the appropriate level for your presentation. Aim to make your poster accessible to a broad audience. Since a poster is a *visual* display, you must pay particular attention to the presentation of information: work that may have taken hours to prepare can be ruined in a few minutes by the ill-considered arrangement of items (Fig. 14.1). Begin by making a draft sketch of the major elements of your poster. It is worth discussing your intended design with someone else, as constructive advice at the draft stage will save a lot of time and effort when you prepare the final version (or consult Simmonds and Reynolds, 1994).

Layout

One approach is to divide the poster into several smaller areas, perhaps six or eight in all, and prepare each as a separate item on a piece of card. Alternatively, you can produce a single large poster on one sheet of paper or card and store it inside a protective cardboard tube. However, a single large poster may bend and crease, making it difficult to flatten out. In addition, photographs and text attached to the backing sheet may work loose; a large printed poster with embedded images is an alternative approach.

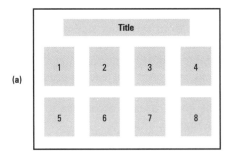

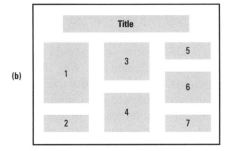

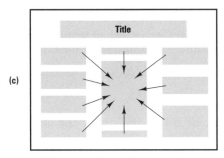

Fig. 14.1 Poster design. (a) An uninspiring design: sub-units of equal area, reading left to right, are not recommended. (b) This design is more interesting and the text will be easier to read (column format). (c) An alternative approach, with a central focus and arrows/tapes to guide the reader.

Subdividing your poster means that each smaller area can be prepared on a separate piece of paper or card, of A4 size or slightly larger, making transport and storage easier. It also breaks the reading matter up into smaller pieces, looking less formidable to a potential reader. By using pieces of card of different colours you can provide emphasis for key aspects, or link text with figures or photographs.

You will need to guide your reader through the poster and headings/sub-headings will help with this aspect. It may be appropriate to use either a numbering system, with large, clear numbers at the top of each piece of card, or a system of arrows (or thin tapes) to link sections within the poster (see Fig. 14.1). Make sure that the relationship is clear and that the arrows or tapes do not cross.

Title

Your chosen title should be concise (no more than eight words), specific and interesting, to encourage people to read the poster. Make the title large and bold – it should run across the top of your poster, in letters at least 4 cm high, so that it can be read from the other side of the room. Coloured spirit-based marker and block capitals drawn with a ruler work well, as long as your writing is readable and neat (the colour can be used to add emphasis). Alternatively, you can print out each word in large font, using a word processor. Details of authors, together with their addresses (if appropriate), should be given, usually across the top of the poster in somewhat smaller lettering than the title.

Text

Write in short sentences and avoid verbosity. Keep your poster as visual as possible and make effective use of the spaces between the blocks of text. Your final text should be double-spaced and should have a minimum capital letter height of 8 mm (minimum font size 36 point), preferably greater, so that the poster can be read at a distance of 1 m. One method of obtaining text of the required size is to photo-enlarge standard typescript (using a good-quality photocopier), or use a high-quality (laser) printer. It is best to avoid continuous use of text in capitals, since it slows reading and makes the text less interesting to the reader. Also avoid italic, 'balloon' or decorative styles of lettering.

> **KEY POINT** Keep text to a minimum – aim to have a maximum of 500 words in your poster.

Subtitles and headings

These should have a capital letter height of 15–20 mm, and should be restricted to two or three words. They can be produced by word processor, photo-enlargement, by stencilling or by hand, using pencilled guidelines (but make sure that no pencil marks are visible on your finished poster).

Colour

Consider the overall visual effect of your chosen display, including the relationship between your text, diagrams and the backing board. Colour can be used to highlight key aspects of your poster. However, it is very

---

Presenting a poster at a formal conference – it can be useful to include your photograph for identification purposes, e.g. in the top right-hand corner of the poster.

Making up your poster – text and graphics printed on good-quality paper can be glued directly onto a contrasting mounting card: use photographic spray mountant or Pritt rather than liquid glue. Trim carefully using a guillotine to give equal margins, parallel with the paper. Photographs should be scanned into an electronic format, or placed in a window mount to avoid the tendency for their corners to curl. Another approach is to trim pages or photographs to their correct size, then encapsulate in plastic film: this gives a highly professional finish and is easy to transport.

Producing composite material for posters – PowerPoint is generally more useful than Word when you wish to include text, graphics and/or images on the same page. It is possible to use PowerPoint to produce a complete poster (Box 14.1), although it can be expensive to have this printed out commercially to A1 or A0 size.

easy to ruin a poster by the inappropriate choice and application of colour. Careful use of two, or at most three, complementary colours and shades will be easier on the eye and should aid comprehension. Colour can be used to link the text with the visual images (e.g. by picking out a colour in a photograph and using the same colour on the mounting board for the accompanying text). For PowerPoint posters, careful choice of colours for the various elements will enhance the final product (Box 14.1). Use coloured inks or water-based paints to provide colour in diagrams and figures, as felt pens rarely give satisfactory results.

Content

The typical format is that of a scientific report (see Box 18.1), i.e. with the same headings, but with a considerably reduced content. Keep references within the text to a minimum – interested parties can always ask you for further information. Also note that most posters have a summary/conclusions section at the end, rather than an abstract.

Introduction

This should give the reader background information on the broad field of study and the aims of your own work. It is vital that this section is as interesting as possible, to capture the interest of your audience. It is often worth listing your objectives as a series of numbered points.

Experimental

Keep this short, and describe only the principal techniques used. You might mention any special techniques, or problems of general interest.

Results

Don't present your raw data: use data reduction wherever possible, i.e. figures and simple statistical comparisons. Graphs, diagrams, histograms and pie charts give clear visual images of trends and relationships and should be used in place of data tables (see p. 471). Final copies of all figures should be produced so that the numbers can be read from a distance of 1 m. Each should have a concise title and legend, so that it is self-contained: if appropriate, a series of numbered points can be used to link a diagram with the accompanying text. Where symbols are used, provide a key on each graph (symbol size should be at least 5 mm). Avoid using graphs straight from a written version, e.g. a project report, textbook or a paper, without considering whether they need modification to meet your requirements.

Conclusions

This is where many readers will begin, and they may go no further unless you make this section sufficiently interesting. This part needs to be the strongest section of your poster, summarising the main points. Refer to your figures here to draw the reader into the main part of your poster. A slightly larger or bolder typeface may add emphasis, though too many different typefaces can look messy. For the reference list, a smaller font can be used.

The poster session

A poster display session may be organised as part of the assessment of your coursework, and this usually means those held at scientific meetings and

Presenting at a scientific meeting – never be tempted to spend the minimum amount of time converting a piece of scientific writing into poster format – the least interesting posters are those where the author simply displays pages from a written communication (e.g. a journal article) on a poster board.

Designing the materials and methods section – photographs or diagrams of apparatus can help to break up the text of this section and provide visual interest. It is sometimes worth preparing this section in a smaller typeface.

Keeping graphs and diagrams simple – avoid composite graphs with different scales for the same axis, or with several trend lines (use a maximum of three trend lines per graph).

Listing your conclusions – a series of numbered points is a useful approach, if your findings fit this pattern.

Consider providing a handout – this is a useful way to summarise the main points of your poster, so that your readers have a permanent record of the information you have presented.

Box 14.1 How to create a poster using PowerPoint

Software such as PowerPoint can be used to produce a high-quality poster, providing you have access to a good colour printer. However, you should avoid the standard templates available on the Web as they encourage unnecessary uniformity and stifle creativity, leading to a less satisfying end result. The following steps give practical advice on creating a poster as a single PowerPoint slide:

1. **Sketch out your plans.** Decide on the main poster elements (images, graphs, tables and text sections) and their relationship with each other and draw out a one-page 'storyboard' (see Fig. 14.1). Think about colours for background, text and graphics (use two or three complementary colours): dark text on a light background is clearer (high contrast), and uses less ink when printing. Also consider how you will link the elements in sequence, to guide readers through your 'story'.

2. **Get your material ready.** Collect together individual files for pictures, figures and tables. Make any required adjustments to images, graphs or tables before you import them into your poster.

3. **Create a new/blank slide.** Open PowerPoint and from *File > New* select *Blank presentation*. Next, choose the *Blank Presentation* option for *New Presentation > New option*. Then use the *File > Page setup* menu to select either *Landscape* or *Portrait* orientation and to set the correct page size (use *Width* and *Height* commands, or select a standard size such as A4, A3, A2, etc.). Right-click on the slide and select *Ruler* and *Guides* (to help position elements within the slide – the horizontal and vertical guidelines can be dragged to different positions at later stages, as required) and also select an appropriate *Background* colour. In general, avoid setting a picture as your background as this tends to detract from the content of the poster. Before going further, save your work. Repeat this frequently and in more than one location (e.g. hard drive and USB memory stick).

4. **Add graphics.** For images, use the drop-down *Insert* menu, select *Picture, From File* and browse to *Insert* the correct file. The *Insert, Object* command performs a similar function for Excel charts (graphs). Alternatively, use the copy-and-paste functions of complementary software. Once inserted, resize using the *sizing handles* in one of the corners (for photographs, take care not to alter one dimension relative to the other, or the image will be distorted). To reposition, put the mouse pointer over the image, left-click and hold, then drag to new location. While the *Drawing* toolbar offers standard shapes and other useful features, you should avoid clipart (jaded and over-used) and poor-quality images from the Web (always use the highest resolution possible) – if you do not have your final images, use blank text boxes to show their position within the draft poster.

5. **Add text.** Use either the *Drawing* toolbar to select a *Text box* and place this on your slide, then either type in your text (use the *Enter* key to provide line spacing within the box) or copy-and-paste text from a word-processed file. You will need to consider the font size for the printed poster (e.g. for an A0 poster (size 1189 × 841 mm), a printed font size of 24 point is appropriate for the main text, with larger fonts for headings and titles. If you find things difficult to read on-screen, use the *Zoom* function (either select a larger percentage in the *Zoom box* on the standard toolbar, or hold down the *Ctrl* key and use the mouse wheel to scroll up (*zoom*) or down (*reduce*). Use a separate text box for each element of your poster and don't be tempted to type too much text into each box – write in succinct phrases, using bullet points and numbered lists to keep text concise (aim for no more than 50 words per text box). Select appropriate font styles and colours using the *Format > Font* menu. For a background colour or surrounding line, right-click and use the *Format Text Box* command (line thickness and colour can then be altered using the *Drawing* toolbar). Present supplementary text elements in a smaller font. For example, details of methodology, references cited.

6. **Add boxes, lines and/or arrows** to link elements of the poster and guide the reader (see Fig. 14.1). These features are available from the *Drawing* toolbar. Note that new inserts are overlaid over older inserts – if this proves to be a problem, select the relevant item and use the *Draw > Order* functions to change its relative position.

7. **Review your poster.** Get feedback from another student, or your tutor, e.g. on a small printed version, or use a projector to view your poster without printing (adjust the distance between projector and screen to give the correct size).

8. **Revise and edit your poster.** Revisit your work and remove as much unnecessary text as possible. Delete any component that is not essential to the message of the poster. Keep graphs simple and clear (p. 471 gives further advice). 'White space' is important in providing structure.

9. **Print the final version.** Use a high-resolution colour printer (this may be costly, so you should wait until you are sure that no further changes are needed).

Coping with questions in assessed poster sessions – you should expect to be asked questions about your poster, and to explain details of figures, methods, etc.

conferences. Staff and fellow students (delegates at conferences) will mill around, looking at the posters and chatting to their authors, who are usually expected to be in attendance. If you stand at the side of your poster throughout the session you are likely to discourage some readers, who may not wish to become involved in a detailed conversation about the poster. Stand nearby. Find something to do – talk to someone else, or browse among the other posters, but remain aware of people reading your poster and be ready to answer any queries they may raise. Do not be too discouraged if you aren't asked lots of questions: remember, the poster is meant to be a self-contained, visual story, without need for further explanation.

A poster display will never feel like an oral presentation, where the nervousness beforehand is replaced by a combination of satisfaction and relief as you unwind after the event. However, it can be a very satisfying means of communication, particularly if you follow these guidelines.

Text reference

Simmonds, D. and Reynolds, L. (1994) *Data Presentation and Visual Literacy in Medicine and Science*. Butterworth-Heinemann, London.

Sources for further study

Alley, M. (2003) *The Craft of Scientific Presentations: Critical Steps to Succeed and Critical Errors to Avoid*. Springer-Verlag, New York.

Briscoe, M.H. (2000) *Preparing Scientific Illustrations: A Guide to Better Posters, Presentations and Publications*, 2nd edn. Springer-Verlag, New York.

Davis, M.F. (2005) *Scientific Papers and Presentations*, 2nd edn. Academic Press, New York.

Gosling, P.J. (1999) *Scientist's Guide to Poster Presentations*. Kluwer, New York.

Hess, G., Tosney, K. and Liegel, L. *Creating Effective Poster Presentations*. Available: http://www.ncsu.edu/project/ posters/NewSite.
Last accessed 20/07/09.

Study exercises

14.1 Design a poster. Working with one or more partners from your year group, decide on a suitable poster topic (perhaps something linked to your current teaching programme). Working individually, make an outline plan of the major elements of the poster, with appropriate sub-headings and a brief indication of the content and relative size of each element (including figures, diagrams and images). Exchange draft plans with your partners and arrange a session where you can discuss their merits and disadvantages.

14.2 Prepare a checklist for assessing the quality of a poster presentation. After reading through this chapter, prepare a 10-point checklist of assessment criteria under the heading 'What makes a good poster presentation?' Compare your list with the one that we have provided (p. 546) – do you agree with our criteria, or do you prefer your own list (and can you justify your preferences)?

14.3 Evaluate the posters in your university. Most universities have a wide range of academic posters on display. Some may cover general topics (e.g. course structures), while others may deal with specific research topics (e.g. poster presentations from past conferences). Consider their good and bad features (if you wish to make this a group exercise, you might compare your evaluation with that of other students, in a group discussion session).

Opportunities for practising speaking skills – these include:

- answering lecturers' questions;
- contributing in tutorials;
- talking to informal groups;
- giving your views at formal (committee) meetings;
- demonstrating or explaining to other students, e.g. during a practical class;
- asking questions in lectures/seminars;
- answering an examiner's questions in an oral exam.

Learning from experience – use your own experience of good and bad lecturers to shape your performance. Some of the more common errors include:

- speaking too quickly;
- reading from notes or from slides and ignoring the audience;
- inexpressive, impersonal or indistinct speech;
- distracting mannerisms;
- poorly structured material with little emphasis on key information;
- factual information too complex and detailed;
- too few or too many visual aids.

Most students feel very nervous about giving talks. This is natural, since very few people are sufficiently confident and outgoing that they look forward to speaking in public. Additionally, the technical nature of the subject matter may give you cause for concern, especially if you feel that some members of the audience have a greater knowledge than you have, e.g. your tutors. However, this is a fundamental method of scientific communication and an important transferable skill, therefore it forms an important component of many courses.

The comments in this chapter apply equally to informal talks, e.g. those based on assignments and project work, and to more formal conference presentations. It is hoped that the advice and guidance given below will encourage you to make the most of your opportunities for public speaking, but there is no substitute for practice. Do not expect to find all of the answers from this, or any other, book. Rehearse, and learn from your own experience.

> **KEY POINT** The three 'Rs' of successful public speaking are: reflect – give sufficient thought to all aspects of your presentation, particularly at the planning stage; rehearse – to improve your delivery; revise – modify the content and style of your material in response to your own ideas and to the comments of others.

Preparing for a spoken presentation

Preliminary information

Begin by marshalling the details needed to plan your presentation, including:

- the duration of the talk;
- whether time for questions is included;
- the size and location of the room;
- the projection/lighting facilities provided, and whether pointers or similar aids are available.

It is especially important to find out whether the room has the necessary equipment for digital projection (e.g. PC, projector and screen, black-out curtains or blinds, appropriate lighting) or overhead projection before you prepare your audio-visual aids. If you concentrate only on the spoken part of your presentation at this stage, you are inviting trouble later on. Have a look around the room and try out the equipment at the earliest opportunity, so that you are able to use the lights, projector, etc. with confidence. For digital projection systems, check that you can load/present your material. Box 15.1 gives practical advice on the use of PowerPoint.

Audio-visual aids

If you plan to use overhead transparencies, find out whether your department has facilities for their preparation, whether these facilities are

Box 15.1 Tips on preparing and using PowerPoint slides in a spoken presentation

Microsoft PowerPoint can be used to produce high-quality visual aids, assuming a computer and digital projector are available in the room where you intend to speak. The presentation is produced as a series of electronic 'slides' onto which you can insert images, diagrams and text. When creating your slides, bear the following points in mind:

- **Plan the structure of your presentation.** Decide on the main topic areas and sketch out your ideas on paper. Think about what material you will need (e.g. pictures, graphs) and what colours to use for background and text.

- **Choose slide layouts according to purpose.** Once PowerPoint is running, from the *Insert* menu select *New Slide > Choose an Autolayout*. You can then add material to each new slide to suit your requirements.

- **Select your background with care.** Many of the pre-set background templates available within the *Format* menu (*Apply design template* option) are best avoided, since they are over-used and fussy, diverting attention from the content of the slides. Conversely, flat, dull backgrounds may seem uninteresting, while brightly coloured backgrounds can be garish and distracting. Choose whether to present your text as a light-coloured font on a dark background (more restful but perhaps less engaging if the room is dark) or a dark-coloured font on a light background (more lively).

- **Use visual images throughout.** Remember the familiar maxim 'a picture is worth ten thousand words'. A presentation composed entirely of text-based slides will be uninteresting: adding images and diagrams will brighten up your talk considerably (use the *Insert* menu, *Picture* option). Images can be taken with a digital camera, scanned in from a printed version or copied and pasted from the Web, but you should take care not to break copyright regulations. 'Clipart' is copyright-free, but should be used sparingly as most people will have seen the images before and they are rarely wholly relevant. Diagrams can be made from components created using the *Drawing* toolbar while graphs and tables can be imported from other programs, e.g. Excel (Box 14.1 gives further specific practical advice on adding graphics, saving files, etc.).

- **Keep text to a minimum.** Aim for no more than 20 words on a single slide (e.g. four/five lines containing a few words per line). Use headings and sub-headings to structure your talk: write only key words or phrases as 'prompts' to remind you to cover a particular point during your talk – never be tempted to type whole sentences as you will then be reduced to reading these from the screen during your presentation, which is boring.

- **Use a large, clear font style.** Use the *Slide Master* option within the *View* menu to set the default font to a non-serif style such as Arial, or Comic Sans MS, and an appropriate colour. Default fonts for headings and bullet points are intentionally large, for clarity. Do not reduce these to anything less than 28 point font size (preferably larger) to cram in more words: if you have too much material, create a new slide and divide up the information.

- **Animate your material.** The *Slide Show* menu provides a *Custom Animation* function that enables you to introduce the various elements within a slide, e.g. text can be made to *Appear* one line at a time, to prevent the audience from reading ahead and help maintain their attention.

- **Don't overdo the special effects.** PowerPoint has a wide range of features that allow complex slide transitions and animations, additional sounds, etc. but these quickly become irritating to an audience unless they have a specific purpose within your presentation.

- **Always edit your slides before use.** Check through your slides and cut out any unnecessary words, adjust the layout and animation. Remember the maxim 'less is more' – avoid too much text; too many bullet points; too many distracting visual effects or sounds.

When presenting your talk:

- **Work out the basic procedures beforehand.** Practise, to make sure that you know how to move forwards and backwards in your slideshow, turn the screen on and off, hide the mouse pointer, etc.

- **Don't forget to engage your audience.** Despite the technical gadgetry, *you* need to play an active role in the presentation, as explained elsewhere in this chapter.

- **Don't go too fast.** Sometimes, new users tend to deliver their material too quickly: try to speak at a normal pace and practise beforehand.

- **Consider whether to provide a handout.** PowerPoint has several options, including some that provide space for notes (e.g. Fig. 4.3). However, a handout should not be your default option, as there is a cost involved.

Testing the room – if possible, try to rehearse your talk in the room in which it will be presented. This will help you to make allowance for layout of equipment, lighting, acoustics and sight lines that might affect the way you deliver your talk. It will also put you more at ease on the day, because of the familiarity of the surroundings.

Using audio-visual aids – don't let the equipment and computer gadgetry distract you from the essential rules of good speaking (Box 15.2): remember that *you* are the presenter.

Pitching your talk at the right level – the general rule should be: 'do not overestimate the background knowledge of your audience'. This sometimes happens in student presentations, where fears about the presence of 'experts' can encourage the speaker to include too much detail, overloading the audience with facts.

Getting the introduction right – a good idea is to have an initial slide giving your details and the title of your talk, and a second slide telling the audience how your presentation will be structured. Make eye contact with all sections of the audience during the introduction.

available for your use, and the cost of materials. Adopt the following guidelines:

- Keep text to a minimum: present only the key points, with up to 20 words per slide/transparency.
- Make sure the text is readable: try out your material beforehand.
- Use several simpler figures rather than a single complex graph.
- Avoid too much colour on overhead transparencies: blue and black are easier to read than red or green.
- Don't mix slides and transparencies as this is often distracting.
- Use spirit-based pens for transparencies: use alcohol for corrections.
- Transparencies can be produced from typewritten or printed text using a photocopier, often giving a better product than pens. Note that you must use special heat-resistant acetate sheets for photocopying.

Electronic presentation software (e.g. PowerPoint) can replace these specialist requirements, as long as the necessary facilities are available for your talk (see below).

Audience

You should consider your audience at the earliest stage, since they will determine the appropriate level for your presentation. If you are talking to fellow students you may be able to assume a common level of background knowledge. In contrast, a research lecture given to your department, or a paper at a meeting of a scientific society, will be presented to an audience from a broader range of backgrounds. An oral presentation is not the place for a complex discussion of specialised information: build up your talk from a low level. The speed at which this can be done will vary according to your audience. As long as you are not boring or patronising, you can cover basic information without losing the attention of the more knowledgeable members in your audience.

Content

While the specific details in your talk will be for you to decide, most spoken presentations share some common features of structure, as described below.

Introductory remarks

It is vital to capture the attention of your audience at the outset. Consequently, you must make sure your opening comments are strong, otherwise your audience will lose interest before you reach the main message. Remember it takes a sentence or two for an audience to establish a relationship with a new speaker. Your opening sentence should be some form of preamble and should not contain any key information. For a formal lecture, you might begin with 'Thank you for that introduction. My talk today is about...' then restate the title and acknowledge other contributors, etc. You might show a transparency or

What to cover in your introduction – You should:

- explain the structure of your talk;
- set out your aims and objectives;
- explain your approach to the topic.

Allowing time for slides – as a rough guide you should allow at least two minutes per illustration, although some diagrams may need longer, depending on content. Make a note of the halfway point, to help you check timing/pace.

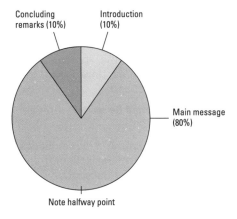

Concluding remarks (10%)

Introduction (10%)

Main message (80%)

Note halfway point

Fig. 15.1 Pie chart showing time allocation for a typical presentation.

Using slides – check that the lecture theatre has a lectern light, otherwise you may have problems reading your notes when the lights are dimmed.

Managing your time when speaking – avoid looking at your watch as it gives a negative signal to the audience. Use a wall clock, if one is provided, or take off your watch and put it beside your notes, so you can glance at it without distracting your audience.

slide with the title printed on it, or an introductory photograph, if appropriate. This should provide the necessary settling-in period.

After these preliminaries, you should introduce your topic. Begin your story on a strong note – avoid timid or apologetic phrases.

Opening remarks are unlikely to occupy more than 10% of the talk. However, because of their significance, you might reasonably spend up to 25% of your preparation time on them.

> **KEY POINT** Make sure you have practised your opening remarks, so that you can deliver the material in a flowing style, with less chance of mistakes.

The main message

This section should include the bulk of your experimental results or literature findings, depending on the type of presentation. Keep details of methods to the minimum needed to explain your data. This is *not* the place for a detailed description of equipment and experimental protocol (unless it is a talk about methodology). Results should be presented in an easily digested format.

> **KEY POINT** Do not expect your audience to cope with large amounts of data; use a maximum of six numbers per slide. Remember that graphs and diagrams are usually better than tables of raw data, since the audience will be able to see the visual trends and relationships in your data (p. 471).

Present summary statistics (Chapter 63) rather than individual results. Show the final results of any analyses in terms of the statistics calculated, and their significance, rather than dwelling on details of the procedures used. Figures should not be crowded with unnecessary detail. Every diagram should have a concise title and the symbols and trend lines should be clearly labelled, with an explanatory key where necessary. When presenting graphical data (Chapter 60) always 'introduce' each graph by stating the units for each axis and describing the relationship for each trend line or data set.

> **KEY POINT** Use summary slides at regular intervals, to maintain the flow of the presentation and to emphasise the main points.

Take the audience through your story step-by-step at a reasonable pace. Try not to rush the delivery of your main message due to nervousness. Avoid complex, convoluted story-lines – one of the most distracting things you can do is to fumble backwards through PowerPoint slides or overhead transparencies. If you need to use the same diagram or graph more than once then you should make two (or more) copies. In a presentation of experimental results, you should discuss each point as it is raised, in contrast to written text where the results and discussion may be in separate sections. The main message typically occupies approximately 80% of the time allocated to an oral presentation (Fig. 15.1).

Box 15.2 Hints on presenting your talk

Notes

Many accomplished speakers use abbreviated notes for guidance, rather than reading from a prepared script. When writing your talk:

- **Prepare a first draft as a full script** – write in spoken English, keeping the text simple and avoiding an impersonal style. Aim to *talk* to your audience, not read to them.

- **Use note cards with key phrases and words** – it is best to avoid using a full script at the final presentation. As you rehearse and your confidence improves, a set of cards may be a more appropriate format for your notes.

- **Consider the structure of your talk** – keep it as simple as possible and announce each subdivision, so your audience is aware of the structure.

- **Mark the position of slides/key points, etc.** – each note card should contain details of structure, as well as content.

- **Memorise your introductory/closing remarks** – you may prefer to rely on a full written version for these sections in case your memory fails.

- **Use notes** – write on only one side of the card/paper, in handwriting large enough to be read easily during the presentation. Each card or sheet must be clearly numbered, so that you do not lose your place.

- **Rehearse your presentation** – ask a friend to listen and to comment constructively on parts that were difficult to follow.

- **Use 'split times' to pace yourself** – following rehearsal, note the time at which you should arrive at key points of your talk. These timing marks will help you keep to time during the 'real thing'.

Image

Ensure that the image you project during your talk is appropriate for the occasion:

- **Consider what to wear** – aim to be respectable without 'dressing up', otherwise your message may be diminished.

- **Develop a good posture** – it will help your voice projection if you stand upright, rather than slouching or leaning over the lectern.

- **Project your voice** – speak towards the back of the room.

- **Make eye contact** – look at members of the audience in all parts of the room. Avoid talking to your notes, to the screen or to only one section of the audience.

- **Deliver your talk with expression** – arm movements and subdued body language will help maintain the interest of your audience. However, you should avoid extreme gestures (it may work for some TV personalities, but it isn't recommended for the beginner!).

- **Try to identify and control any distracting repetitive mannerisms** (e.g. repeated empty phrases, fidgeting with pens, keys, etc.) as this will distract your audience. Practising in front of a mirror may help.

- **Practise your delivery** – use the comments of your friends to improve your performance.

Questions

Many speakers are worried by the prospect of questions after their oral presentation. Once again, the best approach is to prepare beforehand:

- **Consider what questions you may be asked** – prepare brief answers.

- **Do not be afraid to say 'I don't know'** – your audience will appreciate honesty, rather than vacillation, if you don't have an answer for a particular question.

- **Avoid arguing with a questioner** – suggest a discussion afterwards rather than becoming involved in a debate about specific details.

- **If no questions are forthcoming you may pose a question yourself, and then ask for opinions from the audience** – if you use this approach you should be prepared to comment briefly if your audience has no suggestions. This will prevent the presentation from ending in an embarrassing silence.

Final remarks – make sure you give the audience sufficient time to assimilate your final slide: some of them may wish to write down the key points. Alternatively, you might provide a handout, with a brief outline of the aims of your study and the major conclusions.

Concluding remarks

Having captured the interest of your audience in the introduction and given them the details of your story in the middle section, you must now bring your talk to a conclusion. Do not end weakly, e.g. by running out of steam on the last slide. Provide your audience with a clear 'take-home message', by returning to the key points in your presentation. It is often appropriate to prepare a slide or overhead transparency listing your main conclusions as a numbered series.

Signal the end of your talk by saying 'finally ...', 'in conclusion ...', or a similar comment and then finish speaking after that sentence. Your audience will lose interest if you extend your closing remarks beyond this point. You may add a simple end phrase (for example, 'thank you') as you put your notes into your folder, but do not say 'that's all folks!', or make any similar offhand remark. Finish as strongly and as clearly as you started.

Sources for further study

Alley, M. (2003) *The Craft of Scientific Presentations: Critical Steps to Succeed and Critical Errors to Avoid.* Springer-Verlag, New York.

Capp, C.C. and Capp, G.R. (1989) *Basic Oral Communication*, 5th edn. Prentice Hall, Harlow.

Matthews, C. and Marino, J. (1999) *Professional Interactions: Oral Communication Skills of Science, Technology and Medicine.* Pearson, Harlow.

Study exercises

15.1 **Prepare a checklist for assessing the quality of an oral presentation**. After reading through this chapter, prepare a 10-point checklist of assessment criteria under the heading 'What makes a good oral presentation?'. Compare your list with the one that we have provided (p. 546) – do you agree with our criteria, or do you prefer your checklist? (Can you justify your preferences?)

15.2 **Evaluate the presentation styles of other speakers**. There are many opportunities to assess the strengths and weaknesses of academic 'public speakers', including your lecturers, seminar speakers, presenters of TV documentaries, etc. Decide in advance how you are going to tackle the evaluation (e.g. with a quantitative marking scheme, or a less formal procedure).

15.3 **Rehearse a talk and get feedback on your performance**. There are a number of approaches you might take, including: (i) recording and reviewing your presentation using a digital movie camera; or (ii) giving your talk to a small group of fellow students and asking them to provide constructive feedback.

Written communication is an essential component of all sciences. Most courses include writing exercises in which you will learn to describe ideas and results accurately, succinctly and in an appropriate style and format. The following features/aspects are common to all forms of scientific writing.

Organising your time

Making a timetable at the outset helps ensure that you give each stage adequate attention and complete the work on time (e.g. Fig. 16.1). To create and use a timetable:

1. Break down the task into stages.

2. Decide on the proportion of the total time each stage should take.

3. Set realistic deadlines for completing each stage, allowing some time for slippage.

4. Refer to your timetable frequently as you work: if you fail to meet one of your deadlines, make a serious effort to catch up as soon as possible.

> **KEY POINT** The appropriate allocation of your time to reading, planning, writing and revising will differ according to the task in hand (see Chapters 17–19).

Organising your information and ideas

Before you write, you need to gather and/or think about relevant material (Chapters 8 and 9). You must then decide:

- what needs to be included and what doesn't;

- in what order it should appear.

Start by jotting down headings for everything of potential relevance to the topic (this is sometimes called 'brainstorming'). A spider diagram (Fig. 16.2) or a Mind Map (Fig. 4.2) will help you organise these ideas. The next stage is to create an outline of your text (Fig. 16.3). Outlines are valuable because they:

- force you to think about and plan the structure;

- provide a checklist so nothing is missed out;

- ensure the material is balanced in content and length;

- help you organise figures and tables by showing where they will be used.

> **KEY POINT** A suitable structure is essential to the narrative of your writing, and should be carefully considered at the outset.

In an essay or review, the structure of your writing should help the reader to assimilate and understand your main points. Subdivisions of the topic could simply be related to the physical nature of the subject

---

Time management – practical advice is given in Chapter 2.

Monday:	morning	Lectures (University)
	afternoon	Practical (University)
	evening	Initial analysis and brainstorming (Home)
Tuesday:	morning	Lectures (University)
	afternoon	Locate sources (Library)
	evening	Background reading (Library)
Wednesday:	morning	Background reading (Library)
	afternoon	Squash (Sports hall)
	evening	Planning (Home)
Thursday:	morning	Lectures (University)
	afternoon	Additional reading (Library)
	evening	Prepare outline (Library)
Friday:	morning	Lab class (University)
	afternoon	Write first draft (Home)
	evening	Write first draft (Home)
Saturday:	morning	Shopping (Town)
	afternoon	Review first draft (Home)
	evening	Revise first draft (Home)
Sunday:	morning	Free
	afternoon	Produce final copy (Home)
	evening	Proof read and print essay (Home)
Monday:	morning	Final read-through and check Submit essay (deadline midday)

Fig. 16.1 Example timetable for writing a short essay.

Creating an outline – an informal outline can be made simply by indicating the order of sections on a spider diagram (as in Fig. 16.2).

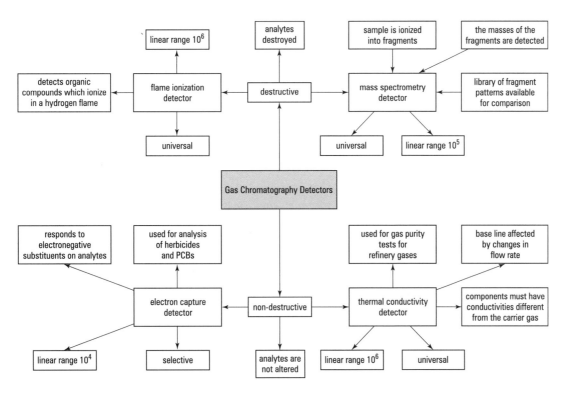

Fig. 16.2 Spider diagram showing how you might 'brainstorm' an essay with the title 'Detectors for Gas Chromatography'. Write out the essay title in full to form the spider's body, and as you think of possible content, place headings around this to form its legs. Decide which headings are relevant and which are not and use arrows to note connections between subjects, if required. This may influence your choice of order and may help to make your writing flow because the links between paragraphs will be natural. You can make an informal outline directly on a spider diagram by adding numbers indicating a sequence of paragraphs (as shown). This method is best when you must work quickly, as with an essay written under exam conditions.

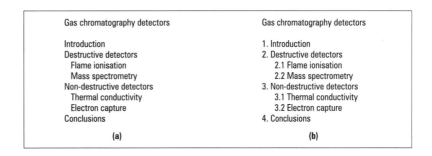

Fig. 16.3 Formal outlines. These are useful for a long piece of work where you or the reader might otherwise lose track of the structure. The headings for sections and paragraphs are simply written in sequence with the type of lettering and level of indentation indicating their hierarchy. Two different forms of formal outline are shown, a minimal form (a) and a numbered form (b). Note that the headings used in an outline are often repeated within the essay to emphasise its structure. The content of an outline will depend on the time you have available and the nature of the work, but the most detailed hierarchy you should reasonably include is the subject of each paragraph.

matter (e.g. components of a gas chromatograph) and should proceed logically (e.g. injection port, column, etc.). A chronological approach is good for evaluation of past work (e.g. the development of the concept of aromaticity), whereas a step-by-step comparison might be best for certain exam questions (e.g. 'Discuss the differences between solid phase extraction and soxhlet extraction in the recovery of pesticides'). There is little choice about structure for practical and project reports (see p. 127).

Writing

Adopting a scientific style

Your main aim in developing a scientific style should be to get your message across directly and unambiguously. While you can try to achieve this through a set of 'rules' (see Box 16.1), you may find other requirements driving your writing in a contradictory direction. For instance, the need to be accurate and complete may result in text littered with technical terms, and the flow may be continually interrupted by references to the literature. The need to be succinct also affects style and readability through the use of, for example, stacked noun-adjectives (e.g. 'ring opening metathesis polymerisation') and acronyms (e.g. 'ROMP'). Finally, style is very much a matter of taste and each tutor, examiner, supervisor or editor will have pet loves and hates which you may have to accommodate. Different assignments will need different styles; Box 16.2 gives further details.

Developing technique

Improving your writing skills – you need to take a long-term view if you wish to improve this aspect of your work. An essential preliminary is to invest in and make full use of a personal reference library (see Box 16.3).

Writing is a skill that can be improved, but not instantly. You should analyse your deficiencies with the help of feedback from your tutors, be prepared to change work habits (e.g. start planning your work more carefully), and willing to learn from some of the excellent texts that are available on scientific writing (p. 120).

Getting started

A common problem is 'writer's block' – inactivity or stalling brought on by a variety of causes. If blocked, ask yourself these questions:

- Are you comfortable with your surroundings? Make sure you are seated comfortably at a reasonably clear desk and have minimised the possibility of interruptions and distractions.

- Are you trying to write too soon? Have you clarified your thoughts on the subject? Have you done enough preliminary reading?

Talking about your work – discussing your topic with a friend or colleague might bring out ideas or reveal deficiencies in your knowledge.

- Are you happy with the underlying structure of your work? If you haven't made an outline, try this. If you are unhappy because you can't think of a particular detail at the planning stage, just start writing – it is more likely to come to you while you are thinking of something else.

- Are you trying to be too clever? Your first sentence doesn't have to be earth-shattering in content or particularly smart in style. A short statement of fact or a definition is fine. If there will be time for revision, first get your ideas down on paper and then revise grammar, content and order later.

Writing with a word processor – use the dynamic/interactive features of the word processor (Chapter 13) to help you get started: first make notes on structure and content, then expand these to form a first draft and finally revise/improve the text.

- Do you really need to start writing at the beginning? Try writing the opening remarks after a more straightforward part. For example, with

Box 16.1 How to achieve a clear, readable style

Words and phrases

- Choose short, clear words and phrases rather than long ones: e.g. use 'build' rather than 'fabricate'; 'now' rather than 'at the present time'. At certain times, technical terms must be used for precision, but don't use jargon if you don't have to.

- Don't worry too much about repeating words, especially when introducing an alternative might subtly alter your meaning.

- Where appropriate, use the first person to describe your actions ('We decided to'; 'I conclude that'), but not if this is specifically discouraged by your supervisor or department.

- Favour active forms of writing ('the observer completed the survey in ten minutes') rather than a passive style ('the survey was completed by the observer in ten minutes').

- Use tenses consistently. Past tense is always used for materials and methods ('samples were taken from ...') and for reviewing past work ('Smith (1990) concluded that ...'). The present tense is used when describing data ('Fig. 1 shows ...'), for generalisations ('Most authorities agree that ...') and conclusions ('To conclude, ...').

- Use statements in parentheses sparingly – they disrupt the reader's attention to your central theme.

- Avoid clichés and colloquialisms – they are usually inappropriate in a scientific context.

Punctuation

- Try to use a variety of types of punctuation, to make the text more interesting to read.

- Decide whether you wish to use 'closed' punctuation (frequent commas at the end of clauses) or 'open' punctuation (less frequent punctuation) and be consistent.

- Don't link two sentences with a comma. Use a full stop, this is an example of what *not* to do.

- Pay special attention to apostrophes, using the following rules:
  - To indicate possession, use an apostrophe before an 's' for a singular word (e.g. the solution's temperature was ...) and after the s for a plural word ending in s (e.g. the solutions' temperatures were = the temperatures of the solutions were). If the word has a special plural (e.g. woman → women) then use the apostrophe before the s (the women's temperatures were ...).
  - When contracting words, use an apostrophe (e.g. do not = don't; it's = it is), but remember that contractions are generally *not* used in formal scientific writing.
  - Do *not* use an apostrophe for 'its' as the possessive form of 'it' (e.g. 'the university and its surroundings'). Note that 'it's' is reserved for 'it is'. This is an exception to the general rule and a very common mistake.
  - Never use an apostrophe to indicate plurals. Even for abbreviations, the accepted style is now to omit the apostrophe for the plural (e.g. write 'the SPEs were').

Sentences

- Don't make them overlong or complicated.

- Introduce variety in structure and length.

- If unhappy with the structure of a sentence, try chopping it into a series of shorter sentences.

Paragraphs

- Get the paragraph length right – five sentences or so. Do *not* submit an essay that consists of a single paragraph, nor one that contains single sentence paragraphs.

- Make sure each paragraph is logical, dealing with a single topic or theme.

- Take care with the first sentence in a paragraph (the 'topic' sentence); this introduces the theme of the paragraph. Further sentences should then develop this theme, e.g. by providing supporting information, examples or contrasting cases.

- Use 'linking' words or phrases to maintain the flow of the text within a paragraph (e.g. 'for example'; 'in contrast'; 'however'; 'on the other hand').

- Make your text more readable by adopting modern layout style. The first paragraph in any section of text is usually *not* indented, but following paragraphs may be (by the equivalent of three character spaces). In addition, the space between paragraphs should be slightly larger than the space between lines. Follow departmental guidelines if these specify a format.

- Group paragraphs in sections under appropriate headings and sub-headings to reinforce the structure underlying your writing.

- Think carefully about the first and last paragraphs in any piece of writing: these are often the most important as they respectively set the aims and report the conclusions.

Note: If you're not sure what is meant by any of the terms used here, consult a guide on writing (see sources for further study).

Box 16.2 Using appropriate writing styles for different purposes (with examples)

Note that courses tend to move from assignments that are predominantly descriptive in the early years to a more analytical approach towards the final year (see Chapter 5). Also, different styles may be required in different sections of a write-up, e.g. descriptive for introductory historical aspects, becoming more analytical in later sections.

Descriptive writing

This is the most straightforward style, providing factual information on a particular subject and is most appropriate:

- in essays where you are asked to 'describe' or 'explain' (p. 123)

- when describing the results of a practical exercise, e.g.: 'The experiment shown in Figure 1 confirmed that the reaction was strongly influenced by temperature, as the rate observed at 80°C was more than double that seen at 20°C.'

However, in literature reviews and essays where you are asked to 'discuss' (p. 123) a particular topic, the descriptive approach is mostly inappropriate, as in the following example, where a large amount of specific information from a single scientific paper has been used, without any attempt to highlight the most important points:

'In a study carried out between July and October 2008, a total of 250 soil samples were collected, stored and then subsequently analysed. The results obtained indicated that high levels (>150 mg/kg) of Pb were obtained in 75% of the samples; negligible levels of Cd, i.e. <0.1 mg/kg, were found in the same samples (Black and White, 2009).'

In the most extreme examples, whole paragraphs or pages of essays may be based on descriptive factual detail from a single source, often with a single citation at the end of the material, as above: such essays often score low marks in essays where evidence of deeper thinking is required (Chapter 5).

Comparative writing

This technique is an important component of academic writing, and it will be important to develop your comparative writing skills as you progress through your course. Its applications include:

- answering essay questions and assignments of the 'compare and contrast' type (p. 123)

- comparing your results with previously published work in the Discussion section of a practical report.

To use this style, first decide on those aspects you wish to compare and then consider the material (e.g. different literature sources) from these aspects – in what ways do they agree or disagree with each other? One approach is to compare/contrast a different aspect in each paragraph. At a practical level, you can use 'linking' words and phrases to help orientate your reader, as you move between aspects where there is agreement and disagreement. These include, for agreement: 'in both cases'; 'in agreement with'; 'is also shown by the study of'; 'similarly'; 'in the same way', and for disagreement: 'however'; 'although'; 'in contrast to'; 'on the other hand'; 'which differs from'. The comparative style is fairly straightforward, once you have decided on the aspects to be compared. The following brief example compares two different studies using this style:

'While Black and White (2009) reported high levels of Pb in 75% of the soil samples, previous work by Grey and Gray (2005) indicated Pb levels >2000 mg kg^{-1} in selected "hot-spots" on the same site.'

Comparative text typically makes use of two or more references per paragraph.

Analytical writing

Typically, this is the most appropriate form of writing for:

- a review of scientific literature on a particular topic;

- an essay where you are asked to 'discuss' (p. 123) different aspects of a particular topic;

- evaluating a number of different published sources within the Discussion section of a final-year project dissertation.

By considering the significance of the information provided in the various sources you have read, you will be able to take a more critical approach. Your writing should evaluate the importance of the material in the context of your topic (see also Chapter 9). In analytical writing, you need to demonstrate critical thinking (p. 59) and personal input about the topic in a well-structured text that provides clear messages, presented in a logical order and demonstrating synthesis from a number of sources by appropriate use of citations (p. 50). Detailed information and relevant examples are used only to explain or develop a particular aspect, and not simply as 'padding' to bulk up the essay, as in the following example:

'Historically, lead has been mined in selected areas in Northern England: a limited study on this site identified elevated lead levels in 188 samples (Black and White, 2009), while a previous study had identified significant lead levels in isolated samples (Grey and Gray, 2005).'

Analytical writing is based on a broad range of sources, typically with several citations per paragraph.

Box 16.3 How to improve your writing ability by consulting a personal reference library

Using dictionaries

We all know that a dictionary helps with spelling and definitions, but how many of us use one effectively? You should:

- Keep a dictionary beside you when writing and always use it if in any doubt about spelling or definitions.

- Use it to prepare a list of words which you have difficulty in spelling: apart from speeding up the checking process, the act of writing out the words helps commit them to memory.

- Use it to write out a personal glossary of terms. This can help you memorise definitions. From time to time, test yourself.

Not all dictionaries are the same! Ask your tutor or supervisor whether he/she has a preference and why. Try out the *Oxford Advanced Learner's Dictionary*, which is particularly useful because it gives examples of use of all words and helps with grammar, e.g. by indicating which prepositions to use with verbs.

Using a thesaurus

A thesaurus contains lists of words of similar meaning grouped thematically; words of opposite meaning always appear nearby.

- Use a thesaurus to find a more precise and appropriate word to fit your meaning, but check definitions of unfamiliar words with a dictionary.

- Use it to find a word or phrase 'on the tip of your tongue' by looking up a word of similar meaning.

- Use it to increase your vocabulary.

Roget's Thesaurus is the standard. Collins also publishes a combined dictionary and thesaurus.

Using guides for written English

These provide help with the use of words.

- Use guides to solve grammatical problems such as when to use 'shall' or 'will', 'which' or 'that', 'effect' or 'affect', 'can' or 'may', etc.

- Use them for help with the paragraph concept and the correct use of punctuation.

- Use them to learn how to structure writing for different tasks.

---

reports of laboratory work, the Experimental section may be the easiest place to start.

- Are you too tired to work? Don't try to 'sweat it out' by writing for long periods at a stretch: stop frequently for a rest.

Revising your text

Wholesale revision of your first draft is strongly advised for all writing, apart from in exams. When using a word processor, this can be a simple process. Where possible, schedule your writing so you can leave the first draft to 'settle' for at least a couple of days. When you return to it fresh, you will see more easily where improvements can be made. Try the following structured revision process, each stage being covered in a separate scan of your text:

1. Examine content. Have you included everything you need to? Is all the material relevant?

2. Check the grammar and spelling. Can you spot any 'howlers'?

3. Focus on clarity. Is the text clear and unambiguous? Does each sentence really say what you want it to say?

Revising your text – to improve clarity and shorten your text, 'distil' each sentence by taking away unnecessary words and 'condense' words or phrases by choosing a shorter alternative.

Learning from others – ask a colleague to read through your draft and comment on its content and overall structure.

4. Be succinct. What could be missed out without spoiling the essence of your work? It might help to imagine an editor has set you the target of reducing the text by 15%.

5. Improve style. Could the text read better? Consider the sentence and paragraph structure and the way your text develops to its conclusion.

Common errors

These include:

- Problems over singular and plural words ("the data is"; "the results shows").

- Verbose text ("One definition that can be employed in this situation is given in the following sentence.")

- Misconstructed sentences ("Health and safety regulations should be made aware of . . .").

- Misuse of punctuation, especially commas and apostrophes (for examples, see Box 16.1).

- Poorly-constructed paragraphs (for advice, see Box 16.1).

Sources for further study

Burchfield, R.W. (ed.) (2004) *Fowler's Modern English Usage*, revised 3rd edn. Oxford University Press, New York.

Clark, R. *The English Style Book. A Guide to the Writing of Scholarly English*. Available: http://www.litencyc.com/stylebook/stylebook.php Last accessed: 20/07/09.

Daintith, J. (ed.) (2008) *A Dictionary of Chemistry*, 6th edn. Oxford University Press, Oxford.

Ebel, H.F., Bliefert, C. and Russey, W.E. (2004) *The Art of Scientific Writing: from student reports to professional publications in chemistry and related fields*, 2nd edn. Wiley, Chichester.

Kane, T.S. (1994) *The New Oxford Guide to Writing*. Oxford University Press, New York.
[This is excellent for the basics of English – it covers grammar, usage and the construction of sentences and paragraphs]

Lim, K.F. (2003) *The Chemistry Style Manual*. Available: http://www.heacademy.ac.uk/assets/ps/documents/practice_guides/practice_guides/ps0068_chemistry_style_manual_dec_2004.pdf Last accessed 04/03/2010.
[A free download for personal use]

Lindsay, D. (1995) *A Guide to Scientific Writing*, 2nd edn. Longman, Harlow.

McMillan, K.M. and Weyers, J.D.B. (2006) *The Smarter Student: Skills and Strategies for Success at University*. Pearson, Harlow.

Palmer, R. (2004) *Studying for Success*. Routledge Education, Abingdon, Oxford.

Partridge, E. (1978) *You Have a Point There*. Routledge, London.
[This covers punctuation in a very readable manner]

Pechnick, J.A. and Lamb, B.C. (1994) *How to Write about Biology*. Harper Collins, London.

Tichy, H.J. (1988) *Effective Writing for Engineers, Managers and Scientists*, 2nd edn. Wiley, New York.
[This is strong on scientific style and clarity in writing]

16.1 'Brainstorm' an essay title. Pair up with a partner in your class. Together, pick a suitable essay title from a past exam paper. Using the spider diagram or another technique, individually 'brainstorm' the title. Meet afterwards, compare your ideas, and discuss their relative merits and disadvantages.

16.2 Improve your writing technique. From the following checklist, identify the *three* weakest aspects of your writing, either in your own opinion or from essay/assignment feedback:

- grammar;
- paragraph organisation;
- presentation of work;
- punctuation;
- scientific style;
- sentence structure/variety;
- spelling;

- structure and flow;
- vocabulary.

Now either borrow a book from a library or buy a book that deals with your weakest aspects of writing. Read the relevant chapters or sections and for each aspect write down some tips that should help you in future.

16.3 Improve your spelling and vocabulary with two lists. Create a pair of lists and pin these up beside your desk. One should be entitled *Spelling Mistakes* and the other *New Words*. Now, whenever you make a mistake in spelling or have to look up how to spell a word in a dictionary, add the problem word to your spelling list, showing where you made the mistake. Also, whenever you come across a word whose meaning is unclear to you, look it up in a dictionary and write the word and its meaning in the 'new words' vocabulary list.

The function of an essay is to show how much you understand about a topic and how well you can organise and express your knowledge.

Organising your time

The way you should divide your time when producing an essay depends on whether you are writing it for in-course assessment or under exam conditions (Fig. 17.1). Essays written over a long period with access to books and other resources will probably involve a research element, not only before the planning phase but also when writing (Fig. 17.1a). For exams, it is assumed that you have revised appropriately (Chapter 5) and essentially have all the information at your fingertips. To keep things uncomplicated, the time allocated for each essay should be divided into three components – planning, writing and reviewing (Fig. 17.1b), and you should adopt time-saving techniques whenever possible (Box 6.2).

Making a plan for your essay

Dissect the meaning of the essay question or title

Read the title very carefully and think about the topic before starting to write. Consider the definitions of each of the important nouns (this can help in approaching the introductory section). Also think about the meaning of the verb(s) used and try to follow each instruction precisely (see Table 17.1). Don't get side-tracked because you know something about one word or phrase in the title: consider the whole title and all its ramifications. If there are two or more parts to the question, make sure you give adequate attention to each part.

Consider possible content and examples

Research content using the methods described in Chapters 8 and 9. If you have time to read several sources, consider their content in relation to the essay title. Can you spot different approaches to the same subject? Which do you prefer as a means of treating the topic in relation to your title? Which examples are most relevant to your case, and why?

Construct an outline

Every essay should have a structure related to its title.

> **KEY POINT** Most marks for essays are lost because the written material is badly organised or is irrelevant. An essay plan, by definition, creates order and, if thought about carefully, should ensure relevance.

Your plan should be written down (but scored through later if written in an exam book). Think about an essay's content in three parts:

1. The introductory section, in which you should include definitions and some background information on the context of the topic being considered. You should also tell your reader how you plan to approach the subject.

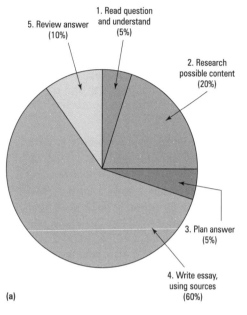

(a)

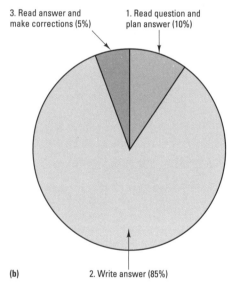

(b)

Fig. 17.1 Typical division of time for an essay written as part of an in-course assessment (a) or under exam conditions (b).

Considering essay content – it is rarely enough simply to lay down facts for the reader – you must analyse them and comment on their significance (see p. 118).

Ten Golden Rules for essay writing – these are framed for in-course assessments (p. 31), though many are also relevant to exams (see also Box 6.2).

1. Read the question carefully, and decide exactly what the assessor wants you to achieve in your answer.
2. Make sure you understand the question by considering all aspects – discuss your approach with colleagues or a tutor.
3. Carry out the necessary research (using books, journals, the Web), taking appropriate notes. Gain an overview of the topic before getting involved with the details.
4. Always plan your work in outline before you start writing. Check that your plan covers the main points and that it flows logically.
5. Introduce your essay by showing that you understand the topic and stating how you intend to approach it.
6. As you write the main content, ensure it is relevant by continually looking back at the question.
7. Use headings and sub-headings to organise and structure your essay.
8. Support your statements with relevant examples, diagrams and references where appropriate.
9. Conclude by summarising the key points of the topic, indicating the present state of knowledge, what we still need to find out and how this might be achieved.
10. Always review your essay before submitting it. Check grammar and spelling and confirm that you have answered *all* aspects of the question.

Table 17.1 Instructions often used in essay questions and their meanings. When more than one instruction is given (e.g. compare and contrast; describe and explain), make sure you carry out *both* or you may lose a large proportion of the available marks (see also Table 5.1)

Account for:	give the reasons for
Analyse:	examine in depth and describe the main characteristics of
Assess:	weigh up the elements of and arrive at a conclusion about
Comment:	give an opinion on and provide evidence for your views
Compare:	bring out the similarities between
Contrast:	bring out dissimilarities between
Criticise:	judge the worth of (give both positive and negative aspects)
Define:	explain the exact meaning of
Describe:	use words and diagrams to illustrate
Discuss:	provide evidence or opinions about, arriving at a balanced conclusion
Enumerate:	list in outline form
Evaluate:	weigh up or appraise; find a numerical value for
Explain:	make the meaning of something clear
Illustrate:	use diagrams or examples to make clear
Interpret:	express in simple terms, providing a judgement
Justify:	show that an idea or statement is correct
List:	provide an itemised series of statements about
Outline:	describe the essential parts only, stressing the classification
Prove:	establish the truth of
Relate:	show the connection between
Review:	examine critically, perhaps concentrating on the stages in the development of an idea or method
State:	express clearly
Summarise:	without illustrations, provide a brief account of
Trace:	describe a sequence of events from a defined point of origin

2. The middle of the essay, where you develop your answer and provide relevant examples. Decide whether a broad analytical approach is appropriate or whether the essay should contain more factual detail.

3. The conclusion, which you can make quite short. You should use this part to summarise and draw together the components of the essay, without merely repeating previous phrases. You might mention such things as: the broader significance of the topic; its future; its relevance to other important areas of chemistry. Always try to mention both sides of any debate you have touched on, but beware of 'sitting on the fence'.

> **KEY POINT** Use paragraphs to make the essay's structure obvious. Emphasise them with headings and sub-headings unless the material beneath the headings would be too short or trivial.

Start writing

- Never lose track of the importance of content and its relevance. Repeatedly ask yourself: 'Am I really answering this question?' Never waffle just to increase the length of an essay. Quality, rather than quantity, is important.

Using diagrams – give a title and legend to each diagram so that it makes sense in isolation and point out in the text when the reader should consult it (e.g. 'as shown in Fig. 1 . . .' or 'as can be seen in the accompanying diagram, . . .').

Learning from lecturers' and tutors' comments – ask for further explanations if you don't understand a comment or why an essay was less successful than you thought it should have been.

- Illustrate your answer appropriately. Use examples to make your points clear, but remember that too many similar examples can stifle the flow of an essay. Use diagrams where a written description would be difficult or take too long. Use tables to condense information.

- Take care with your handwriting. You can't get marks if your writing is illegible. Try to cultivate an open form of handwriting, making the individual letters large and distinct. If there is time, make out a rough draft from which a tidy version can be copied.

Reviewing your answer

Make sure that you leave enough time to:

- re-read the question to check that you have answered all points;

- re-read your essay to check for errors in punctuation, spelling and content. Make any corrections obvious. In an exam, don't panic if you suddenly realise you've missed a large chunk out as the reader can be redirected to a supplementary paragraph if necessary.

Sources for further study

Anon. *Yahoo! Directory: Writing > Essays and Research Papers*. Available: http://dir.yahoo.com/Social_Science/Communications/Writing/Essays_and_Research_Papers Last accessed: 20/07/09. [An extensive directory of web resources]

Anon. (2004) *Essay and Report Writing Skills*. Open University, Milton Keynes.

Ebel, H.F., Bliefert, C. and Russey, W.E. (2004) *The Art of Scientific Writing: from student reports to professional publications in chemistry and related fields*, 2nd edn. Wiley, Chichester.

Good, S. and Jensen, B. (1995) *The Student's Only Survival Guide to Essay Writing*. Orca Book Publishers, Victoria, BC.

Lim, K.F. (2003) *The Chemistry Style Manual* http://www.heacademy.ac.uk/assets/ps/documents/practice_guides/practice_guides/ps0068_chemistry_style_manual_dec_2004.pdf Last accessed 04/03/2010. [A free download for personal use]

Palmer, R. (2004) *Studying for Success*. Routledge Education, Abingdon, Oxford.

Study exercises

17.1 Practise dissecting essay titles. Use past exam papers, or make up questions based on learning objectives for your course and your lecture notes. Take each essay title and carefully 'dissect' the wording, working out exactly what you think the assessor expects you to do (see e.g. Table 17.1).

17.2 Write essay plans under self-imposed time limits. Continuing from study exercise 17.1, outline plans for essays from a past exam paper. Allow yourself a maximum of 5 minutes per outline. Within this time your main goal is to create an essay plan. To do this, you may need to 'brainstorm' the topic. Alternatively, if you allocate 10 minutes per essay, you may be able to provide more details, e.g. list the examples you could describe.

17.3 Practise reviewing your work carefully. For the next assignment you write, review it fully as part of the writing process. This will require you to finish the first draft about one week before the hand-in date, e.g. by setting yourself an earlier deadline than the submission date. This exercise is best done with a word-processed essay. Don't worry if it is a little over the word limit at this stage.

(a) Print out a copy of the essay. Do not look at it for at least two days after finishing this version.

(b) Review 1: spelling, grammar and sense. Read through the draft critically (try to imagine it had been written by someone else) and correct any obvious errors that strike you. Does the text make sense? Do sentences/ paragraphs flow smoothly?

(c) Review 2: structure and relevance. Consider again the structure of the essay, asking yourself whether you have really answered the question that was set (see study exercise 17.1). Are all the parts in the right order? Is anything missed out? Have you followed precisely the instruction(s) in the title? Are the different parts of the essay linked together well?

(d) Review 3: shorten and improve style. Check the word count. Shorten the essay if required. Look critically at phrasing and, even if the essay is within the word limit, ask yourself whether any of the words are unnecessary or whether the text could be made more concise, more precise or more apt.

Typical structure of scientific reports – this usually follows the 'IERaD' acronym: **I**ntroduction, **E**xperimental, **R**esults and **D**iscussion.

Practical reports, project reports, theses and scientific papers differ greatly in depth, scope and size, but they all have the same basic structure. Some variation is permitted, however (see Box 18.1), and you should always follow the advice or rules provided by your department.

Additional parts may be specified: for project reports, dissertations and theses, a Title page is often required and a List of Figures and Tables as part of the Contents section. When work is submitted for certain degrees, you may need to include certain declarations and statements made by the student and supervisor. In scientific papers, a list of Key Words is often added following the Abstract: this information may be combined with words in the title for computer cross-referencing systems.

> **KEY POINT** Department, school or faculty regulations may specify a precise format for producing your report or thesis. Obtain a copy of these rules at an early stage and follow them closely, to avoid losing marks.

Options for discussing data – the main optional variants of the general structure include combining *Results and Discussion* into a single section and adding a separate *Conclusions* section.

- The main advantage of a joint *Results and Discussion* section is that you can link together different experiments, perhaps explaining why a particular result led to a new hypothesis and the next experiment. However, a combined Results and Discussion section may contravene your department's regulations, so you should check before using this approach.
- The main advantage of having a separate *Conclusions* section is to draw together and emphasise the chief points arising from your work, when these may have been 'buried' in an extensive *Discussion* section.

Practical and project reports

These are exercises designed to make you think more deeply about your experiments and to practise and test the skills necessary for writing up research work. Special features are:

- Introductory material is generally short and, unless otherwise specified, should outline the aims of the experiment(s) with a minimum of background material.
- Experimental may be provided by your supervisor for practical reports. If you make changes to this, you should state clearly what you did. With project work, your lab notebook (see p. 210) should provide the basis for writing this section.
- Great attention in assessment will be paid to presentation and analysis of data. Take special care over graphs (see p. 479 for further advice). Make sure your conclusions are justified by the evidence you present.

Theses and dissertations

These are submitted as part of the examination for a degree following an extended period of research. They act to place on record full details about your experimental work and will normally only be read by those with a direct interest in it – your examiners or colleagues. Note the following:

- You are allowed scope to expand on your findings and to include detail that might otherwise be omitted in a scientific paper.
- You may have problems with the volume of information that has to be organised. One method of coping with this is to divide your thesis into chapters, each having the standard format (as in Box 18.1). A General Introduction can be given at the start and a General Discussion at the end. Discuss this with your supervisor.

Oral assessments – there may be an oral exam (*viva voce*) associated with the submission of a thesis or dissertation. The primary aim of the examiners will be to ensure that you understand what you did and why you did it.

Box 18.1 The structure of reports of experimental work

Undergraduate practical and project reports are generally modelled on this arrangement or a close variant of it, because this is the structure used for nearly all research papers and theses. The more common variations include Results and Discussion combined into a single section and Conclusions appearing separately as a series of points arising from the work. In scientific papers, a list of Key Words (for computer cross-referencing systems) may be included following the Abstract. Acknowledgements may appear after the Contents section, rather than near the end. Department or faculty regulations for producing theses and reports may specify a precise format; they often require a Title page to be inserted at the start and a List of Figures and Tables as part of the Contents section, and may specify declarations and statements to be made by the student and supervisor.

Part (in order)	Contents/purpose	Checklist for reviewing content
Title	Explains what the project was about	Does it explain what the text is about succinctly?
Authors plus their institutions	Explains who did the work and where; also where they can be contacted now	Are all the details correct?
Abstract/Summary	Synopsis of methods, results and conclusion of work described. Allows the reader to grasp quickly the essence of the work	Does it explain why the work was done? Does it outline the whole of your work and your findings?
List of Contents	Shows the organisation of the text (not required for short papers)	Are all the sections covered? Are the page numbers correct?
Abbreviations	Lists all the abbreviations used (but not those of SI, chemical elements or standard chemical terms)	Have they all been explained? Are they all in the accepted form? Are they in alphabetical order?
Introduction	Orientates the reader, explains why the work has been done and its context in the literature, why the methods used were chosen, why the experimental conditions were chosen. Indicates the central hypothesis behind the experiments	Does it provide enough background information and cite all the relevant references? Is it of the correct depth for the readership? Have all the technical terms been defined? Have you explained why you investigated the problem? Have you outlined your aims and objectives? Have you explained your methodological approach? Have you stated your hypothesis?
Experimental	Explains how the work was done. Should contain sufficient detail to allow another competent worker to repeat the work	Is each experiment covered and have you avoided unnecessary duplication? Is there sufficient detail to allow repetition of the work? Are proper scientific names and authorities given for all organisms? Have you explained where you got them from? Are the correct names, sources and grades given for all chemicals?
Results	Displays and describes the data obtained. Should be presented in a form which is easily assimilated (graphs rather than tables, small tables rather than large ones)	Is the sequence of experiments logical? Are the parts adequately linked? Are the data presented in the clearest possible way? Have SI units been used properly throughout? Has adequate statistical analysis been carried out? Is all the material relevant? Are the figures and tables all numbered in the order of their appearance? Are their titles appropriate? Do the figure and table legends provide all the information necessary to interpret the data without reference to the text? Have you presented the same data more than once?
Discussion/ Conclusions	Discusses the results: their meaning, their importance; compares the results with those of others; suggests what to do next	Have you explained the significance of the results? Have you compared your data with other published work? Are your conclusions justified by the data presented?
Acknowledgements	Gives credit to those who helped carry out the work	Have you listed everyone that helped, including any grant-awarding bodies?
Literature Cited (Bibliography)	Lists all references cited in appropriate format: provides enough information to allow the reader to find the reference in a library	Do all the references in the text appear on the list? Do all the listed references appear in the text? Do the years of publications and authors match? Are the journal details complete and in the correct format? Is the list in alphabetical order, or correct numerical order?

Choosing between graphs and tables – graphs are generally easier for the reader to assimilate, while tables can be used to condense a lot of data into a small space.

Repeating your experiments – remember, if you do an experiment twice, you have repeated it only once.

Presenting your results – remember that the order of results presented in a report need not correspond with the order in which you carried out the experiments: you are expected to re-arrange them to provide a logical sequence of findings.

Using the correct tense – always use the past tense to describe the methodology used in your work, since it is now complete. Use the present tense only for generalisations and conclusions.

Steps in the production of a practical report or thesis

Choose the experiments you wish to describe and decide how best to present them

Try to start this process before your lab work ends, because at the stage of reviewing your experiments, a gap may become apparent (e.g. a missing control) and you might still have time to rectify the deficiency. Irrelevant material should be ruthlessly eliminated, at the same time bearing in mind that negative results can be extremely important (see p. 220). Use as many different forms of data presentation as are appropriate, but avoid presenting the same data in more than one form. Relegate large tables of primary data to an appendix and summarise the important points within the main text (with a cross-reference to the appendix). Make sure that the experiments you describe are representative: always state the number of times they were repeated and how consistent your findings were.

Make up plans or outlines for the component parts

The overall structure of practical and project reports is well defined (see Box 18.1), but individual parts will need to be organised as with any other form of writing (see Chapter 16).

Write

The Experimental section is often the easiest to write once you have decided what to report. Remember to use the past tense and do not allow results or discussion to creep in. There may be minor variations in style, but the one shown in Box 18.2 will be suitable in the majority of cases. The Results section is the next easiest as it should only involve description. At this stage, you may benefit from jotting down ideas for the Discussion – this may be the hardest part to compose as you need an overview both of your own work and of the relevant literature. It is also liable to become wordy, so try hard to make it succinct. The Introduction shouldn't be too difficult if you have fully understood the aims of the experiments. Write the Abstract and complete the list of references at the end. To assist with the latter, it is a good idea as you write to jot down the references you use or to pull out their cards from your index system.

Revise the text

Once your first draft is complete, try to answer all the questions given in Box 18.1. Show your work to your supervisors and learn from their comments. Let a friend or colleague who is unfamiliar with your subject read your text; they may be able to pinpoint obscure wording and show where information or explanation is missing. If writing a thesis, double-check that you are adhering to your institution's thesis regulations.

Prepare the final version

Markers appreciate neatly produced work but a well-presented document will not disguise poor science! If using a word processor, print the final version with the best printer available. Make sure figures are clear and in the correct size and format.

Box 18.2 Writing experimental procedures

The main purpose of the methods described in the experimental section of a laboratory report, project report, thesis or paper is to communicate sufficient information to allow an experienced chemist to repeat your experiments. One of the goals of writing laboratory reports is to provide you with practice in writing in the generally accepted style required for more professional publications. The following points should be noted:

- Always write in the third person, past tense.

- Do not copy word for word the instructions given in the experiment protocol. You are in a learning situation in the laboratory and the protocol may contain information, which may be new to you, but is general knowledge to experienced chemists.

- Condensing the experimental protocol for your report will help you to see the important steps in the experiment.

- All sentences begin with a capital letter not a number or bracket.

The following examples illustrate the differences between the instructions of the experiment protocol and the accepted style required for the experimental section.

Example 1 A preparative experiment: the synthesis of methyl 2,4-dimethylbenzoate

Experiment protocol
'In a round-bottom flask (100 mL) place 2,4-dimethylbenzoic acid (3.0 g, 0.02 mol), anhydrous potassium carbonate (3.3 g, 0.024 mol) and a small magnetic flea. In the fume cupboard and wearing protective gloves, carefully weigh out dimethylsulphate (2.8 g. 0.022 mol) into a glass sample tube (10 mL) using a Pasteur pipette to transfer the liquid. Using the Pasteur pipette, transfer the dimethylsulphate to the reaction flask and use anhydrous propanone (10 mL) to rinse the sample tube. Add the rinsings to the reaction flask and add more dry propanone (10 mL). Fit the flask with a reflux condenser and boil the mixture under reflux for 3 hours using an oil bath on a stirrer hot plate in the fume cupboard. Allow the reaction mixture to cool to room temperature and pour into water (100 mL) washing the reaction flask with a few millilitres of water. Extract the aqueous solution three times with dichloromethane (20 mL), dry the dichloromethane ($MgSO_4$), filter off the drying agent, remove the solvent on the rotary evaporator and record the weight of the crude product. Recrystallise and charcoal the crude ester from ethanol and dry in a vacuum desiccator. Record the weight and melting point of the purified ester and obtain and interpret infrared and

^{1}H–NMR spectra. Check the purity of your product using TLC (SiO_2 plates and CH_2Cl_2 as eluent) and calculate the percentage yield of the product.'

Experimental
A mixture of 2,4-dimethylbenzoic acid (3.0 g, 0.02 mol), dimethylsulphate (2.8 g, 0.022 mol) and anhydrous potassium carbonate (3.3 g, 0.024 mol) in dry propanone (20 mL) was boiled under reflux (3h), cooled, poured into water (100 mL) and extracted with dichloromethane (3 × 20 mL). Removal of the dried ($MgSO_4$) organic solvent gave a white solid (2.3 g), which was recrystallised from ethanol, using charcoal to improve the colour, to yield white needles of methyl 2,4-dimethylbenzoate (2.28 g). The infrared (Nujol) and ^{1}H–NMR ($CDCl_3$) spectra were recorded and TLC (SiO_2/CH_2Cl_2) showed the product to be pure. The melting point was determined and the % yield calculated.

Note 1. Experimental gives reagents, solvents, quantities, times, yields, etc., and sufficient detail for the experiment to be repeated by a proficient chemist. Details of standard techniques such as weighing liquids, setting up apparatus, recrystallisation, drying the product, etc., are 'understood' by the experimentalist from experience and training.

Note 2. The weights and volumes used are quoted to one decimal place, since this is the level of accuracy required for preparative experiments which results from the techniques used, distillation, recrystallisation, extraction, etc., and the non-quantitative conversion of the reactants to products may be more significant than errors in weighing.

Note 3. All analytical data such as IR and NMR spectra, TLC, melting point and yield calculations are entered in the results section.

Note 4. The % yield for the product represents a comparison with the theoretical yield of the reaction and the practical yield. Calculation of the theoretical yield based on:

(a) the molar quantities of the reactants used;

(b) the number of moles of each reactant required to make 1 mole of product;

(c) the assumption that reactions go 100%;

(d) the 'limiting quantity' of one of the reactants.

To calculate the theoretical yield of a reaction, it is essential that you recognise the reactant, which is the limiting quantity.

If a reaction requires 1 mole of reactant A and 1 mole of reactant B to give 1 mole of product AB, i.e.:

$$A + B \rightarrow AB$$

Box 18.2 Writing experimental procedures (continued)

if we use A (1 mol) and B (1.5 mol), then only 1 mol of AB can be formed and there is 0.5 mol of B in excess and unreacted. Therefore the limiting quantity is the amount of reactant A (1 mol). The excess of reactant B may be necessary to ensure complete conversion of A into AB, i.e. 100% reaction. In the example above, the limiting quantity is the amount of 2,4-dimethylbenzoic acid (0.02 mol) and only 0.02 mol of the methyl ester can be formed ($164 \times 0.02 = 3.28$ g). Therefore:

$$\% \text{ yield} = \frac{\text{reaction yield}}{\text{theory yield}} \times 100 = \frac{2.28}{3.28} \times 100 = 70\%$$

Example 2 A quantitative experiment: standardisation of sodium thiosulphate solution

Experiment protocol
'Prepare a standard solution of potassium iodate by dissolving potassium iodate (about 1.34 g, accurately weighed) in distilled water (100 mL), quantitatively transferring the solution to a volumetric flask (250.00 mL) making up to the mark using distilled water and mixing well. Pipette an aliquot (25.00 mL) of the solution into a conical flask (250 mL) and add sulphuric acid (50 mL, 1 M). Weigh out potassium iodide (1 g), add it to the conical flask and swirl until it has all dissolved. Titrate the liberated iodine (brown solution) with the sodium thiosulphate solution until a pale straw colour is reached. Add iodine indicator (two drops) or freshly prepared starch solution (two drops) and continue the titration until the colour changes from blue–black to colourless. If the solution does not turn blue–black when you add the iodine indicator or starch, you have overshot the endpoint. Repeat the experiment until consistent results are obtained. Calculate the molarity of the sodium thiosulphate solution.'

Experimental
Potassium iodate (1.3402 g) was dissolved in distilled water (100 mL), transferred to a volumetric flask (250.00 mL) and made up to the mark using distilled water. An aliquot (25.00 mL) was transferred to a conical flask (250 mL), sulphuric acid (50 mL, 1 M) and potassium iodide (1 g) were added and the mixture swirled to effect solution. The iodine liberated was titrated with the sodium thiosulphate solution to a pale straw colour. Iodine indicator (two drops) was then added and the titration continued to a blue–black to colourless endpoint. The experiment was repeated until consistent results were obtained and the concentration of the sodium thiosulphate solution calculated.

Note 1. The differences in accuracy, indicating the equipment you must use, are shown by the decimal point quoted in the quantities.

Note 2. Titrations should be repeated to give consecutive results to within one or two drops of titrant. Do not average widely differing results.

Note 3. Balance readings, burette readings and calculations should be included in the results section.

Example 3 Reaction kinetics: determination of rate constant and energy of activation using titrimetry

Experiment protocol
'The following solutions are provided:
A. Potassium persulphate (0.04 M)
B. Sodium thiosulphate (0.01 M)
C. Potassium iodide (0.4 M).

   i. Place solution A (100 mL) and solution C (100 mL) into separate conical flasks and suspend them in a thermostat bath at 25 °C.

  ii. Mix solutions A and C (50 mL of each) in a stoppered flask and immerse in hot water until the end of the experiment.

 iii. After about 15 minutes from step i, mix the solutions A and C and start the clock. This mixture must be kept in the thermostat bath at 25 °C, throughout the experiment.

 iv. Just before 2 minutes have elapsed, take a sample (10.00 mL) from the flask by pipette and add it to distilled water (200 mL) in a separate flask. This quenches (stops) the reaction.

  v. Take further samples at 4, 6, 9, 13, 18, 24, 32, 44 and 60 minutes and quench in the same way.

 vi. Titrate each quenched solution with sodium thiosulphate, including a sample of the 'hot-water' sample. Use a small amount of freshly prepared starch indicator solution and titrate from blue to colourless. The titres for the samples are the values (T) and that for the 'hot-water' sample is T_∞.

 vii. Now repeat the whole experiment using a thermostat bath set at 35–40°C. Make an accurate record of the temperature. You do not need to repeat the 'hot-water' sample since this will serve for both experiments. Since this higher temperature reaction is faster, there is no need to take samples at 44 and 60 minutes.

viii. For each temperature plot a graph of $-\ln(T_\infty - T)$ versus time (s).'

Experimental
Solutions (100 mL) of potassium persulphate (0.04 M) and potassium iodide (0.4 M) were equilibrated (0.25 h) in a constant temperature bath (25 °C). The two

solutions were mixed in a conical flask (250 mL) in the constant temperature bath and the clock started. After 2 minutes, an aliquot (10.00 mL) of the mixture was quenched with distilled water (200 mL) and the sampling process repeated after 4, 6, 9, 13, 18, 24, 32, 44 and 60 minutes. Each sample was titrated with sodium thiosulphate solution (0.01 M), using iodine indicator, to a colourless end-point and the values recorded (T). The experiment was then repeated at a known temperature between 35 °C and 40 °C but the

samples at 44 and 60 minutes were not taken. Solutions (50 mL) of the potassium persulphate and potassium iodide were mixed and kept in a water bath (60–70°C) for 2 hours. An aliquot (10.00 mL) of this solution was quenched in distilled water (200 mL) and titrated (T_∞) with the sodium thiosulphate solution. A graph of $-\ln(t_\infty - T)$ versus time (s) was plotted.

Note 1. Only experimental detail is given. Calculations, results and theory are in the appropriate sections.

Submit your work

Your department will specify when to submit a thesis or project report, so plan your work carefully to meet this deadline or you may lose marks. Tell your supervisor early of any circumstances that may cause delay. And check to see whether any forms are required for late submission, or evidence of extenuating circumstances.

Producing a scientific paper

Scientific papers are the means by which research findings are communicated to others. Peer-reviewed papers are published in journals; each covers a well-defined subject area and publishes details of the format they expect.

> **KEY POINT** Peer review is an important component of the process of scientific publication; only those papers whose worth is confirmed by the peer-review process will be published.

It would be very unusual for an undergraduate to submit a paper on his or her own – this would normally be done in collaboration with your project supervisor, and only then if your research has satisfied appropriate criteria. However, it is important to understand the process whereby a paper comes into being (Box 18.3), as this can help you understand and interpret the primary literature.

Definition

Peer review – the process of evaluation and review of a colleague's work. In scientific communication, a paper is reviewed by two or more expert reviewers for comments on quality and signi-ficance as a key component of the validation procedure.

Box 18.3 Steps in producing a scientific paper

Scientific papers are the lifeblood of any science and it is a major landmark in your scientific career to publish your first paper. The main steps in doing this should include the following:

Assessing potential content

The work must be of an appropriate standard to be published and should be 'new, true and meaningful'. Therefore, before starting, the authors need to review their work critically under these headings. The material included in a scientific paper will generally be a subset

of the total work done during a project, so it must be carefully selected for relevance to a clear central hypothesis – if the authors won't prune, the referees and editors of the journal certainly will.

Choosing a journal

There are thousands of journals covering chemistry and each covers a specific area (which may change through time). The main factors in deciding on an appropriate journal are the range of subjects it covers, the quality of its content and the number and geographical

Box 18.3 Steps in producing a scientific paper (continued)

distribution of its readers. The choice of journal always dictates the format of a paper since authors must follow to the letter the journal's 'Instructions to Authors'.

Deciding on authorship

In multi-author papers, a contentious issue is often who should appear as an author and in what order they should be cited. Where authors make an equal contribution, an alphabetical order of names may be used. Otherwise, each author should have made a substantial contribution to the paper and should be prepared to defend it in public. Ideally, the order of appearance will reflect the amount of work done rather than seniority. This may not always happen in practice!

Writing

The paper's format will be similar to that shown in Box 18.1 and the process of writing will include outlining, reviewing, etc., as discussed elsewhere in this chapter. Figures must be finished to an appropriate standard and this may involve preparing digital images of them.

Submitting

When completed, copies of the paper are submitted to the editor of the chosen journal with a simple covering letter. This is often done electronically by uploading all files on to the publishers' website. A delay of one to two months usually follows while the manuscript is sent to two or more anonymous referees who will be asked by the editor to check that the paper is novel, scientifically correct and that its length is justified.

Responding to referees' comments

The editor will send on the referees' comments to the authors, who will then have a chance to respond. The editor will decide on the basis of the comments and replies to them whether the paper should be published. Sometimes quite heated correspondence can result if the authors and referees disagree.

Checking proofs and waiting for publication

If a paper is accepted, it will be sent off to the typesetters. The next the authors see of it is the proofs (first printed version in style of journal), which have to be corrected carefully for errors and returned. Eventually, the paper will appear in print, but a delay of six months following acceptance is not unusual. Nowadays, papers are often available electronically, *via* the Web, in PDF format – see p. 51 for advice on how to cite 'online early' papers using the DOI system.

Sources for further study

Berry, R. (2004) *The Research Project: How to Write it*, 5th edn. Routledge, London.

Davis, M. (2005) *Scientific Papers and Presentations.* Academic Press, London.

Day, R.A. and Gastel, B. (2006) *How to Write and Publish a Scientific Paper*, 6th edn. Cambridge University Press, Cambridge.

Lobban, C.S. and Schefter, M. (1992) *Successful Lab Reports: A Manual for Science Students.* Cambridge University Press, Cambridge.

Luck, M. (1999) *Your Student Research Project.* Gower, London.

Luey, B. (2002) *Handbook for Academic Authors*, 4th edn. Cambridge University Press, Cambridge.

Valiela, I. (2001) *Doing Science: Design, Analysis and Communication of Scientific Research.* Oxford University Press, Oxford.
[Covers scientific communication, graphical presentations and aspects of statistics]

18.1 Write a formal 'Experimental' section. Adopting the style of a research paper (i.e. past tense, all relevant detail reported such that a competent colleague could repeat your work), write out the 'Experimental' details for a practical you have recently carried out. Ask a colleague or tutor to comment on what you have written.

18.2 Describe a set of results in words. Again adopting the style of a research paper, write a paragraph describing the results contained in a particular table or graph. Ask a colleague or tutor to comment on your description, to identify what is missing or unclear.

18.3 Write an abstract for a paper. Pair up with a colleague. Each of you should independently choose a different research paper in a current journal. Copy the paper, but mask over the abstract section, having first counted the words used. Swap papers. Now, working to the same number of words as in the original, read the paper and provide an abstract of its contents. Then compare this with the real abstract. Compare your abstracts.

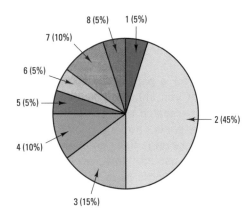

Fig. 19.1 Pie chart showing how you might allocate time for a literature survey:
1. select a topic;
2. scan the literature;
3. plan the review;
4. write first draft;
5. leave to settle;
6. prepare a structured review of text;
7. write final draft;
8. produce top copy.

Creating a glossary – one barrier to developing an understanding of a new topic is the jargon used. To overcome this, create your own glossary. You may wish to cross-reference a range of sources to ensure the definitions are reliable and context-specific. Remember to note your sources in case you wish to use the definition within your review.

Using index cards – these can help you organise large numbers of references. Write key points and author information on each card – this helps when considering where the reference fits into the literature. Arrange the cards in subject piles, eliminating irrelevant ones. Order the cards in the sequence you wish to write in. Use of bibliographic software (p. 50) is often used instead of index cards. The software allows information to be retained direct from e-journals; it is also possible to upload a pdf copy of the research journal article directly into the same software.

The literature survey or review is a specialised form of essay which summarises and reviews the evidence and concepts concerning a particular area of research.

> **KEY POINT** A literature review should *not* be a simple recitation of facts. The best reviews are those which analyse information rather than simply describe it.

Making up a timetable

Figure 19.1 illustrates how you might divide up your time for writing a literature survey. There are many subdivisions in this chart because of the size of the task: in general, for lengthy tasks, it is best to divide up the work into manageable chunks. Note also that proportionately less time is allocated to writing itself than with an essay. In a literature survey, make sure that you spend adequate time on research and revision.

Selecting a topic

You may have no choice in the topic to be covered, but if you do, carry out your selection as a three-stage process:

1. Identify a broad subject area that interests you.

2. Find and read relevant literature in that area. Try to gain a broad impression of the field from books and general review articles. Discuss your ideas with your supervisor.

3. Select a relevant and concise title. The wording should be considered very carefully as it will define the content expected by the reader. A narrow subject area will cut down on the amount of literature you will be expected to review, but will also restrict the scope of the conclusions you can make (and *vice versa* for a wide subject area).

Scanning the literature and organising your references

You will need to carry out a thorough investigation of the literature before you start to write. The key problems are as follows:

- Getting an initial toehold in the literature. Seek help from your supervisor, who may be willing to supply a few key papers to get you started. Hints on expanding your collection of references are given on p. 47.

- Assessing the relevance and value of each article. This is the essence of writing a review, but it is difficult unless you already have a good understanding of the field. Try reading earlier reviews in your area and discussing the topic with your supervisor or other academic staff.

- Clarifying your thoughts. Subdividing the main topic and assigning your references to these smaller subject areas may help you gain a better overview of the literature.

Deciding on structure and content

The general structure and content of a literature survey are described below.

The *Chemical Society Reviews* series (available in most university libraries) provides good examples of appropriate style for reviews of the chemical sciences.

Introduction

The introduction should give the general background to the research area, concentrating on its development and importance. You should also make a statement about the scope of your survey; as well as defining the subject matter to be discussed, you may wish to restrict the period being considered.

Defining terms – the introduction is a good place to explain the meaning of the key terms used in your survey or review.

Main body of text

The review itself should discuss the published work in the selected field and may be subdivided into appropriate sections. Within each portion of a review, the approach is usually chronological, with appropriate linking phrases (e.g. 'Following on from this, ...'; 'Meanwhile, Bloggs (2009) tackled the problem from a different angle ...'). However, a good review is much more than a chronological list of work done. It should:

- allow the reader to obtain an overall view of the current state of the research area, identifying the key areas where knowledge is advancing;

- show how techniques are developing and discuss the benefits and disadvantages of using particular organisms or experimental systems;

- assess the relative worth of different types of evidence – this is the most important aspect (see Chapter 9). Do not be intimidated from taking a critical approach as the conclusions you may read in the primary literature aren't always correct;

- indicate where there is conflict in findings or theories, suggesting if possible which side has the stronger case;

- indicate gaps in current knowledge.

Balancing opposing views – even if you favour one side of a disagreement in the literature, your review should provide a balanced and fair description of all the published views of the topic. Having done this, if you do wish to state a preference, give reasons for your opinion.

You do not need to wait until you have read all the sources available to you before starting to write the main body. Word processors allow you to modify and move pieces of text at any point and it will be useful to write paragraphs about key sources, or groups of related papers, as you read them. Try to create a general plan for your review as soon as possible. Place your draft sections of text under an appropriate set of subheadings that reflects your plan, but be prepared to rearrange these and re-title or re-order sections as you proceed. Not only will working in this way help to clarify your thoughts, but it may help you avoid a last-minute rush of writing near to the submission date.

Conclusions

The conclusions should draw together the threads of the preceding parts and point the way forward, perhaps listing areas of ignorance or where the application of new techniques may lead to advances.

References, etc.

The References or Literature Cited section should provide full details of all papers referred to in the text (see p. 50). The regulations for your department may also specify a format and position for the title page, list of contents, acknowledgements, etc.

Source for further study

Rudner, L.M. and Schafer, W.D. (1999) How to write a scholarly research report. *Practical Assessment, Research & Evaluation*, **6** (13). Available: http://pareonline.net/ getvn.asp?v=6&n=13 Last accessed: 20/07/09.

Study exercises

19.1 Summarise the main differences between a review and a scientific paper. From the many subject areas in the *Chemical Society Reviews* series (find *via* your library's periodical indexing system), pick one that matches your subject interests, and within this find a review that seems relevant or interesting. Read the review and write down *five* ways in which the writing style and content differ from those seen in primary scientific papers.

19.2 Gather a collection of primary sources for a topic. From the journal section of the library, select an interesting scientific paper published about 5–10 years ago. First, work *back* from the references cited by that paper: can you identify from the text or the article titles which are the most important and relevant to the topic? List *five* of these, using the proper conventions for citing articles in a reference list (see Chapter 8). Note that each of these papers will also cite other articles, always going back in time. Now using the Science Citation Index or a similar system (e.g. the Web of Science website at http://wos.mimas.ac.uk or Google Scholar at http://scholar.google.com/), work *forward* and find out who has cited your selected article in the time since its publication. Again list the *five* most important articles found.

19.3 Write a synopsis of a review. Again using one of the *Chemical Society Reviews* series as a source, allow yourself just *five* single-sentence bullet points to summarise the key points reported in a particular review.

Fundamental laboratory techniques

Developing practical skills – these will include:

- observing and measuring
- recording data
- designing experiments
- analysing and interpreting data
- reporting/presenting.

> **SAFETY NOTE** Mobile phones – these should never be used in a lab class, as there is a risk of contamination from hazardous substances. Always switch off your mobile phone before entering a laboratory.

Using textbooks in the lab – take this book along to the relevant classes, so that you can make full use of the information during the practical sessions.

> **SAFETY NOTE** If in doubt over any part of the practical procedure – ASK! There is no such thing as a silly question in the laboratory.

Presenting results – while you don't need to be a graphic designer to produce work of a satisfactory standard, presentation and layout are important and you will lose marks for poorly presented work.

All knowledge and theory in science has originated from practical observation and experimentation: this is equally true for disciplines as diverse as analysis and synthesis. Laboratory work is an essential part of all chemistry courses and often accounts for a significant proportion of the assessment marks. The skills and abilities developed in practical classes will continue to be useful throughout your course and beyond, some within science and others in any career you choose (see Chapter 1).

Being prepared

> **KEY POINT** You will get the most out of laboratory work if you prepare well. Do not go into a practical session assuming that everything will be provided, without any input on your part.

The main points to remember are:

- Read any handouts in advance: make sure you understand the purpose of the practical and the particular skills involved. Does the practical relate to, or expand upon, a current topic in your lectures? Is there any additional preparatory reading that will help?

- Take along appropriate textbooks, to explain aspects in the practical.

- Consider what safety hazards might be involved, and any precautions you might need to take, before you begin (p. 143).

- Listen carefully to any instructions and note any important points: adjust your schedule/handout, as necessary.

- During the practical session, organise your bench space – make sure your lab book is adjacent to, but not within, your working area. You will often find it easiest to keep clean items of glassware, etc., on one side of your working space, with used equipment on the other side.

- All chemical waste (solid or liquid) should be disposed of in the appropriate containers provided (consult the demonstrator or lecturer-in-charge).

- Write up your work as soon as possible and submit it on time or you may lose marks.

- Catch up on any work you have missed as soon as possible – preferably before the next practical session.

Basic requirements

Recording practical results

An A4 loose-leaf ring binder offers flexibility, since you can insert laboratory handouts, and lined and graph paper, at appropriate points. The danger of losing one or more pages from a loose-leaf system is the main drawback. Bound books avoid this problem, although those containing alternating lined/graph or lined/blank pages tend to be wasteful – it is often better to paste sheets of graph paper into a bound book, as required.

All experimental observations and data should be recorded in a notebook in ink at the time they are made because it is easy to forget when you are busy.

A good-quality HB pencil or propelling pencil is recommended for making diagrams etc. as mistakes are easily corrected with a vinyl eraser. Buy a black, spirit-based (permanent) marker to label experimental glassware, sample tubes, etc. Fibre-tipped fine line drawing/lettering pens are useful for preparing final versions of graphs and diagrams for assessment purposes. Use a clear ruler (with an undamaged edge) for graph drawing, so that you can see data points/information below the ruler as you draw.

Calculators

These range from basic machines with no pre-programmed functions and only one memory, to sophisticated programmable minicomputers with many memories. The following may be helpful when using a calculator:

- Power sources. Choose a battery-powered machine, rather than a mains-operated or solar-powered type. You will need one with basic mathematical/scientific operations including powers, logarithms (p. 493), roots and parentheses (brackets), together with statistical functions such as sample means and standard deviations (Chapter 63).

- Mode of operation. Calculators fall into two distinct groups. The older system used by, for example, Hewlett Packard calculators is known as the reverse Polish notation: to calculate the sum of two numbers, the sequence is 2 [enter] 4 + and the answer 6 is displayed. The more usual method of calculating this equation is as $2 + 4 =$, which is the system used by the majority of modern calculators. Most newcomers find the latter approach to be more straightforward. Spend some time finding out how a calculator operates, e.g. does it have true algebraic logic ($\sqrt{}$ then number, rather than number then $\sqrt{}$)? How does it deal with scientific notation (p. 493)?

- Display. Some calculators will display an entire mathematical operation (e.g. '2 + 4 = 6'), while others simply display the last number/operation. The former type may offer advantages in tracing errors.

- Complexity. In the early stages, it is usually better to avoid the more complex machines, full of impressive-looking, but often unused pre-programmed functions – go for more memory, parentheses or statistical functions rather than engineering or mathematical constants. Programmable calculators may be worth considering for more advanced studies. However, it is important to note that such calculators are often unacceptable for exams.

Presenting more advanced practical work

In some practical reports and in project work, you may need to use more sophisticated presentation equipment. Word processing may be essential and computer-based graphics packages can be useful. Choose easily-read fonts such as Arial or Times New Roman for project work and posters and consider the layout and content carefully (p. 103). Alternatively, you could use fine line drawing pens plus dry-transfer lettering and symbols, such as those made by Letraset®, although this approach is usually more time consuming and less flexible than computer-based systems.

Using calculators for numerical problems – Chapter 62 gives further advice.

Using calculators – take particular care when using the exponential key 'EXP' or 'EE'. Pressing this key produces $10^{something}$. For example if you want to enter 2×10^{-4}, the order entry is 2, EXP, −, 4 not 2, ×, 10, EXP, −, 4.

Using inexpensive calculators – many unsophisticated calculators have a restricted display for exponential numbers and do not show the 'power of 10', e.g. displaying 2.4×10^{-5} as 2.4^{-05}, or 2.4E−05, or even 2.4−05.

Presenting graphs and diagrams – ensure these are large enough to be easily read: a common error is to present graphs or diagrams that are too small, with poorly chosen scales (see p. 473).

Printing on acetates – standard overhead transparencies are not suitable for use in laser printers or photocopiers: you need to make sure that you use the correct type.

To prepare overhead transparencies for oral presentations, you can use spirit-based markers and acetate sheets. An alternative approach is to print directly from a computer-based package, using a laser printer and special acetates, or directly to 35 mm slides. You can also photocopy on to special acetates. The use of Microsoft PowerPoint® as a presentation package has become more important in recent years. It is not uncommon to find a computer and presenter available for student use. Advice on content and presentation is given in Chapter 15.

Source for further study

Bennett, S.W. and O'Neale, K. (1999) *Progressive Development of Practical Skills in Chemistry. A guide to early-undergraduate experimental work.* Royal Society of Chemistry, Cambridge.

Study exercises

20.1 Consider the value of practical work. Spend a few minutes thinking about the purpose of practical work within a specific part of your course (e.g. a particular first year module) and then write a list of the six most important points. Compare your list with the generic list we have provided on p. 547, which is based on our experience as lecturers – does it differ much from your list, which is drawn up from a student perspective?

20.2 Make a list of items required for a particular practical experiment. This exercise is likely to be most useful if you can relate it to an appropriate practical session on your course. However, we have given a model list for a recrystallisation of an impure compound from water as an example.

20.3 Check your calculator skills. Carry out the following mathematical operations, using either a hand-held calculator or a PC with appropriate 'calculator' software.

(a) $5 \times (2 + 6)$
(b) $(8.3 \div [6.4 - 1.9]) \times 24$ (to 4 significant figures)
(c) $(1 \div 32) \times (5 \div 8)$ (to 3 significant figures)
(d) $1.2 \times 10^5 + 4.0 \times 10^4$ in scientific notation (see p. 493)
(e) $3.4 \times 10^{-2} - 2.7 \times 10^{-3}$ in 'normal' notation (i.e. conventional notation, not scientific format) and to 3 decimal places.

(See also numerical exercises in Chapter 62)

Health and Safety Legislation – in the UK, the **Health and Safety at Work. Act 1974** provides the main legal framework for health and safety. The **Control of Substances Hazardous to Health (COSHH) Regulations 2002** impose specific legal requirements for risk assessment wherever hazardous chemicals or biological agents are used, with Approved Codes of Practice for the control of hazardous substances, carcinogens and biological agents, including pathogenic microbes.

Definitions

Hazard – the ability of a substance to cause harm.

Risk – the likelihood that a substance might be harmful under specific circumstances.

Risk – is often associated with the quantity of chemical to be used, e.g. there is a much greater risk when using a large volume of flammable solvent than a few millilitres, even though the hazard is the same.

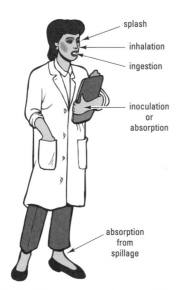

splash
inhalation
ingestion
inoculation
or
absorption
absorption
from
spillage

Fig. 21.1 Major routes of entry of harmful substances into the body.

Health and safety law requires institutions to provide a working environment that is safe and without risk to health. Where appropriate, training and information on safe working practices must be provided. Students and staff must take reasonable care to ensure the health and safety of themselves and of others, and must not misuse any safety equipment.

> **KEY POINT** All practical work must be carried out with safety in mind, to minimise the risk of harm to yourself and to others – safety is everyone's responsibility by law.

Risk assessment

The most widespread approach to safe working practice involves the use of risk assessment, which aims to establish:

1. The intrinsic chemical and physical hazards, together with any maximum exposure limits (MELs) or occupational exposure standards (OESs), where appropriate. All chemical manufacturers provide data sheets listing the hazards associated with particular chemical compounds.

2. The risks involved, by taking into account the amount of substance to be used, the way in which it will be used and the possible routes of entry into the body (Fig. 21.1). In this regard, it is important to distinguish between the intrinsic hazards of a particular substance and the risks involved in its use in a particular exercise.

3. The persons at risk and the ways in which they might be exposed to hazardous substances, including accidental exposure (spillage).

4. The steps required to prevent or control exposure. Ideally, a non-hazardous or less hazardous alternative should be used. If this is not feasible, adequate control measures must be used, e.g. a fume cupboard or other containment system. Personal protective equipment (e.g. lab coats, safety glasses) must continue to be used in addition to such containment measures. A safe means of disposal will be required.

The outcome of the risk assessment process must be recorded and appropriate safety information must be passed on to those at risk. For most practical classes, risk assessments will have been carried out in advance by the person in charge and the information necessary to minimise the risks to students may be given in the practical schedule. You will be asked to carry out risk assessments to familiarise yourself with the process and sources of information. Make sure you know how your department provides such information and that you have read the appropriate material before you begin your practical work. You should also pay close attention to the person in charge at the beginning of the practical session, as they may emphasise the major hazards and risks. In project work, you will need to be involved in the risk assessment process along with your supervisor, before you carry out any laboratory work.

SAFETY NOTE

Protective clothing is worn as a first barrier to spillage of chemicals on to your body.

Lab coats are for protection of you and your clothing.

Eye protection special spectacles with side pieces to protect you from your own mistakes and those of your colleagues. If you wear spectacles, eye protection with prescription lenses and side pieces is available from your optician, an expensive but worthwhile investment. Otherwise goggles can be worn over spectacles.

Contact lenses should not be worn in the laboratory. Chemicals can get under the lens and damage the eye before the lens can be removed. It is often very difficult to remove the contact lens from the eye after a chemical splash.

Shoes should cover the feet: no open-toed sandals, for example.

Long hair should be tied back and hats (e.g. baseball caps) should not be worn.

LABORATORY RISK ASSESSMENT

This sheet **must** be completed **before** commencing each experiment

Name:

Experiment: Synthesis of *N*-phenylethanamide   Date:

1. Hazard and Risk Codes Enter below the correct Hazard Code and Risk Code for each reagent, solvent, product and by product (letter and number in the relevant boxes)

REAGENT AND INSTRUMENTS	A H	A R	C H	C R	T H	T R	F H	F R	W H	W R	M H	M R	Others H	Others R	H	R
Aminobenzene (aniline)	2	2	2	2	2	2	1	1	1	1	1	1				
Ethanoic anhydride	2	2	1	1	2	2	2	1	2	1	1	1				
N-phenylethanamide	1	1	1	1	2	1	1	1	1	1	1	1				
Ethanoic acid (dilute aqueous solution)	1	1	1	1	1	1	1	1	1	1	1	1				

(HAZARD (H) and RISK (R) CODES — Others (insert))

A = Corrosive/irritant   M = Microbiological hazard   1 = Low/no hazard/risk
C = Carcinogenic   R = Radioactive   2 = Moderate hazard/risk
T = Toxic   I = Instrument hazard   3 = High hazard/risk
F = Flammable   X = Explosive   4 = Special high category
W = Violent reaction with water/acid/bases   O = Oxidizing agents

2. Precautions: containment and protection

Stage of Experiment (including disposal)	Containment Code	Personal Protection	Additional Information
Weighing out chemicals	3	Gloves	

Containment code   1 = Open Lab   2 = Restricted Lab (no naked flames)   3 = Fume Cupboard   4 = Glove Box/Safety Cabinet

Personal Protection   Insert all requirements additional to coat and glasses (e.g. gloves, visor, safety screen, etc.)

Additional Information   For example, disposal/specified waste container, sink and water, etc.

3. Signatures

Student: _____   Supervisor: _____   Date: _____

Fig. 21.2 An example of a laboratory hazard assessment form.

Any new materials synthesised during the project should be treated with the utmost respect. An example of a risk assessment is shown in Fig. 21.2.

In addition to specific risk assessments, most institutions will have a safety handbook, giving general details of safe working practices, together with the names and telephone numbers of safety personnel, first aiders, hospitals, etc. Make sure you read this and abide by any instructions.

Basic rules for laboratory work

- Wear appropriate protective clothing at all times – a clean lab coat (buttoned up), eye protection, appropriate footwear – and ensure your hair does not constitute a hazard.

- Never smoke, eat or drink in any laboratory, because of the risks of contamination by inhalation or ingestion (Fig. 21.1).

Fig. 21.3 Warning labels for specific chemical hazards.

- Never work alone in a laboratory.

- Make sure that you know what to do in case of fire, including exit routes, how to raise the alarm, and where to gather on leaving the building. Remember that the most important consideration is human safety: do not attempt to fight a fire unless it is safe to do so.

- All laboratories display notices telling you where to find the first aid kit and who to contact in case of accident/emergency. Report all accidents, even those appearing insignificant – your department will have a reporting procedure to comply with safety legislation.

- Know the warning symbols for specific chemical hazards (Fig. 21.3).

- Never touch chemicals unless they are known to have minimal hazard: use a spatula to transfer and manipulate solids, and pipettes for liquids – see p. 146.

- Never mouth pipette any liquid. Use a pipette filler (see p. 147).

- Take care when handling glassware – see p. 151 for details.

- Use a fume cupboard for hazardous chemicals. Make sure that it is working and then open the front only as far as necessary: many fume cupboards are marked with a maximum opening.

- Always use the minimum quantity of any hazardous materials.

- Work in a logical, tidy manner and minimise risks by thinking ahead.

- Alway clear up spillages, especially around balances, infrared sample preparation areas, etc., for the next worker.

- Always clear up at the end of each session. This is an important aspect of safety, encouraging a responsible attitude towards laboratory work.

Sources for further study

Anon. (2003) *Safety in Academic Chemistry Laboratories. Accident prevention for college and university students,* 7th edn, Vol. 1 (Student copy). American Chemical Society.

Anon. *SIRI MSDS Index*. Available: http://www.hazard.com/msds Last accessed 05/03/10. [Online access to Materials Safety Data Sheets (MSDS) for manufacturers' chemicals].

Cartwright, H. *Hands-on Science Project: Chemical Safety Data Base*. Available: http://www.ptcl.chem.ox.ac.uk/msds Last accessed 05/03/10. [Online access to student-friendly MSDS for a restricted range of common chemicals].

Day, R. and Rowland, E. (2003) *Health, Safety and Environmental Legislation*. Royal Society of Chemistry, Cambridge.

Urben, P.G. (2006) *Bretherick's Handbook of Reactive Chemical Hazards*, 7th edn, Vols 1 and 2. Butterworth-Heinemann, London.

Warren, D. (2001) *Health, Safety and Risk*. Royal Society of Chemistry, Cambridge.

Study exercises

21.1 Test your knowledge of safe working procedures. After reading the appropriate sections of this book, can you remember the following:

(a) The four main steps involved in the process of risk assessment?

(b) The major routes of entry of harmful substances into the body?

(c) The warning labels for the major chemical hazard symbols (either describe them or draw them from memory?

(d) The international symbol for radioactivity?

21.2 Locate the relevant health and safety features in a laboratory. Find each of the following in one of the main laboratories used as part of your course (draw a simple location map, if this seems appropriate):

(a) fire exit(s);

(b) fire-fighting equipment;

(c) first-aid kit;

(d) eye-wash station;

(e) waste flammable solvent container;

(f) waste chlorinated solvent container;

(g) broken glass container.

21.3 Investigate the health and safety procedures in operation at your university. Can you find out the following:

(a) your university's procedure in case of fire;

(b) the colour coding for fire extinguishers available in your department and the recommendations for use;

(c) the accident reporting procedure used in your department;

(d) your department's Code of Safe Practice relating to project work?

21.4 Carry out risk assessments for specific chemical hazards. Look up the hazards associated with the use of the following chemicals and list the appropriate protective measures required to minimise the risk during use in a lab class:

(a) ethanol to be used as a recrystallisation solvent for a solid (about 10 g);

(b) sodium oxalate to be used to make a volumetric standard solution (250.00 mL; 0.1 M);

(c) sodium hydroxide, used in solid form to prepare a dilute solution for neutralisation.

Reading any volumetric scale – make sure your eye is level with the bottom of the liquid's meniscus and take the reading from this point.

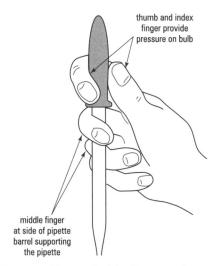

thumb and index finger provide pressure on bulb

middle finger at side of pipette barrel supporting the pipette

Fig. 22.1 How to hold a Pasteur pipette.

Measuring and dispensing liquids

The equipment you should choose to measure out liquids depends upon the volume to be dispensed, the accuracy required and the number of times the job must be repeated (Table 22.1).

Table 22.1 Criteria for choosing a method for measuring out a liquid

Method	Best volume range	Accuracy	Usefulness for repetitive measurement
Pasteur pipette	1–5 mL	Low	Convenient
Conical flask/beaker	25–5000 mL	Very low	Convenient
Measuring cylinder	5–2000 mL	Medium	Convenient
Volumetric flask	5–2000 mL	High	Convenient
Burette	1–100 mL	High	Convenient
Glass pipette	1–100 mL	High	Convenient
Mechanical pipettor	5–1000 μL	High*	Convenient
Syringe	0.5–20 μL	Medium**	Convenient
Microsyringe	0.5–50 μL	High	Convenient
Weighing	Any (depends on accuracy of balance	Very high	Inconvenient

*If calibrated correctly and used properly (see p. 149).
**Accuracy depends on width of barrel: large volumes less accurate.

Conical flasks, beakers, measuring cylinders and volumetric flasks measure the volume of liquid contained in them, while burettes, pipettes, pipettors, syringes and microsyringes mostly measure the volume delivered from them: think about the requirements of the experiment.

Certain liquids may cause problems:

- High-viscosity liquids are difficult to dispense: allow time for the liquid to transfer.

- Organic solvents may evaporate rapidly, making measurements inaccurate: work quickly; seal containers quickly.

- Solutions prone to frothing (e.g. surfactant solutions) are difficult to measure and dispense: avoid forming bubbles; do not transfer quickly.

Pasteur pipettes

Hold correctly during use (Fig. 22.1) – keep the pipette vertical, with the middle finger gripping the barrel to support the pipette while the thumb and index finger provide controlled pressure on the bulb, and squeeze gently to provide individual drops.

To prevent liquid being sucked into the bulb and hence cross-contamination:

- Ensure that the capacity of the bulb does not exceed that of the barrel.

- Do not remove the tip of the pipette from the liquid while drawing up the liquid; the inrush of air may splash the liquid into the bulb. This is

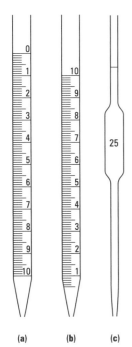

Fig. 22.2 Glass pipettes: (a) graduated pipette, reading from zero to shoulder; (b) graduated pipette, reading from maximum to tip, by gravity; (c) bulb (volumetric) pipette, showing volume on bulb.

> **Glass pipettes** – always check that the pipette is a 'drain-down' type. There may be old 'blow-out' pipettes lurking in the back of drawers.

> **Using rubber bulb pipette fillers** – information on their use is given in Chapter 41 (p. 302).

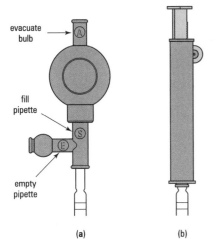

Fig. 22.3 Pipette fillers: (a) rubber-bulb type; (b) Pi-Pump®.

particularly true when you lose patience trying to draw up viscous liquids.

● Do not lay the pipette on its side during use.

Conversely, if volatile liquids such as dichloromethane (DCM), ethanol, propanone (acetone) or diethylether (ether), for example, are to be dispensed, the warmth of the glass pipette will cause the liquid to squirt from the pipette without any pressure on the bulb. To prevent this, suck up the liquid several times into the pipette so as to cool the glass and then dispense as normal.

Conical flasks and beakers

These have approximate graduations and should only be used for measuring volumes of solutions/liquids where accuracy is unimportant.

Measuring cylinders and volumetric flasks

These must be used on a level surface (the laboratory bench) so that the scale is horizontal; you should first fill with solution until just below the desired mark, then fill slowly (e.g. using a Pasteur pipette) until the bottom of the meniscus is level with the mark. Remember to allow time for the solution to run down the walls of the vessel and to bend down so that your eyes are level with the graduation mark(s) and the meniscus.

→ Just look up.

Burettes

These must be mounted vertically in a clamp – don't over-tighten the clamp (see p. 166) – or in a burette holder, on a stand. First ensure that the tap is closed and, using a funnel, add a little of the solution to be dispensed, rinse the burette and discard the washings through the tap: this is vital in titrations where a little water in the burette will alter the concentration of the solution. Refill the burette with solution, open the tap and allow the liquid to fill the barrel below the tap, then take a meniscus reading, noting the value in your notebook. Dispense the solution via the tap and measure the new meniscus reading. The volume dispensed is the difference between the two readings.

Pipettes

There are various designs, including graduated and bulb (volumetric) pipettes (Fig. 22.2). Take care to look at the volume scale before use: some graduated pipettes empty from full volume to zero, others from zero to full volume; some scales refer to the shoulder of the tip, others to the tip by gravity. Never blow out volumetric (bulb) pipettes, just touch the tip against the inside wall of the vessel.

Rinse out pipettes with a little of the solution to be delivered before commencing the accurate measurement. To prevent cross-contamination, never draw the solution into the pipette filler.

> **KEY POINT** For safety reasons, it is no longer permissible to mouth pipette – various aids (pipette fillers) are available, such as the rubber-bulb and Pi-Pump® (Fig. 22.3).

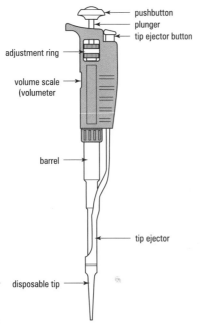

Fig. 22.4 A pipettor – the Gilson Pipetman®.

Pipettors (autopipettors)

There are two basic types:

1. Air displacement pipettors. For routine work with dilute aqueous solutions. One of the most widely used is the Gilson Pipetman® (Fig. 22.4). Box 22.1 gives details on its use.

2. Positive displacement pipettors. For non-standard applications, including dispensing viscous, dense or volatile liquids where an air displacement pipettor might create aerosols leading to errors.

Air displacement and positive displacement pipettors may be:

*   Fixed volume: capable of delivering a single factory-set volume.

*   Adjustable: where the volume delivered is determined by the operator across a particular range of values.

*   Pre-set: movable between a limited number of values.

*   Multichannel: able to deliver several replicate volumes at the same time.

Whichever type of these routine but expensive devices you use, you must ensure that you understand the operating principles of the volume scale and the method for changing the volume delivered – some pipettors are easily misread.

A pipettor must be fitted with the correct disposable tip before use and each manufacturer produces different tips to fit particular models. Specialised tips are available for particular applications.

If you accidentally draw liquid into the barrel, seek assistance from your demonstrator/supervisor since the barrel will need to be cleaned before further use (to prevent cross-contamination) and unskilled dismantling of the device will cause irreparable damage.

Syringes

Syringes should be used by placing the tip of the needle into the solution and slowly drawing the plunger up to the required point on the scale. Check the barrel to make sure no air bubbles have been drawn up, and expel the solution slowly, touching the needle tip on the side of the vessel to remove any adhering solution. If there is air in the barrel, fill past the mark, invert the syringe and push the plunger to the mark so that the air and a little of the solution are expelled into a waste collection vessel. Then dispense the solution. The use of syringes for dispensing air-sensitive reagents is described in Chapter 37.

Microsyringes should always be cleaned before and after use by repeatedly drawing up and expelling pure solvent. The dead space in the needle can occupy up to 4% of the nominal syringe volume. Some microsyringes have a fine wire attached to the plunger, which fills the dead space. Never pull the plunger out of the barrel.

Balances

These can be used to weigh accurately (p. 162) how much liquid you have dispensed. Convert mass to volume using the equation:

$$\text{Mass/density} = \text{volume}$$

Box 22.1 Using a pipettor to deliver accurate, reproducible volumes of liquid

A pipettor can be used to dispense volumes with accuracy and precision, by following this stepwise procedure:

1. **Select a pipettor that operates over the appropriate range.** Most adjustable pipettors are accurate only over a particular working range and should not be used to deliver volumes below the manufacturer's specifications (minimum volume is usually 10–20% of maximum value). Do not attempt to set the volume above the maximum limit, or the pipettor may be damaged.

2. **Set the volume to be delivered.** In some pipettors, you 'dial up' the required volume. Types like the Gilson Pipetman® have a system where the scale (or 'volumeter') consists of three numbers, read from top to bottom of the barrel, and adjusted using the black knurled adjustment ring (Fig. 22.4). This number gives the first three digits of the volume scale and thus can only be understood by establishing the maximum volume of the Pipetman®, as shown on the push-button on the end of the plunger (Fig. 22.4). The following examples illustrate the principle for two common sizes of Pipetman®:

P1000 Pipetman®
(maximum volume 1000 μL)
if you dial up

the volume is set at 1000 μL

P20 Pipetman®
(maximum volume 20 μL)
if you dial up

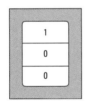

the volume is set at 10.0 μL

3. **Fit a new disposable tip to the end of the barrel.** Make sure that it is the appropriate type for your pipettor and that it is correctly fitted. Press the tip on firmly using a slight twisting motion – if not, you will take up less than the set volume and liquid will drip from the tip during use. Tips are often supplied in boxes, for ease of use: if sterility is important, make sure you use appropriate sterile technique at all times. *Never, ever, try to use a pipettor without its disposable tip.*

4. **Check your delivery.** Confirm that the pipettor delivers the correct volume by dispensing volumes of distilled water and weighing on a balance, assuming $1\,mg = 1\,\mu L = 1\,mm^3$. The value should

be within 1% of the selected volume. For small volumes, measure several 'squirts' together, e.g. 20 'squirts' of $5\,\mu L = 100\,mg$. If the pipettor is inaccurate (p. 209) giving a biased result (e.g. delivering significantly more or less than the volume set), you can make a temporary correction by adjusting the volumeter scale down or up accordingly (the volume *delivered* is more important than the value *displayed* on the volumeter), or have the pipettor recalibrated. If the pipettor is imprecise (p. 209), delivering a variable amount of liquid each time, it may need to be serviced. After calibration, fit a clean (sterile) tip if necessary.

5. **Draw up the appropriate volume.** Holding the pipettor *vertically*, press down on the plunger/push-button until a resistance (spring-loaded stop) is met. Then place the end of the tip in the liquid. Keeping your thumb on the plunger/push-button, release the pressure slowly and evenly: watch the liquid being drawn up into the tip, to confirm that no air bubbles are present. Wait a second or so, to confirm that the liquid has been taken up, then withdraw the end of the tip from the liquid. Inexperienced users often have problems caused by drawing up the liquid too quickly/carelessly. If you accidentally draw liquid into the barrel, seek assistance from your demonstrator or supervisor as the barrel will need to be cleaned before further use.

6. **Make a quick visual check on the liquid in the tip.** Does the volume seem reasonable? (e.g. a 100 μL volume should occupy approximately half the volume of a P200 tip). The liquid will remain in the tip, without dripping, as long as the tip is fitted correctly and the pipettor is not tilted too far from a vertical position.

7. **Deliver the liquid.** Place the end of the tip against the wall of the vessel at a slight angle (10–15° from vertical) and press the plunger/push-button slowly and smoothly to the first (spring-loaded) stop. Wait a second or two, to allow any residual liquid to run down the inside of the tip, then press again to the final stop, dispensing any remaining liquid. Remove from the vessel with the plunger/push-button still depressed.

8. **Eject the tip.** Press the tip ejector button if present (Fig. 22.4). If the tip is contaminated, eject directly into an appropriate container, e.g. a labelled container for hazardous solutions (p. 142). For repeat delivery, fit a new tip if necessary and begin again at step 5 above. Always make sure that the tip is ejected before putting a pipettor on the bench.

e.g. a liquid $(9.0\,g)$ of density $(1.2\,g\,mL^{-1}) = 7.5\,mL$. Densities of common solvents and common chemicals can be found in Haynes (2010). You will also need to know the liquid's temperature, since density is temperature dependent.

Holding and storing liquids

Test tubes

Both 'normal' and the much smaller 'semi-micro' test tubes are used for small-scale reactions and tests, e.g. qualitative analysis (p. 289) or solvent selection for recrystallisation (p. 240).

Beakers

Beakers are used for general purposes, e.g. heating a non-volatile solvent while the solute dissolves, 'working up' a reaction where liquid/solid products need to be accessible for manipulation (stirring with a glass rod), or titrations using electrodes where a wide opening is essential (see p. 413). The volume graduations on the side are inaccurate and should only be used where approximations will suffice. The lip on the beaker is specifically designed to aid quantitative transfer of solutions (see p. 159).

Conical (Erlenmeyer) flasks

These can be used for general purposes, but they have more specialist applications. The narrow mouth and sloping shoulders reduce losses on stirring/swirling and evaporation and make them easier to seal. The absence of a lip does not favour quantitative transfer: useful in manual titrations (p. 301) and recrystallisations (p. 243). Volume markings are approximate.

Bottles and vials

These can be used when the solution needs to be sealed for safety, storage or to prevent evaporation or oxidation. They usually have a screwtop, plastic cap or stopper or a ground-glass stopper and come in various styles and sizes: from 2.5 L glass bottles used for storing large volumes of solutions to small plastic-capped vials (5 mL) for saving small amounts of reaction products.

Seal the vessels in an appropriate manner, using a stopper, cap or sealing film such as Parafilm® or Nescofilm®, bearing in mind the nature of the contents – sealing film should only be used for water solutions since it dissolves in some organic solvents and plasticisers may be extracted. Do not use corks, they are not air-tight. Do not use rubber bungs to seal containers containing organic solvents, they can swell even over a short period of time making removal very difficult.

You should clearly label all stored solutions (see p. 160) including all relevant hazard information.

Creating specialised apparatus

Glassware systems incorporating ground-glass connections, such as Quickfit®, are essential for setting up combinations of standard glass components for reactions, distillation, etc. In project work you may need

Volume accuracy – the experimental protocol may give an indication of the equipment needed to measure the volume of the liquid required. Terms like 25.00 mL and 500.00 mL imply the use of a pipette or volumetric flask but 10 mL and 50 mL imply the use of a measuring cylinder.

Storing light-sensitive chemicals – use a brown-glass vessel or wrap aluminium foil around a clear vessel *and* its stopper.

to adapt standard forms of glassware for a special need. It may be necessary to contact a glassblowing service to make special items to order.

Choosing between glass and plastic containers

Bear in mind the following points:

- Reactivity. Plastic vessels often distort at relatively low temperature, may be inflammable, may dissolve in certain organic solvents and may be affected by prolonged exposure to ultraviolet (UV) light.

- Opacity. Both glass and plastic absorb light in the UV range of the electromagnetic spectrum (Table 22.2). Quartz should be used where this is important, e.g. in cells for UV spectrophotometry (see p. 334) or photochemistry.

- Contamination. Some plasticisers may leach from vessels, especially with some organic solvents, such as DCM. Glass may adsorb ions and other molecules and then leach them into solutions, especially under acidic or alkaline conditions. Pyrex® glass is stronger than ordinary soda glass (rarely found except in specific items such as Pasteur pipettes and melting point tubes, but check if you are not sure) and can withstand temperatures up to 500 °C.

- Rigidity and resilience. Plastic vessels are not recommended where volume is critical as they may distort through time. Glass vessels are more easily broken than plastic.

- Disposability. Plastic items may be cheap enough to make them disposable, an advantage where there is a risk of chemical contamination.

Cleaning glass and plastic

In quantitative analytical work, beware of contamination arising from prior use of chemicals or inadequate rinsing following washing. A thorough rinse with distilled or deionised water immediately before use will remove dust and other soluble deposits, but ensure that the rinsing solution is not left in the vessel. For analyses on the 'μg scale' and below, you should clean glass and plastic containers by immersion in nitric acid (10% v/v) overnight and then rinsing with a large volume of distilled or deionised water. The clean vessels should be stored either upside down or covered with Clingfilm®, to prevent dust contamination.

For general work, 'strong' basic detergents (e.g. Decon® or Pyroneg®) are good for solubilising acidic deposits and an acid wash will remove remaining basic residues. A rinse with ethanol or propanone (acetone) will remove many organic deposits.

Safety with glass

Many minor accidents in the laboratory are due to lack of care with glassware. You should follow these general precautions:

- Wear eye protection at all times.

- Don't use chipped or cracked glassware and examine the equipment for 'star' cracks – it may break under very slight strains and should be disposed of in the broken glassware bin. All laboratories will have a

Table 22.2 Spectral cutoff values for glass and plastics (λ_{50} = wavelength at which transmission of electromagnetic radiation is reduced to 50%)

Material	λ_{50} (nm)
Routine glassware	340
Pyrex® glassware	292
Polycarbonate	396
Acrylic	342
Polyester	318
Quartz	220

SAFETY NOTE Special cleaning of glass – for an acid wash use dilute acid, rinse with tap water (three times) to remove the washing solution and then rinse thoroughly at least three times with distilled or deionised water. To remove acidic deposits, wash with KOH/ethanol solution followed by rinsing with deionised water. Glassware, which must be exceptionally clean, should be washed in a chromic acid bath, but this must only be made up and used under supervision.

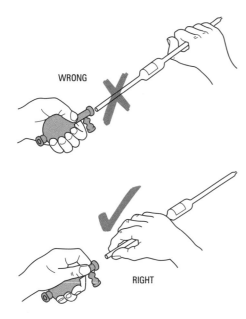

Fig. 22.5 Handling glass tubing.

waste bin dedicated to broken glass. Never put broken glass into other bins.

- If heating glassware, use a 'soft' Bunsen flame (half-open air vent) or 'wave' the flame around the heating point – this avoids creating a hot spot where cracks may start. Always use special heat-resistant gloves or rubber 'fingers' (see p. 176) when handling hot glassware.

- When clamping glassware (see p. 166) ensure that the clamp has a cork, rubber or plastic 'cushion' in the jaws to prevent breakages. There must be no metal–glass contact and you must not over-tighten the clamp.

- Take care when attaching rubber or plastic tubing to glass tubes, condensers, etc., and inserting thermometers and glass tubes into screwcap adapters (see p. 184). Always hold the tube and the 'hole' close together (Fig. 22.5) and wear thick gloves where appropriate.

- Don't force bungs too firmly into bottles (see p. 150) they can be difficult to remove. If you need a tight seal, use a screwtop bottle, with a rubber or plastic seal, Parafilm® or ground-glass jointware, such as Quickfit®.

- Never carry large bottles (>1 L) by their necks – carry them in a bottle basket.

- Dispose of broken glass thoroughly and with great care – use disposable paper towels, tongs or dust-pan and brush and thick gloves. Always put pieces of broken glass in the correct bin.

Text reference

Haynes, W.M. (ed.) (2010) *CRC Handbook of Chemistry and Physics,* 91st edn. CRC Press, Boca Raton.

Sources for further study

Anon. *CHEMnet Base.* Available: http://www.chemnetbase.com Last accessed: 05/03/10. [Online access to the *CRC Handbook of Chemistry and Physics*]

Beram, J.A. (2009) *Laboratory Manual for Principles of General Chemistry,* 8th edn. John Wylie & Sons, Chichester.

Study exercises

22.1 Decide on the appropriate methods and equipment for the following procedures:

(a) Preparing one litre of ethanol at approximately 70% v/v in water for use as a general-purpose reagent.

(b) Adding 25.00 mL of concentrated hydrochloric acid to water (100 mL).

(c) Adding 10 µL of propanone to a volumetric flask (100.00 mL) to produce an aqueous solution calibration standard for chromatography.

(d) Titration of an unknown solution of sodium hydroxide (approximate concentration 0.1 M) with sulphuric acid (0.5 M).

22.2 Write a protocol for calibrating and using a pipettor. After reading this chapter, prepare a streetwise protocol explaining how to use a pipettor to deliver a specific volume, say 500 µL (e.g. using a Gilson Pipetman or an alternative if your department does not use this type). Ask another student to evaluate your protocol and provide you with feedback – either by reading through your protocol or by trying it out with a pipettor as part of a class exercise (check with a member of staff before you attempt this in a laboratory).

Finding out about chemicals The *Merck Index* (O'Neil *et al.*, 2006) and the *CRC Handbook of Chemistry and Physics* (Haynes, 2010) are useful sources on the chemical and physical properties of elements and compounds, including melting and boiling points, solubility and toxicity, etc. Manufacturers' catalogues now include hazard data and disposal procedures.

Table 23.1 Representative risk assessment information for a practical exercise in organic chemistry: the synthesis of *N*-phenylethanamide (acetanilide)

Substance	Hazards/comments
Aminobenzene	Toxic, harmful by skin absorption. Wear gloves, dispense in fume cupboard
Ethanoic anhydride	Corrosive, flammable, toxic, reacts with water. Wear gloves, dispense in fume cupboard

Using chemicals responsibly – be considerate to others: always return storeroom chemicals promptly to the correct place. Report when supplies are getting low to the person responsible for looking after the store. If you empty an aspirator or wash bottle, fill it up from the appropriate source.

Molar solutions – you will find that chemists talk about '0.1 Molar solutions' or you may see '0.1 M' as a concentration written on flasks or in books and journals. The term 'Molar' (abbreviated to M) means number of moles per litre. Hence an aqueous solution of hydrochloric acid (0.1 M) has a concentration of $0.1\,mol\,L^{-1}$ equivalent to 3.65 g of hydrogen chloride per litre of solution.

Using chemicals

Safety aspects

In practical classes, the person in charge has the responsibility to inform you of any hazards associated with the use of chemicals. In project work, your first duty when using an unfamiliar chemical is to find out about its properties, especially those relating to safety. For routine practical procedures, a risk assessment may have been carried out by a member of staff and the relevant safety information may be included in the practical schedule: an example is shown in Table 23.1. In project work, your first duty when using an unfamiliar chemical is to find out about its properties, especially those relating to safety. Your department must provide the relevant information to allow you to do this. If your supervisor has filled out the form, read it carefully before signing.

KEY POINT Before you use any chemical you MUST find out whether safety precautions need to be taken, and complete the appropriate forms confirming that you appreciate the risks involved.

Essential safety points when handling chemicals are:

- Treat all chemicals as potentially dangerous.
- Wear a lab coat, with the buttons fastened, at all times.
- Wear eye protection at all times.
- Make sure you know where safety devices such as eye bath, fire extinguisher, first aid kit are kept before you start work in the lab.
- Wear gloves for toxic, irritant or corrosive chemicals and carry out procedures with them in the fume cupboard.
- Use appropriate aids such as spatulae, pipette fillers, Pasteur pipettes etc., to minimise risk of contact.
- Label all solutions, samples, etc., appropriately (see p. 161).
- Extinguish all naked flames when working with flammable substances.
- Never drink, eat or smoke where chemicals are being handled.
- Report all spillages and clean them up appropriately.
- Dispose of chemicals in the correct manner.

Selection

Chemicals are supplied in varying degrees of purity and this is always stated on the manufacturer's containers. Suppliers differ in the names given to the grades and there is no conformity in purity standards. Very pure chemicals cost more, often very much more, and should only be used when the situation demands. If you need to order a chemical, your department will have a defined procedure for doing this.

Preparing solutions

Solutions are usually prepared with respect to their molar concentrations (e.g. $mol\,L^{-1}$, $mol\,dm^{-3}$ or $mol\,m^{-3}$) or mass concentrations (e.g. $g\,L^{-1}$ or $kg\,m^{-3}$): both can be regarded as an amount (usually mass) per unit volume, in accordance with the relationship:

$$\text{concentration} = \frac{\text{amount}}{\text{volume}} \qquad [23.1]$$

The most important aspect of eqn [23.1] is to recognise clearly the units involved, and to prepare the solution accordingly: for molar concentrations you will need the relative molecular mass of the chemical, so that you can calculate the mass of substance required. Further advice on concentrations and interconversion of units is given on p. 186.

In general there are two levels of accuracy required for the preparation of solutions:

<table>
<tr><td>1.</td><td>General-purpose solutions – solutions of chemicals used in qualitative and preparative procedures (p. 156) when the concentration of the chemical need not be known to more than one or two decimal places. For example:</td></tr>
</table>

(a) solutions used in extraction and washing processes, e.g. hydrochloric acid ($0.1\,mol\,L^{-1}$), sodium hydroxide (2 M), sodium carbonate (5% w/v);

(b) solutions of chemicals used in preparative experiments where the techniques of purification – distillation, recrystallisation, filtration, etc. – introduce intrinsic losses of substances that make accuracy to any greater level meaningless.

<table>
<tr><td>2.</td><td>Analytical solutions – solutions used in quantitative analytical procedures (p. 158) when the concentration needs to be known to an accuracy of four decimal places (e.g. $0.0001\,mol\,L^{-1}$). For example in:</td></tr>
</table>

(a) volumetric procedures (titrations) and gravimetric analysis, where the concentrations of standard solutions of reagents and compounds to be analysed need to be accurately known;

(b) spectroscopy, e.g. quantitative UV and visible spectroscopy, atomic absorption spectroscopy and flame photometry;

(c) electrochemical measurements: pH titrations, conductance measurements and polarography;

(d) chromatographic methods.

The procedures for weighing and the glassware used in the preparation of solutions differ according to the level of accuracy required.

Preparation of general-purpose solutions

Box 23.1 shows the steps involved in making up general-purpose aqueous solutions.

The concentration you require is likely to be defined by the protocol you are following and the grade of chemical and supplier may also be specified. To avoid waste, think carefully about the volume of solution you require, though it is always advisable to err on the high side because you may spill some, make a mistake when dispensing or need to repeat part of

---

Percentage concentration – you may find that the concentration of a solution is expressed in percentage terms. Thus sodium carbonate (5% w/v) – the symbol *w* indicates *weight* of solute and *v* is the *volume* of solution. The resulting solution is a general-purpose dilute aqueous solution of sodium carbonate prepared from sodium carbonate (5 g) made up to 100 mL in water and used for neutralising acid.

The levels of accuracy of solution preparation required are usually indicated in the protocol or by the nature of the experiment. Look for phrases such as 'accurately weighed' which means to four decimal places on an analytical balance, together with quantitative transfer. Volumes quoted as 250.00 mL, 100.00 mL, 25.00 mL imply the use of volumetric flasks and pipettes. Volumes given in μL imply the use of pipettors or syringes.

Box 23.1 How to make up an aqueous solution of known concentration from a solid chemical

1. **Find out or decide the concentration of chemical required** and the degree of purity necessary.

2. **Decide on the volume of solution required.**

3. **Find out the relative molecular mass of the chemical (M_r).** This is the sum of the atomic (elemental) masses of the component element(s) and can usually be found on the container. If the chemical is hydrated, i.e. has water molecules associated with it, these must be included when calculating the mass required.

4. **Work out the mass of chemical that will give you the *concentration* desired in the *volume* required,** bearing in mind the quoted percentage purity of the chemical.

   Example 1: Suppose your procedure requires you to prepare 250 mL of 0.1 mol L^{-1} sodium chloride solution.

   (a) Begin by expressing all volumes in the same units, either millilitres or litres (e.g. 250 mL as 0.25 L).

   (b) Calculate the number of moles required from eqn [23.1]: 0.1 = amount (mol) ÷ 0.25. By rearrangement, the required number of moles is thus 0.1 × 0.25 = 0.025 mol.

   (c) Convert from mol to g by multiplying by the relative molecular mass (M_r for NaCl = 58.44 g mol^{-1}).

   (d) Therefore, you need to make up 0.025 × 58.44 = 1.46 g up to 250 mL of solution, using distilled water.

   Example 2: Suppose you are required to make up 100 mL of sodium carbonate (2 M).

   (a) Convert 2 M into mol L^{-1}; concentration required = 2 mol L^{-1}.

   (b) Express all volumes in the same units: therefore 100 mL = 0.1 L.

   (c) Calculate the number of moles required from eqn [23.1]: 2 = amount (mol) ÷ 0.1. By re-arrangement, the required number of moles is thus 2 × 0.1 = 0.2 mol.

   (d) Convert from mol to g by multiplying by the M_r but note from the container that the compound is $Na_2CO_3.10H_2O$. Therefore the M_r required

   must include the water of crystallisation and $M_r = 286.14$ g mol^{-1}.

   (e) Therefore, you need to make up 0.2 × 286.14 = 57.2 g up to 100 mL of solution using distilled water.

5. **Weigh out the required mass of chemical to an appropriate accuracy.** If the mass is too small to weigh with the desired degree of accuracy, consider the following options:

   (a) Make up a greater volume of solution.

   (b) Make up a more concentrated solution, which can be diluted at a later stage.

   (c) Weigh the mass first, and calculate what volume to make the solution up to afterwards using eqn 23.1.

6. **Add the chemical to a beaker or conical flask and then add a little less water than the final volume required.** If some of the chemical sticks to the weighing receptacle, use some of the water to wash it off. For accurate solutions, see p. 158 for accurate weighing and quantitative transfer.

7. **Stir and, if necessary, heat the solution to ensure all the chemical dissolves.** You can determine visually when this has happened by observing the disappearance of the crystals or powder. Allow the solution to cool, if heated.

8. **Make up the solution to the desired volume.** If the concentration needs to be accurate, use a volumetric flask (see p. 158 for accurate weighing and quantitative transfer); if a high degree of accuracy is not required, use a measuring cylinder.

   (a) Pour the solution from the beaker into the measuring vessel using a funnel to avoid spillage, using water to rinse out the vessel.

   (b) Make up the volume so that the meniscus comes up to the appropriate measurement line. If accuracy is not a major concern, the graduation marks on the beaker or conical flask may be used to establish the approximate volume.

9. **Transfer the solution to a reagent bottle or conical flask and label the vessel clearly, including hazard information, where appropriate.** Do not use water in this final transfer since you will alter the concentration of the solution by dilution.

the experiment. Choose one of the standard volumes for vessels, as this will make measuring out easier.

Use distilled or deionised water to make up aqueous solutions and stir with a clean Pyrex® glass rod or magnetic stirrer bar ('flea') until all the chemical is dissolved. Magnetic stirrers are a convenient means of stirring solutions but precautions should be taken to prevent losses by splashing. Add the flea to the empty beaker or conical flask, add the chemical and then some water. Place the vessel centrally on the stirrer plate, switch on the stirrer and gradually increase the speed of stirring. When the crystals or powder have dissolved, switch off the stirrer and remove the flea with a magnet. Take care not to contaminate your solution when you do this and rinse the flea into the solution with distilled water. In general it is convenient to use glass rods with beakers – ease of access for stirring – and magnetic fleas with conical flasks – lower losses through splashing – but often it is a matter of your preference and laboratory skills.

'Obstinate' solutions may require heating, but only do this if you know that the chemical will not be damaged at the temperature used. Use a stirrer–heater to keep the solution mixed as you heat it. Allow the solution to cool to room temperature before you finalise its volume.

Preparation of analytical solutions

The key features in the preparation of solutions for analytical purposes are:

- Make sure that you have the most accurate available knowledge of masses of the chemicals used.

- Ensure that you have the most accurate available knowledge of the volumes of solutions used.

To achieve these features exact techniques of weighing and solution transfer must be used and the procedure is illustrated in the following example.

'Prepare a standard solution (250.00 mL) of ammonium ferrous sulphate (approximately 0.1 M), which is to be used to determine the concentration of a solution of potassium permanganate by titration.'

You must be aware of the following embedded information:

- This is a quantitative experiment, therefore requiring an analytical solution to be prepared.

- You must use a 250.00 mL volumetric flask, which you should note is calibrated at 20 °C.

- You must weigh accurately, to four decimal places, the mass of the chemical.

- It is almost impossible to weigh the exact mass of chemical for a specific concentration. For example, the mass of $(NH_4)_2FeSO_4.6H_2O$ required to prepare 250.00 mL of 0.1 M solution is 9.8035 g and you cannot weigh out this exact mass. However, you *can* weigh out a known mass to four decimal places accurately. From this you can then calculate the exact concentration of the chemical in solution, since you will know both mass and volume to a high degree of accuracy.

Box 23.2 shows the method for the preparation of the standard solution. The main practical point is that you must not lose, by splashing or failure to transfer by inadequate rinsing, *any* of the solution being prepared in the beaker and you must transfer *all* of the solution, by repeated rinsing, into the volumetric flask. Therefore it is good practice

A **standard solution** is one in which the solute is weighed out to an accuracy of 4 decimal places and is made up in a volumetric flask.

A **stock solution** is one from which dilutions are made.

Box 23.2 How to make up an aqueous solution of known concentration from a solid chemical for use in quantitative analysis

Example: Suppose you are to prepare a standard solution (250.00 mL) of ammonium ferrous sulphate (approximately 0.1 M), which is to be used to determine the concentration of a solution of potassium permanganate.

1. **This is a quantitative experiment so the ammonium ferrous sulphate must be of the highest purity available to you.**

2. **Work out the mass of chemical that will give you the *concentration* desired in the *volume* required.**

   (a) Convert 1.0 M into $mol\,L^{-1}$; concentration required $= 1.0\,mol\,L^{-1}$.

   (b) Express all volumes in the same units: therefore 250.00 mL $= 0.25$ L.

   (c) Calculate the number of moles required from eqn [23.1]: $1.0 =$ amount (mol) $\div 0.25$. By rearrangement, the required number of moles is thus $1.0 \times 0.25 = 0.025$ mol.

   (d) Convert from mol to g by multiplying by the M_r, but note from the container that the compound is $(NH_4)_2FeSO_4.6H_2O$. Therefore the M_r required must include the water of crystallisation and $M_r = 392.14\,g\,mol^{-1}$.

   (e) Therefore, you need to weigh out $0.025 \times 392.14 = 9.8035$ g of $(NH_4)_2FeSO_4.6H_2O$.

3. **Place a clean, dry weighing boat or appropriately sized sample tube onto a simple two-decimal-place balance** (see p. 162) and zero (tare) the balance and weigh about 9.80 g of the chemical.

4. **Carefully transfer the sample tube plus chemical to a four-decimal-place analytical balance** (see p. 163) and record the accurate mass: say 11.9726 g.

5. **Remove the sample and container from the balance and tip the contents into a clean, dry beaker (400 mL)**, ensuring that there is no spillage outside the beaker. *Do not attempt to wash out the sample tube with water.*

6. **Immediately reweigh the sample tube on the analytical balance**: say 2.1564 g. This is the mass of the container together with a few crystals of the chemical which have remained in the container. However, you now know exactly the mass of the chemical in the beaker: $11.9726 - 2.1564 = 9.8162$ g of $(NH_4)_2FeSO_4.6H_2O$.

7. **Add deionised or distilled water** (about 100 mL) to the beaker and stir the mixture gently with a clean Pyrex® glass rod until all the solid has dissolved. *Do not splash or spill any of this solution* or you cannot calculate its concentration. Remove the glass rod from the solution, rinsing it with a little distilled water into the solution.

8. **Clamp a clean volumetric flask** for support (see p. 166) and place a clean, dry filter funnel in the top supported by a ring. Carefully pour the solution into the volumetric flask, ensuring no spillage of solution by using the technique illustrated in Fig. 23.1 and pouring slowly so that no air-lock is formed and no solution runs down the side of the beaker. When the addition is complete, *do not move the beaker from its position over the funnel.*

9. **Rinse the inside of the beaker several times with a distilled water wash bottle** to transfer all of the solution into the volumetric flask, paying particular attention to the 'spout' and glass rod. Then place the beaker aside and lift the funnel from the flask while rinsing it with distilled water. You have now achieved a *quantitative transfer*. Swirl the liquid in the flask to prevent density gradients.

10. **Make the solution up to the mark using distilled water**, stopper the flask and mix thoroughly by gentle inversion (10 times) of the flask while holding the stopper in place.

    You now have a solution (250.00 mL), which contains $(NH_4)_2FeSO_4.6H_2O$ (9.8162 g).

    The concentration of this solution is expressed as:

    250.00 mL of the solution contains 9.8162 g of $(NH_4)_2FeSO_4.6H_2O$

    Therefore:

    1000.00 mL of solution contains

    $$(4 \times 9.8162) = 39.2648\,g \text{ of } (NH_4)_2FeSO_4.6H_2O$$

    The concentration of the solution is

    $39.2648\,g\,L^{-1} = 39.2648 \div 392.14 =$

    $0.1001\,mol\,L^{-1} = 0.1001\,M$

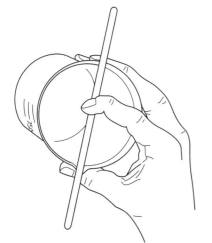

Fig. 23.1 Pouring a solution using a glass rod.

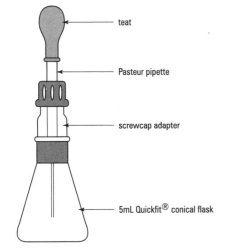

teat

Pasteur pipette

screwcap adapter

5mL Quickfit® conical flask

Fig. 23.2 A weighing bottle.

Making a dilution – use the relationship $[C_1]V_1 = [C_2]V_2$ to determine volume or concentration (see p. 187).

Using the correct volumes for dilutions – it is important to distinguish between the volumes of the various liquids: a one-in-ten dilution is obtained using one volume of stock solution plus nine volumes of diluent $(1 + 9 = 10)$.

to use only a glass rod to stir the solution gently to dissolve the solid and to use the glass rod, as shown in Fig. 23.1, to pour the solution into the filter funnel. This technique, with practice, prevents losses of solution down the side of the beaker via the spout; rinsing with water can be achieved by use of a wash bottle squirted directly into the beaker.

You should not use a flea to stir a solution in the preparation of a standard solution, since this introduces more washing steps – washing the flea and the 'flea extractor' – and you still need to use the glass rod for quantitative transfer.

Procedure required with analytical solutions prepared from liquids

Many experiments in analytical chemistry, such as chromatography and spectroscopy, require the preparation of a standard solution of a liquid organic compound. Therefore you must know accurately the mass of the liquid. The compound can be dispensed by the methods described in Chapter 22, provided that the pipette, syringe, etc., is accurate, and thus the mass = volume × density, bearing in mind the temperature factor.

Alternatively you can use a weighing bottle as shown in Fig. 23.2. The liquid is placed in the bottle, weighed accurately and then the approximate amount required is added to the volumetric flask containing some solvent. The volumetric flask is stoppered immediately, the weighing bottle reweighed and the weight of liquid dispensed is calculated. The volumetric flask is then made up to the mark and stoppered. You now know the concentration of the standard solution to four decimal places.

Preparing dilutions

Making a single dilution

In analytical work, you may need to dilute a standard solution to give a particular mass concentration or molar concentration. Use the following procedure.

1. Transfer an appropriate volume of standard solution to a volumetric flask, using appropriate equipment (Table 22.1).

2. Make up to the calibration mark with solvent – add the last few drops from a Pasteur pipette until the bottom of the meniscus is level with the calibration mark.

3. Mix thoroughly, either by repeated inversion (holding the stopper firmly) or by prolonged stirring, using a magnetic stirrer. Make sure that you add the magnetic flea *after* the volume adjustment step.

For general-purpose work using dilute aqueous solutions where the higher degree of accuracy is not required, it may be acceptable to substitute conical flasks, beakers or test tubes for volumetric flasks and use measuring cylinders for volume measurements. In such cases you would calculate the volumes of 'stock' solutions (usually 'bench' reagents) and diluent required, with the assumption that the final volume is determined by the individual volumes of stock solution and diluent used. Thus a two-fold dilution would be prepared by using one volume of stock solution and one volume of diluent. The dilution factor is obtained from the initial concentration of the stock solution and the final concentration of the diluted solution. The dilution factor can be used to calculate the volumes and stock and diluent required in a particular instance. For example, suppose you wanted to prepare 100 mL of a solution of NaOH at 0.1 mol L^{-1}. Using the bench reagent, commonly containing 2.0 mol L^{-1} (2.0 M), the dilution factor is $0.1 \div 2.0 = 0.05 = 1/20$ (a twenty-fold dilution). Therefore the amount of stock solution required is 1/20th of 100 mL = 5 mL and the amount of diluent needed is 19/20th of 100 mL = 95 mL.

Preparing a dilution series

Dilution series are used in a wide range of procedures including the preparation of standard curves for the calibration of analytical instruments (p. 343). A variety of different approaches can be used but the most common is a *linear dilution series.*

In a linear dilution series the concentrations are separated by an equal amount, e.g. a series containing cadmium at 0, 0.2, 0.4, 0.6, 0.8, 1.0 mmol L^{-1} might be used to prepare a calibration curve for atomic absorption spectroscopy (p. 343) when assaying polluted soil samples. Use $[C_1]V_1 = [C_2]V_2$ to calculate the volume of standard solution for each member of the series and pipette or syringe the calculated volume into an appropriately sized volumetric flask as described above. Remember to label clearly each diluted solution as you prepare it, since it is easy to get confused. The process is outlined in Box 23.3.

> **KEY POINT** Make all the dilutions from the working stock solution to the required solution. Do not make a solution of lower dilution from one already prepared: if you have made an error in the first dilution, it will be repeated for the second dilution.

Storing chemicals and solutions

Sealing flasks – think carefully about the sealing system for a flask to be stored at low temperature. Cooling will reduce the volume of vapour (including air) in the flask and create a partial vacuum. Rubber bungs can be irremovable after cooling (another good reason for never using them) and even ground-glass joints can seize up. Plastic stoppers, screwtops or lightly greased glass stoppers, as appropriate, are recommended.

Chemicals which decompose easily (labile chemicals) may be stored in a fridge or freezer. Take special care when using chemicals which have been stored at low temperature: the container and its contents must be allowed to warm up to room temperature before use, otherwise water will condense onto the chemical. This may render accurate weighing impossible and you may ruin the chemical.

Chemicals and solutions to be stored at low temperatures must be in stoppered or sealed vessels. Do not store aqueous solutions below 0 °C since freezing can occur and, with the resulting expansion of the volume, the vessel may crack. Solutions containing flammable solvents should only be stored in specialised 'spark-proof' fridges: consult your laboratory instructor.

You must be aware of the particular problems of storing solutions in flasks with ground-glass joints. If you are using aqueous solutions you should lightly grease the joint and stopper with petroleum jelly, since the water will not dissolve the grease as it is poured from the flask. The stopper can be removed easily and the solution will be uncontaminated.

Greasing joints – if you are using solutions of NaOH or KOH you *must* grease the ground-glass joint and stopper since the surfaces are attacked by strong alkalis.

Conversely, if you are using solutions made up from organic solvents, you should *not* grease the joints since the organic solvent will dissolve the grease as you pour it from the flask and contaminate the solution. Moreover, you should not allow the solution to come in contact

---

Box 23.3 How to make up a linear dilution series for use in quantitative analysis

The experimental protocol states: 'Prepare a standard solution (250.00 mL; 0.01 M) of cadmium ions using cadmium nitrate and use this solution to produce a linear dilution series of solutions (100.00 mL) of accurately known concentrations of approximately 0.0, 0.2, 0.4, 0.6, 0.8, 1.0 mmol L^{-1}'.

1. **Calculate the amount of cadmium nitrate required for the standard solution:** cadmium nitrate is supplied as the tetrahydrate $Cd(NO_3)_2.4H_2O$; $M_r = 308.47$ g mol^{-1}. Therefore, using eqn [23.1], you should calculate 250.00 mL of an 0.01 M solution of cadmium ions requires $0.01 \times 0.25 = 0.0025$ mol $= 0.0025 \times 308.47 = 0.7712$ g of $Cd(NO_3)_2.4H_2O$. *Remember*: this solution will contain 0.0025 moles of 'cadmium nitrate' or 0.0025 moles of cadmium ions and 0.005 moles of nitrate ions.

2. **Make the standard solution** by the quantitative method described in Box 23.2 and calculate its concentration to four decimal places.

3. **Calculate the volume of solution required for the dilution series** using $[C_1]V_1 = [C_2]V_2$, where $V_1 =$ volume (mL) of standard solution required; $C_1 =$ concentration of standard solution; $V_2 =$ volume of diluted solution (100.00 mL) and $C_2 =$ concentration of diluted solution.

4. **Express the concentrations in the same units,** the most convenient in this case being mol L^{-1}. Therefore, $C_1 = 0.01 M = 1 \times 10^{-2}$ mol L^{-1} and for the diluted solution of concentration 0.2 mmol L^{-1}, $C_2 = 0.2 \times 10^{-3}$ mol L^{-1}. By rearrangement

$$V_1 = \{[C_2]V_2\} \div [C_1]$$

$$= \frac{0.2 \times 10^{-3} \text{ mol L}^{-1} \times 100.00 \text{ mL}}{1 \times 10^{-2} \text{ mol L}^{-1}} = 2.00 \text{ mL}$$

5. **Transfer the standard solution (2.00 mL) to the volumetric flask (100.00 mL)** and make up to the mark with distilled water.

6. **Repeat the calculation for each of the other diluted solutions as required,** but note that a short cut is possible *in this case*: since you require stock solution (2.00 mL) for the diluted solution of concentration 0.2 mmol L^{-1}, you will need 4.00 mL for the 0.4 mmol L^{-1} solution etc. Use pure distilled water for the solution of concentration 0.0 mol L^{-1}.

7. **Calculate the exact concentrations of the diluted solutions** using $[C_1]V_1 = [C_2]V_2$, since the concentration of the standard solution is most unlikely to be exactly 0.0100 mol L^{-1} (see Box 23.2). For example, if the concentration of the standard solution $[C_1]$ is actually 0.009 87 mol L$^{-1} = 9.87 \times 10^{-3}$ mol L^{-1}, then for the dilute solution of approximate concentration 0.2 mmol L^{-1}, the actual concentration $[C_2]$ is:

$$[C_2] = \{V_1 \times [C_1]\} \div V_2$$

$$= \frac{0.2 \text{ mL} \times 9.87 \times 10^{-3} \text{ mol L}^{-1}}{100.00 \text{ mL}}$$

$$= 2 \times 9.87 \times 10^{-5} \text{ mol L}^{-1} = 0.1974 \text{ mmol L}^{-1}.$$

Note: It is much simpler to measure out whole-number volumes (2.00 mL, 4.00 mL, etc.) using a pipette and produce diluted solutions of accurately known concentrations (but not necessarily whole numbers) rather than to try to produce whole-number concentrations by measuring out non-whole-number volumes.

---

with the ungreased joints, since the solvent will evaporate and leave the solute to 'weld' the stopper to the flask. Fill the flask with solution, using a filter funnel with the stem of the funnel positioned well below the joint. See p. 182 for use of ground-glass jointware.

KEY POINT Always label all stored chemicals clearly with the following information: the name (if a solution, state solute(s) and concentration(s)), plus any relevant hazard warning information, the date made up, and your name.

Weighing – *never* weigh anything directly onto a balance's pan: you may contaminate it for others. Use an appropriate weighing container such as a weighing boat, sample tube, weighing paper, conical flask, beaker.

'Weighing paper' – it is common practice to put a piece of paper onto the pan of general-purpose balances. The mass of the paper is then 'tared off' before the weighing container is placed on the balance pan. The paper protects the balance pan from corrosion by spillages and also allows you to discard easily any material spilt without affecting the weighing.

(a)

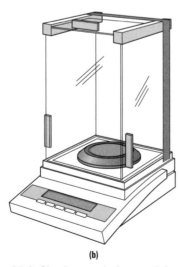

(b)

Fig. 23.3 Single-pan balance: (a) general purpose, two decimal places; (b) analytical, four decimal places.

Balances and weighing

Electronic single-pan balances with digital readouts are now favoured over mechanical types and are common in most laboratories. There are essentially two types of balance:

1. General purpose balances which weigh to the nearest 0.01 g with a capacity of about 300 g. Chemicals may be dispensed for weighing, into a suitable weighing container, directly onto these balances.

2. Analytical four-figure balances for quantitative work, which weigh to the nearest 0.0001 g (0.1 mg) and have a maximum capacity of about 100 g. Chemicals must not be transferred onto the balance at any time and analytical balances must only be used for weighing by difference.

Both types are illustrated in Fig. 23.3 and you should familiarise yourself with their operation before use.

General-purpose balances

The most useful feature of this type of balance is the electronic zero facility (self-taring), which means the mass of the weighing container can be subtracted automatically before weighing chemicals.

To operate a standard self-taring balance:

1. Check that it is level, using the adjustable feet to centre the bubble in the spirit level (usually at the back of the machine). For relatively accurate work or when using in a fume cupboard, make sure that the draught shield is in place.

2. Ensure that the balance is switched on: the display should be lit.

3. Place an empty weighing container (see p. 163) centrally on the balance pan and allow the reading to stabilise. *If the object is larger than the pan, take care that no part rests on the body of the balance or the draught shield as this will invalidate the reading.* Press the tare bar to bring the reading to zero.

4. Place the chemical or object carefully in the weighing vessel:
   (a) Solid chemicals should be dispensed with a suitably sized clean spatula.
   (b) Non-volatile liquids should be dispensed using a Pasteur pipette but take the weighing container off the balance pan before dispensing; then reweigh the liquid plus container. Repeat until the desired weight is obtained.

5. Allow the reading to stabilise and make a note of the reading.

6. If you have added excess chemical, take great care when removing it. Remove the container from the balance, remove the solid (with a spatula) or liquid (with a Pasteur pipette) and reweigh.

7. If you need to clean any deposit accidentally left on or around the balance, switch off the balance.

Take care not to exceed the limits for the balance: while most have devices to protect against overloading, you may damage the mechanism.

Analytical balances

These are delicate precision instruments and as such are likely to be found away from the open laboratory in draught-free conditions on a vibration-dampened surface. Analytical balances are maintained to the highest specifications and should need no adjustments on your part, such as levelling and zero adjustment. The key points for using an analytical balance are summarised below:

- No chemicals must be transferred within the weighing compartment of the balance.

- If it has a 'locking' function, the balance pan must always be 'locked' when placing and removing objects onto and from the balance pan.

- The doors of the balance must always be closed when taking measurements.

The procedure for weighing a solid chemical for the preparation of an analytical standard solution is shown in Box 23.4.

Weighing containers

These come in various materials, shapes and sizes: from glass weighing boats to beakers and even special glazed paper. The weighing container to be used depends on several factors:

- The amount of chemical to be weighed.

- The properties of the chemical to be weighed: is it solid, liquid, volatile, corrosive, deliquescent, hygroscopic?

- How and into what type of vessel it is to be transferred.

- The accuracy to which it is to be weighed.

Some of the common types of weighing container are shown in Fig. 23.4.

For analytical procedures, only weighing boats, weighing bottles or glass or plastic sample tubes should be used. Weighing boats are used to transfer a solid directly into a volumetric flask via the neck of the weighing boat: this procedure is recommended when the chemical is known to be totally soluble in the solvent and allows you to omit the solution preparation stage in a beaker or conical flask (see Box 23.2). You must ensure that the neck of the weighing boat will fit well inside the ground-glass joint of the neck of the volumetric flask so that all the chemical can be washed down the sides of the volumetric flask and does not stick to the ground-glass joint during the quantitative transfer.

For general-purpose work, weighings can be made directly into pre-weighed or 'tared' conical flasks or beakers, again to avoid a transfer stage. Much more common is the use of disposable plastic weighing dishes of the appropriate size. The edges of these dishes can be squeezed together to form a 'funnel' to prevent losses when transferring the solid. Remember that plastic disposable dishes may dissolve in organic solvents such as propanone (acetone), toluene, etc., and should not be used for low-melting organic solids or liquids. Watch- and clock-glasses should be avoided if you wish to transfer the solid into narrow-necked vessels such as conical flasks or sample tubes since it very difficult to direct the solid into the narrow opening of the vessel from the large 'flat' surface of the watch- or clock-glass. In such cases, or when large amounts of solid are

Using a balance – It is poor experimental technique to use large containers to weigh out small masses: you are attempting to measure small differences between large numbers. For small masses, use a small weighing container (Fig. 23.4).

(a)

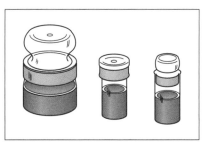

(b)

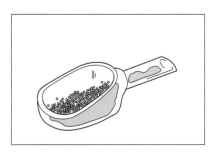

(c)

Fig. 23.4 Weighing containers: (a) plastic weighing dishes; (b) weighing bottles; (c) weighing boat.

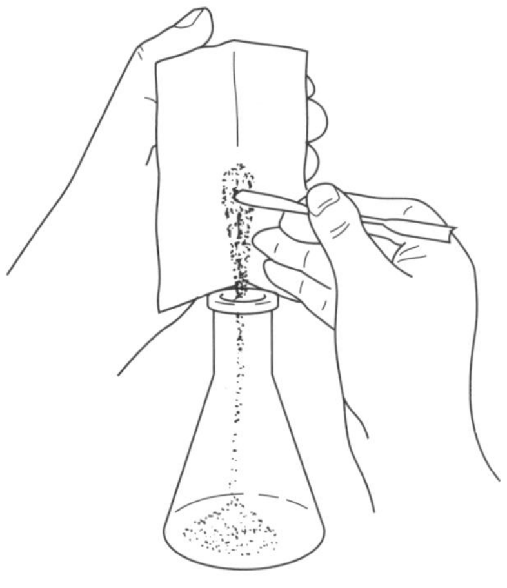

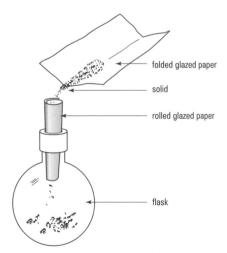

Fig. 23.5 Transferring a solid using glazed paper.

Fig. 23.6 Transferring a solid to a narrow-necked flask.

Box 23.4 **How to weigh out a sample of a solid for use in quantitative analysis**

1. **Place the clean, dry weighing boat or sample tube on a general-purpose two-decimal-place balance** and zero the balance.

2. **Weigh out the calculated amount of chemical** within the accuracy of the balance.

3. **Check the zero reading on the analytical balance** by pressing the bar/button with the balance doors closed.

4. **Relock the balance pan** by pressing the bar/button.

5. **Carefully transfer the weighing boat or sample tube to the balance pan of the analytical balance** (for very accurate work use tweezers or fine tongs since the sweat from your fingers will contribute to the weight recorded) and close the balance door.

6. **Release the balance pan by pressing the bar/button**, allow the balance to stabilise and record the weight of the chemical and container. If the last decimal place 'cycles' between two or three numbers, determine the mid-point of the 'cycle' and record this value as the weight.

7. **Lock the balance pan by pressing the bar/button,** remove the sample container and transfer the solid to your volumetric flask, beaker or conical flask by pouring, but do not wet the weighing boat or sample tube with solvent.

8. **Replace the weighing container on the analytical balance pan,** close the balance door and weigh the container. Again decide on the mid-point weight if the last decimal place 'cycles' and record this value as the weight of the 'empty' weighing container.

9. **Lock the balance pan by pressing the bar/button** and remove the weighing container from the balance.

10. **Subtract the weight of the 'empty' weighing container from that of the weighing container plus sample** and you now know the mass of chemical, to an accuracy of four decimal places, which has been transferred into your volumetric flask, beaker or conical flask.

to be transferred, it is advisable to use a wide-necked filter funnel called a 'powder funnel'.

In many preparative experiments, which are carried out on a small scale (involving 1 g to 10 g of solids), the most useful weighing container is special glazed paper, provided that the chemicals do not react with the paper. A creased square of glazed paper is 'tared' on the balance pan and the solid weighed out directly onto it. The chemical can then be allowed to flow down the crease into the vessel (Fig. 23.5). Furthermore, when attempting to transfer small amounts of solid in vessels with narrow-bore ground-glass joints (see p. 182) it is important not to allow the solid to contact the joint, because the joint will not seal correctly. Use a filter funnel or roll a piece of glazed paper into a funnel, insert the stem of the paper funnel to below the joint and then run in the solid from the creased weighing paper (Fig. 23.6). Paper used in this manner is much cheaper than proprietary weighing dishes and is a useful method of recycling out-of-date manufacturers' catalogues!

folded glazed paper

solid

rolled glazed paper

flask

Text references

Haynes, W.M. (ed.) (2010) *CRC Handbook of Chemistry and Physics,* 91st edn. CRC Press, Boca Raton.

O'Neil, M.J., Smith, A. and Henkelmann, P.E. (2006) *The Merck Index: An Encyclopaedia of Chemicals, Drugs and Biologicals,* 14th edn. Merck & Co. Inc., Whitehouse Station.

Sources for further study

Anon. *CHEMnet Base.* Available: http://www.chemnetbase.com Last accessed: 05/03/10. [Online access to the *CRC Handbook of Chemistry and Physics*]

Anon. *SIRI MSDS Index.* Available: http://www.hazard.com/msds Last accessed 05/03/10. [Online access to Materials Safety Data Sheets (MSDS) for manufacturers' chemicals]

Cartwright, H. *Hands-on Science Project: Chemical Safety Data Base.* Available: http://www.ptcl.chem.ox.ac.uk/msds Last accessed 05/03/10.

[Online access to student-friendly MSDS for a restricted range of common chemicals]

Furniss, B.A., Hannaford, A.J., Smith, P.W.G. and Tatchell, A.R. (1989) *Vogel's Textbook of Practical Organic Chemistry,* 5th edn. Longman, Harlow, Essex.

Mendham, J., Denney, R.C., Barnes, J.D. and Thomas, M.J.K. (2000) *Vogel's Textbook of Quantitative Chemical Analysis,* 6th edn. Prentice Hall, Harlow, Essex.

Urben, P.G. (2006) *Bretherick's Handbook of Reactive Chemical Hazards,* 7th edn. Vols. 1 and 2. Butterworth-Heinemann, London.

Study exercises

23.1 Practise the calculations involved in preparing specific volumes of aqueous solutions of known concentrations. What mass of substance would be required to prepare each of the following (answer in each case to four decimal places):

(a) 250.00 mL of sodium chloride (0.05 M) from NaCl?

(b) 100.00 mL of potassium iodate (0.02 M) from KIO_3?

(c) 50.00 mL of sodium thiosulphate (0.05 M) from $Na_2S_2O_3.5H_2O$?

(d) 250.00 mL of copper ions (0.1 M) from $CuSO_4.5H_2O$?

(e) 100.00 mL of potassium ions (0.05 M) from K_2SO_4?

23.2 Practise the calculations involved in dilutions (answer in each case to four decimal places).

(a) If you added sodium chloride solution (1.00 mL; 0.4 M) to a volumetric flask (10.00 mL) and made up to the mark with water, what would be the concentration of the diluted solution?

(b) Calculate the volume a solution of copper (II) sulphate (0.1 M) required to produce 500.00 mL of 0.02 M solution.

(c) What would be the concentration of a solution of Fe^{2+} ions if 10.00 mL is diluted to 250.00 mL to give a concentration of 0.001 M?

(d) You are provided with a solution of $KMnO_4$ (0.02 M); to what volume must 5.00 mL of this solution be diluted to give a concentration of 0.001 M?

Clamps and support stands

When carrying out experiments it is vital that all apparatus is held in place securely during the procedure. It is essential that you know how to assemble supporting and securing equipment to the highest possible standards of safety. The most common types of supporting and securing equipment are shown in Fig. 24.1.

Support stands

These are also known as 'retort stands' and comprise an aluminium or steel rod screwed into a heavy metal base. Always check that the base sits level and that the rod is tightened fully in place.

Clamp holders

These are also described as 'clamp bosses' or 'bosses'. Make sure that the locking screws move freely and are not distorted. When you attach the clamp holder to the support stand, tighten the screw firmly and ensure that the open 'slot' to be used for the clamp is pointing upwards (Fig. 24.2).

Clamps

General-purpose clamps are used for securing glassware – therefore make sure that the inner surfaces of the clamp 'jaws' and the 'fingers' are covered with cork or rubber to provide a cushion for the glass: there must be no metal to glass contact in case you overtighten the clamp and crush the glass. Tighten the clamp firmly and ensure that the clamped glassware does not move.

Conical flasks should be clamped at the neck and ground-glass jointware should be clamped at the joint – this usually has the greatest thickness of glass.

> **KEY POINT** Take particular care when using parallel-sided separatory funnels and chromatography columns (Fig. 24.3), where clamping in the middle of the funnel can be the same as squeezing the middle of a large-diameter glass tube. Clamp at the ground-glass joint using a 'well-cushioned' clamp.

In most clamps, only *one* of the jaws moves when turning the screw. When you use the clamp in a horizontal position, make sure that the movable jaw is at the *top* (see p. 257).

Burette clamps are specially designed to hold the burette vertically. Springs hold the burette at two points about 5 cm apart – again check for the presence of a rubber or plastic 'cushion' at the points of contact – to prevent slipping and lateral movement. Since the burette clamp slides down the rod of the support stand, then provided the support stand is vertical, the burette will be vertical.

Support rings

These metal rings come in various diameters to support filter funnels and separatory funnels. Often these support rings are coated in plastic to provide the cushion between metal and glass.

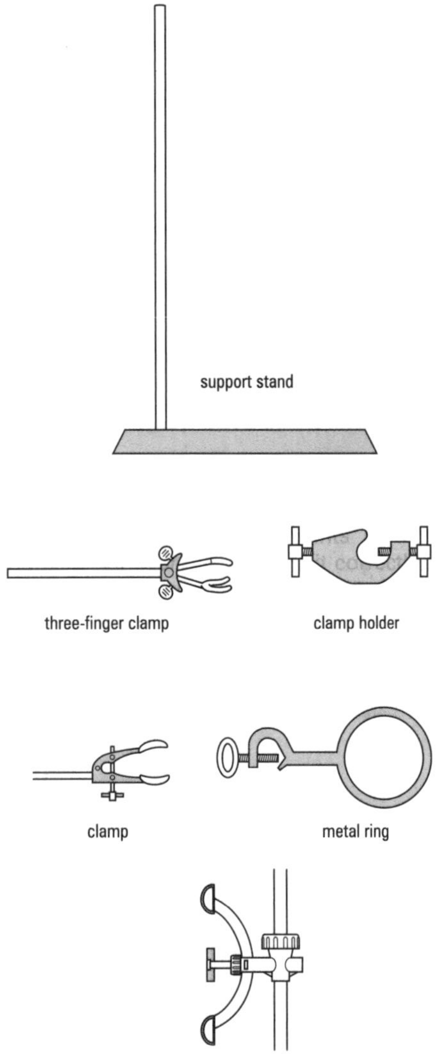

Fig. 24.1 Clamps and supporting equipment.

Using support rings – make sure that the tap on the separating funnel will go through the ring.

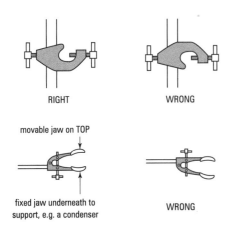

RIGHT   WRONG

movable jaw on TOP

fixed jaw underneath to
support, e.g. a condenser   WRONG

Fig. 24.2 Right and wrong ways of using support stands, clamp holders and clamps.

Gravity filtration to obtain a solid – there are a few occasions when these rules do not apply, e.g. when the solid is to be decomposed by heat and the filter paper destroyed, a process known as 'ashing'. Some gravimetric analyses, such as the determination of sulphate as barium sulphate, require retention of the precipitate from gravity filtration since $BaSO_4$ is too fine to be collected on a vacuum filtration system. $BaSO_4$ is thermally stable up to 600 °C, so the filter paper can be burned away.

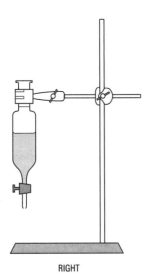

RIGHT

Fig. 24.3 Clamping a parallel-sided funnel.

If your support ring is metal, you can make a 'cushion' by finding a piece of thin-walled rubber tubing of the same bore as the metal of the ring, cutting it to a length equivalent to the circumference of the ring and then cutting down the length of the rubber tubing. You can then slide the tubing around the ring to provide the 'cushion'.

> **SAFETY NOTE** When using clamps, support rings and support stands make sure that the clamped/supported apparatus is always in position above the base of the support stand (Fig. 24.4) to prevent the stand toppling over.

Cork rings

These are used to hold round-bottom flasks on flat surfaces while manipulations are being carried out. Since they are light in weight they can be used to hold round-bottom flasks on a general-purpose balance.

Filtration

Filtration is the physical separation of a solid from a liquid and is a process encountered in experimental procedures such as gravimetric analysis (p. 294), recrystallisation (p. 238) and solvent drying (p. 181). In principle, the mixture of the solid and liquid is passed through a porous material, filter paper or sintered glass, and the solid is trapped on the porous material while the liquid passes through.

The type of filtration equipment you select for use depends upon which of the two components, the solid or the liquid, you are trying to isolate. In general:

- If you wish to isolate the liquid – *use gravity filtration.*

- If you wish to isolate the solid – *use suction (vacuum) filtration*

Gravity filtration

In gravity filtration you need to pass the liquid through the porous material and retain all the unwanted solid in the filter. In general, the best material to use is a filter paper of the appropriate porosity to trap all the solid particles and with the greatest surface area to allow the liquid to pass through quickly. The apparatus required for gravity filtration is shown in Fig. 24.5. The filter funnels are usually made of glass, but if organic solvents are not involved in the filtration, plastic funnels can be used. Glass filter funnels with the pipe cut off are known as 'stemless' filter funnels and have a specific use in hot filtration (p. 244).

The key to successful gravity filtration is the fluted filter paper. A fluted filter paper decreases the area of contact between the filter paper and the funnel, thus allowing rapid filtration. If you use 'traditional' cone-folded filter paper, note that all sides of the paper are touching the sides of the funnel and on half the filter paper the liquid has to pass through three thicknesses of paper, all of which slow the rate of filtration. Slow filtration can lead to disaster in hot filtration during recrystallisation (p. 246).

Since filter funnels and filter papers come in different sizes, choose a filter paper of diameter just less than twice the diameter of the funnel. When fluted, the filter paper will be just below the rim of the funnel. There are many ways to fold (flute) a filter paper, but one of the simplest is shown in Box 24.1.

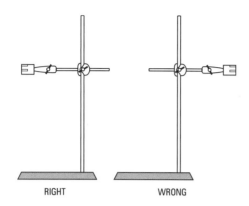

RIGHT   WRONG

Fig. 24.4 Correct use of support stands.

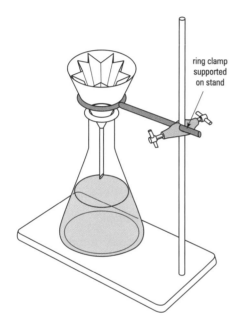

ring clamp
supported
on stand

Fig. 24.5 Gravity filtration.

Box 24.1 How to flute a filter paper for gravity filtration

1. **Fold the filter paper in half (a)**, open it out then fold into quarters (b), open it out and then fold into eighths (c) and (d), all in the same direction.
2. **Turn the paper over** and fold each sector in half (e); you are creating sixteenths but with each fold in the opposite direction to (a), (b), (c) and (d).
3. **Finally, fold the paper into a cone (g)** ensuring that all the folds are sharp and that the base of the cone comes to a sharp point.
4. The flutes ensure that the filter paper has minimum contact with the filter funnel and the sharp point ensures that the liquid flows rapidly out of the cone and out of the funnel.
5. If your cone point is blunt it will cover the stem of the funnel and so all the liquid must pass through this part of the filter paper, slowing the filtration.

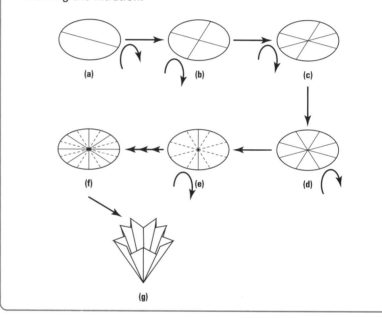

Filtering solids – if you allow the solid to settle you will have difficulty pouring the thick slurry of solid and liquid from the bottom of the beaker or conical flask into the filter cone and you will need to use more filtrate to complete the filtration effectively.

To filter the mixture, swirl the suspension of the solid in the liquid so that there is a fairly even distribution of solid in the liquid, and then pour the mixture into the filter cone, making sure that you do not pour any of the mixture outside the filter paper otherwise you will need to repeat the filtration, and do not overfill the filter cone. Transfer all the mixture in this way and finally wash the last bit of solid and liquid into the filter cone with a *small amount* of filtered solution and then *a little pure solvent*.

Suction filtration

This technique is used for the isolation of a *solid* from a suspension of a solid in a liquid and relies on producing a partial vacuum in the receiving flask. The essential components of a suction filtration system are:

- A ceramic funnel containing a flat perforated plate: there are two types based on size and shape called Büchner funnels or Hirsch funnels. When you are filtering, the perforated plate is covered by a filter paper.

Filtering hot mixtures – *never* attempt to use suction filtration on a *hot* mixture of solid and liquid. As the liquid filters through into the vacuum it may boil under the reduced pressure and be drawn into the pressure tubing. If the liquid is saturated with the solid, the evaporating liquid will deposit the solid in the holes of the perforated plate and block them.

Filtering charcoal – *never* attempt to remove finely divided charcoal, used in decolorisation during recrystallisation or as a catalyst support, by suction filtration. It is a very fine powder and will *always* leak into the filtrate. Filter off charcoal by gravity filtration.

- A receiver flask with a side arm for attachment of the vacuum source. Büchner flasks are conical flasks made from thickened glass, and Hirsch tubes (also known as side-arm boiling tubes or test tubes depending upon size) are capable of withstanding weak vacuum, e.g. a water pump.

- A flexible seal between the ceramic funnel and the receiving vessel: a Büchner collar or filter seal.

- A source of vacuum, usually a water pump (water aspirator) which is connected to the receiving flask by thick walled rubber tubing (pressure tubing). Usually there will be a trap between the water pump and the receiving flask.

The various types of these components are shown in Fig. 24.6: typical apparatus is shown in Fig. 24.7 and the general procedure for suction filtration is described in Box 24.2.

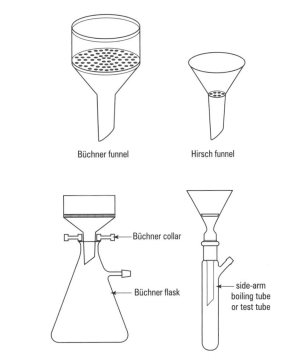

Büchner funnel   Hirsch funnel

Büchner collar

Büchner flask

side-arm boiling tube or test tube

Fig. 24.6 Equipment for suction filtration.

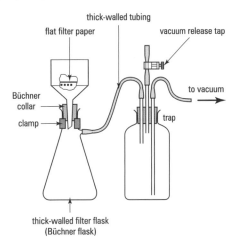

thick-walled tubing

flat filter paper   vacuum release tap

Büchner collar

clamp   to vacuum

trap

thick-walled filter flask (Büchner flask)

Fig. 24.7 Suction filtration using a Büchner funnel.

Box 24.2 Isolation of a solid by suction filtration

1. **Select the appropriate size of apparatus based on the amount of solid you expect to isolate and the volume of liquid to be collected in the receiver flask.** Consider the following points:

   A. There is no point in using a large Büchner funnel for a small amount of solid since you will collect a layer of solid 'one molecule thick' and be unable to scrape it from the filter paper cleanly. If there is too much solid for the size of the funnel, you will have to repeat the filtration with a second set of apparatus or the solid may not suck dry quickly.

   B. If you use a side-arm boiling tube to try to collect 100 mL of liquid, you will overfill the tube and liquid: (i) will flow into the pressure tubing, contaminating it for your fellow students; (ii) may fill the intermediate trap, if there is one, and you will need to dismantle and clean it; (iii) may be sucked into the water pump causing corrosion and loss of performance.

2. **Clean and dry all the apparatus to be used.**

3. **Clamp the receiving vessel to a support stand:** pressure tubing is heavy and even large Büchner flasks will fall over: do not think that a test tube rack will hold a side-arm boiling tube safely.

4. **Place the correct-sized Büchner collar in the neck of the receiving flask:** it should sit well into the neck and fit the funnel to form a good seal.

5. **Place the funnel into the collar/seal:** note that the funnel has a 'point' at the bottom of the stem. Make sure that this 'point' is as far away as possible from the vacuum attachment side arm of the receiver flask, since the filtering liquid runs off this 'point' and if the point is near the vacuum inlet, the liquid may be drawn into the side arm and then into the trap or water pump (see **1B** above).

6. **Select a filter paper, which fits exactly over the perforation in the base of the funnel.** The filter paper should not fold or crease up the sides of the funnel because the solid will be sucked round the edge of the paper into the receiver flask. If the paper does not fit exactly, trim to size with scissors.

7. **Place the paper into the funnel and wet it with a few drops of liquid** – the same liquid which is to be used in the filtration.

8. **Switch on the tap for the water pump to provide gentle suction.** If your system has a trap, don't forget to close the tap on the trap and connect the rubber tubing to the side arm of the receiver. Do not force the rubber tubing too far onto the side arm – you may need to pull it off quickly if something goes wrong

(see **1B** and **5**). The filter paper will be pulled down onto the perforated plate by the vacuum.

9. **Turn on the tap to the water pump to the *maximum water flow*.** If you do not do this, the water pump is not working at its maximum efficiency and the vacuum created in your filtration system may cause water to be sucked into a trap, or receiving flask, from the water pump. This is called 'suck-back'.

10. **Swirl the mixture to be filtered and then slowly pour it into the Büchner or Hirsch funnel at such a rate so that the filtration is rapid.** Note that the rate of filtration may slow as the 'cake' of solid on the filter becomes thicker.

11. **To transfer the last of the solid/liquid from its beaker or conical flask into the funnel use a little of the filtrate in the receiving flask.** Release the vacuum by opening the tap on the trap or pull off the vacuum tubing, but *do not turn off the tap on the water pump* (there is a possibility of 'suck-back' (see **9** above)). Dismantle the apparatus, pour a little of the filtrate into the beaker or conical flask, reassemble the apparatus and continue the filtration. Repeat until all the material has been filtered. Use the filtrate to wash down any of the solid sticking to the sides of the funnel onto the filter 'cake' – it will not dry quickly on the sides of the funnel.

12. **Release the vacuum, by pulling the vacuum tubing from the flask or opening the tap on the trap and turn down the water pressure on the water pump.** Transfer the filtrate to a clean beaker or conical flask. Add a little pure, ice-cold solvent to the filter cake and reconnect the vacuum to provide gentle suction. This will wash the solid. Turn up the vacuum to maximum and suck air through the solid to dry it as much as possible. If 'cracks' appear in the filter 'cake', close them by pressing gently with a clean spatula and repeat until no more filtrate appears to be sucked out.

13. **When drying is complete, release the vacuum, turn off the water tap and remove the filter funnel from the apparatus.** The solid is best removed as a complete 'cake' by lifting the edge of the filter paper with spatula, inverting the funnel over a watch-glass or clock-glass and the cake should fall out. Peel the filter from the top of the 'cake', break up the 'cake' using a spatula and dry it appropriately.

14. **Evaporate the filtrate to half volume (see p. 271)** and cool to obtain a second crop of crystals.

15. **Wash out and clean all the apparatus and dispose of the liquid filtrate safely.**

Sintered-glass funnels – *never* use a sintered-glass funnel to remove finely divided charcoal. It is *always* absorbed into the pores of the sinter and almost impossible to remove easily.

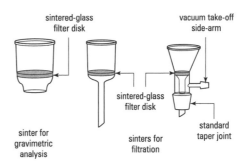

Fig. 24.8 Typical sintered-glass funnels.

Removing charcoal from a cold solution by suction filtration – cover the filter paper with a 'filter aid' such as Celite®. This absorbs the fine particles.

SAFETY NOTE *Never* use gas burners to heat flammable chemicals in open containers, in particular solvents, which are usually used in relatively large volumes.

SAFETY POINT *Before you start heating* a liquid or solution you must *always* take *one* of the following 'anti-bumping' precautions:

- Add one or two 'boiling stones' or 'anti-bumping granules'; these can be filtered off later in the process.

- Add a Pyrex® glass rod to the beaker or conical flask. The rod must be longer than the container so that it can be removed and rinsed before the solution is used further.

- Add a 'boiling stick': these are thin pieces of wood sold as 'wooden applicators', but you must be sure that nothing will be extracted from the wood into your solution.

- Stir the liquid or solution with a magnetic 'flea' (see p. 174) which should be removed before further processing of the chemicals.

- Stir the liquid or solution with a mechanical stirrer (see p. 267).

- Use an air or inert gas (nitrogen) capillary bleed during vacuum distillation (see p. 258).

Instead of a filter paper on a porous plate, sintered-glass can be used as the porous material for filtration. Sintered-glass funnels come in various types and sizes (Fig. 24.8) with different porosity (size of holes) of the sintered glass. Sintered glass is also used in crucibles (Fig. 24.8) in gravimetric analysis (p. 294).

When sintered-glass funnels are used instead of Büchner or Hirsch funnels the solid is collected directly on the sintered glass: no filter paper is used. As a result cleaning sintered-glass funnels is a major problem if the solid has been drawn into the pores of the sintered-glass. Therefore if you are to use a sintered glass funnel, check with your instructor on the appropriate method for cleaning the funnel, before and after use, so that your product will not be contaminated. On the other hand, if particle sizes are large enough to prevent this problem, sintered-glass funnels are very effective in suction filtration.

Heating

In the laboratory you will be required to heat chemicals in dissolution of a solid, promotion of reaction (reflux), distillation of pure compounds and mixtures, extraction, coagulation of precipitates, drying solid compounds, etc. Your choice of heat source depends upon several factors:

- First and foremost, the *flammability* and *volatility* of the chemical and solvent.

- The operation to be carried out, e.g. simple preparation of a solution, reflux or distillation.

- The temperature required for the process.

- The amount of chemical or solvent to be heated.

Bumping

Before you attempt to heat any liquid or solution you must take precautions to prevent 'bumping'. This is when the liquid suddenly boils without any warning and results in hot liquid and vapour shooting uncontrollably out of the container. 'Bumping' can occur during simple heating in a test tube, conical flask or beaker or in more complex situations such as reflux and distillation. It is necessary to provide a point in the liquid or solution where vaporisation of the liquid can occur in a controlled manner.

Heating a test tube – you must 'wave' the test tube in the flame to prevent localised heating, which will cause the liquid to 'bump' out of the tube. Also use an appropriate anti-bumping device and make sure that the tube is not pointing at anyone.

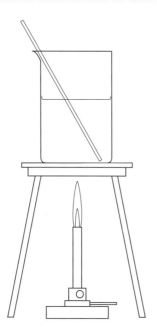

Fig. 24.10 Heating an aqueous solution using a Bunsen burner.

Tubing for gas burners – this must be of medium wall thickness so that it does not kink or compress easily. With thin-walled tubing, you could accidentally lean on the tubing, cutting off the gas supply, which extinguishes the burner. When you release the constriction, gas will then flow into the laboratory.

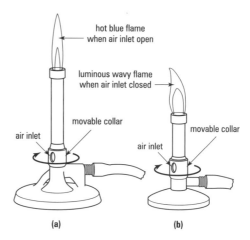

Fig. 24.9 (a) Bunsen burner; (b) microburner.

KEY POINT If you forget to take 'anti-bumping' precautions you MUST allow the liquid to cool down before you attempt the 'anti-bumping' process, otherwise the liquid will boil uncontrollably out of the flask.

Burners

Gas burners come in two common forms: large burners called Bunsen burners and small burners known as microburners (Fig. 24.9). Bunsen burners are commonly used for heating aqueous solutions in flat-bottomed Pyrex® vessels supported on a tripod and wire gauze (Fig. 24.10) but for many other heating applications Bunsen burners do not provide adequate control. Microburners may be used for direct heating of round-bottom or pear-shaped glassware in small-scale operations where good control of the heating rate is required, such as distillation or determination of melting point (see p. 233). When using a microburner for heating make sure that you do not create a 'hot spot', which may result in uneven heating of the liquid and 'bumping', by 'waving' the flame around the flask starting just below the level of the liquid and working down to the bottom of the flask and back again.

Microburners are also useful for heating boiling tubes and test tubes, sealing the ends of melting point tubes (see p. 235), making micropipettes for chromatography (see p. 376) and bending the ends of Pasteur pipettes for special purposes (see p. 260).

To use a burner, first make sure that the gas piping, is attached securely to both the burner and the gas tap, is of the correct type of rubber tubing, and is not damaged. Close the movable collar and light the gas with a gas igniter: do not use a splint or a piece of burning paper in case you cause a fire in the waste bin when disposing of the paper. Open the collar to produce a hot blue flame and adjust the gas flow to give the required size of flame. If your work is interrupted, close the collar a little to produce a luminous flame. Finally, when the operations are complete, turn off the gas and do not pick up the burner by the barrel, or put it into a cupboard, until it has cooled.

The advantages of the burner are that the heat source can be removed instantly from the apparatus and that the flame is visible: in

Do not confuse a *water bath*, which is a general-purpose heating device, with a *constant temperature bath*, which is a precision device used to control the temperature of the liquid in it (usually water, but not always) to within 0.5 °C.

Using a 'multiple hole' water bath – make sure all the other 'holes' are covered otherwise the steam will escape through them and heating your flask will be very slow.

Using hot plates – *never* wrap the power cable round the heating plate. It may be hot and melt the flex, exposing the wires.

contrast you often cannot distinguish between a cold and hot metal surface. The disadvantages are those of an open flame.

Steam baths and water baths

These are heat sources, which have a maximum temperature of 100 °C; they are safe to use even with most flammable chemicals and solvents and they differ only in the way the steam is produced.

Water baths are the more common of the two, and the steam is generated by heating water with an electric element – just like a kettle. The element may have a thermostatic control, which can control the temperature of the water to some extent. Most water baths have a constant level device on the side of the bath, which supplies water to the bath to a fixed level above the heating element and prevents the water bath from boiling dry. Water baths are 'single hole' or 'multiple hole' types, and the holes are covered by concentric metal or plastic rings, which allows you to vary the size of the hole.

When you are to use a water bath, make sure that water is flowing into and out of the bath via the constant level device – check that water is flowing from the pipe into the drain. Turn on the controller to the level you require – the power can be turned down once the bath is boiling.

A steam bath looks like the 'single hole' water bath except that there is no heating element and no constant level device. Steam baths require piped steam as their source of heat usually provided by a steam line, which is a permanent supply in the laboratory.

Beakers and conical flasks sit firmly on the rings, while round-bottom and pear-shaped flasks should have about half the surface of the flask immersed in the steam (Fig. 24.11).

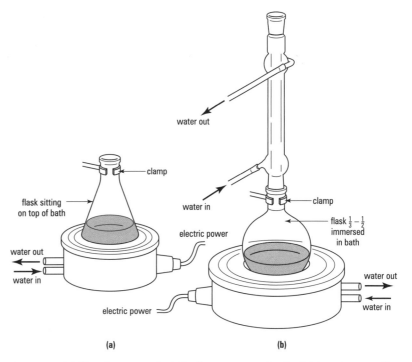

Fig. 24.11 (a) Heating a conical flask on a water bath; (b) heating a reflux set-up on a water bath.

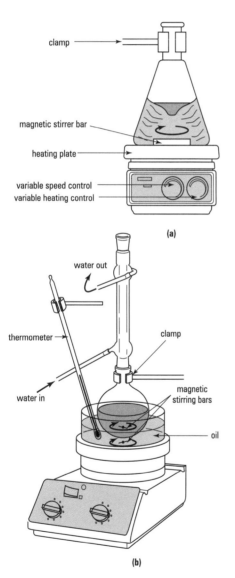

Fig. 24.12 (a) A stirrer hot plate. (b) Using a stirrer hot plate with an oil bath to heat a round-bottom flask.

The main advantage of a water bath is the minimal risk of fire, while the major disadvantages are the maximum temperature available (~100 °C) and the special precautions needed if anhydrous reaction conditions are required: remember that steam will condense down the *inside* of reflux condensers.

Hot plates and stirrer hot plates

These consist of a flat metal or ceramic plate, which is heated electrically, and varies in size for use by an individual or by several people at the same time. The small versions normally have a built-in magnetic stirrer, which can be used to stir the liquid with a magnetic 'flea'.

Hot plates of both types should only be used for heating flat-bottom vessels such as beakers or conical flasks and only when the liquid being heated is non-flammable. The vapour of a flammable liquid may 'run' down the outside of the vessel and ignite on the hot metal of the heating surface. Since the contact area between the heating surface and a round-bottom flask is very small, your attempts to heat these flasks effectively will require excessive temperatures of the heating surface, which increases the dangers due to lack of control of the heating process. Therefore round-bottom flasks should only be heated using an oil bath (below) or a mantle (p. 175).

The flat exposed heating plate is extremely dangerous when hot: *always* check that the plate is cool by passing your hand over the plate without touching it or by placing a drop of water on the plate. If you have to pick up a hot plate, hold it by the sides and do not touch the plate; it may burn. Typical uses of hot plates are illustrated in Fig. 24.12a.

Oil baths

These are mostly used to heat round-bottom flasks at temperatures above 100 °C. The oil bath, containing the heating fluid, is usually a non-ferrous metal or Pyrex® dish and heated on a stirrer hot plate, and the temperature of the bath is measured with a thermometer. The oil bath should never be more than half-full, to allow a margin of safety for thermal expansion of the oil, and stirred with a magnetic 'flea' to ensure even heating. The equipment used in a typical oil bath is shown in Fig. 24.12b.

The nature of the oil used in the bath depends upon the temperature range required and a selection of liquids is shown in Table 24.1.

You are most likely to encounter paraffin oil baths during your laboratory work and the following safety points should be considered:

• Paraffin oil discolours rapidly with prolonged heating. If the oil is dark, replace it with fresh oil. Dispose of the old oil in an appropriate manner (check with laboratory staff).

Table 24.1 Oil bath liquids

Material	Usable range (°C)	Comments
Paraffin oil (mineral oil)	0–200	Flammable, cheap, produces acrid smoke above 220 °C
Ethylene glycol	0–150	Flammable, cheap, low flash point
Polyethylene glycol 400	0–250	Water soluble
Silicone oil	0–250	Expensive
Glycerol	0–250	Water soluble

- Check that there is no water in the bottom of the oil bath: look for a separate layer or globules of liquid in the bottom of the bath. If you heat the bath above 100 °C, the water will boil and may spatter hot oil over you and the apparatus. Dispose of the contaminated oil into the appropriate waste container, clean the bath with paper towels to absorb the water and refill with fresh oil once *completely* dry.

- If the oil bath is a Pyrex® dish, check the dish carefully for cracks and 'star' cracks because you do not do want the dish of hot oil to break.

- Support the stirrer hot plate on a 'labjack' so that you can quickly remove the heat source if the reaction goes wrong (see mantles, p. 175).

- When the heating process is finished, allow the bath to cool and raise the flask, let the oil drain from it into the bath and then wipe the flask with a cloth or paper towel. Otherwise your hands, gloves, apparatus, compounds, etc. may become contaminated with oil.

Electric heating mantles

These are used for heating round-bottom flasks *only* and come in various sizes. Always used a heating mantle appropriate to the size of the flask you are going to heat, since you need to *control* the heating process. The flask should fit snugly into the mantle with the top half of the flask above the case of the mantle. If the mantle is too small, heating will be inefficient, whereas if the mantle is too big, the flask will be overheated and decomposition of the contents may occur.

Electric heating mantles comprise an electric heating element wrapped in a glass fibre covering, protected by an earth screen and enclosed in an aluminium or, more commonly, a polypropylene case to allow handling at moderate temperatures. Heating control is provided either by a regulator built into the heating mantle (Fig. 24.13a) or by an external controller, which is connected to the mantle by a plug.

Some mantles, 'stirrer mantles', have a built-in magnetic stirrer just like a stirrer hot plate and can be used to mix the liquid using a magnetic flea or bar (Fig. 24.13b). Stirrer mantles have *two* controls on the side: make sure that you know the function of each, since one controls the extent of heating and the other the stirrer speed.

When using mantles make the following safety checks:

- Make sure that the heating element is not damaged or worn. If in doubt consult your instructor and get a replacement.

- Plug in and test the mantle controls ensuring that both heater and stirrer are working. If fumes are given off from the heating elements someone has spilt chemicals into the mantle: switch off, report the fault to your instructor and obtain a replacement.

- Mantles are relatively slow to react to changes in the heater control setting and it is easy to 'overshoot' the desired temperature. Therefore always make small incremental changes in the heating control and if a temperature below the boiling point of the liquid is required, make sure that a thermometer is incorporated in the apparatus.

- When using a mantle with complex apparatus such as for distillation (p. 255), support the mantle on a 'labjack' so that it can be removed quickly if overheating occurs (Fig. 24.14).

> **SAFETY NOTE** *Never* connect an electric heating mantle, requiring an external controller, directly to the mains electricity supply.

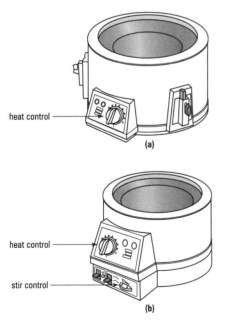

heat control

(a)

heat control

stir control

(b)

Fig. 24.13 Mantles: (a) heating mantle; (b) stirrer mantle.

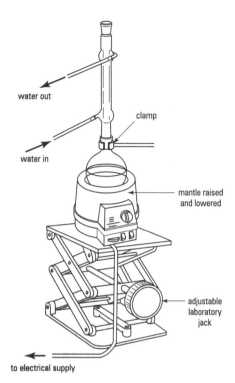

water out

clamp

water in

mantle raised
and lowered

adjustable
laboratory
jack

to electrical supply

Fig. 24.14 Heating using a stirrer mantle.

Fig. 24.15 Rubber 'fingers'.

SAFETY NOTE *Never* attempt to lift and manipulate a volume of liquid/solution that you cannot carry *easily*; if in doubt divide equally between two flasks.

- If the mantle is not equipped with a stirrer, remember to add anti-bumping granules (p. 171) to the liquid.

Hot-air guns

These can be used instead of Bunsen burners or microburners provided that the temperature required is not too high. The main uses of hot-air guns are for drying glassware and as a heat source for distillation of liquids at relatively moderate temperatures up to about 120 °C.

Hot-air guns produce heated air, usually at two temperatures, and cold air. As with a burner, the heat transferred to the flask being heated can be controlled by 'waving' the hot air stream around the flask (see p. 172).

Remember that the hot-air gun has a hot-wire heating element; therefore do not use it in the presence of flammable vapours. The nozzle of the hot-air gun will become very hot and can cause burns or even ignite some solvents for some time after it has been switched off. You should switch the gun to the cold-air mode for a few minutes after you have finished heating and place it in a 'holster' made from a support ring before finally turning off the gun.

Handling hot glassware

The safety precautions necessary for handling hot glassware depend upon:

- The temperature of the glassware.

- The type of glassware: test tube, beaker, conical flask, round-bottom flask, etc.

- The size of the glassware.

- The manipulation being carried out.

Normally you do not need any hand protection to handle glassware at temperatures up to 50 °C. For general-purpose work, such as removing glassware from the drying oven, assembling hot glassware and manoeuvring hot beakers and conical flasks to and from a burner, steam bath or hot plate, heat-resistant gloves are suitable and should be available in the laboratory. Where more intricate processes are required, such as hot filtration, then 'rubber fingers' made from medium-wall rubber tubing (Fig. 24.15) give adequate protection up to about 120 °C and are less cumbersome than insulated gloves. 'Rubber fingers' are useful for small volumes, up to 150 mL, of liquids when the flask or beaker can be easily held by one hand. If larger volumes are being manipulated then two hands are required and heat-resistant gloves are essential.

The following specific techniques should be noted:

- *Test tubes*: should be held by a wooden test tube holder (Fig. 24.16), which provides adequate insulation and grip. You should *never* use folded pieces of paper or metal tongs.

- *Conical flasks*: are often clamped to a support stand during heating and you should *never* attempt to use the clamp as a device to hold the flask when removed from the support stand. If you place the flask on the laboratory bench with the clamp attached it will fall over because of the weight of the clamp. Furthermore, you will have little control

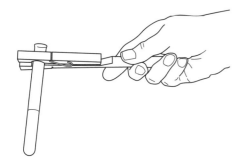

Fig. 24.16 Holding a test tube.

Cooling reactions – the heat from exothermic reactions is absorbed by the cooling medium, otherwise the reaction rate will increase rapidly with the rising temperature and may result in violent boiling or even explosion.

Controlling temperature – temperature control may be necessary to achieve the desired reaction. For example, chemicals may react to give different products at different temperatures.

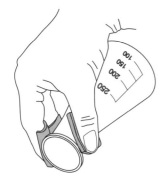

Fig. 24.17 Pouring a hot solution.

over the pouring process. Use 'rubber fingers' or an insulated glove and *never* use folded pieces of paper or metal tongs (Fig. 24.17).

- *Beakers*: these have specific problems since they have no narrow neck which can be gripped for lifting. Small beakers of volumes up to 400 mL capacity can easily be gripped in one hand protected by an insulated glove or 'rubber fingers'.

- *Round-bottom flasks*: small flasks of capacity up to 250 mL should be held at the neck, gripped in one hand protected by an insulated glove or 'rubber fingers' and when moving and pouring from larger flasks they should be held by the neck and supported underneath. Do not use a clamp round the neck of the flask as a support.

Cooling

During laboratory work you will be required to carry out experiments at temperatures below room temperature. The most common situations where cooling is required are:

- Cooling solutions during recrystallisation.

- Completion of precipitation in quantitative (gravimetric) analysis and preparations.

- Cooling exothermic reactions.

- Carrying out reactions at low temperatures.

There are three cooling media commonly used in the laboratory: crushed ice, solid carbon dioxide (Dry Ice®, Drikold®, Cardice®) and liquid nitrogen. You are unlikely to use liquid nitrogen in the undergraduate laboratory – if it is required you must consult your demonstrator about the special safety protocols required for its use.

The most suitable containers for cooling baths are plastic bowls (ice baths), Pyrex® dishes (solid CO_2 baths) and Dewar flasks (solid CO_2 and liquid nitrogen baths). If Pyrex® dishes are to be used below −20 °C, an insulated container can be prepared by placing a smaller Pyrex® dish inside a larger one and filling the space between with an insulating material such as cotton wool, cork chips or polyurethane foam chips. Remember that foam chips will dissolve if they come into contact with many organic solvents.

If the temperature of the liquid or solution being cooled is critical, *do not assume* that the temperature of the liquid or solution is the same as that of the cooling bath: place a thermometer in the flask and remember that for temperatures lower than −5 °C you should use an alcohol thermometer (red thread) or a thermocouple-type thermometer (after checking that the probe will not react with the contents of the flask).

Ice baths

A slurry of crushed ice and water can be used to give a cooling bath in the range 0 °C to 5 °C. Pure crushed ice does not give good contact with the glassware and inefficient cooling results.

If temperatures below 0 °C are required, mixtures of crushed ice and various inorganic salts can be used as shown in Table 24.2. Note that these mixtures contain no liquid and therefore cooling is inefficient and the temperatures indicated in the table are the lowest attainable under ideal conditions.

Table 24.2 Ice–salt mixtures

Salt	Ratio (salt : ice)	Temperature
$CaCl_2.6H_2O$	1 : 2.5	−10 °C
NH_4Cl	1 : 4	−15 °C
NaCl	1 : 3	−20 °C
$CaCl_2.6H_2O$	1 : 0.8	−40 °C

Solid CO_2 baths

Solid CO_2, when mixed with organic solvents, provides cooling media of temperatures ranging from −15 °C to −100 °C. Some common mixtures together with the minimum achievable temperatures are shown in Table 24.3. The CO_2 and the organic solvent form a 'slush', which gives excellent contact with flasks and, therefore, efficient cooling.

Table 24.3 Solid CO_2– solvent mixtures

Solvent	Temperature	Comments
Ethylene glycol	−15 °C	Ice/NH_4Cl cheaper
Acetonitrile	−40 °C	Toxic, flammable
Chloroform	−60 °C	Toxic
Ethanol	−72 °C	Flammable
Acetone	−78 °C	Flammable
Diethyl ether	−100 °C	Highly flammable

Solid CO_2 is supplied as large hard blocks or small quantities can be prepared from cylinders of liquid CO_2 as a 'snow'. Skin contact with solid CO_2 will cause frostbite and it *must* be handled with *insulated gloves*. The cooling bath must be an insulated container, which will need to be topped up with solid CO_2 at regular intervals to maintain the temperature, or, if prolonged cooling is required, a Dewar flask in which the coolant will maintain its temperature for 12 hours or so.

To prepare a solid CO_2 cooling bath:

- Choose the appropriate solvent and remember to take into account the hazards associated with its use.

- Break the solid CO_2 into small pieces. The CO_2 'snow' can be broken with a spatula, but the hard blocks should be wrapped in cloth and then broken into pieces with a wooden or polyethylene mallet.

- Half fill the bath with the solvent and then, using an insulated glove, add small pieces of the solid CO_2 until the mixture stops 'boiling' and then add a little more solid CO_2 and stir with a glass rod to give a slurry.

- Use an alcohol or thermocouple thermometer to check the temperature of the bath.

- Top up the cooling bath with solid CO_2 if the temperature begins to rise.

SAFETY NOTE If the cooling bath is more than half-full of solvent, it will 'boil' out of the bath as you add the first few lumps of solid CO_2.

> **KEY POINT** When using an internal thermometer to measure the temperature of a liquid or solution which is being stirred with a magnetic flea or stirring bar, ensure that the thermometer bulb does not come into contact with it.

To prevent the condensation of water into your flask, you should have an inert gas flowing through it (see p. 277) and prepare the cold bath around the flask and its contents so that slow cooling occurs. Sudden immersion of a relatively 'hot' flask into the cold bath will cause the bath to 'boil' and air (containing water vapour) will be sucked into the apparatus despite the inert atmosphere. Alternatively a 'loosely packed' $CaCl_2$ guard tube (see p. 266) will suffice if cooling is not too rapid.

Using cooling baths – remember that a cooling bath will condense water from the atmosphere and therefore lose its effectiveness over a period of time.

Cooling probes

These are rigid or flexible metal probes, which are connected to a refrigeration compressor. The probe is placed in the cooling bath and covered with a suitable solvent, which is then cooled to the temperature desired. Cooling probes are commonly found in constant temperature baths, when a temperature below ambient temperature is required, and probes can be used instead of solid CO_2 to produce temperatures down to $-100\,°C$. Cooling probes are expensive pieces of equipment; therefore you will find them dedicated to a specific experiment and they are not usually available for basic laboratory operations.

Drying

During your laboratory course it will be necessary to dry glassware, analytical standard compounds (see p. 300), chemicals you have synthesised, crucibles used in gravimetric analysis (see p. 295) and solvents. Drying solvents is described on p. 278.

Drying glassware

For most general laboratory applications glassware can be dried in an electric oven between $80\,°C$ and $90\,°C$ or by rinsing the glassware with a small amount of water-miscible solvent, such as acetone or ethanol, and then evaporating the solvent using a compressed-air jet. Remember to remove all plastic components, taps and stoppers from the glassware *before* you put it in the oven.

If glassware is required for anhydrous reactions, it must be heated in the oven above $100\,°C$, assembled while hot and allowed to cool while a stream of inert gas is passed through it (see p. 277).

Drying solids

Here the term 'drying' means removal of a solvent, not specifically water, from a solid by evaporation. The rate of evaporation and thus the rate of drying can be increased by one (or all) of the following:

- Heating the chemical.

- Using a drying agent in a closed container to absorb the solvent.

- Reducing the atmospheric pressure.

Only chemicals which are *thermally stable* should be dried by heating. Most inorganic compounds, which are salts with relatively high melting points, can be dried in an electric oven to remove water, whereas organic compounds, many of which have relatively low melting points, need to be treated with more care and the oven temperature should be set between $30\,°C$ and $50\,°C$ *below* the melting point of the chemical. Chemicals must be placed in the oven on a clock-glass or watch-glass and be spread as thinly as possible, to increase the rate of solvent evaporation.

If you cannot dry your compound in the oven, then use a *desiccator*. Desiccators are made from glass or plastic and some, vacuum desiccators, are equipped with a tap to allow evacuation as shown in Fig. 24.18. The bottom of the desiccator is filled with a drying agent (desiccant) and the chemical, on a watch-glass or clock-glass, is placed on the mesh shelf above and the desiccator closed by sliding the lid onto the desiccator to provide an air-tight seal. The desiccant absorbs the solvent from the

> **SAFETY NOTE** *Never* place chemicals in the oven on a piece of filter paper. If your chemical melts it will run through the paper and may contaminate the samples of fellow students. If it is on a watch-glass it may be recovered if it has not decomposed.

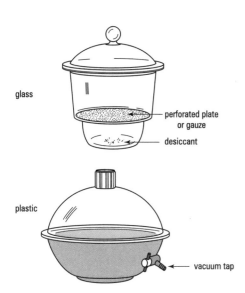

glass

perforated plate or gauze

desiccant

plastic

vacuum tap

Fig. 24.18 Desiccators.

SAFETY NOTE Using corrosive acids – P_2O_5 and concentrated H_2SO_4 should be avoided unless there is no suitable alternative. Consult your instructor for their disposal.

Table 24.4 Drying agents for desiccators

Solvent to be removed	Drying agent	Comments
H_2O	Silica gel	
	$CaCl_2$	
	solid KOH	Corrosive
	P_2O_5	Corrosive
	Conc. H_2SO_4	Corrosive liquid
EtOH, MeOH	$CaCl_2$	
Hydrocarbons	Paraffin wax	

'atmosphere' in the desiccator as it evaporates from the solid. The nature of the desiccant depends upon the solvent to be removed (Table 24.4).

The most common drying agents for removal of water are anhydrous $CaCl_2$ and self-indicating silica gel. The $CaCl_2$ should have the appearance of 'chalky' lumps. Self-indicating silica gel is blue in the 'active' state and pink when its capacity for water absorption is 'exhausted'. The water can be removed from the pink silica gel by heating in an oven above 100 °C and restoration of the blue colour indicates reactivation.

The rate of drying can be increased by evacuating the desiccator and vacuum desiccators are specially designed for this purpose. The principal steps for the use of a vacuum desiccator are as follows and it is essential that you follow the order of the operations:

- Check that the appropriate desiccant is present and active.

- Check that the desiccator seals perfectly: ensure that the ground-glass edges to the lid are greased lightly or, if the desiccator has a rubber gasket, carry out a trial evacuation to ensure that the vacuum seals the desiccator by gently pressing the lid onto the gasket – listen for air being sucked around the seal.

- Place the sample onto a watch- or clock-glass or a beaker covered with tissue paper (secure with an elastic band) and place it on the shelf.

- Place the lid on the desiccator and open the tap and cover the desiccator with an appropriately sized safety cage (Fig. 24.19) to prevent injury from flying glass in the case of an implosion.

Using vacuum desiccators – *never* switch off the vacuum supply before disconnecting the pipe from the desiccator since you will suck water or oil into the supply pipe (see p. 170).

Using vacuum desiccators – *never* disconnect the vacuum supply with the tap on the desiccator open. Air will rush into the desiccator and blow your dry compound around the inside.

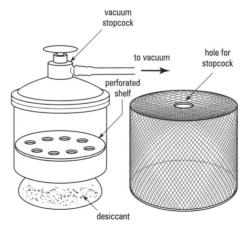

Fig. 24.19 Vacuum desiccator (with mesh safety cage).

Environmental note   Using water pumps for prolonged drying – this uses too much water: evacuate the desiccator, close the tap and disconnect and turn off the water pump. Check periodically that the vacuum is preserved using the filter paper technique. Re-evacuate if necessary.

Drying solvents – the drying agent used for solutions or pure liquids is not usually suitable for drying solvents for inert atmosphere reactions.

Molecular sieves are synthetic calcium and sodium aluminosilicates, which have 'holes' of specific sizes to allow the absorption of molecules of similar dimensions. Types 3A and 4A, with 0.3 nm and 0.4 nm pores respectively, are used for drying.

Drying solutions and liquids – note that phrases such as 'drying *over* magnesium sulphate' mean that the $MgSO_4$ is *added* to the solution.

- Connect the tap to an operating source of vacuum: a water pump (p. 170) or vacuum pump (p. 258) and open the tap slowly to evacuate the desiccator.

- When drying appears complete, close the tap on the dessicator and then disconnect the vacuum supply.

- Place a small piece of filter paper on the end of the tap and open the tap slowly. The filter paper will stick to the tap as air is drawn slowly through it. When the air has completely filled the desiccator, the filter paper will fall off and it is safe to open the desiccator.

If you need to heat the compound under vacuum, then you will need to use a vacuum oven (for large quantities of solids). The principles of operation of these pieces of equipment are similar to those of a vacuum desiccator, except that an electric heater is incorporated. Always allow the apparatus to cool to room temperature before releasing the vacuum.

Drying liquids

This usually means removing water from a liquid chemical or a solution of a chemical in a water-immiscible solvent. You will always need to dry solutions after a liquid–liquid extraction (p. 249) and you may need to dry liquids after evaporation (p. 271) or distillation (p. 255). In both cases the liquid is placed in direct contact with the solid drying agent, i.e. the drying agent is added to the liquid or solution. Ideally the drying agent should be totally insoluble in the liquid, should not react with it, absorb the water quickly and efficiently, and be easily filtered off. A list of the common drying agents is given in Table 24.5.

You must remember that the drying agent will absorb some of the liquid or solvent being dried as well as the water. If you wish to dry a small volume of liquid, it is better to dissolve it in a low-boiling water-immiscible solvent and dry the solution by the procedure described in Box 24.3.

Table 24.5   Drying agents for liquids and solutions

Drying agent	Capacity	Speed	Efficiency	Comments
$MgSO_4$	High	Fast	Good	Best general use
Na_2SO_4	High	Slow	Poor	Useful
$CaCl_2$	High	Slow	Poor	Reacts with O and N compounds
$CaSO_4$	Low	Fast	Good	Useful
K_2CO_3	High	Fast	Good	Reacts with acidic compounds
Molecular sieve*	Moderate	Fast	Good	Must be activated at 300 °C

Capacity: amount of water taken up.

Speed: rate of water absorption.

Efficiency: extent of drying after treatment.

*Do not throw away. Can be regenerated by heating >300 °C.

Jointed glassware

This type of glassware, commonly known as Quickfit®, comprises a complete range of components fitted with standard-taper ground-glass joints. The joints are fully interchangeable with those of the same size and apparatus for a whole range of experiments can be assembled from

---

Box 24.3 How to dry a solution over magnesium sulphate

1. **Place the solution to be dried in a clean, dry conical flask.** The flask should not be more than half-full.

2. **Add small quantities of MgSO$_4$ (between 0.1 g and 1.0 g depending upon the volume of solvent) and swirl the conical flask between each addition.** At first the MgSO$_4$ will 'stick' to the sides and bottom of the flask where it contacts with the water, but on further additions it will eventually form a free-flowing powder in the liquid and the solution will appear very clear and bright.

3. **Allow the mixture to stand for 10 minutes.**

4. **Gravity filter the dried solvent layer through a fluted filter paper into a clean, dry flask.** The fluted filter paper should contain a small amount of fresh MgSO$_4$, as a safety precaution, in case a few drops of water are floating in the surface of a denser solvent than water.

5. **Rinse the MgSO$_4$ in the conical flask with a few millilitres of pure dry solvent and filter it,** to ensure that you recover all the solute, and then rinse the MgSO$_4$ on the filter paper.

6. **Remove the solvent** by rotary evaporation (p. 271) or distillation (p. 255).

---

the simple components without the need to use rubber bungs, corks, etc. Where there is a mismatch between the sizes of the joints of the pieces of glassware, reduction and expansion adapters can be used. A typical range of jointed glassware is illustrated in Fig. 24.20.

The ground-glass joint on the glassware is classified according to the diameter of the joint at its widest point (internal diameter) and the length of the ground-glass portion of the joint. Thus a 14/23 joint has a maximum internal diameter of 14 mm and a length of 23 mm. Other common joint sizes you will frequently encounter are 19/26, 24/29 and 35/39. The joint size is always etched into glass on the side of or near to the joint. For obvious reasons, joints are categorised as 'female' and 'male'.

Care of jointed glassware

Jointed glassware is much more expensive than ordinary glassware because of the precision required in fabricating the joints. If the joints 'seize' and cannot be separated the glassware cannot be used again and you may have the problem of a stoppered flask containing a volatile organic solvent, which somebody has to open! If this happens, consult your instructor for help and further advice.

There are two main causes of 'seized' joints:

1. Using solutions of potassium hydroxide or sodium hydroxide in water or other solvents, which attack the glass.

2. Trapping chemicals, including solids and solutions of solids, in the ground-glass joints.

If you are using jointed glassware with strong alkalis (NaOH, KOH), you *must* grease the joints. In most cases a simple hydrocarbon-based grease, such as petroleum jelly, will suffice, since it is easily removed from the joints by wiping with a cloth wet with a hydrocarbon solvent (petroleum spirit, b.pt. 60–80 °C). Avoid silicone-based grease, since this is difficult to remove, soluble in some organic solvents and may contaminate your reaction products.

To grease a joint, put a small smear of grease on the *upper* part of the 'male' joint, push it into the 'female' joint with a twisting movement

---

SAFETY NOTE Do not attempt to use non-standard ground-glass joints in the standard jointware, it will not fit correctly. For example, ground-glass stoppers from volumetric flasks do not seal Quickfit® separatory funnels.

Greasing joints – you *must* grease all the joints when carrying out a *vacuum distillation*.

Separating joints – *always* separate ground-glass joints as soon as you have finished with the apparatus and wipe the joints clean.

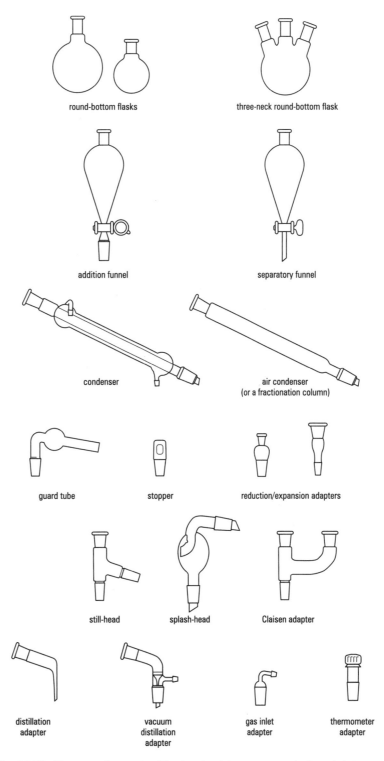

round-bottom flasks

three-neck round-bottom flask

addition funnel

separatory funnel

condenser

air condenser
(or a fractionation column)

guard tube

stopper

reduction/expansion adapters

still-head

splash-head

Claisen adapter

distillation
adapter

vacuum
distillation
adapter

gas inlet
adapter

thermometer
adapter

Fig. 24.20 Glass equipment with standard-taper ground-glass joints.

Environmental note If you break a piece of jointed glassware, *do not* throw the item into the broken-glass bin. The glass blower may be able to re-use it.

and the joint should become 'clear' from the top to about half-way down. If more than half the joint has become 'clear', you have used too much grease: separate the joints, clean with a solvent-soaked cloth and repeat the process.

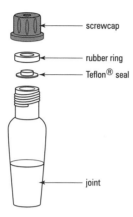

Fig. 24.21 The screwcap adapter.

screwcap

rubber ring

Teflon® seal

joint

To avoid trapping chemicals in the ground-glass joints, fill flasks etc. using a long-stemmed filter funnel or paper cone, which extends past the joint into the flask (see p. 164).

Screwcap adapters

Screwcap or thermometer adapters allow you to place thermometers, glass tubes or air bleeds into jointed glassware flasks. The screwcap adapter works by using the screwcap to compress a rubber ring round the thermometer or glass tube and thus hold it in place. The flexibility of the system allows the height of the thermometer/glass tube to be varied. The adapters come in different joint sizes and varying hole sizes to accommodate different-diameter thermometers, tubes, Pasteur pipettes, etc. The component parts of a screwcap adapter are shown in Fig. 24.21.

To use the screwcap adapter with a thermometer:

- *Always* disassemble the adapter to ensure that the rubber ring and the Teflon® seal are present. If they are missing, get replacements before use. The Teflon® seal is to protect the rubber ring from t and solvent vapours.

- Ease the rubber ring onto the thermometer (see p. 152) and slide the Teflon® seal on *below* the ring.

- Slide the screwcap over the top of the thermometer and then screw the whole assembly onto the base of the adapter and tighten the screw slightly, just enough to hold the thermometer.

- Trial fit the adapter and thermometer into the apparatus and adjust the height of the thermometer by loosening the screwcap and carefully sliding the thermometer up or down as required. When satisfied with the fit, re-tighten the screwcap.

- Check for final fit and tighten the screwcap firmly, but do not over-tighten.

Joint clips

Plastic joint clips or Keck® clips (Fig. 24.22a) are used for holding ground-glass joints firmly together and may be used to replace clamps and support stands at certain points when building apparatus (see p. 257)

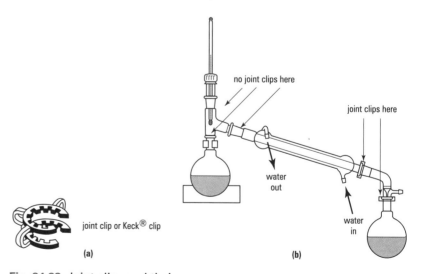

no joint clips here

joint clips here

water out

water in

joint clip or Keck® clip

(a)

(b)

Fig. 24.22 Joint clips and their use.

and are essential when using rotary evaporators (p. 272). The main weakness of these otherwise useful devices is that they soften at about 130 °C and this may allow the joints to separate. Therefore they should never be used at the 'hot end' of a distillation, for example. The clip should be used to hold a distillation adapter on the end of a water condenser, or the flasks onto a fraction collector, but *never* on the distilling flask or to hold the condenser onto the still head (Fig. 24.22b).

When using joint clips always:

- Check that you are using the appropriate size of clip for the joints being held. The clips are often colour coded.

- Check that the clip is not cracked or split.

- Check that the wide 'lower jaw' of the clip fits under the rim of the 'female' joint and the 'upper jaw' fits round the male joint.

- Support the joints with your hand as you push the clip into place. If in doubt use a protective insulated glove.

Sources for further study

Brown, T., LeMay, H., Bursten, B., Murphy, C., Woodward, P., Nelson, J. and Kemp, K. (2008) *Laboratory Experiments for Chemistry*, 11th edn. Prentice Hall, Harlow, Essex.

Furniss, B.A., Hannaford, A.J., Smith, P.W.G. and Tatchell, A.R. (1989) *Vogel's Textbook of Practical Organic Chemistry*, 5th edn. Longman, Harlow, Essex.

Harwood, L.M., Moody, C.J. and Percy, J.M. (1999) *Experimental Organic Chemistry*, 2nd edn. Blackwell Science Ltd., Oxford.

Mendham, J., Denney, R.C., Barnes, J.D. and Thomas, M.J.K. (2000) *Vogel's Textbook of Quantitative Chemical Analysis*, 6th edn. Prentice Hall, Harlow, Essex.

Pass, G. and Sutcliffe, H. (1979) *Practical Inorganic Chemistry*. Kluwer Academic Publishers, Netherlands.

Sharp, J.T., Gosney, I. and Rowley, A.G. (1989) *Practical Organic Chemistry*. Chapman and Hall, London.

Suib, S.L. and Tanaka, J. (1999) *Experimental Methods in Inorganic Chemistry*. Prentice Hall, Harlow, Essex.

Zubrick, J.W. (2007) *The Organic Chem Lab Survival Manual. A student's guide to techniques,* 7th edn. John Wiley & Sons Ltd, Chichester.

Study exercises

24.1 **Write down the apparatus you would need to carry out the following operations, giving your reasons:**

(a) Separation of a mixture of soil and water to allow you to measure the nitrate content of the soil. Remember, nitrates are water soluble.

(b) Isolation of solid, water insoluble *N*-phenylethanamide from the reaction mixture which comprises *N*-phenylethanamide and very dilute ethanoic acid.

(c) Removal of anti-bumping granules from a solution of *N*-phenylethanamide in hot water.

(d) Heating a suspension of *N*-phenylethanamide in cold water so as to dissolve it for recrystallisation.

(e) Heating a solution in toluene (b.pt. 111 °C, flammable).

(f) Cooling a reaction mixture to −10 °C.

Preparing solutions – practical advice is given on p. 154.

Definitions

Electrolyte – a substance that dissociates, either fully or partially, in water to give two or more ions.

Relative atomic mass (A_r) – the mass of an atom relative to $^{12}C = 12$.

Relative molecular mass (M_r) – the mass of a compound's formula unit relative to $^{12}C = 12$.

Mole (of a substance) – the equivalent in mass to relative molecular mass in grams. Note this is a pragmatic rule rather than a definition.

Do not confuse the solubility of a chemical with its strength as an electrolyte. Ethanoic acid is completely soluble with water in all proportions, yet it is a weak electrolyte because it is only partially dissociated. Barium hydroxide is very insoluble in water, but the small quantity which does dissolve (see K_s below) is dissociated completely into Ba^{2+} and OH^- ions; thus it is a strong electrolyte.

Expressing solute concentrations – you should use SI units wherever possible. However, you are likely to meet non-SI concentrations and you must be able to deal with these units too.

Example A 1.0 molar solution of NaCl would contain 58.44 g NaCl (the molecular mass) per litre of solution.

A solution is a homogeneous liquid, formed by the addition of solutes to a solvent. The behaviour of solutions is determined by the type of solutes involved and by their proportions, relative to the solvent. Many laboratory exercises involve calculation of concentrations, e.g. when preparing an experimental solution at a particular concentration, or when expressing data in terms of solute concentration. Make sure that you understand the basic principles set out in this chapter before you tackle such exercises.

Solutes can affect the properties of solutions in several ways, as follows.

Electrolytic dissociation

This occurs where a substance dissociates to give charged particles (ions). For a strong electrolyte, e.g. Na^+Cl^-, dissociation is essentially complete. In contrast, a weak electrolyte, e.g. ethanoic acid, will be only partly dissociated, depending upon the pH and temperature of the solution (p. 199).

Osmotic effects

These are the result of solute particles lowering the effective concentration of the solvent (water). These effects are particularly relevant to biological systems since membranes are far more permeable to water than to most solutes. Water moves across biological membranes from the solution with the higher effective water concentration to that with the lower effective water concentration (osmosis).

Ideal/non-ideal behaviour

This occurs because solutions of real substances do not necessarily conform to the theoretical relationships predicted for dilute solutions of so-called ideal solutes. It is often necessary to take account of the non-ideal behaviour of real solutions, especially at high solute concentrations (see Haynes (2010) for appropriate data).

Concentration

In SI units (p. 214) the concentration of a solute is expressed in $mol\,m^{-3}$, which is *essential* for calculating specific parameters for substances (e.g. p. 217), but which is *inconvenient* when dealing with solutions in the laboratory. A cubic metre (m^3) of water weighs approximately 1 ton! A common unit of volume used in chemistry is the litre (L): this is a non-SI unit and is converted to the SI unit of volume (m^3) using $1.0\,L = 10^{-3}\,m^3$. The concentration of a solute is usually symbolised by square brackets, e.g. [NaCl]. Details of how to prepare solutions are given on pp. 156, 158.

A number of alternative ways of expressing the relative amounts of solute and solvent are in general use, and you may come across these terms in your practical work or in the literature.

Molarity

This is the term used to denote molar concentration, [C], expressed as moles of solute per litre volume of solution ($mol\,L^{-1}$). This non-SI term continues to find widespread usage, in part because of the familiarity of working scientists with the term, but also because laboratory glassware is

Box 25.1 Useful procedures for calculations involving molar concentrations

1. **Preparing a solution of defined molarity.** For a solute of known relative molecular mass (M_r), the following relationship can be applied:

$$[C] = \frac{\text{mass of solute}/M_r}{\text{volume of solution}} \quad [25.1]$$

So, if you wanted to make up 200 mL (0.2 L) of an aqueous solution of NaCl ($M_r = 58.44$ g) at a concentration of 500 mmol L^{-1} (0.5 mol L^{-1}), you could calculate the amount of NaCl required by inserting these values into eqn [25.1]:

$$0.5 = \frac{\text{mass of solute}/58.44}{0.2}$$

which can be re-arranged to

$$\text{mass of solute} = 0.5 \times 0.2 \times 58.44 = 5.844\,\text{g}$$

The same relationship can be used to calculate the concentration of a solution containing a known amount of a solute, e.g. if 21.1 g of NaCl were made up to a volume of 100 mL (0.1 L), this would give:

$$[\text{NaCl}] = \frac{21.1/58.44}{0.1} = 3.61\,\text{mol L}^{-1}$$

2. **Dilutions and concentrations.** The following relationship is very useful if you are diluting (or concentrating) a solution:

$$[C_1]V_1 = [C_2]V_2 \quad [25.2]$$

where $[C_1]$ and $[C_2]$ are the initial and final concentrations, while V_1 and V_2 are their respective volumes: each pair must be expressed in the same units. Thus, if you wanted to dilute 200 mL of 0.5 mol L^{-1} NaCl to give a final molarity of 0.1 mol L^{-1}, then, by substitution into eqn [25.2]:

$$0.5 \times 200 = 0.1 \times V_2$$

Thus $V_2 = 1000$ mL (in other words, you would have to add water to 200 mL of 0.5 mol L^{-1} NaCl to give a final volume of 1000 mL to obtain a 0.1 mol L^{-1} solution).

3. **Interconversion.** A simple way of interconverting amounts and volumes of any particular solution is to divide the amount and volume by a factor of 10^3: thus a molar solution of a substance contains 1 mol L^{-1}, which is equivalent to 1 mmol mL^{-1}, or 1 μmol μL^{-1}, or 1 nmol nL^{-1}, etc. You may find this technique useful when calculating the amount of substance present in a small volume of solution of known concentration, e.g. to calculate the amount of NaCl present in 50 μL of a solution with a concentration (molarity) of 0.5 mol L^{-1} NaCl:

(a) this is equivalent to a concentration of 0.5 μmol μL^{-1};

(b) therefore 50 μL will contain $50 \times 0.5\,\mu$mol = 25 μmol.

The 'unitary method' (p. 495) is an alternative approach to these calculations.

calibrated in millilitres and litres, making the preparation of molar and millimolar solutions relatively straightforward. However, the symbols in common use for molar (M) and millimolar (mM) solutions are at odds with the SI system and many people now prefer to use mol L^{-1} and mmol L^{-1} respectively, to avoid confusion. Box 25.1 gives details of some useful approaches to calculations involving molarities.

Molality

This is used to express the concentration of solute relative to the *mass* of solvent, i.e. mol kg^{-1}. Molality is a temperature-independent means of expressing solute concentration, rarely used except when the osmotic properties of a solution are of interest (p. 190).

Example A 0.5 molal solution of NaCl would contain $58.44 \times 0.5 = 29.22$ g NaCl per kg of water.

Per cent composition (% w/w)

This is the solute mass (in g) per 100 g solution. The advantage of this expression is the ease with which a solution can be prepared, since it simply requires each component to be pre-weighed (for water, a volumetric measurement may be used, e.g. using a measuring cylinder)

Example A 5% w/w NaOH solution contains 5 g NaOH and 95 g water (= 95 mL water, assuming a density of 1 g mL^{-1}) to give 100 g of solution.

and then mixed together. Similar terms are parts per thousand (‰), i.e. $mg\,g^{-1}$, and parts per million (ppm), i.e. $\mu g\,g^{-1}$.

Per cent concentration (% w/v and % v/v)

For solutes added in solid form, this is the number of grams of solute per 100 mL solution. This is more commonly used than per cent composition, since solutions can be accurately prepared by weighing out the required amount of solute and then making this up to a known volume using a volumetric flask. The equivalent expression for liquid solutes is % v/v.

The principal use of mass/mass or mass/volume terms (including $g\,L^{-1}$) is for solutes whose molecular mass is unknown (e.g. polymers), or for mixtures of certain classes of substance (e.g. total salt in sea water). You should *never* use the per cent term without specifying how the solution was prepared, i.e. by using the qualifier w/w, w/v or v/v. For mass concentrations, it is often simpler to use mass per unit volume, e.g. $mg\,L^{-1}$, $\mu g\,\mu L^{-1}$, etc.

Parts per million concentration (ppm)

This is a non-SI weight per volume (w/v) concentration term commonly used in quantitative analysis such as flame photometry, atomic absorption spectroscopy and gas chromatography, where low concentrations of solutes are to be analysed. The term ppm is equivalent to the expression of concentration as $\mu g\,mL^{-1}$ ($10^{-6}\,g\,mL^{-1}$) and a 1.0 ppm solution of a substance will have a concentration of $1.0\,\mu g\,mL^{-1}$ ($1.0 \times 10^{-6}\,g\,mL^{-1}$). A typical procedure for calculations in terms of ppm is shown in Box 25.2.

Parts per billion (ppb) is an extension of this concentration term as $ng\,mL^{-1}$ ($10^{-9}\,g\,mL^{-1}$) and is commonly used to express concentrations of very dilute solutions. For example, the allowable concentration of arsenic in water may be 0.05 ppm, but it is more conveniently expressed as 50 ppb.

Activity (a)

This is a term used to describe the *effective* concentration of a solute. In dilute solutions, solutes can be considered to behave according to ideal (thermodynamic) principles, i.e. they will have an effective concentration equivalent to the actual concentration. However, in concentrated solutions ($\geqslant 0.5\,mol\,L^{-1}$), the behaviour of solutes is often non-ideal, and their effective concentration (activity) will be less than the actual concentration [C]. The ratio between the effective concentration and the actual concentration is called the activity coefficient (γ) where

$$\gamma = \frac{a}{[C]} \qquad [25.3]$$

Equation [25.3] can be used for SI units ($mol\,m^{-3}$), molarity ($mol\,L^{-1}$) or molality ($mol\,kg^{-1}$). In all cases, γ is a dimensionless term, since a and [C] are expressed in the same units. The activity coefficient of a solute is effectively unity in dilute solution, decreasing as the solute concentration increases (Table 25.1). At high concentrations of certain ionic solutes, γ may increase to become greater than unity.

Example A 5% w/v KOH solution contains 5 g KOH in 100 mL of solution. A 5% v/v glycerol solution would contain 5 mL glycerol in 100 mL of solution.

Note that when water is the solvent this is often not specified in the expression, e.g. a 20 % v/v ethanol solution contains 20 mL ethanol made up to 100 mL of solution using water.

Note that ppm may be a weight/weight (w/w) expression. The origin of the term ppm derives from a solution whose concentration is 1 ppm if it contains 1 g of solute for each million (10^6) g of solvent.

Table 25.1 Activity coefficient of NaCl solutions as a function of molality. Data from Robinson and Stokes (2002)

Molality	Activity coefficient at 25 °C
0.1	0.778
0.5	0.681
1.0	0.657
2.0	0.668
4.0	0.783
6.0	0.986

Box 25.2 How to convert ppm into mass of chemical required

Example: Suppose you are asked to prepare an aqueous solution of sodium ions (250.00 mL) of approximate, but accurately known, concentration of 10 ppm from either sodium chloride or anhydrous sodium carbonate.

1. **Convert the ppm concentration into $g L^{-1}$.** Thus 1.0 ppm $= 1.0 \times 10^{-6} g mL^{-1}$ and hence a solution of 10 ppm $= 10 \times 10^{-6} g mL^{-1} = 10^{3} \times 10 \times 10^{-6} g L^{-1} = 10 \times 10^{-3} g L^{-1}$.

2. **Convert the concentration from $g L^{-1}$ to $mol L^{-1}$.** The A_r for sodium ion is 23 g and for a litre of 10 ppm solution you need $10 \times 10^{-3} \div 23 = 0.435 \times 10^{-3}$ mol of sodium ions.

3. **Convert the number of moles per litre into moles in the volume required (250.00 mL).** Since 1.0 litres of 10 ppm solution of sodium ions requires 0.435×10^{-3} mol of sodium ions, then 250.00 mL (0.25 L) of solution will need $0.25 \times 0.435 \times 10^{-3}$ mol $= 0.1087 \times 10^{-3}$ mol of sodium ions.

4. **Calculate the mass of either sodium chloride or sodium carbonate required to make up the solution:**

   (a) Sodium chloride (NaCl), $M_r = 58.5$: therefore you need to weigh out $58.5 \times 0.1087 \times 10^{-3} = 6.359 \times 10^{-3}$ g of sodium chloride to be made up to 250.00 mL for a 10 ppm solution of sodium ions.

   (b) Sodium carbonate (Na_2CO_3), $M_r = 106$: you *must* note that each 'molecule' of sodium carbonate contains *two* sodium ions; thus the number of moles of sodium carbonate required for a 10 ppm solution of sodium ions is $0.1087 \times 10^{-3} \div 2 = 0.054\,35 \times 10^{-3}$ mol. You must therefore weigh out $106 \times 0.054\,35 \times 10^{-3} = 5.7611 \times 10^{-3}$ g of sodium carbonate to be made up to 250.00 mL for a 10 ppm solution of sodium ions.

5. **Decide how you are to prepare these solutions** using the procedures outlined in Boxes 23.1, 23.2 and 23.3, since the calculation shows that you will need to weigh out small masses of chemicals, which are at the limit of accuracy of an analytical balance.

Example A solution of NaCl with a molality of $0.5 \, mol \, kg^{-1}$ has an activity coefficient of 0.681 at 25 °C and a molal activity of $0.5 \times 0.681 = 0.340 \, mol \, kg^{-1}$.

KEY POINT Activity is often the correct expression for theoretical relationships involving solute concentration (e.g. where a property of the solution is dependent on concentration). However, for most practical purposes, it is possible to use the *actual* concentration of a solute rather than the activity, since the difference between the two terms can be ignored for dilute solutions.

Equivalent mass (equivalent weight)

Equivalence and normality are outdated terms, although you may come across them in older texts. The magnitude of an equivalent mass (equivalent weight) can be simply identified from the balanced equation for the reaction being considered. Remember that the equivalent mass can *change*, depending on the reaction, as the following reactions illustrate.

For:

$$HCl + NaOH \rightarrow NaCl + H_2O$$

1 mol of HCl reacts with 1 mol of NaOH, the equivalent mass of HCl is $M_r = 36.5$ and the equivalent mass of NaOH is also its $M_r = 40$.

For:

$$H_2SO_4 + 2NaOH \rightarrow Na_2SO_4 + 2H_2O$$

since 1 mol of H_2SO_4 reacts with 2 mol of NaOH, the equivalent mass of H_2SO_4 is $M_r \div 2 = 98 \div 2 = 49$, while the equivalent mass of NaOH is still $M_r = 40$.

For:

$$5FeSO_4 + KMnO_4 \rightarrow Fe_2(SO_4)_3 + 2MnSO_4$$

since 1 mol of $KMnO_4$ reacts with 5 mol of $FeSO_4$, then the equivalent mass of $KMnO_4$ is $M_r \div 5 = 158 \div 5 = 31.6$, and that of $FeSO_4$ is still $M_r = 152$.

But, for:

$$H_2SO_4 + Na_2CO_3 \rightarrow Na_2SO_4 + CO_2 + H_2O$$

since the reaction is 1:1, the equivalent masses of H_2SO_4 and Na_2CO_3 could be their M_r values, 98 and 106 respectively.

As a result of this possible confusion, the concept of equivalent mass (weight) is rarely used.

Normality

A 1 normal solution (1 N) is one that contains one equivalent mass of a substance per litre of solution. The general formula is:

$$\text{normality} = \frac{\text{mass of substance per litre}}{\text{equivalent mass}} \qquad [25.4]$$

The use of normality is now obsolete.

Osmolarity

This non-SI expression is used to describe the number of moles of osmotically active solute particles per litre of solution (osmol L^{-1}). The need for such a term arises because some molecules dissociate to give more than one osmotically active particle in aqueous solution.

Osmolality

This term describes the number of moles of osmotically active solute particles per unit mass of solvent (osmol kg^{-1}). For an ideal solute, the osmolality can be determined by multiplying the molality by n, the number of solute particles produced in solution (e.g. for NaCl, $n = 2$). However, for real solutes, a correction factor (the osmotic coefficient, ϕ) is used:

$$\text{osmolality} = \text{molality} \times n \times \phi \qquad [25.5]$$

If necessary, the osmotic coefficients of a particular solute can be obtained from tables (e.g. Table 25.2): non-ideal behaviour means that ϕ may have values > 1 at high concentrations. Alternatively, the osmolality of a solution can be measured using an osmometer.

Osmotic pressure

This is based on the concept of a membrane permeable to water, but not to solute molecules. For example, if a sucrose solution is placed on one side and pure water on the other, then a passive driving force will be created and water will diffuse across the membrane into the sucrose solution, since the effective water concentration in the sucrose solution will be lower. The tendency for water to diffuse into the sucrose solution could be counteracted by applying a hydrostatic pressure equivalent to the passive driving force. Thus, the osmotic pressure of a solution is the excess hydrostatic pressure required to prevent the net flow of water into a vessel containing the solution. The SI unit of osmotic pressure is the pascal, Pa $(= kg\,m^{-1}\,s^{-2})$. Older sources may use atmospheres, or bars, and conversion factors are given in Box 27.1 (p. 208). Osmotic pressure and osmolality can be interconverted using the expression 1 osmol kg^{-1} = 2.479 MPa at 25 °C.

Example Under ideal conditions, 1 mol of NaCl dissolved in water would give 1 mol of Na^+ ions and 1 mol of Cl^- ions, equivalent to a theoretical osmolarity of 2 osmol L^{-1}.

Example A 1.0 mol kg^{-1} solution of NaCl has an osmotic coefficient of 0.936 at 25 °C and an osmolality of $1.0 \times 2 \times 0.936 = 1.872$ osmol kg^{-1}.

Table 25.2 Osmotic coefficients of NaCl solutions as a function of molality. Data from Robinson and Stokes (2002)

Molality	Osmotic coefficient at 25 °C
0.1	0.932
0.5	0.921
1.0	0.936
2.0	0.983
4.0	1.116
6.0	1.271

Example A 1.0 mol kg^{-1} solution of NaCl at 25 °C has an osmolality of 1.872 osmol kg^{-1} and an osmotic pressure of $1.872 \times 2.479 = 4.641$ MPa.

The use of osmotic pressure has been criticised as misleading, since a solution does not exhibit an 'osmotic pressure' unless it is placed on the other side of a selectively permeable membrane from pure water!

Colligative properties and their use in osmometry

Several properties vary in direct proportion to the effective number of osmotically active solute particles per unit mass of solvent and can be used to determine the osmolality of a solution. These colligative properties include freezing point, boiling point and vapour pressure.

An osmometer is an instrument which measures the osmolality of a solution, usually by determining the freezing point depression of the solution in relation to pure water, a technique known as cryoscopic osmometry. A small amount of sample is cooled rapidly and then brought to the freezing point (Fig. 25.1), which is measured by a temperature-sensitive thermistor probe calibrated in $mosmol\ kg^{-1}$. An alternative method is used in vapour pressure osmometry, which measures the relative decrease in the vapour pressure produced in the gas phase when a small sample of the solution is equilibrated within a chamber.

Solubility

The extent to which a solute will dissolve in a solvent is called its solubility. The solubility of a chemical is conventionally expressed as the maximum number of grams of a chemical that will dissolve in 100 g of solvent but conversion to $mol\ L^{-1}$ or $g\ L^{-1}$ is simple and may be appropriate for some applications (see below). Since solubility is temperature dependent, is always quoted at a specific temperature. With a very few exceptions, increasing the temperature of a solvent increases the solubility of the solute.

Saturated solutions

For practical purposes, a saturated solution is one in which no more solute will dissolve. For example, the solubility of sodium chloride in water is 35.6 g per 100 g at 25 °C and 39.1 g per 100 g at 100 °C and both solutions are saturated solutions at their respective temperatures. If the 100 °C

Using an osmometer – it is vital that the sample holder and probe are clean, otherwise small droplets of the previous sample may be carried over, leading to inaccurate measurement.

Insolubility – no solute can be shown to be completely insoluble in a given solvent, but for practical purposes, a compound which has less than 0.01% (w/w) solubility in a solvent can be considered to be insoluble in that solvent.

Variation of solubility – the solubility of a chemical may vary in different solvents. For example, NaCl is soluble in water but insoluble in DCM whereas for naphthalene the opposite is true.

Saturated solutions – theoretically, a saturated solution is one in which the solution is in dynamic equilibrium with the undissolved solute.

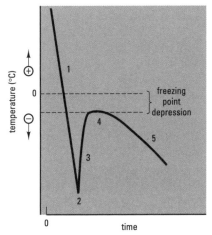

Fig. 25.1 Temperature responses of a cryoscopic osmometer. The response can be subdivided into:
1. initial supercooling
2. initiation of crystallisation
3. crystallisation/freezing
4. plateau, at the freezing point
5. slow temperature decrease

solution is cooled to 25 °C, then 3.5 g of NaCl crystals will precipitate from the solution, because the solution at 25 °C requires only 35.6 g of NaCl for saturation. This process is the basis of purification of compounds by recrystallisation (see p. 238).

Solubility product

In dilute aqueous solutions, it has been demonstrated experimentally for poorly soluble ionic salts (solubilities less than $0.01 \, \text{mol L}^{-1}$) that the mathematical product of the total molar concentrations of the component ions is a constant at constant temperature. This product, K_s is called the *solubility product*. Thus for a saturated solution of a simple ionic compound AB in water, we have the dynamic equilibrium:

$$\text{AB}_{\text{solid}} \rightleftharpoons \text{A}^+_{\text{(aq)}} + \text{B}^-_{\text{(aq)}}$$

where AB represents the solid which has not dissolved, in equilibrium with its ions in the aqueous saturated solution. Then:

$$K_s = [\text{A}^+] \times [\text{B}^-]$$

For example, silver chloride is a solid of solubility 0.000 15 g per 100 mL of water in equilibrium with silver cations and chloride ions. Then:

$$K_s = [\text{Ag}^+] \times [\text{Cl}^-]$$

The solubility of AgCl is $0.0015 \, \text{g mL}^{-1}$ (10 × solubility per 100 g, assuming that the density of water is $1.0 \, \text{g mL}^{-1}$) and therefore the solubility of AgCl is $0.0015 \div 143.5 = 1.05 \times 10^{-5} \, \text{mol L}^{-1}$. Thus the saturated solution contains $1.05 \times 10^{-5} \, \text{mol L}^{-1}$ of Ag^+ ions and $1.05 \times 10^{-5} \, \text{mol L}^{-1}$ of Cl^- ions and the solubility product K_s is

$$K_s = (1.05 \times 10^{-5}) \times (1.05 \times 10^{-5}) = 1.1 \times 10^{-10} \, \text{mol}^2 \, \text{L}^{-2}$$

If the solid does not have a simple 1:1 ratio of its ionic components, e.g. $PbCl_2$, then the solubility product is given by:

$$K_s = [\text{Pb}^{2+}] \times [\text{Cl}^-]^2$$

In general terms, the solubility product for a compound $M_y N_x$, is given by

$$K_s = [\text{M}^+]^y \times [\text{N}^-]^z$$

The practical effects of solubility products are demonstrated in the detection of anions and cations by precipitation (p. 289) and in quantitative gravimetric analysis (p. 294). For example, if dilute aqueous solutions of silver nitrate (solubility 55.6 g per 100 g of water) and sodium chloride (solubility 35.6 g per 100 g of water) are mixed, an immediate white precipitate of AgCl is produced because the solubility product of AgCl has been exceeded by the numbers of Ag^+ and Cl^- ions in the solution, even though the ions come from different 'molecules'. A saturated solution of AgCl is formed and the excess AgCl precipitates out. The solubility product of the other combinations of ions is not exceeded and thus sodium and nitrate ions remain in solution. Even if the concentration of Ag^+ is extremely low, the solubility product for AgCl can be exceeded by the addition of an excess of Cl^- ions, since it is the multiplication of these two concentrations which defines the solubility product. Thus soluble chlorides can be used to detect the presence of Ag^+ ions and, conversely, soluble silver salts can be used to detect Cl^- ions, both quantitatively and qualitatively.

Solubility – remember to use mass = volume × density when converting solubilities from grams of solute per 100 g of solvent to g L^{-1}, when using solvents other than water.

Reactions of ions in solution

There are essentially only four basic reactions of ions in solution:

1. Acid–base reactions.

2. Precipitation reactions.

3. Complexation reactions

4. Reduction–oxidation (redox) reactions.

Acid–base, precipitation and complexation reactions are all examples of exchange (metathesis) reactions in which ions in solution 'exchange partners', for example:

$$A^+Y^- + B^+Z^- \rightarrow A^+Z^- + B^+Y^-$$

Metathesis reactions are really equilibria between the ionic species, which are displaced to the right (to the reaction product) by a feature which defines the classification of the reaction type.

Acid–base reactions

The most common acid–base reactions are exemplified by the neutralisation reaction between hydrogen ions and hydroxide ions; for example, the reaction between dilute hydrochloric acid and dilute sodium hydroxide:

$$H^+Cl^-_{(aq)} + Na^+OH^-_{(aq)} \rightarrow H\text{-}OH_{(liq)} + Na^+Cl^-_{(aq)}$$

Since water is essentially a covalent compound (see p. 198) its formation effectively removes H^+ and OH^- from the equilibrium and drives the reaction to completion. Other examples of this general type of reaction include the removal of a molecule as a gas, such as reactions of acids with carbonates and bicarbonates, where unstable H_2CO_3 decomposes to H_2O and CO_2.

Precipitation reactions

In these reactions between ions, one substance is removed from the ionic equilibrium by precipitation (see solubility product, p. 192) and drives the equilibrium to the right (see p. 192).

Complexation reactions

A complex ion is formed by the reaction of a metal cation, in particular transition metals, with an electron donor molecule (ligand), which can be neutral or have a negative charge. The cation can accept an electron pair and the ligand donates an electron pair to form a covalent donor (co-ordinate) bond between the ligand and the metal ion. The ligands are said to co-ordinate with the metal ion to give a complex. Many ligands are more powerful electron donors than water and thus the addition of a ligand to an aqueous solution of a metal cation displaces the equilibrium towards the more stable complex ion (see p. 310 for stability constants and complexes). The effects of complex formation are illustrated in Box 25.3.

The overall effect of complex formation is to 'remove' a hydrated metal ion from the mixture of ions in solution by displacing the equilibrium in favour of the complex, cf. the similar process in the formation of water in acid–base titrations and precipitation reactions.

Box 25.3 An example of complex formation

If an aqueous solution of ammonia is added to an aqueous solution of copper (II) sulphate the following changes are observed.

A. On addition of the ammonia solution to the pale-blue copper solution a white precipitate forms.
B. As addition is continued, the white precipitate dissolves and a royal-blue solution is formed, which does not change on further addition of ammonia solution.

These changes can be explained as follows:

1. Ammonia solution is an equilibrium mixture, which lies well to the left. Consequently a dilute solution of ammonia contains a little OH^- and lots of free NH_3:

$$NH_3 + H_2O \rightleftharpoons NH_4^+ + OH^-$$

2. Copper (II) sulphate comprises the $Cu(H_2O)_4^{2+}$ ion and SO_4^{2-} ions in solution.

3. As the ammonia solution is added, the solubility product of $Cu(OH)_2$ is exceeded, even by the low concentration of OH^- ions and the white solid, $Cu(OH)_2$, precipitates from the saturated solution (see p. 192).

4. As addition of the ammonia solution is continued, the free NH_3 molecules displace the water molecules from the pale-blue $Cu(H_2O)_4^{2+}$ complex ion to form the royal-blue $Cu(NH_3)_4^{2+}$ complex, which is more stable than the water complex (larger stability constant).

5. Since the insoluble $Cu(OH)_2$ is in equilibrium with the $Cu(H_2O)_4^{2+}$, which is being removed as the $Cu(NH_3)_4^{2+}$ complex, the $Cu(OH)_2$ reverts to $Cu(H_2O)_4^{2+}$ which then forms the $Cu(NH_3)_4^{2+}$ complex. Thus the white precipitate dissolves leaving the royal-blue solution of the $Cu(NH_3)_4^{2+}$ complex.

Reduction–oxidation (redox) reactions

The concepts of oxidation and reduction are defined in terms of complete electron transfer from one atom, ion or molecule of a chemical to another:

- Chemical oxidised – chemical loses electron(s).

- Chemical reduced – chemical gains electron(s).

This approach is generally applicable to most reactions and avoids complications of the older definitions involving hydrogen and oxygen. You should realise that if a chemical is oxidised during a reaction, then another *must* be reduced: oxidation and reduction always occur together. Furthermore:

- Oxidising agent – gains electron(s) and is therefore reduced.

- Reducing agent – loses electron(s) and is therefore oxidised.

The following reaction between magnesium metal and dilute acid illustrates these concepts:

$$Mg_{(s)} + 2H^+_{(aq)} \rightarrow Mg^{2+}_{(aq)} + H_{2(g)}$$

Magnesium metal has lost two electrons in forming Mg^{2+} ions and has therefore been *oxidised*. The two protons have each gained an electron to form hydrogen atoms (and then one hydrogen molecule) and have been *reduced*. Since magnesium metal has been oxidised, it is a *reducing agent* and because H^+ has gained an electron, it is an *oxidising agent*.

The stoichiometry of a redox reaction is defined by the number of electrons transferred between the oxidising agent and the reducing agent since the number of electrons lost by the reducing agent *must* equal the number of electrons gained by the reducing agent, e.g.

$$2Mg_{(s)} + O_{2(g)} \rightarrow 2MgO_{(s)}$$

Box 25.4 The use of oxidation numbers to identify redox systems

The oxidation number is a hypothetical charge assigned to atoms in molecules and ions using a set of specific rules. Since redox reactions involve transfers of electrons, identification of the atoms which change oxidation number will show the atoms, ions or molecules which are specifically involved in the redox process.

Rules for oxidation numbers

1. **For an atom in its elemental form, the oxidation number is *always* 0.** Thus Cl in Cl_2 has an oxidation number 0, as does Na metal, and carbon in charcoal, graphite or diamond.

2. **For any monatomic ion, the oxidation number is the same as the charge on the ion.** Thus Na^+ has an oxidation number of +1, Cl^- is −1, Al^{3+} is +3, S^{2-} is −2, etc.

3. **Non-metals usually have negative values,** but there are some exceptions:

   (a) The oxidation number of fluorine is *always* −1 in *all* compounds.
   (b) The oxidation number of oxygen is always −2, except when bonded to fluorine (OF_2), in peroxides (O_2^{2-}), where each oxygen atom is −1 and superoxides (O_2^-), where each oxygen atom is $-\frac{1}{2}$.
   (c) The oxidation number of the other halogens is always −1, except when bonded to atoms of greater electronegativity, e.g. Cl in ClF_3 is +3, Br in BrCl is +1, etc.
   (d) The oxidation number of hydrogen is always +1, except when bonded to electropositive metals, when it is −1, e.g. in HCl it is +1 in NH_3 it is +1 and in NaH, MgH_2 and AlH_3 it is −1.

4. **The sum of the oxidation numbers of all atoms in a neutral compound is zero,** e.g. in $KClO_4$, K is +1

(rule **2**), four oxygen atoms, $4 \times -2 = -8$ (rule **3b**); therefore Cl must be +7 (rule **3c**).

5. **The sum of the oxidation numbers of all the atoms in a polyatomic ion is equal to the charge on the ion,** e.g. in CO_3^{2-} ion, each oxygen is −2 (rule **3b**); thus $3 \times -2 = -6$. Since the charge on the CO_3^{2-} ion is 2−, then carbon must be +4.

6. **If the oxidation number of an atom becomes more positive during the reaction**, it has lost electrons and has been *oxidised*.

   If the oxidation number of an atom becomes more negative during the reaction, it has gained electrons and has been *reduced*.

Example: If you consider the unbalanced equation for the reaction shown on p. 194:

$$KMnO_4 + H_2O_2 + H_2SO_4 \rightarrow MnSO_4 + K_2SO_4 + O_2 + H_2O$$

you can now calculate that the only atoms which have changed oxidation number are *manganese*, which has changed from +7 in MnO_4^- to +2 as Mn^{2+} in $MnSO_4$, and *oxygen*, which has changed from −1 in H_2O_2 (rule **3b**) to 0 in O_2. Thus Mn has gained electrons and been *reduced* and oxygen has lost electrons and been *oxidised*. Furthermore, the Mn atom has gained five electrons and the O_2^{2-} ion has lost two electrons so five molecules of H_2O_2 should react with two molecules of $KMnO_4$.

The two partial ionic reactions can now be identified:

For reduction $\quad MnO_4^- \rightarrow Mn^{2+}$

For oxidation $\quad H_2O_2 \rightarrow O_2$

and the equation balanced as shown in Box 25.5.

So that you can work out titrations involving redox reactions, you will find it necessary to balance redox equations, and while it is easy for simple reactions such as those above, more complex redox reactions, such as the one below, require more thought and work.

$$2KMnO_4 + 5H_2O_2 + 3H_2SO_4 \rightarrow 2MnSO_4 + K_2SO_4 + 5O_2 + 8H_2O$$

Such problems can be broken down into several simple steps, each with its own set of rules:

- Identify the atoms, ions or molecules which have been oxidised and reduced.

- Identify the ionic half-reactions for the species being oxidised and reduced and combine them.

- Balance the ionic half-reactions and combine them to give a balanced equation for the reaction.

The species which are oxidised and reduced can be identified using the concept of *oxidation numbers*. The rules for determining oxidation numbers and examples are given in Box 25.4 and the application of ionic half-reactions to balance redox equations is shown in Box 25.5. Note that the result of the use of partial ionic equations gives a balanced ionic equation for the redox reaction.

> **KEY POINT** In simple acid–base, precipitation and complexation reactions, no change of oxidation number occurs at any of the atoms involved.

Box 25.5 How to balance redox equations from partial ionic equations using the ion–electron method

Example: You are to produce a balanced equation from the partial ionic equations deduced in Box 25.4.

1. **Balance the atom which changes oxidation number** in each partial ionic equation:

$MnO_4^- \rightarrow Mn^{2+}$ no change necessary in either equation since Mn and O are balanced

$H_2O_2 \rightarrow O_2$ on each side of the equation

2. **Balance the oxygen atoms** on each side of each equation.
   (a) **If the reaction occurs in acid or neutral solution,** for each O atom deficient, add one molecule H_2O to the side deficient.
   (b) **If the reaction occurs in alkaline solution,** for each O deficient add *two* OH^- to the side deficient and one molecule of H_2O to the other.

   Your reaction occurs in acid solution, so:

   $MnO_4^- \rightarrow Mn^{2+} + 4H_2O$
   $H_2O_2 \rightarrow O_2$

3. **Balance the hydrogen** by addition of H^+ to the side deficient:

   $8H^+ + MnO_4^- \rightarrow Mn^{2+} + 4H_2O$
   $H_2O_2 \rightarrow O_2 + 2H^+$

4. **Balance the charge** on each side of the equation by the addition of electrons, each electron having a charge of -1:

$5e^- + 8H^+ + MnO_4^- \rightarrow Mn^{2+} + 4H_2O$
$H_2O_2 \rightarrow O_2 + 2H^+ + 2e^-$

5. **Balance the electrons in each equation**, since number of electrons gained by oxidising agent *must* equal number of electrons lost by reducing agent. Therefore multiply top equation by 2 and bottom equation by 5:

$10e^- + 16H^+ + 2MnO_4^- \rightarrow 2Mn^{2+} + 8H_2O$
$5H_2O_2 \rightarrow 5O_2 + 10H^+ + 10e^-$

6. **Add the equations together:**

$10e^- + 16H^+ + 5H_2O_2 + 2MnO_4^-$
$\rightarrow 2Mn^{2+} + 5O_2 + 10H^+ + 8H_2O + 10e^-$

7. **Cancel terms on opposite sides of the new equation:**

$6H^+ + 5H_2O_2 + 2MnO_4^- \rightarrow 2Mn^{2+} + 5O_2 + 8H_2O$

This *ionic equation* is sufficient to work out the mole ratio of the reacting species, i.e. 5 moles of H_2O_2 will react with 2 moles of MnO_4^-. All the other ions, K^+ and SO_4^{2-}, remain in solution and are unchanged by the reaction. If the fully balanced equation is required, the ions can be added to the ionic equation at the end of the process and the numbers adjusted:

$3H_2SO_4 + 5H_2O_2 + 2KMnO_4$
$\rightarrow 2MnSO_4 + 5O_2 + K_2SO_4 + 8H_2O$

Text references

Haynes, W.M. (ed.) (2010) *CRC Handbook of Chemistry and Physics*, 91st edn. CRC Press, Boca Raton.

Robinson, R.A. and Stokes, R.H. (2002) *Electrolyte Solutions*. Dover Publications, New York.

Sources for further study

Burrows, A., Holman, J., Parsons, A., Pilling, G. and Price, G. (2009) *Chemistry3: Inorganic, Organic and Physical Chemistry*. Oxford University Press.

Mendham, J., Denney, R.C., Barnes, J.D. and Thomas, M.J.K. (2000) *Vogel's Textbook of Quantitative Chemical Analysis*, 6th edn. Prentice Hall, Harlow, Essex.

O'Neil, M.J., Smith, A. and Henkelmann, P.E. (2006) *The Merck Index: An Encyclopaedia of Chemicals, Drugs and Biologicals*, 14th edn. Merck & Co. Inc., Whitehouse Station.

Study exercises

25.1 Practise calculations involving molar concentrations (see also study exercises 23.1 and 23.2). What mass of substance would be required to prepare each of the following aqueous solutions (answer in grams, to four decimal places in each case):

(a) 1000.00 mL of 1.0 M sodium chloride solution?

(b) 250.00 mL of 0.2004 M $KMnO_4$ solution?

(c) 400 mL of sodium hydroxide at 5% w/v?

(d) 300 mL of potassium nitrate at 10% w/w?

25.2 Practise expressing concentrations in different ways. Express all answers to four decimal places.

(a) What is 4.000 g L^{-1} sodium hydroxide expressed in terms of molarity?

(b) What is 0.1 mol L^{-1} $K_2Cr_2O_7$ expressed in g L^{-1}?

(c) What is 5% v/v ethanol, expressed in terms of molarity? (Density of ethanol at 25 °C = 0.7892 g mL^{-1}).

(d) What is 150 mmol L^{-1} glucose expressed in terms of per cent concentration (% w/v)?

25.3 Using the concepts of 'oxidation numbers' and 'partial ionic equations', balance the following redox reactions which all take place in acid solution.

(a) $K_2Cr_2O_7 + FeSO_4 + H_2SO_4$
$\rightarrow Cr_2(SO_4)_3 + Fe_2(SO_4)_3 + K_2SO_4 + H_2O$

(b) $Na_2S_2O_3 + I_2 \rightarrow Na_2S_4O_6 + NaI$

(c) $KIO_3 + KI + H_2SO_4 \rightarrow K_2SO_4 + I_2 + H_2O$

(d) $(COOH)_2 + KMnO_4 + H_2SO_4$
$\rightarrow K_2SO_4 + MnSO_4 + CO_2 + H_2O$

pH is a measure of the amount of hydrogen ions (H^+) in a solution. It is usual to think of aqueous solutions as containing H^+ ions (protons), though protons actually exist in their hydrated form, as hydronium ions (H_3O^+). The proton concentration of an aqueous solution $[H^+]$ is affected by several factors:

Definitions

Acid – a compound that acts as a proton donor in aqueous solution.

Base – a compound that acts as a proton acceptor in aqueous solution.

Conjugate pair – an acid together with its corresponding base.

Alkali – a compound that liberates hydroxyl ions when it dissociates. Since hydroxyl ions are strongly basic, this will reduce the proton concentration.

Ampholyte – a compound that can act as both an acid and a base. Water is an ampholyte since it may dissociate to give a proton and a hydroxyl ion (amphoteric behaviour).

- Ionisation (dissociation) of water, which liberates protons and hydroxyl ions in equal quantities, according to the reversible relationship:

$$H_2O \rightleftharpoons H^+ + OH^- \qquad [26.1]$$

- Dissociation of acids, according to the equation:

$$H\text{–}A \rightleftharpoons H^+ + A^- \qquad [26.2]$$

where H–A represents the acid and A^- is the corresponding conjugate base. The dissociation of an acid in water will increase the amount of protons, reducing the amount of hydroxyl ions as water molecules are formed (eqn [26.1]). The addition of a base (usually, as its salt) to water will decrease the amount of H^+, owing to the formation of the conjugate acid (eqn [26.2]).

- Dissociation of alkalis, according to the relationship:

$$X^+OH^- \rightleftharpoons X^+ + OH^- \qquad [26.3]$$

where X^+OH^- represents the undissociated alkali. Since the dissociation of water is reversible (eqn [26.1]), in an aqueous solution the production of hydroxyl ions will effectively act to 'mop up' protons, lowering the proton concentration.

Many compounds act as acids, bases or alkalis: those which are almost completely ionised in solution are usually called strong acids or bases, while weak acids or bases are only slightly ionised in solution (p. 186).

In an aqueous solution, most of the water molecules are not ionised. In fact, the extent of ionisation of pure water is constant at any given temperature and is usually expressed in terms of the ion product (or ionisation constant) of water, K_w:

$$K_w = [H^+][OH^-] \qquad [26.4]$$

Example The pH of 0.02 mol L^{-1} HCl can be calculated as follows: HCl is a strong acid giving $[H^+] = [Cl^-] = 0.02$ mol L^{-1}. Therefore pH $= -\log_{10}(0.02) = 1.7$.

where $[H^+]$ and $[OH^-]$ represent the molar concentration (strictly, the activity) of protons and hydroxyl ions in solution, expressed as mol L^{-1}. At 25 °C, the ion product of pure water is 10^{-14} mol^2 L^{-2} (i.e. 10^{-8} mol^2 m^{-6}). This means that the concentration of protons in solution will be 10^{-7} mol L^{-1} (10^{-4} mol m^{-3}), with an equivalent concentration of hydroxyl ions (eqn [26.1]). Since these values are very low and involve negative powers of 10, it is customary to use the pH scale, where:

Example The pH of a solution is 6.4. Therefore the $[H^+] = 10^{-pH}$, i.e. 3.98×10^{-7} mol L^{-1}.

$$pH = -\log_{10}[H^+] \qquad [26.5]$$

and $[H^+]$ is the proton activity (see p. 188).

Table 26.1 Effects of temperature on the ion product of water (K_w), H^+ ion concentration and pH at neutrality. Values calculated from Haynes (2010)

Temp. (°C)	K_w (mol² L⁻²)	[H^+] at neutrality (nmol L⁻¹)	pH at neutrality
0	0.11×10^{-4}	33.9	7.47
4	0.17×10^{-4}	40.7	7.39
10	0.29×10^{-4}	53.7	7.27
20	0.68×10^{-4}	83.2	7.08
25	1.01×10^{-4}	100.4	7.00
30	1.47×10^{-4}	120.2	6.92
37	2.39×10^{-4}	154.9	6.81
45	4.02×10^{-4}	199.5	6.70

KEY POINT While pH is strictly the negative logarithm (to the base 10) of H^+ activity, in practice H^+ concentration in mol L⁻¹ (equivalent to kmol m⁻³ in SI terminology) is most often used in place of activity, since the two are virtually the same, given the limited dissociation of H_2O. The pH scale is not SI: nevertheless, it continues to be used widely in chemistry.

The value where an equal amount of H^+ and OH^- ions are present is termed neutrality: at 25 °C the pH of pure water at neutrality is 27.0. At this temperature, pH values below 27.0 are acidic while values above 27.0 are alkaline. However, the pH of a neutral solution changes with temperature (Table 26.1), owing to the enhanced dissociation of water with increasing temperature. This must be taken into account when measuring the pH of any solution and when interpreting your results.

Always remember that the pH scale is a logarithmic one, not a linear one: a solution with a pH of 3.0 is not twice as acidic as a solution of pH 6.0, but a thousand times as acidic (i.e. contains 1000 times the amount of H^+ ions). Therefore, you may need to convert pH values into proton concentrations before you carry out mathematical manipulations (see Box 63.2). For similar reasons, it is important that pH change is expressed in terms of the original and final pH values, rather than simply quoting the difference between the values: a pH change of 0.1 has little meaning unless the initial or final pH is known.

Measuring pH

pH electrodes

Accurate pH measurements can be made using a pH electrode, coupled to a pH meter. The pH electrode is usually a combination electrode, comprising two separate systems: an H^+-sensitive glass electrode and a reference electrode which is unaffected by H^+ ion concentration (see Fig. 26.1). When this is immersed in a solution, a pH-dependent voltage between the two electrodes can be measured using a potentiometer. In most cases, the pH electrode assembly (containing the glass and reference electrodes) is connected to a separate pH meter by a cable, although some hand-held instruments (pH probes) have combination electrodes and meter within the same assembly, often using an H^+-sensitive field effect transistor in place of a glass electrode, to improve durability and portability.

Box 26.1 gives details of the steps involved in making a pH measurement with a glass pH electrode and meter.

pH indicator dyes

These compounds (usually weak acids) change colour in a pH-dependent manner. They may be added in small amounts to a solution, or they can be used in paper strip form. Each indicator dye usually changes colour over a restricted pH range (Table 26.2): universal indicator dyes/papers make use of a combination of individual dyes to measure a wider pH range. Dyes are not suitable for accurate pH measurement as they are affected by other components of the solution including oxidising and reducing agents and salts. However, they are useful for:

- estimating the approximate pH of a solution;
- determining a change in pH, e.g. at the end-point of a titration.

Table 26.2 Properties of some pH indicator dyes

Dye	Acid–base colour change	Useful pH range
Thymol blue (acid)	Red–yellow	1.2–6.8
Bromophenol blue	Yellow–blue	1.2–6.8
Methyl orange	Red–yellow	2.8–4.0
Congo red	Blue–red	3.0–5.2
Bromocresol green	Yellow–blue	3.8–5.4
Methyl red	Red–yellow	4.3–6.1
Litmus	Red–blue	4.5–8.3
Chlorophenol red	Yellow–red	4.8–6.3
Bromocresol purple	Yellow–purple	5.2–6.8
Bromothymol blue	Yellow–blue	6.0–7.6
Neutral red	Red–yellow	6.8–8.0
Phenol red	Yellow–red	6.8–8.2
1-Naphthol-phthalein	Yellow–blue	7.2–8.6
Phenol-phthalein	None–red	8.3–10.0

Box 26.1 Using a glass pH electrode and meter to measure the pH of a solution

The following procedure should be used whenever you make a pH measurement: consult the manufacturer's handbook for specific information, where necessary. Do not be tempted to miss out any of the steps detailed below, particularly those relating to the effects of temperature, or your measurements are likely to be inaccurate.

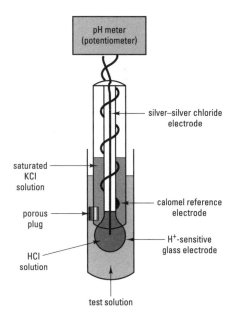

Fig. 26.1 Measurement of pH using a combination pH electrode and meter. The electrical potential difference recorded by the potentiometer is directly proportional to the pH of the test solution.

1. **Stir the test solution thoroughly before you make any measurement**: it is often best to use a magnetic stirrer. Leave the solution for sufficient time to allow equilibration at lab temperature.

2. **Record the temperature of every solution you use**, including all calibration standards and samples, since this will affect K_w, neutrality and pH.

3. **Set the temperature compensator on the meter to the appropriate value.** This control makes an allowance for the effect of temperature on the electrical potential difference recorded by the meter: it does *not* allow for the other temperature-dependent effects mentioned elsewhere. Basic instruments have no temperature compensator, and should only be used at a specified temperature, either 20 °C or 25 °C, otherwise they will not give an accurate measurement. More sophisticated systems have automatic temperature compensation.

4. **Rinse the electrode assembly with distilled water** and gently dab off the excess water onto a clean tissue: check for visible damage or contamination of the glass electrode (consult a member of staff if the glass is broken or dirty). Also check that the solution within the glass assembly is covering the metal electrode.

5. **Calibrate the instrument**: set the meter to 'pH' mode, if appropriate, and then place the electrode assembly in a standard solution of known pH, usually pH 7.00. This solution may be supplied as a liquid, or may be prepared by dissolving a measured amount of a calibration standard in water: calibration standards are often provided in tablet form, to be dissolved in water to give a particular volume of solution. Adjust the calibration control to give the correct reading. Remember that your calibration standards will only give the specified pH at a particular temperature, usually either 20 °C or 25 °C. If you are working at a different temperature, you must establish the actual pH of your calibration standards, either from the supplier, or from literature information.

6. **Remove the electrode assembly from the calibration solution and rinse again with distilled water**: dab off the excess water. Basic instruments have no further calibration steps (single-point calibration), while the more refined pH meters have additional calibration procedures.

If you are using a basic instrument, you should check that your apparatus is accurate over the appropriate pH range by measuring the pH of another standard whose pH is close to that expected for the test solution. If the standard does not give the expected reading, the instrument is not functioning correctly: consult a member of staff.

If you are using an instrument with a slope control function, this will allow you to correct for any deviation in electrical potential from that predicted by the theoretical relationship (at 25 °C, a change in pH of 1.00 unit should result in a change in electrical potential of 59.16 mV) by performing a two-point calibration. Having calibrated the instrument at pH 7.00, immerse in a second standard at the same temperature as that of the first standard, usually buffered to either pH 4.00 or pH 9.00, depending upon the expected pH of your samples. Adjust the slope control until the exact value of the second standard is achieved (Fig. 26.2). A pH electrode and meter calibrated using the two-point method will give accurate readings over the pH range from 3 to 11: laboratory pH electrodes are not accurate outside this range, since the theoretical relationship between electrical potential and pH is no longer valid.

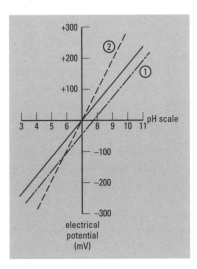

Fig. 26.2 The relationship between electrical potential and pH. The solid line shows the response of a calibrated electrode while the other plots are for instruments requiring calibration: 1 has the correct slope but incorrect isopotential point (calibration control adjustment is needed); 2 has the correct isopotential point but incorrect slope (slope control adjustment is needed).

7. **Once the instrument is calibrated, measure the pH of your solution(s)**, making sure that the electrode assembly is rinsed thoroughly between measurements. You should be particularly aware of this requirement if your solutions contain organic biological material, e.g. soil, tissue fluids, protein solutions, etc., since these may adhere to the glass electrode and affect the calibration of your instrument. If your electrode becomes contaminated during use, check with a member of staff before cleaning: avoid touching the surface of the glass electrode with abrasive material. Allow sufficient time for the pH reading to stabilise in each solution before taking a measurement: for unbuffered solutions, this may take several minutes, so do not take inaccurate pH readings due to impatience!

8. **After use, the electrode assembly must not be allowed to dry out**. Most pH electrodes should be stored in a neutral solution of KCl, either by suspending the assembly in a small beaker, or by using an electrode cap filled with the appropriate solution (typically $1.0\,mol\,L^{-1}$ KCl buffered at pH 7.0). However, many labs simply use distilled water as a storage solution, leading to loss of ions from the interior of the electrode assembly. In practice, this means that pH electrodes stored in distilled water will take far longer to give a stable reading than those stored in KCl.

9. **Switch the meter to zero (where appropriate), but do not turn off the power**: pH meters give more stable readings if they are left on during normal working hours.

   Problems (and solutions) include: inaccurate and/or unstable pH readings caused by crosscontamination (rinse electrode assembly with distilled water and blot dry between measurements); development of a protein film on the surface of the electrode (soak in 1% w/v pepsin in $0.1\,mol\,L^{-1}$ HCl for at least an hour); deposition of organic or inorganic contaminants on the glass bulb (use an organic solvent, such as acetone, or a solution of $0.1\,mol\,L^{-1}$ disodium ethylenediaminetetraacetic acid, respectively); drying out of the internal reference solutions (drain, flush and refill with fresh solution, then allow to equilibrate in $0.1\,mol\,L^{-1}$ HCl for at least an hour); cracks or chips to the surface of the glass bulb (use a replacement electrode).

Definition

Buffer solution – one which resists a change in H^+ concentration (pH) on addition of acid or alkali.

Potassium hydrogen phthalate (KHP) is the mono potassium salt of a weak organic dibasic acid.

Buffers

Rather than simply measuring the pH of a solution, you may wish to *control* the pH, during EDTA complexation titrations (see p. 310) or preparative experiments involving carbonyl compounds, and one of the most effective ways to control pH is to use a buffer solution.

A buffer solution is usually a mixture of a weak acid and its conjugate base. Added protons will be neutralised by the anionic base while a reduction in protons, e.g. due to the addition of hydroxyl ions, will be counterbalanced by dissociation of the acid (eqn [26.2]); thus the conjugate pair acts as a 'buffer' to pH change.

The British standard for the pH scale is an aqueous solution of potassium hydrogen phthalate (0.05 M), which has a pH of 4.001 at 20 °C and is often used as a calibration solution for pH meters.

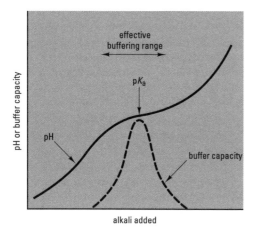

Fig. 26.3 Theoretical pH titration curve for a buffer solution. pH change is lowest and buffer capacity is greatest at the pK_a of the buffer solution.

Table 26.3 pK_a values at 25 °C of some acids and bases (upper section) and some large organic zwitterions (lower section) commonly used in buffer solutions. For polyprotic acids, where more than one proton may dissociate, the pK_a values are given for each ionisation step. Only the trivial acronyms of the larger molecules are provided: their full names can be obtained from the catalogues of most chemical suppliers

Acid or base	pK_a value(s)
Acetic acid	4.8
Carbonic acid	6.1, 10.2
Citric acid	3.1, 4.8, 5.4
Glycylglycine	3.1, 8.2
Phthalic acid	2.9, 5.5
Phosphoric acid	2.1, 7.1, 12.3
Succinic acid	4.2, 5.6
TRIS*	8.3
Boric acid	9.2
MES	6.1
PIPES	6.8
MOPS	7.2
HEPES	7.5
TRICINE	8.1
TAPS	8.4
CHES	9.3
CAPS	10.4

*Note that this compound is hygroscopic and should be stored in a desiccator.

Buffer capacity and the effects of pH

The extent of resistance to pH change is called the buffer capacity of a solution. The buffer capacity is measured experimentally at a particular pH by titration against a strong acid or alkali: the resultant curve will be strongly sigmoidal, with a plateau where the buffer capacity is greatest (Fig. 26.3). The mid-point of the plateau represents the pH where equal quantities of acid and conjugate base are present, and is given the symbol pK_a, which refers to the negative logarithm (to the base 10) of the acid dissociation constant, K_a, where

$$K_a = \frac{[H^+][A^-]}{[HA]} \qquad [26.6]$$

By re-arranging eqn [26.6] and taking negative logarithms, we obtain:

$$pH = pK_a + \log_{10}\frac{[A^-]}{[HA]} \qquad [26.7]$$

This relationship is known as the Henderson–Hasselbalch equation and it shows that the pH will be equal to the pK_a when the ratio of conjugate base to acid is unity, since the final term will be zero. Consequently, the pK_a of a buffer solution is an important factor in determining the buffer capacity at a particular pH. In practical terms, this means that a buffer solution will work most effectively at pH values about one unit either side of the pK_a.

Selecting an appropriate buffer

When selecting a buffer, you should be aware of certain limitations to its use. Citric acid and phosphate buffers readily form insoluble complexes with divalent cations, while phosphate can also act as a substrate, activator or inhibitor of certain enzymes. Both of these buffers contain biologically significant quantities of cations, e.g. Na$^+$ or K$^+$. TRIS (Table 26.3) is often toxic to biological systems: owing to its high lipid solubility it can penetrate membranes, uncoupling electron transport reactions in whole cells and isolated organelles. In addition, it is markedly affected by temperature, with a 10-fold increase in H$^+$ concentration from 4 °C to 37 °C. A number of zwitterionic molecules (possessing both positive and negative groups) have been introduced to overcome some of the disadvantages of the more traditional buffers. These newer compounds are often referred to as 'Good buffers', to acknowledge the early work of Dr N.E. Good and co-workers: HEPES is one of the most useful zwitterionic buffers, with a pK_a of 27.5 at 25 °C.

These zwitterionic substances are usually added to water as the free acid: the solution must then be adjusted to the correct pH with a strong alkali, usually NaOH or KOH. Alternatively, they may be used as their sodium or potassium salts, adjusted to the correct pH with a strong acid, e.g. HCl. Consequently, you may need to consider what effects such changes in ion concentration may have in a solution where zwitterions are used as buffers.

Fig. 26.4 shows a number of traditional and zwitterionic buffers and their effective pH ranges. When selecting one of these buffers, aim for a pK_a which is in the direction of the expected pH change (Tables 26.2 and 26.3). For example, HEPES buffer would be a better choice of buffer

Table 26.4 Preparation of sodium phosphate buffer solutions for use at 25 °C. Prepare separate stock solutions of (a) disodium hydrogen phosphate and (b) sodium dihydrogen phosphate, both at $0.2\,mol\,L^{-1}$. Buffer solutions (at $0.1\,mol\,L^{-1}$) are then prepared at the required pH by mixing together the volume of each stock solution shown in the table, and then diluting to a final volume of 100 mL using distilled or deionised water

Required pH (at 25 °C)	Volume of stock (a) Na₂HPO₄ (mL)	Volume of stock (b) NaH₂PO₄ (mL)
6.0	6.2	43.8
6.2	9.3	40.7
6.4	13.3	36.7
6.6	18.8	31.2
6.8	24.5	25.5
7.0	30.5	19.5
7.2	36.0	14.0
7.4	40.5	9.5
7.6	43.5	6.5
7.8	45.8	4.2
8.0	47.4	2.6

than PIPES for use at pH 27.2 for experimental systems where a pH increase is anticipated, while PIPES would be a better choice for where acidification is expected.

Preparation of buffer solutions

Having selected an appropriate buffer, you will need to make up your solution to give the desired pH. You will need to consider two factors:

1. The ratio of acid and conjugate base required to give the correct pH.

2. The amount of buffering required; buffer capacity depends upon the absolute quantities of acid and base, as well as their relative proportions.

In most instances, buffer solutions are prepared to contain between $10\,mmol\,L^{-1}$ and $200\,mmol\,L^{-1}$ of the conjugate pair. While it is possible to calculate the quantities required from first principles using the Henderson–Hasselbalch equation, there are several sources which tabulate the amount of substance required to give a particular volume of solution with a specific pH value for a wide range of traditional buffers (e.g. Perrin and Dempsey, 1974). For traditional buffers, it is customary to mix stock solutions of acidic and basic components in the correct proportions to give the required pH (Table 26.4). For zwitterionic acids, the usual procedure is to add the compound to water, and then bring the solution to the required pH by adding a specific amount of strong alkali or acid (obtained from tables). Alternatively, the required pH can be obtained by dropwise addition of alkali or acid, using a meter to check the pH, until the correct value is reached. When preparing solutions of zwitterionic buffers, the acid may be relatively insoluble. Do not wait for it to dissolve fully before adding alkali to change the pH – the addition of alkali will help bring the acid into solution (but make sure it has all dissolved before the desired pH is reached).

Finally, when preparing a buffer solution based on tabulated information, always confirm the pH with a pH meter before use.

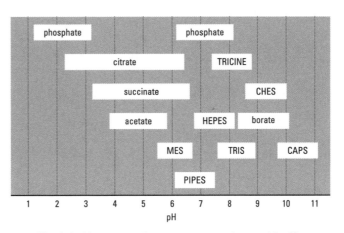

Fig. 26.4 Useful pH ranges of some commonly used buffers.

Text references

Haynes, W.M. (ed.) (2010) *CRC Handbook of Chemistry and Physics*, 90th edn. CRC Press, Boca Raton.

Sources for further study

Clark, J. (2000) *Calculations in AS/A Level Chemistry*. Longman, Harlow, Essex.

Galster, H. (1991) *pH Measurement: Fundamentals, Methods, Applications, Instrumentation*. Wiley, New York.

Radiometer (2006) *pH Theory and Practice: a Radiometer Analytical Guide*.

Perrin, D.D. and Dempsey, B. (1974) *Buffers for pH and Metal Ion Control*. Chapman and Hall, London.

Available: http://www.radiometer-analytical.com/all_resource_centre.asp?code=112 Last accessed 05/03/10.

Rilbe, H. (1996) *pH and Buffer Theory – a New Approach*. Wiley, New York.

Study exercises

26.1 Practise interconverting pH values and proton concentrations. Express all values to four significant figures.

(a) What is a pH 7.4 expressed as $[H^+]$ in mol L^{-1}?

(b) What is a pH 4.1 expressed as $[H^+]$ in mol L^{-1}?

(c) What is the pH of a solution of $[H^+]$ at 2×10^{-5} mol L^{-1}?

(d) What is the pH of a solution of $[H^+]$ at $2 \times 10^{-12.5}$ mol L^{-1}?

26.2 Practise using the Henderson–Hasselbalch equation. What are the relative proportions of the deprotonated (A^-) and protonated (HA) forms of each substance at the following pH values:

(a) ethanoic acid ($pK_a = 4.8$) for use in an experiment at pH 3.8;

(b) boric acid ($pK_a = 9.2$) for use in an experiment at pH 9.5;

(a) HEPES ($pK_a = 7.5$) for use in an experiment at pH 8.1?

The investigative approach

Working with discontinuous variables – note that while the original data values must be integers, derived data and statistical values do not have to be whole numbers. Thus, it is perfectly acceptable to express the mean number of children per family as 2.4.

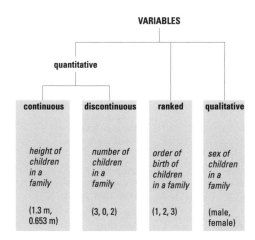

Fig. 27.1 Examples of the different types of variables as used to describe some characteristics of families.

The term data (singular = datum, or data value) refers to items of information, and you will use different types of data from a wide range of sources during your practical work. Consequently, it is important to appreciate the underlying features of data collection and measurement.

Variables

Variables (Fig. 27.1) can be classified as follows:

Quantitative variables

These are characteristics whose differing states can be described by means of a number. They are of two basic types:

- Continuous variables, such as length; these are usually measured against a numerical scale. Theoretically, they can take any value on the measurement scale. In practice, the number of significant figures of a measurement is directly related to the precision of your measuring system; for example, volumes a pipette beaker measured with *Vernier callipers* will provide readings of greater precision than a *millimetre ruler*. Many of the variables measured in sciences are continuous and quantitative, e.g. mass, temperature, time, amount of product formed by an enzyme.

- Discontinuous (discrete) variables; these are always obtained by counting and therefore the data values must be whole numbers (integers), with no intermediate values.

Ranked variables

These provide data which can be listed in order of magnitude (i.e. ranked). A familiar example is the abundance of an organism in a sample, which is often expressed as a series of ranks, e.g. rare = 1, occasional = 2, frequent = 3, common = 4 and abundant = 5. When such data are given numerical ranks, rather than descriptive terms, they are sometimes called 'semi-quantitative data'. Note that the difference in magnitude between ranks need not be consistent. For example, regardless of whether there was a one-year or a five-year gap between offspring in a family; their ranks in order of birth would be the same.

Qualitative variables (attributes)

These are non-numerical and descriptive; they have no order of preference and, therefore, are not measured on a numerical scale nor ranked in order of magnitude, but are described in terms of categories. e.g. the detection of the presence or absence of a chemical by a colour test or precipitate.

Variables may be independent or dependent. Usually, the variable under the control of the experimenter (e.g. time) is the independent variable, while the variable being measured is the dependent variable (p. 222). Sometimes it is inappropriate to describe variables in this way and they are then referred to as interdependent variables.

The majority of data values are recorded as direct measurements, readings or counts, but there is an important group, called derived (or computed), which result from calculations based on two or more data values, e.g. ratios, percentages, indices and rates.

Measurement scales

Variables may be measured on different types of scale:

- Nominal scale: this classifies objects into categories based on a descriptive characteristic. It is the only scale suitable for qualitative data.

- Ordinal scale: this classifies by rank. There is a logical order in any number scale used.

- Interval scale: this is used for quantitative variables. Numbers on an equal unit scale are related to an arbitrary zero point.

- Ratio scale: this is similar to the interval scale, except that the zero point now represents an absence of that character (i.e. it is an absolute zero). In contrast to the interval scale, the ratio of two values is meaningful (e.g. a temperature of 200 K is twice that of 100 K).

The measurement scale is important in determining the mathematical and statistical methods used to analyse your data. Table 27.1 presents a summary of the important properties of these scales. Note that you may be able to measure a characteristic in more than one way, or you may be able to convert data collected in one form to a different form. For instance, you might measure light in terms of the photon flux density

> **Example** A **nominal scale** for temperature is not feasible, since the relevant descriptive terms can be ranked in order of magnitude.
>
> An **ordinal scale** for temperature measurement might use descriptive terms, ranked in ascending order, e.g. cold = 1, cool = 2, warm = 3, hot = 4.
>
> The **Celsius scale** is an interval scale for temperature measurement, since the arbitrary zero corresponds to the freezing point of water (0 °C).
>
> The **Kelvin scale** is a ratio scale for temperature measurement since 0 K represents a temperature of absolute zero (for information, the freezing point of water is 273.15 K on this scale).

Table 27.1 Some important features of scales of measurement

	Measurement scale			
	Nominal	**Ordinal**	**Interval**	**Ratio**
Type of variable	Qualitative (Ranked)* (Quantitative)*	Ranked (Quantitative)*	Quantitative	Quantitative
Examples	Species Sex Colour	Abundance scales Reproductive condition Optical assessment of colour development	Fahrenheit temperature scale Date (BC/AD)	Kelvin temperature scale Weight Length Response time Most physical measurements
Mathematical properties	Identity	Identity Magnitude	Identity Magnitude Equal intervals	Identity Magnitude Equal intervals True zero point
Mathematical operations possible on data	None	Rank	Rank Addition Subtraction	Rank Addition Subtraction Multiplication Division
Typical statistics used	Only those based on frequency of counts made: contingency tables, frequency distributions, etc. Chi-square test	Non-parametric methods, sign tests. Mann–Whitney U-test	Almost all types of test, t-test, analysis of variance (ANOVA), etc. (check distribution before using, Chapter 64)	Almost all types of test, t-test, ANOVA, etc. (check distribution before using, Chapter 64)

*In some instances (see text for examples).

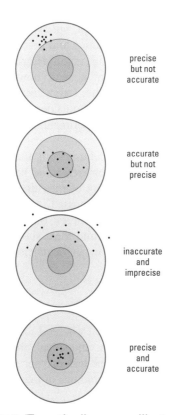

Fig. 27.2 'Target' diagrams illustrating precision and accuracy.

precise but not accurate

accurate but not precise

inaccurate and imprecise

precise and accurate

Minimising errors – determine early in your study what the dominant errors are likely to be and concentrate your time and effort on reducing these.

Working with derived data – special effort should be made to reduce measurement errors because their effects can be magnified when differences, ratios, indices or rates are calculated.

between particular wavelengths of the EMR spectrum (ratio scale), or simply as 'blue' or 'red' (nominal scale); you could find out the dates of birth of individuals (interval scale) but then use this information to rank them in order of birth (ordinal scale). Where there are no other constraints, you should use a ratio scale to measure a quantitative variable, since this will allow you to use the broadest range of mathematical and statistical procedures (Table 27.1).

Accuracy and precision

Accuracy is the closeness of a measured or derived data value to its true value, while precision is the closeness of repeated measurements to each other (Fig. 27.2). A balance with a fault in it (i.e. a bias, see below) could give precise (i.e. very repeatable) but inaccurate (i.e. untrue) results. Unless there is bias in a measuring system, precision will lead to accuracy and it is precision that is generally the most important practical consideration, if there is no reason to suspect bias. You can investigate the precision of any measuring system by repeated measurements of individual samples.

Absolute accuracy and precision are impossible to achieve, due to both the limitations of measuring systems for continuous quantitative data and the fact that you are usually working with incomplete data sets (samples). It is particularly important to avoid spurious accuracy in the presentation of results; include only those digits that the accuracy of the measuring system implies. This type of error is common when changing units (e.g. inches to metres) and in derived data, especially when calculators give results to a large number of decimal places. Further advice is given on p. 491.

Bias (systematic error) and consistency

Bias is a systematic or non-random distortion and is one of the most troublesome difficulties in using numerical data. Biases may be associated with incorrectly calibrated instruments, e.g. an electrode or syringe, or with experimental manipulations, e.g. decomposition of a chemical during storage. Bias in measurement can also be subjective, or personal, e.g. an experimenter's preconceived ideas about an 'expected' result.

Bias can be minimised by using a carefully standardised procedure, with fully calibrated instruments. You can investigate bias in 'trial runs' by measuring a single variable in several different ways, to see whether the same result is obtained.

To avoid personal bias, 'blind' measurements should be made where the identity of individual samples is not known to the operator, e.g. using a coding system.

Measurement error

All measurements are subject to error, but the dangers of misinterpretation are reduced by recognising and understanding the likely sources of error and by adopting appropriate protocols and calculation procedures.

A common source of measurement error is carelessness, e.g. reading a scale in the wrong direction or parallax errors. This can be reduced greatly by careful recording and may be detected by repeating the measurement.

Other errors arise from faulty or inaccurate equipment, but even a perfectly functioning machine has distinct limits to the accuracy and precision of its measurements. These limits are often quoted in manufacturers' specifications and are applicable when an instrument is new; however, you should allow for some deterioration with age. Further errors are introduced when the subject being studied is open to influences outside your control. Resolving such problems requires appropriate experimental design and representative sampling.

One major influence virtually impossible to eliminate is the effect of the investigation itself: even putting a thermometer in a liquid may change the temperature of the liquid. The very act of measurement may give rise to a confounding variable (p. 222), as discussed in Chapter 29. You should include descriptions of possible sources of errors and estimates of their likely importance in any report and these should not be used as a catch-all excuse for poor technique or inadequacies in your experimental design.

Collecting and recording primary data

When carrying out lab work or research projects, you will need to master the important skills of recording and managing data. Individual observations (e.g. laboratory temperature) can be recorded in the text of your notes, but tables are the most convenient way to collect large amounts of information.

- An accurate and neat record helps when using information later, perhaps for exam purposes or when writing a report.

- It allows you to practise important skills such as scientific writing, drawing diagrams, preparing graphs and tables and interpreting results.

- Analysing and writing up your data as you go along prevents a backlog at the end of your study time.

- You can show your work to a future employer to prove you have developed the skills necessary for writing up properly; in industry, this is vital so that others in your team can interpret and develop your work.

> **KEY POINT** A good set of lab notes should:
> - outline the purpose of your experiment or observation;
> - set down all the information required to describe your experimental section;
> - record all relevant information about your results or observations and provide a visual representation of the data;
> - note your immediate conclusions and suggestions for further experiments.

When preparing a table for data collection, you should:

1. Use a concise title or a numbered code for cross-referencing.

2. Decide on the number of variables to be measured and their relationship with each other and lay out the table appropriately:
   (a) The first column of your table should show values of the independent (controlled) variable, with subsequent columns for the individual (measured) values for each replicate or sample.

Understanding what's expected – especially when taking notes for a lab-based practical, pay special attention to the aims and learning objectives (p. 26) of the session, as these will indicate the sorts of notes you should be taking, including content and diagrams, and the ways in which you should present these for assessment.

Recording primary data – never be tempted to jot down data on scraps of paper: you are likely to lose them, or to forget what individual values mean.

(b) If several variables are measured for the same sample, each should be given a row.

(c) In time-course studies, put the replicates as columns grouped according to treatment, with the rows relating to different times.

3. Make sure the arrangement reflects the order in which the values will be collected. Your table should be designed to make the recording process as straightforward as possible, to minimise the possibility of mistakes. For final presentation, a different arrangement may be best (Chapter 60).

4. Consider whether additional columns are required for subsequent calculations. Create a separate column for each mathematical manipulation, so the step-by-step calculations are clearly visible. Use a computer spreadsheet (p. 87) if you are manipulating lots of data.

5. Use a pen to record data.

6. Take sufficient time to record quantitative data unambiguously – use large, clear numbers, making sure that individual numerals cannot be confused.

7. Record numerical data to an appropriate number of significant figures, reflecting the accuracy and precision of your measurement (p. 209). Do not round off data values, as this might affect the subsequent analysis.

8. Record the actual observations, not your interpretation, e.g. the colour of a particular chemical test, rather than whether the test was positive or negative. Take care not to lose any of the information content of the data: for instance, if you only write down means and not individual values, this will affect your ability to carry out subsequent statistical analyses.

9. Prepare duplicated recording tables/checklists for repeated experiments.

10. Explain any unusual results in a footnote. Don't rely on memory.

Recording details of project work

The recommended system is one where you make a dual record.

Primary record

The primary record is made at the bench and you must concentrate on the detail of materials, methods and results. Include information that would not be used elsewhere, but which might prove useful in error tracing: for example, if you note how a solution was made up (exact volumes and weights used rather than concentration alone), this could reveal whether a miscalculation had been the cause of a rogue result. Note the origin, type and state of the chemicals used. In the experimental section, the basic rule is to record enough information to allow a reasonably competent scientist to repeat your work exactly. You must tread a line between the extremes of pedantic, irrelevant detail and the omission of information essential for proper interpretation – better perhaps to err on the side of extra detail to begin with. An experienced

Designing a table for data collection – make sure there is sufficient space in each column for the values; if in doubt, err on the generous side.

Recording numerical data – write down only those numbers that can be justified by your measurement technique (significant figures).

Choosing a lab notebook – a spiral-bound notebook is good for making a primary record: it lies conveniently open on the bench and provides a simple method of dealing with major mistakes!

Analyse your data as soon as possible – always analyse and think about data immediately after collection as this may influence your subsequent activities.

- A graphical indication of what has happened can be particularly valuable.
- Carry out statistical analyses before moving on to the next experiment because apparent differences among treatments may not turn out to be statistically significant when tested.
- Write down any conclusions you make while analysing your data: sometimes those which seem obvious at the time of doing the work are forgotten when the time comes to write up a report or thesis.
- Note ideas for further studies as they occur to you – these may prove valuable later. Even if your experiment appears to be a failure, suggestions as to the likely causes might prove useful.

worker can tell you which subtle shifts in technique are important (e.g. batch numbers for an important chemical, or when a new stock solution is prepared). Many important scientific advances have been made because of careful observation and record taking and because coincident data were recorded that did not seem of immediate value. Make rough diagrams to show the arrangement of replicates, equipment, etc. If forced to use loose paper to record data, make sure each sheet is dated and taped to your lab book, collected in a ring binder, or attached with a treasury tag. The same applies to traces, printouts and graphs.

The basic order of the primary record should mirror that of a research report (see p. 126), including: the title and date, brief introduction, a comprehensive experimental section, the data and short conclusions.

Secondary record

You should make a secondary record concurrently or later in a bound book and it ought to be neater, in both organisation and presentation. This book will be used when discussing results with your supervisor, and when writing up a report or thesis, and may be part of your course assessment. Writing a second, neater version forces you to consider again details that might have been overlooked in the primary record and provides a duplicate in case of loss or damage. While these notes should retain the essential features of the primary record, they should be more concise and the emphasis should move towards analysis of the experiment. Don't repeat the experimental section for a series of similar experiments; use devices such as 'method as for Expt B4'. A photocopy may be sufficient if the method is derived from a text or article (check with your supervisor). Outline the aims more carefully at the start and link the experiment to others in a series (e.g. 'Following the results of Expt D24, I decided to test whether...'). You should present data in an easily digested form, e.g. as tables of means or as summary graphs. Use appropriate statistical tests (p. 510) to support your analysis of the results. Always analyse and think about data immediately after collecting them as this may influence your subsequent activities. Write down any conclusions: sometimes those which seem obvious at the time of doing the work are forgotten when the time comes to write up a report or thesis. Likewise, ideas for further studies may prove valuable later. Even if your experiment appears to be a failure, suggestions as to the likely causes might prove useful.

Using communal records

If working with a research team, you may need to use their communal databases. These avoid duplication of effort and ensure uniformity in techniques. They may also form part of the legal safety requirements for lab work. They might include:

- a shared notebook of common techniques (e.g. solutions or calibration technique);
- a set of simplified step-by-step instructions for use of equipment;

SAFETY NOTE **Maintaining and consulting communal lab records** – these activities may form a part of the safety requirements for working in a laboratory.

- an alphabetical list of suppliers of equipment and consumables;
- a list of chemicals required by the group and where they are stored;
- the risk assessment sheets for dangerous procedures (p. 143);
- a record of the use and disposal of chemicals and solvents.

Sources for further study

Anon. *Suggestions for Keeping Laboratory Notebooks*. Available: http://otl.stanford.edu/inventors/resources/labnotebooks.html Last accessed 01/07/09. [A Stanford University website which looks at the laboratory notebook from a patent perspective]

Beavon, J.R.G. *Writing the Laboratory Notebook*. Available: http://www.home.clara/rod.beavon/lab_book.htm Last accessed 01/07/09.

Milholland, R. *Guide to Keeping Laboratory Notebooks*. Available: http://www.niehs.gov/health/docs/guide-notebooks.pdf Last accessed 01/07/09.

Purrington, C. *Advice on Keeping a Laboratory Notebook*. Available: http://www.swarthmore.edu/NatSci/cpurrin1/notebookadvice.htm Last accessed 01/07/09.

Shuttleworth, M. (2008) *Choosing Scientific Measurements*. Available: http://www.experiment-resources.com/scientific-measurements.hmtl Last accessed 01/07/09.

Zubrick, J.W. (2007) *The Organic Chem Lab Survival Manual. A student's guide to techniques*, 7th edn. John Wiley & Sons Ltd, Chichester

Dimensionless measurements – some quantities can be expressed as dimensionless ratios or logarithms (e.g. absorbance and pH), and in these cases you do not need to use a qualifying unit.

When describing a measurement, you normally state both a number and a unit (e.g. 'the length is 1.85 metres'). The number expresses the ratio of the measured quantity to a fixed standard, while the unit identifies that standard measure or dimension. Clearly, a single unified system of units is essential for efficient communication of such data within the scientific community. The Système International d'Unités (SI) is the internationally ratified form of the metre–kilogram–second system of measurement and represents the accepted scientific convention for measurements of physical quantities.

Another important reason for adopting consistent units is to simplify complex calculations where you may be dealing with several measured quantities (see p. 489). Although the rules of the SI are complex and the scale of the base units is sometimes inconvenient, to gain the full benefits of the system you should observe its conventions strictly.

The description of measurements in SI involves:

- seven base units and two supplementary units, each having a specified abbreviation or symbol (Table 28.1);

- derived units, obtained from combinations of base and supplementary units, which may also be given special symbols (Table 28.2);

- a set of prefixes to denote multiplication factors of 10^3, used for convenience to express multiples or fractions of units (Table 28.3).

Table 28.1 The base and supplementary SI units

Measured quantity	Name of SI unit	Symbol
Base units		
Length	metre	m
Mass	kilogram	kg
Amount of substance	mole	mol
Time	second	s
Electric current	ampere	A
Temperature	kelvin	K
Luminous intensity	candela	cd
Supplementary units		
Plane angle	radian	rad
Solid angle	steradian	sr

Table 28.3 Prefixes used in the SI

Multiple	Prefix	Symbol	Multiple	Prefix	Symbol
10^{-3}	milli	m	10^{3}	kilo	k
10^{-6}	micro	μ	10^{6}	mega	M
10^{-9}	nano	n	10^{9}	giga	G
10^{-12}	pico	p	10^{12}	tera	T
10^{-15}	femto	f	10^{15}	peta	P
10^{-18}	atto	a	10^{18}	exa	E

Example $10\,\mu g$ is correct, while $10\mu g$, $10\,\mu g.$ and $10\mu\,g$ are incorrect; $2.6\,mol$ is right, but $2.6\,mols$ is wrong.

Table 28.2 Some important derived SI units

Measured quantity	Name of unit	Symbol	Definition in base units	Alternative in derived units
Energy	joule	J	$m^2\,kg\,s^{-2}$	N m
Force	newton	N	$m\,kg\,s^{-2}$	$J\,m^{-1}$
Pressure	pascal	Pa	$kg\,m^{-1}\,s^{-2}$	$N\,m^{-2}$
Power	watt	W	$m^2\,kg\,s^{-3}$	$J\,s^{-1}$
Electric charge	coulomb	C	A s	$J\,V^{-1}$
Electric potential difference	volt	V	$m^2\,kg\,A^{-1}\,s^{-3}$	$J\,C^{-1}$
Electric resistance	ohm	Ω	$m^2\,kg\,A^{-2}\,s^{-3}$	$V\,A^{-1}$
Electric conductance	siemens	S	$s^3\,A^2\,kg^{-1}\,m^{-2}$	$A\,V^{-1}$ or Ω^{-1}
Electric capacitance	farad	F	$s^4\,A^2\,kg^{-1}\,m^{-2}$	$C\,V^{-1}$
Luminous flux	lumen	lm	cd sr	
Illumination	lux	lx	$cd\,sr\,m^{-2}$	$lm\,m^{-2}$
Frequency	hertz	Hz	s^{-1}	
Radioactivity	becquerel	Bq	s^{-1}	
Enzyme activity	katal	kat	$mol\,substrate\,s^{-1}$	

Recommendations for describing measurements in SI units

Basic format

- Express each measurement as a number separated from its units by a space. If a prefix is required, no space is left between the prefix and the unit it refers to. Symbols for units are only written in their singular form and do not require full stops to show that they are abbreviated or that they are being multiplied together.

- Give symbols and prefixes appropriate upper or lower case initial letters as this may define their meaning. Upper case symbols are named after persons but when written out in full they are not given initial capital letters.

- Show the decimal sign as a full point on the line. Some metric countries continue to use the comma for this purpose and you may come across this in the literature: commas should not therefore be used to separate groups of thousands. In numbers that contain many significant figures, you should separate multiples of 10^3 by spaces rather than commas.

> **Example** n stands for nano and N for newtons.

> **Example** 123456.789111 becomes 123 457.

Compound expressions for derived units

- Take care to separate symbols in compound expressions by a space to avoid the potential for confusion with prefixes. Note, for example, that $200\,\text{m s}$ (metre seconds) is different from $200\,\text{ms}$ (milliseconds).

- Express compound units using negative powers rather than a solidus (/): for example, write mol m^{-3} rather than mol/m^3. The solidus is reserved for separating a descriptive label from its units (see p. 471).

- Where there is a choice, select relevant (natural) combinations of derived and base units, e.g. you might choose units of Pa m^{-1} to describe a hydrostatic pressure gradient rather than $\text{kg m}^{-2}\,\text{s}^{-1}$, even though these units are equivalent and the measurements are numerically the same.

Use of prefixes

- Use prefixes to denote multiples of 10^3 (Table 28.3) so that numbers are kept between 0.1 and 1000.

- Treat a combination of a prefix and a symbol as a single symbol. Thus, when a modified unit is raised to a power, this refers to the whole unit including the prefix.

- Avoid the prefixes deci (d) for 10^{-1} and centi (c) for 10^{-2} as they are not strictly SI.

- Express very large or small numbers as a number between 1 and 10 multiplied by a power of 10 if they are outside the range of prefixes shown in Table 28.3.

- Do not use prefixes in the middle of derived units: they should be attached only to a unit in the numerator (the exception is in the unit for mass, kg).

> **Examples** $10\,\mu\text{m}$ is preferred to $0.000\,01\,\text{m}$ or $0.010\,\text{mm}$.
>
> $1\,\text{mm}^2 = 1 \times 10^{-3}\,\text{m}^2 = 1 \times 10^{-6}\,\text{m}^3$ (not one-thousandth of a square metre).
>
> $1\,\text{dm}^3$ (1 litre) is more properly expressed as $1 \times (10^{-1}\,\text{m})^3 = 1 \times 10^{-3}\,\text{m}^3$.
>
> Avogadro's constant is $6.022\,174 \times 10^{23}\,\text{mol}^{-1}$.
>
> State as MW m^{-2} rather than W mm^{-2}.

Note – In this book, we use L and mL where you would normally find equipment calibrated in that way, but use SI units where this simplifies calculations. In formal scientific writing, constructions such as $1 \times 10^{-6}\,m^3$ ($= 1\,mL$) and $1\,mm^3$ ($= 1\,\mu L$) may be used.

KEY POINT For the foreseeable future, you will need to make conversions from other units to SI units, as much of the literature quotes data using imperial, c.g.s. or other systems. You will need to recognise these units and find the conversion factors required. Examples relevant to chemistry are given in Box 28.1. Table 28.4 provides values of some important physical constants in SI units.

Box 28.1 Conversion factors between some redundant units and the SI

Quantity	SI unit/symbol	Old unit/symbol	Multiply number in old unit by this factor for equivalent in SI unit*	Multiply number in SI unit by this factor for equivalent in old unit*
Area	square metre/m^2	acre	4.04686×10^3	0.247105×10^{-3}
		hectare/ha	10×10^3	0.1×10^{-3}
		square foot/ft^2	0.092903	10.7639
		square inch/in^2	645.16×10^{-9}	1.55000×10^6
		square yard/yd^2	0.836127	1.19599
Angle	radian/rad	degree/°	17.4532×10^{-3}	57.2958
Energy	joule/J	erg	0.1×10^{-6}	10×10^6
		kilowatt hour/kWh	3.6×10^6	0.277778×10^{-6}
Length	metre/m	Ångstrom/Å	0.1×10^{-9}	10×10^9
		foot/ft	0.3048	3.28084
		inch/in	25.4×10^{-3}	39.3701
		mile	1.60934×10^3	0.621373×10^{-3}
		yard/yd	0.9144	1.09361
Mass	kilogram/kg	ounce/oz	28.3495×10^{-3}	35.2740
		pound/lb	0.453592	2.20462
		stone	6.35029	0.157473
		hundredweight/cwt	50.8024	19.6841×10^{-3}
		ton (UK)	1.01605×10^3	0.984203×10^{-3}
Pressure	pascal/Pa	atmosphere/atm	101325	9.86923×10^{-6}
		bar/b	100000	10×10^{-6}
		millimetre of mercury/mmHg	133.322	7.50064×10^{-3}
		torr/Torr	133.322	7.50064×10^{-3}
Radioactivity	becquerel/Bq	curie/Ci	37×10^9	27.0270×10^{-12}
Temperature	kelvin/K	centigrade (Celsius) degree/°C	°C $+ 273.15$	K $- 273.15$
		Fahrenheit degree/°F	(°F $+ 459.67$) $\times 5/9$	(K $\times 9/5$) $- 459.67$
Volume	cubic metre/m^3	cubic foot/ft^3	0.0283168	35.3147
		cubic inch/in^3	16.3871×10^{-6}	61.0236×10^3
		cubic yard/yd^3	0.764555	1.30795
		UK pint/pt	0.568261×10^{-3}	1759.75
		US pint/liq pt	0.473176×10^{-3}	2113.38
		UK gallon/gal	4.54609×10^{-3}	219.969
		US gallon/gal	3.78541×10^{-3}	264.172

*In the case of temperature measurements, use formulae shown.

Table 28.4   Some physical constants in SI terms

Physical constant	Symbol	Value and units
Avogadro's constant	N_A	$6.022\,174 \times 10^{23}$ mol^{-1}
Boltzmann's constant	k	$1.380\,626$ J K^{-1}
Charge of electron	e	$1.602\,192 \times 10^{-19}$ C
Gas constant	R	$8.314\,43$ J K^{-1} mol^{-1}
Faraday's constant	F	$9.648\,675 \times 10^4$ C mol^{-1}
Molar volume of ideal gas at STP	V_0	$0.022\,414$ m^3 mol^{-1}
Speed of light *in vacuo*	c	$2.997\,924 \times 10^8$ m s^{-1}
Planck constant	h	$6.626\,205 \times 10^{-34}$ J s
Acceleration due to gravity	g	9.807 m s^{-1}
Atomic mass unit	m_u	$1660\,540\,2 \times 10^{-27}$ kg
Rydberg constant	R_∞	1.097×10^7 m^{-1}
Permitivity of vacuum	ε_0	8.854×10^{-12} F m^{-1}

Note – The other common non-SI unit of volume is the cubic centimetre, cm^3, $(10^{-2}$ m$)^3$. Even though they are not *exactly* the same, mL and cm^3 are used interchangeably, as are cubic decimetre dm$^3 (10^{-1}$ m$)^3 = 10^{-3}$ m^3 and litre (L).

Conversion of non-SI units – the following conversions are useful when dealing with 'traditional' units:

$$1\,L \approx 1\,dm^3 = 1 \times (10^{-1}\,m)^3 = 1 \times 10^{-3}\,m^3$$

$$1\,mL = 1 \times 10^{-3} \times 10^{-3}\,m^3 = 1 \times 10^{-6}\,m^3$$

$$1\,\mu L = 1 \times 10^{-6} \times 10^{-3}\,m^3 = 1 \times 10^{-9}\,m^3$$

Some implications of SI in chemistry

Volume

The SI unit of volume is the cubic metre, m^3, which is rather large for practical purposes. The litre (L) and the millilitre (mL) are technically obsolete, but are widely used and glassware is still calibrated using them.

Mass

The SI unit for mass is the kilogram (kg) rather than the gram (g): this is unusual because the base unit has a prefix applied.

Amount of substance

You should use the mole (mol, i.e. Avogadro's constant, see Table 28.4) to express very large numbers. The mole gives the number of atoms in the atomic mass, a convenient constant.

Concentration

The SI unit of concentration, mol m^{-3}, is not convenient for general laboratory work. It is equivalent to the non-SI term 'millimolar' (mM) while 'molar' (M) becomes kmol m^{-3}. If the solvent is not specified, then it is assumed to be water (see Chapter 25).

Time

In general, use the second (s) when reporting physical quantities having a time element. Hours (h), days (d) and years should be used if seconds are clearly absurd (e.g. samples were taken over a 5-year period). Note, however, that you may have to convert these units to seconds when doing calculations.

Box 28.2 How to interconvert SI units

Example: You are required to calculate the molecular weight of a polymer by measurements of its osmotic pressure in solution. At infinite dilution, measured graphically from your experiments, the equation below applies:

$$\frac{\Pi}{c} = \frac{RT}{M_r}$$

where Π = osmotic pressure at infinite dilution (Pa), R = gas constant ($J\,K^{-1}\,mol^{-1}$), T = temperature (K), c = concentration of solution ($kg\,m^{-3}$) and M_r = molecular weight.

1. **Re-arrange the equation for M_r:**

$$M_r = \frac{RTc}{\Pi}$$

2. **Look at the units and decide which are common:** since the gas constant is expressed in joules, you should convert the osmotic pressure term into joules. The derived unit for pressure is $N\,m^{-2}$ and, since the derived units for N are $J\,m^{-1}$, the full derived unit of pressure is $(J\,m^{-1}) \times m^{-2} = J\,m^{-3}$.

3. **Substitute the units into the equation for M:**

$$M_r = \frac{RTc}{\Pi} = \frac{J\,K^{-1}mol^{-1} \times K \times kg\,m^{-3}}{J\,m^{-3}} = kg\,mol^{-1}$$

4. **Substitute the appropriate numerical values into the equation for M_r:** you know that the units of the calculation will be correct since the molecular weight is the weight of 1 mole of polymer, expressed in kg.

Definitions

STP – Standard Temperature and Pressure = 293.15 K and 101 325 Pa (or 101.325 kPa or 0.101 325 M Pa).

Temperature

The SI unit is the kelvin, K. The degree Celsius scale has units of the same magnitude, °C, but starts at 273.15 K, the melting point of ice at STP. Temperature is similar to time in that the Celsius scale is in widespread use, but note that conversions to K may be required for calculations. Note also that you must not use the degree sign (°) with K and that this symbol must be in upper case to avoid confusion with k for kilo; however, you *should* retain the degree sign with °C to avoid confusion with the coulomb, C.

Interconversion of SI units

You will find that the use of SI units simplifies mathematical manipulations and ensures that you obtain the correct units for the parameter being calculated. Remember that you must convert all units into the appropriate SI units, e.g. masses must be expressed as kg, volumes as m^3 and concentrations as $kg\,m^{-3}$ or $mol\,m^{-3}$, etc., and that you may need to use alternatives in derived units (Table 28.2). The application of these principles is shown in Box 28.2.

Sources for further study

Anon. (2007) *Chem 1 Virtual Textbook: Units of Measure.*
Available: http://chem1.com/acad/webtext/pre/mm1.html
Last accessed 05/03/10.

Aylward, G. and Findlay, T. (2007) *SI Chemical Data*, 6th edn. Wiley, Chichester.

Heslop, R.B. and Wild, G.M. (1975) *SI Units in Chemistry.* Applied Science Publishers, London.

Thompson, A. and Taylor, B.N. (2008) *Guide for the Use of the International System of Units (SI)*.
Available:
http://physics.nist.gov/cuu/pdf/sp811.pdf
Last accessed 05/03/10.

Study exercises

28.1 Practise manipulation of equations and deduction of SI base units in the following examples using the procedures outlined in Box 28.2.

(a) $PV = nRT$
    P = pressure (kg m^{-1} s^{-2}): V = volume (m^3);
    n = number of moles (mol);
    T = temperature (K); R = gas constant (?).

(b) $A = \varepsilon cl$

A = absorbance (dimensionless);
c = concentration (mol L^{-1});
l = length (cm); ε = molar absorptivity (?)

(c) $v = \dfrac{1}{2\pi}\sqrt{\dfrac{k}{\mu}}$

v = frequency (s^{-1}); μ = reduced mass (kg);
$\pi = 3.142$
k = force constant (?)

29 Scientific method and design of experiments

Science is a body of knowledge based on observation and experiment. Scientists attempt to explain their observations in terms of theories and hypotheses. They make predictions from these hypotheses and test them by experiment or further observations. The philosophy and sociology that underlie this process are complex topics (see, e.g. Chalmers, 1999). Any brief description must involve simplifications.

Figure 29.1 models the scientific process you are most likely to be involved in – testing 'small-scale' hypotheses. These represent the sorts of explanation that can give rise to predictions which can be tested by an experiment or a series of observations. For example, you might put forward the hypothesis that the rate of loss of a substance from a sample is dependent on temperature. An experiment could be set up to test this hypothesis, and the results would either confirm or refute the hypothesis.

If confirmed, a hypothesis is retained with greater confidence. If refuted, it is either rejected outright as false, or modified and retested. Alternatively, it might be decided that the experiment was not a valid test of the hypothesis – perhaps because it was later found that the substance was sample dependent.

Nearly all scientific research deals with the testing of small-scale hypotheses. These hypotheses operate within a theoretical framework that has proven to be successful – i.e. is confirmed by many experiments and is consistently predictive. This operating model or 'paradigm' is not changed readily, and, even if a result appears that seems to challenge the conventional view, would not be overturned immediately. The conflicting result would be 'shelved' until an explanation was found after further investigation. In the example used above, a relevant paradigm could be the notion that life processes are ultimately chemical in nature.

Although changes in paradigms are rare, they are important, and the scientists who recognise them become famous. Generally, however, results from hypothesis-testing tend to support and develop ('articulate') this paradigm, enhancing its relevance and strengthening its status.

Where do ideas for small-scale hypotheses come from? They arise from one or more thought processes on the part of a scientist:

- analogy with other systems;

- recognition of a pattern;

- recognition of departure from a pattern;

- invention of new analytical methods;

- development of a mathematical model;

- intuition;

- imagination.

Recently, it has been recognised that the process of science is not an entirely objective one. For instance, the choice of analogy which led to a new hypothesis might well be subjective, depending on past knowledge or understanding. Also, science is a social activity, where researchers put forward and defend viewpoints against those who hold an opposing view; where groups may work together towards a common goal; and where

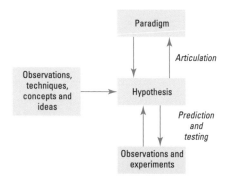

Fig. 29.1 A model of scientific method as used when testing hypotheses on a small scale. Hypotheses can arise as a result of various thought-processes on the part of the scientist, and are consistent with the overlying paradigm. Each hypothesis is testable by experiment or observation, leading to its confirmation or rejection. Confirmed hypotheses act to strengthen the status of the paradigm, but rejected ones do not immediately result in the paradigm's replacement.

effort may depend on externally dictated financial opportunities and constraints. As with any other human activity, science is bound to involve an element of subjectivity.

How are decisions made about whether to accept or reject a hypothesis? This is sometimes clear-cut, where experiments can be set up to result in a binary outcome. In many other cases, the existence of 'natural variation' means that statistical techniques need to be employed (Chapters 63 and 64).

No hypothesis can ever be rejected with certainty. Statistics allow us to quantify as vanishingly small the probability of an erroneous conclusion, but we are nevertheless left in the position of never being 100% certain that we have rejected all relevant alternative hypotheses, nor 100% certain that our decision to reject some alternative hypotheses was correct! However, despite these problems, experimental science has yielded and continues to yield many important findings.

> **KEY POINT** The fallibility of scientific 'facts' is essential to grasp. No explanation can ever be 100% certain as it is always possible for a new alternative hypothesis to be generated. Our understanding of science changes all the time as new observations and methods force old hypotheses to be retested.

Quantitative hypotheses, those involving a mathematical description of the system, have become very important, because they can be formulated concisely by mathematical models. Formulating models is often useful because it forces deeper thought about mechanisms and encourages simplification of the system. A mathematical model:

- is inherently testable through experiment;
- identifies areas where information is lacking or uncertain;
- encapsulates many observations;
- allows you to predict the behaviour of a system.

Remember, however, that assumptions and simplifications required to create a model may result in it being unrealistic. Further, the results obtained from any model are only as good as the information put into it.

The terminology of experimentation

In many experiments, the aim is to provide evidence for causality. If x causes y, we expect, repeatedly, to find that a change in x results in a change in y. Hence, the ideal experiment of this kind involves measurement of y, the dependent (measured) variable, at one or more values of x, the independent variable, and subsequent demonstration of some relationship between them. Experiments therefore involve comparisons of the results of treatments – changes in the independent variable as applied to an experimental subject. The change is engineered by the experimenter under controlled conditions.

Subjects given the same treatment are known as replicates. A 'block' is a grouping of replicates. The blocks are contained in a 'field', i.e. the whole area (or time) available for the experiment (Fig. 29.2). These terms

Deciding whether to accept or reject a hypothesis – this is sometimes clear-cut, as in some areas of genetics where experiments can be set up to result in a binary outcome. In many other cases, the existence of 'chemical variation' means that statistical techniques need to be employed (Chapters 63 and 64).

> **Definition**
>
> **Mathematical model.** An algebraic summary of the relationship between the variables in a system.

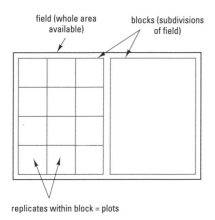

Fig. 29.2 Terminology and physical arrangement of elements in an experiment. Each block should contain the complete range of treatments (treatments may be replicated more than once in each block).

originated from the statistical analysis of agricultural experiments, but they are now used for many other areas of science.

Why you need to control variables in experiments

Interpretation of experiments is seldom clear-cut because uncontrolled variables always change when treatments are given.

Confounding variables

These increase or decrease systematically as the independent variable increases or decreases. Their effects are known as systematic variation. This form of variation can be disentangled from that caused directly by treatments by incorporating appropriate controls in the experiment. A control is really just another treatment where a potentially confounding variable is adjusted so that its effects, if any, can be taken into account. The results from a control may therefore allow an alternative hypothesis to be rejected. There are often many potential controls for any experiment.

The consequence of systematic variation is that you can never be certain that the treatment, and the treatment alone, has caused an observed result, especially when using biological material. By careful design you can, however, 'minimise the uncertainty' involved in your conclusion. Methods available include:

- Ensuring, through experimental design, that the independent variable is the only major factor that changes in any treatment.

- Incorporating appropriate controls to show that potential confounding variables have little or no effect.

- Selecting experimental subjects randomly to cancel out systematic variation arising from biased selection.

- Matching or pairing individuals among treatments so that differences in response due to their initial status are eliminated.

- Arranging subjects and treatments randomly so that responses to systematic differences in conditions do not influence the results.

- Ensuring that experimental conditions are uniform so that responses to systematic differences in conditions are minimised. When attempting this, beware of 'edge effects' where subjects on the periphery of the layout experience substantially different conditions from those in the centre.

Reducing edge effects – One way to do this is to incorporate a 'buffer zone' of untreated subjects around the experiment proper.

Nuisance variables

These are uncontrolled variables which cause differences in the value of y independently of the value of x, resulting in random variation. Experimental science is characterised by the high number of nuisance variables that are found and their relatively great influence on results – some chemical data tend to have large errors! To reduce and assess the consequences of nuisance variables:

- incorporate replicates to allow random variation to be quantified;

- choose subjects that are as similar as possible;

- control random fluctuations in environmental conditions.

Box 29.1 Checklist for designing and performing an experiment

1. Preliminaries

(a) **Read background material** and decide on a subject area to investigate.

(b) **Formulate a simple hypothesis to test** – it is preferable to have a clear answer to one question than to be uncertain about several questions.

(c) **Decide which dependent variable you are going to measure and how** – is it relevant to the problem? Can you measure it accurately, precisely and without bias?

(d) **Think about and plan the statistical analysis of your results** – will this affect your design?

2. Designing

(a) **Find out the limitations on your resources.**

(b) **Choose treatments that alter the minimum of confounding variables.**

(c) **Incorporate as many effective controls as possible.**

(d) **Keep the number of replicates as high as is feasible.**

(e) **Ensure that the same number of replicates is present in each treatment.**

(f) **Use effective randomisation and blocking arrangements.**

3. Planning

(a) **List all the materials you will need** – order any chemicals and make up solutions; obtain the experimental material you require; check equipment is available.

(b) **Organise space and/or time** in which to do the experiment.

(c) **Account for the time taken to apply treatments and record results** – make out a timesheet if things will be hectic.

4. Carrying out the experiment

(a) **Record the results and make careful notes of everything you do** (see p. 126) – make additional observations to those planned if interesting things happen.

(b) **Repeat the experiment** if time and resources allow.

5. Analysing

(a) **Graph data as soon as possible** (during the experiment if you can) – this will allow you to visualise what has happened and make adjustments to the design (e.g. timing of measurements).

(b) **Carry out the planned statistical analysis.**

(c) **Jot down conclusions and new hypotheses** arising from the experiment.

Constraints on experimental design

Box 29.1 outlines the important stages in designing an experiment. At an early stage, you should find out how resources may constrain the design. For example, limits may be set by availability of subject materials, cost of treatment, availability of a chemical or bench space. Logistics may be a factor (e.g. time taken to record or analyse data).

Your equipment or facilities may affect design because you cannot regulate conditions as well as you might desire. For example, you may be unable to ensure that the temperature is constant over an experiment laid out in an open laboratory.

Evaluating design constraints – a good way to do this is by processing an individual subject through the experimental procedures – a 'preliminary run' can help to identify potential difficulties.

Use of replicates

Replicate results show how variable the response is within treatments. They allow you to compare the differences among treatments in the context of the variability within treatments – you can do this *via* statistical tests such as analysis of variance (Chapter 64). Larger sample sizes tend to increase the precision of estimates of parameters and increase the chances of showing a significant difference between treatments, if one exists. For statistical reasons (weighting, ease of calculation, fitting data to certain tests), it is often best to keep the number of replicates even. Remember that the degree of independence of

Deciding the number of replicates in each treatment – try to:

● maximise the number of replicates in each treatment;

● make the number of replicates even.

replicates is important – sub-samples cannot act as replicate samples, they tell you about variability in the measurement method but not in the quantity being measured.

If the total number of replicates available for an experiment is limited by resources, you may need to compromise between the number of treatments and the number of replicates per treatment. Statistics can help here, for it is possible to work out the minimum number of replicates you would need to show a certain difference between pairs of means (say 10%) at a specified level of significance (say $P = 0.05$). For this, you need to obtain a prior estimate of variability within treatments.

Multifactorial experiments

The simplest experiments are those in which one treatment (factor) is applied at a time to the subjects. This approach is likely to give clear-cut answers, but it could be criticised for lacking realism. In particular, it cannot take account of interactions among two or more conditions that are likely to occur in real life. A multifactorial experiment (Fig. 29.3) is an attempt to do this – the interactions among treatments can be analysed by specialised statistics.

Multifactorial experiments are economical on resources because of 'hidden replication'. This arises when two or more treatments are given to a subject because the result acts statistically as a replicate for each treatment. Choice of relevant treatments to combine is important in multifactorial experiments – for instance, an interaction may be present at certain concentrations of a chemical but not at others (perhaps because the response is saturated). It is also important that the measurement scale for the response is consistent, otherwise spurious interactions may occur. Beware when planning a multifactorial experiment that the number of replicates do not get out of hand – you may have to restrict the treatments to 'plus' or 'minus' the factor of interest (as in Fig. 29.3).

Repetition of experiments

Even if your experiment is well designed and analysed, only limited conclusions can be made. Firstly, what you can say is valid for a particular place and time, with a particular investigator, experimental subject and method of applying treatments. Secondly, if your results were significant at the 5% level of probability (p. 511), there is still an approximately one-in-twenty chance that the results did arise by chance. To guard against these possibilities, it is important that experiments are repeated. Ideally, this would be done by an independent scientist with independent materials. However, it makes sense to repeat work yourself so that you can have full confidence in your conclusions. Many scientists recommend that experiments are done three times in total, but this may not be possible in undergraduate work.

> **Definition**
>
> **Interaction.** Where the effect of treatments given together is greater or less than the sum of their individual effects.

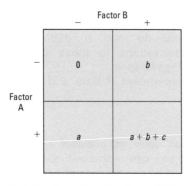

Fig. 29.3 Design of a simple multifactorial experiment. Factors A and B have effects *a* and *b* when applied alone. When both are applied together, the effect is denoted by $a + b + c$.

- If $c = 0$, there is no interaction (e.g. $2 + 2 + c = 4$).
- If c is positive, there is a positive interaction (synergism) between A and B (e.g. $2 + 2 + c = 5$).
- If c is negative, there is a negative interaction (antagonism) between A and B (e.g. $2 + 2 + c = 3$).

Reporting correctly – it is good practice to report how many times your experiments were repeated (in Materials and Methods). In the Results section, you should add a statement saying that the illustrated experiment is representative.

Text reference

Chalmers, A.F. (1999) *What is this Thing called Science?* Open University Press, Buckingham.

Sources for further study

Anon. *Suggestions for Keeping Laboratory Notebooks*. Available:
http://otl.stanford.edu/inventors/resources/labnotebooks.html
Last accessed 01/07/09
[A Stanford University website which looks at the laboratory notebook from a patent perspective]

Beavon, J.R.G. *Writing the Laboratory Notebook*. Available:
http://www.home.clara/rod.beavon/lab_book.htm
Last accessed 01/07/09

Milholland, R. *Guide to Keeping Laboratory Notebooks*. Available:
http://www.niehs.gov/health/docs/guide-notebooks.pdf
Last accessed 01/07/09

Purrington, C. *Advice on Keeping a Laboratory Notebook*. Available:
http://www.swarthmore.edu/NatSci/cpurrin1/notebookadvice.htm
Last accessed 01/07/09

Shuttleworth, M. (2008) *Choosing Scientific Measurements*. Available:
http://www.experiment-resources. com/scientific-measurements.html
Last accessed 01/07/09

Zubrick, J.W. (2007) *The Organic Chem Lab Survival Manual. A student's guide to techniques*, 7th edn. John Wiley & Sons Ltd, Chichester

Study exercises

29.1 Generate random numbers. Produce a list of 20 random whole numbers between 1 and 5 using a spreadsheet. If using Excel, investigate the RAND ( ) and INT functions. The RAND( ) function produces a random number between 0 and 1, so you will need to multiply by a constant factor to scale your final output appropriately. Copy your test formula(e) to several cells to test empirically whether it works.

29.2 Design and plan an experiment. Using one of your practicals, determine the purpose of the experiment and what it aims to achieve. List anything else you could do to make the results more robust.

Research projects are an important component of the final-year syllabus for most degree programmes in chemistry, while shorter projects may also be carried out during courses in earlier years. Project work presents difficulties at many stages but can be extremely rewarding. The assessment of your project is likely to contribute significantly to your degree grade, so all aspects of this work should be approached in a thorough manner.

Deciding on a topic to study

Assuming you have a choice, this important decision should be researched carefully. Make appointments to visit possible supervisors and ask them for advice on topics that you find interesting. Use library texts and research papers to obtain further background information. Perhaps the most important criterion is whether the topic will sustain your interest over the whole period of the project. Other things to look for include:

- Opportunities to learn new skills. Ideally, you should attempt to gain experience and skills that you might be able to 'sell' to a potential employer.

- Ease of obtaining valid results. An ideal project provides a means to obtain 'guaranteed' data for your report, but also the chance to extend knowledge by doing genuinely novel research.

- Assistance. What help will be available to you during the project? A busy lab with many research students might provide a supportive environment should your potential supervisor be too busy to meet you often; on the other hand, a smaller lab may provide the opportunity for more personal interaction with your supervisor.

- Impact. It is not outside the bounds of possibility for undergraduate work to contribute to research papers. Your prospective supervisor can alert you to such opportunities.

- Success. You are doing a research project and it may not always provide a positive result. Negative results are just as useful.

Planning your work

As with any lengthy exercise, planning is required to make the best use of the time allocated. This is true on a daily basis as well as over the entire period of the project. It is especially important not to underestimate the time it will take to write and produce your thesis (see below). If you wish to benefit from feedback given by your supervisor, you should aim to have drafts in his/her hands in good time. Since a large proportion of marks will be allocated to the report, you should not rush its production.

If your department requires you to write an interim report, look on this as an opportunity to clarify your thoughts and get some of the time-consuming preparative work out of the way. If not, you should set your own deadlines for producing drafts of the introduction, materials and methods section, etc.

The Internet as an information source – since many university departments have home pages on the World Wide Web, searches using relevant key words may indicate where research in your area is currently being carried out. Academics usually respond positively to emailed questions about their area of expertise.

Asking around – one of the best sources of information about supervisors, laboratories and projects is past students. Some of the postgraduates in your department may be products of your own system and they could provide an alternative source of advice.

Liaising with your supervisor(s) – this is essential if your work is to proceed efficiently. Specific meetings may be timetabled, e.g. to discuss a term's progress, review your work plan or consider a draft introduction. Most supervisors also have an 'open-door' policy, allowing you to air current problems. Prepare well for all meetings: have a list of questions ready before the meeting; provide results in an easily digestible form (but take your lab notebook along); be clear about your future plans for work.

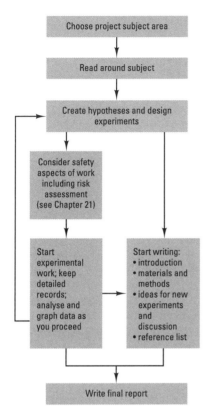

Fig. 30.1 Flowchart showing a recommended sequence of events in carrying out an undergraduate research project.

KEY POINT Project work can be very time consuming at times. Try not to neglect other aspects of your course – make sure your lecture notes are up to date and collect relevant supporting information as you go along.

Getting started

Fig. 30.1 is a flowchart illustrating how a project might proceed; at the start, don't spend too long reading the literature and working out a lengthy programme of research. Get stuck in and do an experiment. There's no substitute for 'getting your hands dirty' for stimulating new ideas:

- even a 'failed' experiment will provide some useful information which may allow you to create a new or modified hypothesis;

- pilot experiments may point out deficiencies in experimental technique that will need to be rectified;

- the experience will help you create a realistic plan of work.

Designing experiments or sampling procedures

Design of experiments is covered in Chapter 29. Avoid being too ambitious at the start of your work! It is generally best to work with a simple hypothesis and design your experiments or sampling around this. A small pilot experiment or test sample will highlight potential stumbling blocks including resource limitations, whether in materials or time or both.

Working in a laboratory environment

During your time as a project student, you are effectively a guest in your supervisor's laboratory.

- Be considerate – keep your 'area' tidy and offer to do your share of lab duties such as calibrating the pH meter, replenishing stock solutions, distilled water, cleaning used glassware, etc.

- Use instruments carefully – they could be worth more than you'd think. Careless use may invalidate calibration settings and ruin other people's work as well as your own.

- Do your homework on techniques you intend to use – there's less chance of making costly mistakes if you have a good background understanding of the methods you will be using.

- Always seek advice if you are unsure of what you are doing.

KEY POINT It is essential that you follow all the safety rules applying to the laboratory. Make sure you are acquainted with all relevant procedures – normally there will be prominent warnings about these. If in doubt, ask!

Brushing up on IT skills – word processors and spreadsheets are extremely useful when producing a thesis. Chapters 13 and 12 detail key features of these programs. You might benefit from attending courses on the relevant programs or studying manuals or texts so that you can use them more efficiently.

Using drawings or photographs – these can provide valuable records of sampling sites or experimental set-ups and could be useful in your report. Plan ahead and do the relevant work at the time of carrying out your research rather than afterwards.

Using a word processor to record your ideas – remember that you can note down your thoughts and any other important information relevant to the Results and Discussion sections of your project in a file that can then form the basis of your first draft (p. 95); that way, you won't forget to include these points in your final report.

Keeping notes and analysing your results

Tidy record keeping is often associated with good research, and you should follow the advice and hints given in Chapter 27. Try to keep copies of all files relating to your project. As you obtain results, you should always calculate, analyse and graph data as soon as you can (see Fig. 30.1). This can reveal aspects that may not be obvious in numerical or readout form. Don't be worried by negative results – these can sometimes be as useful as positive results if they allow you to eliminate hypotheses – and don't be dispirited if things do not work first time. Thomas Edison's maxim 'Genius is one per cent inspiration and ninety-nine per cent perspiration' certainly applies to research work!

Writing the report

The structure of scientific reports is dealt with in Chapter 18. The following advice concerns methods of accumulating relevant information.

Introduction This is a big piece of writing that can be very time-consuming. Therefore, the more work you can do on it early on, the better. You should allocate some time at the start for library work (without neglecting benchwork), so that you can build up a database of references (p. 47). While photocopying can be expensive, you will find it valuable to have copies of key reviews and references handy when writing away from the library. Discuss proposals for content and structure with your supervisor to make sure your effort is relevant. Leave space at the end for a section on aims and objectives. This is important to orientate readers (including assessors), but you may prefer to finalise the content after the results have been analysed!

Experimental You should note as many details as possible *when doing the experiment or making observations*. Don't rely on your memory or hope that the information will still be available when you come to write up. Even if it is, chasing these details might waste valuable time.

Results Show your supervisor graphed and tabulated versions of your data promptly. These can easily be produced using a spreadsheet (p. 87), but you should seek your supervisor's advice on whether the design and print quality is appropriate to be included in your thesis. You may wish to access a specialist graphics program to produce publishable-quality graphs and charts: allow some time for learning its idiosyncrasies! If you are producing a poster for assessment (Chapter 14), be sure to mock up the design well in advance. Similarly, think ahead about your needs for any seminar or poster you will present.

Discussion Because this comes at the end of your thesis, and some parts can only be written after you have all the results in place, the temptation is to leave the discussion to last. This means that it can be rushed – not a good idea because of the weight attached by assessors to your analysis of data and thoughts about future experiments. It will help greatly if you keep notes of aims, conclusions and ideas for future work *as you go along* (Fig. 30.1). Another useful tip is to make notes of comparable data and conclusions from the literature as you read papers and reviews.

Acknowledgements Make a special place in your notebook for noting all those who have helped you carry out the work, for use when writing this section of the report.

References Because of the complex formats involved (p. 50), these can be tricky to type. To save time, process them in batches as you go along – bibliographic software (e.g. Endnote) can help with the organisation of references (p. 50).

> **KEY POINT** Make sure you are absolutely certain about the deadline for submitting your report and try to submit a few days before it. If you leave things until the last moment, you may find access to printers, photocopiers and binding machines is difficult.

Sources for further study

Ebel, H.F., Bliefert, C. and Russey, W.E. (2004) *The Art of Scientific Writing: from Student Reports to Professional Publications in Chemistry and Related Fields*, 2nd edn. Wiley-VCH, Weinheim, Germany.

Jardine, F.H. (1994) *How to do your Student Project in Chemistry*. CRC Press, Boca Raton.

Study exercises

Note: These exercises assume that you have started a research project, or are about to start one, as part of your studies.

30.1 Prepare a project plan. Make a formal plan for your research project, incorporating any milestones dictated by your department, such as interim reports and final submission dates. Discuss your plan with your supervisor and incorporate his or her comments. Refer back to the plan frequently during your project, to see how well you are meeting your deadlines.

30.2 Resolve to write up your work as you go along. Each time you complete an experiment or observation, write up the materials and methods, analyse the data and draw up graphs as soon as you can. While you may reject some of your work at a later stage, you may wish to modify it; this will spread out the majority of the effort and allow time for critical thinking close to the final submission date.

30.3 Devise a computer database for keeping details of your references. Keeping these records up to date will save you a lot of time when writing up. You will need to decide on an appropriate referencing format or find out about the one followed by your department (see Chapter 8).

Laboratory techniques

Melting points are measured (determined) for four reasons:

1. The melting range and upper limit are an indication of the purity of the sample.

2. Comparison of the melting point with the literature may indicate the identity of the compound or confirm that it is not the compound required.

3. If the compound is new, other scientists will need the information.

4. The compound can be identified with reasonable certainty by taking a mixed melting point (p. 237).

Criterion of purity

Pure solid covalent organic compounds and many inorganic complexes incorporating organic ligands have definite melting points. The pure solid will melt reproducibly over a narrow temperature range, usually less than $1\,°C$, and this melting range is known as the melting point. If the compound is not pure, the melting range will increase significantly and the upper end of the melting range will be lowered. Thus the melting point (m.pt.) of a compound is a measure of its purity (p. 236). Other methods are used routinely to estimate purity of solid compounds, such as NMR (p. 441), and the presence of a single 'spot' or a single peak on a chromatogram from thin-layer (p. 376), gas–liquid (p. 370) or high-performance liquid (p. 379) chromatography, but melting point remains the standard measure of purity.

> KEY POINT The term melting point really means the melting range of a chemical and in your laboratory report you should always quote the measured melting range under the heading **'melting point'**.

Melting point apparatus

The equipment for measuring the melting point of a solid varies in complexity from a simple oil bath heated with a microburner to a microscope with a heated stage as shown in Fig. 31.1. The essential components of a melting point apparatus are:

- A sample holder: usually a glass capillary tube sealed at one end in the case of the oil bath and heated block systems, or a pair of microscope slides on an electrically heated plate in the Kofler block.

- A temperature recording device, placed as near to the sample as possible. Usually this is a thermometer but it can be a thermocouple probe with digital readout.

- A heat source with fine control to allow a gradual increase in temperature. These sources vary with the sophistication of the equipment.

  In the undergraduate laboratory you are likely to use only the simpler systems such as the oil bath or heated block apparatus.

Purity of solids – melting points do not vary significantly with changes in atmospheric pressure, whereas the boiling points of pure liquids are not constant: they vary with changes in atmospheric pressure and cannot be used as a measure of purity.

Melting point depression – only impurities, which will dissolve in the compound, will lower its melting point, e.g. reactants, by-products, solvents. Insoluble impurities, e.g. salts, charcoal, filter paper, grit, etc., will not dissolve in the melted compound.

When you synthesise soild compounds in the laboratory – you will always be asked to determine their melting points so that your practical expertise can be assessed.

Thermometers – make sure that you use a partial-immersion thermometer not a total-immersion thermometer. The type is written on the back of the thermometer.

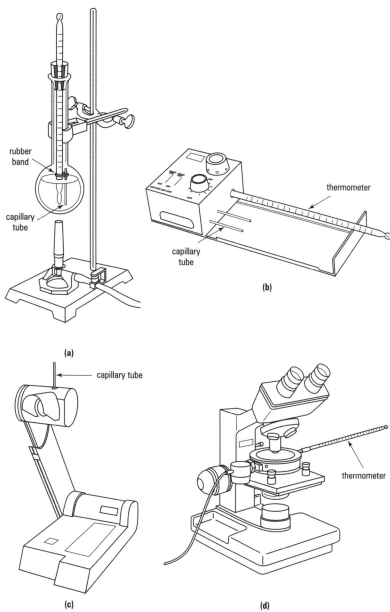

Fig. 31.1 Melting point apparatus: (a) oil bath; (b) heated block – thermometer readout; (c) heated block – digital readout; (d) Kofler hot-stage microscope.

Capillary tubes

Capillary tubes for melting point measurement are available commercially and are supplied open at both ends or closed at one end or closed at both ends. To seal one end of an open capillary tube, just touch the end of the capillary tube onto the outer 'layer' of the hot flame of a microburner (see Fig. 31.2). The end of the tube will collapse in and seal the tube. Make sure that the tube is sealed, i.e. there is not a fine line in the sealed end, and that there is no large globule of glass on the end of the tube, otherwise it may not fit into the hole in the heating block of the melting point apparatus. Similarly, if you push the tube too far into the flame, the tube will bend and therefore not fit into the heating block.

Breaking capillary tubes – if the capillary tube is sealed at both ends, you can break it into two half-sized single-end-sealed melting point tubes by scoring the mid-point of the tube with a glass file and then snapping the tube at the score mark. If you don't score the glass, the edges of the break will be uneven and the tube will be difficult to fill.

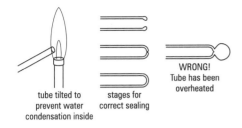

Fig. 31.2 Sealing a melting point capillary tube.

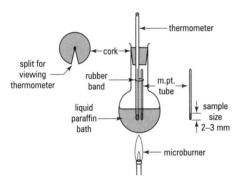

Fig. 31.3 Components of an oil bath melting point apparatus.

If the rubber band comes into contact with the oil it will expand – the capillary tube will drop off into the oil bath and it will discolour the oil so that you will not be able to see when your sample melts.

SAFETY NOTE The 'notch' in the cork is essential: it allows the thermometer to be read over all its length, it allows the thermometer to be gripped by the cork and most importantly, it allows the heated air to escape from the apparatus. **Never** use a cork without the 'notch'.

SAFETY NOTE Mercury vapour is a severe cumulative and chronic hazard and the normal vapour pressure of mercury, at room temperature, is many times above the control limit (CL) of 0.05 mg m^{-3} If you *break a thermometer* or *find* or *suspect* the presence of mercury, inform your instructor *immediately.*

To put the compound into the capillary tube, place a little of the dry compound in a small heap on a watch-glass and press the open end of the tube into the heap, trapping a plug of chemical in the opening. The chemical can be moved to the sealed end by turning the tube over and tapping it on the bench, or by vibrating it by rubbing it against the thread of the screw on a clamp, or dropping it down a long glass tube onto the laboratory bench. Remember: you only need a 2–3 mm length of sample in the bottom of the capillary tube.

Oil bath apparatus

The component parts of a typical oil bath melting point apparatus are shown in Fig. 31.3.

* Check that the mineral oil is clean and contains no water (p. 174) and that the bulb is only two-thirds full, to allow for expansion. Clamp the oil bath to a support stand (p. 166).

* Check that your thermometer is of the appropriate range, that the mercury thread is intact and the glass, in particular the bulb, is not cracked.

* Attach the capillary to the thermometer with a rubber ring, making sure that the compound is next to the thermometer bulb and remember to hold the thermometer near the bulb while attaching the capillary tube (p. 152).

* Press the thermometer into the 'notched' cork, making sure that you can see the thermometer scale, and trial fit the thermometer, sample and cork into the oil bath making sure that the thermometer bulb and sample are in the centre of the oil bath and that the rubber band is not in the oil, and will not be covered by oil, when the oil expands on heating.

* If adjustment is needed, carefully slide the cork up or down the thermometer (p. 152).

* You can attach a melting point capillary to both sides of the thermometer bulb to carry out two separate melting point determinations simultaneously.

Electric heated block apparatus

The heating block usually has three holes, to permit three simultaneous measurements of melting points. Always ensure that:

* The heating block is at room temperature at the outset.

* The light in the heating block works.

* The thermometer is undamaged (as above) and fits snugly into its hole in the heating block.

* All heating controls are set at zero.

* The capillary tubes slide easily into their holes in the heating block.

The usual problems encountered with this equipment are broken capillary tubes or broken thermometer bulbs in the heating block. Consult your instructor in these cases.

Melting point determination

The general procedure is to heat the oil bath with the microburner using the technique described on p. 172, or to use the heating control to give a temperature rise of about 10 °C per minute. When the temperature is about 20 °C below the melting point, the rate of heating must be reduced to about 2 °C per minute and continued at this rate until the compound has melted. The melting point is the *temperature range* from where the first drop of liquid appears to where the last crystal dissolves into the liquid.

Heating too fast – if you record a melting point which is higher than the literature value, you are implying that your compound has a purity >100%, which is impossible. Therefore it must be a different compound to the one expected.

KEY POINTS

- The most common error is heating the sample *too quickly*. There is often a lag between slowing the heating rate and the reduction in temperature increase, resulting in a reading of the melting point which is *too high*.
- If you do not know what the compound is, you will not know its expected melting point. Therefore, you should determine an approximate value and then repeat the procedure to give an accurate measurement, by reducing the heating rate, particularly for the final stage near the melting point. The boost heater on the electrical apparatus can be used for finding the approximate melting point but *not* for accurate determination.
- If you are carrying out several melting point measurements, it is common sense to measure the melting point of the lowest melting compound first – less time for the apparatus to cool to room temperature.
- If you miss the melting point, do not allow the sample to solidify and then retake the melting point with the same sample: some decomposition may have occurred on melting.
- It is normal practice to make at least two measurements of the melting point, one approximate and at least one accurate reading.

Thermometer calibration

Calibrated thermometers – if your compound is only slightly impure and has a melting point 2 °C lower than the literature value, a thermometer reading 10 °C low will give you an error of 12 °C, indicating a low level of purity and hence a low grade or false information to fellow scientists.

Your thermometer may be a major source of error in melting point measurement. Occasionally thermometers for routine laboratory use may not be accurate and may read up to 10 °C high or low. To avoid this problem you should always calibrate your thermometer to determine any error and be able to correct for it.

To calibrate your thermometer you must measure the melting points of a series of very pure compounds, available commercially, having a range of melting points similar to the range over which you will use the thermometer; a general-purpose series is shown in Table 31.1. Having measured the melting points of each of the pure compounds, take the mid-point of each value for the thermometer reading of melting point for each compound and the mid-point of the literature melting point of each compound and plot them graphically using literature temperature as the y-axis and the thermometer reading as the x-axis. The straight-line plot will obey the equation $y = mx + c$, where $y =$ real temperature (literature m.pt.), $x =$ thermometer reading, $m =$ slope and $c =$ intercept. If you use a computer and suitable program, the values of m and c will be calculated and you then solve the equation for using the thermometer

Table 31.1 A typical series of standards for thermometer calibration

Compound	Literature m.pt.
Naphthalene	79–80 °C
Benzoic acid	121 °C
4-Nitroaniline	147 °C
4-Toluic acid	180–182 °C
Anthracene	216–218 °C

reading (*x*-axis values) to find the real temperature of melting (*y*-axis values) to find the true melting range.

Of course, if you break or lose your thermometer, you must calibrate another.

Mixed melting point determination

You can confirm the identity of a compound by determining a mixed melting point. If you prepare a mixture of your unknown chemical and the one you suspect it may be and measure the melting point of the mixture then there are two possible results:

1. The melting point of the mixture is the same as the pure compound, which means that the unknown compound and the known compound are the *same*.

2. The melting point of the mixture is lower than either of the two pure components and the melting range is large. This is because the two compounds are different with the result that one is an impurity in the other.

For example, both benzoic acid and mandelic acid are white crystalline solids which melt at 121 °C. However a 1 : 1 mixture of the two compounds begins to melt at about 80 °C.

The usefulness of mixed melting points is limited in that you must have some idea of the chemical nature of your unknown compound and a sample of the suspected compound must be available.

Sources for further study

Furniss, B.A., Hannaford, A.J., Smith, P.W.G. and Tatchell, A.R. (1989) *Vogel's Textbook of Practical Organic Chemistry*, 5th edn. Longman, Harlow, Essex.

Harwood, L.M., Moody, C.J. and Percy, J.M. (2000) *Experimental Organic Chemistry*, 2nd edn. Blackwell Science Ltd, Oxford.

Haynes, W.M. (ed.) (2010) *CRC Handbook of Chemistry and Physics*, 91st edn. CRC Press, Boca Raton.

Zubrick, J.W. (2007) *The Organic Chem Lab Survival Manual. A student's guide to techniques*, 7th edn. John Wiley & Sons Ltd, Chichester.

Study exercises

31.1 You have prepared a solid crystalline compound which you think is *N*-phenylethanamide (literature m.pt. = 114 °C) and its m.pt. range is 108–110 °C. Draw three possible conclusions from this result.

31.2 You have obtained a sample of a white crystalline compound which you think is benzoic acid (literature m.pt. = 121 °C) and its m.pt. range is found to be 120–128 °C. Draw three possible conclusions from this result.

31.3 You have carried out a synthetic procedure which results in a mixture of 2-nitroaniline (literature m.pt = 92 °C) and 4-nitroaniline (literature m.pt. = 148 °C). Purification by recrystallisation is said to separate the two isomers and your sample, when mixed with pure 4-nitroaniline, has a m.pt. range 147–148 °C. What can you conclude?

Recrystallisation – involves allowing a hot solution of the required compound to cool.

Crystallisation – implies allowing the solvent to evaporate from a solution of the compound. Crystallisation will *not* remove solvent-soluble impurities since they will be deposited as the solvent evaporates.

Limits of purification – crude solids containing only up to 10–15% impurities can be purified by recrystallisation. Otherwise chemical purification or chromatography (p. 378) will be required to produce a compound, which can then be further purified by recrystallisation.

The products from many synthetic preparations are seldom pure and the technique of recrystallisation, which involves dissolving the impure material in a hot solvent and then cooling the solution to produce crystals, is routinely used to purify covalent organic and inorganic solids.

In general there are three types of impurities, which are removed by the recrystallisation process:

1. Insoluble material: anti-bumping granules, pieces of filter paper, traces of drying agents, grit, hair and other materials which may have been present in the starting chemicals.

2. Small quantities of unreacted starting chemicals and/or by-products from side reactions or other isomers.

3. Very small amounts of coloured by-products resulting from oxidation or polymerisation of the chemicals used.

Recrystallisation is designed to remove all these types of impurity and provide a pure product suitable for melting point measurement. Purification by recrystallisation is based on the theory of saturated solutions (p. 191) and a suitable recrystallisation solvent is one in which the chemical to be purified is *insoluble* in the *cold solvent* and *soluble* in the *hot solvent*.

When the crude reaction product is dissolved in the hot solvent the insoluble impurities (type 1 above) can be removed by hot filtration (p. 241). When the hot solution is allowed to cool, the solution becomes saturated with the desired compound and it precipitates from the cold solution. The cold solution does not become saturated with the lower concentration of the contaminants of type 2, which therefore remain in solution. Coloured impurities (type 3) can be removed by absorption using charcoal as described on p. 244.

The recrystallisation process can be divided into three separate steps:

1. Selection of a suitable solvent.

2. Recrystallisation of the crude compound.

3. Drying the purified solid.

> **KEY POINT** Practice in the technique of recrystallisation is important, since the aim of the procedure is to produce the maximum quantity of the highest quality product. Poor technique often results in *low recovery* of *high-quality* product or *high recovery* of *low-quality* product.

Solvents for recrystallisation

You can decide on a suitable solvent for recrystallisation of your crude chemical product in several ways:

- The experimental protocol may tell you which solvent to use.

- If you know the identity of the compound you have made, reference texts may indicate a suitable solvent (e.g. Haynes, 2010; Buckingham and Macdonald, 1995).

- If you are not sure of the identity of the compound you have prepared or if it is a new compound, you must carry out a 'solvent selection' to find out which solvent is the most appropriate (p. 239).

When selecting a suitable solvent for recrystallisation, chemists work to the general rule 'like dissolves like' when considering the polarity of the chemical to be recrystallised and the polarity of the solvent. In general solvents for recrystallisation are classified in terms of polarity and miscibility. Solvent polarity depends upon the overall distortion of the electron clouds in the covalent bonds within the solvent molecules, resulting in a dipole. The greater the dipole, the greater the polarity of the solvent, e.g. trichloromethane has three polarised C–Cl bonds, giving an overall dipole to the molecule and producing a good solvent for many molecules, but in tetrachloromethane all of the C–Cl dipoles cancel out, giving a non-polar solvent with different solvent properties in comparison. An additional feature that adds solvating power is *hydrogen bonding*. Thus water, a polarised molecule, can form hydrogen bonds with oxygen and nitrogen atoms in solutes, dissolving them efficiently.

When you are choosing a solvent for recrystallisation, look for the following general characteristics:

- A high dissolving power for the solute at high temperature and a low dissolving power at room temperature or below, so that a high recovery of purified compound can be achieved.

- A high or negligible dissolving power for the impurities, so that they will either be filtered off or remain in solution.

- A relatively low boiling point, to facilitate drying the purified compound.

The miscibility of solvents with each other must be taken into account when attempting *mixed-solvent recrystallisations* (see p. 240); the properties of some common recrystallisation solvents, which you are likely to encounter in your laboratory work, are shown in Table 32.1. Remember that this is only a general list of solvents; further information on solvent properties can be found in standard textbooks such as Harwood *et al.* (2000, p. 133), Loewenthal (1992, p. 146) and Furniss *et al.* (1989, p. 137).

Yields from recrystallisation – some of the compound that you require will remain dissolved in the solvent, because it has to form a saturated solution. Therefore you can *never* recover 100% of your compound by recrystallisation.

Definitions

Solvents which mix in all proportions, such as water and ethanol, are said to be *miscible*, whereas solvents which do not mix, e.g. water and petrol, are *immiscible*.

Table 32.1 Selected solvent properties

Solvent	b.pt. (°C)	Polarity	Miscibility with water	Comments: class of organic compounds recrystallised
Water	100	V. high	Yes	Always use when suitable: salts, aromatic acids
Ethanol	78	High	Yes	Flammable: alcohols, acids, amides
Propanone	56	High	Yes	Flammable: carbonyl compounds
Ethyl ethanoate	78	Medium	No	Flammable: esters
Dichloromethane	41	Medium	No	Toxic: halogen compounds, ethers
Toluene	110	Low	No	Flammable: hydrocarbons
Light petroleum	40–60	V. low	No	Flammable: hydrocarbons

Solvent selection

To find a suitable solvent for recrystallisation you must carry out a series of tests measuring the solubility of your crude compound in a series of solvents (cold and hot) of varying solvent polarity. This series of tests is called 'solvent selection' and is carried out on a test tube scale but, as your technique improves, you can carry out the tests using semi-micro scale since you will use less of your compound during the process. The procedure for solvent selection at the test tube scale is described in Box 32.1 and modification of the procedure to semi-micro scale requires only a corresponding reduction of the quantities of solvent and solute used.

> **KEY POINT** When carrying out the solvent selection experiments you must always cool the solution after heating. Do not assume that if the compound is insoluble in the cold solvent and dissolves when heated, it will always precipitate on cooling.

Mixed solvents

When no single solvent is found to be suitable for recrystallisation, then a mixed solvent system must be used. There are three essential properties required for a pair of solvents to be used in a mixed-solvent system:

1. The two solvents must be miscible in all proportions over the temperature range to be used.

2. The solute must be insoluble in one of the solvents.

3. The solute must be soluble in the other solvent.

It is an advantage if the two solvents have similar boiling points within 20–30 °C.

Suitable common solvent pairs from the solvents given in Table 32.1 are water/ethanol and dichloromethane/light petroleum (b.pt. 40–60 °C), but many other combinations are possible. One of the most frequently encountered mixed solvent systems is 'aqueous ethanol' (water/ethanol) in which the compound to be recrystallised is insoluble in water and very soluble in ethanol.

You can identify the solubility characteristics of your compound using the solvent selection procedure shown in Box 32.1 and modifications for mixed solvent selection are given in Box 32.2.

Using mixed solvents for recrystallisation – never assume that a mixed solvent system is a mixture of *equal volumes* of the two solvents. The ratio of the two solvents is established practically during the recrystallisation experiment.

The recrystallisation process

Having chosen a suitable solvent system, the process to be used to purify the bulk of your impure compound can be separated into several distinct steps:

- Dissolution of the solid using a single-solvent or a mixed-solvent system.

- Decolorisation using charcoal: even if your compound is white, decolorisation will improve its appearance significantly.

- Hot filtration (p. 244) to remove solvent-insoluble impurities and charcoal.

Box 32.1 How to carry out a solvent selection for recrystallisation of an unknown compound

A suitable range of solvents for general use, in order of decreasing polarity, is: water, ethanol, propanone, ethyl ethanoate, dichloromethane, toluene and light petroleum (b.pt. 40–60 °C).

1. **Clean and dry seven Pyrex® test tubes** to ensure that you will have no problems with contaminated solvents when carrying out the solubility tests.

2. **Add a small sample of the compound under test to each tube,** using just enough compound to cover the bottom of the test tube.

3. **Add about 2.0 mL of a pure solvent to the first tube and observe the effect.** You should look for the following features, which may help in the next recrystallisation stage:

   (a) **The solid does not dissolve, but it is 'wetted' by the solvent.** This implies that the solvent *may* be suitable for use in recrystallisation.

   (b) **The compound dissolves easily.** Therefore the solvent is *unsuitable* for recrystallisation and there is no need to continue tests with this solvent.

   (c) **Most of the compound dissolves but leaves a small amount of insoluble residue.** This means that there are solvent-insoluble impurities present in your compound, but the solvent itself is *unsuitable* for use in recrystallisation.

   (d) **Some colour is released into the solvent and the compound becomes lighter in colour.** This means that there could be a coloured impurity present in your compound and it will be necessary to decolorise the product in the recrystallisation experiment.

4. **Heat the mixture in the test tube** by an appropriate means, bearing in mind the flammability and toxicity of the solvent, to see if the solid dissolves in the hot solvent. For non-flammable solvents, remember to hold the test tube with a holder (see p. 177) and to 'wave' the test tube over the heat source to prevent 'bumping' (p. 171). Flammable solvents should be heated using a steam bath in a fume cupboard: *do not* lower the test tube into the steam bath and leave it there. Instead you must 'wave' the test tube in the steam escaping from the bath to achieve controlled heating. This is particularly important with low-boiling-point flammable or toxic solvents such as propanone, dichloromethane and light petroleum (b.pt. 40–60 °C). You should look for the following results:

   (a) **The solid does not dissolve in the hot solvent,** which is therefore *unsuitable* for recrystallisation and there is no need to continue tests with this solvent.

   (b) **The solid dissolves** and thus the solvent *may be* useful for recrystallisation.

   (c) **Most of the compound dissolves but leaves a small amount of insoluble residue.** This means that there are solvent-insoluble impurities present in your compound and the solvent *may be* suitable for use in recrystallisation.

   (d) **The solid melts and floats on the meniscus at the top of the solvent** giving the *appearance* of having dissolved. This is a common feature of low-melting-point hydrocarbons such as naphthalene and other non-polar aromatic compounds: shake the test tube to see if oily globules are released from the meniscus. If this occurs, the solvent is *unsuitable* for recrystallisation.

5. **Cool the test tube** in an ice-water bath or under a cold stream of water ensuring that no water gets into the test tube. There are several possible results:

   (a) **The compound recrystallises in high yield on cooling:** often there will appear to be more solid than you started with because of the fine crystals produced. This solvent is *suitable*.

   (b) **The compound recrystallises in low yield on cooling:** the solvent is *unsuitable* unless no better alternative can be found.

   (c) **The compound remains in solution after cooling:** the solvent is *unsuitable* or a supersaturated solution has been formed. To check if the formation of a supersaturated solution has occurred, gently scratch the inside of the test tube at the surface of the solution with a Pyrex® rod. The scratches provide points of nucleation for crystal growth and crystals should form rapidly if the solution is supersaturated. Take care when scratching the test tube with the glass rod (see p. 246). If a supersaturated solution is formed, then the solvent is *suitable* for recrystallisation.

6. **Repeat the test using the other solvents** and record your results in tabular form to include your experimental observations and conclusions.

7. **If you have found several suitable solvents,** then select one after considering factors such as flammability, toxicity and boiling point, since you will need to use much larger volumes of solvent in the recrystallisation process, with consequent complications in the equipment to be used (see Table 32.2).

8. **If you have not found a suitable solvent,** then you will need to carry out a *mixed-solvent* recrystallisation and you must find out which combination of solvents will be suitable (see Box 32.2).

Box 32.2 How to carry out a mixed-solvent selection for recrystallisation of an unknown compound

From your solvent selection tests (Box 32.1) you will have discovered the individual solvents in which your compound is soluble (good solvents) and in which it is insoluble (poor solvents), when the solvents are cold. Proceed as follows:

1. **Choose a miscible solvent pair**, in which the solubility of your compound is appropriate.

2. **Place a small amount (about 0.2 g) of the compound in a clean dry Pyrex® test tube** and add a good solvent (about 2.0 mL) in which it is soluble.

3. **Heat the test tube by an appropriate method**, dependent on the solvent used, until the solid has dissolved. Remember that your original solvent selection may have shown that solvent-insoluble impurities are present.

4. **Add a few drops of the poor solvent from a Pasteur pipette**. A slight 'cloudiness' or precipitate should form, since the solubilising power of the good solvent has been decreased by the poor solvent and the solution will have been cooled slightly.

5. **Reheat the solution until the cloudiness or precipitate disappears** and then add a few more drops of the poor solvent to produce a precipitate.

6. **Repeat the heating and solvent addition process** until the point is reached when the precipitate *just* dissolves when the solution is heated. You now have a hot solution of your compound with the correct ratio of the two solvents.

7. **If you have added too much poor solvent and the precipitate will not redissolve on heating**, add enough good solvent to dissolve the precipitate and then continue to add poor solvent and heat as before.

8. **Cool the test tube in an ice–water bath**, to ensure that crystals are formed.

9. **If an oil is formed on cooling**, which may happen if the melting point of the solid is below the boiling points of the solvents used, you should use slightly more of the good solvent (or less of the poor solvent) or try a different combination of solvents.

10. **If crystals do not form on cooling**, you may have formed a supersaturated solution and you should 'scratch' with a Pyrex® glass rod, as described for single solvent selection (Box 32.1).

- Cooling, to produce the crystals.

- Collection of the crystals by suction filtration (p. 167).

- Drying (p. 179).

It is important to remember that for a successful recrystallisation, you need to use equipment of a size appropriate to the amount of solid and the volume of solvent you are likely to use. You can estimate the volume of solvent to be used by extrapolation of the data from your solvent selection tests. In general terms, conical flasks, beakers and round-bottom flasks should never be more than half-full of solution but, on the other hand, using small volumes of solutions in large flasks will result in losses of the compound on the sides of the vessels.

Dissolution

To carry out a single-solvent recrystallisation (Box 32.3) you must get the compound into solution and this is achieved by suspending it in the appropriate cold solvent, found in the solvent selection process, and then heating the mixture to dissolve the solid. The equipment used will depend on the boiling point of the solvent, its flammability and toxicity. Some general systems are shown in Table 32.2.

When heating solvents in conical flasks and beakers you should cover the top of the flask with a clock-glass or watch-glass to prevent excessive evaporation of the solvent, resulting in the formation of crystals

Box 32.3 How to carry out a single-solvent recrystallisation

Examples: Suppose that you have prepared a crude sample (about 4.0 g) of *N*-phenylethanamide (acetanilide) and you are to purify if by recrystallisation from water. The melting point of pure *N*-phenylethanamide is 114 °C (Lide, 2009).

1. **Weigh the crude sample** and retain a few crystals in case seeding is required.

2. **Transfer the solid**, using glazed paper or a solids funnel (p. 164), into a clean, dry conical flask (250 mL).

3. **Add cold water** (about 100 mL) and a glass rod as an anti-bumping device to the flask and then heat the mixture on a hot plate until the compound has dissolved completely. Then add more water (about 10 mL), to ensure that precipitation of the solute does not occur during the following stages.

4. **Remove the flask from the heat** and allow it to cool for 2 minutes.

5. **Add a small amount of decolorising charcoal (about 0.01 g) to the solution**, place a watch-glass on top of the conical flask and heat the mixture gently for 5 minutes.

6. **Prepare another clean, dry conical flask (250 mL)** and add water (about 20 mL) and a glass rod and then heat to boiling on the hot plate with a stemless funnel and fluted filter paper just above the neck (Fig. 32.1), so that the steam heats the funnel and filter paper.

7. **Filter the recrystallisation solution through the filter paper** using hand protection (rubber fingers or an insulated glove) and keep the filter topped up with solution to prevent cooling. At the same time, keep the recrystallisation solution hot during the filtration by putting it back onto the hot plate.

8. **When filtration is complete**, remove the collection flask from the heat, take out the glass rod and clamp the flask in an ice–water bath, covering the top of the flask with a watch-glass.

9. **When the solution is cold** (about 5 °C), collect the solid by suction filtration (Box 24.2), using the filtrate, not fresh water, to transfer the solid completely from the collection flask. If crystals do not form, either add a few crystals of the crude solid to 'seed' the supersaturated solution or 'scratch' with a Pyrex® glass rod to induce recrystallisation.

10. **Rinse the compound on the filter** using a little (about 5 mL) ice-cold water and continue suction, to make the crystals as dry as possible.

11. **Transfer the crystals to a clock-glass** using a spatula and spread them in a thin layer.

12. **Dry the pure compound in the oven** at 70 °C for about 30 minutes and test them with a spatula to check their dryness: they should not stick together.

13. **Allow the crystals to cool**, covering them with another clock-glass to prevent contamination.

14. **Transfer the purified crystals to a 'tared' watch-glass** on a balance to determine their weight and then transfer them to a labelled sample tube using folded glazed paper (p. 164).

15. **Calculate the efficiency of the process:**

$$\% \text{ recovery} = \frac{\text{weight of pure compound}}{\text{weight of crude compound}} \times 100$$

Table 32.2 Solvents for recrystallisation

Solvent	b.pt. (°C)	Glassware	Heat source	Containment
Water	100	Conical flasks, beakers	Burner, hot plate	None
Ethanol	78	Conical flasks	Water bath	Fume cupboard
Propanone	56	Conical flasks	Water bath	Fume cupboard
Ethyl ethanoate	78	Conical flasks	Water bath	Fume cupboard
Dichloromethane	41	Reflux	Water bath	Fume cupboard
Toluene	110	Reflux	Hot plate, mantle	Fume cupboard
Light petroleum	40–60	Reflux	Water bath	Fume cupboard

on the sides of the flask above the surface of the solution. *Do not forget to take the appropriate 'anti-bumping' precautions* (p. 171), because you may need to boil the mixture for several minutes to achieve complete dissolution of the chemical(s). You should use a glass rod, a wooden 'boiling stick' or anti-bumping chips in conical flasks of volume up to 500 mL; magnetic 'fleas' or anti-bumping granules in round-bottom flasks in reflux apparatus (p. 265); magnetic 'fleas' or stirring bars in large-volume glassware (> 500 mL).

Decolorisation

Small amounts of coloured impurities can be removed from your product by absorption on finely divided charcoal, which is then removed in the hot filtration process (p. 244). In general, you should use charcoal in *every* recrystallisation since the colour of white and coloured compounds is improved by 'decolorisation'.

The amount of charcoal used should be about 2% by weight of the sample to be recrystallised. Note the following important SAFETY POINTS:

- Add the charcoal only when the solution has been formed. If you add charcoal to the cold solution, you will not be able to see when all of the compound has dissolved.

- Do not add charcoal to a boiling or a very hot solution otherwise the solution will boil extremely vigorously, usually boiling out of the flask or reflux apparatus.

- To add charcoal to a hot solution, *remove* the flask from the heat source and then let it cool a little (not enough to cause precipitation). Add the charcoal either from a spatula (into a conical flask or beaker), a paper funnel (p. 164) or powder funnel (into a round-bottom flask with a ground-glass joint in reflux apparatus), and then reheat the solution.

Hot filtration

This is a modification of gravity filtration (p. 168), designed to remove solvent-insoluble impurities, charcoal, anti-bumping granules or magnetic 'fleas' from the hot solution before cooling the solution to form the crystals of purified product.

> **KEY POINT** Hot filtration is used to prevent cooling of the solution during the filtration process, which would result in the formation of crystals in the filter paper.

For a successful hot filtration the solution must pass through the filter paper and filter funnel into the collection flask as quickly as possible so that cooling and crystallisation do not occur. The following points should be noted:

- *Always* use a fluted filter paper (p. 168).

- *Always* use a 'stemless' glass filter funnel because cooling and thus crystallisation may occur in the funnel stem causing a blockage.

- *Always* heat the filter funnel and filter paper, either by pre-heating them in an oven or by using boiling solvent in the collecting flask (Fig. 32.1).

- If filtration is rapid, keep the filter cone 'topped up' with the hot solution being filtered, since this keeps the filter cone and filter funnel hot. If you allow the filter cone to empty of liquid, cooling and crystallisation may occur.

Coloured compounds – you should know something about the *colour* of the compound you are trying to purify. There is no point in trying to *remove* the colour from a coloured compound. However, charcoal will improve significantly the appearance of a coloured compound.

Solvent-insoluble impurities – remember that if you have found solvent-insoluble impurities, not *all* your 'compound' will dissolve in the hot solvent. You can confirm the presence of these by adding an excess of hot 'selected' solvent to a small sample of the crude compound. If it does not dissolve completely, solvent-insoluble impurities are present.

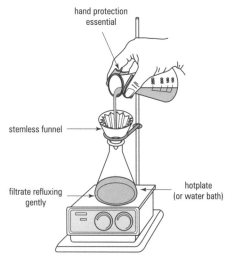

hand protection essential

stemless funnel

filtrate refluxing gently

hotplate (or water bath)

Fig. 32.1 Filtration of a hot solution.

Box 32.4 How to carry out a mixed-solvent recrystallisation

Examples: Suppose that you have prepared a crude sample (e.g. ~ 4.0 g) of *N*-phenylbenzamide (benzanilide). Your solvent selection tests have shown that it is insoluble in water and fairly soluble in cold ethanol. The melting point of pure *N*-phenylbenzamide is 158 °C (Lide, 2009). Proceed as follows:

1. **Weigh the crude sample** and retain a few crystals in case seeding is required.

2. **Transfer the solid**, using glazed paper or a solids funnel (p. 164), into a clean, dry conical flask (250 mL).

3. **Add cold ethanol** (about 25 mL) and a glass rod as an anti-bumping device to the flask and then heat the mixture on a water bath until the compound has dissolved completely.

4. **Add cold water** (about 5 mL) to the hot ethanol solution and a slight precipitate should form, which then redissolves – this is often seen as a 'flash' of white in the solution. Reheat the solution and add more water (5 mL). The precipitate will remain for a little longer and take more time to disappear on reheating.

5. **Repeat the water addition and reheating process**, but note that you will need to reduce the volume of water added at each consecutive addition, since the precipitate will take longer to redissolve as the solvating power of the ethanol is reduced by the water. Eventually, you will reach the situation where the precipitate just redissolves at the boiling point of the solvent mixture. You now have the ideal solvent mixture for recrystallisation of *N*-phenylbenzamide and any slight cooling of the solution will result in its precipitation.

6. **Remove the solution from the heat**, add ethanol (5 mL), to ensure that the *N*-phenylbenzamide remains in solution if it cools a little, add charcoal (about 0.01 g), place a watch-glass on top of the flask and reheat the solution on the water bath for about 5 minutes.

7. **Prepare another clean, dry conical flask (250 mL)** and add ethanol (about 10 mL) and a glass rod and then heat to boiling on the water bath with a stemless funnel and fluted filter paper just above the neck (Box 32.1) so that the ethanol vapour heats the funnel and filter paper.

8. **Filter the recrystallisation solution through the filter paper** using hand protection (rubber fingers or an insulated glove) and keep the filter topped up with solution to prevent cooling. At the same time, keep the recrystallisation solution hot during the filtration by putting it back onto the hot plate.

9. **When filtration is complete**, remove the filter funnel and restart the water addition and reheating process until the ideal solvent ratio is reached once again.

10. **Remove the collecting flask from the heat**, take out the glass rod and clamp the flask in an ice–water bath, covering the top of the flask with a watch-glass.

11. **When the solution is cold** (about 5 °C), collect the solid by suction filtration (Box 24.2), using the filtrate, to transfer the solid completely from the collection flask. If crystals do not form, either add a few crystals of the crude solid to 'seed' the supersaturated solution or 'scratch' with a Pyrex® glass rod to induce recrystallisation.

12. **Rinse the compound on the filter** using a little (about 5 mL) ice-cold water and continue suction, to make crystals as dry as possible.

13. **Transfer the crystals to a clock-glass** using a spatula and spread them out in a thin layer.

14. **Dry the pure compound in the oven** at 70 °C for about 30 minutes and test them with a spatula to check their dryness: they should not stick together.

15. **Allow the crystals to cool**, covering them with another clock-glass to prevent contamination.

16. **Transfer the purified crystals to a 'tared' watch-glass** on a balance to determine their weight and then transfer them to a labelled sample tube using folded glazed paper (p. 164).

17. **Calculate the efficiency of the process:**

$$\% \text{ recovery} = \frac{\text{weight of pure compound}}{\text{weight of crude compound}} \times 100$$

- When attempting a hot filtration with a mixed-solvent system, always ensure that the 'ideal' solvent ratio has not been reached, i.e. there is not enough of the poor solvent to cause immediate precipitation as a result of slight cooling during the hot filtration. The solvent ratio can be adjusted to the 'ideal' ratio for maximum recovery, after filtration and before cooling (Box 32.4).

Cooling

Rapid cooling in an ice–water bath ('crash-crystallisation') usually produces small crystals occluded with mother-liquor, whereas slow cooling by allowing the collection flask to stand on the laboratory bench often produces large well-defined crystals. Remember to:

- cover the top of the collection flask with a watch- or clock-glass to prevent solvent evaporation and entry of dust into the flask: *do not use* rubber bungs or corks since they may be pulled into the flask as it cools (p. 160);

- clamp the flask in place, if you use an ice–water bath, otherwise it may fall over as the ice melts and the volume of water increases;

- make sure that the solution is cold, even after slow cooling, so that maximum precipitation of the solid occurs.

If no crystals appear on cooling, you will have formed a supersaturated solution and, to induce precipitation of the solute, you must provide sites for nucleation and crystal growth. This can be achieved by either *seeding* the solution by adding a few crystals ('dust') of the crude compound or *scratching* the inside of the flask at the surface of the liquid, using a Pyrex® glass rod (Fig. 32.2).

SAFETY NOTE Take great care when 'scratching' a supersaturated solution with a glass rod. Hold the flask or test tube at the *neck*, not at the bottom, and make short scratching move-ments on the side of the flask just above and below the surface of the liquid (Fig. 32.2). If you accidentally break the flask or test tube you will cut your hand if you hold the vessel at the bottom.

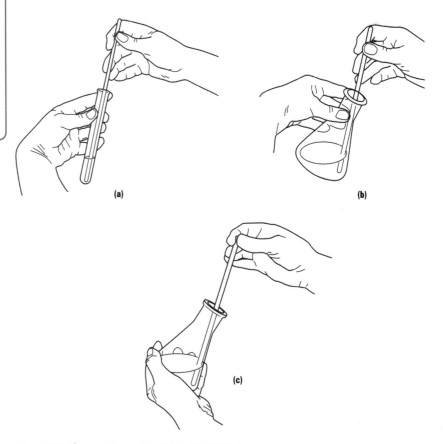

Fig. 32.2 'Scratching': (a) right; (b) right; (c) wrong.

Collection of the crystals

You should collect the purified crystals by suction filtration by the procedure described in Box 24.2 (p. 170). Remember to transfer the crystals from the collecting flask to the filter using a little of the filtrate: *do not use fresh solvent*. The filtrate is a saturated solution of the compound being recrystallised and cannot dissolve any more solute, but fresh solvent will dissolve some of your product resulting in an inefficient recrystallisation process.

Drying

The purified compound should be dried by the appropriate method as described on p. 179. If you do not know the melting point of your compound, you should always carry out a test by placing a small amount on a watch-glass in the oven, before committing the bulk of your chemical.

Detailed procedures for single-solvent and mixed-solvent recrystallisations are shown in Box 32.3 and Box 32.4 respectively and the modifications necessary for the use of other solvent systems can be worked out from the information in Table 32.2.

Problems in recrystallisation

Crystallisation in the filter paper:

prevention – keep everything hot and use a good fluted filter paper;

cure – wash through with hot solvent, evaporate most of the excess and repeat the hot filtration.

Evaporation of excess solvent – remove by rotary evaporation (p. 272) or N_2 blowdown (p. 274). This is the one occasion when water is the less than ideal solvent, since its evaporation is time consuming.

There are three common problems encountered during recrystallisation:

1. The compound crystallises in the filter funnel during hot filtration. This is because the solubility of the solute decreases rapidly with temperature and the slight cooling during hot filtration causes precipitation of the solid, even though you are heating the funnel. The answer is to use more than the minimum amount of solvent and then evaporate off the excess before cooling.

2. The compound does not recrystallise. There are two reasons: you have used too much solvent and you must evaporate off some solvent before cooling, or you have formed a supersaturated solution and you must 'seed' or 'scratch' the solution (see p. 246).

3. The compound precipitates as an oil. This is because compounds with low melting points often come out of a concentrated solution above their melting point. In such cases more solvent should be added and the compound redissolved and cooled so that precipitation is retarded to the temperature at which the crystalline solid comes out of solution. Often 'scratching' the hot solution as it cools can prevent 'oiling out'.

Text references

Buckingham, J. and Macdonald, F. (eds) (1995) *Dictionary of Organic Compounds*, 6th edn. CRC Press, Boca Raton.

Furniss, B.A., Hannaford, A.J., Smith, P.W.G. and Tatchell, A.R. (1989) *Vogel's Textbook of Practical Organic Chemistry*, 5th edn. Longman, Harlow, Essex.

Harwood, L.M., Moody, C.J. and Percy, J.M. (2000) *Experimental Organic Chemistry*, 2nd edn. Blackwell Science Ltd, Oxford.

Haynes, W.M. (ed.) (2010) *CRC Handbook of Chemistry and Physics,* 91st edn. CRC Press, Boca Raton.

Loewenthal, H.J.E. (1992) *A Guide for the Perplexed Organic Experimentalist*, 2nd edn. John Wiley & Sons Ltd, Chichester.

Sources for further study

Keese, R., Brandle, M.P. and Taube, T.P. (2008) *Practical Organic Synthesis: A Student's Guide.* John Wiley & Sons Ltd, Chichester.

Sharp, J.T., Gosney, I. and Rowley, A.G. (1989) *Practical Organic Chemistry*. Chapman and Hall, London.

Smart, L. (ed.) (2002) *Separation, Purification and Identification – The Molecular World.* Open University and Royal Society of Chemistry, Cambridge.

Williamson, K.L. (2006) *Macroscale and Microscale Organic Experiments*, 5th edn. Houghton Mifflin Harcourt, Boston.

Zubrick, J.W. (2007) *The Organic Chem Lab Survival Manual. A student's guide to techniques*, 7th edn. John Wiley & Sons Ltd, Chichester.

Study exercise

32.1 Prepare a list of all the laboratory equipment you would require to recrystallise, from ethanol, an off-white solid ($\approx$4 g) contaminated with a small amount of grit, which should have a m.pt. $\sim$ 140 °C.

33 Solvent extraction

Extraction – making a cup of coffee involves extraction of the flavour chemicals and caffeine from the insoluble vegetable matter using hot water and is an example of liquid–solid extraction.

This technique separates the components of chemical mixtures by using the dissimilar solubility properties of the components of the mixture in different solvents. Extraction is used mainly to purify a reaction product partially before final purification by recrystallisation (p. 238) or distillation (p. 255). The two common types of extraction process used in the laboratory are:

1. Liquid–liquid extraction: this uses two immiscible solvents; the desired compound in solution or suspension in one solvent is extracted into the other solvent. For example, covalent organic compounds are extracted from aqueous solution into dichloromethane, leaving the ionic by-products or reagents in the aqueous phase.

2. Solid–liquid extraction: this involves the use of a solvent to remove solvent-soluble components of a solid mixture.

Liquid–liquid extraction

Several experimental processes in practical chemistry are based on liquid–liquid extraction:

- 'Extraction': where a solid or liquid suspended or dissolved in one solvent is extracted into another. This technique can be used to separate covalent molecules from ionic compounds in an aqueous solution or suspension.

- 'Washing': where ionic species are removed from a non-polar solvent by extraction into water.

- 'Acid–base extraction': where covalent molecules are converted into their salts and thus removed from a non-polar solvent into water, while neutral covalent species will remain in the non-polar solvent, as shown in Table 33.1.

All of these processes involve mixing the two immiscible solvents, one of which contains the mixture, in a separatory funnel (p. 250) and shaking the funnel to promote the extraction process. The immiscible layers are allowed to reform and are then separated.

Table 33.1 Examples of acid–base extraction chemistry

ArCOOH	+	RH	$\xrightarrow[CH_2Cl_2]{NaOH}$	$ArCOO^- Na^+$	+	RH
Acid insoluble in H_2O soluble in CH_2Cl_2		Neutral insoluble in H_2O soluble in CH_2Cl_2		Salt soluble in H_2O		Neutral insoluble in H_2O soluble in CH_2Cl_2
ArNH$_2$	+	RH	$\xrightarrow[CH_2Cl_2]{HCl}$	$ArNH_3^+ Cl^-$	+	RH
Amine insoluble in H_2O soluble in CH_2Cl_2		Neutral insoluble in H_2O soluble in CH_2Cl_2		Salt soluble in H_2O		Neutral insoluble in H_2O soluble in CH_2Cl_2
ArCOOH	+	ArOH	$\xrightarrow[CH_2Cl_2]{Na_2CO_3}$	$ArCOO^- Na^+$	+	ArOH
Acid insoluble in H_2O soluble in CH_2Cl_2		Weak acid insoluble in H_2O soluble in CH_2Cl_2		Salt soluble in H_2O		Weak acid insoluble in H_2O soluble in CH_2Cl_2

Solvent extraction

Extraction calculations – it is necessary to calculate volumes of solvents and number of extractions when attempting to maximise the economics of an industrial-scale extraction process.

Separatory funnels – the coned-shaped funnels are specifically designed for extractions. Only use parallel-sided funnels when no alternative is available.

For liquid–liquid extraction, water is usually the polar solvent. Since most extractions involve getting the required compound into the organic solvent (or removing unwanted ionic chemicals from it), it should have good solvent power for the desired compound and a low boiling point for ease of removal and recovery of the compound. The common organic solvents used in liquid–liquid extraction are diethyl ether (ethoxyethane) b.pt. 34 °C, dichloromethane (DCM) b.pt. 41 °C and ethyl acetate (ethyl ethanoate) b.pt. 77 °C. Dichloromethane is denser than water and forms the lower layer, whereas diethyl ether and ethyl acetate float on water and are the upper layer.

Partition coefficients

The theory of liquid–liquid extraction is based on the equilibrium between the concentrations of dissolved component in the two immiscible liquids, when they are in contact. The equilibrium constant for this process is called the partition coefficient or distribution coefficient and is given by:

$$K = \frac{\text{concentration of solute in liquid 1}}{\text{concentration of solute in liquid 2}} \qquad [33.1]$$

You only need to calculate such quantities if:

- you are carrying out specific experiments to determine partition coefficients, when you will be given specific instructions or references to the appropriate literature;

- the solute has appreciable solubility in both solvents.

The reason calculation is not necessary is that, in the overwhelming majority of extractions you will carry out, the conditions used are designed to ensure that the components will be almost totally soluble in one of the liquids and almost insoluble in the other, since complete separation is required. The number of extractions needed to extract a water-soluble solute into an immiscible organic phase can be calculated from the following relationship:

$$w_n = w_0 \left(\frac{Kv}{Kv + s} \right)^n \qquad [33.2]$$

where K = partition coefficient of the solute, v = volume (mL) of aqueous solution of the solute, s = volume (mL) of immiscible organic solvent, w_0 = weight of solute initially in the aqueous layer, w_n = weight of solute remaining in the aqueous layer after n extractions, and n = number of extractions. Evaluation of this expression shows that, for a fixed volume of solvent, it is more efficient to carry out many small extractions than one big one.

Separatory funnels

These come in a range of sizes from 5 mL to 5000 mL and there are two general types: parallel sided and cone shaped (Fig. 33.1). Cone-shaped separatory funnels are made of thin glass and should be supported in a ring (p. 251). Small-volume cone-shaped funnels (< 100 mL capacity) and parallel-sided separatory funnels should be clamped at the ground-glass joint at the neck (p. 167).

Separatory funnels will have glass or Teflon® taps with a rubber ring and clip or screw cap on the end to prevent the tap slipping from the

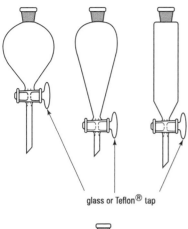

glass or Teflon® tap

Rotaflo® tap

Fig. 33.1 Separatory funnels.

Drying separatory funnels in an oven – *always* disassemble the tap and *do not* place the tap and its plastic components in the oven. Dry them with tissue.

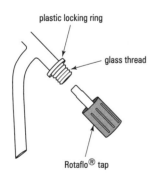

plastic locking ring

glass thread

Rotaflo® tap

Fig. 33.2 A Rotaflo® tap.

barrel, or a Rotaflo® tap. You must ensure that the tap assembly is in good condition by making the following checks before starting work:

- For glass taps: disassemble the tap by first removing the clip and ring or cap from the tap (note the order of the component parts for reassembling). Dry the tap and barrel with tissue, add a light smear of grease to the tap (making sure you do not clog the hole in the tap) and reassemble the tap and fittings, turning the tap to ensure free movement. Support the separatory funnel in position and add some of the organic solvent to be used (2–3 mL) to the funnel, with the tap closed, to check that the tap does not leak. If the tap leaks, disassemble and regrease.

- For Teflon® taps: disassemble the tap, wipe the tap and barrel with clean tissue, reassemble without grease, check for free movement of the tap and for leakage as described above. When you have finished using the funnel, loosen the clip/cap on the tap since Teflon® will flow under pressure and the tap may 'seize' in the barrel.

- For a Rotaflo® tap: unscrew the tap from the funnel and ensure that the plastic locking thread is in place (Fig. 33.2). If it is not present, consult your instructor and obtain a replacement. Dry the barrel of the tap and the tap with a tissue and reassemble. Do not grease the Rotaflo® tap.

The general procedure for using a separatory funnel for extraction is described in Box 33.1 and there are five additional practical tips to aid your success:

1. Label **all** flasks to avoid confusion.

2. ***Never throw away any of the separated liquids until you are absolutely sure of their identity***.

3. ***Always*** transfer solvents into the separatory funnel using a stemmed filter funnel so that solids and liquids will not stick to the inside of the joint and prevent a good seal when you insert the stopper and then invert the funnel.

4. ***Always*** place a ***'safety' beaker*** under the separatory funnel to collect liquid just in case the tap leaks (Fig. 33.3(a)).

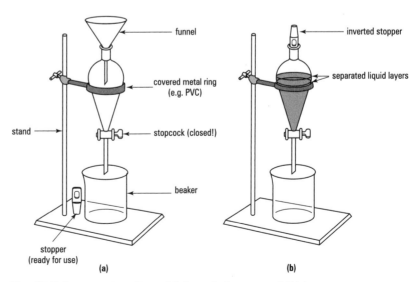

Fig. 33.3 A separatory funnel (a) ready to use and (b) in use.

Box 33.1 How to separate a carboxylic acid and a hydrocarbon using solvent extraction

This is an example of an acid–base extraction. The solid mixture (e.g. 4.0 g for the solvent volumes used below) of benzoic acid and naphthalene is soluble in dichloromethane but benzoic acid will dissolve in dilute aqueous sodium hydroxide (2 M) by forming the sodium salt (sodium benzoate). Naphthalene is insoluble in water.

1. **Dissolve the mixture in a clean, dry beaker in dichloromethane (50 mL).**

2. **Clean and dry the tap** of a separatory funnel (250 mL) and set up as shown in Fig. 33.3(a).

3. **Make sure that the tap is *closed*** and then add the solution containing the mixture, using a stemmed funnel to prevent contamination of the joint, and rinse out the beaker with dichloromethane (∼ 5 mL).

4. **Add sodium hydroxide solution (10 mL) to the separatory funnel**, place the stopper in the separatory funnel and gently invert it and hold it as shown in Fig. 33.4. *Do not shake the separatory funnel* since you do not know how much heat will be produced in the reaction, which will pressurise the separatory funnel.

5. **Open the tap**, to release any pressure caused by the heat of reaction.

6. **Close the tap, shake the mixture once** and open the tap to release any pressure.

7. **Close the tap, shake the mixture twice** and open the tap to release any pressure.

8. **Repeat** until no more vapour is expelled via the tap.

9. **Close the tap**, and replace the separatory funnel in the ring or clamp.

10. **Take out the stopper**, place it upside down in the top of the separatory funnel and allow the solvent layers to separate. The upper layer is the aqueous layer (10 mL compared with 50 mL of dichloromethane). Sometimes a few globules of dichloromethane will 'cling' to the surface of the water layer: these can be released by gently swirling the contents of the separatory funnel.

11. **When the liquids have stopped swirling, open the tap gently** and *slowly* run the dichloromethane lower layer into a clean conical flask and label it 'dichloromethane layer'. Avoid fast emptying of the funnel because a vortex may be formed which will cause the upper layer to run out with the lower layer.

12. **Run the remaining aqueous layer** into a clean, dry conical flask and label it 'sodium hydroxide layer'.

13. **Return the dichloromethane layer** to the separatory funnel and extract it with another portion (10 mL) of sodium hydroxide. Repeat the extraction process for a total of 40 mL (i.e. 4 × 10 mL) of the alkali, collecting all the sodium hydroxide extracts in the same flask.

14. **Finally, extract the dichloromethane with water (20 mL)**, to remove any traces of sodium hydroxide and add these 'washings' to the sodium hydroxide layer' flask.

15. **You now have** a solution of naphthalene in dichloromethane and a solution of sodium benzoate in sodium hydroxide ready for further processing.

16. **If an emulsion forms** – the layers do not have a well defined boundary: add a few drops of methanol to the upper layer down the inside wall of the funnel. This often 'breaks' the emulsion.

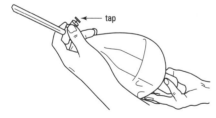

Fig. 33.4 Holding a separatory funnel.

Batch liquid–liquid extraction – the process described is inefficient if the material being extracted has appreciable solubility in both of the solvents used. In these situations a *continuous extraction system* is necessary and you should consult the specialist textbooks, e.g. Furniss *et al.* (1989, p. 160).

5. *Always* take the stopper from the separatory funnel before you attempt to allow liquid to run from the funnel. If you do not remove the stopper from the top of the funnel, a vacuum is formed in the funnel after a little of the liquid has run out. Air will be sucked into the funnel through the outlet stem causing bubbles, which will remix your separated layers. If your funnel is equipped with a Quickfit® stopper, it is good practice to take the stopper out of the top and put it back upside down (Fig. 33.3(b)). This ensures that no vacuum is formed and that organic vapours do not escape easily from the flask.

Solid–liquid extraction

In this process the components of a solid mixture are extracted into a solvent. The 'batch process', analogous to liquid–liquid extraction, involves grinding the solid to a fine powder, mixing it with the appropriate solvent, and filtering off the solid by gravity (p. 167) or

Box 33.2 How to set up a Soxhlet extraction system

1. **Select apparatus of the appropriate size for the amount of solid to be extracted.** Specifically, the Soxhlet thimble should fit below the siphon outlet and the volume of the solvent reservoir should be such that it is never more than half-full when all the solvent has siphoned from the extractor.

2. **Assemble the apparatus as shown in Fig. 33.5,** clamping at the joints at the flask and the *top* of the Soxhlet extractor. The best heat source to use for continuous operation over a long period is a mantle.

3. **Disassemble the apparatus,** leaving the clamps in position.

4. **Fill the flask to about one-third of its volume with solvent,** add some anti-bumping granules (or a magnetic 'flea', if a stirrer-mantle is being used) and clamp it into position in the mantle.

5. *Lightly* **grease the 'male' joint of the Soxhlet extractor** and attach it to the reservoir flask. Clamp the top of the extractor.

6. **Add solvent to the extractor until it siphons.** This ensures that the reservoir will never be dry. Check that the reservoir is now no more than half-full; if it is, replace with a larger flask.

7. **Half-fill the extraction thimble with the solid to be extracted** and plug the top of the thimble with white cotton wool to prevent any solid being carried over into the solvent.

8. **Place the thimble in the extractor.**

9. **Attach a water supply to the reflux condenser,** lightly grease the male joint and attach the condenser to the top of the extractor. Turn on the water, ensuring a steady flow.

10. **Switch on the heater and turn up the power so that the solvent refluxes** and drips into the extractor.

11. **Confirm that everything is running smoothly by watching at least two siphoning cycles** of the extraction and check the apparatus frequently.

12. **When the extraction is complete, allow the apparatus to cool and dismantle it.** Place the extraction thimble in the fume cupboard to allow the solvent to evaporate and the dispose of it appropriately. Gravity filter or decant the solvent in the reservoir flask to remove the anti-bumping granules of magnetic 'flea' and remove the solvent by distillation (p. 255) or rotary evaporation (p. 271).

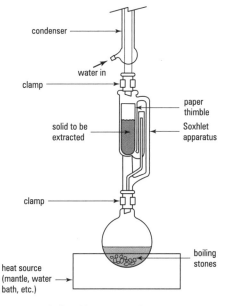

Fig. 33.5 A Soxhlet extraction system.

under vacuum (p. 168) and then evaporating the solvent (p. 271) from the extract solution. However, a more elegant 'continuous extraction process', called Soxhlet extraction, is available when the most appropriate solvent is known.

The apparatus for Soxhlet extraction is shown in Fig. 33.5 and comprises a flask containing the solvent, a Soxhlet extractor and a reflux condenser (p. 265). The solid to be extracted is placed in a porous thimble, made from hardened filter paper, and the solvent is heated so that its vapour flows past the thimble, condenses and fills the extractor with hot solvent to extract the solid. When the extractor is full, the solvent (together with the extracted material) siphons back into the solvent flask and the process is repeated automatically. The advantage of this procedure is that fresh solvent continually extracts the solid, which is concentrated in the flask. The disadvantage is that the compound extracted is kept at the boiling point of the solvent for a prolonged period. Soxhlet extractors come in sizes of 10 mL to 5000 mL, based on the volume of solvent contained in the extractor. The procedure for using a Soxhlet extraction system is described in Box 33.2.

Text reference

Furniss, B.A., Hannaford, A.J., Smith, P.W.G. and Tatchell, A.R. (1989) *Vogel's Textbook of Practical Organic Chemistry*, 5th edn. Longman, Harlow, Essex.

Sources for further study

Harwood, L.M., Moody, C.J. and Percy, J.M. (2000) *Experimental Organic Chemistry,* 2nd edn. Blackwell Science Ltd, Oxford.

Keese, R., Brandle, M.P. and Taube, T.P. (2008) *Practical Organic Synthesis: A Student's Guide.* John Wiley & Sons Ltd, Chichester.

Loewenthal, H.J.E. (1992) *A Guide for the Perplexed Organic Experimentalist*, 2nd edn. John Wiley & Sons Ltd, Chichester.

Sharp, J.T., Gosney, I. and Rowley, A.G. (1989) *Practical Organic Chemistry*. Chapman and Hall, London.

Smart, L. (ed.) (2002) *Separation, Purification and Identification – The Molecular World.* Open University and Royal Society of Chemistry, Cambridge.

Williamson, K.L. (2006) *Macroscale and Microscale Organic Experiments*, 5th edn. Houghton Mifflin Harcourt, Boston.

Zubrick, J.W. (2007) *The Organic Chem Lab Survival Manual. A student's guide to techniques*, 7th edn. John Wiley & Sons Ltd, Chichester.

Study exercise

33.1 Find at least four errors in the diagram below, which illustrates a student's attempt at liquid–liquid extraction.

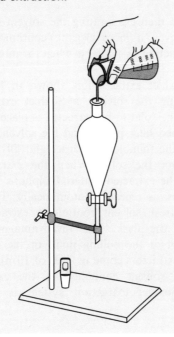

Distillation is used to separate the components of a liquid mixture by vaporising the liquids, condensing the vapours and collecting the liquid condensate. Separation is the result of the differing boiling points of the individual constituents of the mixture and the efficiency of the distillation column. You may be required to *purify* a liquid by *distillation*, which involves the removal of small quantities of impurities, or to *separate* a mixture of liquids by *fractional distillation*, each of which can then be purified by distillation.

You will meet several types of distillation process each applicable to different situations depending on the chemicals to be purified or separated.

- *Simple distillation*: used for separating liquids, boiling *below* 200 °C at atmospheric pressure, from other compounds. For effective separation there should be a difference in the boiling points of the components of at least 80 °C.

- *Fractional distillation*: used for separating components of liquid mixtures, which have boiling points differing by more than 25 °C, at temperatures *below* 200 °C.

- *Vacuum or reduced-pressure distillation*: used for separating liquids boiling *above* 200 °C, when decomposition may occur at the high temperature. The effect of distilling at reduced pressure is to lower the boiling point of a liquid. This technique can be applied to both simple distillation and fractional distillation.

- *Steam distillation*: used for separating mixtures of chemicals such as oils, resins, hydrocarbons, etc., which are essentially insoluble in water and may decompose at their boiling points. Heating the compounds with steam makes them distil *below* 100 °C.

Distillation equipment

Apparatus used for the various types of distillation has several general features:

- Distillation flask: usually round bottom or pear shaped with one or two necks (to allow a vacuum bleed to be fitted).

- Still-head: to hold the thermometer and to channel the vapour into the condenser. For fractional distillation, the fractionating column is fitted between the distillation flask and the still-head.

- Condenser: usually with circulating cold water.

- Take-off adapter: to allow the distillate to run into the collecting vessel. For vacuum distillation, the adapter will have a vacuum inlet tube and could have three 'arms' to allow three fractions to be collected without breaking the vacuum.

- Receiving (collection) vessel: this can be a test tube, a measuring cylinder, a conical flask, or a round-bottom flask with a ground-glass joint.

Working with azeotropes – not all liquid mixtures can be separated by distillation. In some cases an *azeotrope*, a mixture of the liquids of definite composition, which boils at a constant temperature, is formed. For example, an azeotrope containing 95.5% ethanol and 4.5% water boils at 78.15 °C, which is below the boiling point of pure ethanol (78.3 °C). Therefore 100% ethanol cannot be obtained by distillation of ethanol–water mixtures, even though their boiling points are about 22 °C apart.

Using steam distillation – in practice, the decision to use this approach to separate the components of a mixture is based on previous experience. Consult your instructor for advice.

Setting up distillation apparatus – do not allow the support stands to move during the distillation, since this will allow the ground-glass joints connecting the still-head and condenser to separate. The hot vapours will then escape into the laboratory instead of going down the condenser.

Securing distillation components – do not use plastic joint clips on the 'hot end' of a distillation apparatus since they may melt and the joints may separate.

Distillation

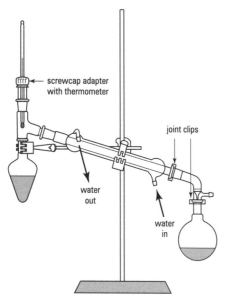

Fig. 34.1 Apparatus for simple distillation.

Heating a distillation flask – unlike when using a microburner, it is difficult to stop the heating process instantly when using an oil bath or mantle on a 'labjack'. Therefore have a clean receiver flask ready to collect the 'tailings' as soon as the temperature begins to rise.

Collecting fractions – as the temperature begins to rise 'between fractions' you will have 2 or 3 seconds to change receiving vessels before the liquid runs from the top to the bottom of the condenser. **Have three or four pre-weighed receivers ready to hand.**

Distillation in fume cupboards – it may be necessary to insulate the fractionating column from the 'wind' by wrapping it in aluminium foil, since the draught prevents equilibration in the column. Don't forget to leave a 'window' in the foil so that you can see the vapour condensing near the top of the column.

No matter what type of distillation you are attempting, it is essential that you assemble the apparatus correctly, since you are dealing with hot, often flammable, liquids and vapours. A typical simple distillation apparatus is shown in Fig. 34.1 and the method of assembly is described in Box 34.1.

> **KEY POINT** You must ensure that all the ground-glass joints are seated properly and the apparatus is clamped firmly so that no movement of the joints will allow vapours to escape.

Simple distillation

The procedure for doing a simple distillation is described in Box 34.2 and you should note the following points:

- Do not distil to dryness, i.e. no liquid remaining in the distillation flask, since this causes overheating and charring (decomposition) of the residue. *Always* leave 1 or 2 mL of liquid in the distillation flask.

- Initially, some liquid may distil while the temperature rises rapidly. This is termed 'forerun' which is often a small amount of solvent from an extraction process (p. 249), for example. Collect and then, when the temperature stabilises, collect the desired compound in a clean receiving vessel.

- Towards the end of the distillation, the temperature may begin to rise again: this will be the higher boiling impurity. Stop heating, quickly remove the receiving flask containing your pure compound and collect these last few drops, termed 'tailings', in a fresh receiving vessel.

Fractional distillation

Simple distillation is not very effective in separating liquids unless their boiling points are at least 80 °C apart and a better separation can be achieved if a fractionating column is used. There are many types available (Fig. 34.2) and the device brings the ascending vapours into contact with the condensing (in the fractionating column) liquid and amounts to a succession of many simple distillations in which the descending liquid strips the high-boiling component from the ascending vapour. Overall, the lower boiling component distils first and cleanly.

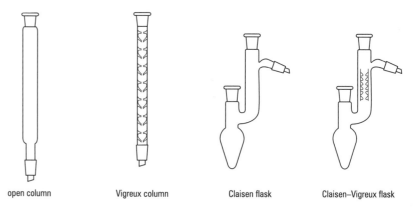

open column   Vigreux column   Claisen flask   Claisen–Vigreux flask

Fig. 34.2 Common fractionating columns.

Box 34.1 How to assemble the apparatus for a simple distillation

In general laboratory work you will usually be distilling small volumes of liquids (~ 25 mL). Standard glass joint-ware apparatus size 14/23 (p. 181) is appropriate. If you are to carry out larger scale distillations, you must consider the weight of the components, specifically the receiver flask, which should be supported on a 'labjack', since a joint clip may not be strong enough to hold a large flask (250 mL or larger).

1. **Clamp the distilling flask firmly to a support stand** ensuring that it is at the correct height to allow the heat source (microburner, oil bath or mantle on a 'labjack') to be removed if necessary.

2. **Insert the still-head** in the top of the flask.

3. **Carefully line up the condenser on a clamp** (attached to the same support stand as the distilling flask (Fig. 34.1), if possible) and adjust the height and angle of the clamp so that the condenser slides onto the still-head joint. Remember to have the non-moving jaw of the clamp at the bottom (p. 167) otherwise you will lift the condenser when you tighten the clamp and break the joint on the still-head or condenser or both. Carefully tighten the clamp and ensure that the joints are 'seated'.

4. **Attach the take-off adapter to the bottom of the condenser with a joint clip.** If you are using a Quickfit® flask as a receiving flask, *you must use a vacuum-type take-off adapter* (p. 183) otherwise you will be distilling in a closed system, which may explode when you begin to heat the distilling flask.

5. **Attach the Quickfit® receiver flask to the take-off adapter with a joint clip** or place the receiver flask underneath the take-off adapter, supported on a 'labjack' or clamped in position. The outlet of the take-off adapter must be just inside the receiving vessel so that no spillage of distillate will occur. If you clamp the receiving vessel in position, use a separate support stand.

6. **Disassemble the apparatus in the reverse order to assembly** by opening the clamps – *do not move the clamps and stands*.

7. **Add the liquid to be distilled to the distillation flask** using a stemmed funnel, together with anti-bumping granules or boiling stick or a magnetic 'flea'. The flask should not be more than 50% full. Reclamp the flask in position.

8. **Lightly grease the 'male' joint on the still-head** and replace it in the flask.

9. **Insert a thermometer into a screwcap adapter** (p. 184) and adjust so that the bulb is just below the outflow from the still-head. Lightly grease the joint on the screwcap adapter and put it into the still-head.

10. **Fit the rubber tubing onto the condenser** (p. 265), lightly grease the joint on the still-head and refit the condenser, clamping it firmly into place.

11. **Connect the lower tube** to the water tap so that the water will flow up the condenser, and upper tube should be routed into the sink. Make sure that there are no kinks in the rubber tubes and, for safety, feed them over the protruding arms at the back of the clamps. Turn on the water tap gently and check that the water flows freely.

12. **Lightly grease the bottom joint of the condenser** and attach the take-off adapter using a joint clip.

13. **Attach the Quickfit® receiving flask to the take-off adapter with a joint clip** (after lightly greasing) or place the receiving vessel underneath the take-off adapter, supported on a 'labjack' or clamped into position. Turn up the water flow to give a steady stream from the condenser.

Box 34.2 How to carry out a simple distillation

1. **Set up the apparatus as described in Box 34.1** and make sure that all the joints in the distillation system are secured properly.

2. *Slowly* **apply the heat source to the distillation** until the liquid is boiling gently.

3. **Increase the heat slowly until the liquid starts to drip into the receiving vessel** at a rate of about one drop every 2 seconds. If the temperature is 'constant' (i.e. it does not vary more than 2–3 °C), collect the liquid and record the temperature range of the distillate.

4. **Remove the heat source**, allowing the apparatus to cool down and the remaining drops of distillate to run out of the condenser into the receiving flask.

5. **Seal and label the receiving flask(s).**

6. **When cool, dismantle the apparatus**, wash it out with an appropriate solvent and dispose of the washings in the correct solvent residues bottle.

Box 34.3 How to carry out a fractional distillation

1. **Set up the apparatus as described Box 34.1 but insert the fractionating column between the distilling flask and the still-head.** For extra stability, clamp the fractionating column at its top joint to support the stand carrying the distilling flask.

2. **Apply the heat source slowly until the liquid begins to boil gently.** Then slowly increase the heat until the column is warmed up and liquid is condensing from the thermometer bulb, *but not distilling over.*

3. **If the temperature is constant, increase the heat slightly until the first component distils over at a rate of about one drop every 2 seconds.** Collect this distillate as the first fraction, as long as the temperature is 'constant' (i.e. it does not vary more than 2–3 °C). Record the temperature range of the distillation.

4. **Change the receiving flask when the temperature begins to rise and the rate of distillation slows.**

5. **Increase the heat slowly** and collect the intermediate fraction until the temperature stabilises again. Record the temperature range of the distillation.

6. **Change the receiving flask** and collect the new fraction (one drop every 2 seconds) for as long as the temperature remains 'constant' (i.e. it does not vary by more than 2–3 °C). Record the temperature of the distillation.

7. **Remove the heat source,** allowing the apparatus to cool down and the remaining drops of distillate to run out of the condenser into the receiving flask.

8. **Seal and label the receiving flask(s).**

9. **When cool, dismantle the apparatus,** wash it out with an appropriate solvent and dispose of the washings in the correct solvent residues bottle.

SAFETY NOTE You must check all flasks and glassware for 'star' cracks and chips. *If in doubt, replace.*

The column packing, usually glass beads, helices or 'fingers', gives a large surface area for contact of the ascending vapours and descending liquid. After the first fraction has distilled, the temperature will rise and the rate of distillation will slow. This is an intermediate fraction containing a little of both components of the mixture. Finally, the temperature will become constant and the pure higher boiling compound will distil. The procedure for fractional distillation is given in Box 34.3.

KEY POINT A successful fractional distillation relies on thermal equilibration of the components in the fractionating column. You must allow the column to be heated by the vapours of the mixture. Take your time!

Working with reduced pressures – distillation flasks and receiving flasks must always be round bottom or pear shaped. Do not use flat-bottom or conical flasks under vacuum.

Measuring reduced pressures – note that despite SI nomenclature for pressure, practical work usually involves pressure measurement in mm of Hg. Atmospheric pressure is about 760 mm Hg. Pressures quoted in 'torr' (seen on some old vacuum equipment) are equivalent to mm Hg.

Moving a mercury manometer – always carry mercury manometers in a vertical position or the mercury may spill out.

Vacuum or reduced-pressure distillation

Distillation at reduced pressure is used to distil liquids with few impurities or to fractionate the components of liquid mixtures with high boiling points, which would decompose if distilled at atmospheric pressure. The modifications to the distillation apparatus (Fig. 34.1) required for reduced-pressure distillation are:

- A vacuum source: this can be a water pump (see p. 168) with an 'anti-suck-back' trap producing a vacuum of 15–25 mm Hg, at best; or a rotary vacuum pump (consult your instructor about its use since it is an expensive piece of equipment and easily contaminated or damaged), which will evacuate down to 0.1 mm Hg. Two-stage dry vacuum pumps produce a vacuum of 1–5 mm Hg, are resistant to organic and acid vapours and are easy to use.

- A manometer to measure the pressure (vacuum) in the apparatus, since the boiling point of a liquid varies with pressure. Two types are in

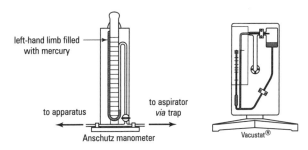

left-hand limb filled
with mercury

to apparatus

to aspirator
via trap

Anschutz manometer

Vacustat®

Fig. 34.3 Manometers for vacuum distillation.

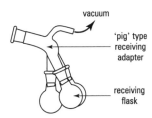

vacuum

'pig' type
receiving
adapter

receiving
flask

Fig. 34.4 'Pig'-type receiving flask adapter.

common use (Fig. 34.3): the Anschutz manometer, which gives a constant reading of the vacuum throughout the distillation, and the Vacustat®, which is used to take a 'sample' of the vacuum at a given instant. Vacustats® are very accurate and are more often used in combination with a rotary oil pump.

- A take-off adapter, which permits the collection of several fractions without stopping the distillation to change the receiving flasks. A receiving adapter, termed a 'pig' (Fig. 34.4), can be rotated on the end of the condenser to collect three fractions.

- Appropriate 'anti-bumping' measures: reduced-pressure distillations are notoriously prone to 'bumping' (p. 171) and anti-bumping granules are ineffective. You can use a magnetic 'flea' in conjunction with a hot plate-stirrer and oil bath; an air bleed, made by pulling out a Pasteur pipette into a fine capillary using a microburner (consult your instructor), inserting it into a screwcap adapter (p. 184) and placing it in the second neck of the distilling flask. The vacuum pulls a fine stream of air into the flask and forms small bubbles which agitate the liquid during distillation; or a wooden boiling stick for small-scale distillations of short duration, since the vacuum will pull air from the stick and agitate the liquid.

- A three-way tap inserted between the vacuum source and the manometer, so that you can control the vacuum applied to the distillation system.

A typical system for reduced-pressure distillation is shown in Fig. 34.5 and the procedure, using a water pump, is described in Box 34.4.

SAFETY NOTE Do not allow air to rush into an Anschutz manometer, otherwise the mercury in the left-hand limb of the manometer will shoot up the tube and may break the glass at the top.

SAFETY NOTE If, during the course of your vacuum distillation using a micro-burner and a boiling stick, the liquid stops boiling and appears 'quiescent', it is about to 'bump' vigorously. Stop heating, allow it to cool, 'break' the vacuum (Box 34.4), and add a new boiling stick.

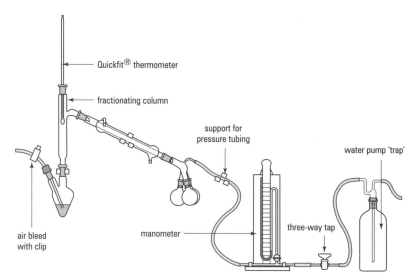

Fig. 34.5 Apparatus for vacuum distillation.

Ending a distillation – complete distillation of a liquid is not possible because of the need to leave a few millilitres in the distilling flask, to prevent overheating and due to the 'hold-up' volume of the flask and fractionating column.

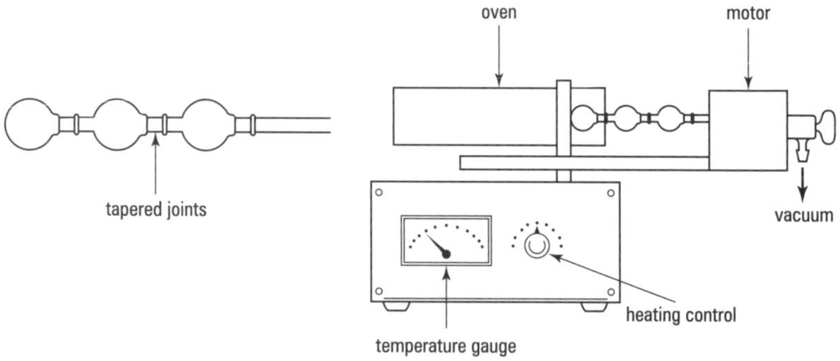

Estimating the boiling point of a liquid at reduced pressure – a useful guide is: *if the pressure is halved, the boiling point is reduced by ~10°C*. For example, if the b.pt is 300°C at 760 mm Hg, it will be approximately 290°C at 380 mm Hg and 190°C at ~1 mm Hg. Alternatively a nomograph (Fig. 34.8) can be used for a more accurate estimation.

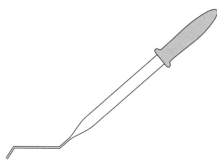

Fig. 34.7 A 'bent' Pasteur pipette.

Fig. 34.6 Kugelrohr distillation apparatus.

Kugelrohr distillation

This is also known as short-path distillation or bulb-to-bulb distillation. It is a procedure for reduced-pressure distillation, which almost eliminates losses owing to the size of the apparatus, and is particularly useful for small volumes of liquids. The liquid sample is placed in a small round-bottom flask, connected to a series of bulbs (Fig. 34.6) and then heated and rotated (to prevent bumping) under vacuum in an electric oven. The liquid distils from the flask inside the oven to a cold bulb outside the oven. Since the distillation path is very short the length of a ground-glass joint losses are minimised. The use of several bulbs as receiver flasks allows a small volume of mixture to be fractionated by varying the temperature in the oven. The distillates can be removed from the bulbs by either washing into another flask with a low-boiling-point solvent or using a 'bent' Pasteur pipette (Fig. 34.7) since the bulbs can only be held horizontally.

Steam distillation

This process can be used to separate water-insoluble covalent compounds from crude reaction mixtures or to isolate volatile natural products, e.g. terpenes from plant tissue. The crude mixture is heated with water and steam and the steam-volatile material co-distils with the steam and is then condensed with the water and collected. You will then need to carry

Box 34.4 How to carry out a reduced-pressure distillation using a water pump

1. **Set up the distillation apparatus as described in Box 34.1**, but use a two-necked distilling flask and include a short fractionating column between the top of the distilling flask and the still-head *or* use a Vigreux flask (Fig. 34.2) *or* use a Claisen still-head (Fig. 34.2).

2. **Connect three Quickfit® round-bottom receiving flasks to the receiving adapter or 'pig' using plastic joint clips** and attach the 'pig' to the bottom of the condenser. Support the receiving flasks on a 'labjack' if they are 100 mL size or larger. Rotation of the 'pig' allows three fractions to be collected without stopping the distillation – this is a major task when working under reduced pressure.

3. **Insert the air bleed into the 'spare' neck of the distilling flask** or into the lower joint on the Vigreux flask or Claisen head and make sure that the tip of the air bleed reaches the bottom of the distilling flask. If you are using boiling sticks as an 'anti-bumping' precaution, add the sticks, making sure that they reach to the bottom of the flask and do not float, and put stoppers in the unused joints.

4. **Insert a Quickfit® thermometer into the remaining 'male' joint in the apparatus.** *Do not use* an ordinary thermometer in a screwcap adapter: it may be sucked into the apparatus and break or crack the flask.

5. **Using thick-walled rubber pressure tubing, connect the water pump** (via the anti-suck-back trap) to the three-way tap and then to the Anschutz manometer. Connect another piece of pressure tubing to the manometer but do not connect it to the 'pig' for the moment.

6. **To check the available vacuum**, turn on the water pump fully, kink or seal the open pressure tubing on the manometer and turn the three-way tap so that a vacuum is created in the manometer. Slowly open the tap on the manometer and the mercury level should rise in one of the manometer 'arms'. When the mercury has stabilised, move the scale so that the zero is level with the lowest mercury level, and read off the upper mercury level. The pressure (vacuum) is the difference in levels in mm. The reading should be between 10 and 20 mm. Now close the tap on the manometer, unkink or unseal the pressure tubing, and turn the three-way tap so that air is admitted into the system.

7. **Connect the pressure tubing from the manometer to the 'pig'.** Pressure tubing is heavy and it should be supported with a clamp and stand, close to the 'pig', to prevent strain on the glassware.

8. *Slowly* **turn the three-way tap to evacuate the apparatus.** As the pressure decreases, bubbles will issue from the air bleed or the boiling stick and low-boiling solvents such as dichloromethane or diethyl ether will begin to boil, causing frothing in the flask. If this happens, stop applying the vacuum via the three-way tap and wait until the frothing has died down and then continue to lower the pressure until the three-way tap is fully open.

9. **Check whether the air bleed is too coarse**, producing large bubbles and vigorous splashing in the distillation flask. If so, place a piece of pressure tubing (about 2 cm long) on the end of the air bleed and constrict the tubing with a screw clip to reduce the air flow through the air bleed to an acceptable rate.

10. *Slowly* **open the tap on the manometer**, allow the mercury levels to stabilise and read the vacuum by moving the zero on the scale to the lower mercury level: the reading should be 15–25 mm or better. If this pressure is not obtained, there must be leaks in the system, which usually occur at the ground-glass joints or rubber-to-glass joints. Close the tap on the manometer, check the sealing of the joints by rotating each one in turn and also check the rubber-to-glass joints by carefully pushing the rubber pressure tubing a little further onto the glass. Open the tap on the manometer and recheck the pressure.

11. *Gently* **heat the distilling flask** and carry out a fractional distillation as described in Box 34.3, collecting the fractions by rotating the 'pig'. Remember to record the temperature *and pressure* at which the fractions distil. If the liquid in the distilling flask bumps over into the condenser, you will need to clean out the apparatus with a solvent, evaporate off the solvent to recover the chemicals and restart the whole process.

12. **When the distillation is complete, close the tap on the manometer** and allow the apparatus to cool. Support the 'pig' and receiving flasks (with your hand or a 'labjack') and slowly open the three-way tap to allow air into the system. Disconnect the pressure tubing from the 'pig' and place the 'pig' and receiving flasks in a safe place. Disconnect all other tubing and apparatus for washing or storage, turn off the water pump and finally, *very gently*, open the tap on the manometer to allow the mercury levels to equalise and then close the tap.

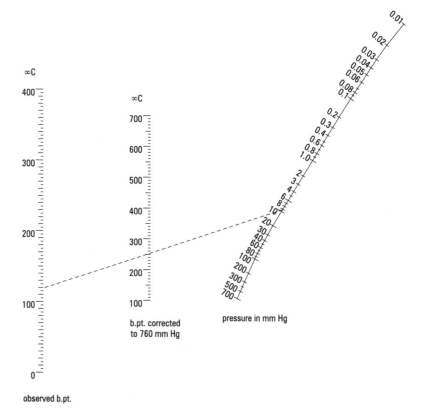

Fig. 34.8 Nomograph for estimating boiling point at reduced pressure. To use it, draw a line between the recorded pressure and the boiling point at 760 mm Hg, and then extend the line to the observed boiling point scale. This point is the boiling point at the reduced pressure. In this example, a liquid b.pt. of 250 °C at 760 mm Hg will boil at 118 °C at 10 mm Hg.

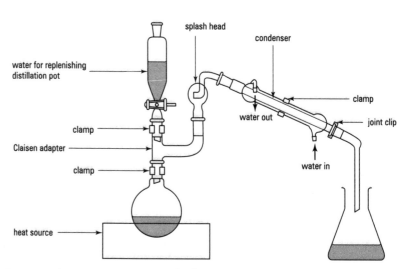

Fig. 34.9 Apparatus for steam distillation.

out an extraction (p. 249) to separate the water and the insoluble component.

The steam required for a steam distillation can be provided by an external source, such as piped steam in the laboratory or steam generated by heating water in a flask, which is then piped into the distilling flask. Steam is very dangerous and the safest way to generate steam is to heat the compound with a vast excess of water in the distilling flask: steam is

---

Box 34.5 How to carry out a steam distillation

1. **Set up the apparatus for distillation** as described in Box 34.1 with the following modifications:

   (a) Use a Bunsen burner with tripod and gauze as the heat source.

   (b) Use a large three-necked flask as the distilling flask, usually 250 mL or 500 mL capacity for most laboratory procedures or a single necked flask with a Claisen head (Fig. 34.9).

   (c) Use a splash-head instead of a still-head since there is no point in recording the distillation temperature and it is more important not to contaminate the distillate by splashing from the distillation flask.

   (d) Insert an addition funnel (a separating funnel with a ground-glass joint on the stem) into the distilling flask and fit a stopper in the remaining neck of the flask.

   (e) Use a single-surface condenser: it is easier to unblock than a double-surface condenser.

   (f) Use a simple take-off adapter leading into a large conical flask since you will be collecting a large volume of water.

2. **Add the compound to be distilled to the flask via the spare neck**, half-fill the distillation flask with water, add a large portion of 'anti-bumping' granules and fill the addition funnel with water.

3. **Heat the flask until steady boiling commences and distillation of an oily emulsion begins.** Then continue the distillation adding water from the addition funnel to maintain the level of water in the distillation flask.

4. **If the distillate is a solid, it may clog and block the condenser.** If this occurs, turn off the condenser water, take the condenser tube off the tap to let the water drain out of the condenser and allow the steam to heat up the condenser and melt the solid, which will then flow into the receiving flask. Then carefully restore the water flow.

5. **The distillation is complete when no more oily emulsion is condensing** (check by collecting a few drops of distillate in a clean, dry test tube). Turn off the heat and allow the apparatus to cool before dismantling.

6. **Separate the product from the water** by extraction into a suitable organic solvent (p. 252).

---

generated *in situ*. The equipment for steam distillation is illustrated in Fig. 34.9 and the procedure is described in Box 34.5.

> **KEY POINT** You must never attempt a distillation in a completely closed system. Always check that the expanding vapours can escape.

Sources for further study

Furniss, B.A., Hannaford, A.J., Smith, P.W.G. and Tatchell, A.R. (1989) *Vogel's Textbook of Practical Organic Chemistry*, 5th edn. Longman, Harlow, Essex.

Harwood, L.M., Moody, C.J. and Percy, J.M. (2000) *Experimental Organic Chemistry*, 2nd edn. Blackwell Science Ltd, Oxford.

Keese, R., Brandle, M.P. and Taube, T.P. (2008) *Practical Organic Synthesis: A Student's Guide.* John Wiley & Sons Ltd, Chichester.

Loewenthal, H.J.E. (1992) *A Guide for the Perplexed Organic Experimentalist*, 2nd edn. John Wiley & Sons Ltd, Chichester.

Sharp, J.T., Gosney, I. and Rowley, A.G. (1989) *Practical Organic Chemistry*. Chapman and Hall, London.

Smart, L. (ed.) (2002) *Separation, Purification and Identification – The Molecular World*. Open University and Royal Society of Chemistry, Cambridge.

Williamson, K.L. (2006) *Macroscale and Microscale Organic Experiments*, 5th edn. Houghton Mifflin Harcourt, Boston.

Zubrick, J.W. (2007) *The Organic Chem Lab Survival Manual. A student's guide to techniques*, 7th edn. John Wiley & Sons Ltd, Chichester.

34.1 An organic liquid has a boiling point of 340 °C at 760 mm Hg. Using the information on p. 260, estimate its **approximate** b.pt. at the following pressures:

(a) 190 mm Hg

(b) 100 mm Hg

(c) 20 mm Hg

(d) 1.0 mm Hg

(e) 0.1 mm Hg

34.2 Use the nomograph (Fig. 34.8) on p. 262 to make an accurate estimation the boiling point of the liquid using the information in **34.1** above.

35 Reflux

When carrying out reactions using volatile or dangerous chemicals or solvents – use a reflux system to keep the vapours in the apparatus even though the mixture is not heated to its boiling point.

Refluxing overnight – you *must* have the approval of your instructor for these operations and complete the necessary documentation for the night-staff. A special laboratory may be available for 'overnight' reactions.

Since the water pressure may change during the night, you must fix the coolant tubes in place, on the condenser and the tap, using copper wire twisted round the rubber tubing or plastic cable ties.

Stirring in pear-shaped flasks – special triangular-shaped 'fleas' are now available for the conical-base tubes used for evaporation and microscale reactions, but they are not yet common in the undergraduate laboratory.

Reflux is one of the most common techniques you will encounter in your chemistry laboratory classes. Since many reactions between covalent compounds are slow processes rather than instantaneous reactions, prolonged heating forces the equilibrium to give an acceptable amount of product. In the reflux process, the reactants are dissolved or suspended in a suitable solvent, the solvent is boiled and then condensed so that it returns to the reaction flask. Once set up, a reaction carried out under reflux can be run for minutes, hours or even days to promote the required reaction. The basic components for a reflux apparatus are:

- a reaction flask;
- a reflux condenser;
- a heat source (see p. 172);
- a coolant source, usually water, for the condenser.

The procedure for setting up a simple reflux apparatus (Fig. 35.1) is given in Box 35.1.

Reaction flasks

Round-bottom or pear-shaped reaction flasks are preferred, but note that stirring with the usual type of magnetic 'flea' is not possible in pear-shaped flasks. The flasks can have multiple necks so that the apparatus can be configured for temperature measurement, addition of solids or liquids, mechanical stirring and inert atmosphere work (p. 276). No matter which arrangement of components is used, always clamp the reaction flask at the neck and keep the heaviest components (such as an addition funnel containing another chemical) vertically above the flask. A condenser will still function at 30° from vertical and it is not very heavy.

Condensers

For general-purpose work, these are usually single-surface or double-surface types (Fig. 35.2): the double-surface condenser is used for low-boiling point solvents such as dichloromethane, diethyl ether or light petroleum (b.pt. 40–60 °C).

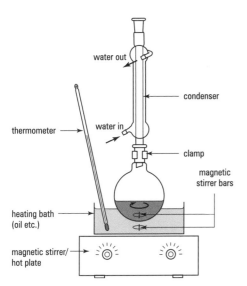

Fig. 35.1 Apparatus for simple reflux.

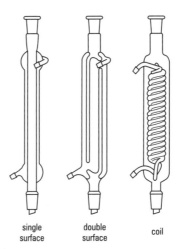

Fig. 35.2 Condensers.

Box 35.1 How to set up a simple reflux apparatus

1. **Choose a round-bottom or pear-shaped Quickfit®
flask** of appropriate size so that it will be no more
than half-full and clamp it to a support stand.

2. **Select the appropriate heat source and anti-
bumping protection**, and adjust the height of the
flask so that the heat source can be removed easily
if something goes wrong.

3. **Choose a condenser of appropriate size** and type so
that it will condense the volume of vapour formed
in the reflux process. For example, do not use a
small condenser with a 14/23 joint on a 250 mL flask,
since it will not cope with the volume of vapour to
be condensed, or a large condenser on a small flask,
where all the solvent may be converted into vapour
before condensation occurs.

4. **Add the liquids/solids and the solvent to the flask**,
using the solids funnel, paper funnel or stemmed filter
funnel (p. 164) so that you do not get chemicals on the
inside of the ground-glass joint. If you do contaminate
the joint, it may not allow the condenser to 'seat'
properly and hot solvent vapour will escape into the
atmosphere. Wipe the joint clean with tissue.

5. **Fit the rubber tubing to the condenser;** the lower tube
is connected to the water tap so that the water flows
up the condenser for the most efficient cooling.

6. **Lightly grease the joint on the condenser** and place
it in the flask, rotating it to ensure a good seal. Do
not clamp the condenser – gravity will keep it in
place – but make sure that it is vertical. You may
need to move the set-up quickly away from the heat
source and it is easier to manipulate if only one
clamp, on the neck of the flask, is present.

7. **Tidy the coolant pipes behind the clamp** ensuring
that there are no kinks, the pipes are not touching
the heat source and the outlet pipe is positioned in
the drain or sink. Turn on the water gently to check
for leaks and, if all is correct, turn up the water to
give a steady flow.

8. **Apply enough heat to bring the liquid to the boil**,
check that the solvent is refluxing at a steady rate and
that the vapour is condensing no higher than one-
third of the length of the condenser. The apparatus
can then be left, with regular monitoring, for the
reaction to proceed.

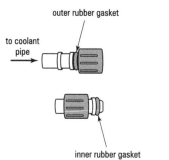

Fig. 35.3 Plastic connectors for condensers.

Refluxing anhydrous reactions – if it is
necessary to exclude atmospheric water
or oxygen or carbon dioxide, guard
tubes are ineffective and the reaction
must be carried out under an inert
atmosphere (p. 276).

SAFETY NOTE Always use a fresh guard
tube because the action of water on the
drying agent may form a solid 'cake' and
seal the guard tube. This will act as a
'stopper' and pressurise the reflux
apparatus when you begin heating and
may cause an explosion. Do not pack the
tube *too* tightly with drying agent.

Rubber tubing for coolant water is attached to the condenser in two ways:

1. If the condenser has glass inlet and outlet pipes with a 'knuckle', wet
the inside of the rubber tube with a little water and slide it onto the
pipe and past the 'knuckle'. The rubber tubing must be a tight fit
otherwise it may slide off over a period of time.

2. Modern condensers have plastic adapters, which can be attached to the
tubing and then screwed on the threaded inlet and outlet pipes. Slide the
rubber tubing onto the moistened 'pipe' on the adapter, and then screw
the adapter onto the condenser. You *must* ensure that the adapter has a
rubber gasket on the inside of the threaded portion (Fig. 35.3),
otherwise it will leak water at the condenser inlet or outlet.

KEY POINT You should always attach rubber tubing to a condenser before fitting it to the apparatus.

Drying tubes

Water can get into your reaction by condensation from the
atmosphere or by condensation of the steam produced in a water
bath. To exclude water, you should fit a guard tube containing a solid
drying agent such as anhydrous calcium chloride or calcium sulphate
to the top of the condenser. A typical guard tube is shown in
Fig. 35.4; use a coarse-sized drying agent rather than a fine powder,
which would 'cake' very quickly as it absorbs moisture.

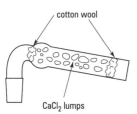

cotton wool

CaCl₂ lumps

Fig. 35.4 A CaCl$_2$ guard tube.

> **SAFETY NOTE** Never attempt to use a pressure-equalising dropping funnel as a separatory funnel because, when you invert the funnel, the solvent will flow down the side arm, past the tap and onto you or the laboratory bench!

Reflux with addition of chemicals

Instead of stopping the reaction and opening the apparatus, you can put in the new chemicals using an addition or 'dropping' funnel. Addition funnels are separatory funnels (see p. 251) with a ground-glass joint on the stem, and there are two types (Fig. 35.5):

1. Addition funnels: when you add a liquid or solution from the funnel to the reaction flask, you must take out the stopper, otherwise a vacuum is formed and the liquid does not flow out (see p. 252). This is a disadvantage when using compounds with irritating or toxic vapours or which are air sensitive. The simplest solution to this problem is to fit a guard tube, instead of a stopper, to the addition funnel and then the liquid or solution will flow easily into the reaction flask.

2. Pressure-equalising dropping funnels: these have a side arm linking the reservoir of the funnel to the inlet stem below the tap. The pressures in the reservoir and the reaction flask are equal, and liquid will flow into the reaction flask even when the stopper is in place in the funnel. Pressure-equalising dropping funnels are very expensive and are normally only used for inert atmosphere reactions (p. 268).

Box 35.2 How to set up the apparatus for reflux with mechanical stirring

1. **Clamp a multineck flask to a heavy support stand** at a height where you can put the heating source (mantle or oil bath) underneath, on a 'labjack'.

2. **Slide the stirring rod through the stirrer gland**, add the stirrer paddle and fit into the clamped joint of the flask. Lift the stirrer rod so that the paddle is not touching the bottom of the flask.

3. **Slide a piece of rubber pressure tubing** (about 40 mm long) half-way onto the drive shaft of the stirrer motor and fix the stirrer motor onto the support stand about 3 mm above the top end of the stirrer rod.

4. **Very carefully line up the centre of the pressure tubing on the motor** with the centre of the stirring rod and ensure that the drive shaft, stirring rod, stirrer gland and flask are aligned and vertical: look at the set-up from several different angles and adjust the clamps as appropriate until you are sure.

5. **Lift the stirring rod and slide it into the rubber tubing**, about 10 mm, and then raise the flask so that the stirrer paddle is about 2 mm above the bottom of the flask. Finally tighten all the clamps firmly.

6. **Make sure that the stirrer motor speed control is set to the minimum speed or zero.** Switch on the power and turn the speed control to the lowest setting. If the stirrer turns smoothly and slowly, all is well. You can increase the speed to check for vibration and 'whip' and then turn the speed down to zero. If the stirrer is reluctant to stir or seems 'stiff', switch off the power and readjust the apparatus.

7. **If the glass stirring rod 'slips' in the rubber tubing**, tighten the tubing round the glass rod with twisted copper wire or a plastic cable tie.

8. **Add the chemicals to the flask** (stemmed funnel) through one of the other necks, grease and fit a reflux condenser and addition funnel (if appropriate). Start the motor and increase the speed to give a steady stirring rate.

9. **Raise the heat source under the flask** and adjust the power to give steady boiling.

10. **When the reaction is complete, remove the heat source and allow the apparatus to cool to room temperature.** Switch off the stirrer and disconnect from the mains and remove the condenser and addition funnel. Carefully lower the reaction flask about 40 mm (the stirrer paddle will be lifted from the bottom of the flask by 40 mm), cut the copper wire or plastic tie holding the top of the stirrer rod in the rubber tube and *carefully* ease the stirrer rod out of the rubber connection. Unclamp the stirrer motor and put it aside. You can now remove the stirrer and stirrer gland from the reaction flask, rinsing the paddle into the flask with a little fresh solvent.

Adding a chemical to a refluxing reaction – many reactions are exothermic, so you should add the new chemical to the reaction at such a rate that the height of the refluxing vapour in the condenser does not change much.

The addition of dry solids to refluxing reactions requires special equipment and you should refer to the appropriate texts (Errington, 1997, p. 125; Harwood *et al.*, 2000, p. 88; Furniss *et al.*, 1989, p. 82). The simplest approach is to dissolve the solid in a small amount of the solvent being used and add it as a solution, using an addition funnel.

Reflux with mechanical stirring

When a magnetic stirrer is unsuitable, e.g. in reactions involving viscous liquids or mixtures of solids and liquids, a mechanical stirrer must be used. A mechanical or overhead stirrer system comprises:

1. An electric variable speed motor connected to the mains supply.

2. A flexible connector, usually a short length of rubber tubing.

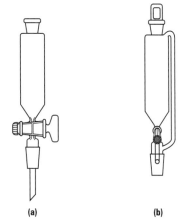

Fig. 35.5 Adding chemicals to a reflux apparatus: (a) addition funnel; (b) pressure-equalising funnel.

Heat sources – in cases where multiple clamps or mechanical stirring are used, the heat source must be mounted on a 'labjack' so that the heat source can be removed quickly if something should go wrong.

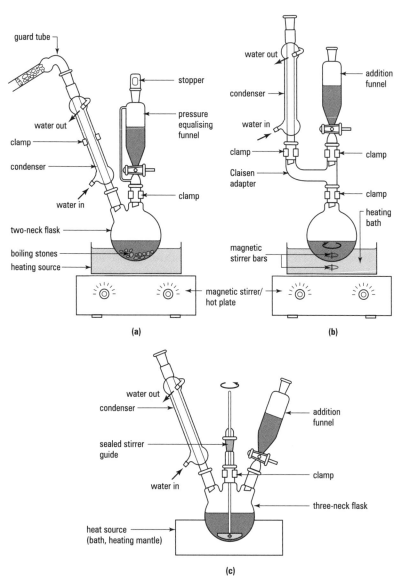

Fig. 35.6 Apparatus arrangements for reflux with addition: (a) heating a reaction mixture to reflux during the addition of a reagent; (b) heating a stirred reaction mixture during the addition of a reagent; (c) heating and overhead stirring of a reaction mixture during the addition of a reagent.

3. A stirrer gland, which fits into the top ground-glass joint of the flask acting as a seal for the refluxing vapour and a guide for the stirrer shaft. There are several types of gland available, but the best is now made from Teflon® and needs no lubrication. If this is not available, a screwcap adapter in which the rubber sealing ring has been lubricated with a touch of silicone oil can be used. Note that the stirrer shaft should rotate in the adapter, not the adapter in the joint of the flask, so do not tighten the screwcap too much.

4. A Teflon® paddle which swivels on the end of the stirrer shaft so that it can pass through the ground-glass joint on the top of the flask.

Setting up the apparatus for reflux with mechanical stirring is a precision task and is described in Box 35.2. The major problems encountered are:

- The weight of the stirrer motor high up on the support stand: use a large support stand with a heavy base or use a support framework, which is screwed to the laboratory bench. Besides the motor's weight, the torque of the motor can cause 'whipping' in the support stand.

- The motor, stirrer gland, stirrer shaft and reaction flask must be absolutely vertical and concentric, otherwise the glass stirrer shaft will snap.

- Since there will always be a little sideways movement when the stirrer is operating, the flask and the motor should be clamped in position *on the same stand*. Condensers and addition funnels should **NOT** be clamped.

A selection of configurations, suitable for most reflux procedures is shown in Fig. 35.6.

Text references

Errington, R.J. (1997) *Advanced Practical Inorganic and Metalorganic Chemistry*. Blackie Academic and Professional, London.

Furniss, B.A., Hannaford, A.J., Smith, P.W.G. and Tatchell, A.R. (1989) *Vogel's Textbook of Practical Organic Chemistry*, 5th edn. Longman, Harlow, Essex.

Harwood, L.M., Moody, C.J. and Percy, J.M. (2000) *Experimental Organic Chemistry*, 2nd edn. Blackwell Science Ltd, Oxford.

Sources for further study

Keese, R., Brandle, M.P. and Taube, T.P. (2008) *Practical Organic Synthesis: A Student's Guide*. John Wiley & Sons Ltd, Chichester.

Loewenthal, H.J.E. (1992) *A Guide for the Perplexed Organic Experimentalist*, 2nd edn. John Wiley & Sons Ltd, Chichester.

Sharp, J.T., Gosney, I. and Rowley, A.G. (1989) *Practical Organic Chemistry*. Chapman and Hall, London.

Smart, L. (ed.) (2002) *Separation, Purification and Identification – The Molecular World*. Open University and Royal Society of Chemistry, Cambridge.

Suib, S.L. and Tanaka, J. (1999) *Experimental Methods in Inorganic Chemistry*. Prentice Hall, Harlow, Essex.

Williamson, K.L. (2006) *Macroscale and Microscale Organic Experiments*, 5th edn. Houghton Mifflin Harcourt, Boston.

Zubrick, J.W. (2007) *The Organic Chem Lab Survival Manual. A student's guide to techniques*, 7th edn. John Wiley & Sons Ltd, Chichester.

Study exercise

35.1 You are to carry out the experiment to convert cyclohexene into 1,2-dibromo-cyclohexane by the dropwise addition of liquid bromine to cyclohexene at room temperature followed by heating to 100 °C for 30 minutes.

Do a Hazard Assessment of the materials involved in the reaction and decide on the apparatus you will use for the synthesis.

Evaporation – the purpose of evaporation is to remove the solvent from a solution. Purification or separation of the components of the solute is by other means, such as recrystallisation or distillation.

Evaporation is the process in which the solvent of a solution is converted into a vapour to leave a solid or liquid solute. There are many applications of evaporation, ranging from the slow evaporation of water from a solution of an ionic compound to leave hydrated crystals, e.g. crystallisation of $CuSO_4.5H_2O$, to the evaporation of large volumes of low-boiling-point solvent under reduced pressure in the extraction of an organic compound. Since crystallisation by evaporation is a specific technique for a relatively small range of compounds, the term evaporation is generally interpreted as the removal of the solvent from a solution.

Evaporation of solvents

There are three commonly used techniques for solvent evaporation:

1. Evaporation from open flasks on a steam bath.

2. Rotary film evaporation.

3. Gas 'blow-down'.

All these techniques have advantages and disadvantages. Where your experimental protocol may simply state 'the solvent is evaporated off', you should select the most appropriate procedure based on:

- the volume of solvent to be removed;

- the amount of solute in solution;

- the relative boiling points of the solvent and solute;

- the next step in the experimental procedure.

Evaporation from open flasks

SAFETY NOTE Clamp the conical flask in position on the steam bath. There is particular risk of the flask falling over when using small conical flasks (< 100 mL) and a glass rod.

This is useful for evaporating small volumes ($\sim 25\,mL$) of low-boiling-point solvents ($< 70\,°C$) from solutions containing a solute which has a boiling point above $110\,°C$. Place the solution in a beaker or conical flask, containing a glass rod or boiling stick, onto a steam bath (maximum temperature achievable is $100\,°C$) in a fume cupboard and evaporate the solvent until boiling ceases. The obvious advantage is simplicity; the disadvantages include environmental concerns of release of solvents in the atmosphere, contamination of the solvent by condensed steam and incomplete solvent removal due to the 'hold-up' volume of the flask.

Rotary film evaporation

Using 'rovaps' – these are communal so make sure that the 'rovap' is clean before you use it and clean it up after use. Empty the solvent collection flask into the appropriate waste solvent bottles.

This method, which is also known as rotary evaporation or 'rovap', is the technique of choice for the removal of large volumes of volatile solvents from solutions, e.g. from extractions and column chromatography (p. 337). Rotary evaporators are now standard communal pieces of equipment in the laboratory and the operating principle is that of a reduced-pressure distillation except that the evaporation flask can be rotated. This rotation reduces the risk of 'bumping', inherent in all reduced-pressure distillations, and spreads the solution in a thin film on the walls of the flask. This effectively

---

Box 36.1 How to use a rotary film evaporator

1. **Check that the apparatus is ready for use by ensuring that:**

   (a) The receiving flask is clipped in place and is empty.

   (b) You have available the correct-size ground-glass joint adapters to connect your flask to the rotating 'barrel' protruding from the motor of the evaporator. Many rotary film evaporators have an 'odd' joint size, usually 29/32, which is not common to the routine ground-glass flasks used in the laboratory. Alternatively, special bulb-shaped flasks with 29/32 joints may be available.

   (c) The rotating barrel is 'clipped' in place in the motor, by pulling it gently. Someone may have had to clean out and reassemble the 'rovap' and, if the barrel is not 'clipped' in place, it will slide out when you attach your flask. If the barrel slides out of the motor when you pull it, consult your instructor.

   (d) The rotating barrel is clean and dry.

   (e) Water is flowing steadily through the condenser. If it is not, adjust the water tap.

   (f) The temperature of the water in the water bath is about 20 °C below the boiling point of the solvent to be removed.

2. **Open the vacuum inlet adapter** at the top of the condenser, and turn the water pump to maximum (p. 170).

3. **Fill the rotating flask half-full or less**, using a stemmed filter funnel. You must not contaminate the joint of the rotating flask with solute, which will be deposited there during evaporation, since you may not be able to remove the flask after evaporation. If the flask is too full it may 'bump', sending solution up into the condenser and receiver. You will then have to dismantle and clean out the equipment with an appropriate solvent to recover your compound.

4. **Raise the apparatus using the lifting mechanism** so that, when the flask is attached, it is not touching the water in the bath. On modern equipment the lifting system is an electric motor controlled by an 'up-down' pressure switch, but on older apparatus the lifting device is either (i) a manual handle with a trigger, which is pulled to lift and released to lock it in place, or (ii) a lever with a twist-grip on the end. To operate the latter mechanism, twist the grip anti-clockwise to release the 'lock', pull the lever down to raise the apparatus and twist the grip clockwise to lock it in place.

5. **Attach the flask to the barrel** and put plastic joint clips on all the joints, while supporting the flask with your hand. If the weight of the flask and contents 'springs' any of the joints, it is too heavy: replace it with a smaller flask or remove some of the solution. *You must not rely on the power of the vacuum to hold your flask in place*.

6. **Turn on the motor**, slowly increasing the speed to the maximum.

7. **Close the vacuum inlet adapter slowly** until it is fully shut and observe the flask for a few seconds. If boiling occurs (liquid is condensed to the receiver flask) continue until boiling stops and then lower the flask so that it just touches the surface of the water, lock it in place and boiling should recommence. As the volume of solution decreases, you may need to lower the flask further into the water bath until all the solvent has been evaporated. If a white coating of frost forms on the flask evaporation may stop, because the flask is too cold: lower the flask into the water bath to warm it and evaporation should begin again.

8. **When evaporation is complete**, raise the flask from the bath, switch the motor off, open the vacuum inlet tap to allow air into the system and allow the flask to cool. Support the flask with your hand, take off the plastic joint clips, put the flask on one side and *only then* turn off the water pump. Turn off the water supply to the condenser.

9. **Unclip the receiving flask**, dispose of the solvent into a waste solvent bottle and reattach the receiving flask to the apparatus.

---

increases the surface area of the solution and increases the rate of evaporation, which is further enhanced by the use of a vacuum.

> **KEY POINT** When using a 'rovap' you must check that the reduced-pressure boiling point of the solute you are trying to isolate is below the temperature of the water bath.

There are many variations in the details of the form of rotary film evaporators and a typical assembly is illustrated in Fig. 36.1. A general guide to the use of a rotary evaporator is given in Box 36.1.

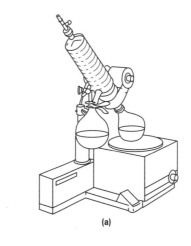

(a)

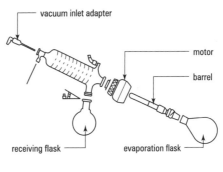

vacuum inlet adapter

motor

barrel

receiving flask

evaporation flask

(b)

Fig. 36.1 (a) Typical examples of a rotary evaporator; (b) exploded view of glassware.

SAFETY NOTES When using rotary film evaporators you should take note of the following:

- Never use flat-bottom flasks or conical flasks under reduced pressure (p. 258).
- Always check your flask for 'star'-cracks.
- Always make sure that your solution has cooled to room temperature before you begin, otherwise it may boil vigorously and 'bump' when you apply the vacuum, before it is lowered into the water bath.
- Do not rush to lower the flask into the water bath: wait to see what happens to the extent of evaporation at room temperature.
- Always have the water bath just warm, not hot, at the start of the procedure. If the water bath is too hot, allow it to cool or add cold water or ice.
- Check that all joints are 'sealed' and that the water pump is producing a vacuum: it will change 'note' as the vacuum is produced, when it is working properly. If there is no vacuum, the solution may not boil and you will overheat it in trying to promote evaporation. The joints may suddenly seal and the solution will then boil vigorously under the reduced pressure and will 'bump' into the condenser and receiving flask.

If it is necessary to evaporate volumes of solvent greater than the capacity of the rotating flask, you can carry out the process batch-wise involving several separate evaporations or the rotary evaporator can be modified for continuous evaporation (Fig. 36.2). A thin Teflon® tube is attached to the vacuum inlet adapter so that it feeds down the condenser into the 'barrel' and another glass tube, dipping

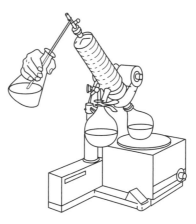

Fig. 36.2 The procedure for continuous solvent removal using a rotary evaporator.

into the solution to be evaporated, is connected to the air inlet on the vacuum adapter. Once the rotary evaporator is operating, the tap on the vacuum adapter is opened a little. Solution is drawn up by the vacuum, runs into the rotating flask and is evaporated. Careful control of the tap allows a constant volume of solution to be sucked into the rotating flask and evaporated without overfilling it.

Gas 'blow-down'

This procedure is useful for removing very small volumes of solvents (about 2 mL) from solutes by blowing a stream of nitrogen over the surface of the solution, while warming the solution gently. The main application of the gas blow-down is in the isolation of small amounts of solute from rotary evaporation or small-scale liquid–liquid extraction, for further analysis by instrumental techniques, where the sample size may be 20 mg or less: for example, infrared spectroscopy (p. 430), NMR spectroscopy (p. 441), gas chromatography (p. 370) or liquid chromatography (p. 379).

The simplest system for evaporation by gas blow-down is shown in Fig. 36.3. A Pasteur pipette is connected by a flexible tube to a cylinder of nitrogen, which has a gas blow-off safety system (p. 276). The sample is placed in a special tube with a conical base, such as a ReactiVial®. Hold the Pasteur pipette and direct a gentle stream of nitrogen towards the side of the tube so that it flows over the surface of the liquid. As the solvent evaporates, the liquid and tube will cool and may condense atmospheric water into the tube. To prevent condensation, clamp the tube in a warm sand bath or above a closed steam bath or in the hole of a purpose-designed aluminium heating

Transferring viscous liquids – it is often difficult to transfer small amounts of viscous liquids from a 'rovap' flask to a small sample tube. Dissolve the liquid in a small amount of dry solvent, transfer a little of this solution (1 or 2 mL) to a suitable small tube and 'blow off' the solvent with nitrogen.

SAFETY NOTE Make sure that you do not put the tip of the Pasteur pipette too close to the liquid surface or you will blow the liquid out of the tube! Test the flow *first*.

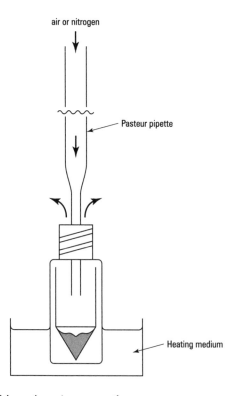

Fig. 36.3 Gas 'blow-down' evaporation.

block. The following points should be noted when using a gas blow-down system:

- Always carry out the operation in a fume cupboard.

- The solute should have negligible vapour pressure at room temperature, otherwise it may co-evaporate with the solvent.

- Do not heat the solution to boiling. Only apply enough heat to prevent condensation of atmospheric water vapour.

Sources for further study

Errington, R.J. (1997) *Advanced Practical Inorganic and Metalorganic Chemistry.* Blackie Academic and Professional, London.

Furniss, B.A., Hannaford, A.J., Smith, P.W.G. and Tatchell, A.R. (1989) *Vogel's Textbook of Practical Organic Chemistry,* 5th edn. Longman, Harlow, Essex.

Harwood, L.M., Moody, C.J. and Percy, J.M. (2000) *Experimental Organic Chemistry,* 2nd edn. Blackwell Science Ltd, Oxford.

Keese, R., Brandle, M.P. and Taube, T.P. (2008) *Practical Organic Synthesis: A Student's Guide.* John Wiley & Sons Ltd, Chichester.

Loewenthal, H.J.E. (1992) *A Guide for the Perplexed Organic Experimentalist,* 2nd edn. John Wiley & Sons Ltd, Chichester.

Sharp, J.T., Gosney, I. and Rowley, A.G. (1989) *Practical Organic Chemistry.* Chapman and Hall, London.

Smart, L. (ed.) (2002) *Separation, Purification and Identification – The Molecular World.* Open University and Royal Society of Chemistry, Cambridge.

Suib, S.L. and Tanaka, J. (1999) *Experimental Methods in Inorganic Chemistry.* Prentice Hall, Harlow, Essex.

Williamson, K.L. (2006) *Macroscale and Microscale Organic Experiments,* 5th edn. Houghton Mifflin Harcourt, Boston.

Zubrick, J.W. (2007) *The Organic Chem Lab Survival Manual. A student's guide to techniques,* 7th edn. John Wiley & Sons Ltd, Chichester.

Study exercise

36.1 Decide on the most appropriate technique for removal of solvent by evaporation in the following examples:

(a) A solution (15 mL) of nitrobenzene (b.pt. 210 °C) in dichloromethane (b.pt. 44 °C).

(b) A solution (500 mL) of naphthalene (m.pt. 80 °C) in ethoxyethane (b.pt. 35 °C).

(c) A solution (2 mL) of an unknown alcohol (b.pt. >150 °C) in ethyl ethanoate (b.pt. 78 °C).

Inert atmosphere reactions – these should be done in the fume cupboard, since most of the solvents and reagents used are flammable and/or toxic.

Nitrogen atmospheres – note that lithium metal reacts slowly with nitrogen.

Use of argon – reactions carried out under argon can be opened to the atmosphere briefly ($\sim5\,$s), for the addition of other chemicals, without degradation of the inert atmosphere.

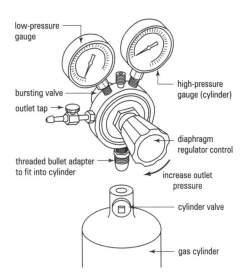

Fig. 37.1 The diaphragm pressure regulator.

SAFETY NOTE Gas cylinders must be supported safely either by clamping to the bench using a special cylinder clamp or in a cylinder trolley.

SAFETY NOTE Hydrogen gas cylinders have special cylinder head regulators with a 'left-hand thread' (tightened by turning anti-clockwise). All 'left-hand thread' fittings are identified by 'notches' cut into the fixing nuts (Fig. 37.2)

During your laboratory work you may need to carry out reactions using chemicals which are described as *air sensitive* or *moisture sensitive*. These compounds may react with water, oxygen, carbon dioxide and even nitrogen (e.g. lithium metal). The most sensitive chemicals may require special apparatus such as glove boxes or vacuum line equipment and you should consult the appropriate specialist literature (Errington, 1997, p. 56). On the other hand, many reactions involving some air-sensitive reagents (e.g. organolithium compounds or hydride reducing agent) can be done on a small scale using standard glassware with appropriate modifications. For simple apparatus for inert atmosphere reactions, the basic requirements are:

- Inert atmosphere, usually nitrogen or argon, piped into the apparatus. Nitrogen is the most commonly used inert gas, whereas argon is more expensive but does have the advantage that it is denser than nitrogen and is not lost from the apparatus as quickly. The inert atmosphere is maintained in the apparatus by the use of a 'bubbler' (see p. 277) on one of the outlets from the glassware – all other outlets must be stoppered or capped with septa.

- Appropriate glassware for the experiment (see Chapter 35) which must be dry.

- Dry solvents and chemicals (p. 278).

- Syringe techniques for dispensing and transferring chemicals to the apparatus (p. 278).

Inert atmosphere

The source of the inert atmosphere is usually a cylinder of nitrogen or argon gas under pressure, which should be placed as close to the apparatus as possible to avoid long 'runs' of connecting rubber tubing.

Gas cylinders

The gas flow rate from the cylinder is controlled by the cylinder head regulating valve (Fig. 37.1). Before you start make sure that the regulator outlet tap is off (turn anti-clockwise until it feels 'free') and then open the valve to the cylinder with the cylinder spanner (turn anti-clockwise) and the cylinder pressure should be indicated on the right-hand pressure dial. Switch on the gas at the regulator (turn slowly clockwise) until there is a reading on the left-hand dial. Use the minimum pressure required to provide a steady flow of gas. The gas flow rate from the regulator can be controlled further by a needle valve on the regulator outlet, if one is fitted. To switch off, reverse the instructions above.

Connection to the apparatus

Use clean, dry, thin-walled rubber tubing and special adapters with ground-glass joints to connect the tubing to your reaction flask or to the inlet pipe of a 'bubbler'. Where a single cylinder supplies several outlets, e.g. in a fume cupboard, the gas flow rate may change markedly when someone turns off one of the outlets, resulting in an increase in gas pressure to your equipment. You should, therefore, fit a gas 'blow-off'

Fig. 37.2 A 'left-hand' thread, fitting.

Inert gas flow rate – only low flow rates are required to provide an inert atmosphere, once the apparatus has been 'swept' with the gas.

Using a gas 'bubbler' – this ensures that your apparatus is not a sealed system, which will pressurise as you introduce the inert gas.

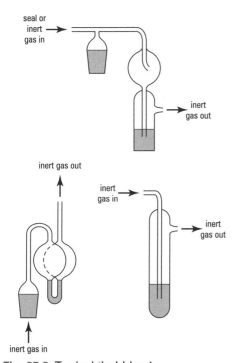

Fig. 37.3 Typical 'bubblers'.

Guard tubes – these absorb relatively little atmospheric water and do not absorb oxygen and carbon dioxide. Always use a gas 'bubbler' to protect the exit from your apparatus.

valve between your gas supply and the apparatus. To do this, fit a glass tube 'T-piece' in the gas line to your apparatus and connect it to a Dreschel bottle containing mineral oil to a depth a little more than that of the mineral oil in the 'bubbler'. If there is a sudden upward change in gas pressure, the gas will be vented through the Dreschel bottle, as well as through your apparatus.

Gas 'bubblers'

The exit of the inert gas from the apparatus must be protected by a gas 'bubbler'. The 'bubbler' allows you to monitor the flow of inert gas through the apparatus and prevents the entry of air into the apparatus. Several designs of gas 'bubbler' are available (Fig. 37.3) and it is usual to connect the 'bubbler' to the apparatus at the top of the condenser. You should make sure that the 'bubbler' contains enough mineral oil to create a seal from the atmosphere and that it has a bulb above the mineral oil to collect any mineral oil, which could be sucked back into your apparatus if there is a sudden contraction in the volume of inert gas in the apparatus. Such changes in volume will occur if you suddenly cool the apparatus without increasing the gas flow to compensate for the resulting reduction in inert atmosphere volume.

Apparatus

Depending upon the type of reaction to be carried out, one of the assemblies shown on p. 280 may be used, with additional modifications for inert gas inlet and outlet. You should consider very carefully what is required: heating or cooling, magnetic or mechanical stirring, temperature measurement, etc. The gas inlet can be either directly into the reaction flask or into the inlet arm of the gas 'bubbler' – it depends on the number of 'necks' available on the reaction flask.

Drying glassware

All equipment to be used should be dried (e.g. in an oven overnight at 125 °C – do not forget to remove all plastic or Teflon® components before placing the glassware in the oven). After drying, the apparatus should be greased, assembled hot, using heat-resistant gloves as protection, and allowed to cool with the inert gas flowing rapidly through it. Once cool, the water connections for the condenser should be fitted – screw-on water connectors (p. 269) are most useful in this context.

Addition of chemicals

Chemicals should be added to the reaction flask using a pressure-equalising dropping funnel (p. 268). Liquids and solid compounds are best added as solutions in the solvent used in the reaction. If the solid is insoluble, a little solvent should be added to the reaction flask, the 'bubbler' outlet sealed, a stopper to the flask opened and the gas flow rate increased. The solid can then be added from a wide-stemmed filter funnel, protected by the inert gas and solvent vapour, so that air does not enter the apparatus. Then, simultaneously unseal the 'bubbler' and restopper the flask, and then turn down the gas flow. Alternatively a solids addition tube (Errington, 1997, p. 124; Harwood *et al.*, 2000, p. 89; Furniss *et al.*, 1989, p. 82) can be used.

Solvents and chemicals

All chemicals and solvents used in inert atmosphere reactions must be dry. Most of these materials provided by suppliers are not dry enough, even solvents which you consider to be immiscible with water, and may contain enough moisture to hinder the reaction or reduce the yield of your product. Therefore you must ensure that all chemicals to be used in the process have been dried to the appropriate levels, as described below.

Solid chemicals

These should be dried by the methods outlined on p. 179. The most common approach is to dry the chemical in an oven and then allow it to cool in a vacuum desiccator (p. 179). Techniques for extremely air-sensitive solids can be found in the specialist literature.

Liquid chemicals

All liquids should be dried by a method appropriate to the amount of water they may contain (p. 181). Generally, the liquid should be dried with a solid drying agent (p. 181) which does not react with the chemical (consult the appropriate literature or your instructor), filtered, distilled (p. 255), then stored over molecular sieves (p. 181) in a bottle capped by a septum and redistilled before use. Alternatively, the liquid can be dissolved in a solvent, the solution dried (p. 181), the solvent removed by evaporation (p. 271) and the liquid distilled and stored as described above.

Solvents

The solvent will have the greatest volume in your reaction and it *must be dry*. Most laboratory-grade solvents, as supplied by manufacturers, contain varying amounts of water and therefore must be dried by the appropriate method before use. If you are required to dry the solvent, you should consult the literature (Errington, 1997; Harwood *et al.*, 2000; Furniss *et al.*, 1989).

Some manufacturers supply dry solvents in 2.5 L quantities for inert atmosphere reactions and HPLC (p. 379). These solvents are relatively expensive but may be economic in terms of time and expense if one-off reactions are required. However, such solvents should be treated with suspicion if the containers are less than half-full, since air and moisture may have been allowed into the container by previous users. If you have any doubts, dry the solvent.

Syringe techniques

Many air-sensitive chemicals are supplied as solutions in nitrogen-filled bottles, which are sealed by a septum, and small volumes (up to 25 mL) of these solutions are best transferred to the apparatus using glass syringes. Similarly, air-sensitive liquids can be added to the reaction using a syringe.

> **KEY POINT** When removing air-sensitive reagents from nitrogen-filled bottles, you must replace the volume of liquid removed with inert gas (nitrogen) from a gas cylinder or balloon, via a needle, otherwise air (water, oxygen and carbon dioxide) will be pulled into the bottle as a result of the vacuum you have created.

Dry solvents – the term also implicitly means carbon dioxide-free and oxygen-free.

Grignard reactions are relatively tolerant – dry solvent can be added to the apparatus using an oven-dried measuring cylinder.

Syringes

Glass, gas-tight syringes with a Luer lock fitting are the most versatile type of syringe and they come in a range of sizes. The Luer lock enables the stainless steel needle to be locked in place on the end of the syringe so that there is no danger of the needle dropping off the syringe during the transfer process (Fig. 37.4). Variations in syringe types include those with Teflon®-tipped pistons (plungers), which are somewhat more expensive.

Before using a syringe, always check that it is working by sucking up a little of the solvent to be used, ensuring that air is not sucked into the syringe either via the Luer lock or down a gap between the syringe and piston. If all is correct, disassemble the syringe and needle, dry in an oven at 120 °C (not if Teflon® tipped) and allow to cool in a desiccator. Once you have transferred the air-sensitive reagent, you must clean out the syringe and needle immediately, by the appropriate method, as air will get into the needle and syringe and decompose the reagent causing the syringe to jam or the needle to block.

Needle-to-tubing connectors

These adapters allow a Luer lock syringe needle to be connected to rubber tubing (Fig. 37.5). An inert gas supply can then be piped, via the needle, into a bottle to allow the transfer of large volumes of solvent or air-sensitive reagents to the apparatus. Alternatively a balloon can be taped to a short piece of thick-walled rubber pressure tubing to provide a supply of nitrogen when withdrawing air-sensitive reagents using a syringe (Fig. 37.6).

Using syringes – always ensure that the syringe piston is the correct one for your syringe, since the components of the syringe are always separated for drying.

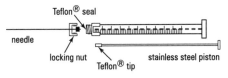

glass barrel   glass piston

glass barrel   Teflon® tip   solid piston

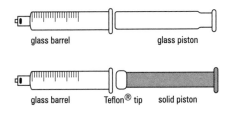

Teflon® seal

needle

locking nut   Teflon® tip   stainless steel piston

Fig. 37.4 Syringes for inert atmosphere work.

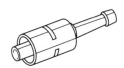

Fig. 37.5 Needle-to-tubing connector.

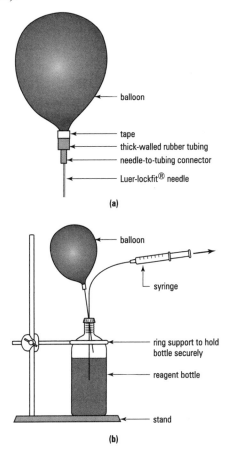

balloon

tape
thick-walled rubber tubing
needle-to-tubing connector
Luer-lockfit® needle

(a)

balloon

syringe

ring support to hold bottle securely

reagent bottle

stand

(b)

Fig. 37.6 Inert atmosphere transfers: (a) balloon and needle; (b) preserving the inert atmosphere while removing reagent.

Working with viscous liquids – attempting to draw the solution up a fine needle creates a strong vacuum in the syringe, which may result in air being pulled into the syringe via the small gap between the syringe barrel and the piston. Use a larger diameter needle.

Syringe needles and cannulae

Stainless steel Luer lock syringe needles come in various lengths and diameters. The length of needle you will need depends on the size of the vessel from which you wish to withdraw the liquid; the diameter required depends on the size of the syringe – you should not use a large-diameter needle with a small-volume syringe – and the viscosity of the solution or liquid. Needle diameters are expressed in 'gauge': the higher the gauge, the narrower the needle diameter. For most inert atmosphere work you should use a needle with a 'non-coring' or 'deflecting' tip (Fig. 37.7),

Fig. 37.7 Needle with non-coring tip for piercing septa.

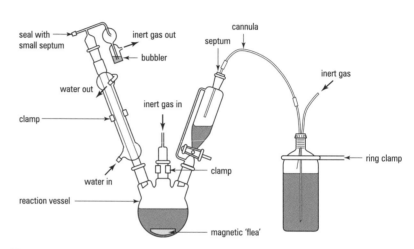

Fig. 37.8 Transfer of air-sensitive reagents using the double-ended needle technique.

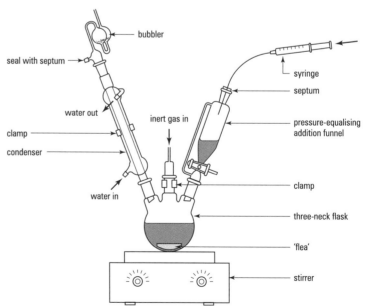

Fig. 37.9 Transferring an air-sensitive reagent to a pressure-equalising dropping funnel.

which ensures that a piece of the septum is not trapped in the needle when you push it through. Cannulae are long, flexible, double-ended needles made from stainless steel or inert plastics, which are used to transfer large volumes of reagents or solvents from one vessel to another under inert gas pressure (Fig. 37.8).

A generic method for transferring an air-sensitive reagent, by syringe, from a bottle to a pressure-equalising dropping funnel is described in Box 37.1.

Box 37.1 How to transfer an air-sensitive reagent using a syringe

1. **Assemble the apparatus (Fig. 37.9) while hot and allow to cool while nitrogen is flowing through it** and then add all the chemicals and solvents as required.

2. **Assemble the syringe and needle, making sure that the needle is locked in place** having first checked that it is air-tight.

3. **Draw a few millilitres of solvent into the syringe**, invert it and squirt the solvent and any air into the waste solvent bottle. Repeat this step three times to ensure that syringe and needle contain only solvent vapour.

4. **Using the syringe, inject a few millilitres of the dry solvent into the pressure-equalising dropping funnel**, either via the septum or by quickly removing the stopper while diverting the gas flow through funnel by putting your finger tip over the 'bubbler' outlet. This ensures that there is an inert atmosphere in the funnel. Replace the stopper and release the gas flow through the 'bubbler'.

5. **Clamp the bottle of air-sensitive reagent to a support stand** so that it cannot fall over while you manipulate the syringe needles.

6. **Remove the needle from the end of a needle-to-tubing connector carrying a balloon.** Connect the inert gas supply using clean, dry rubber tubing and inflate the balloon. Turn off the gas supply, twist the neck of the balloon to stop the gas escaping, reattach the needle, ensuring it is locked in place, and release the neck of the balloon. Dip the end of the needle into a little dry solvent to confirm that nitrogen is being released from the needle – check for bubbles.

7. **Hold the needle near the tip and pierce the septum on the bottle.** Make sure that the needle tip is in the space above the liquid. Support the needle connector and balloon by a clamp on the support stand.

8. **Holding the syringe and the needle near the tip, pierce the septum on the bottle.** Still holding the needle, ease the syringe needle into the space above the liquid.

9. **Draw up some gas into the syringe** and expel it back into the bottle. Repeat three times and then ease the syringe needle into the liquid.

10. **Draw up the required volume of solution into the syringe and carefully ease the needle out of the bottle.** Make sure that you do not press the syringe piston and squirt the reagent out of the syringe!

11. **Inject the solution into the pressure-equalising dropping funnel, either by:**
    (a) holding the syringe needle near the tip, piercing the septum on the pressure-equalising dropping funnel and injecting the reagent; or by
    (b) putting your finger over the 'bubbler' outlet and removing the stopper from the pressure-equalising dropping funnel. You can now inject the solution into the funnel, protected by the nitrogen and solvent vapour coming out of the funnel neck. Replace the stopper and release the gas flow through the 'bubbler'.

12. **Draw a few millilitres of dry solvent into the syringe and inject them into the pressure-equalising dropping funnel.** This rinses any residual reagent from the syringe.

13. **Draw some methanol or another solvent which reacts gently with the reagent to destroy the air-sensitive reagent and squirt it into an excess of water.** To clean the syringe assembly, draw water into the syringe several times and then disassemble it, wash well with propanone (acetone) and water, and then dry in the oven.

14. **Remove the needle–balloon assembly from the reagent bottle**, cover the holes in the septum with a little hydrocarbon grease and screw the bottle cap in place. Place the needle in the oven after washing with propanone (acetone) and then water.

Text references

Errington, R.J. (1997) *Advanced Practical Inorganic and Metalorganic Chemistry*. Blackie Academic and Professional, London.

Furniss, B.A., Hannaford, A.J., Smith, P.W.G. and Tatchell, A.R. (1989) *Vogel's Textbook of Practical Organic Chemistry*, 5th edn. Longman, Harlow, Essex.

Harwood, L.M., Moody, C.J. and Percy, J.M. (2000) *Experimental Organic Chemistry*, 2nd edn. Blackwell Science Ltd, Oxford.

Sources for further study

Keese, R., Brandle, M.P. and Taube, T.P. (2008) *Practical Organic Synthesis: A Student's Guide*. John Wiley & Sons Ltd, Chichester.

Leonard, J., Lygo, B. and Procter, G. (2001) *Advanced Practical Organic Chemistry*, 2nd edn. Nelson Thornes Ltd, Cheltenham.

Loewenthal, H.J.E. (1992) *A Guide for the Perplexed Organic Experimentalist*, 2nd edn. John Wiley & Sons Ltd, Chichester.

Sharp, J.T., Gosney, I. and Rowley, A.G. (1989) *Practical Organic Chemistry*. Chapman and Hall, London.

Smart, L. (ed.) (2002) *Separation, Purification and Identification – The Molecular World*. Open University and Royal Society of Chemistry, Cambridge.

Suib, S.L. and Tanaka, J. (1999) *Experimental Methods in Inorganic Chemistry*. Prentice Hall, Harlow, Essex.

Zubrick, J.W. (2007) *The Organic Chem Lab Survival Manual. A student's guide to techniques*, 7th edn. John Wiley & Sons Ltd, Chichester.

Study exercise

37.1 **Look up and report on the information to be found in the references and sources to dry the solvents below to an appropriate level for inert atmosphere reactions:**

(a) ethoxyethane (diethyl ether)
(b) tetrahydrofuran
(c) hexane.

Traditionally practical chemistry has been focused on making pure samples of target compounds, and the techniques have been devised to aid production of individual samples of high purity. However, more recently it has been a priority for synthetic chemists to develop methods which can make a large number of structurally related compounds simultaneously.

The driving force for this change of emphasis has been a number of areas such as medicinal chemistry where finding the most active compound with the least deleterious effects can be best assessed by making a library of as many slightly differing compounds to the lead compound as possible, and then screening them for suitability. Often the importance of making as many compounds as possible (in what is known as a 'parallel synthesis') outweighs consideration of high purity, and often an acceptable level of purity for library compounds made by combinatorial methods can be lower than 95%, with the proviso that any library compound that has the appropriate properties will be remade at high purity, and testing redone on a high purity sample.

There are many different methods used in what is quite a new branch of synthetic chemistry, with no method having proved to be dominant, and developing new methods, reactions and equipment is an area of ongoing research and development. We will look at two methods of creating a combinatorial library – a solid phase combinatorial method and a parallel synthesis using a multi-component reaction.

Solid phase combinatorial chemistry

Solid phase synthetic methodology has been developed from the pioneering work in the synthesis of proteins (polymers of amino acids) by Bruce Merrifield. Instead of combining molecules and isolating and purifying at each stage – resulting in losses and poor yields overall – Merrifield attached the first molecule to an inert and insoluble polymer bead by a 'linker' and then carried out chemical reactions to attach the second molecule. Since the new structure was still attached to the insoluble polymer, no isolation or purification was necessary. Repetition of the procedure allows the preparation of polymeric structures with defined but complex organisation, e.g. biomolecules such as insulin.

Solid phase synthesis lends itself to automation, since the reaction product is always attached to the insoluble polymer bead, reagents and reactants can be 'washed' past the polymer beads as can rinsing of the product to free it from unreacted molecules. A computer-controlled machine can complete a specific synthesis of a complex molecule by adding the correct amounts of different chemicals and washing the products free of unused reagents and finally detach the desired the final product from the polymer beads. Variation in the order and type of molecules joined up leads to the 'combinatorial library'.

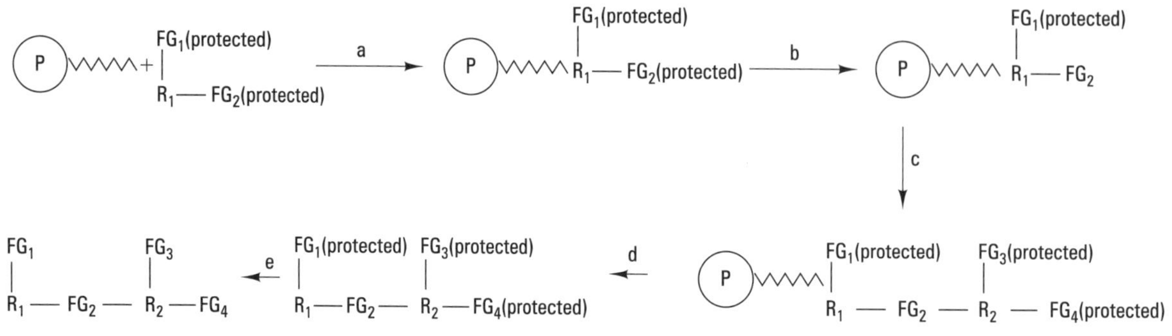

a Combine protected molecule with resin
b Deprotect one functional group
c Combine with new protected molecule
d Remove from polymer stationary phase
e Deprotect all functional groups to reveal new molecule

Fig. 38.1 A general schematic of a solid phase synthesis.

Solid phase synthesis is an extremely versatile process, allowing many variations in chemical structure and entails a lot of very clever organic chemistry:

- different 'linkers' to attach different chemical classes to the polymer (amines, phenols, alcohols, acids, etc.);

- different protecting groups: these groups are attached to functional groups (FGs) on the reacting molecules to prevent reaction during the synthetic process, but can be removed (deprotection) as required at later stages without affecting the overall synthesis;

- removal of the completed molecule from the polymer, without affecting the product molecule.

A general schematic of a section of a solid phase synthesis is shown in Fig. 38.1.

Parallel synthesis using a multi-component reaction

An alternative parallel synthetic method is to use a multi-component reaction where the diversity is created by varying the identity of the reagents in a methodical way, and a microtitre plate (Fig. 38.2) enables many simultaneous reactions to be carried out in a manageable way. Microtitre plates typically have 96 wells (though they can be bought with more or less wells but always laid out in a 2:3 rectangular matrix pattern), each of which is used to be the reaction vessel for one set of reagents. For example, the Ugi reaction (Fig. 38.3) can be used to make a bis-amide using four reagents: a ketone or aldehyde, an amine, an isocyanide and a carboxylic acid. If there were 4 ketones, 4 amines, 3 isocyanides and 4 carboxylic acids available, then it is possible to make

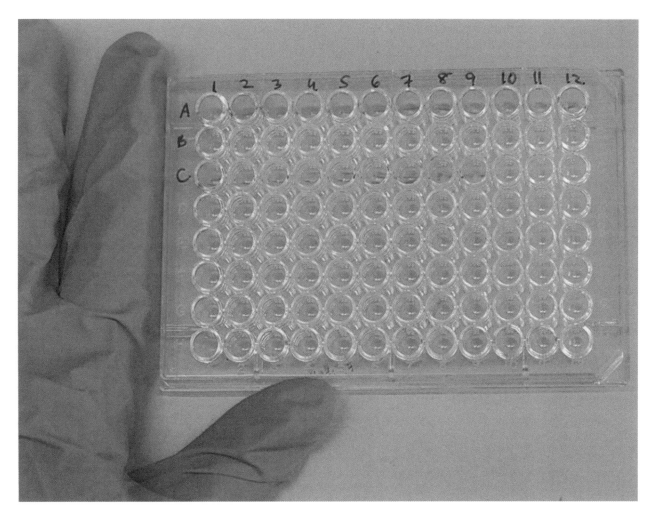

Fig. 38.2 A microtitre plate.

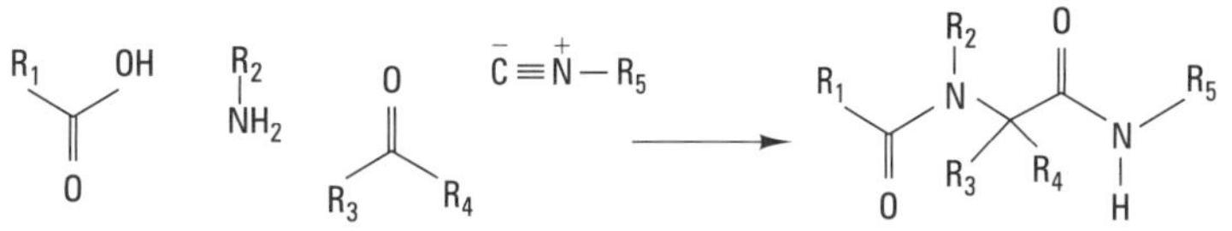

Fig. 38.3 The Ugi reaction.

96 different combinations of components and hence 96 different compounds. Using a 96-well plate, it is possible to arrange the addition of reagents such that each well yields a single component, and the plate itself contains a sample of each of the possible 96 compounds. A further advantage of this method is that many analytical techniques (such as UV/vis absorbance, fluorescence and mass spectrometry) can be operated with robotic sample loaders which can systematically analyse all wells on a microtitre plate.

Text reference

Merrifield, R.B. (1963) *J. Amer. Chem. Soc.,* **85**, 2149.

Sources for further study

Anon. *Journal of Combinatorial Chemistry.* Available: http://www.pubs.acs.org/journal/jcchff Last accessed 05/03/10 [Examples of solid phase combinatorial chemistry]

Bannwarth, W. and Hinzen, B. (eds) (2006) *Combinatorial Chemistry: From Theory to Application,* Wiley-VCH Verlag GmbH and Co., Weinheim, Germany.

De Lue, N. (2001) *Combinatorial Chemistry Moves Beyond Pharmaceuticals.* Available: http://www.pub.acs.org/.../31/i11/html/11delue.html Last accessed 05/03/10

Fassina, G. and Miertus, S. (eds) (2005) *Combinatorial Chemistry: Technologies, Methods and Applications.* CRC Press, Boca Raton, USA.

Fenniri, H. (ed.) (2000) *Combinatorial Chemistry: A Practical Approach.* Oxford University Press, Oxford, UK.

Ganesan, A. (ed.) (2010) *Combinatorial Chemistry: A Primer.* Elsevier Ltd, Amsterdam.

MacLean, D., Baldwin, J.J., Ianov, V.T., Kato, Y., Shaw, A., Schneider, P. and Gordon, E.M. (1999) *Glossary of Terms Used in Combinatorial Chemistry.* Available: http://www.iupac.org/publications/pac/1999/pdf/7112x2349.pdf Last accessed 05/03/10

Miller, B.L. (2010) *Dynamic Combinatorial Chemistry: In Drug Discovery, Bioorganic Chemistry and Materials Science.* John Wiley & Sons Ltd, Chichester.

Reek, J.N.H. and Otto, S. (eds) (2010) *Dynamic Combinatorial Chemistry.* John Wiley & Sons Ltd, Chichester.

Study exercises

38.1 If you were to make a library of tripeptides using a random combinatorial method with 20 amino acids, how many unique compounds would you expect to make?

38.2 You are investigating a multi-component reaction (which uses three reagents, A, B and C) to make a library of compounds. Assuming you have 12 chemicals which can act as A, 5 which can act as B and 8 which can act as C, and that you wish to make all the possible variants, how many 96 well plates would you need to use?

Classical techniques

Qualitative techniques are used to identify cations and anions in aqueous solution by simple reactions, mostly involving the production of a precipitate, evolution of gas or a visual colour change. It is important to make observations accurately and to interpret them in a step-wise manner.

The following basic equipment is required to carry out qualitative analysis:

- Test tubes – in which the reactions are performed. (p. 150)

- Cork or plastic stoppers – for the protection of the contents of test tubes from contamination and for safe storage. (p. 152)

- Test tube rack – this allows test tubes to be stored upright when not in use.

- Test tube holder – this allows individual test tubes to be heated safely. (p. 177)

- A glass rod – this has several functions including the stirring, transfer of solutions, and the break-up of precipitates.

- Watch-glasses these have several functions including the covering of beakers to prevent contamination and as a receptacle for solutions.

- A wash bottle containing distilled water.

- Spatula – for transferring small quantities of solids.

- Pasteur pipettes – for transferring liquids. (p. 146)

- Micro-Bunsen burner – for heating solutions to boiling and for evaporating solutions. (p. 172)

- Evaporation crucible – this is used as a container for solutions when complete evaporation of liquid is required, leaving a solid product.

- Crucible tongs – for removing the crucible from the heat source.

- Centrifuge – for separating precipitates from solution.

- Heated water bath. (p. 173)

Wash bottle – always keep a wash bottle of distilled water handy.

Spatula – never place the spatula in the test solution, it may lead to false-positive tests for iron and chromium.

Table 39.1 Typical reagents for qualitative analysis

2 M NH$_4$OH	Conc. HCl
2 M NaOH	0.1 M HNO$_3$
2 M AgNO$_3$	2 M HNO$_3$
2 M CH$_3$COOH	Conc. HNO$_3$
2 M BaCl$_2$	2 M H$_2$SO$_4$
0.1 M HCl	Conc. H$_2$SO$_4$
2 M HCl	

Reagents

At the start of your experimental work always check that the appropriate reagents are readily available (a list of commonly used reagents is given in Table 39.1). Note that it is essential to use distilled water in all qualitative analysis. Tap water contains ions such as Ca^{2+}, Mg^{2+}, Fe^{2+}, Fe^{3+}, SO_4^{2-} and Cl^- and its use could lead to 'false-positive' results.

Testing for anions and cations

Specific literature containing tests for the determination of anions and cations can be found on page 293. In general, however, the following tips are useful when carrying out qualitative analysis:

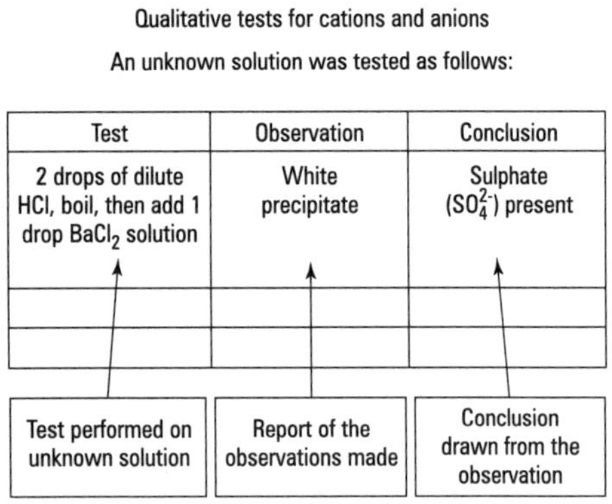

Qualitative tests for cations and anions

An unknown solution was tested as follows:

Test	Observation	Conclusion
2 drops of dilute HCl, boil, then add 1 drop $BaCl_2$ solution	White precipitate	Sulphate (SO_4^{2-}) present

Test performed on unknown solution	Report of the observations made	Conclusion drawn from the observation

Fig. 39.1 Recording your observations in qualitative analysis.

A clear solution is transparent – a 'colourless' solution has no colour.

- Always work tidily to prevent cross-contamination of samples.

- Ensure that all glassware has been cleaned thoroughly in detergent and then rinsed twice with distilled water. Invert the test tubes to drain; never dry the inner surface with towelling or tissue.

- Label test tubes at the start – it may prove difficult to remember what you have done later on.

- Always test solutions with a known composition before you attempt to analyse solutions with an unknown content. This allows you to gain the necessary experience in solution manipulation, observation skills and the interpretation of results.

- The colour of solutions and/or precipitates has to be interpreted from written or oral information. Interpretation of colour can be subjective, so you will need to gain sufficient experience using solutions of known content to establish how a particular colour appears to you.

- Establish a protocol for recording of observations after carrying out different tests (Fig. 39.1).

- Reagents should be added from Pasteur pipettes held with the tip just above the mouth of the test tube. Never put Pasteur pipettes inside test tubes as this can lead to contamination of the reagents.

- Effective mixing of the test solution and added reagents is essential. This can be achieved by holding the test tube between the thumb and index finger of one hand and 'flicking' the tube with the index finger of your other hand. Alternatively, solutions can be mixed by bubbling air from a Pasteur pipette held at the bottom of the test tube.

- Evolved gas can be drawn up into a Pasteur pipette and then bubbled through a test solution, e.g. CO_2 can be drawn into a Pasteur pipette and then 'blown' out through lime water [$Ca(OH)_2$ solution] giving a milky-white solution.

- Solutions can be tested for pH using litmus paper. Never place litmus paper directly into the test solution. Instead, dip a glass rod into the solution, remove, touch the wet glass rod onto the litmus paper and note the colour. Acidic solutions change blue litmus paper to red; alkaline solutions change red litmus paper to blue. Alternatively, universal indicator paper can be used. In this case, the orange paper turns 'reddish' with acidic solutions and 'bluish' with alkaline solutions. By comparing any change in colour with a chart (supplied with the universal indicator paper), the pH of the solution can be estimated.

Centrifugation of solutions

Centrifugation causes particulate material to accumulate at the bottom of the test tube. The procedure for centrifuging your sample is described in Box 39.1. The speed and time of the run will depend on the centrifuge available, but will typically be in the range 5000–10 000 rpm for 5–10 min, respectively. Always allow the centrifuge to stop in its own time, as abruptly halting the centrifuge will disturb light precipitates. After

Box 39.1 How to use a low-speed bench centrifuge

1. **Choose the appropriate test tube size**, with stoppers where necessary. Most low-speed machines have four-place or six-place rotors. Use the correct number of samples to fill the rotor assembly whenever possible.

2. **Fill the tubes to the appropriate level:** do not overfill, or the sample may spill during centrifugation.

3. **Ensure that the rotor is balanced during use.** To achieve this prepare identical test tubes and place these diametrically opposite each other in the rotor assembly. However, for low-speed work, where you are using small amounts of particulate matter in aqueous solution it is sufficient to counterbalance a sample with a second test tube filled with water.

4. **If you are using centrifuges with swing-out rotors**, check that each holder/bucket is correctly positioned in its locating slots on the rotor and that it is able to swing freely. All buckets must be in position on a swing-out rotor, even if they do not contain

sample tubes buckets are an integral part of the rotor assembly.

5. **Load the sample test tubes into the centrifuge.** Make sure that the outside of the centrifuge tubes, the sample holders and sample chambers are dry: any liquid present will cause an imbalance during centrifugation (as well as potentially causing corrosive damage to the rotor). Balanced tubes must be placed opposite each other, use a simple code if necessary, to prevent errors.

6. **Bring the centrifuge up to operating speed** by gentle acceleration. Do not exceed the maximum speed for the rotor and tubes used. If the centrifuge vibrates at any time during use, switch it off and find the source of the problem.

7. **On completion of the run, allow** the rotor to stop spinning, release the lid, and remove all test tubes. If any sample has spilled, make sure you clean it up thoroughly.

8. **Finally,** close the lid (to prevent the entry of dust) and return all controls to zero.

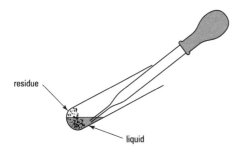

Fig. 39.2 Separation of liquid from a residue using a pipette.

> **SAFETY NOTE** Take care when heating unknown solutions. As well as the risk of burns, some reactions can be violent.

> **SAFETY NOTE** Never point a test tube towards yourself or, for that matter, towards anyone else while evaporation is being carried out.

centrifugation, hold the test tube at an angle so that it is easy to remove the liquid component (or centrifugate) with a Pasteur pipette (Fig. 39.2). You will find that it is difficult to remove all the centrifugate from the precipitate, and to maximise the transfer of centrifugate it is necessary to wash the precipitate. This is carried out as follows:

- Add a small quantity of distilled water to the precipitate.

- Use a glass rod to break up the precipitate and mix thoroughly.

- Recentrifuge the mixture.

- Transfer the liquid obtained to the original centrifugate and store this solution for further analysis.

- Repeat the washing process, but this time discard the centrifugate, and retain the precipitate for further tests.

Heating test tubes and other containers

It is often necessary to heat a solution in a test tube, either to cause precipitation or to dissolve a precipitate. You can carry out this heating effectively and safely by partially immersing the test tube containing the mixture in a simmering boiling-water bath (remember to use a test tube holder!).

Beware – hot glass looks exactly like cold glass.

Table 39.2 Flame tests for cations

Cation	Flame colour
Barium	Apple-green
Calcium	Brick-red**
Copper	Green
Potassium	Lilac*
Sodium	Intense yellow
Strontium	Crimson**
Lead, arsenic, antimony and bismuth	Dull blue

* The colour is often obliterated by trace impurities of sodium present (sodium gives an intense yellow colour). You can overcome this by viewing the colour through cobalt-blue glass which allows the lilac coloration from potassium to be seen.
** Viewing through cobalt-blue glass also allows calcium and strontium to be distinguished. In this case, calcium is light green in colour while strontium appears purple.

It is possible to reduce the volume of the solution in the test tube, i.e. to pre-concentrate the sample, by evaporation. Two different methods can be employed.

1. Transfer the solution to a small evaporating dish. Place the evaporating dish on a wire gauze located on a tripod stand, and apply heat using a micro-Bunsen burner. Note that the volumes of solutions in qualitative analysis are often small, and excessive heating might result in hardening of any residue, making it unusable.

2. Alternatively, evaporate the solution directly in a test tube by gentle heating over a micro-Bunsen burner. Remember to use a test tube holder. Position the test tube at an angle with the tip of the Bunsen burner flame positioned at the upper surface of the liquid. Place a glass rod inside the test tube and rotate constantly. This acts to disperse bubbles of steam that are given off. Extreme caution is required with this method of evaporation, as the steam bubbles can cause the solution to 'bump' out of the test tube (see p. 171). 'Bumping' can result in hot (and maybe toxic) substances being ejected over a surprisingly large distance.

Flame tests

Simple flame tests can be carried out on solid samples. Place a little of the solid on a watch-glass and moisten with a drop of concentrated hydrochloric acid. The purpose of the hydrochloric acid is to produce metal chlorides which are volatile at the temperature of the Bunsen burner.

Pre-clean a platinum or nichrome wire by holding it in the hottest part of the Bunsen flame (just above the central blue cone) until there is no coloured flame from the wire. Cool, then dip the cleaned wire into the moistened solid sample. Place the wire at the edge of the Bunsen flame (Fig. 39.3) and record the colour of the flame from the sample (see Table 39.2).

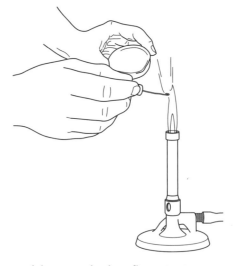

Fig. 39.3 Holding a nichrome wire in a flame test.

Sources for further study

Dean, J.A. and Patnaik, P. (2004) *Dean's Analytical Chemistry Handbook*. McGraw-Hill Co. Inc.

Hardcastle, W.A. (1998) *Qualitative Analysis. A guide to best practice*. Royal Society of Chemistry, Cambridge.

Kramer, B.K. and McCormick, J.M. (2007) *Inorganic Qualitative Analysis*.
Available: http://www.chemlab.truman.edu/ CHEM121Labs/Qual**Analysis**.html
Last accessed 05/03/10.

Lagowski, J.J., Lagowski, J.T. and Sorum, C.H. (2005), *Introduction to Semimicro Qualitative Analysis*, 8th edn. Prentice Hall. Harlow, Essex.

Svehla, G. (1996) *Vogel's Qualitative Inorganic Analysis*, 7th edn. Longman, Harlow, Essex.

Svehla, G. (1989) *Vogel's Textbook of Macro and Semimicro Qualitative Inorganic Analysis*, 5th edn. Longman, Harlow, Essex.

Witten, K.W., Davis R.E. and Peck, M.L. (2006) *A Qualitative Analysis Supplement*. Thomson Brooks/Cole Publishing, Belmont, CA.

Study exercises

39.1 Why is it necessary to use distilled water in qualitative inorganic analysis?

39.2 Analysis of a solid gave the following analysis results:

(a) Treatment of the solid with dilute HCl gave off a gas, which when bubbled through a $Ca(OH)_2$ solution gave a fine white precipitate.

(b) A flame test gave a green flame.

Deduce possible identities for the solid compound.

Gravimetric analysis is the process of converting an element into a definitive compound, isolating this compound from other constituents in a sample and then weighing the compound (Box 40.1). The weight of the element can then be calculated from the formula of the compound and the relative atomic masses of the elements involved. You need to be able to weigh accurately, by difference, a substance to four decimal places (see p. 164).

> **KEY POINT** The essential component of gravimetric analysis is the transformation of the element of interest into a pure stable solid compound, suitable for weighing.

The most common approach for isolating the element is by precipitation from a solution where it is present in ionic form (see p. 191). Ideally, the constituent under investigation is precipitated out of solution as a water-insoluble compound, so that no losses occur when the precipitate is separated by filtration, washed free of soluble impurities and then weighed.

Box 40.1 How to carry out gravimetric analysis

Suppose you wanted to analyse the amount of metal in an alloy. For example, you might want to determine the nickel content, as a w/w percentage (p. 187), in a particular sample of steel.

1. **Select an appropriate solvent for your sample**: in this example, you could dissolve the steel in aqua regia, a combination of concentrated nitric acid and concentrated hydrochloric acid in the volume ratio of 1:3 respectively.

2. **Choose an appropriate precipitant and carry out the precipitation reaction**. Here, an alcoholic solution of dimethylglyoxime could be used to precipitate nickel from a hot solution of aqua regia, by adding a slight excess of aqueous ammonia solution, forming a red precipitate of nickel dimethylglyoximate (Fig. 40.1).

3. **Filter the precipitate through a pre-weighed Gooch crucible**. This should have been previously dried in an oven at 120 °C and stored in a desiccator until required.

4. **Wash the precipitate**: in this example, the nickel dimethylglyoximate can be washed with cold water until qualitative testing shows that the wash solution is free of chloride ions.

5. **Dry the precipitate in an oven**, for example, at 120 °C, and allow to cool in a desiccator.

6. **Determine the weight of the precipitated compound**. Suppose in this example that the nickel had been precipitated from steel (2.0980 g) using dimethylglyoxime (H_2DMG), giving a precipitate of nickel dimethylglyoximate ($Ni(HDMG)_2$) weighing 0.2370 g.

7. **Write out the equation for the reaction and perform the calculation**. In this example, you need to check the relative atomic masses of the elements involved. The relative molecular mass of nickel dimethylglyoximate is 288.91 g mol^{-1} (for structure see Fig. 40.1; A_r, H = 1.01; O = 16.00; C = 12.01; N = 14.01; Ni = 58.69). The equation for the reaction can be summarised as:

$$Ni^{2+} + 2H_2DMG = Ni(HDMG)_2 + 2H^+$$

According to the above equation, for each mole of Ni in the steel sample, 1 mole of precipitate will be formed. Therefore, 0.2370 g of precipitate corresponds to:

0.2370 g $Ni(HDMG)_2$ ÷ 288.95 g mol^{-1} $Ni(HDMG)_2$
= 8.20 × 10^{-4} mol $Ni(HDMG)_2$

The amount of nickel in the steel sample must therefore be:

8.2 × 10^{-4} mol $Ni(HDMG)_2$ × 58.69 g mol^{-1} Ni
= 0.0481 g Ni

The percentage weight of nickel in the steel sample is therefore:

0.0481 g Ni ÷ 2.0980 g sample × 100 = 2.29% w/w

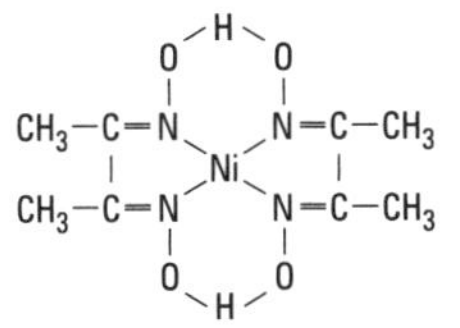

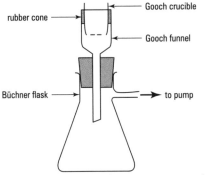

Fig. 40.1 Structure of nickel-dimethyl-glyoxime complex.

Table 40.1 Common precipitants

Precipitant	Ion(s) of interest	Possible interferents
Dimethylglyoxime	Ni^{2+}	Pd^{2+}, Pt^{2+}, Bi^{3+} and Au^{3+}
Cupferron	Sn^{4+}	Cu^{2+} and Pb^{2+}
8-Hydroxyquinoline (oxine)	Al^{3+}	Many metals

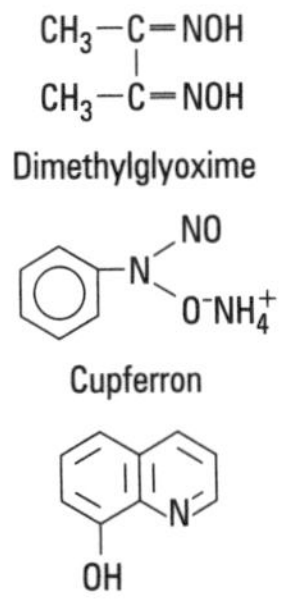

Dimethylglyoxime

Cupferron

8-Hydroxyquinoline

Fig. 40.2 Structures of common precipitants.

Filtering your precipitate – remember that the particle size of your precipitate must be such that it is not lost during the filtering process.

rubber cone
Gooch crucible
Gooch funnel
Büchner flask
to pump

Fig. 40.3 Experimental arrangement for filtration of precipitate.

Precipitation

Inorganic ions can be separated from mixtures using organic reagents (precipitants), with which they form sparingly soluble, often coloured, compounds. The precipitants usually have high molecular weights, so a small quantity of the ion will produce a large amount of precipitate. Ideally, the precipitant should be specific for a particular ion, though this is rarely so. Examples of common precipitants and their target ions are shown in Table 40.1 and their structures are shown in Fig. 40.2.

Dimethylglyoxime is only slightly soluble in water ($0.40\,g\,L^{-1}$) and it is therefore used as a 1% w/v solution in ethanol. Cupferron, the ammonium salt of N-nitroso-N-phenylhydroxylamine, is used as a 5–10% w/v solution in hydrochloric acid or sulphuric acid. Oxine (8-hydroxyquinoline) is almost insoluble in water and is used as either a 2% or a 5% w/v solution in $2\,mol\,L^{-1}$ acetic acid.

When precipitating a compound:

- Mix your reagents slowly, with continuous stirring, to encourage the growth of large crystals of the compound.

- Improve the precipitation process by heating your solutions: ideally, one or both solutions should be heated to just below boiling point.

- Wash your precipitate with a dilute electrolyte solution, to remove any other constituents (it is essential to remove any impurities). Choose a solution that does not interact with the precipitate, and that is volatile at the drying temperature to be used.

- Use the minimum quantity of wash solution because no precipitate is absolutely insoluble. While suitable wash solutions include dilute electrolytes, e.g. ammonium salts, ammonia solution or acids, pure water is rarely used, as it may dissolve the precipitate.

- Test your filtered wash solution for impurities using simple qualitative tests (Chapter 39). Continue until your final washing solution contains no trace of other constituents.

- It is best to wash repeatedly with several small amounts of solution, allowing the precipitate to drain between washings.

Filtration

To carry out this procedure, you will need to assemble a Gooch crucible and funnel on a Büchner flask, clamped for stability using a retort stand (Fig. 40.3). The glass Gooch crucible has a porous disk of sintered ground glass, typically of pore diameter 20–30 µm, which is satisfactory for moderately sized precipitates. Fit the crucible into a Gooch funnel using a rubber cone, put the funnel into a one-holed rubber bung and then into a Büchner flask. The tip of the funnel must project below the side arm of the flask to prevent loss of filtrate down the side arm (see p. 168). Then, connect the Büchner flask to a water pump. Pour your precipitate suspension into the Gooch crucible, using a glass rod (p. 159) to direct the liquid into the centre of the sintered base. The lower end of the glass rod should be close to, but not touching, the sintered-glass base. Never overfill the crucible. The precipitate remaining in the bottom of the beaker should be rinsed out with the filtrate solution: disconnect the pump and pour the filtrate back into the beaker containing the precipitate. The pump should be disconnected by pulling off the vacuum tube from the Büchner flask. On no account turn off the water pump while doing this (p. 170). You may need to rinse the beaker several times, to collect all of the precipitate in the crucible.

Sources for further study

Harris, D.C. (2006) *Quantitative Chemical Analysis*, 7th edn. W.H. Freeman Co., New York.

Mendham, J., Denney, R.C., Barnes, J.D. and Thomas, M.J.K. (2000) *Vogel's Textbook of Quantitative Chemical Analysis*, 6th edn., Prentice Hall, Harlow, Essex.

Rubinson, J.F. and Rubinson, K.A. (1998) *Contemporary Chemical Analysis*. Prentice Hall, Harlow, Essex.

Skoog, D.A., West, D.M. and Holler, F.J. (2004) *Fundamentals of Analytical Chemistry*, 8th edn. Thomson Brooks/Cole, Belmont, CA.

Zang, C. (2007) *Fundamentals of Environmental Sampling and Analysis*. John Wiley & Sons Ltd, Chichester.

Study exercises

40.1 Calculate the salinity of sea water (simply expressed as a % (w/w) of NaCl in water) from the following experimental data: sea water (10.00 mL) was transferred to a tall beaker, and concentrated nitric acid (0.5 mL) and deionised water (200 mL) added. Silver nitrate solution (0.1 M) was added drop-wise from a burette with constant stirring until coagulation of the precipitate began to occur. The suspension was heated to boiling and stirred (5 min) and a few drops of silver nitrate solution added to confirm completeness of precipitation. The suspension was allowed to cool in the dark (30 min) and then filtered through a pre-weighed sintered crucible (porosity 4) using dilute solution of nitric acid [3 mL of 2 M dissolved in deionised water (300 mL)] for transfer and washing. The precipitate and crucible were dried to constant weight to yield silver chloride (0.8329 g).

40.2 Why is deionised water used in the dilution and washing processes in **40.1**?

Volumetric analysis, also known as titrimetric analysis, is a quantitative technique used to determine the amount of a particular substance in a solution of unknown composition.

This requires:

- A standard solution, which is a solution of a compound of accurately known concentration, that reacts with the substance to be analysed.

- The test solution, containing an unknown concentration of the substance to be analysed.

- Some means of detecting the end-point of the reaction between the standard and test solutions, e.g. a chemical indicator or, in the case of potentiometric titrations, a pH electrode (see Chapter 54). Some reactions exhibit a colour change at the end-point without the addition of an indicator.

The volume of standard solution that reacts with the substance in the test solution is accurately measured. This volume, together with a knowledge of concentration of the standard solution and the stoichiometric relationship between the reactants, is used to calculate the amount of substance present in the test solution. Specific examples of the different types of calculations involved are shown in Chapters 42–45.

Classification of reactions in volumetric analysis

There are four main types of reaction

1. Acid–base or neutralisation reactions, where free bases are reacted with a standard acid (or vice versa). These reactions involve the combination of hydrogen and hydroxide ions to form water.

2. Complex formation reactions, in which the reactants are combined to form a soluble ion or compound. The most important reagent for formation of such complexes is ethylenediamine tetra-acetic acid, EDTA (as the disodium salt).

3. Precipitation reactions, involving the combination of reactants to form a precipitate.

4. Oxidation–reduction reactions, i.e. reactions involving a gain (reduction) or loss (oxidation) of electrons. The standard solutions used here are either oxidising agents (e.g. potassium permanganate) or reducing agents [e.g. iron (II) compounds].

What can be measured by titration?

- The concentration of an unknown substance, e.g. $0.900 \, mol \, L^{-1}$.

- Percentage purity, e.g. 56%.

- Water of crystallisation, e.g. $(NH_4)_2SO_4.nH_2O$.

- Percentage of a metal in a salt, e.g. 12% Fe in a salt.

- Water hardness, e.g. determination of the concentration of calcium and magnesium ions.

Examples of the types of calculations used in volumetric analysis are shown in Box 41.1.

Definition

A stoichiometric titration is one with a known reaction path, for which a chemical reaction can be written, and having no alternative or side reactions.

Box 41.1 Types of calculations used in volumetric analysis – titrations

In titrations you react a solution of a known concentration with a solution of an unknown concentration.

If you know the mole ratio of the two reacting chemicals in solution, you can calculate the amount (the number of moles and thus the number of grams) of the solute in the solution of unknown concentration.

Let's look at the reaction between NaOH and HCl:

$$HCl + NaOH = NaCl + H_2O$$

Since the equation is balanced we know that 1 mol (36.5 g) of HCl will react with 1 mol (40 g) of NaOH. We know that a 1.0 M solution of HCl contains 1 mol of HCl in 1000 mL (1 litre) of water. Then:

1000 mL of 1.0 M HCl solution   is equivalent to 1.0 mol of NaOH
                                     is equivalent to 1000 mL of 1.0 M NaOH solution
                                     is equivalent to 40 g of NaOH
                                     is equivalent to 23 g of Na^+ ions
                                     is equivalent to 17 g of OH^- ions

Similarly for the reaction between potassium hydroxide and sulphuric acid:

$$H_2SO_4 + 2KOH = K_2SO_4 + 2H_2O$$

Since *1 mol* of H_2SO_4 reacts with *2 mol* of KOH, then:

1000 mL of 1.0 M H_2SO_4 solution   is equivalent to 2.0 mol of KOH
                                        is equivalent to 2×1000 mL of 1.0 M KOH solution
                                        is equivalent to 2×56 g of KOH
                                        is equivalent to 2×39 g of K^+ ions
                                        is equivalent to 2×17 g of OH^- ions

To work out the results of titrations you *must* always:

- Work out the balanced equation to find out the ratio of moles reacting.

- Decide what you are trying to calculate.

Example: 25.00 mL of sodium hydroxide solution were titrated by 24.00 mL of 0.1 M HCl solution. Calculate the concentration of the sodium hydroxide solution.

- $HCl + NaOH = NaCl + H_2O$

- Concentration of NaOH, i.e. moles of NaOH in 1000 mL, since concentration is $mol\,L^{-1}$.

Now:

1000 mL of 1.0 M HCl solution is equivalent to 1.0 mol of NaOH

but the concentration of HCl is only 0.1 M:

1000 mL of *0.1 M* HCl solution is equivalent to *0.1* $\times$ 1.0 mol of NaOH

but only 24.00 mL of HCl solution were used:

1.0 mL of 0.1 M HCl solution is equivalent to $\dfrac{1.0 \times 0.1 \times 1.0}{1000}$ mol of NaOH

and

24 mL of 0.1 M HCl solution is equivalent to $\dfrac{24 \times 1.0 \times 0.1 \times 1.0}{1000}$ mol of NaOH

$$= 2.4 \times 10^{-3} \text{ mol of NaOH}$$

but 25.00 mL of NaOH solution were used:

25.00 mL of NaOH solution contains 2.4×10^{-3} mol of NaOH

Then

1.0 mL of NaOH solution contains $\dfrac{2.4 \times 10^{-3}}{25}$ mol of NaOH

and

1000 mL of NaOH solution contains $\dfrac{1000 \times 2.4 \times 10^{-3}}{25}$ mol of NaOH

$$= 0.096 \text{ mol of NaOH}$$

Therefore concentration of NaOH solution is *0.096* mol L^{-1}.

Using this set of equations you can calculate directly the mass of NaOH per litre, the mass or moles of sodium ions and the mass or moles of hydroxide ions.

Note: The expression $[C_1]V_1 = [C_2]V_2$ was not used, even though it is applicable in this case.

Problems arise when $[C_1]V_1 = [C_2]V_2$ is used for reactions which are not *1:1, e.g.:*

$$H_2SO_4 + 2KOH = K_2SO_4 + 2H_2O$$

or

$$2MnO_4^- + 16H^+ + 5C_2O_4^{2-} = 2Mn^{2+} + 10CO_2 + 8H_2O$$

or

$$IO_3^- + 5I^- + 6H^+ = 3I_2 + 3H_2O$$

Titrations

The process of adding the standard solution to the test solution is called a titration, and is carried out using a burette (see below). The point at which the reaction between the standard solution and the test substance is just complete is called the equivalence point or the theoretical (or stoichiometric) end-point. This is normally detected by a visible change, either of the standard solution itself or, more commonly, by the addition of an indicator.

Standard solutions

A standard solution can be prepared by weighing out the appropriate amount of a pure reagent and making up the solution to a particular volume, as described on p. 158. The concentration of a standard solution is expressed in terms of molarity (p. 186). A substance used in a primary standard should fulfil the following criteria:

- It should be obtainable in high purity ($>99.9\%$).

- It should remain unaltered in air during weighing (i.e. it should not be hygroscopic).

- It must not decompose when dried by heating or vacuum.

- It should be capable of being tested for impurities.

- It should be readily soluble in an appropriate solvent.

- It must react with the test substance stoichiometrically and rapidly.

Definition

A primary standard should be easy to obtain in a pure form. It should be unaffected in air during weighing, be capable of being tested for impurities and be readily soluble under the conditions used. Finally, the reaction with the standard solution should be stoichiometric and instantaneous.

Preparing a standard solution

The molarity of a solution is the concentration of the solution expressed as $mol\,L^{-1}$. If x g of a substance of molecular weight M_r is dissolved in y mL of distilled water, the moles of substance dissolved $= \dfrac{x}{M_r} = m$.

Therefore, molarity $(mol\,L^{-1}) = \dfrac{m \times 1000}{y}$ [41.1]

Primary standards prepared from solid compounds should be weighed out using the 'weighing by difference' method as described in Chapter 23, and accurately made up to volume using a volumetric flask. Complete transfer of the substance from the weighing vessel to the volumetric flask is best achieved by inserting a funnel into the neck of the flask (Fig. 41.1). As much of the solid as possible should be transferred *via* the funnel. The funnel should be washed with distilled water prior to removal. Distilled water is then added to the flask, with occasional swirling to help to dissolve the solid. This is continued until the meniscus is about 1 cm below the volume mark. At this point a stopper is inserted and the flask is inverted several times to ensure the solid is completely dissolved. Finally, using a Pasteur pipette, distilled water is added up to the volume mark. The solution should be thoroughly mixed before use.

If the solid is not readily soluble in cold water it may be possible to dissolve it by stirring in warm water in a beaker. After allowing the solution to cool to room temperature, it can be transferred to the volumetric flask using a glass rod and filter funnel (Fig. 41.1) followed by several rinses of the glass rod/filter funnel. Finally, the solution is made up to the mark with distilled water.

Filling a burette

- Clamp a clean 50.00 mL burette (p. 147) in a laboratory stand. Place a beaker on a white tile immediately below the outlet of the burette (Fig. 41.2).

- Place a small filter funnel on top of the burette and, with the tap open, carefully pour in the standard solution (or titrant) until it starts to drain into the beaker.

- Close the burette tap, and fill the burette with the standard solution until the meniscus is about 1–2 cm above the zero mark. Remove the funnel.

- Open the tap and allow the solution to drain until the meniscus falls to the zero mark. The burette is then ready for the titration.

Note that to avoid contamination the solution in the beaker should be discarded, rather than recycled.

Using a pipette

A clean 25.00 mL pipette (p. 147) is commonly required together with a suitable pipette filler. Various designs of pipette filler are available. The most common type is based on a rubber-bulb suction device. It is best to evaluate a range of pipette fillers, if available in the laboratory, for ease of use and performance. The pipetting procedure is given in Box 41.2.

For accurate readings – always remember to position your burette vertically.

Titrand – this is the solution of unknown composition in the conical flask. The titrant is the standard solution in the burette.

SAFETY NOTE Never mouth pipette.

Contamination of pipette fillers – this can affect your results detrimentally. The main cause is sucking air into the pipette while filling and the bubbles of liquid shoot into the pipette filler.

Don't lift the pipette out of the liquid while filling.

Ensure that there is more liquid in the beaker than the volume of the pipette.

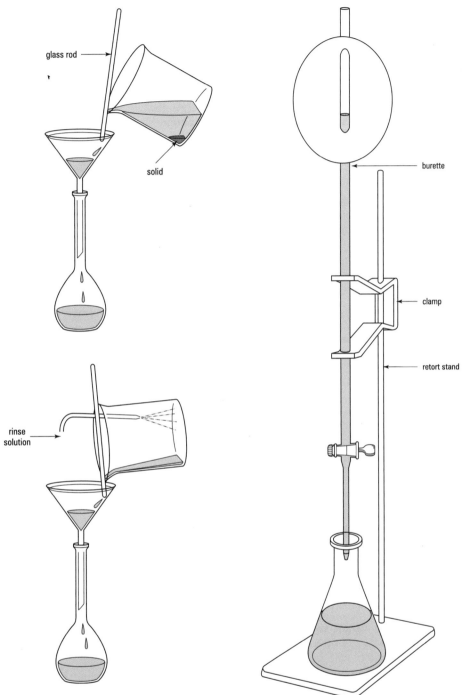

Fig. 41.1 Quantitative transfer of a solid to a volumetric flask.

Fig. 41.2 Apparatus for a titration.

Performing a titration

There are many minor variations in technique in performing titrations dependent upon the type of titration (acid–base, redox, precipitation or back-titration) being carried out. A robust basic procedure which can be applied to the majority of analyses is given in Box 41.3.

Box 41.2 How to fill a pipette

1. **Attach the pipette filler to the pipette** as shown in Fig. 22.5.

2. **Pour the solution of unknown composition (the titrand) into a clean dry beaker making sure that the amount of solution well exceeds the volume of the pipette.** Never place the pipette in the volumetric flask containing the solution as this can lead to contamination of the solution from the external surface of the pipette.

3. **Squeeze the valve 'A' on the pipette filler and then squeeze the bulb to create some 'suction'.** Dip the tip of the pipette into the solution and squeeze the valve 'S'. Draw up the titrand until it is well above the graduation mark (Fig. 41.3(a)). Squeeze valve 'E' to empty the pipette to waste – this rinsing process ensures that the titrand used subsequently will be undiluted and uncontaminated by any residue or liquids in the pipette.

4. **Refill the pipette until the meniscus of the titrand is above the graduation mark.** Carefully raise the pipette to eye level and gently squeeze valve 'E', which allows the titrand to drain slowly back into the beaker. Continue until the bottom of the meniscus is on the graduation mark.

5. **Wipe the outside of the pipette with a tissue (Fig. 41.3(b)).** Be careful not to touch the point of the pipette with the tissue otherwise solution will be lost through capillary action.

6. **Squeeze valve 'E'** to allow the pipette's contents to drain into a conical flask.

7. **Still squeezing valve 'E',** touch the tip of the pipette on the inside of the conical flask to ensure that the correct volume is transferred (Fig. 41.3(c)).

Note: it is normal for a small quantity of solution to remain in the pipette tip. This volume is taken into account when pipettes are calibrated, so DO NOT attempt to 'blow out' the liquid into the conical flask.

Box 41.3 How to carry out a titration

Note: this procedure is applicable to a right-handed person.

1. **Add one or two drops of indicator** to the titrand in a conical flask.

2. **Hold the conical flask in your right hand and control the tap on the burette with your left hand.** The burette should be arranged so that the tap is on the opposite side of the burette to your palm. In this way, your left hand also supports the body of the burette (Fig. 41.4).

3. **Add some titrant by opening the tap.** Where the titrant meets the titrand solution a colour change of the indicator will be observed. Swirl to titrand solution and the original colour will be restored.

4. **Continue adding titrant,** but observe that as the titration proceeds to the end-point the length of time for the original indicator colour to be restored increases and therefore the amount of titrant added must be reduced.

5. **Very close to the end-point** you will be adding the titrant at one drop at a time.

6. **When the new indicator colour 'flashes' through the solution,** you are probably one drop of titrant away from the end-point. Note the volume used (Fig. 41.5) and then continue the titration by drops until the colour change of the indicator is permanent. Do not forget to count the number of drops (see 'Enhancing precision' below).

7. **Refill the burette to the zero mark** using a funnel, ready for the next titration.

8. **Repeat the titration** until consistent results (within 0.2 mL) are obtained.

9. **Do not average analytical results with large variations (>0.2 mL).**

Enhancing precision of a titration

You can increase the precision of your titrations by titrating 'to the nearest drop'. This means that you can measure end-points in a titration to a very small volume of titrant, i.e. one drop. Before you commence the titration set the tap on the burette to deliver a steady series of drops and

Reading a burette – your eye-line should be level with the bottom of the meniscus. Then, record the volume used to one decimal place.

Rough titration – always carry out an initial rough titration to determine the approximate volume of titrant required for the end-point. This allows you to anticipate the end-point in subsequent titrations to determine the accurate volume.

For consistency of results – always perform two or three titrations (or until consistent results are obtained, i.e. titre values within 0.1–0.5 mL).

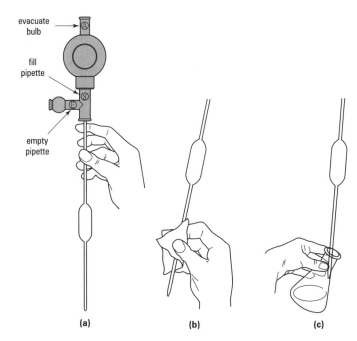

evacuate
bulb

fill
pipette

empty
pipette

(a)   (b)   (c)

Fig. 41.3   Using a pipette.

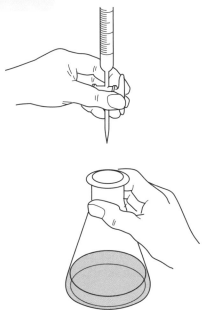

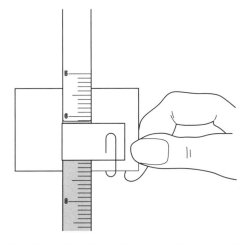

Fig. 41.5   Reading a burette. Place a white card below the level of the meniscus. This allows an accurate reading to be made.

Fig. 41.4   Performing a titration.

Washing the test solution – any distilled water used for washing the test solution from the walls of the conical flask has no effect on the titration or the calculation.

count the number of drops in, say, 1.00 mL; you can then calculate the volume of a drop. After carrying out the first 'rough' titration you can stop the addition of titrant, say, x mL before the end-point and add the titrant by drops until the end-point is reached. The volume of titrant used is then x mL + y drops, and since you have measured the volume of 1 drop you now have a titration 'to the nearest drop'. With practice you can titrate 'to half a drop' by allowing half a drop to form on the burette tip and washing it into the titrand solution with distilled water.

Volumetric analysis – calculating the concentration of a test substance

The calculation should be carried out in a logical order as follows:

1. Write the balanced equation for the reaction between the standard and the test substance.

2. From the stoichiometry of the reaction, determine how many moles of the test substance react with 1 mole of the standard substance. For example, in the reaction between an H_2SO_4 standard solution and an NaOH test solution:

$$H_2SO_4 + 2NaOH \rightarrow Na_2SO_4 + 2H_2O \qquad [41.2]$$

   Therefore 2 moles of NaOH react with 1 mole of H_2SO_4.

3. Calculate the number of moles of standard substance used to reach the end-point of the reaction. This can be determined from knowledge of the concentration of the standard solution $(mol\,L^{-1})$ and the volume of titrant used (mL). Remember to take care with units – in this instance division by a factor of 1000 is required to convert mL to L:

$$\text{Number of moles} = \frac{\text{concentration } (mol\,L^{-1}) \times \text{volume } (mL)}{1000}$$

4. The number of moles of test substance present in the titrand is then obtained from knowledge of the equivalences. In the example given above (point 2) the number of moles of test substance is twice the number of moles of standard substance. Therefore, if X moles of H_2SO_4 are used (as calculated in point 3), 2X moles of NaOH were present in the initial volume of test solution.

5. Finally, the concentration of the test solution can be calculated using the formula:

$$\frac{\text{Concentration of test}}{\text{solution } (mol\,L^{-1})} = \frac{1000 \times \text{amount of test substance } (mol)}{\text{initial volume of test solution } (mL)}$$

Again, the factor of 1000 is used to convert mL to L.

Sources for further study

Christian, G.D. (2004) *Analytical Chemistry*, 6th edn. John Wiley & Sons Ltd, Chichester.

Harris, D.C. (2006) *Quantitative Chemical Analysis*, 7th edn. W.H. Freeman Co., New York.

Jander, G., Jahr, K.-F., Schulze, G. and Simon, J. (2009) *Volumetric Analysis*, 17th edn. Walter de Gruyter Inc, Germany.

Mendham, J., Denney, R.C., Barnes, J.D. and Thomas, M.J.K. (2000) *Vogel's Textbook of Quantitative Chemical Analysis*, 6th edn. Prentice Hall, Harlow, Essex.

Polk, P.J. (2009) *Use of Burets for Acid/Base Titrations*. Available: http://www.podcast.montgomery-college.edu/podcast.php?rcdid=165 Last accessed 05/03/10.

Rubinson, J.F. and Rubinson, K.A. (1998) *Contemporary Chemical Analysis*. Prentice Hall, Harlow, Essex.

Skoog, D.A., West, D.M. and Holler, F.J. (2004) *Fundamentals of Analytical Chemistry*, 8th edn. Thomson Brooks/Cole, Belmont, CA.

Study exercises

41.1 Apply the methodology from Box 41.1 to the following:

i. Sodium carbonate solution (25.00 mL) was titrated by sulphuric acid solution (26.0 mL; 0.1 M). Calculate the concentration of the sodium carbonate solution.

ii. Sodium hydroxide solution (25.00 mL) was titrated by sulphuric acid solution (24.0 mL; 0.05 M). Calculate the concentration of the sodium hydroxide solution.

41.2 Your burette reading for a titration was 25.20 mL plus 8 drops. You have measured that 12 drops = 1.00 mL. What is the total volume of titrant used?

The titration of an acid solution with a standard solution of alkali will determine the amount of alkali which is equivalent to the amount of acid present (or vice versa). The point at which this occurs is called the equivalence point or end-point. For example, the titration of hydrochloric acid with sodium hydroxide can be expressed as follows:

$$NaOH_{(aq)} + HCl_{(aq)} \rightarrow NaCl_{(aq)} + H_2O_{(l)} \qquad [42.1]$$

If both the acid and alkali are strong electrolytes, the resultant solution will be neutral (pH 7). If on the other hand either the acid or alkali is a weak electrolyte the resultant solution will be slightly alkaline or acidic, respectively. In either case, detection of the end-point requires accurate measurement of pH. This can be achieved either by using an indicator dye, or by measuring the pH with a glass electrode (described in Chapter 26).

Acid–base indicators

Typical acid–base indicators are organic dyes that change colour at or near the equivalence or end-point. They have the following characteristics:

- They show pH-dependent colour changes.
- The colour change occurs within a fairly narrow pH range (approximately 2 pH units).
- The pH at which a colour change occurs varies from one indicator to another, and it is possible to select an indicator which exhibits a distinct colour change at a pH close to the equivalence or end-point.

Selected common indicators together with their pH ranges and colour changes are shown in Table 42.1. Examples for thymol blue and phenolphthalein are shown in Fig. 42.1.

Table 42.1 Colour changes and pH range of selected indicators

Indicator	pH range	Colour in acid solution	Colour in alkaline solution
Thymol blue	1.2–6.8	Red	Yellow
Methyl orange	2.8–4.0	Red	Yellow
Methyl red	4.3–6.1	Red	Yellow
Phenol red	6.8–8.2	Yellow	Red
Phenolphthalein	8.3–10.0	Colourless	Pink/red

Neutralisation curves

A plot of pH against the volume of alkali added (mL) is known as a neutralisation or titration curve (Fig. 42.2). The curve is generated by a 'potentiometric titration' in which pH is measured after each addition of alkali (or acid). The significant feature of the curve is the very sharp and sudden change in pH near to the equivalence point of the titration. For a strong acid and alkali this will occur at pH 7. If either the acid or base concentration is unknown, a preliminary 'rough' titration is necessary to find the approximate equivalence point followed by a more accurate titration as described on p. 303. The ideal pH range for an indicator is 4.5–9.5.

thymol blue

red
(<pH 1.7)

yellow
(pH 1.7–8.9)

phenolphthalein

colourless
(<pH 6)

red
(pH 8.3–10)

Fig. 42.1 Examples of indicators used in acid-base titrations: thymol blue and phenolphthalein.

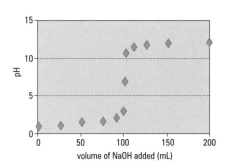

Fig. 42.2 A typical neutralisation curve: 0.1 M HCl with 0.1 M NaOH.

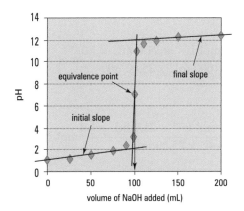

Fig. 42.3 Determination of the equivalence point.

Subscripts – 'aq' is used to represent aqueous, 'l' the liquid state.

Determination of the equivalence point

From the neutralisation curve (Fig. 42.2), the initial and final slopes are drawn (Fig. 42.3) and a parallel line is drawn such that the mid-point is on the curve. This is the equivalence point, producing a titration value of x mL.

Example calculations

Standardisation of a sodium hydroxide solution

Sodium hydroxide solution (25.00 mL) is titrated with a standard solution of hydrochloric acid (21.0 mL; 0.100 M). Calculate the molarity of the sodium hydroxide solution.

Following the sequence in Box 41.1:

1. Write the equation:

$$NaOH_{(aq)} + HCl_{(aq)} \rightarrow NaCl_{(aq)} + H_2O_{(l)} \qquad [42.2]$$

2. Equation [42.2] shows that 1 mole of NaOH requires 1 mole of HCl for neutralisation, i.e. 1 mole of NaOH is equivalent to 1 mole of HCl.

3. *You are trying to find the concentration of NaOH in mol L^{-1}.*

4. 1000 mL of HCl (1.0 M) $\equiv$ 1.0 mol NaOH

But the HCl is only 0.1 M

Self-test: is 0.1 M HCl equivalent to more or less moles of NaOH than 1.0 M HCl?
Answer: less, therefore you must MULTIPLY by 0.1

1000 mL of HCl (0.1 M) $\equiv$ 0.1 mol L^{-1} $\times$ 1.0 mol NaOH

Self-test: is 1.0 mL of 0.1 HCl equivalent to more or less NaOH than 1000 mL?
Answer: less, therefore you must DIVIDE by 1000

$$1.0 \text{ mL of HCl (0.1 M)} \equiv \frac{0.1 \text{ mol L}^{-1} \times 1.0}{1000 \text{ mL}} \text{mol NaOH}$$

But the titration used 21.0 mL of 0.1 M HCl

Self-test: is 21.0 mL of 0.1 HCl equivalent to more or less NaOH than 1.0 mL?
Answer: more, therefore you must MULTIPLY by 21.0

$$21.0 \text{ mL of HCl (0.1 M)} \equiv \frac{0.1 \text{ mol L}^{-1} \times 21.0 \text{ mL} \times 1.0}{1000 \text{ mL}} \text{mol NaOH}$$

Since 25.00 mL of NaOH solution are equivalent to 21.0 mL of 0.1 M HCl

$$\begin{array}{l} \text{25.00 mL of NaOH solution} \\ \text{must contain} \end{array} \equiv \frac{0.1 \text{ mol L}^{-1} \times 21.0 \text{ mL} \times 1.0}{1000 \text{ mL}} \text{mol NaOH}$$

Do the self-test

$$\frac{1.00 \text{ mL of NaOH solution}}{\text{must contain}} \equiv \frac{0.1 \text{ mol L}^{-1} \times 21.0 \text{ mL} \times 1.0}{1000 \text{ mL} \times 25.00 \text{ mL}} \text{mol NaOH}$$

Do the self-test

$$\frac{1000 \text{ mL of NaOH solution}}{\text{must contain}} \equiv \frac{1000 \text{ mL} \times 0.1 \text{ mol L}^{-1} \times 21.0 \text{ mL} \times 1.0}{1000 \text{ mL} \times 25.00 \text{ mL}} \text{mol NaOH}$$

Concentration of NaOH solution = 0.084 mol L^{-1}

Standardisation of a sodium hydroxide solution using potassium hydrogen phthalate (KHP) as a primary standard (p. 299)

An accurately weighed amount (5.1100 g) of potassium hydrogen phthalate (KHC$_8$H$_8$O$_4$) was dissolved in water (250.00 mL). This solution (25.00 mL) required a sodium hydroxide solution (23.5 mL) for equivalence. What is the molarity of the sodium hydroxide solution?
Following the sequence in Box 41.1:

1. Write the equation:

$$NaOH_{(aq)} + KHC_8H_8O_{4(aq)} \rightarrow NaCl_{(aq)} + H_2O_{(l)} \qquad [42.3]$$

2. Equation [42.3] shows that 1 mole of NaOH requires 1 mole of KHP for neutralisation, i.e. 1 mole of NaOH is equivalent to 1 mole of KHP.

3. *You are trying to find the concentration of NaOH in mol L^{-1}.*

4. Calculate the concentration of KHP from equation [25.1]:

$$[C] = \frac{\text{Mass KHP}/M_r}{\text{Volume of solution}}$$

5. $[C] = \dfrac{5.1100/204.22}{250.00} = \textbf{0.100 mol L}^{-1}$

6. 1000 mL of KHP (1.0 M) ≡ 1.0 mol NaOH

   But the KHP is only 0.1 M

Self-test: is 0.1 M KHP equivalent to more or less moles of NaOH than 1.0 M KHP?
Answer: less, therefore you must MULTIPLY by 0.1

   1000 mL of KHP (0.1 M) ≡ 0.1 mol L^{-1} × 1.0 mol NaOH

Self-test: is 1.0 mL of 0.1 KHP equivalent to more or less NaOH than 1000 mL?
Answer: less, therefore you must DIVIDE by 1000

$$1.0 \text{ mL of KHP (0.1 M)} \equiv \frac{0.1 \text{ mol L}^{-1} \times 1.0}{1000 \text{ mL}} \text{mol NaOH}$$

But the titration used 25.00 mL of 0.1 M KHP

Self-test: is 25.00 mL of 0.1 KHP equivalent to more or less NaOH than 1.0 mL?

Answer: more, therefore you must MULTIPLY by 25.00

$$25.00 \text{ mL of KHP (0.1 M)} \equiv \frac{0.1 \text{ mol L}^{-1} \times 25.00 \text{ mL} \times 1.0}{1000 \text{ mL}} \text{mol NaOH}$$

Since 23.5 mL of NaOH solution are equivalent to 25.00 mL of 0.1 M KHP

$$\text{23.5 mL of NaOH solution must contain} \equiv \frac{0.1 \text{ mol L}^{-1} \times 25.00 \text{ mL} \times 1.0}{1000 \text{ mL}} \text{mol NaOH}$$

Do the self-test

$$\text{1.00 mL of NaOH solution must contain} \equiv \frac{0.1 \text{ mol L}^{-1} \times 25.00 \text{ mL} \times 1.0}{1000 \text{ mL} \times 23.5 \text{ mL}} \text{mol NaOH}$$

Do the self-test

$$\text{1000 mL of NaOH solution must contain} \equiv \frac{1000 \text{ mL} \times 0.1 \text{ mol L}^{-1} \times 25.00 \text{ mL} \times 1.0}{1000 \text{ mL} \times 23.5 \text{ mL}} \text{mol NaOH}$$

Concentration of NaOH solution = 0.106 mol L^{-1}

Sources for further study

De Levie, R. (2001) *Aqueous Acid-Base Equilibria and Titrations*. Oxford University Press.

Harris, D.C. (2006) *Quantitative Chemical Analysis*, 7th edn. W.H. Freeman Co., New York.

Jander, G., Jahr, K-F., Schulze, G. and Simon, J. (2009) *Volumetric Analysis*, 17th edn. Walter de Gruyter Inc., Germany.

Mendham, J., Denney, R.C., Barnes, J.D. and Thomas, M.J.K. (2000) *Vogel's Textbook of Quantitative Chemical Analysis*, 6th edn. Prentice Hall, Harlow, Essex.

Rubinson, J.F. and Rubinson, K.A. (1998) *Contemporary Chemical Analysis*. Prentice Hall, Harlow, Essex.

Skoog, D.A., West, D.M. and Holler F.J. (2004) *Fundamentals of Analytical Chemistry*, 8th edn. Thomson Brooks/Cole, Belmont, CA.

Study exercise

42.1 An accurately weighed amount (3.6284 g) of hydrated sodium carbonate ($Na_2CO_3.xH_2O$) was dissolved in water (250.00 mL). An aliquot (25.00 mL) of this solution required hydrochloric acid solution (25.4 mL; 0.100 M) for equivalence. Calculate the number of molecules of water of crystallisation (x) in the original hydrated sodium carbonate.

(HINT: you need to calculate M_r for the original $Na_2CO_3.xH_2O$.)

Complexometric titrations are mainly used to determine the concentration of cations in solution. The method is based on the competition between a metal ion (for example) and two ligands, one of which acts as an indicator and the other is a component of a standard solution.

Some knowledge of the principles of metal–ligand binding is required in order to understand this method.

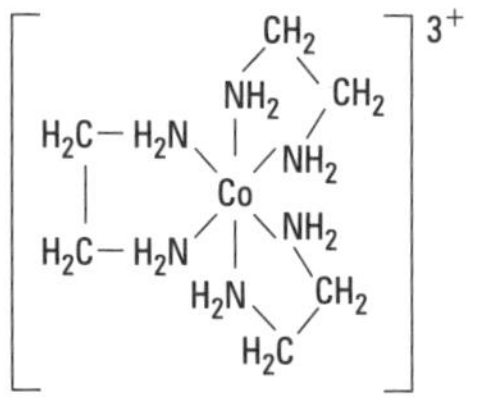

Types of ligand

Ligands are chemical species that co-ordinate with metal ions to form a complex. They are classified on the basis of the number of points of attachment to the central ion.

- Monodentate ligand – here the ligand is bound to the central ion at only one point, e.g. H_2O, NH_3.

- Bidentate ligand – this has two points of attachment to the central ion, e.g. ethylenediamine (en) (Fig. 43.1).

- Multidentate ligand – these have several points of attachment, e.g. ethylenediaminetetra-acetic acid (EDTA), which is a hexadentate ligand (six points of attachment) (Fig. 43.2).

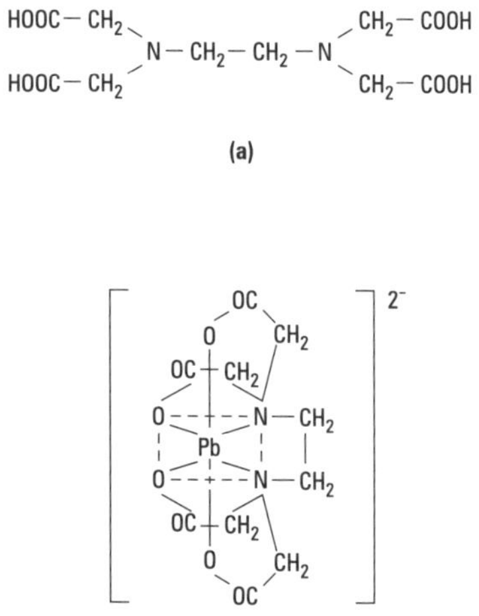

The basis of a complexometric titration involving EDTA

The metal ion under investigation is bound to an indicator in solution (under strict pH control). This solution is then titrated against a standard solution of EDTA. This can be expressed in the form of an equation:

$$\text{Metal–indicator} + \text{EDTA} \rightarrow \text{metal–EDTA} + \text{indicator} \qquad [43.1]$$

For example, if the indicator being used was solochrome black, the metal–indicator solution would be red while the colour of the free indicator would be blue (in the pH range 7–11). The reaction takes place if the EDTA displaces the indicator from the metal–indicator complex. Therefore the metal–EDTA complex must be more stable thermodynamically than the metal–indicator complex.

Stability of complexes

The thermodynamic stability of a species is an indication of the extent to which that species will be formed (under certain conditions and provided that it is allowed to reach equilibrium).

As an example consider the general case of a metal, M, in solution together with a monodentate ligand, L. It is possible to describe this system in terms of step-wise equilibria:

$$M + L = ML \qquad\qquad K_1 = [ML]/[M][L] \qquad [43.2]$$

$$ML + L = ML_2 \qquad\qquad K_2 = [ML_2]/[ML][L] \qquad [43.3]$$

Or, in general terms:

$$ML_{(n-1)} + L = ML_n \qquad K_n = [ML_n]/[ML_{(n-1)}][L] \qquad [43.4]$$

where K_1, K_2, ... K_n are step-wise stability constants.

Fig. 43.1 Structure of $[Co(en)_3]^{3+}$. It is a six-co-ordinate octahedral complex of ethylenediamine (en) with cobalt (III). The complex has three five-membered rings.

(a)

(b)

Fig. 43.2 Structure of EDTA. (a) EDTA contains two donor N atoms and four donor O atoms. It can therefore form a hexadentate complex (b) with a metal ion, e.g. Pb^{2+}.

An alternative approach for expressing the equilibria might be as follows:

$$M + L = ML \qquad \beta_1 = [ML]/[M][L] \qquad [43.5]$$

$$M + L_2 = ML_2 \qquad \beta_2 = [ML_2]/[M][L]^2 \qquad [43.6]$$

Or, in general terms:

$$M + L_n = ML_n \qquad \beta_n = [ML_n]/[M][L]_n \qquad [43.7]$$

where β_1, β_2, ..., β_n are the overall stability constants and are related to the step-wise stability constants as follows:

$$\beta_n = K_1 \times K_2 \times K_n \qquad [43.8]$$

Factors influencing the stability of complexes

The stability of a complex is related to the ability of the metal ion to complex with a given ligand, and to the characteristics of the ligand.

End-points can be determined more easily when a single complex is formed rather than when the complex is formed in a step-wise fashion. This can be achieved by using the aminopolycarboxylic acid, EDTA (Fig. 43.2).

In equations, EDTA can be expressed as H_4Y. The disodium salt Na_2H_2Y is frequently used as a source of the complex-forming ion, H_2Y^{2-}. Thus the typical reaction of EDTA with a metal ion can be written in the following form:

$$M^{2+} + H_2Y^{2-} \rightarrow MY^{2-} + 2H^+ \qquad [43.9]$$

The reaction of a metal ion with EDTA is always in the ratio $1:1$. The stability constants of selected metal–EDTA complexes are given in Table 43.1.

The detection of the end-point in titrations involving EDTA is most commonly achieved using a metal-ion indicator, i.e. a compound that changes its colour when it complexes with a particular metal ion. The structures of selected metal-ion indicators are shown in Fig. 43.3 and the properties of a variety of metal-ion indicators are given in Table 43.2.

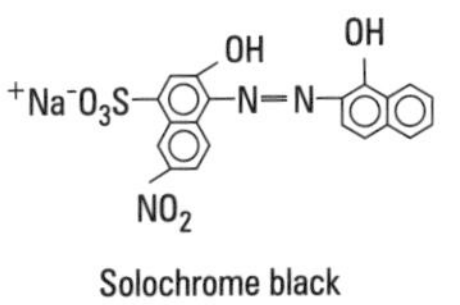

Types of complexometric titration

Direct titration

In this case, the metal ion is titrated with a standard solution of EDTA. The solution containing the metal ion is buffered to an appropriate pH at which the stability constant of the metal–EDTA complex is large. The free indicator has a different colour from that of the metal–indicator complex.

Back titration

In certain circumstances a particular metal ion cannot be titrated directly. This includes situations where:

- The metal ion precipitates in the absence of EDTA.
- The metal ion reacts too slowly with EDTA.
- The metal ion forms an inert complex.
- No suitable indicator is available.

In these cases a back titration is required. This involves addition of a known excess of EDTA to the metal ion (buffered to an appropriate pH). Then, the excess EDTA is titrated with a standard solution of a different

Table 43.1 Stability constants of selected metal–EDTA complexes (expressed as log K)*

Ion	log k	Ion	log k
Mg^{2+}	8.7	Ni^{2+}	18.6
Ca^{2+}	10.7	Cu^{2+}	18.8
Fe^{2+}	14.3	Hg^{2+}	21.9
Co^{2+}	16.3	Sc^{3+}	23.1
Al^{3+}	16.3	Cr^{3+}	24.0
Cd^{2+}	16.6	In^{3+}	24.9

*Ionic strength of solution was 0.1 at 20 °C.
Adapted from *Vogel's Textbook of Quantitative Inorganic Analysis*, 4th edn, J. Bassett, R.C. Denney, G.H. Jeffery and J. Mendham, Longman Scientific and Technical, Harlow, (1978) p. 264.

Solochrome black
(eriochrome black T)

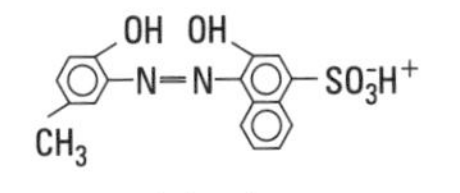

Calmagite

Fig. 43.3 Examples of metal-ion indicators: solochrome black and calmagite.

Table 43.2 Properties of selected indicators

Indicator	Colour of free indicator	Colour of metal-ion complex
Murexide		
< pH 9 (H_4In^-)	Red–violet	orange (Cu^{2+}), yellow (Ni^{2+} and Co^{2+})
pH 9–11 (H_3In^{2-})	Violet	and red (Ca^{2+})
> pH 11 (H_2In^{3-})	Blue	
Solochrome black		
< pH 5 (H_2In^-)	Red	In pH range 7–11 colour change is
pH 7–11 (HIn^{2-})	Blue	blue–red (Mg, Mn, Zn, Cd, Hg, Pb, Cu,
> pH 11.5 (In^{3-})	Orange	Al, Fe, Ti, Co, Ni and Pt metals)
Calmagite		
<pH 5 (H_2In^-)	Red	Same colour change as solochrome
pH 7–9 (HIn^{2-})	Blue	black but clearer and sharper
>pH 11.4 (In^{3-})	Red–orange	
Pyrocatechol violet		
< pH 1.5 (H_4In)	Red	In pH range 2–6, yellow to blue
pH 2–6 (H_3In^-)	Yellow	(Bi and Th); pH 7 violet to blue
pH 7 (H_2In^{2-})	Violet	(Cu^{2+}, Zn^{2+}, Cd^{2+}, Ni^{2+} and Co^{2+})
>pH 10 (In^{4-})	Blue	

metal ion. The choice of a second metal ion is important as it must not displace the analyte metal ion from its EDTA complex.

Practical considerations

- pH adjustment is critical in EDTA titrations. The pH is monitored with a pH meter or pH test paper.

- The metal ion under investigation should ideally be approximately 0.25 mM in a volume of 50–150 mL of solution. Dilution of the metal ion may be necessary to avoid end-point detection problems.

- Do not add excess indicator, as too intense a colour can lead to problems, e.g. masking of the colour change.

- It is sometimes difficult to detect the end-point because the colour change can be slow to develop. Stirring is recommended to assist colour transformation.

- The use of metal-ion indicators to indicate the end-point of complexometric titrations is based on a specific colour change. Some individuals may find it difficult to detect a particular colour change (e.g. those with colour blindness). Alternative approaches for end-point detection are available based on a colorimeter/spectrophotometer (devices for measuring colour, see Chapter 48) or electrochemical detection (see Chapter 54).

Example calculation

A solution of Ni^{2+} (25.0 mL) was titrated with the disodium salt of EDTA (0.1036 mol L^{-1}) at pH 5 and required 20.25 mL for the metal-indicator to change colour. What is the concentration (g L^{-1}) of the Ni^{2+} solution? The A_r of nickel is 58.71 g mol^{-1}.

Metal-ion indicators For a metal-ion indicator to be useful it must be less stable than the corresponding metal–EDTA complex.

1. Write the balanced equation

$$Ni^{2+} + H_2EDTA^{2-} \rightarrow NiEDTA^{2-} + 2H^+ \qquad [43.10]$$

2. Determine the equivalences

1 mole of H_2EDTA^{2-} is equivalent to 1 mole of Ni^{2+}

3. You now have a choice:
   (i) do the calculation in moles and then convert to g L^{-1}

   or

   (ii) work in g

   The calculation below illustrates (ii).

4. 1000 mL of H_2EDTA (1.0 M) $\equiv$ 58.71 g Ni^{2+}

   But H_2EDTA is 0.1036 M

Self-test: is 0.1036 M H_2EDTA equivalent to more or less Ni^{2+} than 1.0 M H_2EDTA?
Answer: less, therefore you must MULTIPLY by 0.1036.

1000 mL of H_2EDTA (0.1036 M) $\equiv$ 0.1036 mol L^{-1} $\times$ 58.71 g mol^{-1} Ni^{2+}

Self-test: is 1.0 mL 0.1036 M H_2EDTA equivalent to more or less Ni^{2+} than 1000 mL M H_2EDTA?
Answer: less, therefore you must DIVIDE by 1000.

1.0 mL of H_2EDTA (0.1036 M) $\equiv \dfrac{1.0\ ML \times 0.1036\ mol\ L^{-1} \times 58.71\ g\ mol^{-1}}{1000\ mL} Ni^{2+}$

But the titration used 20.25 mL of H_2EDTA (0.1036 M)

Self-test: is 20.25 mL 0.1036 M H_2EDTA equivalent to more or less Ni^{2+} than 1.0 mL M H_2EDTA?
Answer: more, therefore you must MULTIPLY by 20.25.

20.25 mL of H_2EDTA (0.1036 M)

$$\equiv \frac{20.25\ mL \times 1.0\ mL \times 0.1036\ mol\ L^{-1} \times 58.71\ g\ mol^{-1}}{1000\ mL} Ni^{2+}$$

Since 25.00 mL of Ni^{2+} solution are equivalent to 20.25 mL of 0.1036 M H_2EDTA solution

25.00 mL of Ni^{2+} solution contains

$$\frac{20.25\ mL \times 1.0\ mL \times 0.1036\ mol\ L^{-1} \times 58.71\ g\ mol^{-1}}{1000\ mL} Ni^{2+}$$

Do the self-test

1.00 mL of Ni^{2+} solution contains

$$\frac{20.25\ mL \times 1.0\ mL \times 0.1036\ mol\ L^{-1} \times 58.71\ g\ mol^{-1}}{25.00\ mL \times 1000\ mL} Ni^{2+}$$

Do the self-test

1000 mL of Ni^{2+} solution contains

$$\frac{1000 \text{ mL} \times 20.25 \text{ mL} \times 1.0 \text{ mL} \times 0.1036 \text{ mol L}^{-1} \times 58.71 \text{ g mol}^{-1}}{1.0 \text{ mL} \times 25.00 \text{ mL} \times 1000 \text{ mL}} Ni^{2+}$$

Concentration of Ni^{2+} solution = 4.927 g L^{-1}

Sources for further study

Christian, G.D. (2004) *Analytical Chemistry*, 6th edn. John Wiley & Sons Ltd, Chichester.

Harris, D.C. (2006) *Quantitative Chemical Analysis*, 7th edn. W.H. Freeman Co., New York.

Jander, G., Jahr, K.-F., Schulze, G. and Simon, J. (2009) *Volumetric Analysis*, 17th edn. Walter de Gruyter Inc., Germany.

Mendham, J., Denney, R.C., Barnes, J.D. and Thomas, M.J.K. (2000) *Vogel's Textbook of Quantitative Chemical Analysis*. 6th edn. Prentice Hall, Harlow, Essex.

Rubinson, J.F. and Rubinson, K.A. (1998) *Contemporary Chemical Analysis*. Prentice Hall, Harlow, Essex.

Skoog, D.A., West, D.M. and Holler F.J. (2004) *Fundamentals of Analytical Chemistry*, 8th edn. Thomson Brooks/Cole, Belmont, CA.

Study exercise

43.1 You are the analyst working in a hospital laboratory. A urine sample from a patient must be analysed for Ca^{2+} and Mg^{2+} ions by the following procedure. The urine sample was diluted to exactly 2.000 L. After buffering to pH = 10, a sample (25.00 mL) required EDTA (24.00 mL; 0.0500 M) for equivalence. In a second sample (50.00 mL), the Ca^{2+} was precipitated as calcium oxalate which was filtered, washed and re-dissolved in acid. To this solution EDTA (25.00 mL; 0.05 M) was added and the resulting solution buffered to pH = 10 and titrated to equivalence with an MgCl$_2$ solution (10.00 mL; 0.0500 M). From these results, calculate the amount of Ca^{2+} and Mg^{2+} (in mg) in the 2.000 L solution.

All reduction–oxidation reactions involve a transfer of electrons. The oxidising agent accepts electrons, and the reducing agent donates electrons. To establish the reaction for a redox titration it is necessary to determine the 'half-equation' for both the oxidising agent and the reducing agent. By adding the two 'half-equations' it is possible to determine the overall equation for the titration (Box 25.4). The basic theory of electrochemistry is described in Chapter 54.

One of the most common oxidants is potassium permanganate which in acidic solution can undergo the following reaction:

$$MnO_4^- + 8H^+ + 5e^- = Mn^{2+} + 4H_2O \qquad [44.1]$$

Unfortunately, potassium permanganate is not obtainable in high enough purity and can undergo decomposition by exposure to sunlight. Therefore it cannot be used as a primary standard (p. 299). However, it can be used in redox titrations provided it is standardised with sodium oxalate (which is available in high purity). The redox reaction involving oxalate is as follows:

$$C_2O_4^{2-} = 2CO_2 + 2e^- \qquad [44.2]$$

The overall reaction between permanganate and oxalate can be obtained by balancing the electrons on each side of the equation. This can be achieved by multiplying eqn [44.1] by 2 and eqn [44.2] by 5, and then combining them as follows:

$$2MnO_4^- + 16H^+ + 5C_2O_4^{2-} = 2Mn^{2+} + 10CO_2 + 8H_2O \qquad [44.3]$$

Another common method for the standardisation of potassium permanganate is to use iron (II):

$$Fe^{2+} = Fe^{3+} + e^- \qquad [44.4]$$

The combined equation is obtained by multiplying eqn [44.4] by 5 and adding to eqn [44.1]:

$$MnO_4^- + 8H^+ + 5Fe^{2+} = Mn^{2+} + 5Fe^{3+} + 4H_2O \qquad [44.5]$$

Potassium permanganate has a major advantage when used for titrations in that it can act as its own indicator.

A list of other common oxidising agents and reducing agents is given in Table 44.1.

Many volumetric procedures involving redox reactions comprise multiple stages which can lead to confusion in your approach to calculation. Typical of these are experiments involving potassium iodate (KIO_3) in which the iodate is reacted with an excess of potassium iodide

Table 44.1 Common oxidising and reducing agents used in redox titrations

Oxidizing agents		Reducing agents	
Ce^{4+}	Ceric	AsO_3^{3-}	Arsenite
$Cr_2O_7^{2-}$	Dichromate	Fe^{2+}	Ferrous
H_2O_2	Hydrogen peroxide	NH_2OH	Hydroxylamine
IO_3^-	Iodate	Sn^{2+}	Stannous
MnO_4^-	Permanganate	$S_2O_3^{2-}$	Thiosulphate

(KI) in acid solution and then the iodine released is titrated with sodium thiosulphate $Na_2S_2O_3$.

Using the principles outlined in Boxes 25.4 and 25.5 you can work out a direct relationship between KIO_3 and $Na_2S_2O_3$ as shown below:

$$IO_3^- + I^- \rightarrow I_2 + H_2O \tag{44.6}$$

Using the Boxes 25.4 and 25.5, identify the two partial ionic equations and process them

$$10\varepsilon + 12H^+ + 2IO_3^- \rightarrow I_2 + 6H_2O \tag{44.7}$$

$$10I^- \rightarrow 5I_2 + 10\varepsilon \tag{44.8}$$

Add eqns [44.7] and [44.8] and divide by 2

$$IO_3^- + 5I^- + 6H^+ \rightarrow 3I_2 + 3H_2O \tag{44.9}$$

Now look at the reaction between I_2 and $Na_2S_2O_3$ using the same methodology;

$$2\varepsilon + I_2 \rightarrow 2I^- \tag{44.10}$$

$$2S_2O_3^{2-} \rightarrow S_4O_6^{2-} + 2\varepsilon \tag{44.11}$$

Add eqns [44.10] and [44.11]

$$2S_2O_3^{2-} + I_2 \rightarrow 2I^- + S_4O_6^{2-} \tag{44.12}$$

Now balance I_2 between eqns [44.9] and [44.12] by multiplying [44.12] by 3

$$6S_2O_3^{2-} + 3I_2 \rightarrow 6I^- + 3 S_4O_6^{2-} \tag{44.13}$$

Now combining eqns [44.9] and [44.13] you can see that:

1 mole of KIO_3 is equivalent to 6 moles of $Na_2S_2O_3$

Example calculation

Standardisation of potassium permanganate with a primary standard, sodium oxalate

An accurately weighed portion of sodium oxalate (0.1550 g) was dissolved in dilute sulphuric acid (250 mL). While maintaining the temperature of the solution above $70\,^\circ C$, it was titrated to equivalence with potassium permanganate solution (18.5 mL). What is the molarity of potassium permanganate?

1. Write the balanced equation for the reaction between the standard and the test substance (using the two half-equations [44.1] and [44.2]):

$$2MnO_4^- + 16H^+ + 5C_2O_4^{2-} = 2Mn^{2+} + 10CO_2 + 8H_2O \tag{44.3}$$

2. Determine the equivalences of the reacting species:

   2 moles of MnO_4^- are equivalent to 5 moles of $C_2O_4^{2-}$.

3. Calculate the number of moles of standard substance (sodium oxalate) used to reach the end-point of the reaction.

   The molecular weight of sodium oxalate is 134 g mol^{-1}. Therefore 0.1550 g of sodium oxalate is equivalent to:

$$\frac{0.1550\,(g)}{134\,(g\,mol^{-1})} = 1.157 \times 10^{-3}\,mol$$

4. Calculate the corresponding number of moles of potassium permanganate present in the volume of titrant added.

From the equation:

$$5 \text{ moles of } Na_2C_2O_4 = 2 \text{ moles of } KMnO_4$$

Therefore,

$$1 \text{ mole of } Na_2C_2O_4 \equiv \frac{2}{5} \text{ moles of } KMnO_4$$

Therefore

$$1.157 \times 10^{-3} \text{ moles of } Na_2C_2O_4 \equiv \frac{1.157 \times 10^{-3} \times 2}{5} \text{ moles of } KMnO_4$$

Therefore

$$18.5 \text{ mL of } KMnO_4 \text{ solution contain} \frac{1.157 \times 10^{-3} \times 2}{5} \text{ moles of } KMnO_4$$

Therefore

$1000 \text{ mL of } KMnO_4$ solution contain

$$\frac{1000 \text{ mL} \times 1.157 \times 10^{-3} \times 2}{18.5 \text{ mL} \times 5} \text{ moles of } KMnO_4$$

Concentration of $KMnO_4$ solution = 0.025 mol L^{-1}

Sources for further study

Christian, G.D. (2004) *Analytical Chemistry,* 6th edn. John Wiley & Sons Ltd., Chichester.

Harris, D.C. (2006) *Quantitative Chemical Analysis,* 7th edn. W.H. Freeman Co., New York.

Jander, G., Jahr, K.F., Schulze, G. and Simon, J. (2009) *Volumetric Analysis,* 17th edn. Walter de Gruyter Inc., Germany.

Mendham, J., Denney, R.C., Barnes, J.D. and Thomas, M.J.K. (2000) *Vogel's Textbook of*

Quantitative Chemical Analysis, 6th edn. Prentice Hall, Harlow, Essex.

Rubinson, J.F. and Rubinson, K.A. (1998) *Contemporary Chemical Analysis.* Prentice Hall, Harlow, Essex.

Skoog, D.A., West, D.M. and Holler, F.J. (2004) *Fundamentals of Analytical Chemistry,* 8th edn. Thomson Brooks/Cole, Belmont, CA.

Study exercise

44.1 Dilute aqueous hydrogen peroxide is sold commercially to the cosmetic and health care industries as '10–Volume Hydrogen Peroxide'. This means that one volume of solution will decompose to give ten volumes of oxygen at STP. From the following analytical data calculate the concentration (% w/v) of '10-Volume Hydrogen Peroxide'.

'10–volume Hydrogen Peroxide' (25.00 mL) was dissolved in water and made up to 250.00 mL. This solution (25.00 mL) was titrated with a $KMnO_4$ solution (48 mL; 0.02 M) to a pale-pink end-point in the presence of dilute H_2SO_4.

Titration curves – plots of concentration of titrand against volume of titrant used.

Table 45.1 Titration of 100 mL of 0.1 M NaCl with 0.1 M AgNO$_3$. (Note that K_s, for AgCl = 1.1×10^{-10})

0.1 M AgNO$_3$ (mL)	pCl$^-$	pAg$^-$
0	0.1	0.0
25	1.2	8.7
50	1.5	8.5
90	2.3	7.7
95	2.6	7.4
98	3.0	7.0
99	3.3	6.7
99.5	3.6	6.4
99.8	4.0	6.0
99.9	4.3	5.7
100	5.0	5.0
100.1	5.7	4.3
100.2	6.0	4.0
100.5	6.4	3.6
101	6.7	3.3
102	7.0	3.0
105	7.4	2.6
110	7.7	2.3
120	8.0	2.0
130	8.1	1.9
140	8.2	1.8
150	8.3	1.7

Adapted from *Vogel's Textbook of Quantitative Inorganic Analysis*, 4th edn, J. Bassett, R.C. Denney, G.H. Jeffery and J. Mendham, Longman Scientific and Technical, Harlow (1978), p. 280.

Precipitation is the term used to describe the process whereby a substance leaves solution rapidly, forming either a crystalline solid or amorphous solid (the precipitate). In the case of a precipitation titration, this process occurs when the analyte forms a precipitate with the titrant. The most common types of precipitation titrations use silver nitrate as the titrant. They are often referred to as argentimetric titrations.

Titration curves used in precipitation reactions usually use a concentration-dependent variable called the '*p* function' rather than the concentration itself. The *p* function for a species X is defined as follows:

$$pX = -log_{10} [X] \tag{45.1}$$

For example, in the titration of 100 mL of 0.1 mol L^{-1} NaCl with 0.1 mol L^{-1} AgNO$_3$ the initial concentration of [Cl$^-$] is 0.1 mol L^{-1}, so by using eqn [45.1] the *p* function is 1 or $pCl^- = 1$.

When 25 mL of 0.1 mol L^{-1} AgNO$_3$ has been added, 75 mL of NaCl remains in a total volume of 125 mL. Therefore, the concentration of the chloride ion is given by

$$[Cl^-] = \frac{75 \text{ mL} \times 0.1 \text{ mol L}^{-1}}{125 \text{ mL}} = 6 \times 10^{-2} \text{ mol L}^{-1} \tag{45.2}$$

and $pCl^- = 1.22$. (Note that the solubility product, K_s, of AgCl is 1.1×10^{-10}, see p. 192.)

Therefore:

$$[Ag^+] \times [Cl^-] = K_s = 1.1 \times 10^{-10} \tag{45.3}$$

or

$$pAg^+ + pCl^- = 9.96 = pAgCl \tag{45.4}$$

It was found above that pCl$^-$ = 1.22, hence pAg$^+$ = 9.96 − 1.22 = 8.74. In a similar manner, the pAg^+ values can be calculated.

At the equivalence point [Ag$^+$] = [Cl$^-$]. Therefore:

$$[Ag^+] = [Cl^-] = \sqrt{K_s} = \sqrt{1.1 \times 10^{-10}} = 1.05 \times 10^{-5} \tag{45.5}$$

$$pAg^+ = -log(1.05 \times 10^{-5}) = 4.98 \tag{45.6}$$

Beyond the equivalence point the situation changes. For 100.1 mL AgNO$_3$ solution:

$$[Ag^+] = \frac{0.1 \text{ mL} \times 0.1 \text{ mol L}^{-1}}{200.1 \text{ mL}} = 5 \times 10^{-5} \text{ mol L}^{-1} \tag{45.7}$$

or $pAg^+ = 4.3$. Therefore,

$$pCl^- = pAgCl - pAg^+ = 9.96 - 4.3 = 5.66$$

Values calculated in this way up to the addition of 150 mL of 0.1 mol L^{-1} AgNO$_3$ are given in Table 45.1 and the titration curve in Fig. 45.1.

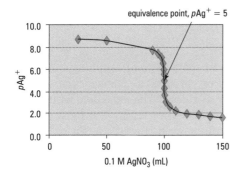

Fig. 45.1 Precipitation titration curve. Initial and final slopes are drawn (see Fig. 42.3) and a parallel line is drawn such that the mid-point is on the curve. This is the equivalence point.

In acid media (pH < 6), the concentration of CrO_4^{2-} is lowered by the following reaction: $CrO_4^{2-} + 2H^+ \rightleftharpoons 2HCrO_4^- \rightleftharpoons Cr_2O_7^{2-} + H_2O$. In alkaline media (pH > 10), $Ag(OH)_{(s)}$ may precipitate.

In all argentimetric titrations strong light (including daylight) should be avoided as it can lead to decomposition of the silver salts.

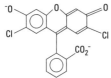

Fig. 45.2 Structure of dichlorofluorescein.

End-point determination

Three techniques are commonly used to determine the end-point in precipitation titrations. They are:

1. potentiometric methods;

2. chemical indicator methods;

3. light-scattering methods, exemplified by turbidimetry or nephelometry.

Only indicator methods will be discussed further. Three types of indicator methods can be applied to determine the end-point of an Ag^+ and a Cl^- titration. These are:

1. Mohr titration, which involves the formation of a coloured precipitate by reaction with the indicator. For example, in the determination of chloride concentration with silver nitrate a small amount of potassium chromate solution is added as an indicator. This results in the formation of a red silver chromate (Ag_2CrO_4) precipitate at the end-point:

$$2Ag^+ + CrO_4^{2-} \rightarrow Ag_2CrO_{4(s)} \tag{45.8}$$
$$\text{(red)}$$

In this case, the precipitate may form slightly after the end-point, but this error can usually be neglected. Also, the titration should be done in neutral or slightly alkaline solution (pH 6.5–9) otherwise silver chromate might not be formed.

2. Volhard titration, which involves the formation of a soluble coloured compound. This approach is exemplified by the quantitative analysis of chlorides, bromides and iodides by back titration. In this case, the halide is titrated with silver:

$$Ag^+ + Cl^- \rightarrow AgCl_{(s)} \tag{45.9}$$

Excess silver ions are then titrated with standard potassium thiocyanate solution in the presence of an iron (III) salt:

$$Ag^+ + SCN^- \rightarrow AgSCN_{(s)} \tag{45.10}$$

When all the Ag^+ has been reacted, the SCN^- reacts with Fe^{3+} to form a red complex, indicating the end-point:

$$Fe^{3+} + SCN^- \rightarrow FeSCN^{2+} \tag{45.11}$$
$$\text{(red)}$$

A problem with the determination of chloride by this approach is that the end-point coloration slowly fades, as AgCl is more soluble than AgSCN. As a consequence the AgCl slowly dissolves to be replaced by the $FeSCN^{2+}$. Two approaches are possible to prevent this secondary reaction from taking place. The most common method is to filter off the AgCl and titrate only the Ag^+ left in solution. Alternatively, add a few millilitres of an immiscible liquid (e.g. nitrobenzene) to the titrand

Table 45.2 Selected applications of precipitation titrations

Analyte	Comments
Cl^-, Br^-	Mohr method: Ag_2CrO_4 used as end-point
Br^-, I^-, AsO_4^-	Volhard method: precipitate removal is unnecessary
Cl^-, CN^-, CO_3^{2-}	Volhard method: precipitate removal is required
Cl^-, Br^-, I^-, SCN^-	Fajans method: titration with Ag^+. Detection with fluorescein, dichlorofluorescein and eosin
F^-	Titration with $Th(NO_3)_4$ to produce ThF_4. End-point detection with alizarin red S

Adapted from: *Quantitative Chemical Analysis*, 4th edn, D.C. Harris, W.H. Freeman, New York (1995), p. 176.

prior to the back titration. The nitrobenzene acts to 'coat' the AgCl precipitate, thereby isolating it from the SCN^-.

3. Fajans titration, which involves the adsorption of a coloured indicator onto the precipitate at the end-point, resulting in a colour change. During this adsorption process a change occurs in the indicator resulting in a change of colour. The indicators used for this are often anionic dyes, e.g. fluorescein or eosin. The most common indicator for AgCl is dichlorofluorescein (Fig. 45.2) (this is greenish yellow in solution but changes colour to pink when it is adsorbed on AgCl).

Selected examples of precipitation titrations are shown in Table 45.2.

Sources for further study

Christian, G.D. (2004) *Analytical Chemistry*, 6th edn. John Wiley & Sons Ltd, Chichester.

Harris, D.C. (2006) *Quantitative Chemical Analysis*, 7th edn. W.H. Freeman Co., New York.

Jander, G., Jahr, K.-F., Schulze, G. and Simon, J. (2009) *Volumetric Analysis*, 17th edn. Walter de Gruyter Inc., Germany.

Mendham, J., Denney, R.C., Barnes, J.D. and Thomas, M.J.K. (2000) *Vogel's Textbook of Quantitative Chemical Analysis*, 6th edn. Prentice Hall, Harlow, Essex.

Rubinson, J.F. and Rubinson, K.A. (1998) *Contemporary Chemical Analysis*. Prentice Hall, Harlow, Essex.

Skoog, D.A., West, D.M. and Holler, F.J. (2004) *Fundamentals of Analytical Chemistry*, 8th edn. Thomson Brooks/Cole, Belmont, CA.

Study exercise

45.1 You are a major manufacturer of fireworks and you suspect that your bulk supplier of potassium nitrate, a white crystalline solid, has been adulterating the potassium nitrate with salt to increase his profits. Your analysis of the 'potassium nitrate' gave the following results: 'potassium nitrate' (4.0124 g) was dissolved in water and made up to 250.00 mL. This solution (25.00 mL) required silver nitrate solution (10.3 mL; 0.1 M) for equivalence using dichlorofluorescein as indicator. Calculate the % (w/w) salt in the 'potassium nitrate'.

Instrumental techniques

Most analytical methods rely on one or more chemical or physical properties of the test substance (the analyte) for detection and/or measurement. There are two principal approaches:

1. Qualitative analysis – where a sample is analysed to determine whether a compound is present or absent. For example, the use of infrared spectroscopy (Chapter 56) and nuclear magnetic resonance spectroscopy (Chapter 57).

2. Quantitative analysis – where the quantity of a particular element or compound in a sample is determined in terms of its concentration (e.g. as $mg\,L^{-1}$). For example, the use of atomic spectroscopy (Chapter 49) and X-ray fluorescence spectroscopy (Chapter 50) for elemental analysis, or gas and liquid chromatography (Chapter 52) for compound analysis.

Your choice of approach will be determined by the purpose of the investigation and by the level of accuracy and precision required. Many of the basic quantitative methods rely on chemical reactions of the analyte and involve assumptions about the nature of the test substance and the lack of interfering compounds in the sample: such assumptions are unlikely to be wholly valid at all times. If you need to make more exacting measurements of a particular analyte, it may be necessary to separate it from the other components in the sample, e.g. extraction of the analyte using solid phase extraction to remove interferences (Chapter 52), using chromatography (Chapters 51–52) or electrophoresis (Chapter 53), and then identify the separated components, e.g. using mass spectrometry (e.g. Chapter 58).

> **KEY POINT** In general, you should aim to use the simplest procedure that satisfies the purpose of your investigation – there is little value in using a complex, time-consuming or costly analytical procedure to answer a simple problem when a high degree of accuracy is not required.

Most of the routine methods based on chemical analysis are destructive since the analyte usually has to be extracted from the matrix in which it is held, for example extracting drugs from blood or urine (Chapter 52) or decomposition of a solid sample using concentrated acids (Chapter 49). However, many analytical methods that are based on physical properties are non-destructive, for example compound identification using Fourier transform infra red (FTIR) spectroscopy (Chapter 56). Non-destructive methods are often preferred, as they allow further characterisation of a particular sample.

Validity and quantitative analysis

Before using a particular procedure, you should consider its possible limitations in terms of:

- measurement errors, and their likely magnitude: these might include processing errors (e.g. in preparing solutions and making dilutions),

---

Definitions

Accuracy The closeness of an individual measurement, or a mean value based on a number of measurements, to the true value.

Concentration range The range of values from the detection limit to the upper concentration at which the technique becomes inaccurate or imprecise.

Detection limit The minimum concentration of an analyte that can be detected at a particular confidence level.

Drift 'Baseline' movement in a particular direction: drift can be a problem during analysis (e.g. when separating compounds by chromatography).

Noise Random fluctuations in a continuously monitored signal.

Precision The extent of mutual agreement between replicate data values for an individual sample.

Quality control Measures in place to ensure that the result meets your laboratory's standard.

Quality assurance Measures in place to monitor and document the performance of a test procedure, e.g. proficiency testing schemes.

Replicate Repeat measurement.

Selectivity The extent to which a method is free from interference due to other substances in the sample.

Sensitivity The ability to discriminate between small differences in analyte concentration.

Validation The process whereby the accuracy and precision of a particular analytical method are checked in relation to specific standards, using an appropriate reference material containing a known amount of analyte.

Selected suppliers of certified reference materials –

UK: LGC – Laboratory of the Government Chemist, London.

USA: NIST – National Institute of Science and Technology, Washington DC.

Certified reference materials can be used for a variety of purposes including –

- establishing metrological traceability of results;
- confirmation of the identity of a material;
- development and validation of new methods of measurement;
- calibration and verification of measurement processes in routine analyses;
- verification of the correct application of standard methods;
- internal quality control schemes;
- defining values for other materials which may then be used as secondary standards or calibrants.

Accreditation – In the UK, analytical science laboratories can be accredited by UKAS (United Kingdom Accreditation Services) to ensure that all analytical procedures are performed to an internationally recognised standard (BS ISO 17025).

instrumental errors (e.g. a gas chromatography instrument that has not been set up correctly), calibration errors (e.g. converting a digital readout to an analyte concentration) and errors due to the presence of interfering substances (e.g. fatty acids in blood samples);

- sampling errors: these may occur if the material used for analysis is not representative, e.g. elemental analysis of a soil sample or drug composition of a biological fluid (see Prichard and Barwick, 2007).

The reliability of a particular method can be assessed by measuring 'standards' (sometimes termed 'controls'). These are often prepared in the laboratory by adding a known amount of analyte, or reference material, to a sample matrix. For example, when analysing a blood sample, controls should be prepared using real blood, such as horse blood or human transfusion blood (this is often termed 'spiking' a sample). The reference material used for spiking must be pure and supplied from a recognised source. These are available from commercial suppliers who will also provide a certificate of analysis indicating the exact concentration and purity of the compound. In most instances, several standards (including a 'blank' or zero) are analysed to construct a calibration curve (see Chapter 60), which is then used to convert sample measurements to amounts of analyte.

The use of certified reference materials (CRMs) is particularly important when establishing (validating) new methods or comparing methods. CRMs are obtained from recognised suppliers and can either be analysed directly or extracted/decomposed and then analysed. As well as the actual material all CRMs have a certificate which provides details of element/compound content, in appropriate units, and an estimate of uncertainty of the content, e.g. Pb-content of 12.5 ± 0.3 mg/kg. The results obtained within the laboratory can then be compared with the certificate values. Ideally agreement between measured and certified values for each analyte should be obtained before continuing with the selected experimental approach.

CRMs can be obtained for a whole variety of analytes in a wide range of matrices (chemical, biological and foodstuffs). Care should be taken in matching both concentrations of analytes and matrix between samples and the chosen CRM.

Validation of a particular method is particularly important in the pharmaceutical, environmental or food analysis laboratory, where the results of the analysis have important implications. Such laboratories operate strict validation procedures which include: (i) adherence to standard operating procedures (SOPs); (ii) calibration of assays using CRMs containing known amounts of analyte and traceable to a national reference laboratory; (iii) effective quality assurance and quality control systems; (iv) detailed record-keeping, covering all aspects of the analysis and recording of results. Such rigour is often required for legal reasons and consumer protection, although the general principles of standardisation, calibration, assessment of performance and record-keeping are equally valid.

Proficiency testing schemes

These are used by laboratories carrying out analytical measurements and will give a snapshot of a laboratory's performance and quality systems at

A proficiency testing scheme should test the:

- organisation
- quality system
- quality audits and reviews
- staff
- equipment
- measurement traceability
- methods and procedures
- environment
- handling of samples
- records
- complaints
- sub-contracting and purchasing

based on NAMAS criteria available at http://www.smtl.co.uk/MDRC/NAMAS/about-namas.html

Criteria for the selection of a particular analytical method –

- the required level of accuracy and precision
- the number of samples to be analysed
- the amount of each sample available for analysis
- the physical form of the samples
- the expected concentration range of the analyte in the samples
- the sensitivity and detection limit of the technique
- the likelihood of interfering substances
- the speed of the analysis
- the ease and convenience of the procedure
- the skill required by the operator
- the cost and availability of the equipment.

any one point of time. By reviewing the performance over a period of time, the analytical quality of the laboratory can be determined.

Reporting analytical results

Chemical analysis demands both accuracy and precision (p. 209). In order to report the presence of, for example, a drug in a blood sample, you have to be certain that the drug is present. In order to do so, a combination of analytical procedures should be used. GC–MS (Chapter 52) used for screening the blood sample may identify the specific drug using a combination of the retention time and the mass spectrum of the drug. Using this procedure, an internal standard (p. 329) is added to the blood sample prior to extraction. This ensures that (i) the extraction process is working satisfactorily and (ii) the instrument is operating correctly. If a drug has been identified using this process, a reference standard is analysed which should elute at the same retention time ($\pm 2\%$, Anon., 2002) of the drug in the case sample. Occasionally, after the extraction process, the extract will have to be derivatised prior to analysis by GC–MS, for example morphine is usually derivatised using N-methyl-N-trimethylsilyltrifluoroacetamide (MSTFA). If a drug has been derivatised, it can still be identified by the combination of retention time and mass spectrum in comparison to a derivatised reference standard. Once the drug has been identified, the presence of the drug can either be confirmed or quantified, usually by a technique based on a different chemical principle to that used for screening, such as HPLC (Chapter 52) or LC–MS (Chapter 58). It is only after the process of identification, quantification (if appropriate) and confirmation that the drug can be reported.

Text references

Anon. (2002) *Forensic Toxicology Laboratory Guidelines*. Society of Forensic Toxicologists, SOFT.

Prichard, E. and Barwick, V. (2007) *Quality Assurance in Analytical Chemistry*. Wiley, Chichester.

Sources for further study

Anon. (2004) *Guidance on Analytical Methods Validation*. Available: http://www.fda.gov/cber/gdlns/methval.htm Last accessed 15/12/04. [US FDA guidance/details of reference standards, procedures for method validation, etc.]

Anon. (2004) *Valid Analytical Measurement Homepage*. Available: http://www.vam.org.uk Last accessed: 15/12/04.

Barwick, V., Burke, S., Lawn, R., Roper, P. and Walker, R. (2001) *Applications of Reference Materials in Analytical Chemistry*. RSC, Cambridge.

Burgess, C. (2000) *Valid Analytical Methods and Procedures*. Royal Society of Chemistry, Cambridge.

Chan, C.C., Lee, Y.C., Lam, H. and Zhang, X-M. (eds) (2004) *Analytical Method Validation and Instrument Performance Verifications*. Wiley, Chichester.

Currell, G. (2000) *Analytical Instrumentation. Performance and Characteristics of Quality*. Wiley, Chichester.

Funk, W., Dammann, V. and Donnevert, G. (2007) *Quality Assurance in Analytical Chemistry*. Wiley, Chichester.

Kellner, R., Mermet, J.M., Otto, M., Valcarcel, M. and Widner, H.M. (2004) *Analytical Chemistry: A Modern Approach to Analytical Science*, 2nd edn. Wiley, Chichester.
[Covers all modern analytical topics.]

Konieczka, P. and Namiesnik, J. (2009) *Quality Assurance and Quality Control in the Analytical Chemical Laboratory. A Practical Approach*. CRC Press, Boca Raton.

Prichard, E. and Barwick, V. (2007) *Quality Assurance in Analytical Chemistry*. Wiley, Chichester.
[Gives detailed coverage of all topics in this chapter.]

Ratliff, T.A. (2003) *The Laboratory Quality Assurance System. A manual of quality procedures and forms*, 3rd edn. Wiley, Chichester.

Schwedt, G. (1998) *The Essential Guide to Analytical Chemistry*. Wiley, Chichester.

Stoeppler, M., Wolf, W.R. and Jenks, P.J. (eds) (2001) *Reference Materials for Chemical Analysis*. Wiley, Chichester.

Study exercises

46.1 Test your knowledge of quality in analytical measurements – explain the meaning of the following terms and why they are important in quantitative chemical analysis:

(a) accuracy
(b) precision
(c) quality control
(d) quality assurance
(e) replicate
(f) detection limit.

46.2 Offer your opinion – discuss with your colleagues whether or not all analytical chemistry laboratories should be accredited to UKAS standards.

46.3 Based on your knowledge of an instrumental analytical technique that you have used consider the following issues:

(a) What physical form must the sample be in for the technique to accept the sample?
(b) For quantitative analysis what is the expected concentration range for the calibration?
(c) Does the technique suffer from any known interferences?
(d) How would you dilute or pre-concentrate the analyte in the sample?

There are many instances where it is necessary to measure the quantity of a test substance using a calibrated procedure. You are most likely to encounter this approach in one or more of the following practical exercises:

- Quantitative spectrophotometric assay (Chapter 48).

- Atomic absorption spectroscopic analysis of metal ions in quantitative analysis of metal ions in solution using atomic spectroscopy (Chapter 49) or electroanalytical techniques (Chapter 54).

- Quantitative chromatographic analysis (e.g. GC or HPLC Chapters 51 and 52).

- Quantitative element analysis of solids using XRF (Chapter 50).

> **KEY POINT** In most instances, calibration involves the establishment of a relationship between the measured response (the 'signal') and one or more 'standards' containing a known amount of substance.

In some instances, you can measure a signal due to an inherent property of the substance (e.g. the absorption of UV light p. 333), whereas in other cases you will need to react it with another substance to see the result (e.g. an acid–base titration, visualised using an indicator p. 306).

The different types of calibration curve

By preparing a set of solutions (termed 'standards'), each containing either (i) a known *amount* or (ii) a specific *concentration* of the substance, and then measuring the response of each standard solution, the underlying relationship can be established in graphical form as a 'calibration curve', or 'standard curve'. This can then be used to determine either (i) the amount or (ii) the concentration of the substance in one or more test samples. Alternatively, the response can be expressed solely in mathematical terms: an example of this approach is the determination of chlorophyll pigments in plant extracts by measuring absorption at particular wavelengths, and then applying a formula based on previous (published) measurements for purified pigments.

There are various types of standard curve: in the simplest cases, the relationship between signal and substance will be linear, or nearly so, and the calibration will be represented best by a straight-line graph (see Box 47.1). In some instances (Fig. 47.1(a)), you will need to transform either the x values or y values, in order to produce a linear graph. In other instances, the straight-line relationship may only hold up to a certain value (the 'linear dynamic range') and beyond this point the graph may curve (e.g. in quantitative spectrophotometry the Beer–Lambert relationship often becomes invalid at high absorbance, giving a curve, Fig. 47.1(b)). Some calibration curves are sigmoid (Fig. 47.1(c)). Finally, the signal may *decrease* in response to an increase in the substance (Fig. 47.1(d), e.g. radioimmunoassay), where an inverse sigmoid calibration curve is obtained. In some practical classes, you may be told that the relationship is expected to be linear, curvilinear, or

Understanding quantitative measurement – Chapter 46 contains details of the basic principles of valid measurement, while Chapters 48–59 deal with some of the specific analytical techniques used in chemistry. The use of internal standards is covered on p. 386.

Calibrating laboratory apparatus – this is important in relation to validation of equipment, e.g. when determining the accuracy and precision of a pipettor by the weighing method: see p. 149.

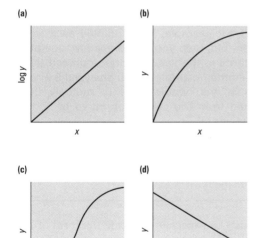

Fig. 47.1 Types of calibration curve.

Box 47.1 The stages involved in preparing and using a calibration curve

1. **Decide on an appropriate test method** – for example, in a project, you may need to research the best approach to the analysis of a particular compound in your sample.

2. **Select either (a) amount or (b) concentration, and an appropriate range and number of standards** – in practical classes, this may be given in your schedule, along with detailed instructions on how to make up the standard solutions. In other cases, you may be expected to work this out from first principles (Chapters 23, 49 and 52 give worked examples) – aim to have evenly spaced values along the x axis.

3. **Prepare your standards very carefully** – due attention to detail is required: for example, you should ensure that you check the calibration of pipettors beforehand, using the weighing method (p. 149). Don't forget the 'zero standard' plus any other controls required, for example to test for interference due to other chemical substances. Your standards should cover the range of values expected in your test samples.

4. **Analyse the standards and the unknown (test) samples** – preferably all at the same time, to avoid introducing error due to changes in the sensitivity or drift in the zero setting of the instrument with time. It is a good idea to measure all of your standard solutions at the outset, and then measure your test solutions, checking that the 'zero standard' and 'top standard' give the same values after, say, every six test measurements. If the remeasured standards do not fall within a reasonable margin of the previous value, then you will have to go back and recalibrate the instrument, and repeat the last six test measurements. If your test samples lie outside the range of your standards, you may need to repeat the assay using diluted test samples (extrapolation of your curve may not be valid, see p. 479).

5. **Draw the standard curve, or determine the underlying relationship** – Figure 47.2 gives an example of a typical linear calibration curve, where the spectrophotometric absorbance of a series of standard solutions is related to the amount of substance. When using Excel® or graphics packages, it is often appropriate to use type linear

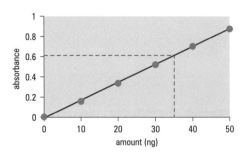

Fig. 47.2 Typical calibration curve for spectrophotometric analysis.

regression (p. 518) to produce a linear trend line (also termed the 'line of best fit') and you can then quote the value of r^2, which is a measure of the 'fit' of the measurements to the line (see p. 520). In chemical analysis the value of r^2 should normally be as close to 1.00 as possible. However, you should take care not to use a linear plot when the underlying relationship is clearly non-linear (p. 479) and you must consider whether the assumptions of the regression analysis are valid (e.g. for transformed data).

6. **Determine the amount or concentration in each unknown sample** – either by reading the appropriate value from the calibration curve, or by using the underlying mathematical relationship, i.e. $y = a + bx$ (p. 494). Make sure you draw any horizontal and vertical construction lines very carefully – students often lose marks unnecessarily by submitting poorly drawn construction lines within practical reports.

7. **Correct for dilution or concentration, where appropriate** – for example, if you diluted each test sample by ten-fold, then you would need to multiply by 10 to determine the value for the undiluted test sample. As another example, if you analysed 0.2 mL of test sample, you would need to multiply the value obtained from the calibration curve by 5, to give the value per mL.

8. **Quote your test results to an appropriate number of significant figures** – this should reflect the accuracy of the method used (see p. 209), not the size of your calculator's display.

whatever, while in others you may be expected to decide the form of the standard curve as part of the exercise.

KEY POINT You should always aim for a linear regression value (r^2) > 0.99 in your calibration curve

Practical considerations

Amount or concentration?

This first step is often the most confusing for new students. It is vital that you understand the difference between *amount* of substance (e.g. mg, ng, etc.), and *concentration* (the amount of substance per unit volume, e.g. mmol L^{-1}, μg mL^{-1}, mol m^{-3}, % w/v, etc.) before you begin your practical work. Essentially, you have to choose whether to work in terms of either (i) the total amount of substance in your assay vessel (e.g. test tube, or cuvette) or (ii) the final concentration of the substance in your assay vessel, which is independent of the volume used. Either way, this is usually plotted on the x (horizontal) axis and the measured response on the y (vertical) axis.

Choice of standards

In your early practical classes, you may be provided with a stock solution (p. 157), from which you then have to prepare a specified number of standard solutions. In such cases, you will need to understand how to use dilutions to achieve the required amounts or concentrations (p. 159). In later work and projects, you may need to prepare your standards from chemical reagents in solid form, where the important considerations are purity and solubility (pp. 156, 158). In analytical chemistry it is often important to be able to trace the original standard or stock solution back to national or international standards (p. 324).

How many standards are required?

This may be given in your practical schedule, or you may have to decide what is appropriate (e.g. in project work and research). If the form and working range of the standard curve is known in advance, this may influence your choice – for example, linear calibration curves can be established with fewer standards than curvilinear relationships. Replication of each standard solution is a good idea, since it will give you some information on the variability involved in preparing and analysing the standards. Consider whether it is best to plot mean values on your standard curve, or whether you should plot the individual values (if one value appears to be well off the line, you have made an error, and you may need to check and repeat).

Preparing your standards

It is extremely important to take the greatest care to measure out all chemicals and liquids very accurately, to achieve the best possible standard curve. The grade of volumetric flask used and temperature of the solution also affect accuracy (grade A apparatus is best). You may also consider what other additives might be required in your standard solutions. For example, do your test samples have high levels of potentially interfering substances, and should these also be added to your standards? Also consider what controls and blank solutions to prepare.

Dealing with interfering substances – one approach is to use the method of 'standard additions', where the standards all contain a fixed additional amount of the sample (p. 344; see also Dean, 1997). Internal standards can also be used to detect such problems.

> **KEY POINT** The validity of your standard curve depends upon careful preparation of standards, especially in relation to accurate dispensing of the volumes of any stock solution and diluting liquid – the results for your test samples can only be as good as your standard curve!

Your pipetting skills are really important. Chapter 22 gives more details on the correct use of pipettors. It is also worth checking that your pipette is correctly calibrated prior to use.

Preparing the calibration curve and determining the amount of the unknown (test) sample(s)

This is described in step-wise fashion within Box 47.1. Check you understand the requirements of graph drawing, especially in relation to plotted curves (p. 471) and the mathematics of straight line graphs (p. 494). Spreadsheet programs such as Microsoft Excel can be used to produce a regression line for a straight line calibration plot (p. 518). Examples of how to do this are provided in Box 47.2.

Box 47.2 How to use a spreadsheet (Microsoft Excel 2007) to produce a linear regression plot

In the example shown below, the following simple data set has been used:

Concentration $\mu g\ mL^{-1}$	Peak area
0	0
10	1002
20	2054
30	3089
40	4100
50	5007

Using the Trendline feature. This quick method provides a line of best fit on an Excel chart and can also provide a set of equation values for predictive purposes.

1. **Create a graph (chart) using the data above.** Enter the data in two columns in your spreadsheet, select the data array (highlight using left mouse button) and then, using the Insert icon, select Scatter and then the icon Scatter only with markers.

2. **Add a trend line.** Right-click on any of the data points on your graph, and select the Add Trendline menu. Choose the Linear trend line option, but do not click OK at this stage. Select: (i) Display equation on chart and (ii) Display R-squared value on chart. Now click OK. The equation (shown in the form $y = bx + a$) gives the slope and intercept of the line of best fit, while the R-squared value (coefficient of determination, p. 518) gives the proportional fit to the line (the closer this value is to 1, the better the fit of the data to the trend line).

3. **Modify the graph to improve its effectiveness.** For a graph that is to be used elsewhere (e.g. in a lab write-up or project report), adjust the display to remove the default background and gridlines and change the symbol shape. Right-click on the trend line and use the Format Trendline > Line style menu to adjust the weight of the line to make it thinner or thicker. Drag and move the equation panel if you would like to alter its location on the chart. Fig. 47.3 shows a calibration curve produced in this way for the data presented above.

4. **Add a title and axes labels.** Click on the Layout icon > Chart title (to add a title) and Layout icon > Chart axis (horizontal or vertical to add a label to the x and y-axis respectively).

5. **Use the regression equation to estimate unknown (test) samples.** By rearranging the equation for a straight line and substituting a particular y-value, you can predict the amount/concentration of substance (x-value) in a test sample. This is more precise than simply reading the values from the graph using construction lines. If you are carrying out multiple calculations, the appropriate equation, $x = (y - a)/b$, can be entered into a spreadsheet, for convenience.

6. The resultant calibration graph is shown in Fig. 47.3.

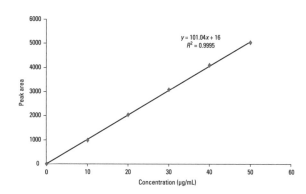

$y = 101.04x + 16$
$R^2 = 0.9995$

Fig. 47.3 Calibration curve showing line of best fit and details of linear regression equation.

Text reference

Dean, J.D. (1997) *Atomic Absorption and Plasma Spectroscopy*, 2nd edn. Wiley, Chichester. [Chapter 1 deals with calibration, and covers the principle of standard additions.]

Sources for further study

Brown, P.J. (1994) *Measurement, Regression, and Calibration*. Clarendon Press, Oxford. [Covers advanced methods, including curve fitting and multivariate methods.]

Christian, G.D. (2003) *Analytical Chemistry*, 6th edn. Wiley, Chichester.

Harris, D.C. (2006) *Quantitative Chemical Analysis*, 6th edn. W.H. Freeman.

Kellner, R., Mermet, J.M., Otto, M., Valcarcel, M. and Widmer, H.M. (2004) *Analytical Chemistry: A Modern Approach to Analytical Science*, 2nd edn. Wiley, Chichester. [Covers all modern analytical topics.]

Mark, H. (1991) *Principles and Practice of Spectroscopic Calibration*. Wiley, New York.

Miller, J.N. and Miller, J.C. (2000) *Statistics and Chemometrics for Analytical Chemistry*, 4th edn. Prentice Hall, Harlow. [Gives detailed coverage of calibration methods and the validity of analytical measurements.]

Prichard, E. and Barwick, V. (2007). *Quality Assurance in Analytical Chemistry*. Wiley, Chichester.

Schwedt, G. (1998) *The Essential Guide to Analytical Chemistry*. Wiley, Chichester.

Study exercises

47.1 Determine unknowns from a calibration curve produced in Excel. The following data are for a set of calibration standards for chlorophenol in a sample extract.

Concentration (mg L^{-1})	Peak area
0	0
2	14 567
4	30 124
6	45 623
8	60 021
10	71 209
15	112 458

Using PC-based software (e.g. Excel), fit a trend line (linear regression) and determine the chlorophenol content of the following extracted water samples with the following peak areas:
(a) 8 741, (b) 23 478, (c) 38 500.

Give your answers to 3 significant figures in each case.

47.2 Identify the errors in a calibration curve. The figure below shows a calibration curve of the type that might be submitted in a practical write-up. List the errors and compare your observations with the list given on p. 473.

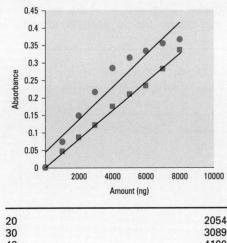

20	2054
30	3089
40	4100
50	5007

(continued)

47.3 Using the Trendline feature. This quick method provides a line of best fit on an Excel chart and can also provide a set of equation values for predictive purposes.

1. **Create a graph (chart) of your data.** Enter the data in two columns within your spreadsheet, select the data array (highlight using left mouse button) and then, using the 'Insert' icon, select 'Scatter' and then the icon 'Scatter only with markers'.

2. **Add a trend line.** Right-click on any of the data points on your graph, and select the Add Trendline menu. Choose the Linear trend line option, but do not click OK at this stage. Select: (i) Display equation on chart and (ii) Display R-squared value on chart. Now click OK. The equation (shown in the form $y = bx + a$) gives the slope and intercept of the line of best fit, while the R-squared value (coefficient of determination, p. 518) gives the proportional fit to the line (the closer this value is to 1, the better the fit of the data to the trend line).

3. **Modify the graph to improve its effectiveness.** For a graph that is to be used elsewhere (e.g. in a lab write-up or project report), adjust the display to remove the default background and gridlines and change the symbol shape. Right-click on the trend line and use the Format Trendline >line style menu to adjust the Weight of the line to make it thinner or thicker. Drag and move the equation panel if you would like to alter its location on the

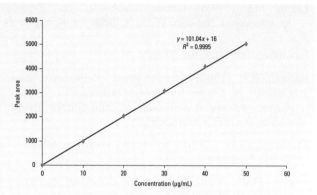

Fig. 47.4 Calibration curve showing line of best fit and details of linear regression equation.

chart. Fig. 47.4 shows a typical calibration curve produced in this way.

4. **Add a title and axes labels.** Click on the Layout icon >chart title (to add a title) and Layout icon >chart axis (horizontal or vertical to add a label to the x and y axis respectively).

5. **Use the regression equation to estimate unknown (test) samples.** By rearranging the equation for a straight line and substituting a particular y-value, you can predict the amount/concentration of substance (x-value) in a test sample. This is more precise than simply reading the values from the graph using construction lines. If you are carrying out multiple calculations, the appropriate equation, $x = (y - a)/b$, can be entered into a spreadsheet, for convenience.

Spectroscopic techniques – can be used to:

- tentatively identify compounds, by determining their absorption or emission spectra;
- quantify substances, either singly or in the presence of other compounds, by measuring the signal strength at an appropriate wavelength;
- determine molecular structure;
- follow reactions, by measuring the disappearance of a substance, or the appearance of a product as a function of time.

The absorption and emission of electromagnetic radiation (Fig. 48.1) of specific energy (wavelength) are characteristic features of many molecules, involving the movement of electrons between different energy states, in accordance with the laws of quantum mechanics. Electrons in atoms or molecules are distributed at various energy levels, but are mainly at the lowest energy level, usually termed the ground state. When exposed to energy (e.g. from electromagnetic radiation), electrons may be excited to higher energy levels (excited states), with the associated absorption of energy at specific wavelengths giving rise to an absorption spectrum. One quantum of energy is absorbed for a single electron transition from the ground state to an excited state. On the other hand, when an electron returns to its ground state, one quantum of energy is released; this may be dissipated to the surrounding molecules (as heat) or may give rise to an emission spectrum. The energy change (ΔE) for an electron moving between two energy states, E_1 and E_2, is given by the equation:

$$\Delta E = E_1 - E_2 = h\upsilon \qquad [48.1]$$

where h is the Planck constant (p. 217) and υ is the frequency of the electromagnetic radiation expressed in Hz or s^{-1}). Frequency is related to wavelength (λ, usually expressed in nm) and the speed of electromagnetic radiation, c (p. 217) by the expression:

$$\upsilon = c \div \lambda \qquad [48.2]$$

UV/visible spectrophotometry

This is a widely used technique for measuring the absorption of radiation in the visible and UV regions of the spectrum. A spectrophotometer is an instrument designed to allow precise measurement at a particular wavelength, while a colorimeter is a simpler instrument, using filters to measure broader wavebands (e.g. light in the green, red or blue regions of the visible spectrum).

Principles of light absorption

Two fundamental principles govern the absorption of light passing through a solution:

- The absorption of light is exponentially related to the number of molecules of the absorbing solute that are encountered, i.e. the solute concentration [C].

- The absorption of light is exponentially related to the length of the light path through the absorbing solution, l.

These two principles are combined in the Beer–Lambert relationship (sometimes referred to simply as 'Beer's Law'), which is usually expressed in terms of absorbance (A) – the logarithm of the ratio of the incident light (I_0) to the emergent light (I):

$$A = \varepsilon l[C] \qquad [48.3]$$

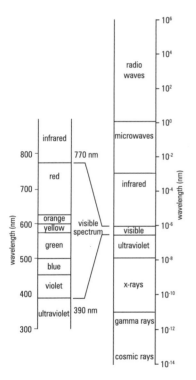

Fig. 48.1 The electromagnetic spectrum.

Definitions

Absorbance (A) – this is given by:

$A = \log_{10}(I_0/I)$.

Usually shown as A_x where 'x' is the wavelength, in nanometres.

---

where A is absorbance, ε is a constant for the absorbing substance and the wavelength, termed the absorption coefficient or absorptivity, and [C] is expressed either as mol L^{-1} or g L^{-1} (see p. 186) and l is given in cm. This relationship is extremely useful, since most spectrophotometers are constructed to give a direct measurement of absorbance (A), sometimes also termed extinction (E), of a solution (older texts may use the outdated term optical density, OD). Note that for substances obeying the Beer–Lambert relationship, A is linearly related to [C]. Absorbance at a particular wavelength is often shown as a subscript (e.g. A_{550} represents the absorbance at 550 nm). The proportion of light passing through the solution is known as the transmittance (T), and is calculated as the ratio of the emergent and incident light intensities.

Some instruments have two scales:

- an exponential scale from zero to infinity, measuring absorbance;

- a linear scale from 0 to 100, measuring (per cent) transmittance.

For most practical purposes, the Beer–Lambert relationship applies and you should use the absorbance scale.

UV/visible spectrophotometer

The principal components of a UV/visible spectrophotometer are shown in Fig. 48.2. High intensity tungsten bulbs are used as the light source in basic instruments, capable of operating in the visible region (i.e. 400–700 nm). Deuterium lamps are used for UV spectrophotometry (200–400 nm); these lamps are fitted with quartz envelopes, since glass does not transmit UV radiation.

A major improvement over the simple colorimeter is the use of a diffraction grating to produce a parallel beam of monochromatic light from the (polychromatic) light source. In practice the light emerging from such a monochromator is not of a single wavelength, but is a narrow band of wavelengths. This bandwidth is an important characteristic, since it determines the wavelengths used in absorption measurements – the bandwidth of basic spectrophotometers is around 5–10 nm while research instruments have bandwidths of less than 1 nm.

Bandwidth is affected by the width of the exit slit (the slit width), since the bandwidth will be reduced by decreasing the slit width. To obtain accurate data at a particular wavelength setting, the narrowest possible slit width should be used. However, decreasing the slit width also reduces the amount of light reaching the detector, decreasing the signal-to-noise ratio. The extent to which the slit width can be reduced depends upon the sensitivity and stability of the detection/amplification system and the presence of stray light.

Most UV/visible spectrophotometers are designed to take cuvettes with an optical path length of 10 mm. Disposable plastic cuvettes are suitable for routine work in the visible range using aqueous and alcohol-based solvents, while glass cuvettes are useful for other organic solvents. Glass cuvettes are manufactured to more exacting standards, so use optically matched glass cuvettes for accurate work, especially at low absorbances (<0.1), where any differences in the optical properties of cuvettes for reference and test samples will be pronounced. Glass and plastic absorb UV light and quartz cuvettes must be used at wavelengths below 300 nm.

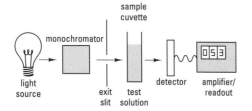

Fig. 48.2 Components of a UV/visible spectrophotometer.

Using plastic disposable cuvettes – These are adequate for work in the near-UV region as well as the visible range.

Handling cells – never handle the cells by the polished sides.

Examples – the molar absorptivity of phenol is 6.20×10^3 L mol^{-1} cm^{-1} at 210 nm. For a test solution giving an absorbance of 0.21 in a cell with a light path of 5 mm, using eqn [48.3] this is equal to a concentration of:

$0.21 = 6.20 \times 10^3 \times 0.5 \times [C]$

$[C] = 0.000067.7$ mol L^{-1} (or 67.7 μmol L^{-1})

SAFETY NOTE – never balance full cells on the instrument.

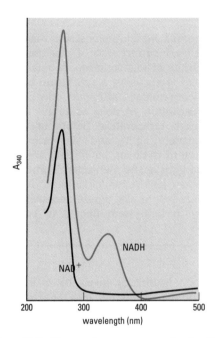

Fig. 48.3 Absorption spectra of nicotinamide adenine dinucleotide in oxidised (NAD$^+$) and reduced (NADH) form. Note the 340 nm absorption peak (A$_{340}$), used for quantitative work.

Before taking a measurement, make sure that cuvettes are clean, unscratched, dry on the outside, filled to the correct level and in the correct position in their sample holders. Unwanted material can accumulate on the inside faces of glass/quartz cuvettes, so remove any deposits using acetone on a cotton bud, or soak overnight in 1 mol L^{-1} nitric acid. Corrosive and hazardous solutions must be used in cuvettes with tightly fitting lids, to prevent damage to the instrument and to reduce the risk of accidental spillage.

Basic instruments use photocells similar to those used in simple colorimeters or photodiode detectors. In many cases, a different photocell must be used at wavelengths above and below 550–600 nm, due to differences in the sensitivity of such detectors over the visible waveband. The detectors used in more sophisticated instruments give increased sensitivity and stability when compared to photocells.

Digital displays are increasingly used in preference to needle-type meters, as they are not prone to parallax errors and misreading of the absorbance scale. Some digital instruments can be calibrated to give a direct readout of the concentration of the test substance.

Types of UV/visible spectrophotometer

Basic instruments are single beam spectrophotometers in which there is only one light path. The instrument is set to zero absorbance using a blank solution, which is then replaced by the test solution, to obtain an absorbance reading. An alternative approach is used in double beam spectrophotometers, where the light beam from the monochromator is split into two separate beams, one beam passing through the test solution and the other through a reference blank. Absorbance is then measured by an electronic circuit which compares the output from the reference (blank) and sample cuvettes. Double beam spectrophotometry reduces measurement errors caused by fluctuations in output from the light source or changes in the sensitivity of the detection system, since reference and test solutions are measured at the same time (Box 48.1). Recording spectrophotometers are double beam instruments, designed for use with a chart recorder, either by recording the difference in absorbance between reference and test solutions across a predetermined waveband to give an absorption spectrum (Fig. 48.3), or by recording the change in absorbance at a particular wavelength as a function of time (e.g. in an enzyme assay).

Quantitative spectrophotometric analysis

A single (purified) substance in solution can be quantified using the Beer–Lambert relationship (eqn [48.3]), provided its absorptivity is known at a particular wavelength (usually at the absorption maximum for the substance, since this will give the greatest sensitivity). The molar absorptivity is the absorbance given by a solution with a concentration of 1 mol L^{-1} ($= 1$ kmol m^{-3}) of the compound in a light path of 1 cm. The appropriate value may be available from tabulated spectral data (e.g. Anon., 1963), or it can be determined experimentally by measuring the absorbance of known concentrations of the substance (Box 48.1) and plotting a standard curve (see Chapter 60). This should confirm that the relationship is linear over the desired concentration range and the slope of the line will give the molar absorptivity.

Box 48.1 How to use a UV/visible spectrophotometer

1. **Switch on and select the correct lamp** for your measurements (e.g. deuterium for UV, tungsten for visible light).

2. **Allow up to 15 min for the lamp to warm up** and for the instrument to stabilise before use.

3. **Select the appropriate wavelength:** on older instruments a dial is used to adjust the monochromator, while newer machines have microprocessor-controlled wavelength selection.

4. **Select the appropriate detector:** some instruments choose the correct detector automatically (on the basis of the specified wavelength), while others have manual selection.

5. **Choose the correct slit width** (if available): this may be specified in the protocol you are following, or may be chosen on the manufacturer's recommendations.

6. **Insert appropriate reference blank(s):** single beam instruments use a single cuvette, while double beam instruments use two cuvettes (a matched pair for accurate work). The reference blanks should match the test solution in all respects apart from the substance under test, i.e. they should contain all reagents apart from this substance. *Make sure that the cuvettes are positioned correctly, with their polished (transparent) faces in the light path, and that they are accurately located in the cuvette holder(s).*

7. **Check/adjust the 0% transmittance:** most instruments have a control which allows you to zero the detector output in the absence of any light (termed 'dark current' correction). Some microprocessor-controlled instruments carry out this step automatically.

8. **Set the absorbance reading to zero:** usually via a dial, or digital readout.

9. **Analyse your samples:** replace the appropriate reference blank with a test sample, allow the absorbance reading to stabilise (5–10 s) and read the absorbance value from the meter/readout device. For absorbance readings greater than 1 (i.e. <10% transmission), the signal-to-noise ratio is too low for accurate results. Your analysis may require a calibration curve or you may be able to use the Beer–Lambert relationship (eqn [48.3]) to determine the concentration of test substance in your samples.

10. **Check the scale zero at regular intervals** using a reference blank (e.g. after every 10 samples).

11. **Check the reproducibility of the instrument:** measure the absorbance of a single solution several times during your analysis. It should give the same value.

Problems (and solutions): inaccurate/unstable readings are most often due to incorrect use of cuvettes, for example dirt, fingerprints or test solution on outside of cuvette (wipe the clear faces using a soft tissue before insertion into the cuvette holder and handle only by the opaque faces), condensation (if cold solutions aren't allowed to reach room temperature before use), air bubbles (which scatter light and increase the absorbance; tap gently to remove), insufficient solution (causing refraction of light at the meniscus), particulate material in the solution (check for 'cloudiness' in the solution and centrifuge before use, where necessary) or incorrect positioning in light path (locate in correct position).

Measuring absorbances in colorimetric analysis – if any final solution has an absorbance that is too high to be read with accuracy on your spectrophotometer (e.g. A > 2), it is bad practice to dilute the solution so that it can be measured. This dilutes both the sample molecules and the colour reagents to an equal extent. Instead, you should dilute the original sample and reassay.

The specific absorptivity is the absorbance given by a solution containing 10 g L^{-1} (i.e. 1% w/v) of the compound in a light path of 1 cm. This is useful for substances of unknown molecular weight (e.g. proteins or nucleic acids), where the amount of substance in solution is expressed in terms of its mass, rather than as a molar concentration. For use in eqn [48.3], the specific absorptivity should be divided by 10 to give the solute concentration in g L^{-1}.

This simple approach cannot be used for mixed samples where several substances have a significant absorption at a particular wavelength. In such cases, it may be possible to estimate the amount of each substance by measuring the absorbance at several wavelengths.

Fluorescence

With most molecules, after electrons are raised to a higher energy level by absorption of electromagnetic radiation, they soon fall back to the ground state by radiationless transfer of energy (heat) to the solvent.

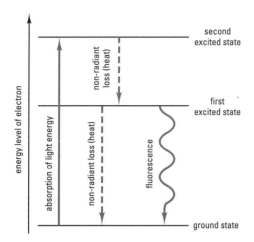

Fig. 48.4 Energy levels and energy transitions in fluorescence.

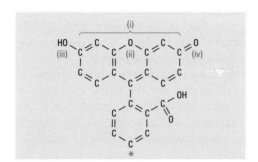

Fig. 48.5 Fluorescein – a widely used fluorescent label, showing (i) a planar conjugated system of fused rings; (ii) heteroatoms within the conjugated structures; (iii) an electron-donating group; and (iv) an electron-attracting group. In fluorogenic enzyme substrates, linkage is usually *via* one of the two hydroxyl groups, while in fluoroscein-labelled proteins, linkage is *via* an isothiocyanate group (N=C=S) on the lowermost ring (*)

Table 48.1 Examples of compounds with intrinsic fluorescence

Drugs
Aspirin, morphine, barbiturates, propanalol, ampicillin, tetracyclines

Vitamins
Riboflavin, vitamins A, B6 and E, nicotinamide

Pollutants
Naphthalene, anthracene, benzopyrene

However, with some molecules, the events shown in Fig. 48.4 may occur, i.e. electrons may lose only part of their energy by non-radiant routes and the rest may be emitted as electromagnetic radiation, a phenomenon known as fluorescence. Since not all of the energy that was absorbed is emitted (due to non-radiant loss), the wavelength of the fluorescent light is longer than the absorbed light (longer wavelength = lower energy). Thus, a fluorescent molecule has both an absorption spectrum and an emission spectrum. The difference between the excitation wavelength (λ_{ex}) and the emission wavelength (λ_{em}), measured in nm, is known as the Stokes shift, and is fundamental to the sensitivity of fluorescence techniques. The existence of a Stokes shift means that emitted light can be detected against a low background, independently of the excitation wavelength.

Most fluorescent molecules have the following features:

- A highly conjugated system (alternating double and single bonds), involving aromatic or heterocyclic rings, usually containing O or N (as heteroatoms).

- A condensed system of fused rings, with one or more heteroatoms.

- Electron-donating groups such as –OH, –OCH$_3$, –NH$_2$ and –NR$_2$, together with electron-attracting groups elsewhere in the molecule, in conjugation with the electron-donating groups.

- A rigid, planar structure.

Figure 48.5 illustrates many of these features for fluorescein, used in a range of applications including visualisation of nucleic acids, fluorescent antibody tests, etc.

Fluorescence spectrophotometry

The principal components of a fluorescence spectrophotometer (fluorimeter) are shown in Fig. 48.6. The instrument contains two monochromators, one to select the excitation wavelength and the other to monitor the light emitted, usually at 90° to the incident beam (though light is actually emitted in all directions). As an example, the wavelengths used to measure the highly fluorescent compound aminomethylcoumarin are 388 nm (excitation) and 440 nm (emission). Some examples of molecules with intrinsic fluorescence are given in Table 48.1.

Compared with UV/visible spectrophotometry, fluorescence spectroscopy has certain advantages, including:

- Enhanced sensitivity (up to 1000-fold), since the emitted light is detected against a background of zero, in contrast to spectrophotometry where small changes in signal are measured against a large 'background' (see eqn [48.3]).

- Increased specificity, because not one, but two specific wavelengths are required for a particular compound.

However, there are also certain drawbacks:

- Not all compounds show intrinsic fluorescence, limiting its application. However, some non-fluorescent compounds may be coupled to fluorescent dyes, or fluorophores (e.g. alcohol ethoxylates may be coupled to naphthoyl chloride).

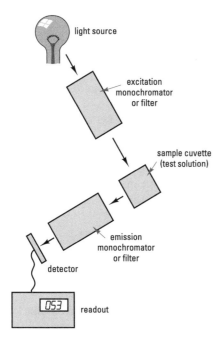

Fig. 48.6 Components of a fluorimeter (fluorescence spectrophotometer). Note that sample cuvettes for fluorimetry must have clear sides all round.

SAFETY NOTE – Caution is needed when using strong (concentrated) acids always work in a fume cupboard, wear gloves to protect your hands from acids burns, and always rinse affected areas with large amounts of water.

Safe working in atomic spectroscopy – the use of high pressure gas cylinders can be particularly hazardous. Always consult a member of staff before using such apparatus.

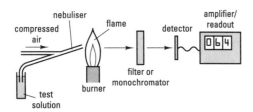

Fig. 48.7 Components of a flame photometer.

• The light emitted can be less than expected due to quenching, i.e. when substances in the sample (e.g. oxygen) either interfere with energy transfer, or absorb the emitted light (in some instances, the sample molecules may self-quench if they are present at high concentration).

The sensitivity of fluorescence has made it invaluable in techniques in which specific antibodies are linked to a fluorescent dye, including:

• fluorescence immunoassay (FIA);

• immunohistochemistry, which requires the use of a fluorescence microscope, for example using fluorescent antibodies, or fluorescent *in situ* hybridisation (FISH) for nucleic acid detection.

Phosphorescence and luminescence

A phenomenon related to fluorescence is phosphorescence, which is the emission of light following inter-system crossing between electron orbitals (e.g. between excited singlet and triplet states). Light emission in phosphorescence usually continues after the exciting energy is no longer applied and, since more energy is lost in inter-system crossing, the emission wavelengths are generally longer than with fluorescence. Phosphorescence has limited applications in forensic science.

Luminescence (or chemiluminescence) is another phenomenon in which light is emitted, but here the energy for the initial excitation of electrons is provided by a chemical reaction rather than by electromagnetic radiation. An example is the action of the enzyme luciferase, extracted from fireflies, which catalyses the following reaction:

$$\text{luciferin} + \text{ATP} + O_2 \implies \text{oxyluciferin} + \text{AMP} + \text{PP}_i + CO_2 + \text{light} \qquad [48.4]$$

The light produced is either yellow-green (560 nm) or red (620 nm). This system can be used in the analysis of ATP (e.g. to determine ATP concentration in a biological sample). Measurement can be performed using the photomultiplier tubes of a scintillation counter to detect the emitted light, with calibration of the output using a series of standards of known ATP content.

Atomic spectroscopy

Atoms of certain metals will absorb and emit radiation of specific wavelengths when heated in a flame, in direct proportion to the number of atoms present. Atomic spectrophotometric techniques measure the absorption or emission of particular wavelengths of UV and visible light, to identify and quantify such metals.

Flame atomic emission spectrophotometry (or flame photometry)

The principal components of a flame photometer are shown in Fig. 48.7. A liquid sample is converted into an aerosol in a nebuliser (atomiser) before being introduced into the flame, where a small proportion (typically less than 1 in 10 000) of the atoms will be raised to a higher energy level, releasing this energy as light of a specific wavelength, which is passed through a filter to a photocell detector. Flame photometry is

---

Box 48.2 How to use a flame photometer

1. **Allow time for the instrument to stabilise.** Switch on the instrument, light the flame and wait at least 5 min before analysing your solutions.

2. **Check for impurities in your reagents.** For example, if you are measuring Na^+ in an acid digest of some material, for e.g., soil, check the Na^+ content of a reagent blank, containing everything except the soil, processed in exactly the same way as the samples. Subtract this value from your sample values to obtain the true Na^+ content.

3. **Quantify your samples using a calibration curve.** Calibration standards should cover the expected concentration range for the test solutions – your calibration curve may be non-linear (especially at concentrations above 1 mmol L^{-1}, i.e. 1 mol m^{-3}).

4. **Analyse all solutions in duplicate,** so that repeatability can be assessed.

5. **Check your calibration.** Make repeated measurements of a standard solution of known concentration after every six or seven samples, to confirm that the instrument calibration is still valid.

6. **Consider the possibility of interference.** Other metal atoms may emit light which is detected by the photocell, since the filters cover a wider waveband than the emission line of a particular element. This can be a serious problem if you are trying to measure low concentrations of a particular metal in the presence of high concentrations of other metals (e.g. Na^+ in sea water), or other substances which form complexes with the test metal, suppressing the signal (e.g. phosphate).

---

used to measure the alkali metal ions K^+, Na^+ and Ca^{++} in biological fluids and water samples (Box 48.2).

When using a flame photometer:

- Allow time for the instrument to stabilise. Switch on the instrument, light the flame and wait at least 5 min before analysing your solutions.

- Check for impurities in your reagents. For example, if you are measuring K^+ in an acid digest of some biological material, check the K^+ content of a reagent blank, containing everything except the biological material, processed in exactly the same way as the samples. Subtract this value from your sample values to obtain the true K^+ content. If using acid digestion, always work within a fume hood and wear gloves and safety glasses at all times. Rinse any spillages with a large volume of water.

- Quantify your samples using a calibration curve (Chapter 60). Calibration standards should cover the expected concentration range for the test solutions – your calibration curve may be non-linear (especially at concentrations above 1 mmol L^{-1}, i.e. 1 mol m^{-3} in SI units).

- Analyse all solutions in duplicate, so that reproducibility can be assessed.

- Check your calibration. Make repeated measurements of a standard solution of known concentration after every six or seven samples, to confirm that the instrument calibration is still valid.

- Consider the possibility of interference. Other metal atoms may emit light which is detected by the photocell, since the filters cover a wider waveband than the emission line of a particular element. This can be a serious problem if you are trying to measure low concentrations of a particular metal in the presence of high concentrations of other metals

Plotting calibration curves in quantitative analysis – do not force your calibration line to pass through zero if it clearly does not. There is no reason to assume that the zero value is any more accurate than any other reading you have made.

(e.g. Na$^+$ in sea water), or other substances which form complexes with the test metal, suppressing the signal (e.g. phosphate).

Atomic absorption spectroscopy

This technique is applicable to a broad range of metal ions, including those of Pb, Cu, Zn, etc. It relies on the absorption of light of a specific wavelength by atoms dispersed in a flame. The appropriate wavelength is provided by a hollow cathode lamp, coated with the element to be analysed, focused through the flame and onto the monochromator detector. When the sample is introduced into the flame, it will decrease the light detected in direct proportion to the amount of metal present. Practical advantages over flame photometry include:

- improved sensitivity,

- increased precision,

- decreased interference.

Variants of this method include flameless atomic absorption spectroscopy and atomic fluorescence spectroscopy, both of which are more sensitive than the flame atomic absorption technique. Chapter 49 gives further details on the practical applications of atomic spectroscopy.

Text reference

Anon. (1963) *Tables of Spectrophotometric Absorption Data for Compounds used for the Colorimetric Detection of Elements (International Union of Pure and Applied Chemistry)*. Butterworth-Heinemann, London.

Sources for further study

Christian, G.D. (2003) *Analytical Chemistry*, 6th edn. Wiley, Chichester.

Gore, M.G. (ed.) (2000) *Spectrophotometry and Spectrofluorimetry: A Practical Approach*, 2nd edn. Oxford University Press, Oxford.

Harris, D.A. (1996) *Light Spectroscopy*. Bios, Oxford.
[Gives practical guidance on techniques, applications and interpretation of results.]

Harris, D.C. (1995) *Quantitative Chemical Analysis*, 4th edn. Freeman, New York.

Kellner, R. (1998) *Analytical Chemistry*. Wiley, Chichester.

Kellner, R., Mermet, J.M., Otto, M., Valcarcel, M. and Widmer, H.M. (2004) *Analytical Chemistry: A Modern Approach to Analytical Science*, 2nd edn. Wiley, Chichester.
[Covers all modern analytical topics.]

McMohan, G. (2008) *Analytical Instrumentation: A Guide to Laboratory, Portable and Miniaturized Instruments*. Wiley, Chichester.

Rouessac, F. and Rouessac, A. (2007) *Chemical Analysis: Modern Instrumentation Methods and Techniques*, 2nd edn. Wiley, Chichester.

Schwedt, G. (1997) *The Essential Guide to Analytical Chemistry*. Wiley, Chichester.

Schwedt, G. (1998) *The Essential Guide to Analytical Chemistry*. Wiley, Chichester.

Skoog, D.A., West, D.M. and Holler, F.J. (1996) *Fundamentals of Analytical Chemistry*, 7th edn. Saunders, Orlando.

Study exercises

48.1 Write a protocol for using a spectrophotometer. After reading this chapter, prepare a detailed stepwise protocol explaining how to use one of the spectrophotometers in your Department. Ask another student or a tutor to evaluate your protocol and provide you with feedback.

48.2 Use the Beer–Lambert relationship in quantitative spectrophotometric analysis. Calculate the following (express your answer to 3 significant figures):

(a) The concentration (μgmL^{-1}) of pentachlorophenol in a test solution giving an absorbance at 300 nm (A_{300}) of 0.57 in a cuvette of path length 5 mm, based on an absorptivity of 20 L g^{-1} cm^{-1}.

(b) The amount (ng) of pentachlorophenol in a 50 μL sub-sample from a test solution where A_{300} = 0.31 in a cuvette of path length 1 cm, based on an absorptivity of 20 L g^{-1} cm^{-1}.

48.3 Determine the molar absorptivity of a substance in aqueous solution. A solution of p-nitrophenol containing 8.8 μgmL^{-1} gave an absorbance of 0.535 at 404 nm in a cuvette of path length 1 cm. What is the molar absorptivity of a p-nitrophenol at 404 nm, expressed to 3 significant figures? (Note: M_r of p-nitrophenol is 291.27.)

All spectroscopic equipment is costly – The use of such equipment must always be done under guidance from a demonstrator or technician. All equipment in this section has an inherent risk due to its use of mains electricity.

SAFETY NOTE In atomic spectroscopy, the use of high-pressure gas sources, e.g. cylinders, can be particularly hazardous. Always consult a demonstrator or technician before use.

Atomic spectroscopy is a quantitative technique used for the determination of metals in samples. Atomic spectroscopy is characterised by two main techniques: atomic absorption spectroscopy and atomic emission spectroscopy. Atomic absorption spectroscopy (AAS) is normally carried out with a flame (FAAS), although other devices can be used. Atomic emission spectroscopy (AES) is typified by the use of a flame photometer (p. 338) or an inductively coupled plasma. The flame photometer is normally used for elements in groups I and II of the Periodic Table only, i.e. alkali and alkali earth metals.

In both AAS and AES the substance to be analysed must be in solution. In order to do quantitative analysis, i.e. determine how much of the metal is present, the preparation of analytical standard solutions is necessary. While the concentration range over which the technique can be used may be different, for various instruments, the principles associated with the preparation of analytical standard solutions are the same (Boxes 49.1–5).

Atomic Absorption Spectroscopy

The components of an atomic absorption spectrometer are a radiation source, an atomisation cell, a sample introduction system, a method of wavelength selection and a detector (Fig. 49.1).

Radiation source

The main radiation source for AAS is the hollow-cathode lamp (HCL). The HCL (Fig. 49.2) emits radiation characteristic of a particular element. The choice of HCL for AAS is simple. For example, if you are analysing for lead, you will need a lead-coated HCL. It is normal to pre-warm the HCL for about 10 min prior to use. This can be done either by using a separate pre-heater unit, capable of warming up several HCLs simultaneously, or by inserting the HCL in the AAS instrument and switching on the current. The lamp is typically operated at an electric current between 2 and 30 mA.

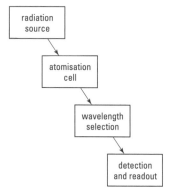

Fig. 49.1 Components of an atomic absorption spectrometer.

Box 49.1 How to prepare a 1000 μg mL^{-1} stock solution of a metal ion from a metal salt

Stock solutions can be prepared directly from reagent-grade chemicals. It is important to use only reagent-grade chemicals of the highest purity (e.g. AnalaR®). This includes the water to be used – distilled and deionised – MilliQ water. (Note: many reagents (solids and liquids) contain metallic impurities in trace amounts. While you can minimise this risk of contamination by using the highest-purity reagents, it is essential to run 'reagent blanks', especially for elemental determinations trace levels.)

1. **Determine the M_r of the metal salt.** For example, the M_r of $Pb(NO_3)_2$ = 331.20 g mol^{-1}.

2. **Determine the A_r of the metal.** The A_r for Pb is 207.19 g mol^{-1}.

3. **Establish the ratio of M_r to A_r:**

$$\frac{331.20}{207.19} = 1.5985 \text{ g of } Pb(NO_3)_2 \text{ in 1 litre}$$

4. **Accurately weigh out (p. 19) the metal salt.** In this case, weigh 1.5985 g of $Pb(NO_3)_2$.

5. **Quantitatively transfer the metal salt to a pre-cleaned 100 mL beaker** and dissolve in 1% v/v HNO_3 (AnalaR® or equivalent).

6. **Quantitatively transfer the dissolved metal salt to a 1 L volumetric flask** and make up to the graduation mark with 1% v/v HNO$_3$ (AnalaR® or equivalent).

Often, a certified stock standard with a single or multi-element composition can be purchased, usually at a concentration (per element) of 1000 mg L^{-1} (1000 μg mL^{-1}).

Box 49.2 How to prepare a set of five calibration solutions in the concentration range 0–10 μg mL^{-1} (mg L^{-1})

Assuming that we are starting with a 1000 μg mL^{-1} stock solution of a particular metal (e.g. lead) then you will need the following: six 100.00 mL grade A volumetric flasks; two 100 mL beakers; and a graduated pipette (0–10.00 mL).

1. **Ensure that all the glassware is clean** (see p. 151).

2. **Transfer ≈15 mL of the stock solution into one of the pre-cleaned beakers.**

3. **Quantitatively transfer 10.00 mL of the stock solution** into a 100.00 mL volumetric flask. Then, dilute to 100.00 mL with 1% v/v HNO$_3$ (high purity).

4. **Determine the concentration of this new solution.** Remember that we started with an initial 1000 μg mL^{-1} Pb stock solution.

$$\frac{1000\,\mu g}{mL} \times 10\ mL \equiv 10\ 000\ \mu g\ Pb$$

10 000 μg Pb was placed in a 100.00 mL volumetric flask, so:

$$\frac{10\ 000\,\mu g}{100\ mL} \equiv 100\ \mu g\ mL^{-1}\ Pb$$

You now have a 100 μg mL^{-1} 'working' stock solution of Pb.

5. **Transfer ≈15 mL of the working stock solution into the other pre-cleaned beaker.**

6. **Quantitatively transfer 2.00 mL of the solution into a 100.00 mL volumetric flask** and dilute to 100.00 mL with 1% v/v HNO$_3$ (high purity). Label the flask as the 2 μg mL^{-1} Pb calibration solution.

7. **Similarly transfer 0, 4.00, 6.00, 8.00 and 10.00 mL volumes into separate volumetric flasks** and dilute to 100.00 mL with the nitric acid and label as 0, 4, 6, 8 and 10 μg mL^{-1} Pb calibration solutions.

8. **Take the 0, 2, 4, 6, 8 and 10 μg mL^{-1} Pb calibration solutions** for FAAS analysis.

Sample/standard dilutions – all dilutions should be done using appropriate glassware or plastic ware. Typically, this involves the use of grade A pipettes for the transfer of known volumes of liquids and grade A volumetric flasks for subsequent dilutions.

SAFETY NOTE – Caution is needed when using strong (concentrated) acids. When using concentrated acids always work in a fume cupboard. Wear gloves to protect your hands from 'acid burns'. Always rinse affected areas with copious amounts of water.

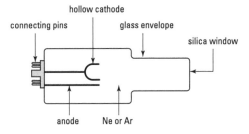

Fig. 49.2 Components of a hollow-cathode lamp (HCL).

Atomisation cell

Several types of atomisation cell are available: flame, graphite furnace, hydride generation and cold vapour. Flame is the most common. In the pre-mixed laminar flame, the fuel and oxidant gases are mixed before they enter the burner (the ignition site) in an expansion chamber. The more commonly used flame in FAAS is the air–acetylene flame (temperature, 2500 K), while the nitrous oxide-acetylene flame (temperature, 3150 K) is used for refractory elements (e.g. Al). Both are formed in a slot burner positioned in the light path of the HCL (Fig. 49.3).

In the graphite furnace atomiser, a small volume of sample (5–100 μL) is introduced onto the inner surface of a graphite tube (or onto a platform placed within the tube) through a small opening (Fig. 49.4). The graphite tube is arranged so that light from the HCL passes directly through the centre. Passing an electric current through the tube allows the operator to program a heating cycle, with several stages (Fig. 49.5) including the elimination of water from the sample (drying), removal of the sample matrix (ashing), atomisation of the analyte (analysis), and removal of extraneous material (cleaning). An internal gas flow of inert gas (N$_2$ or Ar) during the drying and ashing stages removes any extraneous material.

Hydride generation is a sample introduction technique exclusively for elements that form volatile hydrides (e.g. As, Se, Sn). An acidified sample solution is reacted with sodium borohydride solution, liberating the gaseous hydride in a gas–liquid separator. The generated hydride is then transported to an atomisation cell using a carrier gas. The atomisation cell is normally an electrically heated or flame-heated quartz tube. Using

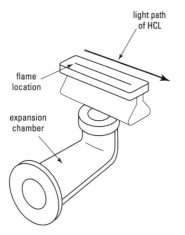

Fig. 49.3 Components of a slot burner for FAAS.

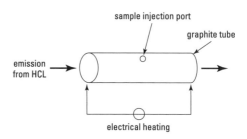

Fig. 49.4 Schematic diagram of a graphite furnace atomiser.

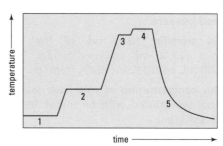

Fig. 49.5 Heating cycle for a graphite furnace atomiser. 1. drying; 2. ashing; 3. analysis; 4. cleaning; 5. cooling

---

Box 49.3 How to analyse a sample using the method of standard additions in FAAS

The method of standard additions is used when the sample matrix may cause difficulties, for example chemical interferences, in sample concentration determination. Standard additions allows any adverse effects to be overcome by incorporating a known amount of the sample in the calibration solutions.

1. **Prepare a 1000 μg mL^{-1} stock solution** (see Box 49.1).

2. **Then, prepare a 100 μg mL^{-1} working stock solution** (see Box 49.2).

3. **You will also need to have prepared the sample.** If the sample is a solid you will need to digest the sample (see Box 49.7).

4. **An estimate of the metal concentration in the sample is required prior to carrying out standard additions** so that the linear relationship between signal (absorbance) and concentration is maintained.

5. **You can then prepare the standard addition solutions.** This is most easily done as in Table 49.1.

6. **Analyse the samples using FAAS.**

7. **Plot the graph.** The graphical output should appear as shown in Fig. 49.6.

8. **The graph should contain several features:** it must have a linear response (signal against concentration); it does not pass through the origin; and extrapolation of the graph is required until it intersects the x-axis (e.g. 2.9 μg mL^{-1}).

9. **Determine the concentration of the metal in the original sample.** This can be done by taking into account the dilutions involved in the standard additions method and any dilutions used to prepare the sample (see dilution factor, Box 49.5).

Table 49.1 Standard additions solutions

Volumetric flask (100.00 mL capacity)	Volume of 100 μg mL^{-1} working stock solution (mL)	Volume of aqueous sample solution (mL)
1	0	10
2	1	10
3	3	10
4	5	10
5	7	10

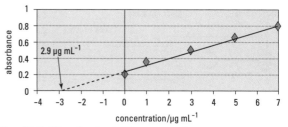

Fig. 49.6 Standard additions graph.

Box 49.4 Sample size and certified reference materials

If a linear calibration graph (plot of concentration against absorbance) has been prepared for lead in FAAS with the concentrations 0, 2, 4, 6, 8 and 10 μg mL^{-1}, the absorbance for the digested sample needs to fall within the linear portion of the graph. This is controlled by two (non-instrumental) factors: the weight of the sample digested and the final volume that the digested sample is made up to. As the volume of the digested sample is limited by the availability of volumetric flasks (10.00, 25.00, 50.00, 100.00 or 250.00 mL are most commonly used, with the 50.00 and 100.00 mL volumetric flasks the most common) it is often easier to alter the sample size. In order to have a representative sample, a minimum sample size is often recommended. For example, if using a certified reference material (CRM) the supplier will recommend a minimum sample size to ensure homogeneity (e.g. not <0.5 g for a powdered solid steel or alloy sample, or not <1.0 g for a powdered biological sample such as citrus leaves). Often the maximum sample size is limited by the cost of the CRM. If using a 'real' sample then it is best to take a larger sample size, since a CRM has usually been tested and prepared to a high specification with respect to drying, milling and shelf-life time. A typical minimum sample size for a soil might be 5.00 g. It is important if using 'real' samples to consider the following additional factors:

- Sampling – how it is to be done? How will a representative sample be arrived at?
- Storage of sample – what containers will be used for storage of sample? Be aware of contamination for the storage container and from the implements used to sample and transfer the sample.
- Lifetime of stored sample – how long will the sample remain stable? Is preservation of the sample necessary?

Note: CRMs can be obtained from appropriate suppliers, for example the Laboratory of the Government Chemist (LGC) in the UK or the National Institute for Science and Technology (NIST) in the USA. In addition to the CRM, a certificate is provided that contains information on the concentration of various metals within the sample as well as their variation, normally quoted as one standard deviation either side of the mean value (e.g. 2.5 $\pm$ 0.3 μg g^{-1} Pb). CRMs are used to test the accuracy of a new method or to enable a quality control scheme to be operated by a commercial laboratory (see also Chapter 46). In practical work they are useful for assessing student performance in preparing and analysing a sample.

Box 49.5 Analysis of a sample: dilution factor

A sample was weighed (0.4998 g) and digested in concentrated nitric acid (20 mL). After cooling, the digested sample was quantitatively transferred into a 100.00 mL volumetric flask and made up with ultrapure water and then analysed for lead by FAAS. Let us suppose that the absorbance obtained corresponds to a concentration of 3.4 μg mL^{-1}. What is the concentration of lead in the original sample?

The method of calculation is most appropriately done as follows:

- Calculate the dilution factor. This can be done if the final volume of the sample and its original weight are known. In this case 100 mL and 0.4998 g.
- You then multiply the concentration from the graph with the dilution factor:

$$\frac{3.4\,\mu g}{mL} \times \frac{100\ mL}{0.4998\ g} = 680\,\mu g\,g^{-1}$$

Note:

- The volume of acid used is irrelevant in the calculation – only the final volume in the volumetric flask matters.
- The units cancel (mL on top line cancels with mL on the bottom line) leaving you with units of μg g^{-1} (μg/g).
- Alternatively, the units can be expressed in mg kg^{-1} (mg/kg), i.e. 680 mg kg^{-1} or % w/w, i.e. 0.068% w/w (see p. 187). (10 000 μg g^{-1} $\equiv$ 1% w/w or for aqueous samples 10 000 μg mL^{-1} $\equiv$ 1% w/v.)

arsenic as an example it is possible to write the following equation for the generation of arsine (AsH$_3$):

$$3BH_4^- + 3H^+ + 4H_3AsO_3 \rightarrow 3H_3BO_3 + 4AsH_3 + 3H_2O \qquad [49.1]$$

Cold vapour generation is the term exclusively reserved for mercury. Mercury in a sample is reduced to elemental mercury by tin (II) chloride (eqn 49.2):

$$Sn^{2+} + Hg^{2+} \rightarrow Sn^{4+} + Hg^0 \qquad [49.2]$$

and the mercury vapour produced is transported to an atomisation cell by a carrier gas. The atomisation cell consists of a long-path glass absorption cell located in the path of the HCL. Mercury is monitored at a wavelength of 253.7 nm.

Sample introduction into the flame

Samples are almost exclusively introduced into flames as liquids. Solid samples need to be converted to aqueous solutions using methods such as decomposition (see p. 352). Once in the aqueous form the sample is introduced into the flame using a nebuliser–expansion chamber.

The pneumatic concentric nebuliser (see also p. 349) consists of a stainless steel tube through which a Pt/Ir capillary tube is located. The aqueous sample is drawn up through the capillary tube by the action of the oxidant gas (air) escaping through the exit orifice that exists between the outside of the capillary tube and the inside of the stainless steel tube. The action of the escaping air and aqueous sample is sufficient to form a coarse aerosol in a process termed the Venturi effect. The typical uptake rate of the nebuliser is between 3 and 6 mL min^{-1}.

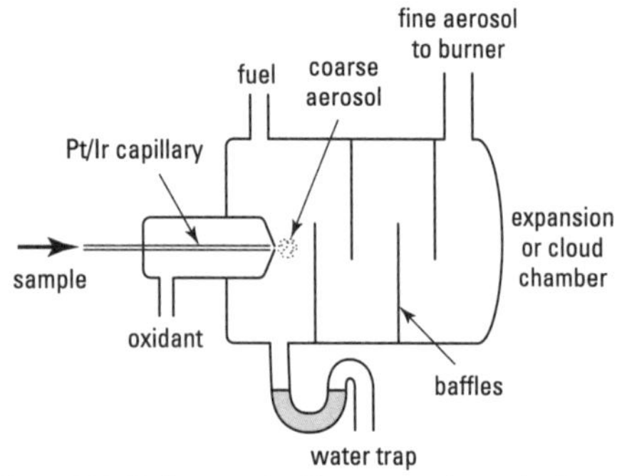

The expansion chamber (Fig. 49.7) has two functions. The first is concerned with aerosol generation the objectives of which are:

- to convert the aqueous sample solution into a coarse aerosol using the oxidant gas;

- to disperse the coarse aerosol further into a fine aerosol, by interaction with baffles located within the chamber;

- to condense any residual aerosol particles, which then go to waste.

The second function involves the safe pre-mixing of the oxidant and fuel gases before they are introduced into the laminar flow burner.

Wavelength selection and detection

As AAS is used to monitor one metal at a time, the spectrometer used is termed a monochromator. Two optical arrangements are possible; single and double beam. The latter is preferred as it corrects for fluctuations in the HCL caused by warm-up, drift and source noise, thus leading to improved precision in the absorbance measurement. A schematic diagram of the optical arrangement is shown in Fig. 49.8. The attenuation of the HCL radiation by the atomic vapour is detected by a photomultiplier tube (PMT), a device for proportionally converting photons of light to electric current.

Background correction methods

One of the main practical problems with the use of AAS is the occurrence of molecular species that coincide with the atomic signal. One approach to remove this molecular absorbance is by the use of background correction methods. Several approaches are possible, but the most common is based on the use of a continuum source, D_2. In the atomisation cell (e.g. flame) absorption is possible from both atomic species and from molecular species (unwanted interference). By measuring the absorption that occurs from the radiation source (HCL) and comparing it with the absorbance that occurs from the continuum

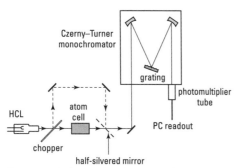

Fig. 49.7 Schematic diagram of a nebuliser – expansion chamber for FAAS.

Fig. 49.8 Schematic diagram of the optical arrangement for AAS.

source (D_2) a corrected absorption signal can be obtained. This is because the atomic species of interest absorb the specific radiation associated with the HCL source, whereas the absorption of radiation by the continuum source for the same atomic species will be negligible.

Interferences in the flame

Interferences in the flame can be classified into four categories: chemical, ionisation, physical and spectral.

Chemical interferences occur when the analyte forms a thermally stable compound with a molecular or ionic species present in the sample solution. Examples include the suppression of alkaline earth metals due to the presence of phosphate, silicate or aluminate in the sample solution in the air–acetylene flame. The most well-known example of this is the absorption signal suppression that occurs for Ca at 422.7 nm owing to increasing amounts of phosphate. This signal suppression is due to the formation of calcium pyrophosphate, a thermally stable compound in the flame.

Ionisation interferences occur most commonly for alkali and alkaline earth metals. The low ionisation potential of these metals can lead to their ionisation in the relatively hot environment of the flame. If this occurs, no absorption signal is detected, since FAAS is a technique for measuring atoms not ions. This process can be prevented by the addition of an ionisation suppressor or 'buffer' (e.g. an alkali metal such as Cs). Addition of excess Cs leads to its ionisation in the flame in preference to the metal of interest (e.g. Na). This process is termed the 'mass action' effect.

Physical interferences are due to the effects of the sample solution on aerosol formation within the spray chamber. The formation of an aerosol is dependent upon the surface tension, density and viscosity of the sample solution. This type of interference can be controlled by the matrix matching of sample and standard solutions, i.e. add the same sample components to the standard solution, but without the metal of interest. If this is not possible, it is then necessary to use the method of standard additions (Box 49.3).

Spectral interferences are uncommon in AAS owing to the selectivity of the technique. However, some interferences may occur, for example the resonance line of Cu occurs at 324.754 nm and has a line coincidence from Eu at 324.753 nm. Unless the Eu is 1000 times in excess, however, it is unlikely to cause any problems for Cu determination. In addition to atomic spectral overlap, molecular band absorption can cause problems, for example calcium hydroxide has an absorption band on the Ba wavelength of 553.55 nm while Pb at 217.0 nm has molecular absorption from NaCl. Molecular band absorption can be corrected for using background correction techniques (see p. 346). The operation of a flame atomic absorption spectrometer is described in Box 49.6.

Atomic Emission Spectroscopy

The main components of an atomic emission spectrometer are an atomisation and ionisation cell, a method of sample introduction, the spectrometer and detector. In contrast to AAS, no radiation source is required.

Flame photometry (see also p. 338) is almost exclusively used for the determination of alkali metals because of their low excitation potential

Box 49.6 How to operate a flame atomic absorption spectrometer

You should only operate an FAAS system under direct supervision. The instrument should be located under a fume extraction hood. The spectrometer requires approximately 20 min to warm up before switching the gases on and using the instrument.

1. **Adjust the operating wavelength and slit width of the monochromator.** This is done by consulting standard operating conditions, for example for lead see Table 49.2.

2. **Decide what wavelength is to be used for the analysis.** For lead the maximum sensitivity is achieved by selecting 217.0 nm.

3. **Adjust the wavelength selector to the appropriate wavelength.**

4. **Adjust the gain control** until the energy meter reading reaches a maximum.

5. **Adjust the wavelength selector** for maximum signal reading. You are now ready to ignite the air–acetylene flame.

6. **Turn on the fume extraction hood.** This allows toxic gases to be safely removed from the laboratory environment.

7. **Turn on the air supply** such that the oxidant flow meter is at the desired setting.

8. **Turn on the acetylene supply** such that the fuel flow meter is at the desired setting.

9. **Press the ignite button (or flame button).** The flame should light instantaneously with a 'pop'.

10. **After establishing the flame,** insert the aspirator tube into distilled water. Allow the flame to stabilise for up to 1 minute by aspirating distilled water, prior to analysis.

11. **After completing your analysis,** shut off the acetylene first (by closing the cylinder valve) and vent the acetylene gas line while the air is still on. Then, shut off the air compressor and allow the air line to vent.

12. **Finally, switch off the fume extraction hood.**

Table 49.2 Standard operating conditions for lead

Wavelength (nm)	Slit (nm)	Characteristic concentration (mg L^{-1})
283.3	0.7	0.45
217.0	0.7	0.19
205.3	0.7	5.4
202.2	0.7	7.1
261.4	0.7	11.0
368.3	0.7	27.0
364.0	0.7	67.0

Note: recommended flame: air–acetylene, oxidising (lean, blue).

Using a flame photometer – make sure distilled water is available to aspirate into the flame once it is ignited.

Contamination risk – wipe the outside of the aspirator tube with a clean tissue in between samples/standards to prevent contamination.

SAFETY NOTE – Once the flame is ignited the instrument should not be left unattended.

(e.g. sodium 5.14 eV and potassium 4.34 eV). This simplifies the instrumentation required and allows a cooler flame (air–propane, air–butane or air–natural gas) to be used in conjunction with a simpler spectrometer (interference filter). The use of an interference filter allows a large excess of light to be viewed by the detector. Thus, the expensive photomultiplier tube is not required and a cheaper detector can be used, for example a photodiode or photoemissive detector. The sample is introduced using a pneumatic nebuliser as described for FAAS (p. 346). Flame photometry is therefore a simple, robust and inexpensive technique for the determination of potassium (766.5 nm) or sodium (589.0 nm) in clinical or environmental samples. The technique suffers from the same type of interferences as in FAAS. The operation of a flame photometer is described on p. 338.

Inductively coupled plasma

A radio frequency inductively coupled plasma (ICP) is formed within the confines of three concentric glass tubes or plasma torch (Fig. 49.9). Each concentric glass tube has a tangentially arranged entry point through which argon gas enters the intermediate (plasma) and external (coolant) tubes. The inner tube consists of a capillary tube through which the

Be prepared – ensure all standards, blanks and samples are readily and easily accessible prior to ignition.

SAFETY NOTE – Check that the drain is full of water prior to use.

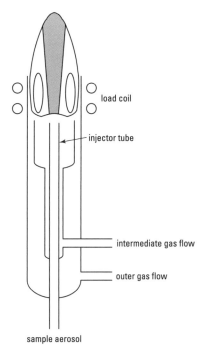

load coil

injector tube

intermediate gas flow

outer gas flow

sample aerosol

Fig. 49.9 Schematic diagram of an inductively coupled plasma.

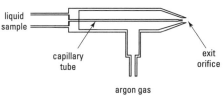

liquid sample

capillary tube

exit orifice

argon gas

Fig. 49.10 Schematic diagram of a pneumatic nebuliser.

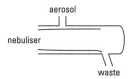

aerosol

nebuliser

waste

Fig. 49.11 Schematic diagram of a spray chamber.

aerosol is introduced from the sample introduction system. Located around the plasma torch is a coil of water-cooled copper tubing. Power input to the ICP is achieved through this copper, load or induction coil, typically in the range 0.5–1.5 kW at a frequency of 27 or 40 MHz.

Initiation of the plasma is achieved as follows. The carrier gas flow is first switched off and a spark added momentarily from a Tesla coil (attached to the outer edge of the plasma torch). The spark, a source of 'seed' electrons, causes ionisation of the argon gas. The co-existence of argon, argon ions and electrons constitutes a plasma located within the confines of the plasma torch but protruding from the top in the shape of a bright white luminous bullet. In order to introduce the sample aerosol into the ICP (7000–10 000 K) the carrier gas is switched on and punches a hole into the centre of the plasma creating the characteristic doughnut or toroidal shape. The emitted radiation is viewed laterally (side-on) through the luminous plasma.

Sample introduction

The most common method of liquid sample introduction in ICP–AES is the nebuliser. The nebuliser operates in the same manner as that used for FAAS but there are differences in its construction material and manufactured tolerance (the nebuliser for ICP–AES generates a finer aerosol, but is more inefficient). The pneumatic nebuliser consists of a concentric glass tube through which a capillary tube passes (Fig. 49.10). The sample is drawn up through the capillary by the action of the argon carrier gas escaping through the exit orifice that exists between the outside of the capillary tube and the inside of the glass concentric tube. The typical uptake rate of the nebuliser is between 0.5 and 4 mL min^{-1}. In common with FAAS, a means to reduce the coarse aerosol generated to a fine aerosol is required. In ICP–AES terminology this device is called a spray chamber (Fig. 49.11).

Spectrometers

The nature of the ICP is such that all elemental information from the sample is contained within it. The only limitation is whether it is possible to observe all the elemental information at the same time or one element at once. This limitation is associated not with the ICP but with the type of spectrometer used to view the emitted radiation. A monochromator allows measurement of one wavelength, corresponding to one element at a time, while a polychromator allows multiwavelength or multielement detection. The former can perform sequential multielement analysis, while the latter carries out simultaneous multielement analysis. The typical wavelength coverage required for a spectrometer is between 167 nm (Al) and 852 nm (Cs).

Detectors

The most common detector for AES is the photomultiplier tube (see p. 346). An alternative approach for the detection of multielement (multiwavelength) information is the charged-coupled device (CCD). A CCD is essentially an array of closely spaced metal–insulator–semiconductor diodes formed on a wafer of semiconductor material. Incident light striking the CCD is converted into an electrical signal.

Interferences in ICP–AES

Interferences for AES can be classified into two main categories, spectral and matrix interferences. Spectral interference can occur as a result of an interfering emission line from either another element or the argon source gas, or from impurities within or entrained into the source, for example molecular species such as N_2. Such interferences can be eliminated or reduced either by increasing the resolution of the spectrometer or by selecting an alternative spectral emission line.

Matrix interferences are often associated with the sample introduction process. For example, pneumatic nebulisation can be affected by the dissolved-solids content of the aqueous sample, which affects the uptake rate of the nebuliser and hence the sensitivity of the assay. Matrix effects in the plasma source typically involve the presence of easily ionisable elements (EIEs, e.g. alkali metals) within the plasma source.

Inductively coupled plasma mass spectrometry

The inductively coupled plasma has been developed as an ion source for mass spectrometry (see also Chapter 58). The plasma is operated in horizontal mode and is positioned at the interface of a mass spectrometer. Most common mass spectrometers for ICP–MS are based on a quadrupole instrument. Key to the success of ICP–MS was the development of an interface (Fig. 49.12) that allows an ICP operating at atmospheric pressure to be linked to a mass spectrometer operating under high vacuum.

The ICP operates in much the same way as in AES, and with the same approach to sample introduction. However, the inherent sensitivity of ICP–MS has made it a very useful addition to the methods available for trace metal analysis (Fig. 49.13). Typical sensitivities for metals by ICP–MS are in the trace (ng ml^{-1}) to ultratrace (pg mL^{-1}) range. This ability to measure metals at low concentrations can cause problems, particularly with the grade of reagents used to prepare the standards and the water supply to prepare samples and standards.

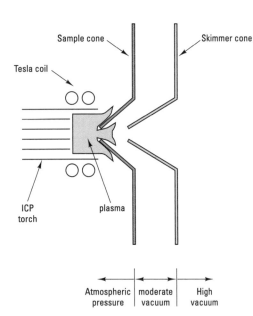

Fig. 49.12 Schematic diagram of an inductively coupled plasma mass spectrometer interface.

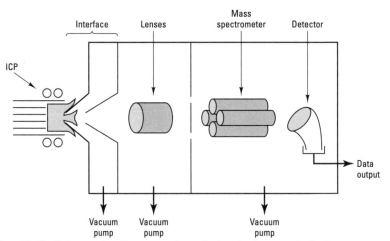

Fig. 49.13 Schematic diagram of an inductively coupled plasma mass spectrometry system.

Quantitative analysis in ICP–MS is achieved by measurement of element isotopes. Approximately 70% of elements in the Periodic Table have more than one stable isotope. For example, lead (Pb) has four isotopes with mass/charge ratios of 204, 206, 207 and 208 which have % abundances of 1.4, 24.1, 22.1 and 52.4, respectively. It should therefore be obvious that in order to achieve the largest response for Pb you should choose the isotope with the largest abundance, i.e. 208. However, a mass spectrometer offers additional advantages, including the ability to measure all isotopes very quickly. An ICP–MS can therefore measure almost all elements in the Periodic Table very quickly. ICP–MS can also use the isotopic information present for an element to provide quantitative information. The typical approach to quantitation involves preparing a calibration graph (see Chapter 47), however ICP–MS can also quantify samples using isotope dilution analysis (IDA). Isotope dilution analysis requires an enriched artificial isotopic standard of the element to be quantified, i.e. a different isotopic abundance to that normally found in nature.

Two classes of interferences occur in ICP–MS:

1. isobaric interferences;

2. molecular interferences (polyatomic and doubly charged species).

Isobaric interferences occur as a result of direct overlap of isotopes from one element with another. These interferences (Table 49.3) are well known and can be compensated for either by selecting an alternative isotope or by applying a correction based on the isotopic abundance. Molecular interferences, and in particular polyatomic interferences, can be troublesome and result from interactions between the element of interest and other species present, for example argon plasma gas, or the type of acid used to prepare the sample digest. It is therefore possible to produce species, such as $ArCl^+$ or, more correctly in this example, $^{40}Ar^{35}Cl^+$. This may have resulted from the presence of chlorine in the sample matrix or the acid used to digest the sample (e.g. HCl).

The other molecular interference, doubly charged species, can also cause problems. For example, barium has isotopes at mass/charge ratios that include 130, 132, 134, 136 and 138 amu that can form doubly charged species at mass/charge ratios of 65, 66, 67, 68 and 69 amu respectively.

One approach to reduce or eliminate molecular interferences is via a collision–reaction cell (Dean, 2005). The use of a collision–reaction cell can allow for either neutralisation of chemical ionisation species or

Table 49.3 Examples of isobaric interferences

Element							Atomic mass unit (amu)						
	108	109	110	111	112	113	114	115	116	117	118	119	120
Pd	26.5		11.7										
Ag		48.2											
Cd	0.9		12.5	12.8	24.1	12.2	28.7		7.5				
In						4.3		95.7					
Sn					1.0		0.6	0.4	14.5	7.7	24.2	8.6	32.6
Te													0.09

interferent/analyte ion mass/charge ratio shifts. These charges are affected by the introduction of reagent gases (e.g. H_2, He, NH_3 or CH_4) into the collision–reaction cell.

Decomposition techniques for solid inorganic samples

Conversion of a solid matrix into a liquid matrix involves the decomposition of the sample. One of the major problems in preparing solid samples for trace element analysis is the potential risk of contamination. Contamination can arise from several sources: the grade of reagents used; the vessels used for digestion and the subsequent dilution of the sample; and human involvement.

In order to minimise the risk of contamination you should take the following measures:

- Use the highest purity of reagents and acids, including the water used for sample dilution.

- Use sample blanks in the analytical procedure, to identify the base level of impurity in the reagents.

- Soak sample vessels in an acid leaching bath (e.g. 10% v/v nitric acid) for at least 24 hours, followed by rinsing in copious amounts of ultrapure water.

- Store cleaned volumetric flasks with their stoppers inserted; cover beakers with Clingfilm® or store upside down to protect from dust.

- In addition to the wearing of a laboratory coat and safety glasses, it may be necessary to wear 'contaminant'-free gloves and a close-fitting hat.

Decomposition involves the liberation of the analyte (metal) of interest from an interfering matrix using a reagent (mineral/oxidising acids or fusion flux) and/or heat. An important aspect in the decomposition of an unknown sample is the sample size (Box 49.4). You need to consider two aspects. Firstly, the dilution factor required to convert the solid sample to an aqueous solution (Box 49.5), and, secondly, the sensitivity of the analytical instrument (e.g. FAAS or ICP-MS).

Acid digestion

This involves the use of mineral or oxidising acids and an external heat source to decompose the sample matrix. The choice of an individual acid or combination of acids depends upon the nature of the matrix to be decomposed. For example, the digestion of a matrix containing silica, SiO_2 (e.g. a geological sample), requires the use of hydrofluoric acid (HF). A summary of the most common acids used for digestion and their application is shown in Table 49.4.

Once you have chosen an appropriate acid, place your sample into an appropriate vessel for the decomposition stage. Typical vessels include an open glass beaker or boiling tube for conventional heating or for microwave heating, a PTFE or Teflon® PFA (perfluoroalkoxyvinylether) vessel. A typical microwave system operates at 2.45 GHz with up to 14 sample vessels arranged on a rotating carousel; commercial systems have additional features such as: a PTFE-lined cavity; a safety vent (if the

Table 49.4 Common acids* used for digestion

Acid(s)	Boiling point (°C)	Comments
Hydrochloric acid (HCl)	110	Useful for salts of carbonates, some oxides and some sulphides. A weak reducing agent; not generally used to dissolve organic matter
Hydrofluoric acid (HF)	112	For digestion of silica-based materials only. Cannot be used with glass containers (use plasticware). In addition to laboratory coat and safety glasses, extra safety precautions are needed, e.g. gloves. In case of spillages, calcium gluconate gel is required for treatment of skin contact sites and should be available during use; evacuate to hospital immediately if skin is exposed to liquid HF
Nitric acid (HNO_3)	122	Useful for the digestion of metals, alloys and biological samples. Oxidising attack on many samples not dissolved by HCl; liberates trace metals as the soluble nitrate salt
Sulphuric acid (H_2SO_4)	338	Useful for releasing a volatile product; good oxidising properties for ores, metals, alloys, oxides and hydroxides. Often used in combination with HNO_3. Note: Sulphuric acid must never be used in PTFE vessels (melting point 327 °C)
Hydrochloric/nitric acids (HCl/HNO_3)	–	A 3 : 1 v/v mixture of HCl and HNO_3 is called aqua regia. It forms a reactive intermediate, NOCl. Useful for digesting metals, alloys, sulphides and other ores

*All concentrated acids should be used only in a fume cupboard.

Box 49.7 How to acid-digest a sample using a hot plate

1. **Accurately weigh your sample into a beaker (100 mL).** For digestion of a powdered metal sample 0.5000 g is appropriate (for details on how to weigh accurately see p. 158).

2. **Add 20 mL of concentrated acid(s)** (see Table 49.4).

3. **Cover the beaker with a watch glass.** This is done to prevent the loss of sample and to minimise the risk of contamination.

4. **Place the beaker on a pre-heated hot plate.**

5. **Reflux the sample for approx. 30 min to 1 hour;** depending on the nature of the sample a coloured, clear solution should result.

6. **Remove the beaker from the heat and allow to cool.** This may take several minutes. Retain the watch-glass cover during this stage to reduce airborne contamination.

7. **Wash the watch-glass cover** into the beaker to 'capture' any splashes of solution.

8. **Dilute the digested sample** with deionised, distilled water.

9. **Quantitatively transfer the diluted, digested sample** to a 100.00 mL volumetric flask (see p. 159). Make up to the graduation mark with de-ionised, distilled water.

10. **Prepare a sample blank using the same procedure,** i.e. perform all of the above tasks but without adding the actual sample.

11. **Prepare samples in at least duplicate.** For statistical work on the results, at least seven sample digests and two sample blanks are recommended.

---

pressure inside a vessel is excessive the vent will open, allowing the contents to go to waste); and an ability to measure both the temperature and pressure inside the digestion vessels. The procedure for acid digestion of a sample is shown in Box 49.7.

Other methods of sample decomposition

The use of acid(s) and heat is probably the most common approach to the decomposition of samples. However, several alternatives exist including dry ashing and fusion.

Dry ashing involves heating the sample in air in a muffle furnace at 400–800 °C to destroy the sample matrix (e.g. soil). After decomposition, the sample residue is dissolved in acid and quantitatively transferred to a volumetric flask prior to analysis. The method may lead to the loss of volatile elements (e.g. Hg, As).

Some substances, such as silicates and oxides, are not always destroyed by the direct action of acid and heat. In these situations an alternative approach is required. Fusion involves the addition of a 10-fold excess of a suitable reagent (e.g. lithium metaborate or tetraborate) to a finely ground sample. The mixture is placed in a metal crucible (e.g. Pt), and then heated in a muffle furnace at 900–1000 °C. After heating (from several minutes to several hours) a clear 'melt' should result, indicating completeness of the decomposition. After cooling, the melt is dissolved in HF (Table 49.4). This process can lead to a higher risk of contamination.

Text references and sources for further study

Cullen, M. (2003) *Atomic Spectroscopy in Elemental Analysis*. Wiley, Chichester.

Dean, J.R. (1997) *Atomic Absorption and Plasma Spectroscopy*, 2nd edn. ACOL series, Wiley, Chichester.

Dean, J.R. (2005) *Practical Inductively Coupled Plasma Spectroscopy*. Wiley, Chichester.

Ebdon, L., Evans, H., Fisher, A. and Hill, S. (1998) *An Introduction to Atomic Absorption Spectrometry*. Wiley, Chichester.

Hill, S.J. (2006) *Inductively Coupled Plasma Spectrometry and its Applications*, 2nd edn. Wiley, Chichester.

Holland, J.G. and Tanner, S.D. (2003) *Plasma Source Mass Spectrometry: Applications and Emerging Technologies*. Royal Society of Chemistry, Cambridge.

Kellner, R., Mermet, J.M., Otto, M., Valcarcel, M. and Widmer, H.M. (2004) *Analytical Chemistry: A Modern Approach to Analytical Science*, 2nd edn. Wiley, Chichester.
[Covers all modern analytical topics.]

Lajunen, L.H.J. and Peramaki, P. (2004) *Spectrochemical Analysis by Atomic Absorption and Emission*, 2nd edn. Royal Society of Chemistry, Cambridge.

Schmidt, W. (2005) *Optical Spectroscopy in Chemistry and Life Sciences: An Introduction*. Wiley, Chichester.

Taylor, H. (2000) *Inductively Coupled Plasma–Mass Spectrometry: Practices and Techniques*. Academic Press, London.

Vandecasteele, C. and Block, C.B. (1993) *Modern Methods of Trace Element Determination*. Wiley, Chichester.

Study exercises

49.1 Determine the concentration of metal ions based on atomic spectroscopy of test and standard solutions. The following data represent a set of calibration standards for K^+ in aqueous solution, measured by flame photometry:

Absorbance of standard solutions containing K^+ at up to 0.5 mmol L^{-1}

K^+ concentration (mmol L^{-1})	Absorbance
0	0.000
0.1	0.155
0.2	0.279
0.3	0.391
0.4	0.537
0.5	0.683

Draw a calibration curve using the above data and use this to estimate the amount of K^+ in a test sample prepared by digestion of 0.482 g of sample in a final volume of 25 ml of solution, giving an absorbance of 0.429 when measured at the same time as the standards shown above. Express your answer in mmol K^+ (g sample)$^{-1}$, to 3 significant figures.

49.2 Determine unknowns from a calibration curve. The following data are for a set of calibration standards of Zn, measured by atomic absorption spectroscopy.

Absorbance measurements for a series of standard solutions containing different amounts of zinc:

Zinc concentration (μg mL^{-1})	Absorbance
0	0.000
1	0.082
2	0.174
3	0.257
4	0.340
5	0.408
6	0.463
7	0.511
8	0.543
9	0.561
10	0.575

Draw a calibration curve by hand using graph paper and estimate the concentration of zinc in the following water samples:

(a) an undiluted sample, giving an absorbance of 0.157
(b) a 20-fold dilution, giving an absorbance of 0.304
(c) a five-fold dilution, giving an absorbance of 0.550.

Give your answer to 3 significant figures in each case.

Terminology in XRF – It is common practice to refer to an atom with shells (Fig. 50.1) of electrons, i.e. K, L, M, N, etc., instead of the modern approach using *s*, *p*, *d* and *f* as descriptors.

Understanding the relationship between energy and wavelength – The following equation applies:

$$E = h \times c/\lambda$$

where *E* is the energy, *h* is Planck's constant, *c* is the velocity of light and λ is the wavelength.

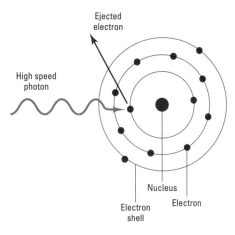

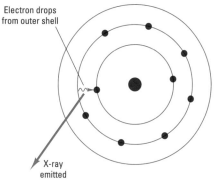

Fig. 50.1 Operating principle of X-ray fluorescence spectroscopy. Simplified diagrams showing (a) ejection of an electron and (b) the X-ray emitted.

X-ray fluorescence spectrometry (XRF) can be applied to determine the elemental composition of a wide range of objects of importance in chemical sciences. Its value arises from its non-destructive nature and potential for rapid identification of elements present in samples. The multi-element nature of XRF allows 'elemental fingerprints' to be generated from samples of known or unknown authenticity. Typical applications areas include paint, glass, pottery and ceramics, metals and alloys, soil, plastics, and fabrics. XRF can also be used to identify elements present in drug samples that may give clues as to the manufacturing processes involved and thereby help to further characterise the samples.

X-rays are part of the electromagnetic spectrum (p. 333) with wavelengths between 0.001 and 10 nm. They are produced when high-energy electrons decelerate or when electron transitions occur in the inner shells of atoms. The irradiation of matter with high-energy photons can lead to the ejection of an electron from an inner shell (e.g. the K shell) of an atom (Fig. 50.1a) and formation of an ion. This vacancy in the inner shell is filled almost immediately by an electron from a higher energy level (Fig. 50.1b). The difference in energy between the two energy levels is released in the form of an X-ray. This energy difference between the two specific orbitals always has the same characteristic energy. Therefore, by determining the energy (or wavelength) of the X-ray emitted by a particular element, it is possible to determine the identity of that element. In terms of identification, if the transition is to a K shell, the X-ray produced is described as a K X-ray, if to an L shell, an L X-ray results, and so on. Each X-ray can be further classified as, for example, K_α, K_β, indicating that the energy transition has taken place from the L and M shell respectively (Fig. 50.2). The number of X-rays per unit time at a particular energy (or wavelength) can be counted to allow either qualitative or quantitative analysis to be undertaken.

> **KEY POINT** The energy of an emitted X-ray is specific to a particular element and allows unequivocal identification while the strength of the signal allows quantification.

Instrumentation

An XRF spectrometer requires a source of X-rays (to excite the atoms in the sample), a sample holder, and a spectrometer to measure the energy (or wavelength) and intensity of the radiation emitted by the sample. Instrumentally two types of XRF can be identified: energy-dispersive and wavelength-dispersive XRF. Energy dispersive X-ray fluorescence (EDXRF) relies on the detector and associated electronics to resolve spectral peaks due to differences in the energy of the generated X-rays. A schematic diagram of an EDXRF is shown in Fig. 50.3. In wavelength dispersive XRF (WDXRF) a diffractive device such as a crystal is used to investigate the element of interest. A schematic diagram of a WDXRF is shown in Fig. 50.4. This chapter will focus on EDXRF only, since this is the most widely used method in analytical science. The analytical

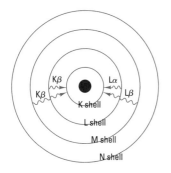

Fig. 50.2 Identification of K and L spectral lines.

Desirable properties of an X-ray source –
- long-term power stability
- low power output requirements
- purity of spectral output
- long life
- small size.

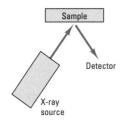

Fig. 50.3 Schematic diagram of an EDXRF system.

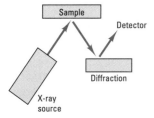

Fig. 50.4 Schematic diagram of an WDXRF system.

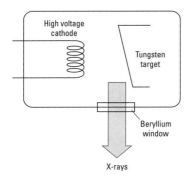

Fig. 50.5 X-ray tube (side window).

performance of EDXRF can be improved by the introduction of additional components, including source filters or secondary targets. In the case of a secondary target, the X-ray tube excites the secondary target. The secondary target fluoresces and excites the sample, and finally the detector measures X-rays from the sample. In addition, detector filters are sometimes positioned between the sample and the detector to remove unwanted X-rays.

Sample chambers in XRF can be operated in air. However, as air absorbs low-energy X-rays from elements below atomic number 20 (e.g. calcium) purges are often used. The two most common purge methods are the vacuum system and helium purge. Vacuum systems are preferred for analysis of solids or pressed pellets, while helium is preferred for analysis of liquids or powdered materials.

X-ray source

To generate X-rays you need:

- A source of electrons.

- A means of accelerating the electrons.

- A target, to stop the electrons.

X-ray sources are available in a variety of forms, for example side window X-ray tubes (Fig. 50.5), end window X-ray tubes, and radioisotopes. In the case of X-ray tubes – the most common source of X-rays for laboratory-based instruments – the applied voltage determines which elements can be excited. Also, the more power is applied, then the lower the detection limits achievable.

Detectors

Several types of detectors are available for XRF, including:

- Si(Li) detectors.

- PIN (positive–intrinsic–negative) diodes.

- Silicon drift detectors.

- Proportional counters.

- Scintillation detectors.

For EDXRF the most common detector has been the Si(Li) detector (Fig. 50.6).

The principle of operation of a detector for XRF is as follows:

1. A detector is composed of a non-conducting or semiconducting material between two charged electrodes.

2. X-ray radiation ionises the detector material causing it to become conductive, momentarily.

3. The newly freed electrons are accelerated towards the detector anode to produce an output pulse.

4. The ionised semiconductor produces electron–hole pairs, the number of pairs produced being proportional to the X-ray photon energy.

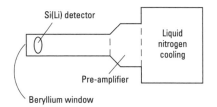

Fig. 50.6 Schematic diagram of a Si(Li) detector.

Evaluating spectra

EDXRF can be used to analyse, for example, the chemical composition of glass either quantitatively or qualitatively. It is important to be able to differentiate between peaks due to the elements of interest and other spectral anomalies including interferences. The types of anomalies found in XRF are complex and varied, but need to be recognised in order to distinguish them from elemental peaks.

Elemental K and L spectral peaks

These are the most common elemental peaks observed in EDXRF spectra. For example, the L shell electron transition to fill a vacancy in the K shell results in the production of K_α radiation. This is the most frequent transition and hence produces the most intense peak. Whereas, when an M shell electron transition occurs to fill a vacancy in the K shell it results in the production of K_β radiation, and so on (Fig. 50.2). The ratio of signal intensities between K_α and K_β is normally 20 : 1.

Similarly, if an M shell electron transition occurs to fill a vacancy in the L shell, it results in the production of L_α radiation. Whereas, an N shell electron transition to fill a vacancy in the L shell produces L_β radiation, and so on (Fig. 50.2). In addition to the elemental peaks, other peaks can also appear in spectra.

Scatter

When some of the source X-rays strike the sample they are scattered back at the detector (often referred to as 'backscatter'). Two types of scatter can be identified:

- Rayleigh scatter – X-rays from the X-ray tube or target strike the atom without promoting fluorescence. In this scenario, energy is not lost in the collision process. As a result this type of scatter appears as a source peak in the line spectrum. It is sometimes referred to as 'elastic' scatter.

- Compton scatter – X-rays from the X-ray tube or target strike the atom without promoting fluorescence. In this scenario energy is lost in the collision process, and scatter appears as a source peak in the line spectrum, but slightly lower in energy than the Rayleigh scatter. Compton scatter is often referred to as 'inelastic' scatter.

Escape peaks

In normal operation, X-rays strike the sample and promote elemental fluorescence. However, escape peaks result from the fact that some silicon (Si) fluorescence at the surface of the detector escapes and is not collected by the detector. The result is a peak that appears in the spectra at an energy that corresponds to silicon, i.e. 1.74 keV.

Sum peaks

Sum peaks result when two photons strike the detector at exactly the same time. In this situation, fluorescence is captured by the detector, and recognised as a single photon but at twice its normal energy. Sum peaks can be observed in spectra at twice the energy for the element under investigation, i.e. $2 \times$ element keV.

Bremsstrahlung

The process of electrons colliding with atoms in the object under investigation results in deceleration of electrons and production of an X-ray photon. The resultant continuum of energy, often called *Bremsstrahlung* radiation, appears as a broad band across many energies.

Interferences

Interferences can be divided into three categories:

1. Spectral interferences.

2. Environmental interferences.

3. Matrix interferences.

Spectral interferences

Spectral interferences are peaks in the spectrum, from other sources, that overlap with the spectral peak of the element to be analysed. Examples include K and L line overlaps for sulphur and molybdenum, chlorine and rhodium, and arsenic and lead. In addition, adjacent element overlap can occur, examples being aluminium and silicon, sulphur and chlorine, and potassium and calcium. In these situations it is the resolution of the detector that determines the significance of the overlap.

Environmental interferences

Lighter elements, such as those between sodium and chlorine in the Periodic Table, emit weak X-rays, whose signal can be reduced by air. The remedy is to either (a) purge the instrument with an inert gas such as helium (as helium is less dense than air, it results in less attenuation of the signal) or (b) evacuate air from the sample chamber via a vacuum pump. The removal of air from the sample chamber also has additional benefits, such as the elimination of spectral interferences resulting from argon which is present in small quantities in air, has a spectral overlap with chlorine.

Matrix interferences

Two types of matrix interferences can result in absorption or enhancement effects. In absorption, any element can absorb or scatter the fluorescence of the element of interest, whereas in enhancement characteristic X-rays of one element can excite another element in the same sample resulting in signal enhancement. These matrix interferences can be mathematically corrected by the use of influence coefficients, or alpha corrections. This is demonstrated in Fig. 50.7 where the incoming source X-ray causes iron in the sample to fluoresce. The resultant iron fluorescence is sufficient in energy to cause calcium to fluoresce. In this situation calcium is detected, but iron is not. The resultant signal responses are proportional to the concentrations of both calcium and iron.

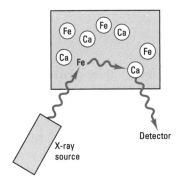

Fig. 50.7 Absorption-enhancement effects in XRF.

> **Box 50.1 How to avoid problems with liquid samples in XRF**
>
> 1. **Reduce evaporation of liquid samples by preparing and analysing samples immediately.** Evaporation can be reduced by placing a cover over the cup holder, though this can lead to bulging of the window film resulting in poor reproducibility of measurement. Some manufacturers produce baffled cups to help to reduce evaporation.
>
> 2. **Mixtures or immiscible liquids can give rise to stratification problems.** In order to assist in their analysis it may be necessary to separate the two liquids and analyse them separately. Alternatively, mix the solution rapidly to form an emulsion and then analyse immediately.
>
> 3. **If precipitation occurs, remove the liquid (supernatant) from the precipitate using a pipette.** This then allows analysis of both liquid and solid fractions. Alternatively, rapidly mix the liquid sample and the precipitate prior to analysis.

Sample preparation

XRF is often regarded as requiring minimal or no sample preparation. However, for reproducible results, consideration needs to be given to the type and form of sample to be analysed. Often the sample to be analysed can be placed directly in a sample cup holder in the XRF instrument. A typical sample cup is normally 2–4 cm in diameter, and is no higher than it is wide. In addition, the sample cup holder can be obtained in a variety of configurations, including as a single open-ended cup (the obvious benefit being that it requires no cover on the cup) or a double open-ended cup (allows flexibility in terms of selecting the cover for the sample, e.g. Mylar^{TM} film). You should always use covers for solution or powder samples, to prevent contamination and/or loss of material.

The most common window (i.e. sample support) film is Mylar^{TM}. This has the combined benefits of low cost and high tensile strength, allowing it to be produced in a thin form (down to 1.5 μm), and thereby leading to highly reproducible results. However, Mylar^{TM} has poor resistance to acids, preventing its use in many applications where acid may have been used in the preparation of the sample. Other materials used include polypropylene, polycarbonate, polyimide (Kapton^{TM}) and Teflon^{TM}. It is also possible to use cups with solid beryllium windows for analysis of very light elements.

Sample preparation for liquid samples

Liquid samples can be analysed directly by three-quarters filling the sample cup and placing it in the EDXRF spectrometer. However, problems can arise due to the liquid sample evaporating, stratifying (forming layers) and/or precipitating (see Box 50.1). In addition, the liquid sample itself may react with the window cup film or be absorbed by it. In order to minimise these effects, it is appropriate to prepare all liquid samples immediately before analysis.

Alternative procedures for liquid samples include the addition of a solidifying agent to the liquid sample (e.g. cellulose, alumina or gelatin) to form a solid support. Alternatively, the sample can be presented as a thin film by applying the liquid sample to the surface of a support material (e.g. filter paper or the sample cup itself). The liquid sample can

---

Box 50.2 How to prepare a loose powder sample for XRF analysis

1. **Dry and grind the loose powder sample** to a particle size corresponding to 400 mesh (15–35 μm) or better.

2. **Mix a portion of the dried powder with a binder,** for example paraffin or cellulose (1 : 1 w/w). The binder helps to hold the finished pellet together.

3. **Clean the die.** This can be done by wiping with methanol or another solvent.

4. **Insert the backing (i.e. an aluminium cap) into the die and accurately weigh the sample added,** for example 5–10 g. It is important to keep the weight constant to allow consistent results.

5. **Place a polished pellet over the sample** to produce a smooth finish.

6. **Insert the plunger and position the die in the press.** Press the pellet at a pressure of 10–20 tonnes maintained for approximately 60 s.

7. **Remove the pellet from the die,** taking care not to crack it in the process. The pellet is then ready for analysis.

---

then be analysed directly, wet, in the case of the filter paper, or dry by evaporating the sample directly in the cup. A variation on this approach is to use an ion-exchange resin to pre-concentrate the elements from the liquid sample, filter the resin (now containing the elements) and analyse this directly.

Sample preparation for solid samples

Solid objects can be placed directly into the sample chamber of the XRF spectrometer. However, several factors can influence the analysis of solid samples including surface roughness, particle shape and size, homogeneity, particle distribution, and mineralistion.

Loose powders can simply be analysed by filling a sample cup to approximately three-quarters without any need for additional sample preparation. However, while this approach will give results, it has significant shortcomings due in part to the heterogeneity of most samples and to variation in particle size of most loose powders. The most effective approach for loose powder samples is to press them into a pellet. This is most effectively done using a hydraulic press capable of delivering pressures ranging from 10 to 50 tonnes. The press uses a die to contain and form the sample during pressing (see Box 50.2). The only remaining disadvantage with pelletised samples is that there are still matrix effects due to the grain size being larger than the X-rays.

Environmental application

An environmental soil sample was subjected to EDXRF. The soil sample was prepared by air-drying it for 48 h prior to grinding and sieving. The sample was prepared as indicated in Box 50.2. The pelletised soil sample was then analysed. The results, shown in Fig. 50.8 as a plot of energy against signal, identify the range of elements present in the sample. By calibration of the EDXRF the elements identified can be converted into quantitative data.

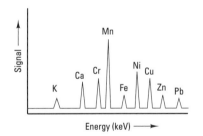

Fig. 50.8 Representative EDXRF trace of a soil sample.

Sources for further study

Beckhoff, B., Kanngleber, B., Langhoff, N., Wedell, R. and Wolff, H. (2006) *Handbook of Practical X-Ray Fluorescence Analysis*. Springer, Berlin.

Buhrke, V.E., Jenkins, R. and Smith, D.K. (1998) *A Practical Guide for the Preparation of Specimens of X-Ray Fluorescence and X-Ray Diffraction Analysis*. Wiley, Chichester.

Christian, G.D. (2003) *Analytical Chemistry*, 6th edn. Wiley, Chichester.

Jenkins, R. (1999) *X-ray Fluorescence Spectrometry*, 2nd edn. Wiley, Chichester.

Kellner, R., Mermet, J.M., Otto, M., Valcarcel, M. and Widmer, H.M. (2004) *Analytical Chemistry: A Modern Approach to Analytical Science*, 2nd edn. Wiley, Chichester.
[Covers all modern analytical topics.]

Rouessac, F. and Rouessac, A. (2007) *Chemical Analysis: Modern Instrumentation Methods and Techniques*, 2nd edn. Wiley, Chichester.

Schwedt, G. (1998) *The Essential Guide to Analytical Chemistry*. Wiley, Chichester.

Vandecasteele, C. and Block, C.B. (1993) *Modern Methods for Trace Element Determination*. Wiley, Chichester.

Study exercises

50.1 Explain the principle of X-ray fluorescence spectroscopy. Ask a colleague to listen to your explanation and provide feedback.

50.2 Test your knowledge. What are the main types of interferences associated with XRF and explain how they occur and how to avoid them.

50.3 Write a protocol for analysing a sample of soil. After reading this chapter, prepare a detailed stepwise protocol explaining how to prepare the soil sample and analyse it by XRF. Ask another student to evaluate your protocol and provide you with written feedback – either simply by reading through your protocol, or by trying it out as part of a class exercise. (Check with a member of staff before you attempt this in a laboratory.)

Chromatography is used to separate the individual components of a mixture on the basis of differences in their physical characteristics, for example molecular size, shape, charge, volatility, solubility and/or adsorption properties. The essential components of a chromatographic system are:

- A stationary phase, where a solid, a gel or an immobilised liquid is held by a support matrix.

- A chromatographic bed: the stationary phase may be packed into a glass or metal column, spread as a thin layer on a sheet of glass or plastic, or adsorbed on cellulose fibres (paper).

- A mobile phase, either a liquid or a gas which acts as a solvent, carrying the sample through the stationary phase and eluting from the chromatographic bed.

- A delivery system to pass the mobile phase through the chromatographic bed.

- A detection system to visualise the test substances.

The individual substances in the mixture interact with the stationary phase to different extents, as they are carried through the system, enabling separation to be achieved.

> **KEY POINT** In a chromatographic system, those substances which interact strongly with the stationary phase will be retarded to the greatest extent, while those which show little interaction will pass through with minimal delay, leading to differences in distances travelled or elution times.

Chromatography is subdivided according to the mechanism of interaction of the solute with the stationary phase.

Adsorption chromatography

This is a form of solid–liquid chromatography. The stationary phase is a porous, finely divided solid which adsorbs molecules of the mixture on its surface by dipole–dipole interactions, hydrogen bonding and/or van der Waals' interactions (Fig. 51.1). The range of adsorbents is limited to polystyrene-based resins for non-polar molecules and silica, aluminium oxide and calcium phosphate for polar molecules. Most adsorbents must be activated by heating to 110–120 °C before use, since their adsorptive capacity is significantly decreased if water is adsorbed on the surface. Adsorption chromatography can be carried out in column (p. 375) or thin-layer (p. 376) form, using a wide range of organic solvents.

Partition chromatography

This is based on the partitioning of a substance between two liquid phases, in this instance the stationary and mobile phases. Substances which are more soluble in the mobile phase will pass rapidly through the system while those which favour the stationary phase will be retarded

Chromatography is often a three-way compromise between:
1. separation of analytes;
2. time of analysis;
3. volume of eluent.

Selecting a separation method – it is often best to select a technique that involves direct interaction between the substance(s) and the stationary phase (e.g. ion-exchange or affinity chromatography), owing to their increased capacity and resolution compared with other methods (e.g. partition or gel permeation chromatography) where the analytes are not bound to the stationary phase.

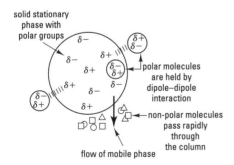

Fig. 51.1 Adsorption chromatography (polar stationary phase).

Chromatography – basic principles

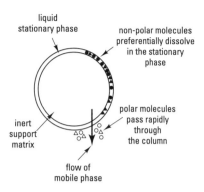

Fig. 51.2 Liquid–liquid partition chromatography, e.g. reversed-phase HPLC.

Maximising resolution in IEC – keep your columns as short as possible. Once the sample components have been separated, they should be eluted as quickly as possible from the column in order to avoid band broadening resulting from diffusion of sample ions in the mobile phase.

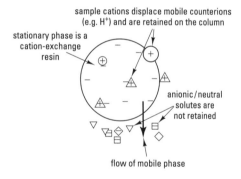

Fig. 51.3 Ion-exchange chromatography (cation exchanger).

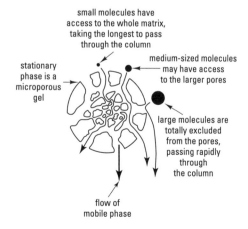

Fig. 51.4 Gel permeation chromatography.

(Fig. 51.2). In normal phase partition chromatography the stationary phase is a polar solvent, usually water, supported by a solid matrix (e.g. cellulose fibres in paper chromatography) and the mobile phase is an immiscible, non-polar organic solvent. For reversed-phase partition chromatography the stationary phase is a non-polar solvent (e.g. a C_{18} hydrocarbon, such as octadecylsilane) which is chemically bonded to a porous support matrix (e.g. silica), while the mobile phase can be chosen from a wide range of polar solvents, usually water or an aqueous buffered solution containing one or more organic solvents (e.g. acetonitrile). Solutes interact with the stationary phase through non-polar interactions and so the least polar solutes elute last from the column. Solute retention and separation are controlled by changing the composition of the mobile phase (e.g. % v/v acetonitrile). Reversed-phase high-performance liquid chromatography (RPHPLC, p. 379) is used to separate a broad range of non-polar, polar and ionic molecules, including environmental compounds (e.g. phenols) and pharmaceutical compounds (e.g. steroids).

Ion-exchange chromatography (IEC)

Here, separations are carried out using a column packed with a porous matrix which has a large number of ionised groups on its surfaces, i.e. the stationary phase is an ion-exchange resin. The groups may be cation or anion exchangers, depending upon their affinity for positive or negative ions. The net charge on a particular resin depends on the pK_a of the ionisable groups and the pH of the solution, in accordance with the Henderson–Hasselbalch equation (p. 202).

For most practical applications, you should select the ion-exchange resin and buffer pH so that the test substances are strongly bound by electrostatic attraction to the ion-exchange resin on passage through the system, while the other components of the sample are rapidly eluted (Fig. 51.3). You can then elute the bound components by raising the salt concentration of the mobile phase, either stepwise or as a continuous gradient, so that exchange of ions of the same charge occurs at oppositely charged sites on the stationary phase. Weakly bound sample molecules will elute first, while more strongly bound molecules will elute at a higher concentration.

Computer-controlled gradient formers are available: if two or more components cannot be resolved using a linear salt gradient, an adapted gradient can be used in which the rate of change in salt concentration is decreased over the range where these components are expected to elute. IEC can be used to separate mixtures of a wide range of anionic and cationic compounds. Electrophoresis (Chapter 53) is an alternative means of separating charged molecules.

Gel permeation chromatography (GPC) or gel filtration

Here, the stationary phase is in the form of beads of a cross-linked gel containing pores of a discrete size (Fig. 51.4). The size of the pores is controlled so that at the molecular level, the pores act as 'gates' that will exclude large molecules and admit smaller ones (Table 51.1). However, this gating effect is not an all-or-nothing phenomenon: molecules of intermediate size partly enter the pores. A column packed with such beads will have within it two effective volumes that are potentially

Table 51.1 Fractionation ranges of selected GPC media

M_r	Medium
50–1 000	Sephadex G15, Biogel P-2
1 000–5 000	Sephadex G-25
1 500–30 000	Sephadex G-50, Biogel P-10
4 000–150 000	Sephadex G-100
5 000–250 000	Sephadex G-200
20 000–1 500 000	Sephacryl S 300
60 000–20 000 000	Sepharose 4B

Using a gel permeation system – keep your sample volume as small as possible, in order to minimise band broadening due to dilution of the sample during passage through the column.

Example Biospecific molecules used in affinity chromatography include:

- enzymes and inhibitors/cofactors/substrates;
- hormones and receptor proteins;
- antibodies and antigens;
- complementary base sequences in DNA and RNA.

Elution of substances from an affinity system – make sure that your elution conditions do not affect the interaction between the ligand and the stationary phase, or you may elute the ligand from the column.

Remember that you cannot quantify a particular analyte without first identifying it: the presence of a single peak on a chromatogram does not prove that a single type of analyte is present.

available to sample molecules in the mobile phase, i.e. V_i, the volume surrounding the beads and V_{ii}, the volume within the pores. If a sample is placed at the top of such a column, the mobile phase will carry the sample components down the column, but at different rates according to their molecular size. A very large molecule will have access to all of V_i but to none of V_{ii}, and will therefore elute in the minimum possible volume (the 'void volume', or V_0, equivalent to V_i). A very small molecule will have access to all of V_i and all of V_{ii}, and therefore it has to pass through the total liquid volume of the column (V_t, equivalent to $V_i + V_{ii}$) before it emerges. Molecules of intermediate size have access to all of V_i but only part of V_{ii}, and will elute at a volume between V_0 and V_t, in order of decreasing size depending on their access to V_{ii}.

Cross-linked dextrans (e.g. Sephadex®), agarose (e.g. Sepharose®) and polyacrylamide (e.g. Bio-gel®) can be used to separate mixtures of macro-molecules, particularly enzymes, antibodies and other globular proteins. Selectivity in GPC is solely dependent on the stationary phase, with the mobile phase being used solely to transport the sample components through the column. Thus, it is possible to estimate the molecular mass of a sample component by calibrating a given column using molecules of known molecular mass and similar shape. A plot of elution volume (V_e) against $\log_{10}$ molecular mass is approximately linear. A further application of GPC is the general separation of components of low molecular mass and high molecular mass, for example 'desalting' a protein extract by passage through a Sephadex® G-25 column is faster and more efficient than dialysis.

Affinity chromatography

Affinity chromatography allows biomolecules to be purified on the basis of their biological specificity rather than by differences in physico-chemical properties, and a high degree of purification (more than 1000-fold) can be expected. It is especially useful for isolating small quantities of material from large amounts of contaminating substances. The technique involves the immobilisation of a complementary binding substance (the ligand) onto a solid matrix in such a way that the specific binding affinity of the ligand is preserved. When a biological sample is applied to a column packed with this affinity support matrix, the molecule of interest will bind specifically to the ligand, while contaminating substances will be washed through with the buffer (Fig. 51.5). Elution of the desired molecule can be achieved by changing the pH or ionic strength of the buffer, to weaken the non-covalent interactions between the molecule and the ligand, or by addition of other substances that have greater affinity for the ligand.

The chromatogram

A plot of the detector response present at the column outlet as a function of time is called a chromatogram (Fig. 51.6). The time from injection of the sample until the peak elutes from the column is called the retention time, t_r. The amount of compound present for a given peak can be quantified by measuring the peak height or area (most useful) and comparing it with the response for a known amount of the same compound.

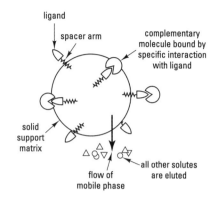

Fig. 51.5 Affinity chromatography.

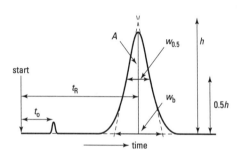

Fig. 51.6 Peak characteristics in a chromatographic separation, i.e. a chromatogram. For symbols, see eqns [51.1] and [51.3].

The aim of any chromatographic system is to resolve a number of components in a sample mixture, i.e. to ensure that individual peaks do not overlap or coincide. To achieve this you need to consider several important factors: capacity factor, separation factor or selectivity, column efficiency and asymmetry factor.

Capacity factor, k' This is a more useful measure of peak retention that retention time, as it is independent of column length and flow rate. To calculate k', you need to measure column dead time, t_o. This is the time it takes an unretained component to pass through the column without any interaction with the stationary phase. It is the time taken from the point of sample injection until the first disturbance in the base line caused by the unretained component. The capacity factor for other components can then be calculated according to the following equation:

$$k' = \frac{t_R - t_o}{t_o} \qquad [51.1]$$

Separation factor, α The separation factor, or selectivity, identifies when the peaks elute relative to each other. It is defined for two peaks as the ratio of the capacity factors ($k_2' > k_1'$):

$$\alpha = \frac{k_2'}{k_1'} = \frac{t_{R,2} - t_o}{t_{R,1} - t_o} \qquad [51.2]$$

where $t_{R,1}$ and $t_{R,2}$ are the retention times of peak 1 and peak 2, respectively. If two peaks are present the separation factor must be greater than one to achieve an effective separation.

Column efficiency (plate number), N An additional parameter used to characterise a separation system is the plate number, N. It represents, in general terms, the narrowness of the peak and is often calculated using one of the following equations:

$$N = 5.54 \left(\frac{t_R}{w_{0.5}} \right)^2 \qquad [51.3]$$

$$N = 16 \left(\frac{t_R}{w_b} \right)^2 \qquad [51.4]$$

$$N = 2\pi \left(\frac{t_{R.h}}{A} \right)^2 \qquad [51.5]$$

Where t_R is the retention time of the peak, $w_{0.5}$ and w_b are the peak widths at half height and base, respectively, and h and A are the peak height and peak area, respectively (Fig. 51.6).

For a compound emerging from a column of length L, the number of theoretical plates, N, can be expressed as:

$$N = \frac{L}{H} \qquad [51.6]$$

where H is the plate height (or height equivalent to a theoretical plate). In general, chromatographic columns with larger values of N give the narrowest peaks and generally better separation.

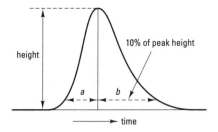

Fig. 51.7 Peak asymmetry.

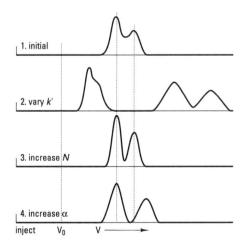

Fig. 51.8 A multicomponent chromatogram. Separation of many compounds, some well resolved, e.g. peaks at 12–13 min, and others that are not, e.g. peaks at 24–25 min.

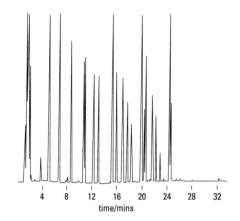

Fig. 51.9 Influence of k', α and N on resolution.

Asymmetry factor, A_s The plate number, N, assumes that the peak shape is Gaussian, but in practice this is rare. It is more likely that the peak is asymmetrical, i.e. it 'tails'. This is quantified using the asymmetry factor, A_s, calculated as shown in Fig. 51.7.

A vertical line is drawn between the peak maximum and the base line. At 10% of the peak height, the width of the peak to the leading edge and the trailing edge is measured (a and b in Fig. 51.7). The asymmetry factor is then calculated as follows:

$$A_s = \frac{b}{a} \qquad [51.7]$$

In general, A_s values between 0.9 and 1.2 are acceptable. If $A_s > 1$ peak tailing is in evidence; if $A_s < 1$ peak fronting is evident. The practical impact of peak tailing or fronting is that adjacent peaks are not as well separated as they would be if they were symmetrical, leading to difficulties in peak quantitation.

Resolution

It is often important to be able to separate a large number of compounds. A visual inspection of the chromatogram (Fig. 51.8) will usually indicate whether the separation is appropriate. It is desirable that the valley between adjoining peaks returns to the base line and resolution is a quantitative measure of the separation. The influence of k', α and N on resolution, R, is shown in the following expression:

$$R = \frac{\sqrt{N}}{4} \times \frac{k'}{k'+1} \times \frac{\alpha - 1}{\alpha} \qquad [51.8]$$

Three conditions must be satisfied in order to achieve some degree of resolution:

1. Peaks have to be retained on the column ($k' > 0$).

2. Peaks have to be separated from each other ($\alpha > 1$).

3. The column must develop some minimum value of N.

These different effects and their influence on resolution are shown in Fig. 51.9, using high-performance liquid chromatography (HPLC) as an example (see Chapter 52).

1. Initial conditions result in inadequate separation of the two components.

2. Effect of varying the capacity factor, k': from an initial mobile phase of 50% methanol : 50% water (v/v) two scenarios are possibile. Firstly, on the left-hand side, the influence of increasing the percentage of organic solvent (70% methanol : 30% water) allows a faster through-put, but the peaks are unresolved. Secondly, on the right-hand side, the percentage organic solvent is reduced (30% methanol : 70% water) allowing the components to remain in the system for a longer time, giving some separation, but causing peak broadening. This is the easiest change to make and will affect resolution. As a guide, a two- to three-fold change in k', will result for each 10% change in mobile phase composition.

3. Effect of increasing the plate number, N: reducing the particle size of the HPLC packing from 5 μm to 3 μm allows a more efficient

separation. It should be noted that the retention times of the peaks are not altered (from the initial chromatogram) provided the stationary phase is not altered. Alternatively N can be increased by placing columns in series with one another. However, you should note from eqn [51.8] that R has a square-root dependence on N, i.e. a four-fold increase in N is required to double R.

4. Increase separation factor, α: resolved peaks can be obtained by changing the mobile phase (e.g. methanol to acetonitrile) or the column stationary phase (e.g. C_{18} to C_8). Unfortunately this is the least predictable approach.

Detectors

After separating the components of the mixture it is necessary to detect them. A description of a range of detectors suitable for chromatography is described in Chapter 52. As chromatography is often used as a quantitative technique it is essential to be familiar with the following terms:

- Universal detector: this responds to all compounds eluting from the column, irrespective of their composition.

- Selective/specific detector: this responds to certain elements or functional groups. This is a useful approach if the components of the mixture are known.

- Sensitivity: the ratio of detector signal to sample size (or detector response per amount of sample).

- Minimum detectable level (MDL): the amount of sample in which the peak height is at least twice the noise height.

- Linear dynamic range: the concentration range of the sample that is detectable and where the detector response is linear (between the MDL and detector saturation).

Sources for further study

Barry, E.F. and Grob, R.L. (2007) *Columns for Gas Chromatography: Performance and Selection.* Wiley, Chichester.

Dean, J.R. (2003) *Methods for Environmental Trace Analysis.* Wiley, Chichester.

Hanai, T. (1999) *HPLC: A Practical Guide.* Royal Society of Chemistry, Cambridge.

Kellner, R., Mermet, J.M., Otto, M., Valcarcel, M. and Widmer, H.M. (2004) *Analytical Chemistry: A Modern Approach to Analytical Science*, 2nd edn. Wiley, Chichester.
[Covers all modern analytical topics.]

Kromidas, S. (2000) *Practical Problem Solving in HPLC.* Wiley, Chichester.

McNair, H.M. and Miller, J.M. (2009) *Basic Gas Chromatography*, 2nd edn. Wiley, Chichester.

Meyer, V. (2010) *Practical High-Performance Liquid Chromatography*, 5th edn. Wiley, Chichester.

Miller, J.M. (2009) *Chromatography: Concepts and Contrasts*, 2nd edn. Wiley, New York.

Rouessac, F. and Rouessac, A. (2007) *Chemical Analysis: Modern Instrumentation Methods and Techniques*, 2nd edn. Wiley, Chichester.

Schwedt, G. (1998) *The Essential Guide to Analytical Chemistry.* Wiley, Chichester.

Synder, L.R., Kirkland, J.J. and Glajch, J.L. (1997) *Practical HPLC Method Development*, 2nd edn. Wiley, New York.

Snyder, L.R., Kirkland, J.J. and Dolan, J.W. (2009) *Introduction to Modern Liquid Chromatography.* Wiley, Chichester.

Study exercises

51.1 Calculate the capacity factor, resolution and number of theoretical plates of two components from a chromatogram. Quinaldine and nicotine have retention times of 5.9 and 6.2 min, respectively on a 30 cm × 0.25 mm id × 0.25 μm film thickness DB5 column. If the peak width of quinaldine is 0.16 min and for nicotine is 0.18 min, calculate

(a) Capacity factor for quinaldine and nicotine
(b) Column Resolution
(c) Average number of theoretical plates in the column (column efficiency, N) per compound.

NOTE: the retention time of the unretained component is 1.0 min.

51.2 Test your knowledge of chromatographic theory – define the following terms:

(a) Dead time (t_o)
(b) Retention time (t_R)
(c) Capacity factor (k)
(d) Separation factor (α)
(e) Column efficiency (N).

51.3 Calculate the resolution and efficiency of two compounds. Compounds X and Y have retention times of 18.40 and 20.63 min, respectively, on a 30 cm column. If the peak widths at the peak bases are 1.11 and 1.21 min, respectively, calculate:

(a) The resolution factor for the two peaks.
(b) The efficiency of each peak.

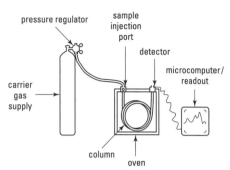

Fig. 52.1 Components of a GC system.

Gas chromatography

In gas chromatography (GC), a gaseous solute (or the vapour from a volatile liquid) is carried by the gaseous mobile phase. In gas–liquid partition chromatography, the stationary phase is a non-volatile liquid coated on the inside of the column or on a fine support. In gas–solid adsorption chromatography, solid particles that adsorb the solute act as the stationary phase.

The typical components of a gas chromatograph are shown in Fig. 52.1. A volatile liquid is injected through a septum into a heated port, which volatilises the sample. A gaseous mobile phase carries the sample through the heated column, and the separated components are detected and recorded. Two types of column are available: packed and capillary. Open tubular capillary columns offer higher resolution, shorter analysis time and greater sensitivity than packed columns, but have lower capacity for the sample.

Sample injection

Samples are injected onto the 'top' of the column, through a sample injection port containing a gas-tight septum. The two common sample injection methods for capillary GC are:

1. **Split/splitless injector**: in the split mode only a portion of the injected sample (typically, 1 part in 50) reaches the column. The rest is vented to waste. A split injector is used for concentrated samples (> 0.1 mg mL^{-1} for FID; see p. 373). In the splitless mode all the sample volume injected passes through to the column. It is used, in this mode, for trace samples (< 0.1 mg mL^{-1} for FID).

2. **Cold on-column injector:** all the sample is injected onto the column. It is used for thermally unstable compounds and high-boiling solvents.

In both cases a syringe (1 μL) is used to inject the sample. Examples of each type of injection system are shown in Fig. 52.2. The procedure for injection of a sample is shown in Fig. 52.3. In Fig. 52.3(a) the syringe (see p. 371) is filled with the sample/standard solution (typically 0.5 μL). Then the outside of the syringe is wiped clean with a tissue (Fig. 52.3(b)). The syringe is placed into the injector of the gas chromatograph (Fig. 52.3(c)) and, finally, the plunger on the syringe is depressed to inject the sample (Fig. 52.3(d)). The procedure for the preparation of a series of calibration solutions is shown in Box 52.1.

The column

Modern GC uses capillary columns (internal diameter 0.1–0.5 mm) up to 60 m in length. The stationary phase is generally a cross-linked silicone polymer, coated as a thin film on the inner wall of the fused silica (SiO_2) capillary: at normal operating temperatures, this behaves in a similar manner to a liquid film, but is far more robust. Common stationary phases for GC are shown in Fig. 52.4. The mobile phase ('carrier gas') is usually nitrogen or helium. Selective separation is achieved as a result of the differential partitioning of individual compounds between the carrier gas and silicone polymer phases. The separation of most organic

---

Types of capillary column

- Wall-coated open tubular (WCOT) column: liquid stationary phase on inside wall of column.
- Support-coated open tubular (SCOT) column: liquid stationary phase coated on solid support attached to inside wall of column.
- Porous layer open tubular (PLOT) column: solid stationary phase on inside wall of column.

Applications of gas–liquid chromatography – GLC is used to separate volatile, non-polar compounds: sub-stances with polar groups must be converted to less polar derivatives prior to analysis, in order to prevent adsorp-tion on the column, resulting in pool resolution and peak tailing.

Analysing compounds by GC in the split mode – make sure no hazardous materials enter the laboratory atmosphere through the split vent. A charcoal split-vent trap may be required to eliminate potential hazards.

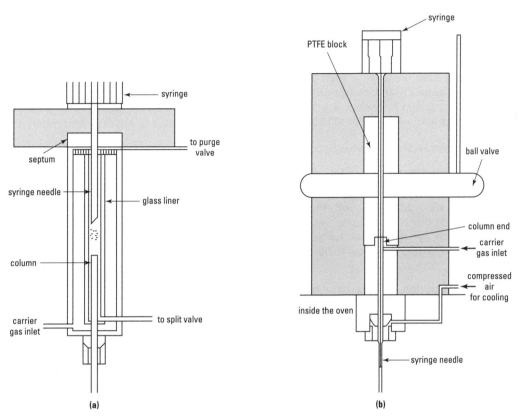

Fig. 52.2 Sample introduction in GC: (a) split/splitless injector; (b) on-column injector.

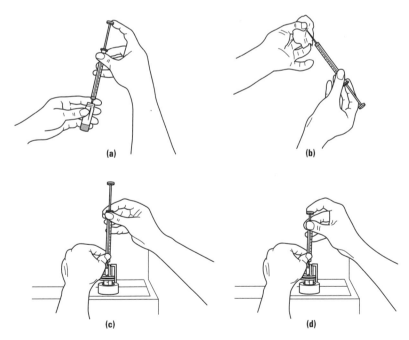

Fig. 52.3 Sample injection in GC. (a) Fill the syringe, (b) wipe clean the outside of the syringe needle, (c) place the syringe needle into the injector and (d) depress the plunger on the syringe to inject the sample.

Box 52.1 How to prepare a set of five calibration solutions in the concentration range 0–10 μg mL^{-1} (mg L^{-1})

Assuming that we are starting with a 1000 μg mL^{-1} stock solution of a particular organic compound (e.g. 2-chlorophenol) you will need the following: 6 × 10.00 mL grade A volumetric flasks and a syringe (0–100.00 μL).

1. **Ensure that all the glassware is clean** (see p. 151).

2. **Add ≈9 mL of organic solvent** (e.g. dichloromethane) to a 10.00 mL with dichloromethane.

3. **Quantitatively transfer 20.00 μL of the stock solution** into the 10.00 mL volumetric flask. Inject the solution from the syringe below the surface of the dichloromethane. Then, dilute to 10.00 mL with dichloromethane.

4. **What is the concentration of this new solution?** Remember that we started with an initial 1000 μg mL^{-1} 2-chlorophenol stock solution.

$$\frac{1000\,\mu g}{mL} \times 20 \times 10^{-3}\ mL = 20\ \mu g\ \text{2-chlorophenol}$$

$$[52.1]$$

so 20 μg 2-chlorophenol was placed in the 10.00 mL volumetric flask. So,

$$\frac{20\,\mu g}{10\ mL} = 2\ \mu g\ mL^{-1}\ \text{2-chlorophenol} \qquad [52.2]$$

You now have a 2 μg mL^{-1} calibration solution of 2-chlorophenol.

5. **Similarly transfer 0, 40.00, 60.00, 80.00 and 100.00 μL volumes into separate volumetric flasks** and dilute to 10.00 mL with dichloromethane and label as 0, 4, 6, 8 and 10 μg mL^{-1} 2-chlorophenol calibration solutions.

6. **Take the 0, 2, 4, 6, 8 and 10 μg mL^{-1} 2-chlorophenol calibration solutions** to the chromatograph for analysis.

100% dimethylsiloxane: the least polar bonded phase. Used for boiling point separations (solvents, petroleum products, etc.). Typical names: DB–1, HP–1, Rtx–1

95% dimethylsiloxane–5% diphenylypolysiloxane: a non-polar phase. Used for separation of environmental samples, e.g. polycyclic aromatic hydrocarbons. Typical names: DB–5, HP–5, Rtx–5

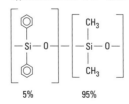

Fig. 52.4 Common stationary phases for capillary GC.

molecules is influenced by the temperature of the column, which may be constant during the analysis ('isothermal' – usually 50–250 °C) or, more commonly, may increase in a pre-programmed manner (e.g. from 50 °C to 250 °C at 10 °C per min).

Selecting an appropriate column for capillary GC is a difficult task and one which is usually left to the technician. However, it is important to be aware of some general issues and what influence they can have on the separation. The column internal diameter can affect both resolution and speed of analysis. Smaller internal diameters columns (0.25 mm i.d.) can provide good resolution of early eluting peaks (Fig. 52.5(a)). However, the problem is that the analysis times of the eluting components may be longer and that the linear dynamic range may be restricted. In contrast, larger internal diameter columns (0.53 mm i.d.) provide less resolution for early eluting compounds (Fig. 52.5b), but this is reflected in shorter analysis times and a greater linear dynamic range. This type of column may provide sufficient resolution for the analysis of complex mixtures. Fig. 52.5 illustrates the effects of column internal diameter.

Another important column effect is the length of the column and the influence this can have on the resolution of eluting components. It was previously shown (p. 367) that resolution was influenced by k', α and N. Substituting eqn [51.6] into eqn [51.8] produces the following equation:

$$R = \frac{1}{4}\sqrt{\frac{L}{h}} \times \frac{k'}{k'+1} \times \frac{\alpha - 1}{\alpha} \qquad [52.3]$$

The importance of this equation can be shown by considering the influence on resolution, R, of column length, L. Under isothermal analysis conditions, i.e. the same column temperature, the retention of eluting compounds is more dependent upon column length. For example, doubling the column length doubles the analysis times and increases the resolution by 41%. This is shown in Fig. 52.6 for the analysis of phenols. In contrast, under temperature-programmed analysis (e.g. 130 °C to 250 °C at 4 °C min⁻¹) the retention time of eluting components is more dependent on temperature. For example, doubling the column length has minimal effect on analysis times. This is shown in Fig. 52.7 for the analysis of bacterial acid methyl esters.

GC detectors

The output from the GC column is monitored by a detector. The most commonly used detectors for GC analysis of organic molecules are as follows.

The flame ionisation detector (FID) is particularly useful for the analysis of a broad range of organic molecules. It involves passing the exit gas stream from the column through a hydrogen flame that has a potential of more than 100 V applied across it (Fig. 52.8). Most organic compounds, on passage through this flame, produce ions and electrons that create a small current across the electrodes, and this is amplified for measurement purposes. The FID is very sensitive (typically down to $\approx$0.1 pg), with a linear response over a wide concentration range. One drawback is that the sample is destroyed during analysis.

The thermal conductivity detector (TCD) is based on changes in the thermal conductivity of the gas stream brought about by the presence of separated sample molecules. The detector elements are two electrically heated platinum wires, one in a chamber through which only the carrier gas flows (the reference detector cell), and the other in a chamber that takes the gas flow from the column (the sample detector cell). In the presence of a constant gas flow, the temperature of the wires (and therefore their electrical resistance) is dependent on the thermal conductivity of the gas. Analytes in the gas stream are detected by temperature-dependent changes in resistance based on the thermal conductivity of each separated molecule; the size of the signal is directly related to concentration of the analyte.

The advantages of the TCD include its applicability to a wide range of organic and inorganic molecules and its non-destructive nature, since the sample can be collected for further study. Its major limitation is its low sensitivity (down to $\approx$10 ng), compared with other systems.

The electron capture detector (ECD) is highly sensitive (Fig. 52.9) and is useful for the detection of certain compounds with electronegative functional groups (e.g. halogens, peroxides and quinones). The gas stream from the column passes over a β-emitter such as ⁶²Ni, which provides electrons that cause ionisation of the carrier gas (e.g. nitrogen). When carrier gas alone is passing the β-emitter, its ionisation results in a constant current flowing between two electrodes placed in the gas flow. However, when electron-capturing sample molecules are present in the gas flow, a decrease in current is detected. An example of the application of the ECD is in detecting and quantifying chlorinated pesticides.

Mass spectrometry (see also p. 459) used in conjunction with GC provides a powerful tool for identifying the components of complex

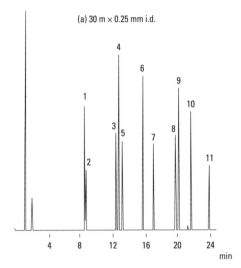

(a) 30 m × 0.25 mm i.d.

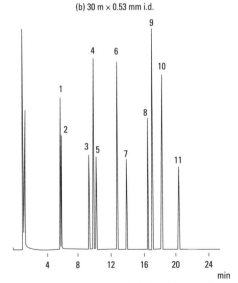

(b) 30 m × 0.53 mm i.d.

Fig. 52.5 Influence of GC column internal diameter on separation: 1. phenol; 2. 2-chlorophenol; 3. 2-nitrophenol; 4. 2,4-dimethylphenol; 5. 2,4-dichlorophenol; 6. 4-chloro-3-methylphenol; 7. 2,4,6-trichlorophenol; 8. 2,4-dinitrophenol; 9. 4-nitrophenol; 10. 2-methyl-4,6-dinitrophenol; 11. pentachlorophenol.

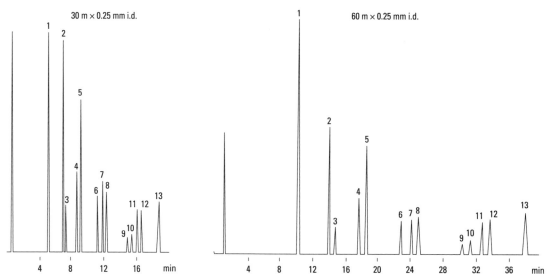

Fig. 52.6 Influence of column length on analysis time. Analysis of phenols under isothermal conditions: 1. phenol; 2. *o*-cresol; 3. 2,6-xylenol; 4. *p*-cresol; 5. *m*-cresol; 6. *o*-ethylphenol; 7. 2,4-xylenol; 8. 2,5-xylenol; 9. 2,3-xylenol; 10. *p*-ethylphenol; 11. *m*-ethylphenol; 12. 3,5-xylenol; 13. 3,4-xylenol.

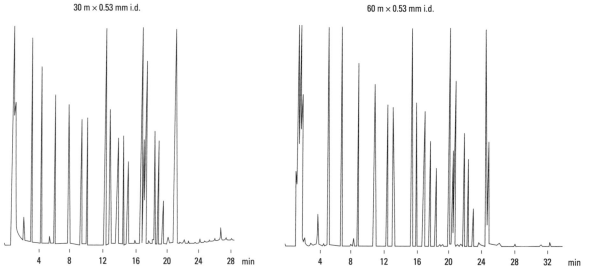

Fig. 52.7 Influence of column length on analysis time. Analysis of bacterial acid methyl esters under temperature-programmed conditions.

Detectors – the most appropriate detector depends on the type of chromatography and the application: ideally, the detector should show high sensitivity, a low detection limit and minimal noise or drift. These terms are defined in Chapter 51.

mixtures, for example environmental pollutants, synthetic products (Fig. 52.10). The procedure requires computer control of the instrument and for data storage/analysis. Compounds eluting from the column are bombarded by electrons (electron impact, EI, mode) causing fragmentation and production of charged species. These charged species are separated by the mass spectrometer on the basis of their mass-to-charge ratio. Ions passing through the mass spectrometer are detected by an electron multiplier tube. The mass spectrometer can be used in two

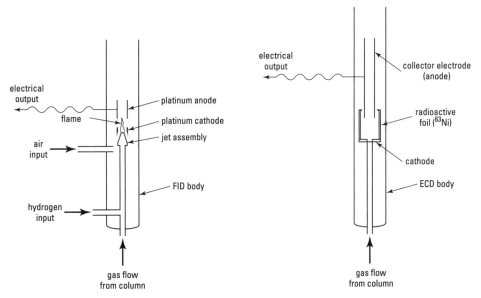

Fig. 52.8 Components of a flame ion-isation detector (FID).

Fig. 52.9 Components of an electron capture detector (ECD).

modes (p. 463): total ion and selected ion monitoring. In the former mode, the complete mass spectrum of each of the components of the mixture eluting from the column is recorded. In the latter mode, only ions of specified mass-to-charge ratios are detected. Selected ion monitoring offers increased sensitivity and selectivity.

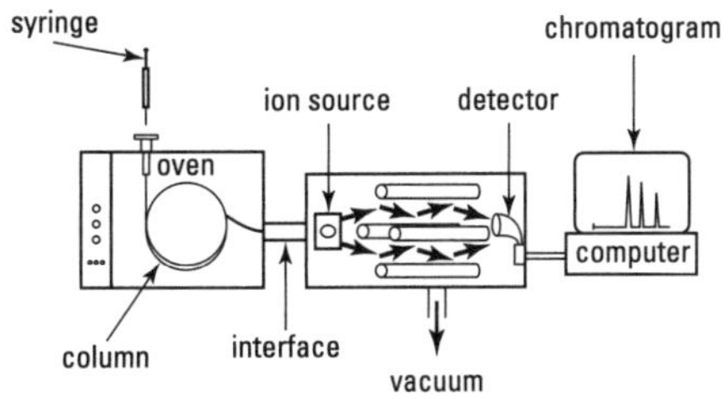

Liquid chromatography

The basic chromatographic system comprises a stationary phase (adsorbant), usually alumina, silica gel or cellulose, through which a mobile phase travels (elutes). Separation of a mixture of compounds is achieved by a combination of the differing 'adsorption' and solubility characteristics of the components on the stationary phase and in the mobile phase respectively.

Liquid chromatography is used both as an analytical method to determine the complexity of mixtures and the purity of compounds, and as a preparative system for the separation of mixtures. Liquid chromatography is divided into two general types:

1. Thin-layer chromatography (TLC): in which a glass or plastic plate is coated with a thin layer of the stationary phase and the mobile phase *ascends* the plate by capillary action. TLC is essentially an analytical tool and preparative TLC has been largely superseded by flash chromatography.

2. Column chromatography: in which the stationary phase is packed into a glass column and the mobile phase is passed *down* the column, either by gravity (gravity chromatography) or under low pressure from a pump or nitrogen cylinder (flash chromatography). These are the preparative systems.

Fig. 52.10 Schematic diagram of a GCMS instrument.

Using TLC plates – do not touch the surface of the TLC plates with your fingers. Hold them by the edges to prevent contamination.

Using TLC plates – a plate (2 cm x 5 cm) will hold three sample 'spots'.

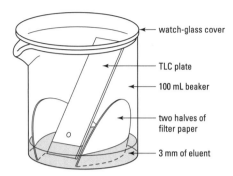

Fig. 52.11 The developing tank for TLC.

watch-glass cover

TLC plate

100 mL beaker

two halves of filter paper

3 mm of eluent

Solutions of the mixture – the mixture must be applied to the plate as a solution. If the solvent for the solution is not the same as the eluent to be used, you must evaporate the solvent from the plate, before placing it in the eluent.

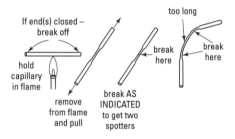

Fig. 52.12 How to make micropipettes.

too long

If end(s) closed – break off

break here

break here

hold capillary in flame

remove from flame and pull

break AS INDICATED to get two spotters

Thin-layer chromatography

The essential components of a TLC system are:

- The stationary phase comprising the layer of adsorbant on a solid backing – the chromatoplate. Aluminium or plastic-backed chromatoplates are now the norm having replaced glass plates, which needed to be prepared 'in-house'. The chromatoplates (20 cm × 20 cm) can be cut down to the more useful size (2 cm × 5 cm) for analytical work, using a guillotine. The adsorbant often contains a fluorescent compound (ZnS) to enable visualisation of the compounds after elution.

- The development tank: for plates of (2 cm × 5 cm) a clean, dry beaker (100 mL) covered with a watch-glass is ideal. The eluting solvent should be about 3 mm deep and filter paper should be placed in the tank to saturate the tank atmosphere with solvent vapour (Fig. 52.11).

- The application system: a micropipette or a microsyringe to place the solution of the mixture on the chromatoplate. Micropipettes (Fig. 52.12) are the more common and Box 52.2 gives the instructions for their preparation.

- The eluent: finding the eluent, which will give the best separation of the components of the mixture, is by experiment – you may need to try several solvents of differing polarity (Table 52.1) or mixtures of solvents to find the best eluent.

- A visualisation system to be able to see colourless separated components on the chromatogram. If the plate contains a fluorescer, it can be viewed under UV light ($\lambda = 254$ nm) in a special box or cabinet. The ZnS in the stationary phase fluoresces green, whereas the 'spots' of separated compounds appear dark. Alternatively, the plate can be placed in a sealed jar containing a few iodine crystals. The iodine vapour stains the plate light brown and the 'spots' dark brown.

Box 52.2 How to make micropipettes for TLC

1. **Heat the middle of an open-ended melting point tube at the tip of the hot flame of a microburner until it begins to sag.** If the melting point tube is sealed at one or both ends, carefully break off the sealed end(s) wearing gloves for protection.

2. **Quickly remove the tube from the flame and pull gently, forming a short capillary.** Do not pull the tube while it is in the flame.

3. **Allow the tube to cool and then break in the centre of the capillary.** You now have two micropipettes. If the capillary is too long, break it near to each end and *immediately* dispose of the fine waste glass into the broken-glass bin. *Do not leave* the waste glass on the laboratory bench.

4. **Make at least 10 micropipettes** and store them in a plastic-capped sample tube for future use.

Table 52.1 The elutropic series of solvents for chromatography

Non-polar	Light petroleum (b.pt. 40–60 °C)
	Cyclohexane
	Toluene
	Dichloromethane
	Diethylether (ether)
	Ethyl ethanoate (ethyl acetate)
	Propanone (acetone)
	Ethanoic acid (acetic acid)
Polar	Methanol

You can express the movement of an individual compound up the TLC plate in terms of its R_f (relative frontal mobility) value, where:

$$R_f = \text{distance moved by compund/distance moved by solvent} \quad [52.4]$$

The R_f value is a constant for a particular substance and eluent system on a specific stationary phase, but variations in chromatographic conditions adsorbant, eluent (in particular solvent mixtures), temperature and atmosphere make the application of R_f values to absolute identification rather problematical. Usually an authentic sample is run alongside the unknowns in the mixture (Fig. 52.13) or on top of the mixture – 'double spotting' – as shown in Fig. 52.14, to enable identification. The general procedure for running a TLC plate is described in Box 52.3.

Gravity chromatography

This is used for the preparative scale separation of mixtures of compounds, where a sample of the mixture is separated by percolation down a column of adsorbant by a suitable eluent. For effective separation the components of the mixture should have a difference in R_f value of at least 0.3. There are many variations in detail of equipment and technique such as adsorbant, column packing (dry or slurry), sample application (including pre-adsorption on a small sample of the stationary phase) and fraction collection, many of which are a matter of personal choice based on personal experience. A typical arrangement is shown in Fig. 52.15(a) and for a detailed description of how to carry out gravity chromatography you should consult specialist texts such as Errington (1997, p. 163), Harwood *et al.* (2000, p. 175) or Furniss *et al.* (1989, p. 209).

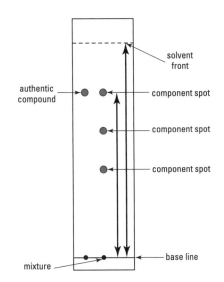

Fig. 52.13 A thin-layer chromatogram.

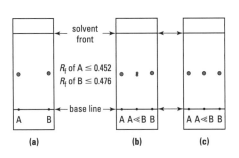

Fig. 52.14 Double-spotting technique: (a) compounds A and B with close R_f values; (b) figure '8' of double spot shows that A and B are different; (c) single spot for double spot shows that A and B could be the same.

Box 52.3 How to run a TLC

1. **Prepare the TLC development tank using a clean, dry beaker, as shown in Fig. 52.11,** and allow it to equilibriate for 10 minutes.

2. **Prepare the plastic-backed TLC plate** by drawing a fine line (the base line) in *pencil* about 1 cm above the bottom. Take care not to scrape off any of the stationary phase. Put three pencil dots on the base line – one in the centre and the others equidistant on either side, but no closer than 3 mm to the edges of the plate.

3. **Dissolve the mixture (1–3 mg) in two or three drops of a suitable volatile solvent** (dichloromethane or ether are the most common), in a small sample tube.

4. **Dip the tip of a micropipette into the solution** and capillary action will draw the solution into the pipette.

5. **Touch the tip of the micropipette onto one of the pencil spots on the base line.** Capillary action will draw the solution from the micropipette onto the plate as a spot. Do not allow the spot to be more than 2 mm in diameter. Put the micropipette back into the sample tube containing the mixture.

6. **Spot other samples** (e.g. reference compounds) onto the plate as appropriate, *using a new micropipette* in each case.

7. **Evaporate the solvent from the plate** by waving it in the air, holding the plate by the edges.

8. **Lower the plate into the developing tank,** holding it by the edges and make sure that *the eluent does not* cover the base line. If it does, discard the plate, prepare another and empty some eluent from the tank.

9. **Put the lid on the tank and allow the eluent to rise up the plate** to about 1 cm from the top of the plate.

10. **Remove the chromatoplate from the tank** and quickly mark the height reached by the eluent, using a pencil.

11. **Wave the chromatoplate in the air** to evaporate the eluent from the plate.

12. **Visualise the chromatogram by either placing the dry chromatoplate in the UV cabinet and using a pencil to draw round the spots** (*remember to wear gloves when your hands are in the UV cabinet*) or **putting the plate in the iodine jar until the dark spots develop.**

Problems with thin-layer chromatography

Overloading the chromatoplate with sample. TLC is an extremely sensitive technique and it is easy to put too much sample on the plate. The sample solution must not be too concentrated and you must not repeat applications of solutions on the same spot. The result is non-separation of the mixture and a 'smear' up the plate. Dilute the solution or don't put so much on the plate.

Putting the spots of sample too close together. The separated spots 'bleed' into each other and you can't tell from which sample they originate.

Putting the spots too close to the edge of the plate. This results in inaccurate R_f values (spots travel faster up the edge of the plate) and 'bleeding'.

Contamination, which produces unexpected spots. Make sure all apparatus is clean, solvents are clean and use a fresh micropipette for each application.

Flash chromatography

Flash chromatography or medium pressure chromatography has now almost completely replaced gravity chromatography for the preparative scale separation of mixtures. The use of smaller and more uniform particle size adsorbants (alumina or silica) and the use of medium pressure *via* a nitrogen or air cylinder, a small air pump or even a pressure ball to pump the eluent through the column gives more efficient (R_f difference of components down to 0.15) and much faster (minutes rather than hours) separations but at the expense of the use of much greater volumes of eluent. A typical arrangement of equipment is shown in Fig. 52.15(b), and Box 52.4 gives instructions on how to set up and run a flash column based on our experiences. The references (p. 377) provide a more comprehensive insight into the methodology.

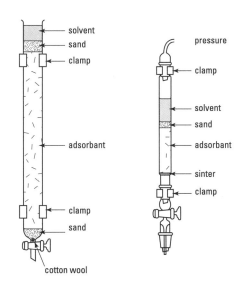

(a)　　　　　**(b)**

Fig. 52.15 Column chromatography: (a) gravity chromatography; (b) flash chromatography.

SAFETY NOTE Iodine vapour is toxic and the iodine tank should be stored in the fume cupboard.

UV visualisation – if you use an eluent such as toluene, which absorbs in the UV region, you must allow all the eluent to evaporate or you will see only a dark plate.

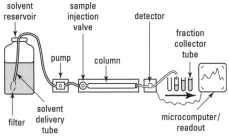

Fig. 52.16 Components of an HPLC system.

KEY POINTS

1. Before attempting a preparative mixture separation by gravity or flash chromatography, you must always analyse the mixture by TLC to establish the stationary phase and eluent parameters for effective separation and to determine the R_f values of the components of the mixture.

2. You must analyse by TLC all the fractions collected from the column to ensure that there is no 'overlap' of mixture components.

3. Some chromatographers prefer to use dry packing for gravity chromatography and slurry packing for flash chromatography: the method used is often based on experience to achieve the desired separation of components.

High-performance liquid chromatography

High-performance liquid chromatography (HPLC) uses high pressure to force the mobile phase through a closed column packed with micrometre-sized particles. This allows rapid separation of complex mixtures. Several operating modes of HPLC are possible. These are:

- **Normal phase (NPHPLC)**: the sample should be soluble in a hydrophobic solvent (e.g. hexane) and should be non-ionic. The mobile phase is non-polar while the stationary phase is polar (e.g. silica, cyano, amino).

- **Reversed phase (RPHPLC)**: the sample should be soluble in water or a polar organic solvent (e.g. methanol) and should be non-ionic. The mobile phase is polar while the stationary phase is non-polar (e.g. C18 (ODS), C_8 (octyl), phenyl).

- **Size exclusion chromotography (SEC)**: this is used when the major difference between compounds in a mixture is their molecular weight. It is normally used for compounds with molecular weights greater than 2000. The mobile phase should be a strong solvent for the sample. Aqueous SEC is called gel filtration chromatography (GFC) and is used for separation of proteins and other biomolecules, while organic SEC is called gel permeation chromatography (GPC) and is used for the separation of polymers.

- **Ion exchange chromotography (IEC)**: it is used when compounds are ionic, or potentially ionic (e.g. anions, cations, organic acids and bases, amino acids, catecholamines, peptides). The mobile phase is typically a buffer and the choice of pH is critical. Two types can be differentiated: SAX (Strong-Anion eXchange) and SCX (Strong-Cation eXchange).

The essential components of an HPLC system are a solvent delivery system, a method of sample introduction, a column, a detector and an associated readout device (Fig. 52.16).

Box 52.4 How to prepare and run a flash column

SAFETY NOTES

1. Flash alumina and silica are extremely fine and *MUST* be handled/transferred in the fume hood while you are wearing a dust mask, since they are extremely harmful and tend to disperse in the air.

2. The column must be wrapped in plastic webbing or adhesive tape to prevent glass flying in case of explosion when in use.

3. The pressure inlet must NOT be wired into place.

1. **Prepare at least 30 clean and dry, numbered test tubes in racks for fraction collection.** Once you start the chromatographic process you will not have time to prepare more.

2. **Clamp into a vertical position** a Pyrex®, jointed chromatography column containing a No. 4 sinter and mark the half height point.

3. **Prepare a fluted filter paper** (see Box 24.1) and puncture a very small hole in the point.

4. **Place the filter paper in a stemmed filter funnel** in the top of the column and add the silica.

5. **As the silica dribbles through into the column,** tap the sides of the column with a piece of thick-walled rubber tubing to ensure even packing until the silica is about 2 cm below the half height mark.

6. **Carefully add eluent to the top of the silica column,** either by using a long Pasteur pipette or by clamping a log glass rod down the centre of the column, almost but not touching the top of the adsorbant, and running eluent down the glass rod. Try not to disturb the top of the stationary phase as you fill the column with eluent.

7. **Rinse the top joint** with a little eluent to wash any particles of adsorbant down on to the column.

8. **Switch on the air pump and hold the joint in the top of the column as the eluent pumps down.** The column becomes opaque as the solvent passes through it and becomes warm.

9. **Stop pumping,** by removal of the pressure joint, when the eluent is about 2 cm from the top of the

silica and allow the column to cool. If eluent continues to drip from the bottom of the column, with no pressure, replace the amount being lost by addition with the Pasteur pipette. AT NO STAGE SHOULD THE ELUENT BE ALLOWED TO GO BELOW THE TOP OF THE ADSORBANT/SAND.

10. **Add more eluent to the column** so that it is 75% full and then add enough acid-washed dry sand, using the fluted filter paper technique, to produce a layer 1–2 cm deep on top of the silica.

11. **Pump the eluent down until it is about 1 cm above the sand layer.** The sand is there to prevent disturbance to the flat top of the silica which will result in uneven separation of the mixture.

12. **Dissolve the mixture to be separated in the minimum of eluent** and add it to the eluent above the sand using the technique described in section 6.

13. **Pump the eluent down** to 1 cm above the sand, add another 5 mL of eluent and pump down again to 1 cm above the sand. The mixture is now adsorbed on the top of the column.

14. **Fill the column with eluent (as in section 6)** and pump down to about 1 cm above the sand, collecting the eluent from the bottom of the column as fraction 1, or if you can see the components eluting, collect them as separate fractions.

15. **Repeat the elution** process until all the required fractions have been collected.

16. **Run TLC** on all the fractions collected to ensure that efficient separation has been effected.

NOTE With the system described above, one pumped elution is equivalent to one 'pass of solvent' through the column. This becomes important when a gradient elution (changing to eluent mixtures of increasing polarity) is required.

Solvent delivery system

This should fulfil certain requirements:

- It should be chemically inert.
- It should be capable of delivering a wide flow-rate range.

- It should be able to withstand high pressures.

- It should be able to deliver high flow-rate precision.

- It should have a low internal volume.

- It should provide minimum flow pulsation.

Although several systems are available that meet these requirements, the most common is the reciprocating or piston pump. The choice of solvent delivery system depends on the type of separation to be performed:

- **Isocratic separation:** a single solvent (or solvent mixture) is used throughout the analysis.

- **Gradient elution separation:** the composition of the mobile phase is altered using a microprocessor-controlled gradient programmer, which mixes appropriate amounts of two different solvents to produce the required gradient.

The main advantages of gradient HPLC are that you can control mobile-phase composition. This allows you to resolve closely related compounds and provide faster elution of strongly retained compounds thereby producing reduced analysis times and faster method development time. However, these advantages have to be compared with some disadvantages, such as the initial higher cost of the equipment compared with an isocratic system. Also, after each gradient run, a re-equilibration of the system is required to return to the initial mobile-phase conditions.

Sample introduction

The most common method of sample introduction in HPLC is via a rotary valve (e.g. a Rheodyne® valve). A schematic diagram of a rotary valve is shown in Fig. 52.17. In the load position, the sample is introduced via a syringe to fill an external loop of volume 5, 10 or 20 μL. While this occurs, the mobile phase passes through the valve to the column. In the inject position, the valve is rotated so that the mobile phase is diverted through the sample loop, thereby introducing a reproducible volume of the sample into the mobile phase. The procedure for injection of a sample is shown in Fig. 52.18. In Fig. 52.18(a) the syringe is filled with the sample/standard solution (typically 1 mL). Then the outside of the syringe is wiped clean with a tissue (Fig. 52.18(b)). The syringe is placed into the Rheodyne® injector of the chromatograph while in the 'load' position (Fig. 52.18(c)) and the plunger on the syringe is depressed to fill the sample loop. Finally, the position of the Rheodyne valve is switched to the 'inject' position to introduce the sample into the chromatograph (Fig. 52.18(d)) and then the syringe is removed from the injection valve. The procedure for the preparation of a series of calibration solutions is shown in Box 52.1.

The column

This is usually made of stainless steel, and all components, valves, etc., are manufactured from materials which can withstand the high pressures involved. The most common form of liquid chromatography is reversed phase HPLC. In RPHPLC the most common column packing material consists of C_{18} or octadecylsilane (ODS). A chemically bonded stationary phase is shown in Fig. 52.19. However, some of the surface silanol

HPLC is a versatile form of chromatography, used with a wide variety of stationary and mobile phases, to separate individual compounds of a particular class of molecules on the basis of size, polarity, solubility or adsorption characteristics.

Preparing samples for HPLC – filter all samples through either a 0.2 μm or a 0.45 μm filter prior to injection.

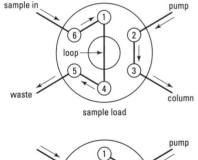

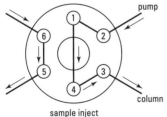

Fig. 52.17 Schematic diagram of a rotary valve.

Always use the highest purity solvents.

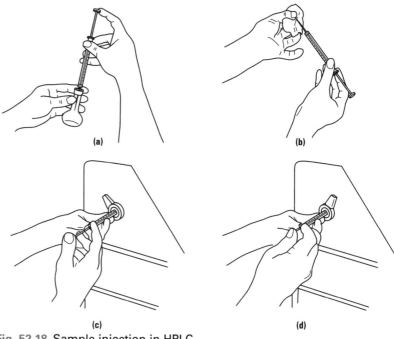

Fig. 52.18 **Sample injection in HPLC.**

ODS bonded group

end-capped silanol

untreated silanol

Fig. 52.19 **A C$_{18}$ stationary phase.**

SAFETY NOTE Always dispose of organic solvent waste in accordance with laboratory procedure (never down the sink).

Using silica-based HPLC columns – these are limited to a pH range of 2–8 (preferably 3–7). At low pH the bonded phase may be removed; at high pH the silica particles may be dissolved.

UV cutoff for organic solvents:

Hexane	195 nm
Acetonitrile	190 nm
Methanol	205 nm
Water	190 nm

groups remain unaffected. These unreacted groups lead to undesirable chromatographic effects, such as peak tailing (p. 367). One approach to remove the unreacted silanol groups is end capping. In this way, the silanol group is reacted with a small silylating group, e.g. trimethyl-chlorosilane. An alternative approach to nullify the action of the silanol groups is to add triethylamine to the mobile phase, which modifies the silica surface while in use.

HPLC detectors

Most HPLC systems are linked to a continuous monitoring detector of high sensitivity, for example phenols may be detected spectrophoto-metrically by monitoring the absorbance of the eluent at 280 nm as it passes through a flow cell. Other detectors can be used to measure changes in fluorescence, current or potential, as described below. Most detection systems are non-destructive, which means that you can collect eluent with an automatic fraction collector for further study.

UV/visible detectors (see also Chapter 48) are widely used and have the advantages of versatility, sensitivity and stability. Such detectors are of two types: fixed wavelength and variable wavelength. Fixed-wavelength detectors are simple to use, with low operating costs. They usually contain a mercury lamp as a light source, emitting at several wavelengths between 254 nm and 578 nm; a particular wavelength is selected using suitable cutoff filters. The most frequently used wavelengths for analysis of organic molecules are 254 nm and 280 nm. Variable wavelength detectors use a deuterium lamp and a continuously adjustable monochromator for wavelengths of 190–600 nm. For both types of detector, sensitivity is in the absorbance range 0.001–1.0 (down to $\approx$1 ng), with noise levels as low as 4×10^{-5}. Note that sensitivity is

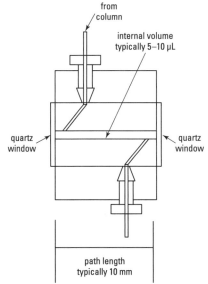

Fig. 52.20 UV detector cell for HPLC.

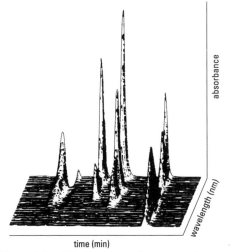

Fig. 52.21 Diode array detector absorption spectra of the eluent from an HPLC separation of a mixture of four steroids, taken every 15 seconds.

Overcoming interference with fluorescence detectors – use a dual flow cell to offset background fluorescence due to components of the mobile phase.

Maximising sensitivity with fluorescence detectors – the concentration of other sample components, e.g. pigments, must not be so high that they cause quenching of fluorescence.

partly influenced by the path length of the flow cell, typically 10 mm (see Fig. 52.20). Monitoring at short-wavelength UV (e.g. below 240 nm) may give increased sensitivity but decreased specificity, since many organic molecules absorb in this range. Additional problems with short-wavelength UV detection include instrument instability, giving a variable base line, and absorption by components of the mobile phase (e.g. organic solvents, which often absorb at <210 nm).

An important development in chromatographic monitoring is diode array detection (DAD). The incident light comprises the whole spectrum of light from the source, which is passed through a diffraction grating and the diffracted light detected by an array of photodiodes. Typical DAD can measure the absorbance of each sample component at 1–10 nm intervals over the range 190–600 nm. This gives an absorbance spectrum for each eluting substance which may be used to identify the compound and give some indication as to its purity. An example of a three-dimensional diode array spectrum is shown in Fig. 52.21.

Many aromatic organic molecules, including some polycyclic aromatic hydrocarbons, show natural fluorescence, or can be made to fluoresce by pre-column or post-column derivatisation with a fluorophore. Fluorescence detection is more sensitive than UV/visible detection, and may allow analysis in the picogram (10^{-12} g) range. A fluorescence detector consists of a light source (e.g. a xenon lamp), a diffraction grating to supply light at the excitation wavelength, and a photomultiplier to monitor the emitted light (usually arranged to be at right angles to the excitation beam). The use of instruments with a laser light source can give an extremely narrow excitation waveband, and increased sensitivity and specificity.

Electrochemical detectors offer very high sensitivity and specificity, with the possibility of detection of femtogram amounts of electroactive compounds such as catecholamines, vitamins, thiols, purines, ascorbate and uric acid. The two main types of detector, amperometric and coulometric, operate on similar principles, i.e. by measuring the change in current or potential as sample components pass between two electrodes within the flow cell. One of these electrodes acts as a reference (or counter) electrode (e.g. calomel electrode), while the other – the working electrode – is held at a voltage that is high enough to cause either oxidation or reduction of sample molecules. In the oxidative mode, the working electrode is usually glassy carbon, while in reductive mode a mercury electrode is used. In either case, a current flow between the electrodes is induced and detected.

Mass spectrometry (p. 460) used in conjunction with chromatographic methods can provide a powerful tool for identifying the components of complex mixtures (e.g. pharmaceuticals). One drawback is the limited capacity of the mass spectrometer – due to its vacuum requirements – compared with the volume of material leaving the chromatography column. Similarly, in HPLC, devices have been developed for solving the problem of large solvent volumes, for example by splitting the eluent from the column so only a small fraction reaches the mass spectrometer.

The computer-generated outputs from the mass spectrometer are similar to chromatograms obtained from other methods, and show peaks corresponding to the elution of particular components. However, it is then possible to select an individual peak and obtain a mass spectrum for the component in that peak to aid in its identification (p. 463). This has helped to identify hundreds of components present in a single sample, including flavour molecules in food, drug metabolites and water pollutants.

Recording and interpreting chromatograms

For analytical purposes, the detector output is usually connected to a computer-based data acquisition and analysis system. This consists of a personal computer (PC) with data acquisition hardware to convert an analogue detector signal to digital format, plus software to control the data acquisition process, store the signal information and display the resulting chromatogram. The software will also detect peaks and calculate their retention times and sizes (areas) for quantitative analysis. The software often incorporates functions to control the chromatographic equipment, enabling automatic operation. In sophisticated systems, the detector output may be compared with that from a 'library' of chromatograms for known compounds, to suggest possible identities of unknown sample peaks.

In simpler chromatographic systems, you may need to use a chart recorder for detector output. Two important settings must be considered before using a chart recorder:

1. The base-line reading – this should be set only after a suitable quantity of mobile phase has passed through the column (prior to injection of the sample) and stability is established. The chart recorder is usually set a little above the edge of the chart paper grid, to allow for base-line drift.

2. The detector range – this must be set to ensure that the largest peaks do not go off the top of the chart. Adjustment may be based on the expected quantity of analyte, or by a trial-and-error process. Use the maximum sensitivity that gives intact peaks. If peaks are still too large on the minimum sensitivity, you may need to reduce the amount of sample used, or prepare and analyse a diluted sample.

Interpreting chromatograms

Make sure you know the direction of the horizontal axis of the chromatogram (usually, either volume or time) – it may run from right to left or vice versa – and make a note of the detector sensitivity on the vertical axis. Ideally, the base line should be 'flat' between peaks, but it may drift up or down owing to a number of factors including:

- changes in the composition of the mobile phase (e.g. in gradient elution);

- tailing of material from previous peaks;

- carry-over of material from previous samples; this can be avoided by efficient cleaning of columns between runs – allow sufficient time for the previous sample to pass through the column before you introduce the next sample;

- loss of the stationary phase from the column (column 'bleed'), caused by extreme elution conditions;

Optimising electrochemical detection – the mobile phase must be free of any compounds that might give a response; all constituents must be of the highest purity.

Interpreting chromatograms – never assume that a single peak is a guarantee of purity: there may be more than one compound with the same chromatographic characteristics.

Problems with peaks – non-symmetrical peaks may result from column overloading, co-elution of solutes, poor packing of the stationary phase, or interactions between the substance and the support material.

Avoiding problems with air bubbles in liquid chromatography – always ensure that buffers are effectively degassed by vacuum treatment before use, and regularly clean the flow cell of the detector.

Degassing your mobile phase solvent – this is an important step and the best approach is to prepare the solvent composition (e.g. 50 : 50 v/v methanol : water, for isocratic RPHPLC) and then filter through a 0.22 μm porosity filter using a Büchner flask arrangement.

- air bubbles (in liquid chromatography); if the buffers used in the mobile phase are not effectively degassed, air bubbles may build up in the flow cell of the detector, leading to a gradual upward drift of the base line, followed by a sharp fall when the accumulated air is released. Small air bubbles that do not become trapped may give spurious small peaks as they pass through the detector.

A peak close to the origin may be due to non-retained sample molecules, flowing at the same rate as the mobile phase, or to artefacts, for example air (GC) or solvent (HPLC) in the sample. Whatever its origin, this peak can be used to measure the void volume and dead time of the column (p. 366). No peaks from genuine sample components should appear before this type of peak.

Peaks can be denoted on the basis of their elution volume (used mainly in liquid chromatography) or their retention times (mainly in GC). If the peaks are not narrow and symmetrical, they may contain more than one component. Where peaks are more curved on the trailing side compared with the leading side (peak tailing, p. 367), this may indicate too great an association between the component and the stationary phase, or overloading of the column.

Optimising chromatographic separations

In an ideal chromatographic analysis the sample molecules will be completely separated, and detection of components will result in a series of discrete individual peaks corresponding to each type of molecule. However, to minimise the possibility of overlapping peaks, or of peaks composed of more than one substance, it is important to maximise the separation efficiency of the technique, which depends on:

- the selectivity, as measured by the relative retention times of the two components (p. 366), or by the volume of the mobile phase between the peak maxima of the two components after they have passed through the column; this depends on the ability of the chromatographic method to separate two components with similar properties;

- the band-broadening properties of the chromatographic system, which influence the width of the peaks; these are mainly due to the effects of diffusion.

The resolution of two adjacent components can be defined in terms of k', α and N, using eqn [51.8]. In practical terms, good resolution is achieved when there is a large 'distance' (either time or volume) between peak maxima, and the peaks are as narrow as possible. The resolution of components is also affected by the relative amount of each substance: for systems showing low resolution, it can be difficult to resolve small amounts of a particular component in the presence of larger amounts of a second component. If you cannot obtain the desired results from a poorly resolved chromatogram, other chromatographic conditions, or even different methods, should be tried in an attempt to improve resolution. For liquid chromatography, changes in the following factors may improve resolution:

- Stationary-phase particle size – the smaller the particle, the greater the area available for partitioning between the mobile phase and the stationary phase. This partly accounts for the high resolution observed with HPLC compared with low-pressure methods.

- The slope of the salt gradient in eluting IEC columns (e.g. using computer-controlled adapted gradients).

- In low-pressure liquid chromatography, the flow rate of the mobile phase must be optimised because this influences two band-broadening effects which are dependent on diffusion of sample molecules: (i) the flow rate must be slow enough to allow effective partitioning between the mobile phase and the stationary phase: and (ii) it must be fast enough to ensure that there is minimal diffusion along the column once the molecules have been separated. To allow for these opposing influences, a compromise flow rate must be used.

- If you prepare your own columns, they must be packed correctly, with no channels present that might result in uneven flow and eddy diffusion.

Quantitative analysis

Most detectors and chemical assay systems give a linear response with increasing amounts of the test substance over a given 'working range'. Alternative ways of converting the measured response to an amount of substance are:

- External standardisation: this is applicable where the sample volume is sufficiently precise to give reproducible results (e.g. HPLC). You measure the peak areas (or heights) of known amounts of the substance to give a calibration factor or calibration curve (Chapter 47) which can be used to calculate the amount of test substance in the sample.

- Internal standardisation: where you add a known amount of a reference substance (not originally present in the sample) to the sample, to give an additional peak in the elution profile. You determine the response of the detector to the test and reference substances by analysing a standard containing known amounts of both substances, to provide a response factor (r), where:

$$r = \frac{\text{peak area (or height) of test substance}}{\text{peak area (or height) of reference substance}} \qquad [52.5]$$

Use this response factor to quantify the amount of test substance (Q_t) in a sample containing a known amount of the reference substance (Q_r), from the relationship:

$$Q_t = \frac{[\text{peak area (or height) of test substance}]}{[\text{peak area (or height) of reference substance}]} \times \frac{Q_r}{r} \qquad [52.6]$$

Internal standardisation should be the method of choice wherever possible, since it is unaffected by small variations in sample volume (e.g. for GC microsyringe injection). The internal standard should be chemically similar to the test substance(s) and must give a peak that is distinct from all other substances in the sample. An additional

---

Quantifying molecules – note that quantitative analysis often requires assumptions about the identity of separated components and that further techniques may be required to provide information about the nature of the molecules present, e.g. mass spectrometry (see Chapter 58).

When using external standardisation – samples and standards should be analysed more than once, to confirm the reproducibility of the technique.

When using an internal standard, you should add an internal standard to the sample at the first stage in the extraction procedure, so that any loss or degradation of test substance during purification is accompanied by an equivalent change in the internal standard, as long as the extraction characteristics of the internal standard and the test substance are very similar.

advantage of an internal standard which is chemically related to the test substance is that it may show up problems due to changes in detector response, incomplete derivatisation, etc. A disadvantage is that it may be difficult to fit an internal standard peak into a complex chromatogram.

Sample preparation for chromatography

The preparation of a sample for subsequent chromatographic analysis is critical to the chemist. Often the key steps in the sample preparation are to ensure that the sample acquired is

- not mislaid or lost,

- converted to a form that is suitable for subsequent chromatographic analysis,

- not contaminated.

Sample preparation is also used for removal of target analyte(s) from a sample matrix, and for their pre-concentration prior to chromatographic analysis.

A range of analytical procedures can be used depending upon whether the sample can be classified as either solid (or semi-solid) or an aqueous solution. In either situation, a range of sample preparation techniques can be used.

Preparation of solid (or semi-solid) samples

The most common approach for recovery of analytes from solid (or semi-solid) samples is Soxhlet extraction (see p. 253 and Fig. 33.5). In addition, several modern techniques can be used, including supercritical fluid extraction, microwave-assisted extraction and pressurised fluid extraction (also known by its trade name of accelerated solvent extraction). These instrumental techniques rely on the use of heat, pressure and solvents to extract organic compounds from solid or semi-solid samples. Supercritical fluid extraction (SFE) exploits the gas-like and liquid-like properties of a supercritical fluid, typically CO_2, to extract organic compounds at temperatures above 31.1 °C at a pressure of 74.8 atm (1070.4 psi). By using combinations of CO_2 mixed with an organic modifier (e.g. methanol), it is possible to extract a range of organic molecules of different polarity. Instrumentally, the system consists of a source of CO_2, which is pumped (after cooling of the pump head) to the extraction cell. A second pump can be added for the organic modifier. The extraction cell is located in an oven while pressure is generated in the system via a back-pressure regulator (Fig. 52.22). Typically, samples are extracted for 10–60 min, depending on the organic compounds present and the temperature and pressure conditions selected, and collected ready for analysis. A procedure for the SFE of organic compounds is described in Box 52.5.

In pressurised microwave-assisted extraction (MAE), an organic solvent and the sample are subjected to radiation from the microwave source (i.e. the magnetron) in a sealed vessel (Fig. 52.23). The sample and solvent are placed into an inert vessel liner (100 mL) made from a

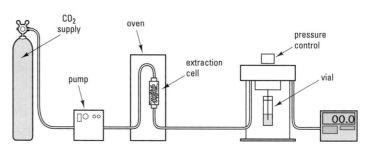

Fig. 52.22 Schematic diagram of a supercritical fluid extraction system.

fluoropolymer and subject to heating for a period of time (thereby resulting in the build up of pressure). In the event of an extraction cell reaching critical conditions, an automatic system allows venting of excess pressure. If any solvent leaks from an extraction vessel a solvent monitoring system will automatically shut off the magnetron but leave the exhaust fan to continue working. Most systems allow up to 14 samples to be extracted simultaneously. A procedure for the extraction of organic compounds by MAE is described in Box 52.6.

Pressurised fluid extraction, available commercially as accelerated solvent extraction, ASE^{TM}, is an automated system capable of processing up to 24 samples sequentially (Fig. 52.24). Each sample is placed in an extraction cell and loaded on a carousel. After setting the extraction conditions, typically a temperature of 100 °C and a pressure of 2000 psi for an extraction time of 10 min, organic solvent is introduced into the extraction cell. Upon completion the extract is collected in a vial (a flow of nitrogen gas is used to remove trace amounts of solvent) and analysed.

Box 52.5 How to operate a typical supercritical fluid extraction system

1. **Turn on the electrical supply** of the SFE system including recirculating water bath. Allow 30 mins for cooling of the CO_2 pump head.

2. **Take an extraction cell and tighten an end cap on one end only** using a wrench and then weigh the cell. Ensure the extraction cell is suitable for its purpose, i.e. able to withstand high pressure and does not leak.

3. **Fill the extraction cell with the sample** mixed 50 : 50 with an inert matrix (e.g. Celite^{TM}), and weigh the cell again.

4. **Tighten the other end cap onto the cell** with the wrench and insert into the oven of the SFE system. This requires the use of a wrench to ensure a suitable connection.

5. **Connect a glass collection vial containing 2 ml of methanol to the outlet** of the back-pressure regulator fitted with a C18 SPE cartridge (p. 395).

6. **Set the SFE operating parameters**: flow rate of liquid CO_2, 2 mL min^{-1} and methanol, 0.2 mL min^{-1}; oven temperature, 60 °C; and, pressure, 250 kg cm^2. Before the extraction commences, pre-heat the extraction cell containing the sample to the pre-set temperature for 10 min, then undergo a static extraction (no flow of CO_2) at the operating conditions for 5 min and finally a dynamic extraction (flow of CO_2 and methanol) for one hour.

7. **Remove the collection vial from the system after the allotted extraction time,** and back-flush the C18 SPE cartridge with fresh methanol (2 mL).

8. **Carefully transfer extract to a volumetric flask.** Ensure all extract is transferred by washing the collection vial with small quantities of solvent.

9. **Analyse the extract using an appropriate technique,** for example gas chromatography.

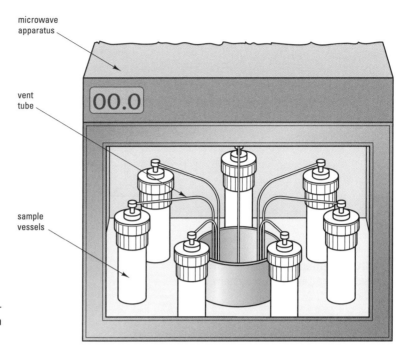

microwave
apparatus

vent
tube

00.0

sample
vessels

Fig. 52.23 Schematic diagram of a pressurised microwave-assisted extraction system.

A procedure for the extraction of organic compounds by ASE™ is described in Box 52.7.

Preparation of aqueous samples

Centrifugation

One of the simplest forms of sample preparation for aqueous samples containing particulates is centrifugation. Particles suspended in a liquid will move at a rate that depends on:

- the applied force – particles in a liquid within a gravitational field (e.g. a stationary test tube) will move in response to the earth's gravity;

Box 52.6 How to operate a typical pressurised microwave-assisted extraction (MAE) system

1. **Take an extraction cell** and then weigh the cell.

2. **Fill each extraction cell with sample**, approximately 2 g, and weigh the cell again.

3. **Add 20–50 mL of organic solvent to each sample.** Typical solvents include dichloromethane, acetone and methanol. Non-polar solvents (e.g. hexane) can be used by mixing them with polar solvents.

4. **Tighten the end cap on to the cell and insert into the microwave oven of the MAE system.** All extraction cells are mounted in a carousel.

5. **Set the MAE operating parameters**: temperature, 200 °C; pressure, 250 psi; extraction time, 10 min. Typically, pressure is continuously measured during

the extraction, while temperature is monitored for all cells every 7 s.

6. **After the allotted extraction time,** remove all the extraction cells on the carousel and allow to cool for approximately 30 min before attempting to open them.

7. **Filter each extract** to remove the sample matrix from the organic solvent containing solvent.

8. **Carefully transfer extract to a volumetric flask.** Ensure that all extract is transferred by washing the collection vial with small quantities of solvent.

9. **Analyse the extract** using an appropriate technique, for example gas chromatography.

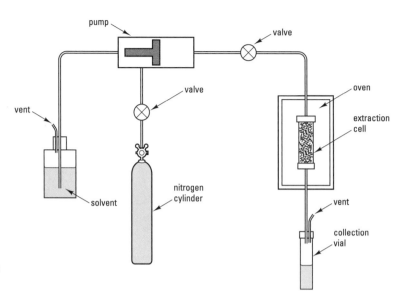

Fig. 52.24 Schematic diagram of an accelerated solvent extraction system.

- the density difference between the particles and the liquid – particles less dense than the liquid will float upwards while particles denser than the liquid will sink;

- the size and shape of the particles;

- the viscosity of the medium.

For most particles (cells, organelles soil or molecules) the rate of flotation or sedimentation in response to the earth's gravity is too slow to be of practical use in separation.

Box 52.7 How to operate a typical pressurised fluid extraction (PFE) system

1. **Ensure the system is connected to the electrical supply** and is ready for operation with a nitrogen supply and organic solvent. Ensure collection vials are in place.

2. **Take an extraction cell** and finger tighten an end cap on one end only and then weigh the cell.

3. **Fill the extraction cell with the sample,** 2–10 g, mixed 50 : 50 with an inert matrix (e.g. Celite™) and weigh the cell again.

4. **Finger tighten the other end cap on to the cell and place in carousel** and start the extraction programme.

5. **Typical PFE operating parameters** are temperature, 100 °C; pressure, 2000 psi; extraction time, 10 min.

6. **After the allotted extraction time,** remove the extract containing collection vial.

7. **Carefully transfer extract to a volumetric flask.** Ensure that all extract is transferred by washing the collection vial with small quantities of solvent.

8. **Analyse the extract** using an appropriate technique, for example gas chromatography.

Working in SI units – to convert RCF to acceleration in SI units, multiply by 9.80 m s^{-2}.

Examples Suppose you wanted to calculate the RCF of a bench centrifuge with a rotor of $r_{av} = 95$ mm running at a speed of 3000 r.p.m. Using eqn [52.7] the RCF would be: $1.118 \times 95 \times (3)^2 = 956$ g.

You might wish to calculate the speed (r.p.m.) required to produce a relative centrifugal field of 2000 g using a rotor of $r_{av} = 85$ mm. Using eqn [52.8] the speed would be: $945.7 \sqrt{(2000 \div 85)} = 4587$ r.p.m.

How to calculate centrifugal acceleration

The acceleration of a centrifuge is usually expressed as a multiple of the acceleration due to gravity ($g = 9.80$ m s^{-2}), termed the relative centrifugal field (RCF, or 'g value'). The RCF depends on the speed of the rotor (n, in revolutions per minute, r.p.m.) and the radius of rotation (r, in mm) where:

$$\text{RCF} = 1.118r\left(\frac{n}{1000}\right)^2 \qquad [52.7]$$

This relationship can be rearranged, to calculate the speed (r.p.m.) for specific values of r and RCF:

$$n = 945.7 \sqrt{\left(\frac{\text{RCF}}{r}\right)} \qquad [52.8]$$

However, you should note that RCF is not uniform within a centrifuge tube: it is highest near the outside of the rotor (r_{max}) and lowest near the central axis (r_{min}). In practice, it is customary to report the RCF calculated from the average radius of rotation (r_{av}), as shown in Fig. 52.26. It is also worth noting that RCF varies as a *squared* function of the speed: thus the RCF will be doubled by an increase in speed of approximately 41% (Table 52.2).

Types of centrifuge and their uses

Low-speed centrifuges

These are bench-top instruments for routine use, with a maximum speed of 3000–6000 r.p.m. and RCF up to 6000 g (Fig. 52.25). Most modern machines also have a sensor that detects any imbalance when the rotor is spinning and cuts off the power supply (Fig. 52.25). However, some of the older models do not, and must be switched off as soon as any vibration is noticed, to prevent damage to the rotor or harm to the operator.

Microcentrifuges (microfuges)

These are bench-top machines, capable of rapid acceleration up to 12 000 r.p.m. and 10 000 g. They are used to sediment small sample volumes (up to 1.5 mL) of larger particles (e.g. precipitates) over short time-scales

Table 52.2 Relationship between speed (r.p.m.) and acceleration (relative centrifugal field, RCF) for a typical bench centrifuge with an average radius of rotation, $r_{av} = 115$ mm

r.p.m.	RCF*
500	30
1000	130
1500	290
2000	510
2500	800
3000	1160
3500	1570
4000	2060
4500	2600
5000	3210
5500	3890
6000	4630

* RCF values rounded to nearest 10.

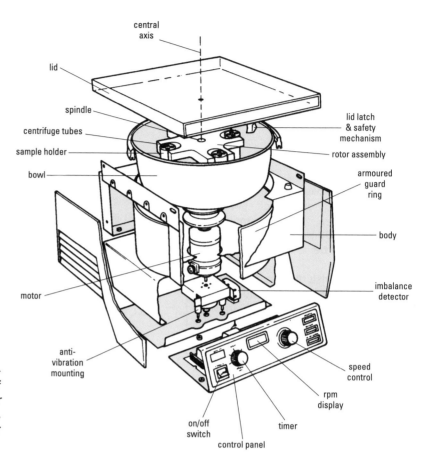

central axis

lid

spindle

centrifuge tubes

sample holder

bowl

motor

anti-vibration mounting

lid latch & safety mechanism

rotor assembly

armoured guard ring

body

imbalance detector

speed control

rpm display

on/off switch

timer

control panel

Fig. 52.25 Principal components of a low-speed bench centrifuge, from diagram of low-speed centrifuge *model MSE Centaur 2*, supplied by Fisher Scientific UK Ltd, reproduced by kind permission of Fisher Scientific UK Ltd.

(typically, 0.5–15 min). Box 52.8 gives details of operation for a low-speed centrifuge.

Rotors

Many centrifuges can be used with tubes of different size and capacity, either by changing the rotor, or by using a single rotor with different buckets/adaptors.

- Swing-out rotors: sample tubes are placed in buckets which pivot as the rotor accelerates (Fig. 52.26(a)). Swing-out rotors are used on many low-speed centrifuges: their major drawback is their extended path length and the resuspension of pellets due to currents created during deceleration.

- Fixed-angle rotors: used in many high-speed centrifuges and microcentrifuges (Fig. 52.26(b)). With their shorter path length, fixed rotors are more effective at pelleting particles than swing-out rotors.

- Vertical tube rotors: used for isopycnic density gradient centrifugation in high-speed centrifuges and ultracentrifuges (Fig. 52.26(c)). They cannot be used to harvest particles in suspension as a pellet is not formed.

Changing a rotor – if you ever have to change a rotor, make sure that you carry it properly (don't knock/drop it), that you fit it correctly (don't cross-thread it, and tighten to the correct setting using a torque wrench) and that you store it correctly (clean it after use and don't leave it lying around).

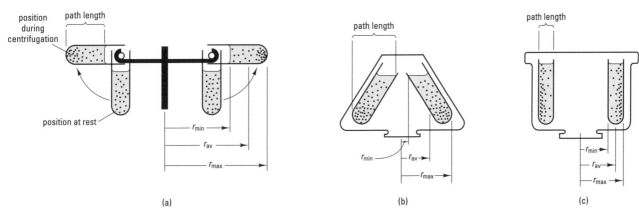

Fig. 52.26 Rotors: (a) swing-out rotor; (b) fixed angle rotor; (c) vertical tube rotor.

Box 52.8 How to use a low-speed bench centrifuge

1. **Choose the appropriate tube size and material for your application**, with caps where necessary. Most low-speed machines have four-place or six-place rotors – use the correct number of samples to *fill* the rotor assembly whenever possible.

2. **Fill the containers to the appropriate level**: do not overfill, or the sample may spill during centrifugation.

3. **It is vital that the rotor is balanced during use.** Therefore, *identical* tubes must be prepared, to be placed opposite each other in the rotor assembly. This is particularly important for density gradient samples, or for samples containing materials of widely differing densities (e.g. soil samples) since the density profile of the tube will change during a run. However, for low-speed work using small amounts of particulate matter in aqueous solution, it is sufficient to counterbalance a sample with a second tube filled with water, or a saline solution of similar density to the sample.

4. **Balance each pair of sample tubes** (plus the corresponding caps, where necessary) to within 0.1 g using a top-pan balance; add liquid dropwise to the lighter tube, until the desired weight is reached. Alternatively, use a set of scales. For small sample volumes (up to 10 mL) added to disposable, lightweight plastic tubes, accurate pipetting of your solution may be sufficient for low-speed use.

5. **For centrifuges with swing-out rotors,** check that each holder/bucket is correctly positioned in its locating slots on the rotor and that it is able to swing freely. All buckets must be in position on a swing-out rotor, even if they do not contain sample tubes – buckets are an integral part of the rotor assembly.

6. **Load the sample tubes into the centrifuge.** Make sure that the outside of the centrifuge tubes, the sample holders and sample chambers are dry: any liquid present will cause an imbalance during centrifugation, in addition to the corrosive damage it may cause to the rotor. For sample holders where rubber cushions are provided, make sure that these are correctly located. Balanced tubes must be placed opposite each other – use a simple code if necessary, to prevent mix-ups.

7. **Bring the centrifuge up to operating speed** by gentle acceleration. Do not exceed the maximum speed for the rotor and tubes used.

8. **If the centrifuge vibrates at any time during use, switch off** and find the source of the problem.

9. **Once the rotor has stopped spinning, release the lid and remove all tubes.** If any sample has spilled, make sure you clean it up thoroughly using a non-corrosive disinfectant (e.g. Virkon®) so that it is ready for the next user.

10. **Close the lid (to prevent the entry of dust) and return all controls to zero.**

Centrifuge tubes

These are manufactured in a range of sizes (from 1.5 mL up to 1000 mL) and materials. The following aspects may influence your choice:

- Capacity. This is obviously governed by the volume of your sample. Note that centrifuge tubes must be completely full for certain applications (e.g. for high-speed work).

- Shape. Conical-bottomed centrifuge tubes retain pellets more effectively than round-bottomed tubes, while the latter may be more useful for density gradient work.

- Maximum centrifugal force. Detailed information is supplied by the manufacturers. Standard Pyrex® glass tubes can only be used at low centrifugal force (up to 2000 g).

- Solvent resistance. Glass tubes are inert, polycarbonate tubes are particularly sensitive to organic solvents (e.g. ethanol, acetone), while polypropylene tubes are more resistant. See manufacturer's guidelines for detailed information.

- Sterilisation. Disposable plastic centrifuge tubes are often supplied in sterile form. Glass and polypropylene tubes can be repeatedly sterilised. Cellulose ester tubes should *not* be autoclaved. Repeated autoclaving of polycarbonate tubes may lead to cracking/stress damage.

- Opacity. Glass and polycarbonate tubes are clear, while polypropylene tubes are more opaque.

- Ability to be pierced. If you intend to harvest your sample by puncturing the tube wall, cellulose acetate and polypropylene tubes are readily punctured using a syringe needle.

- Caps. Most fixed-angle and vertical tube rotors require tubes to be capped, to prevent leakage during use and to provide support to the tube during centrifugation. For low-speed centrifugation, caps must be used for any hazardous samples. Make sure you use the correct caps for your tubes.

Balancing the rotor

For the safe use of centrifuges, the rotor must be balanced during use, or the spindle and rotor assembly may be damaged permanently; in severe cases, the rotor may fail and cause a serious accident.

> **KEY POINT** It is vital that you balance your loaded centrifuge tubes before use. As a general rule, balance all sample tubes to within 1% or better, using a top-pan balance or scales. Place balanced tubes opposite each other.

Safe practice

Given their speed of rotation and the extremely high forces generated, centrifuges have the potential to be extremely dangerous, if used

Balancing tubes – never balance centrifuge tubes 'by eye' – use a balance. Note that a 35 mL tube full of liquid at an RCF of 3000 g has an effective weight greater than a large adult man.

incorrectly. For safety reasons, all centrifuges are manufactured with an armoured casing that should contain any fragments in cases of rotor failure. Machines usually have a safety lock to prevent the motor from being switched on unless the lid is closed and to stop the lid from being opened while the rotor is moving. Don't be tempted to use older machines without a safety lock, or centrifuges where the locking mechanism is damaged/inoperative. Be particularly careful to make sure that hair and clothing are kept well away from moving parts.

Solvent extraction

The most common approaches for preparing aqueous samples for chromatographic analysis involve solvent extraction. Typically, this is done using either liquid–liquid extraction (Chapter 33) or solid–liquid extraction. The most common form of solid–liquid extraction is solid phase extraction.

Solid phase extraction

Solid phase extraction (SPE) is a technique that can be used for clean-up and pre-concentration of aqueous samples. The aqueous sample is passed through a sorbent (typically the same material as the stationary phase in HPLC, see Chapter 52) via gravity or, more likely, with the aid of a vacuum. The sorbent is usually packed in to small tubes or cartridges (Fig. 52.27). The primary function of the sorbent is to retain the analyte(s) in the aqueous sample, but not to retain any extraneous material present. After this pre-concentration and/or clean-up step the analyte(s) are eluted from the sorbent and collected for subsequent analysis.

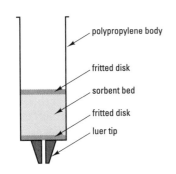

polypropylene body

fritted disk

sorbent bed

fritted disk

luer tip

Fig. 52.27 Solid phase extraction cartridge.

SPE cartridge

The most common arrangement for SPE is the syringe barrel or cartridge. The cartridge itself is usually made of polypropylene with a wide entrance, through which the sample is introduced, and a narrow exit (male luer tip). The sorbent material, ranging in mass from 50 mg to 10 g, is positioned between two frits, at the base (exit) of the cartridge and on top of the sorbent, which act to both retain the sorbent material and to filter out any particulate matter (Fig. 52.27).

Solvent flow through a single cartridge is typically done using a side-arm flask apparatus (Fig. 52.28), whereas multiple cartridges can be simultaneously processed (from 8 to 30 cartridges) using a vacuum manifold (Fig. 52.29). Recent advances in automation have allowed modified autosamplers (devices for sample manipulation) to be used to provide unattended operation of an SPE system with the potential to link the system to the analysis stage. The use of automated SPE allows more samples to be extracted (higher sample throughput) with better precision. In addition, it also allows the scientist to perform other tasks or prepare more samples for analysis.

Types of SPE media

Sorbents for SPE can be classified as normal phase, reversed phase or ion exchange. The most common sorbents are based on silica particles (see

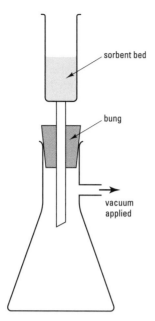

Fig. 52.28 Manifold for a single solid phase extraction cartridge.

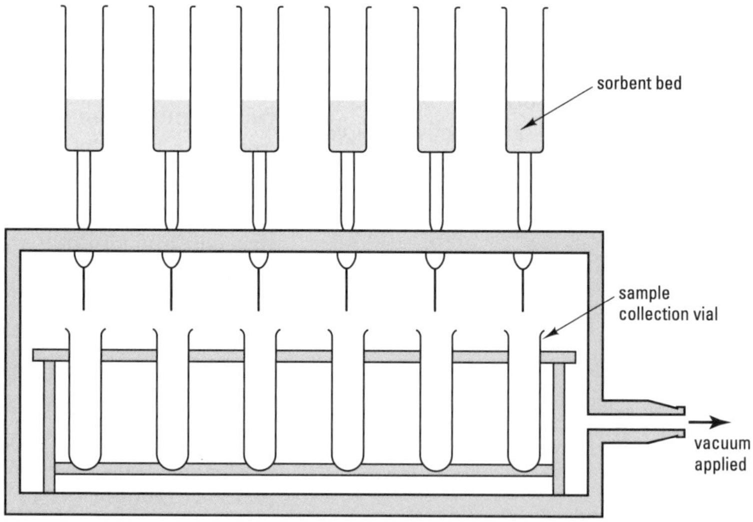

Fig. 52.29 Manifold for multiple solid phase extraction cartridges.

Reversed phase sorbents – these use non-polar sorbents and polar solvents while 'normal' phase sorbents use polar sorbents and non-polar solvents.

Chapter 52) to which functional groups are bonded to surface silanol groups to alter their retentive properties. In addition to silica, some other common sorbents are based on florisil, alumina and macroreticular polymers.

Normal phase sorbents have polar functional groups (e.g. cyano, amino and diol groups) and hence can retain polar analytes (e.g. drugs, phenols). In contrast, reversed phase sorbents have non-polar functional groups (e.g. octadecyl, octyl and methyl groups) and hence can retain non-polar compounds (e.g. polycyclic aromatic hydrocarbons). Ion-exchange sorbents have either cationic or anionic functional groups that attract compounds of the opposite charge in the ionised form. For example, a cation-exchange phase, such as benzenesulfonic acid, will extract an analyte with a net positive charge (e.g. a phenoxyacid herbicide).

Method of SPE operation

The mode of operation of SPE can be divided in to five steps (Box 52.9). Each step is characterised by the nature and type of solvent used which in turn is dependent upon the characteristics of the sorbent and the sample. The five steps are:

1. Wetting the sorbent

2. Conditioning the sorbent

3. Loading the sample

4. Rinsing or washing the sorbent to elute extraneous material

5. Eluting and collecting the analyte of interest.

Box 52.9 How to pre-concentrate a sample using a reversed phase C18 solid phase extraction (SPE) cartridge

1. **Place the SPE cartridge into a vacuum manifold.** Apply the vacuum at a flow rate of 5 mL min^{-1}.

2. **Wet the sorbent** by passing 1.0 mL of methanol or acetonitrile through the cartridge. This solvent will remove impurities from the C18 sorbent and wet its surface.

3. **Condition the sorbent** by passing 1 mL of water or buffer through the sorbent. Do not allow the sorbent to dry out before applying the sample.

4. **Add the sample to the sorbent** in a high-polarity solvent or buffer.

5. **Remove unwanted, extraneous material by washing** the sample-containing sorbent with a high-polarity solvent or buffer. This process may be repeated.

6. **Elute analytes from the cartridge** with a less polar solvent, for example methanol or the HPLC mobile phase (if this is the method of subsequent analysis).

7. **Carefully transfer extract to a volumetric flask.** Ensure that all extract is transferred by washing the collection vial with small quantities of solvent.

8. **Analyse the extract** using an appropriate technique, for example gas chromatography.

9. **Discard the SPE cartridge.**

The choice of solvents for SPE are obviously important in the overall success of this method. Further guidance on solvent selection is found on page 249. In practice, at the wetting stage a solvent is required that will 'activate' the sorbent whereas the conditioning sorbent is required to prepare the sorbent for the aqueous sample. Perhaps the most difficult solvent to select is the rinsing or washing solvent. In this step the function of the solvent is to remove any extraneous material but not the analyte(s) of interest. Finally, the choice of elution solvent is one that can both effectively remove the analyte(s) from the sorbent and can also be compatible with the method of analysis to be used. If the eluting solvent proves to be incompatible with the analytical technique of choice it is possible to carry out a solvent exchange. This can be done by evaporating the analyte(s) containing solvent to dryness, using a solvent evaporation technique (p. 271), and then to reconstitute the analyte(s) in a different solvent. This process can be problematical in that volatile analyte(s) can be lost due to evaporation: it is wise to evaluate the approach on a test sample first.

Solid phase microextraction (SPME)

Solid phase microextraction is a relatively new technique for the preparation of samples for chromatography. It uses a coated fused-silica fibre to retain organic compounds, i.e. to pre-concentrate them from the sample matrix, for example air, aqueous or solid. Desorption of organic compounds normally occurs in the hot injection port of a gas chromatograph (GC), although it is possible to use the mobile phase of a high-performance liquid chromatography (HPLC) system to desorb the organic compounds.

The SPME device consists of a fused silica fibre, coated with a stationary phase and mounted in a syringe-type holder (Fig. 52.30). The holder has two functions:

1. to provide protection for the fibre

2. to allow insertion into the hot environment of the GC injection port (or injection valve of an HPLC) using a needle.

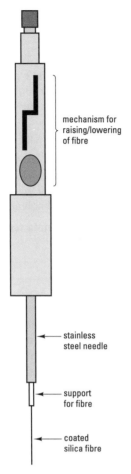

Fig. 52.30 Solid phase microextraction system.

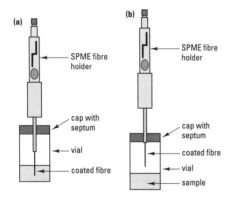

Fig. 52.31 Schematic diagrams representing the two approaches in which SPME can be used (a) direct SPME involving insertion of the fibre directly into the aqueous sample and (b) headspace SPME where the fibre is suspended above the sample.

As samples and standards are normally introduced into chromatographic systems using a syringe (p. 260) the use of an SPME device is straightforward.

When not in use the fused-silica coated fibre is retracted within the protective needle of the holder. In operation, the fibre (~1 cm long) is exposed to organic compounds within their matrix (air, aqueous, solid) for a specified time. SPME can be used in two ways (Fig. 52.31):

1. direct

2. headspace SPME.

In direct SPME the coated silica fibre is exposed to the sample matrix directly (e.g. blood plasma). A procedure for the analysis of an organic compound in aqueous solution by SPME is shown in Box 52.10. Improved response time and signal can be achieved by agitation of the sample vial, agitation of the fibre, and/or stirring or sonication of the sample solution. For gaseous samples, the natural convection of air is usually sufficient to aid diffusion of analyte(s) onto the SPME fibre. In headspace SPME, the process relies on the release of volatile compounds from the sample matrix. This may be achieved by heat, chemical modification or the inherent volatility of the organic compounds. A procedure for the analysis of an organic compound in the headspace above a sample or air by SPME is shown in Box 52.11. After sampling, the fibre is retracted within its holder for protection until inserted in the hot injector of the GC (or mobile phase of the HPLC); desorption of analytes occurs due to the influence of temperature in the case of GC or organic solvent in the case of HPLC.

> **KEY POINT** Prior to sampling, the silica-coated SPME fibre should be cleaned. This is done, for example, by exposing the fibre to the hot injection port of the GC. This is particularly important as the fibre can equally adsorb analytes from the atmosphere as well as the sample and in some cases the atmosphere may be the sample.

> **Box 52.10 How to concentrate a sample of an organic compound in an aqueous sample using direct solid phase microextraction (SPME)**
>
> 1. **Place the sample in a vial.**
>
> 2. **Clean the SPME fibre** by inserting it into the hot injection port (220 °C) of the GC.
>
> 3. **Expose the SPME fibre** to the aqueous sample. Agitate the sample solution by sonication for 10 min.
>
> 4. **Retract the fibre into the SPME holder.**
>
> 5. **Pierce the GC septum with the SPME needle** and then expose the silica-coated fibre to the hot temperature (220 °C) of the injection port for 5 min.
>
> 6. **Start the GC** isothermal or temperature programme for separation and analysis of the organic compounds.

Box 52.11 **How to concentrate a sample of an organic compound in an aqueous sample using headspace solid phase microextraction (SPME)**

1. **Place the sample in a septum-sealed vial.**

2. **Clean the SPME fibre** by inserting it into the hot injection port (220 °C) of the GC.

3. **Pierce the septum-sealed vial** with the needle of the SPME.

4. **Expose the fibre to the headspace above the aqueous sample** for 2 min. Gentle heating of the sample solution (40 °C) may be beneficial.

5. **Retract the fibre into the SPME holder.**

6. **Pierce the GC septum with the SPME needle** and then expose the fibre to the hot temperature (220 °C) of the injection port for 5 min.

7. **Start the GC** isothermal or temperature programme for separation and analysis of the organic compounds.

Purge and trap

A specialist form of sample preparation is used for volatile compounds in aqueous samples, for example BTEX in aqueous samples. The technique, called purge and trap, is widely used for the extraction of alcohol in blood samples and urine followed by gas chromatography. The method involves the introduction of an aqueous sample (e.g. 5 mL urine) into a glass sparging vessel (Fig. 52.32). The sample is then purged with (high purity) nitrogen at a specified flow rate and time. The extracted alcohol is then transferred to a trap (e.g. Tenax^{TM}) at ambient temperature. This is followed by the desorption step. In this step, the trap is rapidly heated to desorb the trapped alcohol in a narrow band. The desorbed alcohol is then transferred via a heated transfer line to the injector of a gas chromatograph for separation and detection.

Solvent evaporation

Often when the sample preparation step is complete additional steps are required prior to analysis. The most common approach at this stage is to remove the organic solvent. In all cases, the evaporation method is slow with a high risk of contamination from the solvent, glassware and any gas used (see Chapter 36).

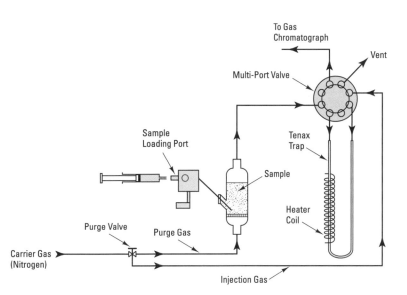

Fig. 52.32 Purge and trap system for the extraction of volatile compounds from aqueous samples.

Text references

Ardrey, R.E. (2003) *Liquid Chromatography – Mass Spectrometry: An Introduction.* Wiley, Chichester.

Barry, E.F. and Grob, R.L. (2007) *Columns for Gas Chromatography: Performance and Selection.* Wiley, Chichester.

Bertholf, R. and Winecker, R. (2007) *Chromatographic Separations in Clinical Chemistry and Toxicology.* Wiley, Chichester.

Bliesner, D.M. (2006) *Validating Chromatographic Methods: A Practical Guide.* Wiley, New York.

Cazes, J. (2005) *Encyclopedia of Chromatography.* CRC Press, Boca Raton.

Dean, J.R. (2010) *Extraction Techniques in Analytical Sciences.* Wiley, Chichester.

Errington, R.J. (1997) *Advanced Practical Inorganic and Metalorganic Chemistry.* Blackie Academic and Professional, London.

Furniss, B.A., Hannaford, A.J., Smith, P.W.G. and Tatchell, A.R. (1989) *Vogel's Textbook of Practical Organic Chemistry*, 5th edn. Longman, Harlow.

Grob, R.L. and Barry, E.F. (2004) *Modern Practice of Gas Chromatography*, 4th edn. Wiley, New York.

Harwood, L.M., Moody, C.J. and Percy, J.M. (2000) *Experimental Organic Chemistry*, 2nd edn. Blackwell Science Ltd, Oxford.

Kellner, R., Mermet, J.M., Otto, M., Valcarcel, M. and Widmer, H.M. (2004) *Analytical Chemistry: A Modern Approach to Analytical Science*, 2nd edn. Wiley, Chichester.
[Covers all modern analytical topics.]

Kromidas, S. (2000) *Practical Problem Solving in HPLC.* Wiley, Chichester.

McMaster, M. (2005) *LC-MS: A Practical User's Guide.* Wiley, New York.
[Covers principles and practice of HPLC systems and MS detectors.]

McMaster, M. (2008) *GC/MS: A Practical User's Guide*, 2nd edn. Wiley, Chichester.

McNair, H.M. and Miller, J.M. (2009) *Basic Gas Chromatography.* 2nd edn. Wiley, Chichester.

Meloan, C.E. (1999) *Chemical Separations: Principles, Techniques and Experiments.* Wiley, Chichester.

Meyer, V. (2010) *Practical High-Performance Liquid Chromatography*, 5th edn. Wiley, Chichester.

Miller, J.M. (2009) *Chromatography: Concepts and Contrasts*, 2nd edn. Wiley, New York.

Sadek, P.C. (2002) *The HPLC Solvent Guide*, 2nd edn. Wiley, Chichester.

Scott, R.P.W. (1996) *Chromatography Detectors: Design, Function and Operation.* Marcel Dekker, New York.

Snyder, L.R., Kirkland, J.J. and Dolan, J.W. (2009) *Introduction to Modern Liquid Chromatography.* Wiley, Chichester.

Subramanian, G. (2006) *Chiral Separation Techniques: A Practical Approach*, 3rd edn. Wiley, Chichester.

Sources for further study

Anon. *Flash Chromatography.* Available: http://www.siggy.che.ucla.edu/voh/136/ **Flash_Chromatography**.pdf
Last accessed 1/11/09
[Alternative procedure for flash chromatography.]

Anon. *Micro Flash Chromatography.* Available: http://www.orgchem.colorado.edu/.../ colchromprocmicroflash.html
Last accessed 1/11/09
[Details of very small scale flash chromatography.]

Harris, D.C. (1995) *Quantitative Chemical Analysis*, 4th edn. Freeman, New York.

Kellner, R. (1998) *Analytical Chemistry.* Wiley, Chichester.

Schwedt, G. (1997) *The Essential Guide to Analytical Chemistry.* Wiley, Chichester.

Skoog, D.A., West, D.M. and Holler, F.J. (1996) *Fundamentals of Analytical Chemistry*, 7th edn. Saunders, Orlando.

Study exercises

52.1 Calculate R_f values from a chromatogram. The figure represents the separation of three pigments by thin-layer chromatography.

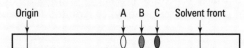

Origin   A B C   Solvent front

Thin-layer chromatographic separation of a mixture of three pigments (A, B and C).

What is the R_F value of each pigment?

Express your answers to 3 significant figures.

52.2 Test your knowledge of detector terminology. Explain what the following acronyms stand for:

(a) FID

(b) TCD

(c) ECD

(d) DAD.

52.3 Check your knowledge of liquid chromatography detectors. Make a list of the various major types of liquid chromatography detector in order, from highest to lowest sensitivity. Which of these methods is most versatile and why?

53 Electrophoresis

Definition

Electrophoretic mobility – the rate of migration of a particular type of molecule in response to an applied electrical field.

KEY POINT Electrophoresis is a separation technique based on the movement of charged molecules in an electric field. Dissimilar molecules move at different rates and the components of a mixture will be separated when an electric field is applied. It is a widely used technique, particularly for the analysis of complex mixtures or for the verification of purity (homogeneity) of isolated molecules.

Understanding electrophoresis – this is, in essence, an incomplete form of electrolysis, since the applied electrical field is switched off well before sample molecules reach the electrodes.

While electrophoresis is mostly used for the separation of charged macromolecules, techniques are available for high resolution separations of small molecules such as amino acids, anions and catecholamines (e.g. by capillary electrophoresis, p. 409).

The electrophoretic mobility of a charged molecule depends on:

- **Net charge** – negatively charged molecules (anions) migrate towards the anode (+), while positively charged molecules (cations) migrate towards the cathode (–); highly charged molecules move faster towards the electrode of opposite charge than those with lesser charge.

- **Size** – frictional resistance exerted on molecules moving in a solution means that smaller molecules migrate faster than large molecules.

- **Shape** – the effect of friction also means that the shape of the molecule will affect mobility, for example globular proteins compared with fibrous proteins.

- **Electrical field strength** – mobility increases with increasing field strength (voltage), but there are practical limitations to using high voltages, especially due to heating effects. It is expressed in terms of electrical potential difference per unit length, as Vm^{-1}.

The combined influence of net charge and size means that mobility (μ) is determined by the charge : density or the charge : mass ratio, according to the formula:

$$\mu = \frac{qE}{r} \qquad [53.1]$$

where q is the net charge on the molecule, r is the molecular radius and E is the field strength.

Electrophoresis and the separation of proteins

The net charge of a sample molecule determines its direction of movement and significantly affects its mobility. The net charge of a biological macromolecule is pH dependent and is determined by the relative numbers of positively and negatively charged groups at a given pH. The degree of ionisation of each group is pH dependent, resulting in a variation of net charge on the molecule at different pH values (Fig. 53.1). Thus, electrophoresis is always carried out at *constant* pH and a suitable buffer must be present along with the sample in order to maintain that pH. For example, if the proteins shown in Fig. 53.1 were subjected to electrophoresis at pH 9.0, and if the proteins were of similar size and shape, then the rate at which protein A (net charge, –3) migrates towards the anode would be faster than that for protein B (net charge, –1).

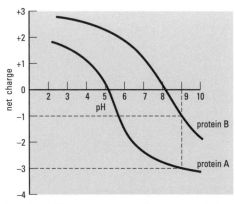

Fig. 53.1 Titration curves for two proteins, A and B, containing different proportions of acidic and basic amino acid residues.

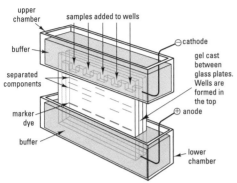

Fig. 53.2 Apparatus for vertical slab electrophoresis (components move downwards from wells, through the gel matrix).

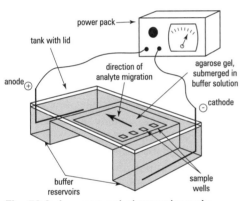

Fig. 53.3 Agarose gel electrophoresis.

Minimising diffusion – make the sample zone as narrow as possible, and fix and/or stain the bands as soon as possible after the run.

Definition

Ohm's law $V = IR$, where V = voltage, I = current and R = resistance.

Optimising electrophoresis – attempting to minimise heat production using very low currents is not practical, since it leads to long separation times and therefore to increased diffusion.

Separation of proteins is usually carried out at alkaline pH, where most proteins carry a net negative charge.

Ionisable groups in nucleic acids include the phosphate of the phosphodiester bond and the purine and pyrimidine bases. Most nucleic acid electrophoresis is carried out at alkaline pH values at which the negatively charged phosphate group predominates. Each nucleotide moiety of nucleic acids contributes one negatively charged phosphate group, so the charge : mass ratio for molecules of different sizes will be constant. Nucleic fragments of different sizes will migrate toward the anode, but separation can only be achieved by running the sample in a gel that is able to act as a 'molecular sieve'.

Basic apparatus

Most types of electrophoresis using a supporting medium (described below) are simple to carry out and the apparatus can be easily constructed, although inexpensive equipment is commercially available. High-resolution techniques such as 2D-electrophoresis and capillary electrophoresis require more sophisticated equipment, both for separation and analysis.

Simple electrophoretic separations can be performed either vertically (Fig. 53.2) or horizontally (Fig. 53.3). The electrodes are normally made of platinum wire, each in its own buffer compartment. In vertical electrophoresis, the buffer solution forms the electrical contact between the electrodes and the supporting medium in which the sample separation takes place. In horizontal electrophoresis electrical contact can be made by buffer-soaked paper 'wicks' dipping in the buffer reservoir and laid upon the supporting medium. The buffer reservoir normally contains a divider acting as a barrier to diffusion (but not to electrical current), so that localised pH changes which occur in the region of the electrodes (as a result of electrolysis) are not transmitted to the supporting medium or the sample. Individual samples are spotted onto a solid supporting medium containing buffer or are applied to 'wells' formed in the supporting medium. The power pack used for most types of electrophoresis should be capable of delivering ≈ 500 V and ≈ 100 mA.

Using a supporting medium

The effects of convection currents (resulting from the heating effect of the applied field) and the diffusion of molecules within the buffer solution can be minimised by carrying out the electrophoresis in a porous supporting medium. This contains buffer electrolytes and the sample is added in a discrete location or zone. When the electrical field is applied, individual sample molecules remain in sharp zones as they migrate at different rates. After separation, post-electrophoretic diffusion of selected molecules (e.g. proteins) can be avoided by 'fixing' them in position on the supporting medium, for example using trichloracetic acid (TCA).

The heat generated during electrophoresis is proportional to the square of the applied current and to the electrical resistance of the medium: even when a supporting medium is used, heat production will lead to zone broadening by increasing the rate of diffusion of sample components and buffer ions. Heat denaturation of sample proteins may also occur. Another problem is that heat will reduce buffer viscosity, leading to a decrease in resistance. If the electrophoresis is run at constant voltage, Ohm's law dictates that as resistance falls, the current will increase, leading to further heat production. This can be avoided by using a power pack that provides constant power. In practice, most electrophoresis equipment incorporates a cooling device; even so, distortions of an electrophoretic zone from the ideal 'sharp, linear band' can often be explained by inefficient heat dissipation.

Types of supporting medium

These can be subdivided into:

- Inert media – these provide physical support and minimise convection: separation is based on charge density only (e.g. cellulose acetate).

- Porous media – these introduce molecular sieving as an additional effect: their pore size is of the same order as the size of molecules being separated, restricting the movement of larger molecules relative to smaller ones. Thus, separation depends on both the charge density and the size of the molecule.

With some supporting media (e.g. cellulose acetate), a phenomenon called electro-endosmosis or electro-osmotic flow (EOF) occurs. This is due to the presence of negatively charged groups on the surface of the supporting medium, attracting cations in the electrophoresis buffer solution and creating an electrical double layer. The cations are hydrated (surrounded by water molecules) and when the electric field is applied, they are attracted towards the cathode, creating a flow of solvent that opposes the direction of migration of anionic biomolecules towards the anode. The EOF can be so great that weak anionic molecules (e.g. antibodies) may be carried towards the cathode.

Where necessary, EOF can be avoided by using supporting media such as agarose or polyacrylamide, but it is not always a hindrance to electrophoretic separation. Indeed, the phenomenon of EOF is used in the high resolution technique of capillary electrophoresis (p. 409).

Agarose

Agarose is the neutral, linear polysaccharide component of agar (from seaweed), consisting of repeating galactose and 3,6-anhydrogalactose subunits (Fig. 53.4). Powdered agarose is mixed with electrophoresis buffer at concentrations of 0.5–3.0% w/v, boiled until the mixture becomes clear, poured onto a glass plate, then allowed to cool until it forms a gel. Gelation is due to the formation of hydrogen bonds both between and within the agarose polymers, resulting in the formation of pores. The pore size depends on the agarose concentration. Low concentrations produce gels with large pores relative to the size of biological macromolecules, allowing them to migrate relatively unhindered through the gel, as determined by their individual charge densities. Low concentrations of agarose gel are suitable for techniques such as isoelectric focusing (p. 407), where charge is the main basis of separation. The smaller pores produced by higher concentrations of agarose may result in molecular sieving.

When agarose gels are used for the separation of DNA, the large fragment size means that molecular sieving is observed, even with low concentration gels. This is the basis of the electrophoretic separation of nucleic acids.

> **Definition**
>
> **Electro-osmotic flow** – the osmotically driven mass flow of water resulting from the movement of ions in an electrophoretic system.

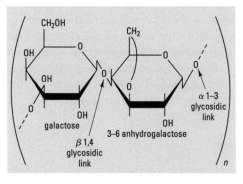

Fig. 53.4 Structure of agarose. Additional sulphate and pyruvyl groups are attached at selected hydroxyls in the polymer.

> **Advantages of polyacrylamide gels** – in addition to their versatility in terms of pore size, these gels are chemically inert, stable over a wide range of pH, ionic strength and temperature, and transparent.

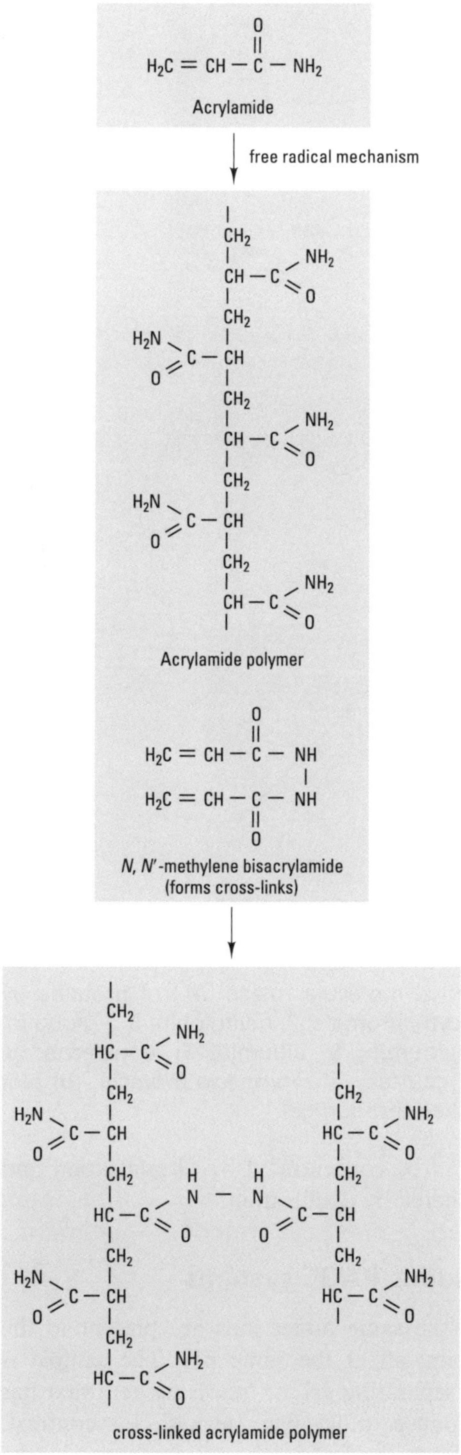

Fig. 53.5 Reactions involved in the formation of polyacrylamide gels.

Polyacrylamide

Polyacrylamide gel electrophoresis (PAGE) has a major role in protein analysis and in separation of smaller DNA fragments. The gel is formed by polymerising acrylamide monomer into long chains and cross-linking these chains using N,N',-methylene bisacrylamide (often abbreviated to 'bis'). The process is shown in Fig. 53.5. In most protocols, polymerisation is initiated by free radicals produced by ammonium persulphate in the presence of N,N,N',N'-tetramethylethylenediamine (TEMED). The photodecomposition of riboflavin can also be used as a source of free radicals.

The formation of polyacrylamide from its acrylamide monomers is extremely reproducible under standard conditions, and electrophoretic separations are correspondingly precise. The pore size, and hence the extent of molecular sieving, depends on the total concentration of monomer (% T), i.e. acrylamide plus bisacrylamide in a fixed ratio. This means that pores in the gel can be 'tailored' to suit the size of biomolecule to be separated: gels containing 3% acrylamide have large pores and are used in methods where molecular sieving should be avoided (e.g. in isoelectric focusing, p. 407), while higher concentrations of acrylamide (5–30% T) introduce molecular sieving to various degrees depending on the size of the sample components (e.g. with 30% acrylamide gels, molecules as small as M_r 2000 may be subject to molecular sieving). Gels of $< 2.5\%$ are necessary for molecular sieving of molecules of $M_r > 10^6$, but such gels are almost fluid and require 0.5% agarose to make them solid. Note that a gel of 3% will separate DNA by molecular sieving, due to the large size of the nucleic acid molecules.

SDS-polyacrylamide gel electrophoresis (SDS–PAGE)

The most widely used PAGE protein separation technique uses an ionic detergent, usually sodium dodecyl sulphate (SDS), which dissociates proteins into their individual polypeptide subunits and gives a uniform net charge along each denatured polypeptide. This technique, known as SDS--PAGE, requires only μg amounts of sample and is quick and easy to carry out. On the other hand, if it is necessary to preserve the native protein conformation and biological activity, non-dissociating conditions are used, i.e. no SDS is added. In SDS–PAGE the sample protein is normally heated to 100 °C for 2 min, in buffer containing 1% (w/v) SDS and 1% (w/v) 2-mercaptoethanol, the latter to cleave any disulphide bonds. The resultant polypeptides bind to SDS in a constant weight ratio, with 1.4 g of SDS per g of protein. As a result, the intrinsic net charge of each polypeptide is 'swamped' by the negative charge imposed by SDS, and there is a uniform negative charge per unit length of polypeptide. Since the polypeptides now have identical charge densities, when they are subject to PAGE (with SDS present) using a gel of appropriate pore size, molecular sieving will occur and they will migrate strictly according to polypeptide size. This not only gives effective separation, but the molecular mass of a given polypeptide can be determined by comparing its mobility to polypeptides of known molecular mass run under the same conditions (Fig. 53.6). Several manufacturers (e.g. Amersham®, Sigma®) supply molecular mass standard kits which may include polypeptides of M_r 11 700 to 212 000 (Table 53.1), together with details of their preparation and use. Where

Preparing polyacrylamide gels – most solutions used for gel preparation can be made in advance, but the ammonium persulphate solution must be prepared immediately before use.

Table 53.1 Molecular masses of standard proteins used in electrophoresis

Protein	M_r	$\log_{10} M_r$
Cytochrome c	11 700	4.068
Myoglobin	11 200	4.236
γ-globulin (light chain)	23 500	4.371
Carbonic anhydrase	29 000	4.462
Ovalbumin	43 000	4.634
γ-globulin (heavy chain)	50 000	4.699
Human albumin	68 000	4.832
Transferrin	77 000	4.886
Myosin (heavy chain)	212 000	5.326

Following the progress of PAGE – add bromophenol blue solution (0.002% w/v) to the sample in the ratio 1 : 25 (dye : sample). This highly ionic, small M_r dye migrates with the electrophoretic front.

Choosing a buffer system – discontinuous systems are more time-consuming to prepare, but have the advantage over continuous systems in that relatively large volumes of dilute sample can be used and good resolution is still obtained.

(a)

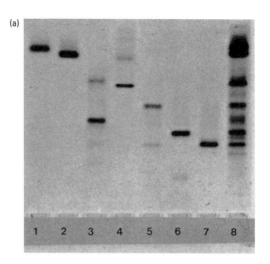

(b)

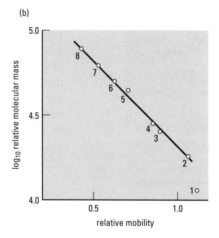

Fig. 53.6 Determination of relative molecular mass (M_r) of proteins by SDS–PAGE: (a) gel samples: 1, cytochrome c; 2, myoglobin; 3, γ-globulin; 4, carbonic anhydrase; 5, ovalbumin; 6, albumin; 7, transferrin; 8, mixture of samples 1–7 (photo courtesy of *Pharmacia Biotech*). (b) plot of log M_r against distance travelled through gel.

necessary, the treated sample can be concentrated by ultrafiltration and the buffer composition can be altered by diafiltration.

Continuous and discontinuous PAGE systems

A continuous system is where the same buffer ions are present in the sample, gel and buffer reservoirs, all at the same pH. The sample is loaded directly onto a gel (the 'separating gel' or 'resolving gel') that has pores small enough to introduce molecular sieving. In contrast, discontinuous systems have different buffers in the gel compared to the reservoirs, both in terms of buffer ions and pH. The sample is loaded onto a large-pore 'stacking gel', previously polymerised on top of a small-pore separating gel (Fig. 53.7). The individual proteins in the sample concentrate into very narrow zones during their migration through the large-pore gel and stack up according to their charge densities, prior to separation in the small-pore gel, giving enhanced results compared with continuous systems.

Choosing a pH for electrophoresis – many proteins have isoelectric points in the range pH 4–7 and in response to electrophoresis with buffers in the region pH 8.0–9.5, most proteins will migrate towards the anode. With nucleic acid electrophoresis using agarose, Tris acetate EDTA (TAE) buffer, pH 8.0, is routinely used to ensure that the DNA fragments are negatively charged.

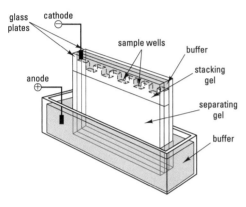

Fig. 53.7 Apparatus for discontinuous electrophoresis.

If your polyacrylamide gels fail to set – polymerisation is inhibited by oxygen, so solutions should be degassed, and the surfaces of the polymerisation mixture exposed to air should be overlayed with water; if your gels still do not polymerise, the most common cause is the use of 'old' ammonium persulphate stock solution. If low pH buffers are used, polymerisation may be delayed because TEMED is required in the free base form.

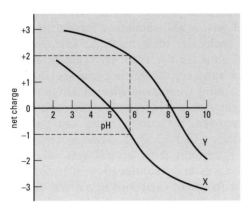

Fig. 53.8 Titration curves for two proteins, X and Y.

Table 53.2 Preparation of gels for PAGE and SDS–PAGE. The gel solutions are made by mixing the components in the proportions and in the order shown. Figures are mL of each solution required to give the stated 90% gel strength

Solution (added in order shown)	PAGE		SDS–PAGE	
	3.5% gel (T = 3.6%)	7.5% gel (T = 7.7%)	5% gel (T = 5.1%)	10% gel (T = 10.2%)
1. Distilled water	19.3	7.5	14.9	—
2. TRIS-glycine buffer, pH 8.9, 0.1 mol L⁻1	33.0	33.0	—	—
3. Imidazole buffer, pH 7.0, 0.1 mol L^{-1} plus 0.2% w/v SDS	—	—	33.0	33.0
4. Acrylamide solution 22.2% w/v and 0.6% w/v bis	10.4	22.2	14.8	29.7
5. Ammonium persulphate solution, 0.15% w/v	3.2	3.2	3.2	3.2
6. TEMED	0.1	0.1	0.1	0.1
Final volume (ml)	66.0	66.0	66.0	66.0

Practical details of the preparation of PAGE and SDS–PAGE gels are given in Table 53.2 (see Westermeier and Barnes, 2001 or Gersten, 1996 for further details).

Isoelectric focusing (IEF)

In contrast to electrophoresis, which is carried out at constant pH, IEF is carried out using a pH gradient. The gradient is formed using small molecular mass ampholytes, which are analogues and homologues of polyamino-polycarboxylic acids that collectively have a range of isoelectric points (pI values) between pH 3 and 10. The mixture of ampholytes, either in a gel or in free solution, is placed between the anode in acid solution (e.g. H_3PO_4), and the cathode in alkaline solution (e.g. NaOH). When an electric field is applied, each ampholyte migrates to its own pI and forms a stable pH gradient which will persist for as long as the field is applied. When a protein sample is applied to this gradient separation is achieved, since individual proteins will migrate to their isoelectric points. The net charge on the protein when first applied will depend on the specific 'titration curve' for that protein (Fig. 53.8). As an example, consider two proteins, X and Y, having pI values of pH 5 and pH 8 respectively, which are placed together on the gradient at pH 6 (Fig. 53.9). At that pH, protein X will have a net negative charge, and will migrate towards the anode, progressively losing charge until it reaches its pI (pH 5) and stops migrating. Protein Y will have a net positive charge at pH 6, and so will migrate towards the cathode until it reaches its pI (pH 8).

Using a polyacrylamide gel as a supporting medium and a narrow pH gradient, proteins differing in pI by 0.01 units can be separated. Even greater resolution is possible in free solution (e.g. in capillary electrophoresis, p. 409). Such resolution is possible because protein molecules that diffuse away from the pI will acquire a net charge (negative at increased pH, positive at decreased pH) and immediately be focused back

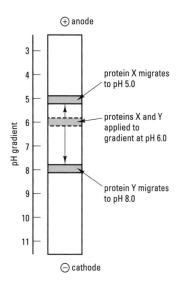

Fig. 53.9 The migration of two proteins, X and Y, in response to a pH gradient.

Avoiding streaking in 2D electrophoresis – ensure that the sample contains no particulate material (e.g. from protein aggregation); filter or centrifuge before use.

Maximising resolution in 2D electrophoresis of proteins – try to minimise nucleic acid contamination of your sample, as they may interact with polypeptides/proteins, affecting their movement in the gel.

Freezing gel strips – be sure to mark the identity and orientation of each gel strip before freezing, e.g. by inserting a fine wire into one end of the strip. Note that if urea is used in the gel strip, it will form crystals on freezing.

to their pI. This focusing effect will continue for as long as the electric field is applied.

A useful variant of IEF is in obtaining *titration curves* for proteins. A pH gradient is set up, and the sample applied in a line at a right angle to the gradient. The net charge on a given protein will vary according to its position on the gradient – when electrophoresis is carried out at right angles to the pH gradient, the protein will migrate at a velocity and direction governed by that charge. When stained, each protein will appear as a continuous curved line, corresponding to its titration curve (Fig. 53.10). This technique can be usefully performed during protein purification, prior to ion-exchange chromatography (p. 364): by obtaining the titration curve for a protein of interest and those of major contaminants, the mobile phase pH that gives optimal separation can be selected.

In IEF, it is important that electro-osmotic flow (EOF, p. 404) is avoided, as this would affect the ability of the proteins to remain stationary at their pIs. For gel IEF, polyacrylamide minimises EOF, while capillary IEF uses narrow bore tubing with an internal polymer coating.

Two-dimensional electrophoresis

The most commonly used version of this high resolution technique involves separating proteins by charge in one dimension using IEF in polyacrylamide gel, followed by separation by molecular mass in the second dimension using denaturing SDS-PAGE (p. 405). The technique allows up to 1000 proteins to be separated from a single sample. Typically, the first dimension IEF run (pH 3–10) is carried out on gel strips of length 7–24 cm. Strips are run at a voltage of 500–3500 V for 1.5 h, then at 3500 V for a further 4 h. Gel strips can then be used immediately, or frozen until required.

It is common for the second-dimension SDS-PAGE separation to be carried out on a discontinuous slab gel 0.5–1.5 mm thick, which includes a low percentage T stacking gel and a separating gel with an exponential gradient of 10–16% T. The separating gel can be prepared in advance, but the stacking gel must be formed shortly before addition of the rod gel from the one dimensional run.

After equilibration with the buffer used in SDS-PAGE, the IEF gel strip is loaded onto the 2D gel (still between the glass plates in which it was formed) and sealed in position using acrylamide or agarose. Before the sealing gel sets, a well should be formed in it at one end to allow addition of molecular mass markers. The second-dimension is run at 100–200 V until the dye front is ≈1 cm from the bottom edge of the slab. After running, the gel is processed for the detection of polypeptides, e.g. using Coomassie Blue or silver stain. Analysis of the complex patterns that result from 2D electrophoresis requires computer-aided gel scanners to acquire, store and process data from a gel, such as that shown in Fig. 53.11. These systems can compare, adjust and match up patterns from several gels, allowing both accurate identification of spots and quantification of individual proteins. Allowance is made for the slight variations in patterns found in different runs, using internal references ('landmarks'), which are

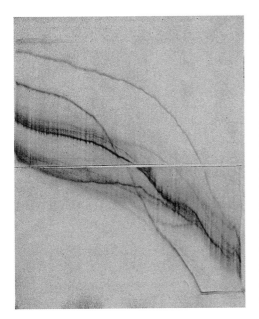

Fig. 53.10 Titration curves of bovine muscle proteins produced by electrofocusing-electrophoresis (photo courtesy of *Pharmacia Biotech*).

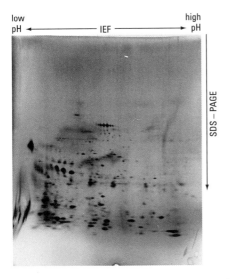

Fig. 53.11 Two-dimensional separation of proteins from 100x concentrated urine (2.5 μg total protein; silver stain. Courtesy of T. Marshall and K.M. Williams).

either added standard proteins or particular spots known to be present in all samples.

Capillary electrophoresis

The technique of capillary electrophoresis (CE) combines the high resolving power of electrophoresis with the speed and versatility of HPLC (p. 379). The technique largely overcomes the major problem of carrying out electrophoresis without a supporting medium, i.e. poor resolution due to convection currents and diffusion. A capillary tube has a high surface area : volume ratio, and consequently the heat generated as a result of the applied electric current is rapidly dissipated. A further advantage is that very small samples (5–10 nl) can be analysed. The versatility of CE is demonstrated by its use in the separation of a range of biomolecules, e.g. amino acids, proteins, nucleic acids, drugs, vitamins, organic acids and inorganic ions; CE can even separate neutral species, e.g. steroids, aromatic hydrocarbons (see Weinberger, 2000).

The components of a typical CE apparatus are shown in Fig. 53.12. The capillary is made of fused silica and externally coated with a polymer for mechanical strength. The internal diameter is usually 25–50 μm, a compromise between efficient heat dissipation and the need for a light path that is not too short for detection using UV/visible spectrophotometry. A gap in the polymer coating provides a window for detection purposes. Samples are injected into the capillary by a variety of means, e.g. electrophoretic loading or displacement. In the former, the inlet end of the capillary is immersed in the sample and a pulse of high voltage is applied. The displacement method involves forcing the sample into the capillary, either by applying pressure in the sample vial using an inert gas, or by introducing a vacuum at the outlet. The detectors used in CE are similar to those used in chromatography (p. 382), e.g. UV/visible spectrophotometric systems. Fluorescence detection is more sensitive, but this may require sample derivatisation. Electrochemical and conductivity detection is also used in some applications, e.g. conductivity detection of inorganic cations such as Na^+ and K^+.

Electro-osmotic flow (EOF), described on page 404, is essential to the most commonly used types of CE. The existence of EOF in the capillary is the result of the net negative charge on the fused silica surface at pH values over 3.0. The resulting solvent flow towards the cathode is greater than the attraction of anions towards the anode, so they will flow towards the cathode (note that the detector is situated at the cathodic end of the capillary). The greater the net negative charge on an anion, the greater is its resistance to the EOF and the lower its mobility. Separated components migrate towards the cathode in the order: (1) cations, (2) neutral species, (3) anions.

Capillary zone electrophoresis (CZE)

This is the most widely used form of CE, and is based on electrophoresis in free solution and EOF, as discussed above. Separations are due to the charge : mass ratio of the sample components, and the technique can be used for almost any type of charged molecule, and is especially useful for peptide separation and confirmation of purity.

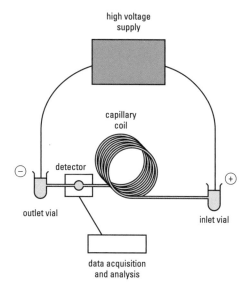

high voltage
supply

capillary
coil

detector

⊖

outlet vial

inlet vial

⊕

data acquisition
and analysis

Fig. 53.12 Components of a capillary electrophoresis system.

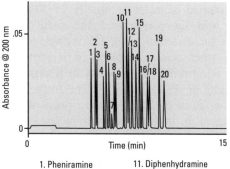

Absorbance @ 200 nm

.05

0

0   Time (min)   15

1. Pheniramine
2. Chlorpheniramine
3. brompheniramine
4. Anileridine
5. Amphetamine
6. Methamphetamine
7. Trifluoperazine
8. Pseudoephedrine
9. Ephedrine
10. Methoxamine

11. Diphenhydramine
12. Dextromethorphan
13. Codeine
14. Hydroxyzine
15. Salbutamol (ES)
16. Metoprolol
17. Trazodone
18. Haloperidol
19. Verapamil
20. Loperamide

Fig. 53.13 MEKC separation of a range of drugs.
Source: http://www.beckman.com/literature/ BioResearch/BR-9515A1.pdf, with permission of Beckman Coulter, Inc.

Distinguishing between stereoisomers – the *R* and *S* convention involves prioritising atoms or groups bonded to a chiral carbon atom (one which has four different atoms or groups attached) in order of their atomic number. With the smallest atom or group pointing away from you, note the size of the three remaining atoms or groups. If

Micellar electrokinetic chromatography (MEKC)

This technique involves the principles of both electrophoresis and chromatography. Its main strength is that it can be used for the separation of neutral molecules as well as charged ones. This is achieved by including surfactants (e.g. SDS, Triton X-100) in the electrophoresis buffer at concentrations that promote the formation of spherical micelles, with a hydrophobic interior and a charged, hydrophilic surface. When an electric field is applied, these micelles will tend to migrate with or against the EOF depending on their surface charge. Anionic surfactants like SDS are attracted by the anode, but if the pH of the buffer is high enough to ensure that the EOF is faster than the migration velocity of the micelles, the net migration is in the direction of the EOF, i.e. towards the cathode. During this migration, sample components partition between the buffer and the micelles (acting as a pseudo-stationary phase); this may involve both hydrophobic and electrostatic interactions. For neutral species it is only the partitioning effect that is involved in separation; the more hydrophobic a sample molecule, the more it will interact with the micelle, and the longer will be its migration time, since the micelle resists the EOF. The versatility of MEKC enables it to be used for separations of molecules as diverse as amino acids, polycyclic hydrocarbons and drugs of abuse. Figure 53.13 shows a MEKC separation of a range of drugs. MEKC is also known as micellar electrokinetic capillary chromatography (MECC).

Chiral capillary electrophoresis (CCE)

Resolution of a pair of chiral enantiomers (optical isomers) represents one of the biggest challenges for separation science, because each member of the pair will have identical physicochemical properties. CE offers an effective method of separating enantiomers by inducing a 'chiral selector' in the electrophoresis medium. The most commonly used chiral selectors are cyclodextrins such as the highly sulphated cyclodextrins (HSCDs) (Fig. 53.14). As the enantiomers migrate along the capillary, one will tend to interact more strongly than the other and its mobility will be reduced relative to the other. Figure 53.15 shows separation of the *R* and *S* forms of amphetamine using 5% HSCD in the electrophoresis buffer. The *R*-form has greater affinity for the HSCD used, so its retention time on the capillary is longer than that of the *S*-form.

Note that HSDCs can also be used in HPLC, but CCE is more effective, with shorter development times and lower reagent costs.

Capillary gel electrophoresis (CGE)

The underlying principle of this technique is directly comparable with that of conventional PAGE, i.e. the capillary contains a polymer that acts as a molecular sieve. As charged sample molecules migrate through the polymer network, larger molecules are hindered to a greater extent than smaller ones and will tend to move more slowly. CGE differs from CZE and MEKC in that the inner surface of the capillary is polymer-coated in order to prevent EOF; this means that for most applications (e.g. polypeptide or oligonucleotide separations) sample components will migrate towards the anode at a rate determined by their size. The

the configuration of increasing atomic number is clockwise, this is termed the (R)-configuration (*L. rectus*); if the order is anticlockwise, this is the (S)-configuration (*L. sinister*). Note that the older, alternative terminology of (D) and (L) stereoisomers is still widely used but the two systems do not always coincide [i.e. (R) is not always D and (S) is not always L].

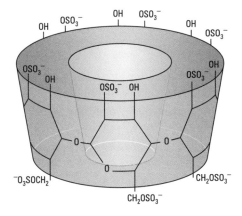

Fig. 53.14 General structure of highly sulphated cyclodextrins (HSCDs). The central cavity of the cyclodextrin (shaded blue) can interact differently with the *R* and *S* isomers of a molecule, enabling separation in CE. Copyright © 1999–2002 Beckman Coulter, Inc. http://www.beckmancoulter.com/products/splashpage/chiral38/default.asp/

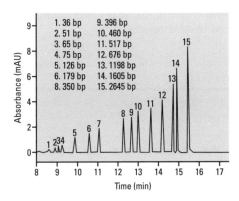

Fig. 53.16 CGE separation of a range of oligonucleotides.
Source: http://www.chem.agilent.com/scripts/LeteraturePDF.asp?iWHID=15729, Publication 5965-9037E, reproduced with permission of Agilent Technologies.

technique also differs from conventional PAGE in that a 'polymer network' is used rather than a gel: the polymer network may be polyacrylamide or agarose. A typical separation of oligonucleotide fragments by CGE is shown in Fig. 53.16.

CGE offers the following advantages over conventional electrophoresis:

- efficient heat dissipation means that a high electrical field can be applied, giving shorter separation times;

- detection of the separated components as they move towards the anodic end of the capillary (e.g. using a UV/visible detector) means that staining is unnecessary;

- automation is feasible.

Capillary isoelectric focusing (CIEF)

This is used mainly for protein separation. Here, the principles of IEF are valid as long as EOF is prevented by using capillaries that are polymer-coated on their inner surface. Sample components migrate to their isoelectric points and become stationary. Once separated (<10 min), the components must be mobilised so that they flow past the detector. This is achieved by changing the NaOH solution in the cathodic reservoir

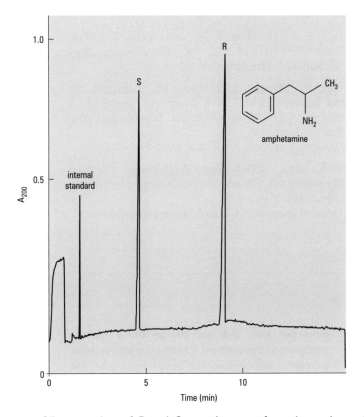

Fig. 53.15 CE separation of *R* and *S* enantiomers of amphetamine using Beckman Coulter highly sulphated gamma cyclodextrin. Copyright © 1999–2002 Beckman Coulter, Inc. http://www.beckmancoulter.com/products/splashpage/chiral38/default.asp/

Choosing a detector for capillary electrophoresis – most types of HPLC detector are suitable for CE and related applications (see Chapter 52).

with an NaOH/NaCl solution. When the electric field is reapplied, Cl^- enters the capillary, causing a decrease in pH at the cathodic end and the subsequent migration of sample components.

Text references

Gersten, D. (1996) *Gel Electrophoresis: Proteins* (Essential Techniques Series). Wiley, New York.

Weinberger, R. (2000) *Practical Capillary Electrophoresis*. Academic Press, New York.

Westermeier, R. and Barnes, N. (2001) *Electrophoresis in Practice: A Guide to Methods and Applications of DNA and Protein Separation*, 3rd edn. VCH, Berlin.

Sources for further study

Anon. *The American Electrophoresis Society Homepage*. Available: http://www.aesociety.org Last accessed: 01/04/07.
[Includes details on electrophoretic techniques including IEF and CE]

Anon. *Cyclodextrin Resource*. Available: http://www.cyclodex.com/index.html Last accessed: 01/04/07.
[Information on cyclodextrin structure, applications, etc.]

Cunico, R.L., Gooding, K.M. and Wehr, T. (1998) *Basic HPLC and CE of Biomolecules*. Bay Bioanalytical, Hercules, CA.

Kellner, R., Mermet, J.M., Otto, M., Valcarcel, M. and Widmer, H.M. (2004) *Analytical Chemistry: A Modern Approach to Analytical Science*, 2nd edn. Wiley, Chichester.
[Covers all modern analytical topics]

Khaledi, M.G. (1998) *High Performance Capillary Electrophoresis: Theory, Techniques and Applications*. Wiley, New York.
[Detailed manual of CE techniques and procedures]

Lunn, G. (2000) *Capillary Electrophoresis Methods for Pharmaceutical Analysis*. Wiley, Chichester.

Palfrey, S.M. (1999) *Clinical Applications of Capillary Electrophoresis*. Humana Press, New Jersey.

Schwedt, G. (1998) *The Essential Guide to Analytical Chemistry*. Wiley, Chichester.

Strenge, M.A. and Lagu, A.L. (2004) *Capillary Electrophoresis of Proteins and Peptides*. Humana Press, New Jersey.

Westermeier, R. (2000) *Practical Capillary Electrophoresis*. Elsevier, Amsterdam.

Westermeier, R. (2004) *Electrophoresis in Practice: A Guide to Methods and Applications of DNA and Protein Separations*, 3rd edn. Wiley-VCH, Berlin.
[Covers the principles underlying IEF]

Westermeier, R. (2005) *Electrophoresis in Practice*. Wiley, Chichester.

Weston, A. and Brown, P.R. (1997) *HPLC and CE: Principles and Practice*. Academic Press, New York.
[Covers practical aspects including applications, optimisation and troubleshooting]

Study exercises

53.1 Find out why the net charge on a protein molecule varies with pH. Identify the amino acids primarily responsible for determining the net charge on a protein molecule and draw simple diagrams to represent the ionisation of their side chains, indicating how you would expect these side chains to be charged at acid, neutral and alkaline pH values.

53.2 Consider the requirements for sample application in PAGE and IEF. Explain why in PAGE the sample is applied in a discrete narrow band, usually at the cathodic end of the gel, while in IEF the sample can be applied at any point along the length of the gel without concern about location or narrowness of the sample zone.

54 Electroanalytical techniques

Electrochemical methods are used to quantify a broad range of different molecules, including ions, gases, metabolites and drugs.

> **KEY POINT** The basis of all electrochemical analysis is the transfer of electrons from one atom or molecule to another atom or molecule in an obligately coupled oxidation–reduction reaction (a redox reaction).

It is convenient to separate such redox reactions into two half-reactions and, by convention, each is written as:

$$\text{oxidised form} + \text{electron(s)} (n\,e^-) \underset{oxidation}{\overset{reduction}{\rightleftharpoons}} \text{reduced form} \qquad [54.1]$$

You should note that the half-reaction is reversible: by applying suitable conditions, reduction *or* oxidation can take place. As an example, a simple redox reaction occurs when metallic zinc (Zn) is placed in a solution containing copper ions (Cu^{2+}), as follows:

$$Cu^{2+} + Zn \rightarrow Cu + Zn^{2+} \qquad [54.2]$$

The half-reactions are (i) $Cu^{2+} + 2e^- \rightarrow Cu$ and (ii) $Zn^{2+} + 2e^- \rightarrow Zn$. The oxidising power of (i) is greater than that of (ii), so in a coupled system, the latter half-reaction proceeds in the opposite direction to that shown above, i.e. as $Zn - 2e^- \rightarrow Zn^{2+}$. When Zn and Cu electrodes are placed in separate solutions containing their ions, and connected electrically (Fig. 54.1), electrons will flow from the Zn electrode to Cu^{2+} via the Cu electrode owing to the difference in oxidising power of the two half-reactions.

By convention, the electrode potential of any half-reaction is expressed relative to that of a standard hydrogen electrode (half-reaction $2H^+ + 2e^- \rightarrow H_2$) and is called the standard electrode potential, E. Table 54.1 shows the values of E^o for selected half-reactions. With any pair of half-reactions from this series, electrons will flow from that having the lowest electrode potential to that of the highest. E^o is determined at pH = 0. It is often more appropriate to express standard electrode potentials at pH 7 for biological systems, and the symbol $E^{o\prime}$ is used: in all circumstances, it is important that the pH is clearly stated.

The arrangement shown in Fig. 54.1 represents a simple galvanic cell where two electrodes serve as the interfaces between a chemical system and an electrical system. For analytical purposes, the magnitude of the potential (voltage) or the current produced by an electrochemical cell is related to the concentration (strictly the activity, *a*, p. 188) of a particular chemical species. Electrochemical methods offer the following advantages:

- excellent detection limits, and wide operating range (10^{-1} to $10^{-8}\,mol\,L^{-1}$);

- measurements may be made on very small volumes (μL) allowing small amounts (pmol) of sample to be measured in some cases;

- miniature electrochemical sensors can be used for certain *in vivo* measurements, e.g. pH, glucose, oxygen content.

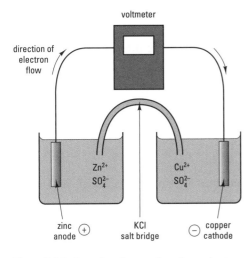

Fig. 54.1 A simple galvanic electrochemical cell. The KCl salt bridge allows migration of ions between the two compartments but prevents mixing of the two solutions.

Table 54.1 Standard electrode potentials* (E^o) for selected half-reactions

Half-reaction	E^o at 25 °C (V)
$Cl_2 + 2e^- \rightleftharpoons 2Cl^-$	+1.36
$O_2 + 4H^+ + 4e^- \rightleftharpoons 2H_2O$	+1.23
$Br_2 + 2e^- \rightleftharpoons 2Br^-$	+1.09
$Ag^+ + e^- \rightleftharpoons Ag$	+0.80
$Fe^{3+} + e^- \rightleftharpoons Fe^{2+}$	+0.77
$I_3^- + 2e^- \rightleftharpoons 3I^-$	+0.54
$Cu^{2+} + 2e^- \rightleftharpoons Cu$	+0.34
$Hg_2Cl_2 + 2e^- \rightleftharpoons 2Hg + 2Cl^-$	+0.27
$AgCl + e^- \rightleftharpoons Ag + Cl^-$	+0.22
$Ag(S_2O_3)_2^{3-} + e^- \rightleftharpoons Ag + 2S_2O_3^{2-}$	+0.01
$2H^+ + 2e^- \rightleftharpoons H_2$	+0.00
$AgI + e^- \rightleftharpoons Ag + I$	−0.15
$PbSO_4 + 2e^- \rightleftharpoons Pb + SO_4^{2-}$	−0.35
$Cd^{2+} + 2e^- \rightleftharpoons Cd$	−0.40
$Zn^{2+} + 2e^- \rightleftharpoons Zn$	−0.76

*From Milazzo *et al*. (1978).

Using a calomel electrode – always ensure that the KCl solution is saturated by checking that KCl crystals are present.

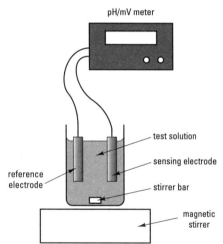

Fig. 54.2 Components of a potentiometric cell.

Potentiometry and ion-selective electrodes

Operating principles

These systems involve galvanic cells (p. 413) and are based on measurement of the potential (voltage) difference between two electrodes in solution when no net current flows between them: no net electrochemical reaction occurs and measurements are made under equilibrium conditions. These systems include methods for measuring pH, ions, and gases such as CO_2 and NH_3. A typical potentiometric cell is shown in Fig. 54.2. It contains two electrodes:

1. a 'sensing' electrode, the half-cell potential of which responds to changes in the activity (concentration) of the substance to be measured; the most common type of indicator electrodes are ion-selective electrodes (ISEs);

2. a 'reference' electrode, the potential of which does not change, forming the second half of the cell.

To assay a particular analyte, the potential difference between these electrodes is measured by an mV meter (e.g. a standard pH meter).

Reference electrodes for potentiometry are of three main types:

1. The standard hydrogen electrode, which is the reference half-cell electrode, defined as 0.0 V at all temperatures, against which values of E^o are expressed. H_2 gas at 1 atmosphere pressure is bubbled over a platinum electrode immersed in an acid solution with an activity of unity. This electrode is rarely used for analytical work, since it is unstable and other reference electrodes are easier to construct and use.

2. The calomel electrode (Fig. 54.3), which consists of a paste of mercury covered by a coat of calomel (Hg_2Cl_2), immersed in a saturated solution of KCl. The half-reaction $Hg_2Cl_2 + 2e^- \rightarrow 2Hg + 2Cl^-$ gives a stable standard electrode potential of +0.24 V.

3. The silver/silver chloride electrode. This is a silver wire coated with AgCl and immersed in a solution of constant chloride concentration. The half-reaction $AgCl + e^- \rightarrow Ag + Cl^-$ gives a stable, standard electrode potential of +0.20 V.

KEY POINT Ion-selective electrodes (ISEs) are based on measurement of a potential across a membrane which is selective for a particular analyte.

An ISE consists of a membrane, an internal reference electrode, and an internal reference electrolyte of fixed activity. The ISE is immersed in a sample solution that contains the analyte of interest, along with a reference electrode. The membrane is chosen to have a specific affinity for a particular ion, and if activity of this ion in the sample differs from that in the reference electrolyte, a potential develops across the membrane that is dependent on the ratio of these activities. Since the potentials of the two reference electrodes (internal and external) are fixed, and the internal electrolyte is of

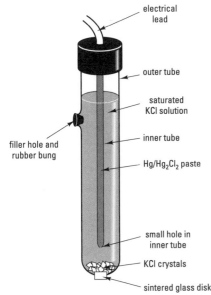

Fig. 54.3 A calomel reference electrode.

constant activity, the measured potential, E, is dependent on the membrane potential and is given by the Nernst equation:

$$E = K + 2.303 \frac{RT}{zF} \log [a] \qquad [54.3]$$

where K represents a constant potential which is dependent on the reference electrode, z represents the net charge on the analyte, $[a]$ the activity of analyte in the sample and all other symbols and constants have their usual meaning (p. 214). For a series of standards of known activity, a plot of E against $\log [a]$ should be linear over the working range of the electrode, with a slope of $2.303\,RT/zF$ (0.059 V at 25 °C). Although ISEs strictly measure *activity*, the potential differences can be approximated to concentration as long as (i) the analyte is in dilute solution (p. 188), (ii) the ionic strength of the calibration standards matches that of the sample, e.g. by adding appropriate amounts of a high ionic strength solution to the standards, and (iii) the effect of binding to sample macromolecules (e.g. proteins, nucleic acids) is minimal. Potentiometric measurements on undiluted biological fluids, e.g. K^+ and Na^+ levels in plasma, tissue fluids or urine, are likely to give lower values than flame emission spectrophotometry, since the latter procedure measures total ion levels, rather than just those in aqueous solution.

All of the various types of membrane used in ISEs operate by incorporating the ion to be analysed into the membrane, with the accompanying establishment of a membrane potential. The scope of electrochemical analysis has been extended to measuring gases and non-ionic compounds by combining ISEs with gas-permeable membranes, enzymes, and even immobilised bacteria or tissues.

Glass membrane electrodes

The most widely used ISE is the glass membrane electrode for pH measurement (p. 198). The membrane is thin glass (50 μm wall thickness) made of silica which contains some Na^+. When the membrane is soaked in water, a thin hydrated layer is formed on the surface in which negative oxide groups (Si-O$^-$) in the glass act as ion-exchange sites. If the electrode is placed in an acid solution, H^+ exchanges with Na^+ in the hydrated layer, producing an external surface potential: in alkaline solution, H^+ moves out of the membrane in exchange for Na^+. Since the inner surface potential is kept constant by exposure to a fixed activity of H^+, a consistent, accurate potentiometric response is observed over a wide pH range. Glass electrodes for other cations (e.g. Na^+, NH_4^+) have been developed by changing the composition of the glass, so that it is predominantly sensitive to the particular analyte, though the specificity of such electrodes is not absolute. The operating principles and maintenance of such electrodes are broadly similar to those for pH electrodes (p. 198).

Gas-sensing glass electrodes

Here, an ISE in contact with a thin external layer of aqueous electrolyte (the 'filling solution') is kept close to the glass membrane by an additional, outer membrane that is selectively permeable to the gas of interest. The arrangement for a CO_2 electrode is shown in Fig. 54.4: in this case the outer membrane is made of CO_2-permeable silicone rubber. When CO_2 gas in the sample selectively diffuses across the membrane

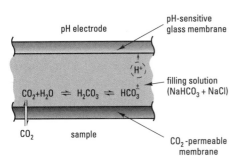

Fig. 54.4 Underlying principles of a gas-sensing electrode.

Using CO_2 electrodes – applications include measurement of blood PCO_2 and in enzyme studies where CO_2 is utilised or released: calibration of the electrode is accomplished using 5% v/v and 10% v/v mixtures of CO_2 in an inert gas equilibrated against the measuring solution.

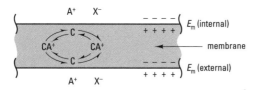

internal solution

external (sample) solution

Fig. 54.5 Underlying principles of a liquid membrane ion-selective electrode. A^+ = analyte; C = neutral carrier ionophore; E_m = surface potential; membrane potential = E_m(internal) − E_m(external).

Definition

Ionophore – a compound that enhances membrane permeability to a specific ion: an ionophore may be incorporated into an ISE to detect that ion.

Definitions

Electrolytic cell – an electrochemical cell in which reactions are driven by the application of an external voltage greater than the spontaneous potential of the cell.

Electrolysis – a non-spontaneous chemical reaction resulting from the application of a potential to an electrode.

---

and dissolves in the filling solution (in this case an aqueous $NaHCO_3/NaCl$ mixture), a change in pH occurs owing to the shift in the equilibrium:

$$CO_2 + H_2O \rightleftharpoons H_2CO_3 \rightleftharpoons H^+ + HCO_3^- \qquad [54.4]$$

The pH change is 'sensed' by the internal ion-selective pH electrode, and its response is proportional to the partial pressure of CO_2 of the solution (PCO_2). A similar principle operates in the NH_3 electrode, where a Teflon® membrane is used, and the filling solution is NH_4Cl.

Liquid and polymer membrane electrodes

In these types of ISEs, the liquid is a water-insoluble viscous solvent containing a soluble ionophore, i.e. an organic ion exchanger, or a neutral carrier molecule, that is specific for the analyte of interest. When this liquid is soaked into a thin membrane such as cellulose acetate, it becomes effectively immobilised. The arrangement of analyte (A^+) and ionophore in relation to this membrane is shown in Fig. 54.5. The potential on the inner surface of the membrane is kept constant by maintaining a constant activity of A^+ in the internal solution, so the potential change measured is that which results from A^+ in the sample interacting with the ionophore in the outer surface of the membrane.

A relevant example of a suitable ionophore is the antibiotic valinomycin, which specifically binds K^+. Other ionophores have been developed for measurement of, for example, NH_4^+, Ca^{2+}, Cl^-. In addition, electrodes have been developed for organic species by using specific ion-pairing reagents in the membrane that interact with ionic forms of the organic compound, e.g. with drugs such as 5,5-diphenylhydantoin.

Solid-state membrane electrodes

These contain membranes made from single crystals or pressed pellets of salts of the analyte. The membrane material must show some permeability to ions and must be virtually insoluble in water. Examples include:

- the fluoride electrode, which uses LaF_3 impregnated with Eu^{2+} (the latter to increase permeability to F^-). A membrane potential is set up when F^- in the sample solution enters spaces in the crystal lattice;

- the chloride electrode, which uses a pressed pellet membrane of Ag_2S and $AgCl$.

Voltammetric methods

Voltammetric methods are based on measurements made using an electrochemical cell in which electrolysis is occurring. Voltammetry, sometimes also called amperometry, involves the use of a potential applied between two electrodes (the working electrode and the reference electrode) to cause oxidation or reduction of an electroactive analyte. The loss or gain of electrons at an electrode surface causes current to flow, and the size of the current (usually measured in mA or μA) is directly proportional to the concentration of the electroactive analyte. The materials used for the working electrode must be good conductors and

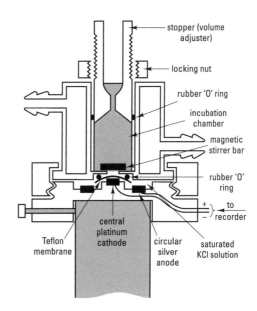

Fig. 54.6 Transverse section through a Clark (Rank) oxygen electrode.

electrochemically inert, so that they simply transfer electrons to and from species in solution. Suitable materials include Pt, Au, Hg and glassy carbon.

Two widely used devices that operate on the voltammetric principle are the oxygen electrode and the glucose electrode. These are sometimes referred to as amperometric sensors.

Oxygen electrodes

The Clark (Rank) oxygen electrode

These instruments measure oxygen in solution using the polarographic principle, i.e. by monitoring the current flowing between two electrodes when a voltage is applied. The most widespread electrode is the Clark type (Fig. 54.6), manufactured by Rank Bros, Cambridge, UK, which is suitable for measuring O_2 concentrations in cell, organelle and enzyme suspensions. Pt and Au electrodes are in contact with a solution of electrolyte (normally saturated KCl). The electrodes are separated from the medium by a Teflon® membrane, permeable to O_2. When a potential is applied across the electrodes, this generates a current proportional to the O_2 concentration. The reactions can be summed up as:

$$4Ag \rightarrow 4Ag^+ + 4e^- \qquad \text{(at silver anode)}$$

$$O_2 + 2e^- + 2H^+ \rightleftharpoons H_2O_2 \qquad \text{(in electrolyte solution; } O_2 \text{ replenished by diffusion from test solution)}$$

$$H_2O_2 + 2e^- + 2H^+ \rightleftharpoons 2H_2O \qquad \text{(at platinum cathode)}$$

Oxygen probes

Clark-type oxygen electrodes are also available in probe form for immersion in the test solution (Fig. 54.7), e.g. for field studies, allowing direct measurement of oxygen status *in situ*, in contrast to chemical assays. The main point to note is that the solution must be stirred

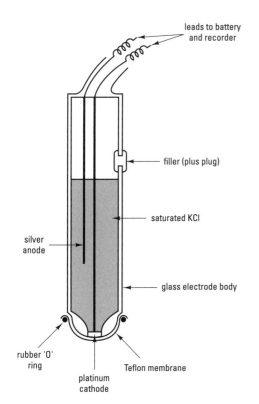

Fig. 54.7 A Clark-type oxygen probe.

during measurement, to replenish the oxygen consumed by the electrode ('boundary layer' effect).

The glucose electrode

The glucose electrode is a simple type of biosensor, whose basic design is shown in Fig. 54.8. It consists of a Pt electrode, overlaid by two membranes. Sandwiched between these membranes is a layer of the immobilised enzyme glucose oxidase. The outer membrane is glucose permeable and allows glucose in the sample to diffuse through to the glucose oxidase layer, where it is converted to gluconic acid and H_2O_2. The inner membrane is selectively permeable to H_2O_2, which is oxidised to O_2 at the surface of the Pt electrode. The current arising from this release of electrons is proportional to the glucose concentration in the sample within the range 10^{-7} to $10^{-3}\,mol\,L^{-1}$.

Electrochemical detectors used in chromatography operate by voltammetric principles and currents are produced as the mobile phase flows over electrodes set at a fixed potential: to achieve maximum sensitivity, this potential must be set at a level that allows electrochemical reactions to occur in all analytes of interest.

Coulometric methods

Here, the charge required to electrolyse a sample completely is measured: the time required to titrate an analyte is measured at constant current and related to the amount of analyte using Faraday's law. There are few chemical applications of this technique, though it is sometimes used for determination of Cl^- in serum and body fluids.

Cyclic voltammetry

The technique provides qualitative information about electrochemical reactions, e.g. the redox behaviour of compounds and the kinetics of electron transfer reactions. In practice, a triangular potential waveform is applied linearly to the working electrode in a unstirred solution. After a few seconds, the ramp is reversed and the potential is returned to its initial value. The process may be repeated several times. The resulting plot of current versus potential is termed a cyclic voltammogram. Fig. 54.9 shows a typical cyclic voltammogram for a reversible redox couple after a single potential cycle. It is assumed that the oxidised form, O, is the only species present at the start. Therefore, the first scan is towards the (more) negative direction, commencing at a value were no reduction occurs. As the applied potential approaches the characteristic $E°$ for the redox process, a catholic current starts to increase, up to a maximum. After exceeding the potential at which the reduction process takes place, the direction of the potential current is reversed. During this stage, reduced molecules R, generated during the initial process, are reoxidised back to O, resulting in an anodic peak.

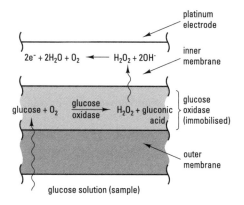

Fig. 54.8 Underlying principles of a glucose electrode.

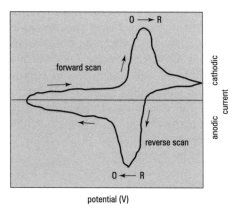

Fig. 54.9 A typical cyclic voltammogram for a reversible $O + ne^- \leftrightarrow R$ redox process.

Sources for further study

Bard, A.J. and Faulkner, L.R. (2001) *Electrochemical Methods*. Wiley, Chichester.

Hamann, C.H., Hamnett, A. and Vielstich, W. (2007) *Electrochemistry*, 2nd edn. Wiley, Chichester.

Kellner, R., Mermet, J.M., Otto, M., Valcarcel, M. and Widmer, H.M. (2004) *Analytical Chemistry: A Modern Approach to Analytical Science*, 2nd edn. Wiley, Chichester.
[Covers all modern analytical topics.]

McMahon, G. (2008) *Analytical Instrumentation: A Guide to Laboratory, Portable and Miniaturized Instruments*. Wiley, Chichester.

Monk, P.M.S. (2001) *Fundamentals of Electro-Analytical Chemistry*. Wiley, Chichester.

Schwedt, G. (1998) *The Essential Guide to Analytical Chemistry*. Wiley, Chichester.

Wang, J. (2006) *Analytical Electrochemistry*, 3rd edn. Wiley, Chichester.

Study exercises

54.1 Test your understanding of the circumstances under which ion-selective electrodes can be used. List the three main assumptions underlying the measurement of ion concentration using an ion-selective electrode.

54.2 Test your knowledge of biosensor design. List the two main functional components of bio-sensor such as the glucose electrode. Research a specific application – note that it should be different from the ones used in this chapter (e.g. using the Web).

54.3 Calculate the oxygen content of specified volumes of water at defined temperatures. Using the information in Table 54.1 and assuming air equilibration at 101.3 kPa, what is the amount of oxygen in each of the following (give all answers to three significant figures):

(a) 4 mL of distilled water at 20 °C (express your answer in µmol);

(b) 20 mL of sea water at 12 °C (express your answer in µmol);

(c) 10 mL of distilled water at 15 °C (express your answer in µmol);

(d) 250 mL of distilled water at 37 °C (express your answer in mg);

(e) 200 mL of sea water at 25 °C (express your answer in mL).

Examples $^{12}_{6}C$, $^{13}_{6}C$ and $^{14}_{6}C$ are three of the isotopes of carbon. About 98.9% of naturally occurring carbon is in the stable $^{12}_{6}C$ form. $^{13}_{6}C$ is also a stable isotope but it only occurs at 1.1% natural abundance. Trace amounts of radioactive $^{14}_{6}C$ are found naturally; this is a negatron-emitting radioisotope (see Table 55.2).

Example ^{226}Ra decays to ^{222}Rn by loss of an alpha particle, as follows:

$$^{226}_{88}Ra \rightarrow \; ^{222}_{86}Rn + \; ^{4}_{2}He^{2+}$$

^{14}C shows beta decay, as follows:

$$^{14}_{6}C \rightarrow \; ^{14}_{7}N + \beta^{-}$$

^{22}Na decays by positron emission, as follows:

$$^{22}_{11}Na \rightarrow \; ^{22}_{10}Ne + \beta^{+}$$

^{55}Fe decays by electron capture and the production of an X-ray, as follows:

$$^{55}_{26}Fe \rightarrow \; ^{55}_{25}Mn + X$$

The decay of ^{22}Na by positron emission (β^{+}) leads to the production of a γ-ray when the positron is annihilated on collision with an electron.

The isotopes of a particular element have the same number of protons in the nucleus but different numbers of neutrons, giving them the same proton number (atomic number) but different nucleon numbers (mass number, i.e. number of protons + number of neutrons). Isotopes may be stable or radioactive. Radioactive isotopes (radioisotopes) disintegrate spontaneously at random to yield radiation and a decay product.

Radioactive decay

There are three forms of radioactivity (Table 55.1) arising from three main types of nuclear decay:

- Alpha decay involves the loss of a particle equivalent to a helium nucleus. Alpha (α) particles, being relatively large and positively charged, do not penetrate far in living tissue, but they do cause ionisation damage and this makes them generally unsuitable for tracer studies.

- Beta decay involves the loss or gain of an electron or its positive counterpart, the positron. There are three subtypes:

  (a) Negatron (β^{-}) emission: loss of an electron from the nucleus when a neutron transforms into a proton. This is the most important form of decay for radioactive tracers. Negatron-emitting isotopes of importance include ^{3}H, ^{14}C, ^{32}P and ^{35}S.

  (b) Positron (β^{+}) emission: loss of a positron when a proton transforms into a neutron. This only occurs when sufficient energy is available from the transition and may involve the production of gamma rays when the positron is later annihilated by collision with an electron.

  (c) Electron capture (EC): when a proton 'captures' an electron and transforms into a neutron. This may involve the production of X-rays as electrons 'shuffle' about in the atom (as with ^{125}I) and it frequently involves electron emission.

- Internal transition involves the emission of electromagnetic radiation in the form of gamma (γ) rays from a nucleus in a metastable state and always follows initial alpha or beta decay. Emission of gamma radiation leads to no further change in atomic number or mass.

Note from the above that more than one type of radiation may be emitted when a radioisotope decays. The main radioisotopes used in chemistry and their properties are listed in Table 55.2.

Table 55.1 Types of radioactivity and their properties

Radiation	Range of maximum energies (MeV*)	Penetration range in air (m)[†]	Suitable shielding material
Alpha (α)	4–8	0.025–0.080	Unnecessary
Beta (β)	0.01–3	0.150–16	Plastic (e.g. Perspex)
Gamma (γ)	0.03–3	1.3–13	Lead

*Note that $1\,MeV = 1.6 \times 10^{-13}\,J$

[†] Distance at which radiation intensity is reduced to half

Table 55.2 Properties of some isotopes used commonly in chemistry. Physical data obtained from Haynes (2010)

Isotope	Emission(s)	Maximum energy (MeV)	Half-life	Main uses	Advantages	Disadvantages
^{3}H	β^-	0.018 61	12.3 years	Suitable for labelling organic molecules in wide range of positions at high specific activity	Relatively safe	Low efficiency of detection, high isotope effect, high rate of exchange with environment
^{14}C	β^-	0.156 48	5715 years	Suitable for labelling organic molecules in a wide range of positions	Relatively safe, low rate of exchange with environment	Low specific activity
^{22}Na	β^+ (90%) + γ, EC	2.842 (β^+)	2.60 years	Transport studies	High specific activity	Hazardous
^{32}P	β^-	1.710	14.3 days	Labelling proteins and nucleotides (e.g. DNA)	High specific activity, ease of detection	Short half-life, hazardous
^{33}P	β^-	0.248	25 days	Labelling nucleotides and proteins	Safer than ^{32}P	Moderate half-life
^{35}S	β^-	0.167	87.2 days	Labelling proteins and nucleotides	Low isotope effect	Low specific activity
^{36}Cl	β^-, β^+, EC	0.709 (β^-) 1.142 (β^+, EC)	300 000 years	Transport studies	Low isotope effect	Low specific activity, hazardous
^{125}I	EC + γ	0.178 (EC)	59.9 days	Labelling proteins and nucleotides	High specific activity	Hazardous
^{131}I	β^- + γ	0.971 (β^-)	8.04 days	Labelling proteins and nucleotides	High specific activity	Hazardous

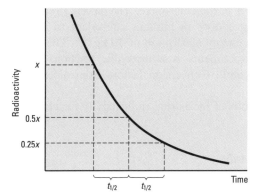

Fig. 55.1 Decay of a radioactive isotope with time. The time taken for the radioactivity to decline from x to $0.5x$ is the same as the time taken for the radioactivity to decline from $0.5x$ to $0.25x$, and so on. This time is the half-life ($t_{1/2}$) of the isotope.

Example For ^{35}S, with a half-life of 87.2 days (Table 55.2), the fraction of radioactivity remaining after 28 days would be worked out as follows: first, from eqn [55.1] $x = (-0.693 \times 28) \div 87.2 = -0.222\,522\,936$, then using eqn [55.1], $f = e^{-0.222522936} = 0.800\,496\,646$ (with appropriate rounding, 80.0% of original activity).

Each radioactive particle or ray carries energy, usually measured in electron volts (eV). The particles or rays emitted by a particular radioisotope exhibit a range of energies, termed an energy spectrum, characterised by the maximum energy of the radiation produced, E_{max} (Table 55.2). The energy spectrum of a particular radioisotope is relevant to the following:

● Safety: isotopes with the highest maximum energies will have the greatest penetrating power, requiring appropriate shielding (Table 55.1).

● Detection: different instruments vary in their ability to detect isotopes with different energies.

● Discrimination: some instruments can distinguish between isotopes, based on the energy spectrum of the radiation produced (p. 422).

The decay of an individual atom (a 'disintegration') occurs at random, but that of a population of atoms occurs in a predictable manner. The radioactivity decays exponentially, having a characteristic half-life ($t_{1/2}$). This is the time taken for the radioactivity to fall from a given value to half that value (Fig. 55.1). The $t_{1/2}$ values of different radioisotopes range from fractions of a second to more than 10^{19} years (see also Table 55.2). If $t_{1/2}$ is very short, as with ^{15}O ($t_{1/2} \approx 2\,min$), then it is generally impractical to use the isotope in experiments because you would need to account for the decay during the experiment and counting period.

To calculate the fraction (f) of the original radioactivity left after a particular time (t), use the following relationship:

$$f = e^x, \text{ where } x = -0.693t/t_{\frac{1}{2}} \quad [55.1]$$

Note that the same units must be used for t and $t_{\frac{1}{2}}$ in this equation.

Table 55.3 Relationships between units of radioactivity. For abbreviations, see text

1 Bq = 1 d.p.s.	1 Sv = 100 rem
1 Bq = 60 d.p.m.	1 Gy = 100 rad
1 Bq = 27 pCi	1 Gy ≈ 100 roentgen
1 d.p.s. = 1 Bq	1 rem = 0.01 Sv
1 d.p.m. = 0.0167 Bq	1 rad = 0.01 Gy
1 Ci = 37 GBq	1 roentgen ≈ 0.01 Gy
1 mCi = 37 MBq	
1 μCi = 37 kBq	

Example If 0.4 mL of a ^{32}P-labelled DNA solution at a concentration of 50 μmol L^{-1} (amount = 0.4 × 50 ÷ 1000 = 0.02 μmol) gave a count of 2490 d.p.m. (= 41.5 Bq), using eqn [55.2] this would correspond to a specific activity of 2490 ÷ 0.02 = 124500 dpm μmol^{-1} (or 2075 Bq μmol^{-1}).

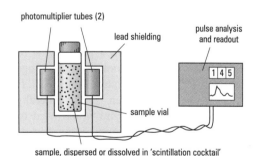

sample, dispersed or dissolved in 'scintillation cocktail'

Fig. 55.2 Components of a scintillation counter. Note that in most modern instruments, all components are enclosed within a single cabinet.

Measuring radioactivity

The SI unit of radioactivity is the becquerel (Bq), equivalent to one disintegration per second (d.p.s.), but disintegrations per minute (d.p.m.) are also used. The curie (Ci) is a non-SI unit equivalent to the number of disintegrations produced by 1 g of radium (37 GBq). Table 55.3 shows the relationships between these units. In practice, most instruments are not able to detect all of the disintegrations from a particular sample, i.e. their efficiency is less than 100% and the rate of decay may be presented as counts min^{-1} (c.p.m.) or counts s^{-1} (c.p.s.). Most modern instruments correct for background radiation and inefficiencies in counting, converting count data to d.p.m. Alternatively, the results may be presented as the measured count rate, although this is only valid where the efficiency of counting does not vary greatly among samples.

KEY POINT The specific activity is a measure of the quantity of radioactivity present in a known amount of the substance:

$$\text{specific activity} = \frac{\text{radioactivity (Bq, Ci, d.p.m., etc.)}}{\text{amount of substance (mol, g, etc.)}} \qquad [55.2]$$

This is an important concept in practical work involving radioisotopes, since it allows interconversion of disintegrations (activity) and amount of substance (see Box 55.1).

Two SI units refer to doses of radioactivity and these are used when calculating exposure levels for a particular source. The sievert (Sv) is the amount of radioactivity giving a dose in humans equivalent to 1 gray (Gy) of X-rays: 1 Gy = an energy absorption of 1 J kg^{-1}. The dose received in most biological experiments is a negligible fraction of the maximum permitted exposure limit. Conversion factors from older units are given in Table 55.3.

The most important methods of measuring radioactivity for chemical purposes are described below.

The Geiger–Müller (G–M) tube

This operates by detecting radiation when it ionises gas between a pair of electrodes across which a voltage has been applied. You should use a hand-held Geiger–Müller tube for routine checking for contamination (although it will not pick up ^{3}H activity). It is not possible to detect low-energy β^- and α particles as they are not able to penetrate the window of the tube. In addition, γ-rays (of medium to high energy) pass through the filling gas causing little ionisation, and hence have low efficiency.

The scintillation counter

This operates by detecting the scintillations (fluorescence 'flashes') produced when radiation interacts with certain chemicals called fluors (Fig. 55.2). In solid (or external) scintillation counters (often referred to as 'gamma counters') the radioactivity causes scintillations in a crystal of fluorescent material held close to the sample. This method is only suitable for radioisotopes producing penetrating radiation.

Liquid scintillation counters are mainly used for detecting beta decay. The sample is dispersed or dissolved in a suitable solvent

Box 55.1 How to determine the specific activity of an experimental solution

Suppose you need to make up a certain volume of an experimental solution, to contain a particular amount of radioactivity. For example, 50 mL of a mannitol solution at a concentration of 25 mmol L^{-1}, to contain 5 Bq μL^{-1} – using a manufacturer's stock solution of ^{14}C-labelled mannitol (specific activity = 0.1 Ci mmol^{-1}).

1. **Calculate the total amount of radioactivity in the experimental solution**, in this example 5 × 1000 (to convert μL to mL) × 50 (50 mL required) = 2.5 × 10^5 Bq (i.e. 250 kBq).

2. **Establish the volume of stock radioisotope solution required**: for example, a manufacturer's stock solution of ^{14}C-labelled mannitol contains 50 μCi of radioisotope in 1 mL of 90% v/v ethanol: water. Using Table 55.3, this is equivalent to an activity of 50 × 37 = 1850 kBq. So, the volume of solution required is 250/1850 of the stock volume, i.e. 0.135 1 mL (135 μL).

3. **Calculate the amount of non-radioactive substance required** as for any calculation involving concentration (see p. 158), e.g. 50 mL (0.05 L) of a 25 mmol L^{-1} (0.025 mol L^{-1}) mannitol (relative molecular mass 182.17) will contain 0.05 × 0.025 × 182.17 = 0.2277 g.

4. **Check the amount of radioactive isotope to be added.** In most cases, this represents a negligible amount of substance, e.g. in this instance, 250 kBq of stock solution at a specific activity of 14.8 × 10^6 kBq mmol^{-1} (converted from 0.4 Ci mmol^{-1} using Table 55.3) is equal to 250/14 800 000 = 16.89 nmol, equivalent to approximately 3 μg mannitol. This can be ignored in calculating the mannitol concentration of the experimental solution.

5. **Make up the experimental solution** by adding the appropriate amount of non-radioactive substance and the correct volume of stock solution.

6. **Measure the radioactivity in a known volume of the experimental solution**. If you are using an instrument with automatic correction to Bq, your sample should contain the predicted amount of radioactivity, e.g. an accurately dispensed volume of 100 μL of the mannitol solution should give a corrected count of 100 × 5 = 500 Bq (or 500 × 60 = 30 000 d.p.m.).

7. **Note the specific activity of the experimental solution**: in this case, 100 μL (1 × 10^{-4} L) of the mannitol solution at a concentration of 0.025 mol L^{-1} will contain 25 × 10^{-7} mol (2.5 μmol) mannitol. Dividing the radioactivity in this volume (30 000 d.p.m.) by the amount of substance (eqn [55.2]) gives a specific activity of 30 000/2.5 = 12 000 d.p.m. μmol^{-1}, or 12 d.p.m. nmol^{-1}. This value can be used:

(a) To assess the accuracy of your protocol for preparing the experimental solution: if the measured activity is substantially different from the predicted value, you may have made an error in making up the solution.

(b) To determine the counting efficiency of an instrument; by comparing the measured count rate with the value predicted by your calculations.

(c) To interconvert activity and amount of substance: the most important practical application of specific activity is the conversion of experimental data from counts (activity) into amounts of substance. This is only possible where the substance has not been metabolised or otherwise converted into another form; e.g. a tissue sample incubated in the experimental solution described above with a measured activity of 245 d.p.m. can be converted to nmol mannitol by dividing by the specific activity, expressed in the correct form. Thus 245/12 = 20.417 nmol mannitol.

Correcting for quenching – find out how your instrument corrects for quenching and check the quench indication parameter (QIP) on the printout, which measures the extent of quenching of each sample. Large differences in the QIP would indicate that quenching is variable among samples and might give you cause for concern.

containing the fluor(s) – the 'scintillation cocktail'. The radiation first interacts with the solvent, and the energy from this interaction is passed to the fluors which produce detectable light. The scintillations are measured by photomultiplier tubes which turn the light pulses into electronic pulses, the magnitude of which is directly related to the energy of the original radioactive event. The spectrum of electronic pulses is thus related to the energy spectrum of the radioisotope.

Modern liquid scintillation counters use a series of electronic 'windows' to split the pulse spectrum into two or three components. This may allow more than one isotope to be detected in a single sample, provided their energy spectra are sufficiently different (Fig. 55.3). A complication of this approach is that the energy spectrum can be altered by pigments and chemicals in the sample, which absorb scintillations or interfere with the transfer of energy to the fluor; this is known as quenching

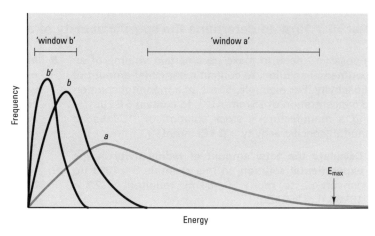

Fig. 55.3 Energy spectra for three radioactive samples, detected using a scintillation counter. Sample *a* is a high energy β-emitter while *b* contains a low energy β-emitter, giving a lower spectral range. Sample *b'* contains the same amount of low energy β-emitter, but with quenching, shifting the spectral distribution to a lower energy band. The counter can be set up to record disintegrations within a selected range (a 'window'). Here, 'window a' could be used to count isotope *a* while 'window b' could give a value of isotope *b*, by applying a correction for the counts due to isotope *a*, based on the results from 'window a'. Dual counting allows experiments to be carried out using two isotopes (double labelling).

(Fig. 55.3). Most instruments have computer-operated quench correction facilities (based on measurements of standards of known activity and energy spectrum) which correct for such changes in counting efficiency.

Many liquid scintillation counters treat the first sample as a 'background', subtracting whatever value is obtained from the subsequent measurements as part of the procedure for converting to d.p.m. If not, you will need to subtract the background count from all other samples. Make sure that you use an appropriate background sample, identical in all respects to your radioactive sample but with no added radioisotope, in the correct position within the machine. Check that the background reading is reasonable (15–30 c.p.m. is a reasonable background for most radioisotopes). Tips for preparing samples for liquid scintillation counting are given in Box 55.2.

Gamma-ray (γ-ray) spectrometry

This is a method by which a mixture of γ-ray-emitting radionuclides can be resolved quantitatively by pulse-height analysis. It is based on the fact that pulse heights (voltages) produced by a photomultiplier tube are proportional to the amounts of γ-ray energy arriving at the scintillant or a lithium-drifted germanium detector. The lithium-drifted germanium detector, which is abbreviated to Ge(Li) – pronounced 'jelly' – provides high resolution (narrow peaks), essential in the analysis of complex mixtures, such as in biological material.

Autoradiography

This is a method where photographic film is exposed to the isotope. It is used mainly to locate radioactive tracers in thin sections of an organism or on chromatography papers and gels, but quantitative

Liquid scintillation counting of high energy β-emitters – β-particles with energies greater than 1 MeV can be counted in water (Čerencov radiation), with no requirement for additional fluors (e.g. ^{32}P).

Box 55.2 Tips for preparing samples for liquid scintillation counting

Modern scintillation counters are very simple to operate; problems are more likely to be due to inadequate sample preparation than to incorrect operation of the machine. Common pitfalls are the following:

- **Incomplete dispersal of the radioactive compound in the scintillation cocktail.** This may lead to underestimation of the true amount of radioactivity present:

  (a) Water-based samples may not mix with the scintillation cocktail – change to an emulsifier-based cocktail. Take care to observe the recommended limits, upper and lower, for amounts of water to be added or the cocktail may not emulsify properly.

  (b) Solid specimens may absorb disintegrations or scintillations: extract radiochemicals using an intermediate solvent like ethanol (ideally within the scintillation vial) and then add the cocktail. Tissue-solubilising compounds such as Soluene are effective, particularly for animal material, but extremely toxic, so the manufacturer's instructions must be followed closely. Radioactive compounds on slices of agarose or polyacrylamide gels may be extracted using a product such as Protosol. Agarose gels can be dissolved in a small volume of boiling water.

(c) Particulate samples may sediment to the bottom of the scintillation vial – suspend them by forming a gel. This can be done with certain emulsifier-based cocktails by adding a specific amount of water.

- **Chemiluminescence.** This is where a chemical reacts with the fluors in the scintillation cocktail causing spurious scintillations, a particular risk with solutions containing strong bases or oxidising agents. Symptoms include very high initial counts which decrease through time. Possible remedies are:

  (a) Leave the vials at room temperature for a time before counting. Check with a suitable blank that counts have dropped to an acceptable level.

  (b) Neutralise basic samples with acid (e.g. acetic acid or HCl).

  (c) Use a scintillation cocktail that resists chemiluminescence, such as Hiconicfluor.

  (d) Raise the energy of the lower counts detected to about 8 keV – most chemiluminescence pulses are weak (0–7 keV). This approach is not suitable for weak emitters, e.g. ^3H.

---

work is possible. The radiation interacts with the film in a similar way to light, silver grains being formed in the developed film where the particles or rays have passed through. The radiation must have enough energy to penetrate into the film, but if it has too much energy the grain formation may be too distant from the point where the isotope was located to identify precisely the point of origin (e.g. high energy β-emitters). Autoradiography is a relatively specialised method and individual lab protocols should be followed for particular isotopes/applications.

Chemical applications for radioactive isotopes

The main advantages of using radioactive isotopes in chemical experiments are:

- Radioactivity is readily detected. Methods of detection are sufficiently sensitive to measure extremely small amounts of radioactive substances.

- Studies can be carried out in synthetic chemistry using radiolabelled compounds, e.g. ^3H or ^{14}C.

- Protocols are simple compared to equivalent methods for chemical analysis.

The main disadvantages are:

- The 'isotope effect'. Molecules containing different isotopes of the same atom may react at slightly different rates and behave in slightly

Investigating the metabolic fate of radiolabelled compounds – you may need to separate individual metabolites before counting, e.g. using chromatography (Chapter 52), or electrophoresis (Chapter 53).

different ways from the natural isotope. The isotope effect is more extreme the smaller the atom, and is most important for ^{3}H-labelled compounds of low molecular mass.

- The possibility of mistaken identity. The presence of radioactivity does not tell you anything about the compound in which the radioactivity is present: it could be different from the one in which it was applied, due to metabolism or spontaneous breakdown of a ^{14}C-containing organic compound.

The main types of experiments are:

- Radiolabelled compounds: the use of radiolabelled compounds in synthetic and tracer studies in important as it allows the scientist to locate the labelled atom, i.e. ^{14}C, ^{3}H, in, for example, chemical synthesis and laboratory environmental fate (degradation) studies. If using radiolabelled compounds several issues arise and these include deciding upon the radionuclide itself, its position in the molecule, the specific activity, the solvent and cost.

- Radio-dating: the age of plant or mineral samples can be determined by measuring the amount of a radioisotope in the sample. The age of the specimen can be found using $t_{1/2}$ by assuming how much was originally incorporated.

- Medical uses: in radiotherapy the use of gamma radiation from ^{60}Co to destroy cancerous cells; ^{24}Na can be introduced into the blood stream to follow the flow of blood and identify obstructions; heart disease can be assessed using ^{201}Tl and ^{99}Tc where the former concentrates in healthy heart tissue and the latter concentrates in abnormal heart tissue.

- Assays: radioisotopes are used in several quantitative detection methods of value to chemists. Radioimmunoassay is a quantitative method for measurement of a substance (the analyte) using antibodies which bind specifically to that analyte. Isotope dilution analysis works on the assumption that introduced radiolabelled molecules will equilibrate with unlabelled molecules present in the sample. The amount of substance initially present can be worked out from the change in specific activity of the radioisotope when it is diluted by the 'cold' material. A method is required whereby the substance can be purified from the sample and sufficient substance must be present for its mass to be measured accurately. Activation analysis is a sensitive technique for the determination of element concentration. It is based upon selectivity inducing radioactivity in some of the atoms of the elements comprising the sample and then selectivity measuring the radiations emitted by the radionuclides. After bombardment with suitable nuclear particles, the induced radionuclides are identified or quantitatively measured. Neutron activation analysis is the most common method of analysis.

Working practices when using radioactive isotopes

By law, undergraduate work with radioactive isotopes must be very closely supervised. In practical classes, the protocols will be clearly outlined, but in project work you may have the opportunity to plan and

Example Carbon dating – living organisms have essentially the same ratio of ^{14}C to ^{12}C as the atmosphere; however, when an organism dies, its ^{14}C/^{12}C falls because the radioactive ^{14}C isotope decays. Since we know the half-life of ^{14}C (5715 years), a sample's ^{14}C/^{12}C ratio will allow us to estimate its age; e.g. if the ratio were exactly 1/8 of that in the atmosphere, the sample is three half-lives old and was formed 17 145 years before present. Such estimates carry an error of the order of 10% and are unreliable for samples older than 50 000 years, for which longer-lived isotopes can be used.

Registering for radioisotope work – in the UK, institutions must be registered for work with specific radioisotopes under the Radioactive Substances Act (1993).

Supervision of work with radioisotopes – in the UK, the *Ionising Radiations Act (1985)* provides details of local arrangements for the supervision of radioisotope work.

carry out your own experiments, albeit under supervision. Some of the factors that you should take into account, based on the assumption that your department and laboratory are registered for radioisotope use, are discussed below:

1. Must you use radioactivity? If not, it may be a legal requirement that you use an alternative method.

2. Have you registered for radioactive work? Normal practice is for all users to register with a local Radiation Protection Supervisor. Details of the project may have to be approved by the appropriate administrator(s). You may have to have a short medical examination before you can start work.

3. What labelled compound will you use? Radioactive isotopes must be ordered well in advance through your department's Radiation Protection Supervisor. Aspects that need to be considered include:

   (a) The radionuclide. With many organic compounds this will be confined to ^{3}H and ^{14}C (but see Table 55.2). The involvement of a significant 'isotope effect' may influence this decision (see p. 425).

   (b) The labelling position. This may be a crucial part of a metabolic study. Specifically labelled compounds are normally more expensive than those that are uniformly ('generally') labelled.

   (c) The specific activity. The upper limit for this is defined by the isotope's half-life, but below this, the higher the specific activity, the more expensive the compound.

4. Are suitable facilities available? You'll need a suitable work area, preferably out of the way of general lab traffic and within a fume cupboard for those cases where volatile radioactive substances are used or may be produced.

In conjunction with your supervisor, decide whether your method of application will introduce enough radioactivity into the system, how you will account for any loss of radioactivity during recovery of the isotope and whether there will be enough activity to count at the end. You should be able to predict approximately the amount of radioactivity in your samples, based on the specific activity of the isotope used, the expected rate of uptake/exchange and the amount of sample to be counted. Use the isotope's specific activity to estimate whether the non-radioactive ('cold') compound introduced with the radiolabelled ('hot') compound may lead to excessive concentrations being administered. Advice for handling data is given in Box 55.1.

Safety and procedural aspects

Make sure the bench surface is one that can be easily decontaminated by washing (e.g. Formica) and always use a disposable surfacing material such as Benchkote. It is good practice to carry out as many operations as possible within a Benchkote-lined plastic tray so that any spillages are contained. You will need a lab coat to be used exclusively for work with radioactivity, safety spectacles and a supply of thin latex or vinyl disposable gloves. Suitable vessels for liquid waste disposal will be

SAFETY NOTE Planning radioisotope work – each new experiment should be planned carefully and experimental protocols laid down in advance so you work as safely as possible and do not waste expensive radioactively labelled compounds.

Carrying out a 'dry run' – consider doing this before working with radioactive compounds, perhaps using a dye to show the movement or dilution of introduced liquids, as this will lessen the risks of accident and improve your technique.

SAFETY NOTE Using Benchkote – the correct way to use Benchkote and similar products is with the waxed surface down (to protect the bench or tray surface) and the absorbent surface up (to absorb any spillage). Write the date in the corner when you put down a new piece. Monitor using a G–M tube and replace regularly under normal circumstances. If you are aware of spillage, replace immediately and dispose of correctly.

CAUTION RADIOACTIVE MATERIAL

Fig. 55.4 Tape showing the international symbol for radioactivity.

required and special plastic bags for solids – make sure you know beforehand the disposal procedures for liquid and solid wastes. Wash your hands after handling a vessel containing a radioactive solution and again before removing your gloves. Gloves should be placed in the appropriate disposal bag as soon as your experimental procedures are complete.

It is important to comply with the following guidelines:

- Read and obey the local rules for safe usage of radiochemicals.

- Maximise the distance between you and the source as much as possible.

- Minimise the duration of exposure.

- Wear protective clothing (properly fastened lab coat, safety glasses, gloves) at all times.

- Use appropriate shielding at all times (Table 55.1).

- Monitor your working area for contamination frequently.

- Mark all glassware, trays, bench work areas, etc., with tape incorporating the international symbol for radioactivity (Fig. 55.4).

- Keep adequate records of what you have done with a radioisotope – the stock remaining and that disposed of in waste form must agree.

- Store radiolabelled compounds appropriately and return them to storage areas immediately after use.

- Dispose of waste promptly and with due regard for local rules.

- Make the necessary reports about waste disposal, etc., to your departmental Radiation Protection Supervisor.

- Clear up after you have finished each experiment.

- Wash thoroughly after using radioactivity.

- Monitor the work area and your body when finished.

Text references and sources for further study

Billington, D., Jayson, G.G. and Maltby, P.J. (1992) *Radioisotopes*. Bios, Oxford.

Choppin, G., Rydberg, J. and Liljenzin, J.O. (2001) *Radiochemistry and Nuclear Chemistry*. Elsevier, Amsterdam.

Kellner, R., Mermet, J.M., Otto, M., Valcarcel, M. and Widmer, H.M. (2004) *Analytical Chemistry: A Modern Approach to Analytical Science*, 2nd edn. Wiley, Chichester.
[Covers all modern analytical topics.]

L'Annunziata, M.F. (ed.) (2003) *Handbook of Radioactivity Analysis*, 2nd edn. Academic Press, San Diego.

L'Annunziata, M. (2007) *Radioactivity: Introduction and History*. Elsevier, Amsterdam.

Haynes, W.M. (ed.) (2010) *CRC Handbook of Chemistry and Physics*, 91st edn. CRC Press, Boca Raton.

Schwedt, G. (1998) *The Essential Guide to Analytical Chemistry*. Wiley, Chichester.

Study exercises

55.1 Carry out a half-life calculation. A rat dropping found in a pyramid in Egypt had a $^{14}C:^{12}C$ ratio that was 57.25% of a modern-day standard. Use this value to estimate the approximate date when the rat visited the pyramid, to the nearest century.

55.2 Practise radioactivity interconversions. Express the following values in the alternative units indicated, with appropriate prefixes as necessary. Answer to three significant figures.

(a) 72 000 d.p.m. as Bq;

(b) 20 μCi as d.p.m.;

(c) 44 400 Bq as μCi;

(d) 6.3×10^5 d.p.m. mol^{-1} as Bq g^{-1}, for a compound with a relative molecular mass of 350;

(e) 3108 d.p.m. as pmol, for a sample of a standard where the specific activity is stated as 50 Ci mol^{-1}.

55.3 Use the concept of specific activity in calculations. A researcher wishes to estimate the rate of uptake of the sugar galactose by carrot cells in a suspension culture. She prepares 250 mL of the cell culture medium containing 10^7 cells per mL and unlabelled galactose at a concentration of 5 mmol L^{-1}. She then 'spikes' this with 5 μL (regard this as an insignificant volume) of radioactive standard containing 55 MBq of ^{14}C-labelled galactose (regard as an insignificant concentration). Answer to two significant figures.

(a) Calculate the specific activity of the galactose in the culture solution in Bq mol^{-1}.

(b) If the total cell sample takes up 79.2×10^5 Bq in a 2-hour period, calculate the galactose uptake rate in mol s^{-1} cell^{-1}.

Definitions

Spectroscopy – any technique involving the production and subsequent recording of a spectrum of electromagnetic radiation, usually in terms of wavelength or energy.

Spectrometry – any technique involving the measurement of a spectrum, e.g. of electromagnetic radiation, molecular masses, etc.

Interpreting spectra – the spectrum produced in UV–vis, IR and NMR spectroscopy is a plot of wavelength or frequency or energy (x-axis) against absorption of energy (y-axis). Convention puts high frequency (high energy, short wavelength) at the left-hand side of the spectrum.

In addition to ultraviolet–visible (UV–vis) spectroscopy (p. 333), there are three other essential techniques that you will encounter during your laboratory course. They are:

1. *Infrared (IR) spectroscopy*: this is concerned with the energy changes involved in the stretching and bending of covalent bonds in molecules.

2. *Nuclear magnetic resonance (NMR) spectroscopy*: this involves the absorption of energy by specific atomic nuclei in magnetic fields and is probably the most powerful tool available for the structural determination of molecules (Chapter 57).

3. *Mass spectrometry (MS)*: this is based on the fragmentation of compounds into smaller units. The resulting positive ions are then separated according to their mass-to-charge ratio (m/z) (Chapter 58).

As with UV–vis spectroscopy, IR and NMR spectroscopy are based on the interaction of electromagnetic radiation with molecules, whereas MS is different in that it relies on high-energy particles (electrons or ions) to break up the molecules. The relationship between the various types of spectroscopy and the electromagnetic spectrum (see p. 333) is shown in Table 56.1.

Infrared spectroscopy

A covalent bond between two atoms can be crudely modelled as a spring connecting two masses and the frequency of vibration of the spring is defined by Hooke's law (eqn [56.1]), which relates the frequency of the vibration (v) to the strength of the spring, expressed as the force constant (k), and to the masses (m_1 and m_2) on the ends of the spring [defined as the reduced mass $\mu = (m_1 \times m_2) \div (m_1 + m_2)$].

$$v = \frac{1}{2\pi}\sqrt{\frac{k}{\mu}}$$

[56.1]

In simple terms, this means that:

- the stretching vibration of a bond between two atoms will increase in frequency (energy) if on changing from a single bond to a double bond

Table 56.1 The electromagnetic spectrum and types of spectroscopy

Type of radiation	Origin	Wavelength	Type of spectroscopy
γ-rays	Atomic nuclei	< 0.1 nm	γ-ray spectroscopy
X-rays	Inner shell electrons	0.01–2.0 nm	X-ray fluorescence (XRF)
Ultraviolet (UV)	Ionisation	2.0–200 nm	Vacuum UV spectroscopy
UV/visible	Valency electrons	200–800 nm	UV/visible spectroscopy
Infrared	Molecular vibrations	0.8–300 μm	IR and Raman spectroscopy
Microwaves	Molecular rotations Electron spin	1 mm to 30 cm	Microwave spectroscopy Electron spin resonance (ESR)
Radio waves	Nuclear spin	0.6–10 m	Nuclear magnetic resonance (NMR)

and then to a triple bond between the same two atoms (masses), i.e. the spring gets stronger. For example,

$$v \text{ for } C{\equiv}C > v \text{ for } C{=}C > v \text{ for } C{-}C$$

- as the masses of the atoms on a bond increases, the frequency of the vibration decreases, i.e the effect of reducing the magnitude of μ; for example,

$$v \text{ for } C{-}H > v \text{ for } C{-}C; \, v \text{ for } C{-}H > v \text{ for } C{-}D; \, v \text{ for } O{-}H > v \text{ for } S{-}H$$

Bonds can also bend, but this movement requires less energy than stretching and thus the bending frequency of a bond is always *lower* than the corresponding stretching frequency. When IR radiation of the same frequency as the bond interacts with the bond it is absorbed and increases the amplitude of vibration of the bond. This absorption is detected by the IR spectrometer and results in a peak in the spectrum. For a vibration to be detected in the IR region the bond must undergo a change in dipole moment when the vibration occurs. Bonds with the greatest change in dipole moment during vibration show the most intense absorption, e.g. $C{=}O$ and $C{-}O$.

Since bonds between specific atoms have particular frequencies of vibration, IR spectroscopy provides a means of identifying the type of bonds in a molecule, e.g. all alcohols will have an O–H stretching frequency and all compounds containing a carbonyl group will have a $C{=}O$ stretching frequency. This property, which does not rely on chemical tests, is extremely useful in diagnosing the functional groups within a covalent molecule.

IR absorption bands – since the frequency of vibration of a bond is a specific value you would expect to see line spectra on the chart. However, each vibration is associated with several rotational motions and bands (peaks) are seen in the spectrum.

IR spectra

A typical IR spectrum is shown in Fig. 56.1 and you should note the following points:

- The x-axis, the wavelength of the radiation, is given in wavenumbers ($\bar{v}$) and expressed in reciprocal centimetres (cm^{-1}). You may still

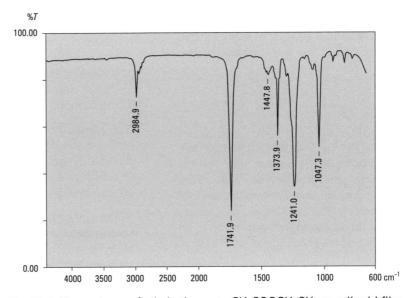

Fig. 56.1 IR spectrum of ethyl ethanoate $CH_3COOCH_2CH_3$ as a liquid film.

The use of wavenumber – this is an old established convention, since high wavenumber = high frequency = high energy = short wavelength. Expression of the IR range, $4000\,cm^{-1}$ to $650\,cm^{-1}$, is in 'easy' numbers and the high energy is found on the left-hand side of the spectrum. Note that IR spectroscopists often refer to wavenumbers as 'frequencies', e.g. 'the peak of the C=O stretching "frequency" is at $1720\,cm^{-1}$'.

see some spectra from old instruments using microns (μ, equivalent to the SI unit 'micrometres', μm, at $1 \times 10^{-6}\,m$) for wavelength; the conversion is given by eqn [56.2]:

$$\text{wavenumber } (cm^{-1}) = 1/\text{wavelength } (cm) = 10\,000/\text{wavelength } (\mu m)$$
[56.2]

- The y-axis, expressing the amount of radiation absorbed by the molecule, is usually shown as % transmittance (p. 334). When no radiation is absorbed (all is transmitted through the sample) we have 100% transmittance and 0% transmittance implies all radiation is absorbed at a particular wavenumber. Since the y-axis scale goes from 0 to 100% transmittance, the absorption peaks are displayed *down* from the 100% line; this is *opposite* to most other common spectra.

- The cells holding the sample usually display imperfections and are not completely transparent to IR radiation, even when empty. Therefore the base line of the spectrum is rarely set on 100% transmittance and quantitative applications of IR spectroscopy are more complex than for UV–vis (p. 336).

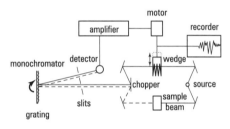

Fig. 56.2 Schematic diagram of a double-beam IR spectrometer.

Using double-beam instruments – you can identify the sample beam by quickly placing your hand in the beam. If the pen records a peak, this is the sample beam, but if the pen moves up, then this is the reference beam.

Using the 100% control – if you use this control to set the base line for the sample, you *must* turn down the 100% control when you remove the sample, otherwise the pen-drive mechanism may be damaged in trying to drive off the top of the chart.

IR spectrometers

There are two general types:

1. Double-beam or dispersive instruments in which the IR radiation from a single source is split into two identical beams. One beam passes through the sample and the other is used as a reference and passes through air or the pure solvent used to dissolve the sample. The difference in intensity of the two beams is detected and recorded as a peak; the principal components of this type of instrument are shown in Fig. 56.2. The important controls on the spectrometer are:

   (a) scan speed: this is the rate at which the chart moves – slower for greater accuracy and sharp peaks;

   (b) wavelength range: the full spectrum or a part of the IR range may be selected;

   (c) 100% control: this is used to set the pen at the 100% transmittance line when no sample is present the base line. It is usual practice to set the pen at 90% transmittance at $4000\,cm^{-1}$ when the sample is present, to give peaks of the maximum deflection.

   You should remember that this is an electromechanical instrument and you should always make sure that you align the chart against the calibration marks on the chart holder. In the more advanced instruments an on-board computer stores a library of standard spectra, which can be compared with your experimental spectrum.

2. Fourier transform IR (FT–IR) spectrometer: the value of IR spectroscopy is greatly enhanced by Fourier transformation, named after the mathematician J.B. Fourier. The FT is a procedure for inter-converting frequency functions and time or distance functions. The IR beam, composed of all the frequencies in the IR range, is passed through the sample and generates interference patterns, which

are then transformed electronically into a normal IR spectrum. The advantages of FT–IR are:

(a) rapid scanning speed – typically four scans can be made per minute, allowing addition of the separate scans to enhance the signal-to-noise ratio and improve the resolution of the spectrum;

(b) simplicity of operation – the reference is scanned first, stored and then subtracted from the sample spectrum;

(c) enhanced sensitivity: the facility of spectrum addition from multiple scans permits detection of smaller quantities of chemicals;

(d) the integral computer system enables the use of libraries of spectra and simplifies spectrum manipulation, such as the subtraction of contaminant or solvent spectra.

The procedures for running IR spectra on double-beam and FT spectrometers are described in Box 56.1.

Box 56.1 How to run an infrared spectrum of a liquid, solid film, mull or KBr disk

A. Double-beam spectrometer

1. **Ensure that the instrument is switched on** and that it has had a few minutes to warm up.

2. **Make sure that the chart is aligned with the calibration marks on the chart bed or chart drum.** Most spectrometers scan from $4000\,cm^{-1}$ to $650\,cm^{-1}$ and the pen should be at the $4000\,cm^{-1}$ mark.

3. **Adjust the 100% transmittance control to about 90%,** if necessary.

4. **Place the sample cell in the sample beam and adjust the 100% transmittance control to 90%,** or the highest value possible.

5. **Select the scan speed.** You must balance the definition required in the spectrum with the time available for the experiment. For most qualitative applications the fastest setting is satisfactory.

6. **Press the 'scan' or 'start' button to run the spectrum.** The spectrum will be recorded and the spectrometer will automatically align itself at the end of the run. *Do not press* any other buttons while the spectrum is running or the instrument may not realign itself at the end of the run.

7. **Adjust the 100% transmittance control to about 50%,** remove the sample cell from the spectrometer and turn the 100% transmittance control to about 90%.

8. **Enter all of the following data on the spectrum:** name, date, compound and phase (liquid film, Nujol® mull, KBr disk, etc.).

B. FT–IR spectrometer

1. **Make sure that the sample compartment is empty** and close the lid.

2. **Select the number of scans;** usually four is adequate for routine work.

3. **Select 'background' on the on-screen menu,** and scan the background. *Do not press* any other buttons or icons while the spectrum is running.

4. **Place the sample cell in the beam,** close the lid, select 'sample' and scan the sample. *Do not press* any other buttons or icons while the spectrum is running.

5. **Select 'customize',** or a similar function, and enter all the data – name, date, compound, phase (liquid film, Nujol® mull, KBr disk, etc.) – on the spectrum.

6. **Select 'print',** to produce the spectrum from the printer.

Problems with IR spectra

These are usually caused by poor sample preparation and the more common faults are:

1. **The large peaks have tips below the bottom of the chart or the large peaks have 'squared tips' near the bottom of the chart:** the sample is too thick; remove some sample from the cell and rerun the spectrum.

2. **The spectrum is 'weak', i.e. few peaks:** the sample is too thin – add more sample or remake the KBr disk.

3. **The base line cannot be adjusted to 90% transmittance:** the NaCl plates or KBr disk are 'fogged', scratched or dirty – replace or remake the KBr disk.

4. **The pen tries to 'go off' the top of the spectrum:** obviously due to some absorption at $4000\,cm^{-1}$ when you were setting the base line. Repeat baseline set-up but at 80% transmittance and bear in mind that dirty plates, above, can be the cause.

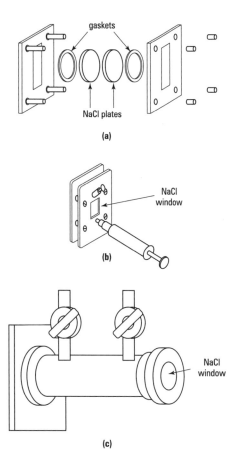

Fig. 56.3 Cells for IR spectroscopy: (a) demountable cell for liquid and solid films and mulls; (b) solution cell; (c) gas cell.

IR spectra of aqueous solutions – special sample cells made from CaF_2 are available for aqueous solutions, but they are expensive and only used in specific applications.

Storing IR sample cells and KBr powder – NaCl cells are always stored in desiccators to prevent 'fogging' by absorption of moisture. KBr powder must be dried in the oven, cooled and kept in a desiccator.

Sample handling

You can obtain IR spectra of solids, liquids and gases by use of the appropriate sample cell (sample holder). The sample holder must be completely transparent to IR radiation; consequently glass and plastic cells cannot be used. The most common sample cells you will encounter are made from sodium chloride or potassium bromide and you cannot use aqueous solutions or very wet samples, otherwise the sample cells will dissolve. A typical range of sample cells is shown in Fig. 56.3 and for routine qualitative work you will regularly use NaCl plates and KBr disks to obtain spectra of solids and liquids. Solution cells and gas cells are utilised in more specialised applications and require specific instructions and training.

Liquid samples

The most convenient way to obtain the IR spectrum of a pure, dry liquid is to make a thin liquid film between two NaCl disks (plates). Since the film thickness is unknown, this procedure is not applicable to quantitative work.

Solid samples

If you were to place a fine powder between two NaCl plates, a usable spectrum would not be obtained because the IR radiation would be scattered by diffraction at the edges of the particles and would not pass through to the detector. There are *three* solutions to this problem:

1. *Mulls*: in which the finely ground solid is mixed with a liquid, usually Nujol® (liquid paraffin) or, less frequently, HCB (hexachloro-1, 3-butadiene). This mulling liquid does not dissolve the chemical but fills the gaps round the edges of the crystals preventing diffraction and scattering of the IR radiation. Remember that these mulling liquids have their own IR spectrum, which is relatively simple, and can be subtracted either 'mentally' or by the computer. The choice of mulling liquid depends upon the region of the IR spectrum of interest: Nujol® is a simple hydrocarbon containing only C–H and C–C bonds, whereas HCB has no C–H bonds, but has C–Cl, C=C and C–C bonds. Examination of the separate spectra of your unknown compound in each of these mulling agents enables the full spectrum to be analysed.

2. *KBr disks*: here the finely ground solid compound is mixed with anhydrous KBr and squeezed under pressure. The KBr becomes fluid and forms a disk containing the solid compound dispersed evenly within it and suitable for obtaining a spectrum. The advantage of the KBr disk technique is the absence of the spectrum from the mulling liquid, but the disadvantages are the equipment required (Fig. 56.4) and the practice required to obtain suitable transparent disks, which are very delicate and rapidly absorb atmospheric moisture.

3. *Thin solid films*: here a dilute solution of the compound in a low-boiling-point solvent such as dichloromethane or ether is allowed to evaporate on a NaCl plate producing a thin transparent film. This method gives excellent results but is slightly limited by solubility factors.

Box 56.2 How to prepare liquid and solid films and mulls

A. Preparing a liquid film

1. **Select a pair of clean NaCl plates from a desiccator,** clean them by wiping with a soft tissue soaked in dichloromethane and place them on the bench on a piece of filter paper or tissue paper to prevent scratching by the bench surface.

2. **Using a glass rod or boiling stick, place a small drop of liquid in the centre of one of the plates.** Do not use a Pasteur pipette, which may scratch the surface of the plate.

3. **Carefully, holding it by the edge, place the other plate on top and see if a thin film spreads between the plates, covering the centres.** Do not press to force the plates together. If there is not enough liquid, carefully separate the plates by lifting at the edge and add another drop of liquid. If there is too much liquid, separate the plates and wipe the liquid from one of them using a soft tissue.

B. Preparing a thin solid film

1. **Dissolve the sample (about 5 mg) in a suitable low-boiling-point solvent (about 0.25 mL),** such as DCM or ether.

2. **Place two drops of the solution onto the centre of a NaCl plate** and allow the solvent to evaporate. Use a Pasteur pipette, but *do not* touch the surface of the plate.

3. **If the resulting thin film of solid does not cover the centre of the plate,** add a little more solution.

4. **Mount the *single* NaCl plate in the spectrometer and run the spectrum.** Note that the NaCl plate can rest on the 'V'-shaped wedge on the sample holder in the spectrometer.

C. Preparing a mull

1. **Grind a small sample of your compound (about 5 mg) using a small agate mortar and pestle for at least 2 minutes.** The powder should be as fine as possible.

2. **Add one drop of mulling agent (Nujol® or HCB) and continue grinding until a smooth paste is formed.**

If the mull is too thick, add another drop of mulling agent, or if it is too thin, add a little more solid. Only experience will give you the correct consistency of the mull and the key to a good spectrum is a mull of the correct fluidity.

3. **Transfer the mull to the centre or along the diameter of an NaCl plate,** on a piece of filter paper or tissue paper to prevent scratching by the bench surface, using a small plastic spatula or a boiling stick.

4. **Carefully, holding it by the edge, place the other plate on top and very gently press to ensure that the mull spreads as a thin film between the plates.** If there is not enough liquid, carefully separate the plates by lifting at the edge and add another drop of mull. If there is too much liquid (poor spectrum), separate the plates and wipe the mull from one of them using a tissue.

C. Setting up the cell holder for liquid films and mulls

1. **Place the back-plate of the cell holder on the bench, position the rubber gasket, place the NaCl plates on the gasket and then put the second gasket on top of the plates.** These gaskets are essential to prevent fracture of the plates when you tighten the locking nuts.

2. **Carefully place the cell holder top-plate on the top gasket, drop the locking nuts into place and carefully tighten each in rotation.** These are safety nuts and if you over-tighten them or if the back- and top-plates are not parallel, they will spring loose to prevent the NaCl plates being crushed.

3. **Transfer the cell holder assembly to the spectro-meter and make sure it is securely mounted in the cell compartment.**

4. **Clean the plates in the fume cupboard by wiping them with a tissue soaked in DCM,** stand them on filter paper or tissue paper to allow the solvent to evaporate and put them in the desiccator. Allow the DCM to evaporate from the tissue swab and dispose of it in the chemical waste.

Handling NaCl plates and KBr disks – NaCl plates are delicate and easily damaged by scratching, dropping or squeezing. Hold them only by the edges and place them on filter paper or tissue when adding chemicals. KBr disks should be handled using tweezers.

When you are recording spectra of mulls, KBr disks and thin solid films air is used as the reference and they are suitable for qualitative analysis only. The procedure for the preparation of liquid and solid films and mulls is described in Box 56.2 and that for KBr disks in Box 56.3.

Attenuated total reflectance (ATR) sample holders

The principle of this technique depends on the fact that when light passes from a dense medium to a less dense medium, and the angle of the incident

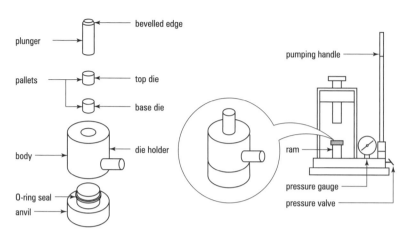

Fig. 56.4 Equipment for preparation of a KBr disk.

Box 56.3 How to prepare a KBr disk

1. **Take spectroscopic-grade KBr powder from the oven** and allow it to cool in a desiccator.

2. **Grind your compound (1–2 mg) in an agate mortar for 2 minutes, then add the KBr (0.2 g) and continue grinding to a fine powder.** Put the KBr powder back into the oven.

3. **Obtain a 'disk kit'** and make sure that:
   (a) it is complete – comprising a plunger, two dies (base and top), a die holder and an anvil, as shown in Fig. 56.4;
   (b) the components are for the same device – they are not interchangeable with another disk kit – and should be numbered.

4. **Press the die holder onto the anvil ensuring a proper fit.**

5. **Lower the base die, numbered-side down, into the die holder** and make sure it slides into a depth of about 50 mm.

6. **Pour the compound/KBr powder mixture, about one-third to one-half of the amount prepared, into the die holder** and tap gently to produce an even layer on the base die.

7. **Lower the top die, numbered-side up, on top of the KBr mixture and make sure it slides down onto the powder.**

8. **Slide the plunger, with the bevelled edge at the top, into the die holder** ensuring that it is touching the top die and press down gently so that the dies slide to the bottom, ensuring that you do not then push off the anvil.

9. **Place the assembled disk kit in the hydraulic press** and tighten the top screw so that it touches the top of the plunger.

10. **Connect the anvil to a source of vacuum**, e.g. a rotary vacuum pump.

11. **Close the hydraulic release valve on the side of the press and gently pump the handle** until the pressure gauge reads between 8 and 10 tons and leave for 30 seconds.

12. **Open the hydraulic release valve gently** and, when the pressure has fallen to zero, disconnect the vacuum from the anvil.

13. **Loosen the top screw** and remove the disk kit from the press.

14. **Turn the disk kit upside down and carefully pull off the anvil.** Make sure that the plunger does not slide out by supporting it in the palm of your hand.

15. **Gently push the plunger and the base die will emerge from the die holder.** Take off the base die leaving the KBr disk exposed.

16. **Carefully slide the KBr disk into the special disk holder** using a microspatula.

17. **Run the IR spectrum immediately**, because the disk will begin to cloud over as it absorbs atmospheric moisture.

18. **Clean the disk kit components with a tissue and check that all parts are present.**

19. **If the dies or the plunger stick in the die holder, tell your instructor.**

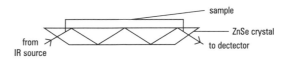

Fig. 56.5 Schematic of an ATR cell.

light is at a critical angle, then the light is reflected back into the dense medium, having penetrated a short distance into the less dense medium (see Fig. 56.5). In effect, the infrared spectrum of the less dense medium is recorded.

The ATR cell is commonly made of infrared transparent zinc selenide (ZnSe) and the major advantage of ATR cells is that spectra are now available from a wide variety of sample types without the need for sample preparation – the sample is simply laid on top of the ATR cell. Paper (with print), fabrics, polymer films, powders, gels and even aqueous solutions can produce high quality infrared spectra.

Interpretation of IR spectra

To identify compounds from their IR spectrum you should know at which frequencies the stretching and bending vibrations occur. A detailed analysis can be achieved using the correlation tables found in specialist textbooks. For interpretation, the spectrum is divided into three regions.

Region 1 (4000–2000 cm^{-1}): this region contains the high frequency vibrations such as C–H, N–H and O–H stretching, together with C=C and C≡N stretching vibrations.

Region 2 (2000–1500 cm^{-1}): this is known as the 'functional group region' and includes the stretching frequencies for C=C, C=O, C=N, N=O and N–H bending vibrations.

Region 3 (1500–650 cm^{-1}): this region contains stretching bands for C–O, C–N, C–Hal and the C–H bending vibrations. It is known as the 'fingerprint region' because it also contains complex low-energy vibrations resulting from the overall molecular structure and these are unique to each different molecule. Fig. 56.6 shows the spectra of 1-propanol and 1-butanol, both of which show almost identical peaks for the O–H, C–H and C–O stretching frequencies and the C–H bending frequencies, but the spectra are different in the number and intensity of the peaks between 1500 and 650 cm^{-1}, resulting from the presence of the additional CH_2 in 1-butanol. Conversely, these highly specific bands in the 'fingerprint' region are useful for identification of molecules by comparison with authentic spectra via a database.

A simple correlation chart indicating the three regions of the spectrum and their associated bond vibrations is shown in Fig. 56.7. You can obtain most diagnostic information from spectral regions 1 and 2, since these are the simplest regions containing the peaks related to specific functional groups, while region 3 is normally used for confirmation of your findings. Another important aspect of the IR spectrum is the relative intensities of the commonly found peaks and you should become familiar with peak sizes. A chart indicating the positions, general shapes and relative intensities of commonly found peaks is shown in Fig. 56.8. When you are attempting to interpret an IR spectrum you should use the approach described in Box 56.4.

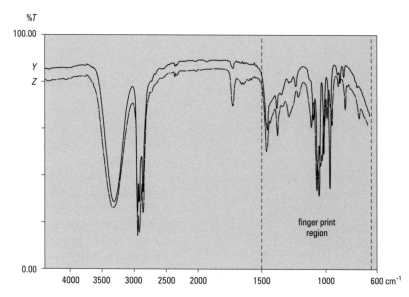

Fig. 56.6 IR spectra of 1-propanol (*Y*) and 1-butanol (*Z*).

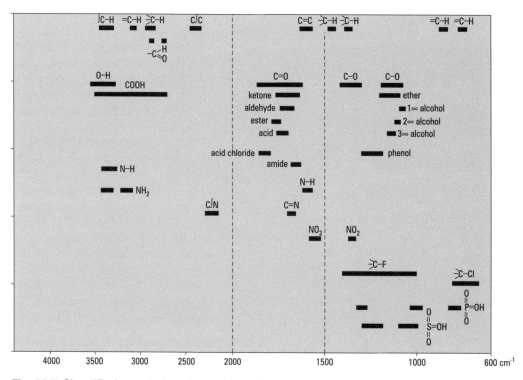

Fig. 56.7 Simplified correlation chart of functional group absorptions.

If you are studying complexes formed from metals and organic ligands, the metal–ligand stretching vibration will occur below 600 cm^{-1} and special IR spectrometers are used to observe this region. However, changes in the IR spectrum of the organic ligand on complexation can be detected in the normal 4000–650 cm^{-1} range.

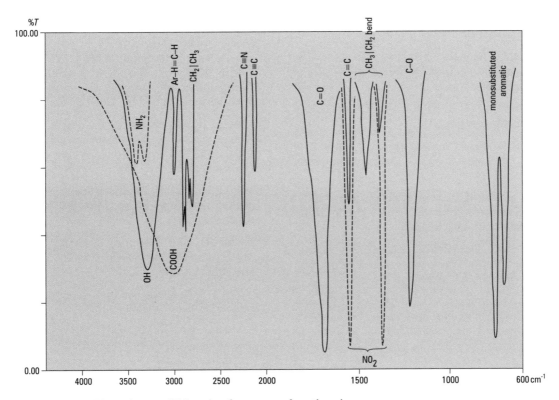

Fig. 56.8 Idealised intensities of some IR bands of common functional groups.

Box 56.4 How to interpret an IR spectrum

1. **Note the conditions under which the spectrum was obtained**, which should be written on the spectrum as 'phase'. If it is a solution or a mull, you will need to identify and 'subtract' the spectrum of the mulling agent or solvent.

2. **Consider carefully the reaction you have carried out.** You should know, from the correlation table, the functional groups and peaks in the starting materials and those expected in the product.

3. **Remember that the absence of peaks may be as useful in interpretation as the presence of peaks.**

4. **Do not attempt to identify all the peaks**, just those which are relevant to your interpretation. Go for the large peaks first.

5. **Many sharp peaks of medium to strong intensity** throughout the spectrum generally indicate an aromatic compound.

6. **Examine region 1 (4000–2000 cm^{-1}).** It is useful to draw a line on the chart at 3000 cm^{-1}: just above the line (3000–3100 cm^{-1}) you will find the stretching frequencies for C_{sp}–H and C_{sp^2}–H indicating

unsaturation, while just below (2980–2800 cm^{-1}) you will find the C_{sp^3}–H stretching frequencies for CH_3, CH_2 and CH in saturated systems. Other bands for O–H, N–H, C≡C and C≡N are obvious.

7. **Examine region 2 (2000–1500 cm^{-1}).** Here you will find C=O stretch, usually the most intense band in the spectrum; C=C and C=N stretches, less intense and sharper; N=O stretch (from NO_2) intense and sharp and with a twin band in region 3; N–H bending vibrations – do not confuse with C=O.

8. **Examine region 3 (1500–650 cm^{-1}).** The large bands here are C–O, C–N, C–Cl, S=O, P=O, N=O (twin from region 2) stretches and C–H 'breathing' bands (900–700 cm^{-1}), which indicate the number and position of substituents on a benzene ring. Medium-intensity peaks of importance include the CH_3 and CH_2 bands at 1460 cm^{-1} and 1370 cm^{-1} from the carbon skeleton which are also found in Nujol®.

9. **Tabulate your results and make the appropriate deductions**, after consulting the detailed correlation table. Remember to correlate the spectroscopic data with the chemical data.

Sources for further study

Anderson, R.J., Bendell, D.J. and Groundwater, P.W. (2004) *Organic Spectroscopic Analysis*. Royal Society of Chemistry. Cambridge.

CD-ROM Abrams, C.B. (1992) *IR Tutor*. Perkin Elmer Ltd, Beaconsfield, UK.

Crews, J., Rodriguez, J. and Jaspars, M. (2010) *Organic Structure Analysis*. Oxford University Press, New York.

Field, L.D., Sternhell, S. and Kalman, J.R. (2008) *Organic Structures from Spectra,* 4th edn. John Wylie & Sons Ltd, Chichester.

Griffiths, P. and De Haseth, J.A. (2007) *Fourier Transform Infrared Spectroscopy*, 2nd edn. John Wylie & Sons Ltd, Chichester.

Pavia, D.L., Lampman, G.M., Kriz, G.S. and Vyvyan, J.A. (2009) *Introduction to Spectroscopy*, 4th edn. Brooks/Cole, Pacific Grove, California.

Shriner, R.L., Hermann, C.K.F., Morrill, T.C., Curtin, D.Y. and Fuson, R.C. (2003) *Systematic Identification of Organic Compounds*, 8th edn. John Wylie & Sons Ltd, Chichester.

Silverstein, R.M., Webster, F.X. and Kiemle, D.J. (2005) *Spectroscopic Identification of Organic Chemicals*, 7th edn. John Wylie & Sons Ltd, Chichester.

Stuart, B.H. (2004) *Infrared Spectroscopy: Fundamentals and Applications*. John Wiley & Sons Ltd, Chichester.

Williams, D. and Fleming, I. (2008) *Spectroscopic Methods in Organic Chemistry*, 6th edn. McGraw-Hill, Maidenhead, UK.

Study exercise

56.1 The following infrared spectra A → D are all run as liquid films and they represent the colouress liquids (i) 1-octanol, (ii) heptane, (iii) benzonitile, (iv) ethyl ethanoate. Deduce the structural information from each of the spectra A → D and hence identify the compounds A → D.

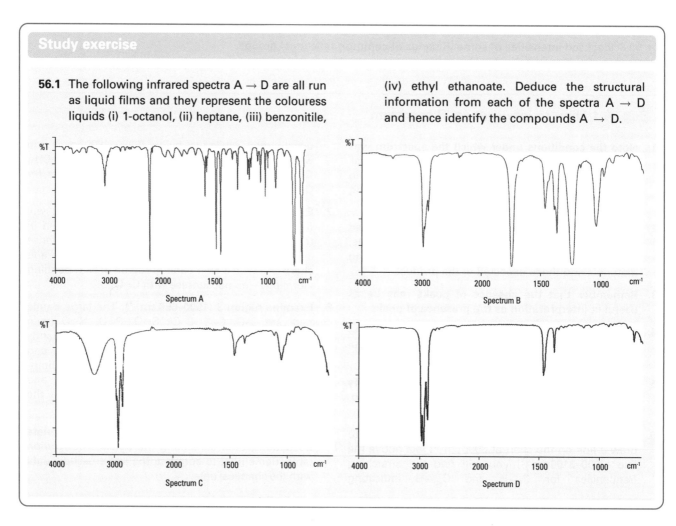

Electromagnetic radiation (typically at radio frequencies of 60–600 MHz) is used to identify compounds in a process known as nuclear magnetic resonance (NMR) spectroscopy. This is possible because of differences in the magnetic states of atomic nuclei, involving very small transitions in energy levels. The atomic nuclei of the isotopes of many elements possess a magnetic moment. When these magnetic moments interact with a uniform external magnetic field, they behave like tiny compass needles and align themselves in a direction 'with' or 'against' the field. The two orientations, characteristic of nuclei with a nuclear spin quantum number $I = \frac{1}{2}$, have two different energies: the orientation aligned 'with' the field has a lower energy than that aligned 'against' the field (Fig. 57.1).

Typical magnetic nuclei of general use to chemists and biochemists are ^1H, ^{13}C, ^{19}F and ^{31}P, all of which have nuclear spin quantum numbers $I = \frac{1}{2}$. The energy difference between the two levels (ΔE) corresponds to a precise electromagnetic frequency (v), according to similar quantum principles for the excitation of electrons (p. 333). When a sample containing an isotope with a magnetic nucleus is placed in a magnetic field and exposed to an appropriate radio frequency, transitions between the energy levels of magnetic nuclei will occur when the energy gap and applied frequency are in *resonance* (i.e. when they are matched exactly in energy). Differences in energy levels, and hence resonance frequencies (v_0), depend upon the magnitude of the applied magnetic field (B_0) and the magnetogyric ratio (γ), according to the equation:

$$v_0 = \gamma B_0 / 2\pi \qquad [57.1]$$

For a given value of the applied field (B_0), nuclei of different elements have different values of the magnetogyric ratio (γ) and will give rise to resonance at various radio frequencies. The principal components of an NMR spectrometer are shown in Fig. 57.2.

For magnetic nuclei in a given molecule, an NMR spectrum is generated because, in the presence of the applied field, different nuclei of the same atoms experience small, different, local magnetic fields depending on the arrangement of electrons, i.e. in the chemical bonds, in their vicinity. The effective field at the nucleus can be expressed as:

$$B = B_0(1 - \sigma) \qquad [57.2]$$

where σ (the shielding constant) expresses the contribution of the small secondary field generated by the nearby electrons. The magnitude of σ depends on the electronic environment of a nucleus, so nuclei of the same

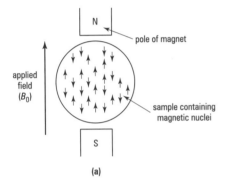

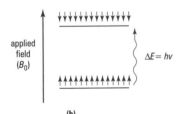

Fig. 57.1 Effect of an applied magnetic field, B_0, on magnetic nuclei. (a) Nuclei in magnetic field have one of two orientations – either with the field or against the field (in the absence of an applied field, the nuclei would have random orientation). (b) Energy diagram for magnetic nuclei in applied magnetic field.

Example For an external magnetic field of 2.5 T (tesla), ΔE for ^1H is 6.6×10^{-26} J and since $\Delta E = hv$, the corresponding frequency (v) is 100 MHz; for ^{13}C in the same field, ΔE is 1.7×10^{-26} J, and v is 25 MHz.

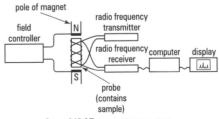

Fig. 57.2 Components of an NMR spectrometer.

isotope give rise to small different resonance frequencies according to the equation:

$$v_0 = \gamma B_0 (1 - \sigma)/2\pi \qquad [57.3]$$

> **KEY POINT** The variation of resonance frequencies with surrounding electron density is crucial to the usefulness of the NMR technique. If it did not occur, *all nuclei* of a single isotope would come into resonance at the same combination of magnetic field and radio frequency and only *one peak* would be observed in the spectrum.

Chemical shift

The separation of resonance frequencies resulting from the different electronic environments of the nucleus of the isotope is called the *chemical shift*. It is expressed in dimensionless terms, as parts per million (ppm), against an internal standard, usually *tetra*methyl*s*ilane (TMS). By convention, the chemical shift is positive if the sample nucleus is less shielded (lower electron density in the surrounding bonds) than the nucleus in the reference and negative if it is more shielded (greater electron density in the surrounding bonds). The chemical shift scale (δ) for a nucleus is defined as:

$$\delta = [(v_{sample} - v_{reference}) \times 10^6]/(v_{reference}) \qquad [57.4]$$

This means that the chemical shift of a specific nucleus in a molecule is at the same δ value, no matter what the operating frequency of the NMR spectrometer.

An NMR spectrum is a plot of chemical shift (δ) as the *x*-axis against absorption of energy (resonance) as the *y*-axis. On the right-hand side of the spectrum at $\delta = 0$ ppm there may be a small peak, which is the reference (TMS). A typical ^{1}H–NMR spectrum is shown in Fig. 57.3.

NMR spectrometers

These can operate at different radio frequencies and magnetic fields and are usually referred to in terms of radio frequency, e.g. 60 MHz, 270 MHz and 500 MHz spectrometers. Spectrometers operating above 100 MHz require expensive superconducting magnets to generate the high

Measuring chemical shifts – ppm is *not* a concentration term in NMR but is used to reflect the small frequency changes that occur relative to the reference standard, measured in proportional terms.

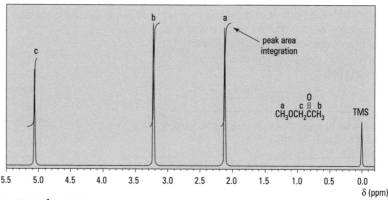

Fig. 57.3 ^{1}H–NMR spectrum of 1-methoxypropanone.

Using deuterated solvents – these are expensive and should not be wasted. $CDCl_3$ is 100 times more expensive than spectroscopic-grade $CHCl_3$ and the others are at least 10–15 times more expensive than $CDCl_3$.

Using $CDCl_3$ – when using this solvent additional peaks can appear in the spectrum. ^1H spectra – a sharp single peak at $\delta_H = 7.26$ ppm due to the presence of $CHCl_3$ as an impurity (Fig. 57.4).

^{13}C spectra – a triplet at $\delta_C = 77.41$ ppm due to coupling between ^{13}C and D $(I = 1)$ (Fig. 57.5).

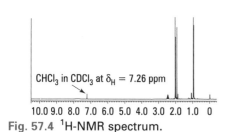

CHCl₃ in CDCl₃ at $\delta_H = 7.26$ ppm

10.0 9.0 8.0 7.0 6.0 5.0 4.0 3.0 2.0 1.0 0

Fig. 57.4 ^1H-NMR spectrum.

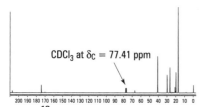

CDCl₃ at $\delta_C = 77.41$ ppm

200 190 180 170 160 150 140 130 120 110 100 90 80 70 60 50 40 30 20 10 0

Fig. 57.5 ^{13}C-NMR spectrum (broad band decoupled).

magnetic fields. In routine laboratory work 60 MHz and 90 MHz instruments are common but 270 MHz machines are becoming more affordable. Increasing the operating frequency of the spectrometer effectively increases the resolution of the chemical shifts of the nuclei under examination. For example, the difference in frequency between 0 and 1δ is 60 Hz in a 60 MHz spectrometer but 270 Hz for a 270 MHz instrument.

Spectrometers can be divided into two types:

1. *Continuous-wave (CW) spectrometers*, which use a permanent magnet or an electromagnet, usually operating at 60 or 90 MHz. In practice the radio frequency is held constant and small electromagnets on the faces of the main magnet (sweep coils) vary the magnetic field over the chemical shift range. The spectrometer sweeps through the spectroscopic region plotting resonances (absorption peaks) on a chart recorder (cf. dispersion IR spectrometers). CW spectrometers are usually dedicated to observation of a specific nucleus such as ^1H.

2. *Fourier transform (FT) spectrometers*, using superconducting magnets containing liquid nitrogen and liquid helium for cooling. Here the magnetic field is held constant and the sample is irradiated with a radio frequency pulse containing all the radio frequencies over the chemical shift region of the nucleus being examined, cf. FT–IR (p. 432). Computer control allows rapid repeat scans to accumulate spectra, presenting the data as a standard CW-type spectrum via FT processing. Simple variation of the radio frequencies permits observation of different nuclei (multinuclear NMR spectrometers). Thus an FT–NMR spectrometer can be used for obtaining ^1H, ^{13}C, ^{19}F, ^{15}N and ^{31}P NMR spectra.

Sample handling

The majority of NMR spectra are obtained from samples in solution and therefore the solvent should preferably not contain atoms of the nuclei being observed (except in the case of ^{13}C–NMR). The most common solvents are those in which the hydrogen atoms have been replaced by deuterium, which is not observed under the conditions under which the spectrum is obtained. $CDCl_3$ (deuterochloroform, chloroform-d) is often the solvent of choice, but others such as dimethylsulphoxide-d^6, $[(CD_3)_2SO]$, propanone-d^6 $[(CD_3)_2CO]$, methanol-d^4 (CD_3OD) and deuterium oxide (D_2O) are in common use.

As it is unlikely that you will be allowed 'hands-on' use of an NMR spectrometer, the best approach you can take to obtain a good spectrum is to ensure good sample preparation. The quality of an NMR spectrum is degraded by:

- inappropriate solvent;
- inappropriate concentration of solute;
- inappropriate solvent volume;
- solid particles in the solution;
- water in the sample (inefficient drying);
- paramagnetic compounds.

Sample preparation for NMR spectroscopy is described in Box 57.1.

Box 57.1 How to prepare a sample for NMR spectroscopy

1. **Make sure that your compound is free from water and solvent (p. 179).**

2. **Test the solubility of your compound in cold CH₂Cl₂.** If it is soluble you can use CDCl₃ as the solvent for the NMR experiment. If it is insoluble, consult your instructor for the availability of other deuterated solvents.

3. **Dissolve your compound CDCl₃ (about 2 mL) in a clean, dry sample tube.** Use about 10 mg of sample for CW–NMR or 5 mg of sample for FT–NMR. Check to see if the solvent contains TMS; if it does not, consult your instructor.

4. **Make a simple filter** in a new Pasteur pipette to remove insoluble material and water (Fig. 57.6). Check that your compound does not react with cotton wool and neutral alumina (alcohols and acids are strongly adsorbed on neutral alumina). If it

does, replace the cotton wool with glasswool and do not use alumina. You *must* wear gloves when handling glasswool.

5. **Put the filter into a suitable clean, dry NMR tube** and, using a clean, dry Pasteur pipette, filter the solution into the NMR tube.

6. **Fill the NMR tube to the appropriate level:** between 30 and 50 mm in height is sufficient.

7. **Cap the NMR tube with the correct-size tube cap**, making sure that it is correctly fitted to prevent oscillation when the tube is spinning in the spectrometer. Make sure that the cap is fitted correctly so that it will not fall off when the tube is in the spectrometer.

8. **Wipe the outside of the tube with a clean, dry tissue** to make sure that the spectrometer will not be contaminated. Cleaning the spectrometer probe is a very difficult task.

---

¹H-NMR spectra – most of the spectra shown in this chapter do not extend over the normal spectral range δ = 0–10 ppm. They are expanded to show the details of coupling patterns.

Interpreting NMR spectra

As a matter of routine in your laboratory work you will be required to interpret ¹H–NMR spectra (also known as proton spectra). ¹³C–NMR spectra are becoming more common, while ¹⁹F and ³¹P spectra may be obtained in specialised experiments. Therefore you should concentrate on the interpretation of ¹H and ¹³C spectra in the first instance.

¹H–NMR spectra

These normally cover the range between $\delta = 0$ and 10 ppm but the range is increased to $\delta = 15$ ppm when acidic protons are present in the molecule. The ¹H–NMR spectrum of a molecule gives three key pieces of information about the structure of a molecule:

1. Chemical shift (δ): the peak positions indicate the chemical (magnetic) environment of the protons, i.e. different protons in the molecule have different chemical shifts.

2. Integration: the relative size of peak area indicates how many protons have the δ value shown.

3. Coupling: the fine structure on each peak (coupling) indicates the number of protons on adjacent atoms.

These three features make ¹H-NMR a powerful tool in structure determination and there are two extreme approaches to it:

1. Prediction of the spectrum of the expected compound from theoretical knowledge and then comparison with the spectrum obtained. You should recognise 'patterns' (e.g. triplet and quartet for an ethyl group; a singlet of peak area six for two identical methyl groups), which were present in the starting materials, but the δ_H values may have changed in the 'new' molecule. There are

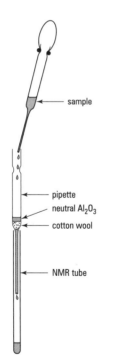

sample

pipette
neutral Al₂O₃
cotton wool

NMR tube

Fig. 57.6 Filtration of solutions for NMR.

Proton chemical shifts – only hydrogen atoms bonded to carbon will be considered in this simplified treatment.

Interpreting NMR spectra: changes of δ – the terms used to indicate the movement of a particular peak with change in its chemical (magnetic) environment are: *upfield* – towards $\delta = 0$ ppm; *downfield* – towards $\delta = 10$ ppm; *shielded* – increased electron density near the proton; *deshielded* – decreased electron density near the proton.

Table 57.1 Chemical shifts of methyl protons

Compound	Chemical shift (ppm)
$(CH_3)_4Si$	0.00
CH_3R	0.90
CH_3I	2.16
CH_3Br	2.65
CH_3Cl	3.10
CH_3OR	3.30
CH_3F	4.26

computer programs, such as g-NMR®, which will simulate the NMR spectrum from a structural formula.

2. Interpretation of the spectrum from correlation tables, but this is very difficult for the inexperienced.

In practice a combination of the two approaches is used with cross-referencing and checking the proposed structure with tabulated δ_H values and reference spectra until a satisfactory answer is found.

> **KEY POINT** Always make sure that your predicted structure is consistent with the spectrum.

Factors affecting chemical shift (δ_H)

The δ values of protons can be predicted to a general approximation from knowledge of the effects which produce variations in chemical shift.

1. The hybridisation of the carbon atom to which the hydrogen atom is attached:
    (a) sp^3 hybridised carbon: peaks occur between $\delta = 0.9$ and 1.5 ppm in simple hydrocarbon systems. The peaks move downfield with change of structure from CH_3 to CH_2 to CH.

    (b) sp hybridised carbon: peaks occur at about $\delta = 1.5-3.5$ ppm in alkynes.

    (c) sp^2 hybridised carbon: in alkenes the resonances occur around $\delta = 4-8$ ppm and the C–H peaks of aromatic rings are found between $\delta = 6$ and 9 ppm. The large downfield shifts of these C_{sp2}–H nuclei result from deshielding of the protons by fields set up by circulation of the π-electrons in the magnetic field. The proton of the aldehyde group (CHO) is particularly deshielded by this effect and is found at $\delta = 9-10$ ppm.

2. Electron attraction or electron release by substituent atoms attached to the carbon atom. Electron attracting atoms, such as N, O, Hal attached to the carbon, attract electron density from the C–H bonds and thus deshield the proton. This results in movement of the chemical shift to higher δ values (Table 57.1). Conversely, electron-releasing groups produce additional shielding of the C–H bonds resulting in upfield shifts of δ values.

3. All the protons in benzene are identical and occur at $\delta = 7.27$ ppm. In substituted aromatic compounds, the overall electron-attracting or re-leasing effect of the substituent(s) alters the δ values of the remaining ring protons making them non-equivalent. The *ortho* protons are affected most.

4. For protons attached to atoms other than carbon: the chemical shifts of protons attached to oxygen increase with increasing acidity of the O–H group; thus $\delta = 1-6$ ppm for alcohols, $4-12$ ppm for phenols and $10-14$ ppm for carboxylic acids. Hydrogens bound to nitrogen (1° and 2° amines) are found at $\delta = 3-8$ ppm. The approximate chemical shift regions are shown in Table 57.2 and Fig. 57.7.

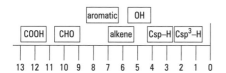

Fig. 57.7 Approximate chemical shift positions in the ^{1}H–NMR spectrum.

A range of chemical shift correlation tables is provided in Tables 57.2, 57.3, 57.4, 57.5 and 57.6.

Table 57.2 Proton chemical shifts of common aalkyl derivatives RX (δ_H ppm)

R	Methyl	Ethyl		n-Propyl			iso-Propyl		t-Butyl
X	CH_3	CH_2	CH_3	α-CH_2	β-CH_2	CH_3	CH	CH_3	CH_3
H	0.23	0.86	0.86	0.91	1.33	0.91	1.33	0.91	0.89
$-CH=CH_2$	1.71	2.00	1.00				1.73		1.02
$-C\equiv CH$	1.80	2.16	1.15	2.10	1.50	0.97	2.59	1.15	1.22
-Ph	2.35	2.63	1.21	2.59	1.65	0.95	2.89	1.25	1.32
-F	4.27	4.36	1.24	4.30	1.68	0.97			
-Cl	3.06	3.47	1.33	3.47	1.81	1.06	4.14	1.55	1.60
-Br	2.69	3.37	1.66	3.35	1.89	1.06	4.21	1.73	1.76
-I	2.16	3.16	1.88	3.16	1.88	1.03	4.24	1.89	1.95
-OH	3.39	3.59	1.18	3.49	1.53	0.93	3.94	1.16	1.22
-O-	3.24	3.37	1.15	3.27	1.55	0.93	3.55	1.08	1.24
-OPh	3.73	3.98	1.38	3.86	1.70	1.05	4.51	1.31	
$-OCOCH_3$	3.67	4.05	1.21	3.98	1.56	0.97	4.94	1.22	1.45
-OCOPh	3.88	4.37	1.38	4.25	1.76	1.07	5.22	1.37	1.58
p-Tosyl	3.70	3.87	1.13	3.94	1.60	0.95	4.70	1.25	
-CHO	2.18	2.46	1.13	2.35	1.65	0.98	2.39	1.13	1.07
$-COCH_3$	2.09	2.47	1.05	2.32	1.56	0.93	2.54	1.08	1.12
-COPh	2.55	2.92	1.18	2.86	1.72	1.02	3.58	1.22	
-COOH	2.08	2.36	1.16	2.31	1.68	1.00	2.56	1.21	1.23
$-COOCH_3$	2.01	2.28	1.12	2.22	1.65	0.98	2.48	1.15	1.16
$-CONH_2$	2.02	2.23	1.13	2.19	1.68	0.99	2.44	1.18	1.22
$-NH_2$	2.47	2.74	1.10	2.61	1.43	0.93	3.07	1.03	1.15
$-NHCOCH_3$	2.71	3.21	1.12	3.18	1.55	0.96	4.01	1.13	
-SH	2.00	2.44	1.13	2.46	1.57	1.02	3.16	1.34	1.43
-S-	2.09	2.49	1.25	2.43	1.59	0.98	2.93	1.25	
$-C\equiv N$	1.98	2.35	1.31	2.29	1.71	1.11	2.67	1.35	1.37
$-NO_2$	4.29	4.37	1.58	4.28	2.01	1.03	4.44	1.53	

Table 57.3 ^{1}H-NMR correlation table for methylene (CH_2) groups

This table gives an estimate of the chemical shift of a CH_2 group depending on the two groups X and Y attached to it

$$X-CH_2-Y$$

The estimated chemical shift δ is: $\delta = 0.23 + \sigma_X + \sigma_Y$

X or Y	σ (ppm)	X or Y	σ (ppm)
-H	0.34	-OC(=O)R	3.01
$-CH_3$	0.68	-OC(=O)Ph	3.27
-C=C	1.32	-C(=O)R	1.50
$-C\equiv C$	1.44	-C(=O)Ph	1.90
-Ph	1.83	-C(=O)OR	1.46
$-CF_3$	1.14	-C(=O) NR_2, -C(=O) NH_2	1.47
-F	3.30	$-C\equiv N$	1.59
-Cl	2.53	$-NR_2$, $-NH_2$	1.57
-Br	2.33	-NHPh	2.04
-I	2.19	-NHC(=O)R	2.27
-OH	2.56	$-NO_2$	3.36
-OR	2.36	-SH, -SR	1.64
-OPh	2.94	$-OSO_2R$	3.13

Table 57.4 ^{1}H-NMR correlation table for methine (CH) groups

This table gives an estimate of the chemical shift of a CH group depending on the three groups X, Y, and Z attached to it:

$$X - CH - Y$$
$$|$$
$$Z$$

The estimated chemical shift δ is: $\quad \delta = 2.50 + \sigma_X + \sigma_Y + \sigma_Z$

X, Y, or Z	σ (ppm)	X, Y, or Z	σ (ppm)
–alkyl	0	–OC(=O)R	2.07
–C=C	0.46	–C(=O)R	0.47
–C≡C	0.79	–C(=O)Ph	1.22
–Ph	0.99	–C(=O)OR	0.47
–F	1.59	–C(=O)NR$_2$, –C(=O)NH$_2$	0.60
–Cl	1.56	–C≡N	0.66
–Br	1.53	–NR$_2$, –NH$_2$	0.64
–OH	1.14	–NHC(=O)R	1.80
–OR	1.14	–NO$_2$	1.84
–OPh	1.79		

Table 57.5 ^{1}H-NMR correlation table for alkenes

This method allows the estimation of the chemical shift of a proton connected to a carbon-carbon double bond:

$$\delta = 5.25 + \sigma_{cis} + \sigma_{trans} + \sigma_{gem}$$

| Substituent | σ (ppm) | | |
	gem	cis	trans
–H	0	0	0
–Alkyl (linear)	0.44	−0.26	−0.29
–Alkyl (ring)	0.71	−0.33	−0.30
–CH$_2$OR	0.67	−0.02	−0.07
–CH$_2$I	0.67	−0.02	−0.07
–CH$_2$Cl	0.72	0.12	0.07
–CH$_2$Br	0.72	0.12	0.07
–CH$_2$Ar	1.05	−0.29	−0.32
–CH$_2$NR$_2$	0.66	−0.05	−0.23
–C≡C	0.50	0.35	0.10
–C=C	0.98	−0.04	−0.21
–C=O	1.10	1.13	0.81
–CO$_2$H	1.00	1.35	0.74
–CO$_2$R	0.84	1.15	0.56
–CHO	1.03	0.97	1.21
–C(=O)NR$_2$	1.37	0.93	0.35
–OR (R = alkyl)	1.18	−1.06	−1.28
–OC(=O)R	2.09	−0.40	−0.67
–Ph	1.35	0.37	−0.10
–Cl	1.00	0.19	0.03
–Br	1.04	0.40	0.55
–NR$_2$ (R = alkyl)	0.69	−1.19	−1.31

Table 57.6 ^{1}H-NMR correlation table for substituted benzenes

This method allows the calculation of a chemical shift of a proton on a phenyl ring depending on the nature of the substituents:

$$\delta = 7.27 + \sigma_{ortho} + \sigma_{meta} + \sigma_{para}$$

Substituent	ortho	meta	para
	σ (ppm)		
–H	0	0	0
–Me	−0.20	−0.12	−0.22
–Et	−0.14	−0.06	−0.17
–CH$_2$OH	−0.07	−0.07	−0.07
–CH$_2$NH$_2$	−0.07	−0.07	−0.07
–CH$_2$Cl	0	0	0
–CF$_3$	0.32	0.14	0.20
–CCl$_3$	0.64	0.13	0.10
–C=C	0.06	−0.03	−0.10
–Ph	0.37	0.20	0.10
–CHO	0.56	0.22	0.29
–COR	0.62	0.14	0.21
–C(=O)N	0.61	0.10	0.17
–CO$_2$H	0.85	0.18	0.27
–CO$_2$R	0.71	0.10	0.21
–C≡C	0.15	0.02	−0.01
–C≡N	0.36	0.18	0.28
–NH$_2$	−0.75	−0.25	−0.65
–NR$_2$ (R = alkyl)	−0.66	−0.18	−0.67
–NHC(=O)R	0.12	−0.07	−0.28
–NO$_2$	0.95	0.26	0.38
–OH	−0.56	−0.12	−0.45
–OR (alkyl)	−0.48	−0.09	−0.44
–OC(=O)R	−0.25	0.03	−0.13
–F	−0.26	0	−0.04
–Cl	0.03	−0.02	−0.09
–Br	0.18	−0.08	−0.04
–I	0.39	−0.21	0

Integration of peak areas

The area of each peak gives the relative number of protons and is produced directly on the spectrum (Fig. 57.8). On CW–NMR spectrometers the height of the peak area integration line must be measured using a ruler, whereas on FT–NMR machines the area is calculated and displayed as a number. You must remember that:

- The areas are *ratios*, not absolute values, and you must find a peak attributable to a specific group to obtain a reference area, e.g. a single peak at $\delta = 1.0$ ppm is likely to be a CH$_3$ group and thus the area displayed or measured is equal to three protons.

Integration of coupled peaks – the area under the singlet, doublet, triplet, quartet, etc., is still that of the type of hydrogen being considered. For example, if the peak for the three protons of a *methyl group* is split into a triplet by an adjacent methylene group, the area of the triplet is *three*.

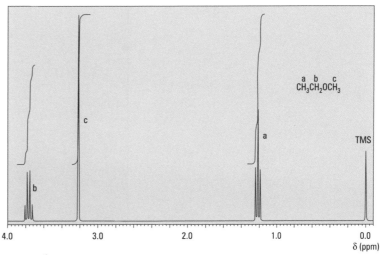

Fig. 57.8 ^{1}H–NMR spectrum of methoxyethane.

- You must ensure that you include integrations from all the fine-structure (coupling) peaks in the peak area.

- Do not expect the peak area integrations to be exact whole numbers, e.g. an area of 2.8 is probably three protons (CH_3), 5.1 is probably five protons (e.g. a C_6H_5 group), but 1.5 is probably a CH_3 and all the peak area integrations must be doubled.

Coupling (spin–spin splitting)

Many ^{1}H–NMR signals do not consist of a single line but are usually associated with several lines (splitting patterns). Protons giving multiline signals are said to be *coupled*. This coupling arises from the magnetic influence of protons on one atom with those on an adjacent atom(s). Thus information about the nature of adjacent protons can be determined and fed into the structural elucidation problem. To a simple first approximation the following three general points are useful in the interpretation of coupling patterns:

1. Aliphatic systems: if *adjacent* carbon atoms have *different types* of protons (a and b), then the protons will couple. If a proton is coupled to n ($n = 1, 2, 3, 4, 5$, etc.) other protons on an adjacent carbon atom, the number of lines observed is $n + 1$, as shown in the examples below.

    $CH_3CH_2OCH_3$ Protons a are coupled to two protons b: $n = 2$;
      a   b   c   therefore the peak for protons a is split into three lines (a triplet).

                           Protons b are coupled to three protons a: $n = 3$; therefore the peak for protons b is split into four lines (a quartet).

                           Protons c have no adjacent protons and therefore are not coupled and give a single line (singlet) (Fig. 57.8).

    $CH_3CHBrCH_2Br$ Protons a are coupled to one proton b: $n = 1$;
      a   b   c   therefore the peak for protons a is split into two lines (doublet)

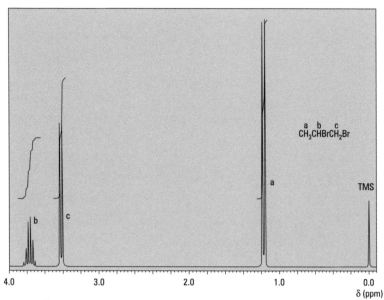

Fig. 57.9 ^{1}H–NMR spectrum of 1,2-dibromopropane.

Protons b are coupled to three protons a and two protons c: $n = 5$; therefore the peak for protons b is split into six lines (sextet).

Protons c are coupled to one proton b: $n = 1$; therefore the peak for protons c is split into two lines (doublet).

Protons a and protons c are not adjacent and do not couple (Fig. 57.9).

The intensity of each peak in the resulting singlet, doublet, triplet, quartet, etc. is calculated from Pascal's triangle (Fig. 57.10).

The separation between the coupled lines is called the coupling constant, J, and, for aliphatic protons CH, CH_2 and CH_3, it is usually ~ 8 Hz.

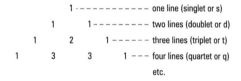

Fig. 57.10 Intensities of coupled peaks from Pascal's triangle.

KEY POINT The $(n + 1)$ rule only applies in systems where the coupling constant (J) between the protons is the same. Fortunately this is common in aliphatic systems.

---

2. Alkene hydrogens: hydrogen atoms on double bonds have different coupling constants depending upon the stereochemistry of the alkene. Alkene hydrogens in the Z (cis) configuration have $J = 5-14$ Hz, whereas those in the E (trans) configuration have $J = 11-19$ Hz (Figs 57.11(a) and (b)).

3. Aromatic hydrogens: coupling of hydrogens, which are non-adjacent, is readily observed in aromatic compounds. Different protons *ortho* to each other couple with $J = 7-10$ Hz, while those in a *meta* relationship have $J = 2-3$ Hz. *Para* coupling ($J = 0-1$ Hz) is not usually seen on the spectrum. The types of aromatic compound you are likely to meet most often are:

   (a) Monosubstituted aromatic compounds, in which three basic patterns are found in the aromatic region of the spectrum. If the substituent

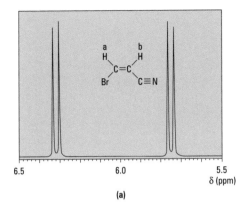

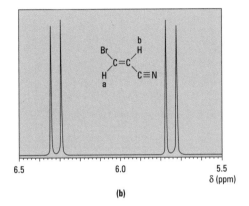

Fig. 57.11 ¹H–NMR spectra of: (a) (Z)-3-bromopropanonitrile; (b) (E)-3-bromopropanonitrile.

exerts a weak electronic effect on the ring, the δ values of the ring protons are similar and the protons appear as a single peak of area five (Fig. 57.12(a)). If the group is strongly electron releasing (OH, NH_2, OCH_3, etc.), the protons appear as complex multiplets (*ortho* and *meta* coupled), below $\delta = 7.27$ ppm of relative areas two to three (Fig. 57.12(b)). If the group is electron attracting (e.g. NO_2, COOH, etc.), then the complex multiplets have $\delta > 7.27$ ppm (Fig. 57.12(c));

(b) *para* disubstituted aromatic compounds, which are of two types. If the substituents are the same, then all the ring protons are identical and a singlet, of relative area four, is seen (Fig. 57.12(d)). If the substituents are different, then the pairs of hydrogens *ortho* to each substituent are different and *ortho*-couple to give what appears to be pair of doublets, each of relative area two (Fig. 57.12(e)).

(c) Increasing numbers of substituents, which decrease the number of aromatic hydrogens and the spectrum becomes simpler. Thus the common 1,2,4-trisubstituted pattern (Fig. 57.12(f)) is recognised easily as an *ortho*-coupled doublet, a *meta*-coupled doublet and a doublet of doublets (coupled *ortho* and *meta*).

The chemical shifts of aromatic protons can be calculated from detailed correlation tables. (Table 57.6)

¹³C-NMR spectra

The ¹³C nucleus has $I = \frac{1}{2}$, like ¹H, and the ¹³C–NMR spectrum of a compound can be observed using a different radio frequency range (in the same magnetic field) to that for ¹H. The ¹³C spectrum will give peaks for each different type of carbon atom in a molecule but the properties of the ¹³C nucleus give some important and useful differences in the spectrum obtained:

- The natural abundance of ¹³C is only 1.1% compared with 98.9% for ¹²C – in any molecule no two adjacent atoms are likely to be ¹³C and therefore coupling between ¹³C nuclei will not be seen, giving a very simple spectrum.

- In a sample of a compound, which contains many molecules, the ¹³C isotope is randomly distributed and all the different carbon atoms in a sample of a compound will be seen in the ¹³C–NMR spectrum.

- The sensitivity of the ¹³C nucleus is low and this, together with its low natural abundance, means that FT–NMR is the only practical system to produce a spectrum by accumulation of spectra by repetitions. Larger sample size in bigger NMR tubes also assist in solving the sensitivity/abundance problem.

- The chemical shift range for ¹³C is greater ($\delta_C = 0{-}250$ ppm) than for ¹H ($\delta_H = 0{-}15$ ppm) giving greater spectral dispersion, i.e. the peaks for carbons with very slight differences in chemical shifts are separated and do not overlap.

- ¹³C nuclei will couple with the ¹H nuclei to which they are directly bonded, e.g. CH_3 will appear as a quartet, CH_2 as a triplet, CH as a doublet, but C with no hydrogen atoms attached will appear as a singlet. This introduction of complexity in the ¹³C–NMR spectrum is removed by broadband decoupling (see p. 453).

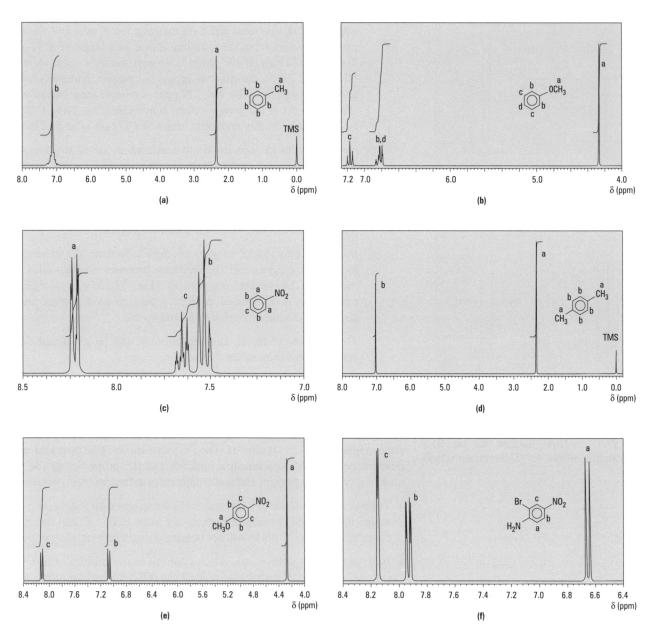

Fig. 57.12 ¹H–NMR spectra of (a) methylbenzene; (b) methoxybenzene; (c) nitrobenzene; (d) 1,4-dimethylbenzene; (e) 4-methoxynitrobenzene; (f) 4-amino-3-bromonitrobenzene (NH₂ protons not shown).

- The peak areas of the different carbon atoms are *not* related to the number of carbon atoms having the same chemical shift, as in the case for ¹H–NMR spectra.

Interpreting ¹³C–NMR spectra

Normally you will be given two ¹³C–NMR spectra (Fig. 57.13). The upper spectrum, which is more complex (more lines) is called the *off-resonance decoupled* spectrum and shows the ¹³C–¹H coupling to enable you to determine which carbon signals are CH₃, CH₂, CH and C. Then overlapping of peaks may make the identification of different carbon atoms difficult. The lower spectrum is a *broadband decoupled* spectrum in

Interpretation of ¹³C–NMR spectra – the spectrum is that of all the *carbon atoms* in the molecule. It is easy to forget that the peaks for carbon atoms carrying no hydrogen atoms are present.

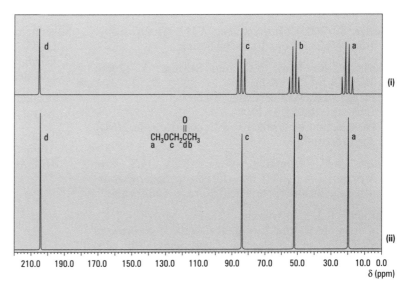

Fig. 57.13 ^{13}C–NMR spectra of 1-methoxypropanone: (i) off-resonance decoupled; (ii) broadband decoupled.

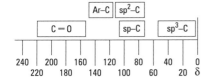

Fig. 57.14 Approximate chemical shift positions in ^{13}C–NMR.

which the molecule is irradiated with a second radio frequency range for the protons in the molecule and effectively removes all the ^{13}C–^{1}H couplings from the spectrum. The resulting simplicity of the spectrum makes identification of the different types of carbon in the molecule relatively easy.

The chemical shifts of ^{13}C atoms (δ_C) vary in the same manner as those of protons (Fig. 57.14):

1. δ_C moves downfield as the hybridisation of the carbon atom changes from sp^3 (0–50 ppm) to sp (75–105 ppm) to sp^2 (100–140 ppm);

2. for sp^3 hybridised carbon: δ_C moves further downfield with the change from CH$_3$ to CH$_2$ to CH to C;

3. for sp^2 hybridised carbon: aromatic carbons occur further downfield ($\delta_C = 115-145$ ppm) than alkene carbon atoms ($\delta_C = 100-140$ ppm);

4. bonding more electronegative atoms to carbon deshields the carbon atom and moves the peaks downfield, e.g CH$_3$–C ($\delta_C \sim 6$ ppm) and CH$_3$–O ($\delta_C \sim 55$ ppm), C=C ($\delta_C \sim 123$ ppm) and C=O ($\delta_C \sim 205$ ppm).

A representative list of chemical shift ranges is given in Table 57.7.

Sources for further study

Anderson, R.J., Bendell, D.J. and Groundwater, P.W. (2004) *Organic Spectroscopic Analysis*. Royal Society of Chemistry, Cambridge.

Breitmaier, E. (2002) *Structure Elucidation by NMR in Organic Chemistry: A Practical Guide*, 3rd revised edn. John Wylie & Sons Ltd., Chichester.

Crews, P., Rodriguez, J. and Jaspars, M. (2010) *Organic Structure Analysis*. Oxford University Press, New York.

Field, L.D., Sternhell, S. and Kalman, J.R. (2008) *Organic Structures from Spectra*, 4th edn. John Wylie & Sons Ltd, Chichester.

Iggo, J.A. (2000) *NMR Spectroscopy in Inorganic Chemistry*. Oxford University Press.

Jacobsen, N.E. (2007) *NMR Spectroscopy Explained: Simplified Theory, Applications and Examples for Organic Chemistry and Structural Biology*. John Wylie & Sons Ltd, Chichester.

Keeler, J. (2005) *Understanding NMR Spectroscopy.* John Wylie & Sons Ltd, Chichester.

Merlic, C.A., Fam, B.C. and Strouse, J. (2000) *Webspectra.* Available: http://www.chem.ucla.edu/~webspectra/ Last accessed 05/03/10 [A selection of problems, with solutions, in NMR spectroscopy.]

Pavia, D.L., Lampman, G.M., Kriz, G.S. and Vyvyan, J.A. (2009) *Introduction to Spectroscopy,* 4th edn. Brooks/Cole, Pacific Grove, California.

Shriner, R.L., Hermann, C.K.F., Morrill, T.C., Curtin, D.Y. and Fuson, R.C. (2003) *Systematic Identification of Organic Compounds,* 8th edn. John Wylie & Sons Ltd, Chichester.

Silverstein, R.M., Webster, F.X. and Kiemle, D.J. (2005) *Spectroscopic Identification of Organic Chemicals,* 7th edn. John Wylie & Sons Ltd, Chichester.

Whittaker, D. (2000) *Interpreting Organic Spectra.* Royal Society of Chemistry, Cambridge.

Williams, D. and Fleming, I. (2008) *Spectroscopic Methods in Organic Chemistry,* 6th edn. McGraw-Hill, Maidenhead, UK.

Study exercises

57.1 Predict the ^{1}H-NMR spectra of the following molecules. *Note:* only the number of different hydrogen atoms needs to be stated and coupling patterns must be deduced.

(i) $CH_3CH_2CH_2Br$;

(ii) $CH_3CHBrCH_3$;

(iii) $CH_3CHBrCHO$;

(iv) $CH_3CH_2OCOCH_2CH_2COOCH_2CH_3$;

(v) $CH_3CH_2OCOCH_2CH_2OCOCH_2CH_3$.

57.2 Predict the ^{13}C-NMR spectra of the following molecules. *Note:* only the number of different carbon atoms needs to be given and the ^{13}C–^{1}H coupling patterns deduced.

(i) $(CH_3)_3CBr$;

(ii) $CH_3OCH_2CH_2OCH_3$;

(iii) $CH_3CH(COOCH_2CH_3)_2$;

(iv) $(CH_3)_2C=C(CH_3)_2$;

(v) $C_6H_5CH_3$.

57.3 Using the information provided in Table 57.3, estimate the δ value for the protons of the CH_2 group in:

57.4 Using the information provided in Table 57.4, estimate the δ value for the proton of the CH group in:

57.5 Using the information provided in Table 57.5, estimate the δ values for the protons of the Ha and Hb in:

57.6 Using the information provided in Table 57.6, estimate the chemical shift of Ha, Hb, Hc and Hd in the following molecule:

57.7 With reference to the molecule shown in Fig. 57.12(f), calculate the δ values for the protons Ha, Hb and Hc to confirm that they correlate with the spectrum.

Mass spectrometry (MS) involves the bombardment of molecules, in the gas phase, with electrons. An electron is lost from the molecule to give a cation, the molecular ion (M^+), which then breaks down in characteristic ways to give smaller fragments, which are cations, neutral molecules and uncharged radicals (Fig. 58.1).

The mixture of molecular ion and fragments is accelerated to specific velocities using an electric field and then separated on the basis of their different masses by deflection in a magnetic or electrostatic field. Only the cations are detected and a mass spectrum is a plot of mass-to-charge ratio (m/z) on the x-axis against the number of ions (relative abundance, RA, %) on the y-axis. A schematic of the components of a mass spectrometer is shown in Fig. 58.2 and an example of a line-graph-type mass spectrum in Fig. 58.3.

There are many types of mass spectrometer, from high-resolution double-focusing instruments, which can distinguish molecular and fragment masses to six decimal places, to 'bench-top' machines with a quadrupole mass detector which can resolve masses up to about $m/z = 500$, but only in whole-number differences. Routinely you are most likely to encounter data from 'bench-top' instruments and therefore only this type of spectrum will be considered.

Sample handling

For low-resolution spectra obtainable from a 'bench-top' MS, samples should be presented in the same form and quantity as demanded for gas chromatographic analysis (p. 370). For high-resolution spectra contamination of any sort must be avoided and samples (typically less than $500\,\mu g$) should be submitted in glass sample tubes with screwcaps containing an aluminium-foil insert. MS is so sensitive that the plasticisers from plastic tubes or plastic push-on caps will be detected, as will contaminating grease from ground-glass joints and taps.

Mass spectra

The standard low-resolution mass spectrum (Fig. 58.3) is computer generated, which allows easy comparison with known spectra in a computer database for identification. The peak at the highest mass number is the molecular ion (M^+), the mass of the molecule minus an electron. The peak at RA = 100%, the base peak, is the most abundant fragment in the spectrum and the computer automatically scales the spectrum to give the most abundant ion as 100%. The mass spectrum of a compound gives the following information about its chemical structure:

- molecular ion mass, which includes information on the number of nitrogen atoms and the presence of chlorine and bromine atoms (see p. 456) – which is not easily obtained from IR and NMR spectra;

- the most stable major fragment (base peak), which can be correlated to the structure of the molecule;

- other important fragment ions, which may give information on the structure;

Understanding mass spectrometry – since this technique does not involve the production and measurement of electromagnetic spectra and is not based on quantum principles, it should not really be referred to as a spectroscopic technique.

Mass-to-charge ratios – in the overwhelming majority of simple cases the ion detected is a monopositive cation; thus $z = 1$ and the peaks seen on a low-resolution spectrometer equate to the mass of the ion.

Determination of exact molecular mass – high-resolution instruments enable the molecular formula of a compound to be determined by summation of the masses of the individual isotopes of atoms, e.g. both ethane and methanal have integral mass values of 30, but the accurate values are 58.046 950 and 58.010 565 respectively.

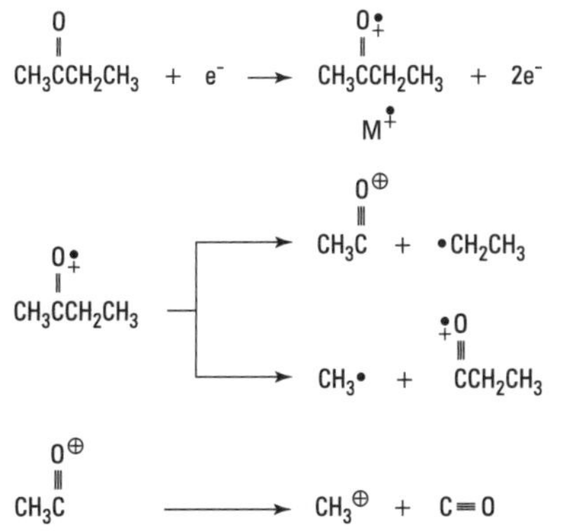

Fig. 58.1 Formation and fragmentation of a molecular ion (M^+).

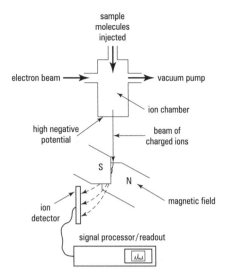

Fig. 58.2 Components of an electron-impact mass spectrometer.

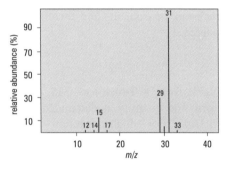

Fig. 58.3 Mass spectrum for methanol; m/z = mass-to-charge ratio.

Identification of isotope peaks – the natural abundance of ^{13}C is 1.1%. For a molecule containing n carbon atoms the probability is that $1.1 \times n\%$ of these atoms will be ^{13}C. Thus the mass spectrum of hexane (six carbons) gives a molecular ion (M^+) at $m/z = 86$ and a peak at $m/z = 87$ ($M + 1$) which is 6.6% the intensity of the M^+ peak.

- the detailed fragmentation pattern, which can be used to confirm a structure by reference to a library database, cf. the 'fingerprint' region in IR spectrometry (p. 437).

Molecular ions

The m/z value of the molecular ion is the summation of all the atomic masses in the molecule, *including the naturally occurring isotopes*. For organic molecules you will find a small peak ($M + 1$) above the apparent molecular ion mass (M^+) value due to the presence of ^{13}C. The importance of isotope peaks is the detection of chlorine and bromine in molecules since these two elements have large natural abundances of isotopes, e.g. $^{35}Cl : ^{37}Cl = 3:1$ and $^{79}Br : ^{81}Br = 1:1$. The mass spectra produced by molecules containing these atoms are very distinctive with peaks at $M + 2$ and even $M + 4$ and $M + 6$ depending on how many chlorine or bromine atoms are present. The identification of the number and type of halogen atoms is illustrated in Box 58.1.

Since the low-resolution mass spectrum produces integer values for m/z, the mass of M^+ indicates the number of nitrogen atoms in the molecule. If m/z for M^+ is an *odd integer*, there is an *odd number* of N atoms in the molecule and, if the value is an *even number*, then there is an *even number* of N atoms.

Base peak

The molecular ion M^+ fragments into cations, radicals, radical cations and neutral molecules of which only the positively charged species are detected. There are several possible fragmentations for each M^+ but the base peak represents the most *energetically favoured* process with the m/z value of the base peak representing the mass of the most *abundant* (and therefore most stable) positively charged species. The fragmentation of M^+ into the base peak follows the simplified rules outlined in Box 58.2, and for a more detailed interpretation you should consult the correlation tables to be found in the specialist texts referred to at the end of the section.

Fragmentation patterns

The mass spectrum of a molecule is unique and can be stored in a computer. A match of the spectrum with those in the computer library is made in terms of molecular weight and the 10 most abundant peaks and a selection of possibilities will be presented. At this point you need to correlate all the information obtained from the spectroscopic techniques described in Chapters 48, 56, 57 and 58 together with the chemistry of the molecule to attempt to identify the structure of the molecule.

When you attempt to interpret the mass spectrum remember that:

- Only the base peak is almost certain to be derived from the molecular ion.

- Some lesser peaks may result from alternative fragmentation pathways, but these may be useful in assigning structural features.

- MS is often used to confirm information from IR and NMR spectra; interpretation of the mass spectrum alone is very difficult, except for the simplest molecules.

Box 58.1 How to identify the number of bromine or chlorine atoms in a molecule from the molecular ion

1. Since Cl and Br have isotopes two mass numbers apart, their presence in a molecule will produce peaks at m/z values above M^+, which are two mass numbers apart, i.e. $M + 2$, $M + 4$, etc.

2. The expression for the number and intensities of these peaks is given by the expansion of the formula:

$$(a + b)^n$$

where a and b are the ratio of the two atom isotopes, and n is the number of atoms.

Example 1: If the molecule contains one chlorine atom then:

$$(a + b)^n = (3 + 1)^1 = 3 + 1$$

Thus the mass spectrum of CH_3Cl would show M^+ at $m/z = 50$ ($CH_3{}^{35}Cl$) and $M + 2$ at $m/z = 52$ ($CH_3{}^{37}Cl$) and the heights of these two peaks will be in the approximate ratio $3:1$ (Fig. 58.4(a)).

Example 2: If the molecule contains two chlorine atoms then:

$$(a + b)^n = a^2 + 2ab + b^2 = (3 + 1)^2 = 9 + 6 + 1$$

Thus the mass spectrum of CH_2Cl_2 would show M^+ at $m/z = 84$ ($CH_2{}^{35}Cl_2$), $M + 2$ at $m/z = 86$ ($CH_2{}^{35}Cl^{37}Cl$) and $M + 4$ at $m/z = 88$ ($CH_2{}^{37}Cl_2$) and the heights of these peaks will be the approximate ratio $9:6:1$ (Fig. 58.4(b)).

Example 3: If the molecule contains one bromine atom then:

$$(a + b)^n = (1 + 1)^1 = 1 + 1$$

Thus the mass spectrum of CH_3CH_2Br would show M^+ at $m/z = 108$ ($CH_3CH_2{}^{79}Br$) and $M + 2$ at $m/z = 110$ ($CH_3CH_2{}^{81}Br$) and the heights of these peaks will be in the approximate ratio $1:1$ (Fig. 58.4(c)).

Example 4: If the molecule contains three bromine atoms then:

$$(a + b)^3 = a^3 + 3a^2b + 3ab^2 + b^3 =$$

$$(1 + 1)^3 = 1 + 3 + 3 + 1$$

Thus the mass spectrum of $CHBr_3$ would show M^+ at $m/z = 250$ ($CH^{79}Br_3$), $M + 2$ at $m/z = 252$ ($CH^{79}Br_2{}^{81}Br$), $M + 4$ at $m/z = 254$ ($CH^{79}Br^{81}Br_2$) and $M + 6$ at $m/z = 256$ ($CH^{81}Br_3$) and the heights of the peaks will be in the approximate ratio $1:3:3:1$ (Fig. 58.4(d)).

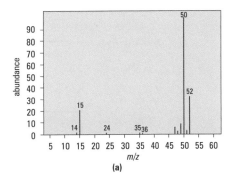

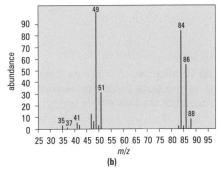

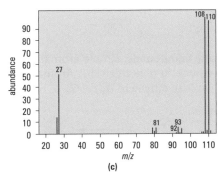

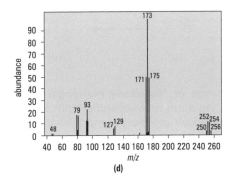

Fig. 58.4 Mass spectra of: (a) CH_3Cl; (b) CH_2Cl_2; (c) CH_3CH_2Br; (d) $CHBr_3$.

Box 58.2 Idealised fragmentation processes for the molecular ion (M$^+$)

1. **α-Cleavage**: this involves breaking the 'next but one bond' to a hetero-atom (N, O, Hal, etc.) in the functional group of a molecule. The following examples illustrate the general principles:

2. **σ-Bonds in alkanes**: C–C bonds break in preference to C–H bonds and the most stable carbocation will be formed as the base peak. For example, 2,2-dimethylpentane will give the stable $(CH_3)_3C^+$ cation as the base peak instead of the less stable propyl cation $CH_3CH_2CH_2^+$.

3. **Aromatic compounds**: simple aromatics cleave to give a phenyl cation, $m/z = 77$, as the base peak which then loses ethyne to give $m/z = 51$. Aromatics with CH_2 next to the ring give the stable tropylium cation $m/z = 91$, and then lose ethyne to $m/z = 65$.

4. **β-Cleavage or McLafferty rearrangement**: this is applied to molecules with a carbonyl group. If there is a hydrogen atom on the carbon atom four away from the carbonyl oxygen (γ carbon atom), a rearrangement of the molecular ion occurs and a neutral alkene is lost from M$^+$. This process occurs concurrently with the α-cleavage:

Interfacing chromatography and mass spectrometry

The use and application of low-cost 'bench-top' mass spectrometers has expanded in recent years. The proliferation of this type of instrument, i.e. a chromatograph coupled to a mass spectrometer, is partly due to the lower capital cost of such instrumentation, but also to the value of the additional analytical information that is possible. This section will consider the coupling of gas chromatography to a mass spectrometer (GC–MS) and liquid chromatography to a mass spectrometer (LC–MS). The key differences between the approaches are also discussed.

Gas chromatography–mass spectrometry (GC–MS)

For specific details on capillary gas chromatography see Chapter 52. The coupling of capillary GC to MS is achieved by a heated transfer line which allows the vapour phase compounds that have been separated by the GC to remain in the gas phase and be transported in the carrier gas, for example helium, directly to the ion source of the MS.

Ionisation sources for GC–MS

The two most common approaches for ionisation of compounds in GC–MS are those based on either chemical ionisation or electron impact. The latter is the most common. In electron impact (EI) mode, electrons produced from a heated tungsten or rhenium filament (cathode) are accelerated towards an anode, colliding with the vaporised sample (X) and producing (positively) charged ions (Fig. 58.5) which can be separated by MS. This can be expressed in the form of the following equation:

$$X_{(g)} + e^- \rightarrow X_{(g)}^+ + 2e^- \qquad [58.1]$$

Alternatively, in chemical ionisation (CI) mode, a reagent gas (e.g. methane) is ionised by electron bombardment to produce a molecular ion (CH_4^+). This molecular ion then reacts with neutral methane to produce a reactant ion (CH_5^+). It is this reactant ion that interacts with the

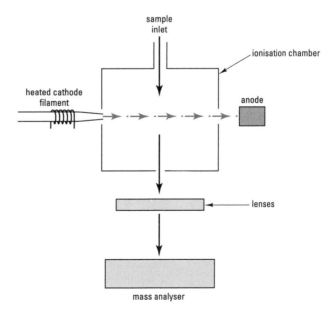

Fig. 58.5 Electron impact ionisation.

compound molecule to produce a (positively) charged ion which can be separated by MS. The difference, in this mode of ionisation, is that the resultant (positively) charged ion has the molecular weight of the compound plus one (i.e. XH_1^+). The chemical ionisation mode can be expressed in the form of the following equations:

$$CH_4 + e^- \rightarrow CH_4^+ + 2e^-$$ [58.2]

$$CH_4^+ + CH_4 \rightarrow CH_5^+ + CH_3^*$$ [58.3]

$$X_{(g)} + CH_5^+ \rightarrow XH_{(g)}^+ + CH_4$$ [58.4]

It is clear from the above that the CI mode is an indirect method of ionisation.

Liquid chromatography–mass spectrometry (LC–MS)

While developments in interface technology have improved considerably in recent years, it is true to say that it went through many developments including moving belt transport interfaces and thermospray. Modern instruments have relied on the use of two approaches both of which allow ionisation of compounds at atmospheric pressure and outside of the MS. The two approaches are electrospray (ES) ionisation and atmospheric pressure chemical ionisation (APCI).

Electrospray (ES) ionisation

A schematic diagram of the electrospray interface is shown in Fig. 58.6. In operation, solvent from the high-performance liquid chromatography system is pumped through a stainless steel capillary tube, which is held at a high potential (3–5 kV). The presence of this electric field causes the solvent to be sprayed from the end of the capillary tube, hence the name. This action causes highly charged solvent and solute ion droplets to be formed. Solvent from these droplets evaporates, assisted by a flow of warm carrier gas (nitrogen). The generated ions (solvent and solute) are transported into the high-vacuum system of the mass spectrometer via a nozzle-skimmer arrangement. The electrospray and nozzle-skimmer arrangement are often positioned at right-angles to one another. By allowing a potential gradient to exist between the electrospray and nozzle-skimmer arrangement, the generated ions are 'pulled' into the mass spectrometer, while at the same time allowing some discrimination between the desirable solute ions and unwanted extraneous material, for example salts present in the buffer of the HPLC mobile phase.

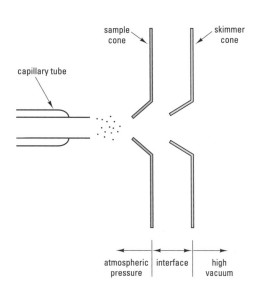

Fig. 58.6 Electrospray ionisation.

Applicability of LC–MS – APCI is more focused on the analysis of low to moderate molecular weight compounds with low to moderate polarity, while ES is focused on large molecular weight compounds of high polarity.

Atmospheric pressure chemical ionisation (APCI)

A schematic diagram of the atmospheric pressure chemical ionisation interface is shown in Fig. 58.7. Its operation is similar to that of the ES ionisation approach except in that in APCI the voltage is not applied to the stainless steel capillary tubing but to a corona pin. Solvent from the HPLC system is pumped through a heated stainless steel capillary tube which is surrounded by a coaxial flow of nitrogen gas. The combination of liquid solvent exiting the capillary tube and the flow of nitrogen gas produces an aerosol. Desolvation takes place easily due to the heat

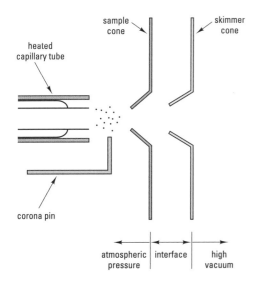

Fig. 58.7 Atmospheric pressure chemical ionisation

Understanding units – 'amu' or atomic mass units are used to represent M_r on mass spectra. An alternative, often used in the biological field, is 'da' or Daltons.

Definition

Plasma – a hot, ionised gas.

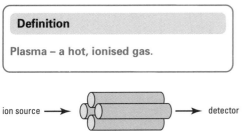

ion source → detector

Fig. 58.8 Quadrupole mass spectrometer.

applied to the solvent via the heated capillary tubing. Located immediately in front of the capillary tube is the probe or corona pin to which is applied a high voltage (2.5–3 kV). In the region around the corona discharge, a plasma is formed due to collisions and charge transfer processes. Therefore this plasma will be made up of solute and solvent ions. In the same manner as in ES ionisation (p. 460) the generated ions (solvent and solute) are transported into the high-vacuum system of the MS.

In ES ionisation and APCI, molecules can form singly charged ions by loss or gain of a proton (hydrogen atom) – i.e. they can form ions represented as $[M + 1]^+$ or $[M - 1]^-$, where M_r = the relative molecular mass of the compound. Therefore, it is possible to operate the mass spectrometer in positive ion mode and determine peaks at m/z ratios of $M + 1$ (e.g. basic compounds typified by amines), or in negative ion mode and determine peaks at m/z ratios of $M - 1$ (e.g. acidic compounds typified by carboxylic acids). Both ES and APCI are regarded as 'soft' ionisation techniques, and as such produce little or no fragmentation patterns. Care is also needed in the interpretation of mass spectra, particularly in the presence of additives (buffer solution) or contaminants. This is because adduct formation is possible. This manifests itself in the form of m/z ratios of $M + 18$ for ammonium adducts or $M + 23$ for sodium adducts.

Types of mass spectrometer

A variety of mass spectrometers are available for the mass/charge separation of charged particles. The most popular are the quadrupole mass spectrometer, ion trap mass spectrometer and the time-of-flight mass spectrometer. While each operates in a different manner, all are capable of separating charged particles on the basis of their m/z ratios.

Quadrupole mass spectrometer

Essentially a quadrupole mass spectrometer consists of four parallel rods (Fig. 58.8). To these rods voltages (both DC and RF) are applied – different voltages are applied to adjacent rods while opposite rods are electrically connected, i.e. have the same voltages applied. By altering the applied voltages, ions of a particular m/z ratio can pass the mass spectrometer to the detector. At the same time, other ions become unstable and are lost. By changing the applied voltages particles of different m/z ratios can pass through the mass spectrometer.

Ion trap mass spectrometer

The ion trap mass spectrometer consists of three cylindrically symmetrical electrodes to which voltages are applied. By altering the applied voltages, ions of increasing m/z ratios leave the ion trap and travel on to the detector (Fig. 58.9).

Time-of-flight mass spectrometer

In a time-of-flight mass spectrometer, charged particles are separated according to their velocity. Essentially, a charged particle accelerated by application of a voltage has a resulting velocity that is characteristic of its m/z ratio. The ability to separate different charged particles can be

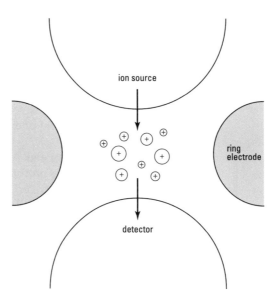

Fig. 58.9 Ion trap mass spectrometer.

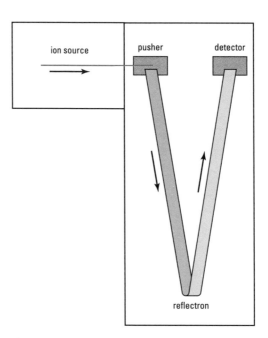

Fig. 58.10 Time-of-flight mass spectrometer.

improved by increasing the flight time of ions. This is achieved via a reflectron. It is not uncommon to find that pre-separation of ions is achieved in a time-of-flight mass spectrometer via an initial quadrupole mass spectrometer (Fig. 58.10).

Detectors for MS

The most common detector of positive ions in chromatography–mass spectrometry is the electron multiplier tube (EMT). The EMT (Fig. 58.11) consists of an open aperture to which is applied a high voltage (3 kV). The positive ions are attracted to the high negative potential of the EMT. For each positive ion that strikes the internal surface of the EMT, the semiconductor coating produces one electron.

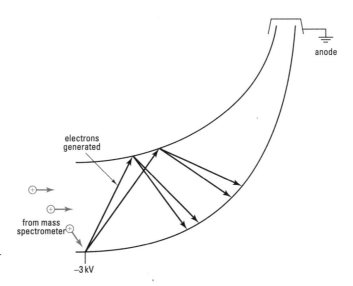

Fig. 58.11 Schematic diagram of an electron multiplier tube.

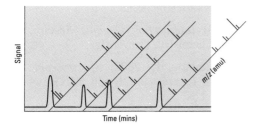

Fig. 58.12 Schematic representation of a typical output from a chromatography–mass spectrometer system.

The generated electrons (negatively charged) are attracted to an area that is less negative than the open aperture. This is achieved by having the narrow end of the device earthed (zero potential). By this process the generated electrons are drawn deeper into the EMT. On their way they strike the internal surfaces of the device producing more secondary electrons. All the generated secondary electrons produced from the initial positive ion are collected and measured as an electric current.

Data acquisition

The main reason that mass spectrometry is linked to chromatographic separation is because of the ability of the mass spectrometer to perform quantitative analysis, and allow mass spectral data to be produced. So, while quantitative analysis is possible for a multitude of other detectors (Chapter 52) it is an additional benefit for the identification of compounds in chemistry. A mass spectrometer produces data that has time, signal intensity and spectral dimensions (Fig. 58.12). Two possible data acquisition modes are possible in mass spectrometry: full scan mode and selected ion monitoring mode.

Full scan mode

In full scan mode, ions produced by the ion source are separated with respect to their m/z ratio by the mass spectrometer scanning the entire mass range, typically 0–400 amu, and a mass spectrum is recorded at the detector. In this manner all ions separated by the mass spectrometer are detected. As the mass spectrometer is coupled up to a chromatographic separation system, all compounds separated with respect to time are monitored in terms of a chromatogram – a plot of signal intensity versus time (p. 366) – and mass spectral information. Depending on the method of ionisation used, it should be possible to identify unknown compounds by their fragmentation patterns or by their molecular weight (see p. 456). The operator is assisted, most notably in GC–MS, by the presence of computer databases that allow searching for particular compounds and comparison of mass spectral information.

Selected ion monitoring (SIM) mode

In contrast to the full scan mode, the SIM mode allows only specified ions to be monitored. This leads to enhanced sensitivity, as the mass spectrometer is not monitoring m/z ratios where no ions are present. The disadvantages of this approach are that only known compounds are monitored in the chromatogram, and no mass spectral information is available. This approach is particularly useful once unknown compounds have been identified via the full scan mode, leading to enhanced sensitivity and selectivity.

Sources for further study

Anderson, R.J., Bendell, D.J. and Groundwater, P.W. (2004) *Organic Spectroscopic Analysis*. Royal Society of Chemistry, Cambridge.

Crews, P., Rodriguez, J. and Jaspars, M. (2010) *Organic Structure Analysis*. Oxford University Press, New York.

Dass, C. (2007) *Fundamentals of Contemporary Mass Spectrometry*. John Wylie & Sons Ltd, Chichester.

Downword, K. (2004) *Mass Spectrometry: A Foundation Course*. Royal Society of Chemistry, Cambridge.

Field, L.D., Sternhell, S. and Kalman, J.R. (2008) *Organic Structures from Spectra*, 4th edn. John Wylie & Sons Ltd, Chichester.

Pavia, D.L., Lampman, G.M., Kriz, G.S. and Vyvyan, J.A. (2009) *Introduction to Spectroscopy*, 4th edn. Brooks/Cole, Pacific Grove, California.

Shriner, R.L., Hermann, C.K.F., Morrill, T.C., Curtin, D.Y. and Fuson, R.C. (2003) *Systematic Identification of Organic Compounds*, 8th edn. John Wylie & Sons Ltd, Chichester.

Silverstein, R.M., Webster, F.X. and Kiemle, D.J. (2005) *Spectroscopic Identification of Organic Chemicals*, 7th edn. John Wylie & Sons Ltd, Chichester.

Watson, J.T. and Sparkman, O.D. (2007) *Introduction to Mass Spectrometry: Instrumentation, Application and Strategies for Data Interpretation*, 4th edn. John Wylie & Sons Ltd, Chichester.

Whittaker, D. (2000) *Interpreting Organic Spectra*. Royal Society of Chemistry, Cambridge.

Williams, D. and Fleming, I. (2008) *Spectroscopic Methods in Organic Chemistry*, 6th edn. McGraw-Hill, Maidenhead, UK.

Study exercises

58.1 You are trying to identify a compound $M_r =$ 126. Infrared, ^{1}H- and ^{13}C-NMR spectroscopy have indicated that it is either $CH_3CH_2COOCH_2CH_2CH_3$ or $CH_3CH_2CH_2COOCH_2CH_3$, but have not provided enough detail for a satisfactory conclusion. Predict the mass spectra of the two compounds from the possible α- and β-cleavages for each molecule so that a distinction can be made.

58.2 Test your knowledge of MS terminology. Explain what the following acronyms stand for:

(a) EI

(b) CI

(c) APCI

(d) ESI

Thermal methods are techniques in which changes in physical and/or chemical properties of a substance are measured as a function of temperature. Several methods of analysis are used:

- Thermogravimetry (TG) is a technique in which a change in the weight of the substance under investigation is monitored with respect to temperature or time.

- Differential thermal analysis (DTA) is a technique for measuring the difference in temperature between the substance under investigation and an inert reference material with respect to temperature or time.

- Differential scanning colorimetry (DSC) is a technique in which the energy necessary to establish a zero temperature difference between the substance under investigation and a reference material is monitored with respect to temperature or time.

When carrying out a thermal analysis procedure it is important to consider and record the following details:

- Sample: a chemical description of the sample, plus its source and any pre-treatment. Also, the purity, chemical composition and formula, if known. Other important items to note are: the particle size, whether the sample has been mixed with a 'binder' (and, if so, what it has been mixed with and in what ratio) and the 'history' of the sample.

- Crucible: the material and design of the sample holder is important. Obviously it is important that the crucible does not react with the sample during heating. In addition, the geometry of the crucible can influence the gas flow.

- Rate of heating: this is very important if you intend to repeat the experiment on a subsequent occasion. Obviously the rate of heating of the sample in the crucible is not instantaneous but depends upon conduction, convection and radiation within the system. Thermal lag is therefore likely to be observed.

- Atmosphere: The nature of the atmosphere surrounding the sample is important in relation to the transfer of heat and the chemistry of the sample reaction. Common sample atmospheres are shown in Table 59.1. In addition, the flow rate of the gas is important: a static system will not remove reaction products from the sample.

- Mass of sample: obviously the amount of sample will have an effect on the heating rate. Also, sample homogeneity may be an issue with very small samples.

Thermogravimetry

The apparatus required for TG analysis is shown in Fig. 59.1. TG is normally carried out on solid samples. Example operating conditions are as follows:

Sample:	calcium oxalate monohydrate
Crucible:	platinum pan
Rate:	$10\,K\,min^{-1}$
Atmosphere:	nitrogen, $20\,mL\,min^{-1}$
Mass:	$10.5\,mg$

Table 59.1 Common sample atmospheres

Gas at 1 atm	Thermal conductivity at 400/K ($mW\,m^{-1}\,K^{-1}$)
Air	33.3
Carbon dioxide	25.1
Helium	190.6
Nitrogen	32.3

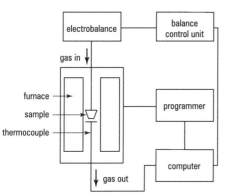

Fig. 59.1 Schematic diagram of a system for thermogravimetry.

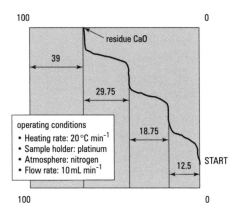

Fig. 59.2 A typical thermal analysis trace for $CaC_2O_4.H_2O$.

The result can be expressed as either a TG curve, a plot of changing weight with respect to temperature or time, or a derivative of the curve, i.e. DTG, where the first derivative of the TG curve is plotted with respect to temperature or time. As well as providing information on the thermal decomposition of inorganic compounds, additional information can be deduced, e.g. sample purity and M_r.

The oxalate hydrates of the alkaline earth metals, e.g. calcium, strontium and barium, are all insoluble. If a calcium salt made acidic with ethanoic acid is treated with sodium oxalate solution, a white precipitate of calcium oxalate monohydrate is formed quantitatively. After washing the precipitate with ethanol it can be analysed. A typical TG curve, for calcium oxalate monohydrate, $CaC_2O_4.H_2O$, is shown in Fig. 59.2. Box 59.1 shows how to interpret a thermal analysis trace for calcium oxalate monohydrate.

Box 59.1 How to interpret a thermal analysis trace

1. **Identify the start position of the trace** (see Fig. 59.2); this is usually indicated by the scale on the trace.

2. **Identify any regions of decomposition**: these are where there is a rapid change in the vertical axis. Three distinct regions of decomposition can be identified in Fig. 59.2: (a) between the start and the first plateau there is a loss of 12.5% (stage 1); (b) between the first and second plateau a loss of 18.75% occurs (stage 2); and (c) between the second plateau and the final residue there is a loss of 29.75% (stage 3).

3. **Determine the M_r of the starting material.** The M_r of $CaC_2O_4.H_2O$ is 146.1.

4. **Using the M_r determine the decomposition loss associated with each region.**

    Stage 1: $146.1 \times 12.5/100 = 18.3$ (18 corresponds to the loss of water)

    $$CaC_2O_4.H_2O_{(s)} \rightarrow CaC_2O_{4(s)} + H_2O_{(v)}$$

    Stage 2: $146.1 \times 18.75/100 = 27.4$ (28.01 corresponds to loss of CO)

    $$CaC_2O_{4(s)} \rightarrow CaCO_{3(s)} + CO_{(g)}$$

    Stage 3: $146.1 \times 29.75/100 = 43.5$ (44.01 corresponds to loss of CO_2)

    $$CaCO_{3(s)} \rightarrow CaO_{(s)} + CO_{2(g)}$$

5. **Determination of the final product.** In this case for $CaC_2O_4.H_2O$ the final residue is CaO ($M_r = 56.08$).

6. **Check the M_r of the original compound:**

    original sample (M_r) = [residue (M_r)/% residue] × 100

    Residue from Fig. 59.2 is 39%. Therefore,

    original sample (M_r) = [56.08/39%] × 100 = 143.8

    Thus the calculated (M_r) of $CaC_2O_4.H_2O$ is 143.8, which is similar to the known M_r of $CaC_2O_4.H_2O$ of 146.1 g mol^{-1}.

7. **Assess the purity of the original material.** The percentage purity of $CaC_2O_4.H_2O$ is calculated as follows:

    143.8 × 100 × 1/146.1 = 98.43%

Applications

As well as inorganic complexes, thermal analysis is applicable to a wide range of substances, e.g. polymers, drugs, soils and coals. It can also be applied to mixtures of, for example, polymer blends.

Degradation of polymers

The effect of heat on polymers varies according to the type of polymer under investigation. In an inert atmosphere, polymeric materials react in two distinct ways: they either depolymerise or carbonise. For example, poly(methyl methacrylate) may degrade back to the monomer.

Soil

The composition of soil is complex and varies with location and geology. Three general stages of soil decomposition on heating can be identified:

1. Loss of moisture and simple organic compounds (between room temperature and 150 °C).

2. Ignition of soil organic matter (between 250 and 550 °C).

3. Presence of minerals e.g. carbonates. The process can be complicated by the presence of hydrated minerals e.g. aluminium and iron oxides, and micas (above 550 °C).

Drugs

The presence of water in both 'free' and 'bound' states in pharmaceuticals can be identified.

Sources for further study

Gabbott, P. (ed.) (2007) *Principles and Applications of Thermal Analysis*. John Wylie & Sons Ltd, Chichester.

Menczel, J.D. and Prime, R.B. (2009) *Thermal Analysis of Polymers, Fundamentals and Applications*. John Wylie & Sons Ltd, Chichester.

Robinson, J.W., Skelly Frame, E.M. and Frame, G.M. (2005) *Undergraduate Instrumental Analysis*, 6th edn. Marcel Dekker, New York.

Skoog, D.A., Holler, F.J. and Crouch, S.R. (2006) *Principles of Instrumental Analysis*, 6th edn. Brooks/Cole, Pacific Grove, California.

Wendlandt, W.W. and Collins, L.W. (1976) *Thermal Analysis*. Academic Press, Elsevier, Amsterdam.

Study exercise

59.1 Use the methodology in Box 59.1 to comment on the thermal decomposition of $CuSO_4.5H_2O$. Solid $CuSO_4.5H_2O$ (1.0 mg) was heated (10 °C min^{-1}) from 30 °C to 400 °C on a thermogravimetric balance and gave the following Tg trace: 60–110 °C, 14.4% weight loss; 120–140 °C, 14.8% weight loss; 240–300 °C, 6.9% weight loss.

Analysis and presentation of data

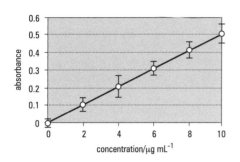

Fig. 60.1 Calibration curve for the determination of lead in soil using FAAS. Vertical bars show standard errors ($n = 3$).

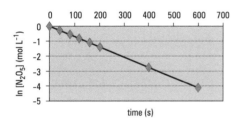

Fig. 60.2 Decomposition of N_2O_5. The first-order rate constant can be determined from the slope of the line.

Graphs can be used to show detailed results in an abbreviated form, displaying the maximum amount of information in the minimum space. Graphs and tables present findings in different ways. A graph (figure) gives a visual impression of the content and meaning of your results, while a table provides an accurate numerical record of data values. You must decide whether a graph should be used, e.g. to illustrate a pronounced trend or relationship, or whether a table (Chapter 61) is more appropriate.

A well-constructed graph will combine simplicity, accuracy and clarity. Planning of graphs is needed at the earliest stage in any write-up as your accompanying text will need to be structured so that each graph delivers the appropriate message. Therefore, it is best to decide on the final form for each of your graphs before you write your text. The text, diagrams, graphs and tables in a laboratory write-up or project report should be complementary, each contributing to the overall message. In a formal scientific communication it is rarely necessary to repeat the same data in more than one place (e.g. as a table and as a graph). However, graphical representation of data collected earlier in tabular format may be applicable in laboratory practical reports.

Practical aspects of graph drawing

The following comments apply to graphs drawn for laboratory reports. Figures for publication, or similar formal presentation, are usually prepared according to specific guidelines, provided by the publisher/organiser.

> **KEY POINT** Graphs should be self-contained – they should include all material necessary to convey the appropriate message without reference to the text. Every graph must have a concise explanatory title to establish the content. If several graphs are used, they should be numbered so they can be quoted in the text.

Criteria for preparing graphs:

- Clarity – show the relationships within the data.
- Economy – leave out superfluous information/text.
- Integrity – present the data without trying to mislead.

Selecting a title – it is a common fault to use titles that are grammatically incorrect. A widely applicable format is to state the relationship between the dependent and independent variables within the title, e.g. 'The relationship between absorbance and concentration'.

- Consider the layout and scale of the axes carefully. Most graphs are used to illustrate the relationship between two variables (x and y) and have two axes at right angles (e.g. Fig. 60.1 and Fig. 60.2). The horizontal axis is known as the abscissa (x-axis) and the vertical axis as the ordinate (y-axis).

- The axis assigned to each variable must be chosen carefully. Usually the x-axis is used for the independent variable (e.g. concentration) while the dependent variable (e.g. signal response) is plotted on the y-axis. When neither variable is determined by the other, or where the variables are interdependent, the axes may be plotted either way round.

- Each axis must have a descriptive label showing what is represented, together with the appropriate units of measurement, separated from the descriptive label by a solidus or 'slash' ($/$), as in Fig. 60.1, or by brackets, as in Fig. 60.2.

- Each axis must have a scale with reference marks ('ticks') on the axis to show clearly the location of all numbers used.

- A figure legend should be used to provide explanatory detail, including a key to the symbols used for each data set.

Remembering which axis is which – a way of remembering the orientation of the x-axis is that 'x' is 'a cross', and it runs 'across' the page (horizontal axis) while 'y' is the first letter of 'yacht', with a large vertical mast (vertical axis).

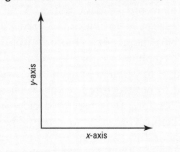

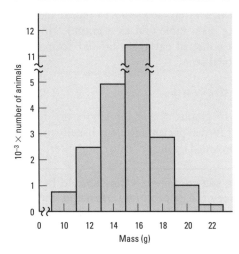

Fig. 60.3 Frequency distribution (histogram) of masses for a range of different soil types (sample size 24 085); the size class interval is 2 g.

Example For a data set where the smallest number on the log axis is 12 and the largest number is 9000, three-cycle log-linear paper would be used, covering the range 10–10 000.

Choosing between a histogram and a bar chart – use a histogram for continuous quantitative variables and a bar chart for discrete variables (see Chapter 27 for details of these types of measurement scale).

Handling very large or very small numbers

To simplify presentation when your experimental data consist of either very large or very small numbers, the plotted values may be the measured numbers multiplied by a power of 10: this multiplying power should be written immediately before the descriptive label on the appropriate axis (as in Fig. 60.3). However, it is often better to modify the primary unit with an appropriate prefix (p. 214) to avoid any confusion regarding negative powers of 10.

Size

Remember that the purpose of your graph is to communicate information. It must not be too small, so use at least half an A4 page and design your axes and labels to fill the available space without overcrowding any adjacent text. If using graph paper, remember that the white space around the grid is usually too small for effective labelling. The shape of a graph is determined by your choice of scale for the x and y axes which, in turn, is governed by your experimental data. It may be inappropriate to start the axes at zero (e.g. Fig. 60.1). In such instances, it is particularly important to show the scale clearly, with scale breaks where necessary, so the graph does not mislead.

Graph paper

In addition to conventional linear (squared) graph paper, you may need the following:

- **Probability graph paper.** This is useful when one axis is a probability scale.

- **Log-linear graph paper.** This is appropriate when one of the scales shows a logarithmic progression, e.g. in chemical kinetics. A plot of $\ln K$ against $1/T$ is used to determine the activation energy (E_a), where K is the rate constant and T is the temperature. Log-linear paper is defined by the number of logarithmic divisions (usually termed 'cycles') covered (e.g. Fig. 60.4) so make sure you use a paper with the appropriate number of cycles for your data. An alternative approach is to plot the log-transformed values on 'normal' graph paper.

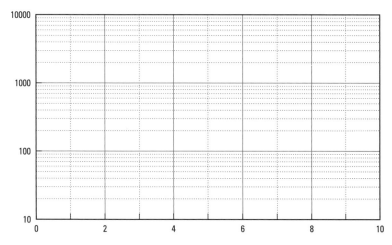

Fig. 60.4 Representation of three-cycle log-linear graph paper, marked up to show a y-axis (log) scale from 10 to 10000 and an x-axis (linear) scale from 0 to 10.

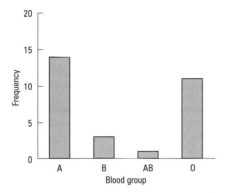

Fig. 60.5 Bar chart, showing the number of students belonging to each ABO blood group ($n = 29$).

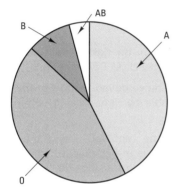

Fig. 60.6 Pie chart: relative abundance of human blood groups.

- **Log-log graph paper**. This is appropriate when both scales show a logarithmic progression.

Types of graph

Different graphical forms may be used for different purposes, including:

- Plotted curves – used for data where the relationship between two variables can be represented as a continuum (e.g. Fig. 60.1).

- Scatter diagrams – used to visualise the relationship between individual data values for two interdependent variables often as a preliminary part of a correlation analysis (p. 518).

- Three-dimensional graphs show the interrelationships of three variables, often one dependent and two independent (e.g. Fig. 66.5). A contour diagram is an alternative method of representing such data.

- Histograms represent frequency distributions of continuous variables (e.g. Fig. 60.3).

- Frequency polygons emphasise the form of a frequency distribution by joining the coordinates with straight lines, in contrast to a histogram. This is particularly useful when plotting two or more frequency distributions on the same graph.

- Bar charts represent frequency distributions of a discrete qualitative or quantitative variable (e.g. Fig. 60.5). An alternative representation is the line chart.

- Pie charts illustrate portions of a whole (e.g. Fig. 60.6).

The plotted curve

This is the commonest form of graphical representation used in chemistry. The key features are outlined below and in checklist form in Box 60.1, while Box 60.2 advises on using Microsoft Excel.

Box 60.1 **Checklist for the stages of drawing a graph**

The following sequence can be used whenever you need to construct a plotted curve: it will need to be modified for other types of graph.

1. **Collect all of the data values and statistical values** (in tabular form, where appropriate).

2. **Decide on the most suitable form of presentation**: this may include transformation to convert data to linear form.

3. **Choose a concise descriptive title**, together with a reference (figure) number and date, where necessary.

4. **Determine which variable is to be plotted on the x-axis and which on the y-axis.**

5. **Select appropriate scales for both axes** and make sure that the numbers and their location (scale marks) are clearly shown, together with any scale breaks.

6. **Decide on appropriate descriptive labels for both axes**, with SI units of measurement, where appropriate.

7. **Choose the symbols for each set of data points** and decide on the best means of representation for statistical values.

8. **Plot the points** to show the coordinates of each value with appropriate symbols.

9. **Draw a trend line for each set of points.** Use a see-through ruler, so you can draw the line to have an equal number of points on either side of it.

10. **Write a figure legend**, to include a key which identifies all symbols and statistical values and any descriptive footnotes.

Box 60.2 How to create and amend graphs within a spreadsheet (Microsoft Excel 2007) for use in coursework reports and dissertations

Microsoft Excel can be used to create graphs of reasonable quality, as long as you know how to amend the default settings so that your graph meets the formal standards required for practical and project reports. As with a hand-drawn graph, the basic stages in graph drawing (Box 60.1) still apply. The following instructions explain how to produce an X–Y graph (plotted curve, p. 47), bar graph (p. 473) pie graph and histogram using Excel 2007, where all types of graphs are termed 'charts'. Earlier versions use broadly similar commands, though not always in the same locations within the software.

Producing an X–Y graph (*Scatter* chart in Excel)

1. **Create the appropriate type of graph for your data.** Enter the numeric values for your X variable data in the cells of a single column and the equivalent values for the Y variable in the adjacent cells of the next column to the right. Then select the whole data array (highlight the appropriate cells by clicking and holding down the left mouse button and dragging the cursor across the cells so that all values are included). Then select the *Insert* tab at the top of the sheet, and select (left-click) the *Scatter* chart from the options provided in the upper ribbon. Note that you should never use the *Line* chart option, as it is based on an X axis that is not quantitative, so all X values will appear as equally-spaced categories, rather than having a true scale). Select the first options from the *Scatter* menu (*Scatter with only Markers*). Once selected, this will produce an embedded scatter chart

of the type show in Fig. 60.7(a). The line is then added later, as described below.

2. **Change the default settings to improve the appearance of your graph.** Consider each element of the image in turn, including the overall size, height and width of the graph (resize by clicking and dragging one of the 'sizing handles' around the edge of the chart). The graph shown in Fig. 60.7(b) was produced by altering the default settings, typically by moving the cursor over the feature and then clicking the right mouse button to reveal an additional menu of editing and formatting options. (Note that the example given below is for illustrative purposes only, and should not necessarily be regarded as prescriptive.)

Example for an X–Y graph (compare Fig. 60.7(a) with Fig. 60.7(b)):

- Unnecessary legend box on right-hand side can be removed using the (right-click) *Delete* option.

- Border to chart can be removed using *Format Chart Area* function (available by right-clicking within chart area).

- Gridlines can either be removed, using the *Delete* function or, if desired (as in Fig. 60.7(b)), changed by clicking on each axis and using the *Add Minor Gridlines* and *Format Gridlines* options to alter the *Colour* and *Style* of the gridlines to make them more like those of conventional graph paper.

(a)

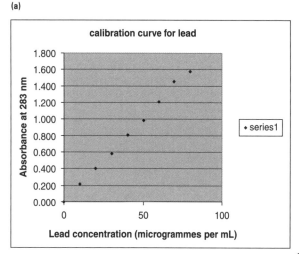

(b)

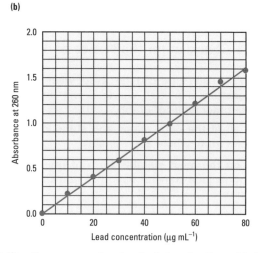

Calibration curve for lead determination. Performed using an atomic absorption spectrometer (on 01.04.09). Values shown are averages of triplicate measurements.

Fig. 60.7 Examples of a plotted curve produced in Microsoft Excel using (a) default settings and (b) modified (improved) settings.

- X and Y axes can be reformatted by selecting each in turn, and using the *Format Axis* menu options to select appropriate scales for major and minor units, style of tick marks, etc. Remember that it is better to use a figure legend in Word, rather than the *Chart Title* option within Excel.

- X and Y axis labels can be added by selecting the *Layout* tab, then *Axis Titles*, then *Primary Horizontal Axis Title* and *Primary Vertical Axis Title* options, which will produce a text box beside each axis into which can be typed the axis label and any corresponding units. This can then be changed from the default font using the *Home* tab options.

- Data point style can be changed by selecting (right-clicking) any data point and following the *Format Data Series* options to choose appropriate styles, colours and fill of the data markers.

- A straight line of best fit can be added by selecting any data point and using the *Add Trendline* option to choose a *Linear* line type with appropriate colour and style (explore other options within the *Format, Layout* and *Design* tabs at the top of the worksheet).

Producing a bar graph (*Column* chart in Excel)

1. **Create the appropriate type of graph for your data.** Enter the category names (for X axis) in one column and the numeric values (for Y axis) in the next column. Select (highlight) the data array, then select the *Insert* tab, and choose the *Column* chart from the options provided. For a standard bar graph, select

the first option from the *Column* menu (*Clustered Column*). Once selected, this will produce an embedded bar graph of the type show in Fig. 60.8(a).

2. **Change the default settings to improve the appearance of your graph.** The bar graph shown in Fig. 60.8(b) was produced by selecting each feature and altering the default settings, as detailed below (illustrative example).

Example for a bar graph (compare Fig. 60.8(a) with Fig. 60.8(b)):

- Unnecessary legend box on right-hand side can be removed using the *Delete* option.

- Border to chart can be removed using *Format Chart Area* function available by right-clicking within chart area).

- Gridlines can either be removed, using the *Delete* function or changed by selecting the gridlines and using the *Format Gridlines* option to alter the *Colour* and *Style*.

- Y axis can be reformatted by selecting the axis, then using the *Format Axis* menu options to select appropriate scales, tick marks, line colour, etc. Note that the X axis should already contain category labels from the spreadsheet cells (modify original cells to update spreadsheet, if necessary).

- X and Y axis labels can be added by selecting the *Layout* tab, then *Axis Titles*, then *Primary Horizontal Axis Title* and *Primary Vertical Axis Title* options, as detailed for the plotted curve (p. 474).

(a)

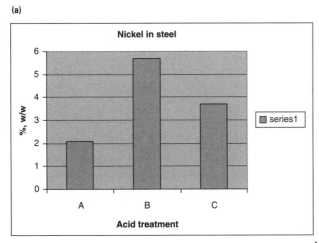

(b)

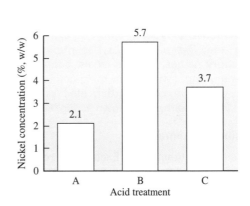

Influence of acid on the determination of nickel in steel using gravimetry. Key: A = HCl, B = aqua regia and C = HNO_3.

Fig. 60.8 Examples of a bar chart produced in Microsoft Excel using (a) default settings and (b) modified (improved) settings.

(continued)

Box 60.2 How to create and amend graphs within a spreadsheet (Microsoft Excel 2007) for use in coursework reports and dissertations (continued)

- Bar colour can be modified using the *Format Data Series* menu, selecting appropriate *Fill* and *Border* colours, e.g. white and black respectively in Fig. 60.8(b).

- Individual Y data values can be shown using the *Add Data Labels* option (other options and adjustments can be made using the *Format, Layout* and *Design* tabs at the top of the worksheet).

Note that for all types of graph, it is better not to use the Chart Title option within Excel, which places the title at the top of the chart (as in Fig. 60.8(a)), but to copy and paste your untitled graph into a word-processed document, such as a Microsoft Word file, and then type a formal figure legend below the graph, as in Fig. 60.8(a) and Fig. 60.8(b)). However, once your graph is embedded into a Word file, it is generally best not to make further amendments – you should go back to the original Excel file, make the required changes and then repeat the copy–paste procedure to reinsert the graph into the Word file.

Producing a pie graph (*Pie* chart in Excel)

1. **Create the appropriate type of graph for your data.** Enter the category names for each part of the pie chart in one column, and the corresponding numbers (counts, fractions or percentages) in the next column. Select (highlight) the data array, then select (left-click) the *Insert* tab, and choose the *Pie* chart from the options provided. For a standard pie graph, select the first option from the menu (*Pie*). Once selected, this will produce an embedded pie graph.

2. **Change the default settings to improve the appearance of your graph.** For example, you can use the *Design* and *Layout* ribbons show the category names, as *Data labels*, adjust colours and shading (e.g. switch from multi-colour to shades of grey), remove chart border, etc., as required (an illustrative example is shown as Fig. 60.9).

Producing a histogram

The histogram function in Excel 2007 requires a little more effort to master, compared with other chart types. Essentially, a histogram is a graphical display of frequencies (counts) for a continuous quantitative variable, where the data values are grouped into classes. It is possible to select the upper limit for each class into which you want the data to be grouped (these are termed 'bin range values' in Excel 2007). An alternative approach is to let the software select the class intervals (bin range values) for you: Excel selects evenly distributed bins between the minimum and maximum values. However, this is

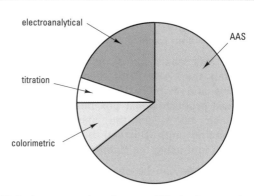

Fig. 60.9 An example of a modified pie graph: Most popular approaches to determine metals in solution.

often less effective than selecting your own class intervals.

To use the Excel histogram function, you will need to make sure that the *Analysis ToolPack* is loaded (check under the *Data* tab and, if not loaded, select via the *Office Button > Excel Options > Add-ins > Manage Excel Add-ins > Analysis ToolPak*. The *Histogram* function should then be available in the *Analysis ToolPak* option on the *Data tab/ribbon*.

The following steps outline the procedure used to create the histograms shown in Fig. 60.10 for the table of data below (concentration of benzo(a)pyrene, in mg kg^{-1}, in 24 soil samples).

7.2	6.5	7.1	8.5	6.6	7.2
7.0	7.3	8.6	9.1	7.5	8.3
7.1	5.7	7.3	7.6	6.9	7.1
8.3	7.6	5.4	8.6	7.9	8.0

1. **Enter the raw data values,** e.g. as a single column of numbers, or as an array, as above.

2. **Decide the class intervals to be used.** Base your choice on the number of data points and the maximum and minimum values (for a small data set such as that shown above, you can do this by visual examination, whereas for a large data set, use the Excel Functions *COUNT, MAX* and *MIN* (find these under the Σ symbol (*More Functions*) on the *Editing* section on the *Home* tab/ribbon, or use the *Descriptive Statistics > Summary statistics* option of the *Data Analysis* component on the *Data* tab/ribbon). A typical histogram would have 4–10 classes, depending on the level of discrimination required. Enter the upper limit for each class (*bin range values*) in ascending order in a separate array of cells, e.g. in a column close to the data values (in

the above example, 6, 7, 8 and 9 were chose – the few data values above the final bin value will be shown on the histogram as a group labelled 'more').

3. **Select the histogram function, then input your data and class interval values.** From the *Data* tab/ribbon, select *Data Analysis > Histogram*. A new window will open: input your data into the *Input Range* box (highlight the appropriate cells by clicking on the first data value and dragging to the final data value while holding down the left mouse button). Next, input the *Bin Range* values into the appropriate box (if this is left empty, Excel will select default bin range values). Most of the remaining boxes can be left empty, though you must click the last box to get a *Chart Output*, otherwise the software will give the numerical counts for each group, without drawing a histogram. Click *OK* and entries will be created within a new worksheet, showing the upper limits of each group (in a column labelled *Frequency*), plus a poorly constructed chart based on Excel 2007 default settings, as shown in Fig. 60.10(a) (note that the default output is a bar chart, rather than a histogram, since there are gaps between the groups).

Example for a histogram (compare Fig. 60.10(a) with Fig. 60.10(b)):

- Chart can be resized to increase height, using the 'sizing handles' at the edges of the chart and border line around graph can be removed using *Format Chart Area > Border Color > No line* (menu available by right-clicking within chart area).

- Title and unnecessary legend box can be removed using the *Delete* option.

- Axis scales can be reformatted using the *Format Axis* menu options (e.g. scales, tick marks, line colour).

- X axis labels (class intervals) can be amended by typing directly into the cells containing the bin range values.

- Axis titles can be changed by typing directly into the axis title box (double-click to access).

- Bar colour can be changed (e.g. to grey, with black outline) using the *Format Data Series > Fill* and *Border Colour* options.

- Bar chart converted to correct histogram format (no gaps between bars) using the Format Data Series > Series Options, setting *Gap Width* to 0%.

- Figure legend can be added below figure in Microsoft Word, following copying and pasting of the Excel histogram into a Word file.

Importing an Excel 2007 chart into a Word 2007 document

One problem encountered with Microsoft Office 2007 products (but not with earlier versions e.g. Office 1997–2003) is that the standard *Cut > Paste* procedure gives a poor quality figure, with grainy appearance and fuzzy lines/text; similar problems occur using the *Insert* tab/ribbon in Word 2007. The simplest approach is to follow the step-wise procedure below:

1. Select your Excel 2007 chart: right-click outside the chart itself, near to the edge, then choose the *Copy* option from the drop-down menu.

2. Open your Word 2007 file, go to the *Home* tab/ribbon and select *Paste special > Microsoft Office*

(a)

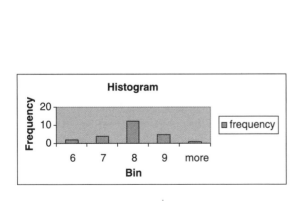

(b)

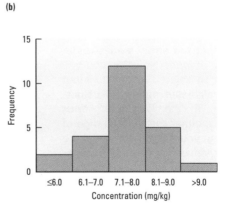

Histogram of benzo(a)pyrene in soil samples (n = 24).

Fig. 60.10 Examples of histogram output from Microsoft Excel using (a) default settings and (b) modified (improved) settings.

(continued)

Box 60.2 How to create and amend graphs within a spreadsheet (Microsoft Excel 2007) for use in coursework reports and dissertations (continued)

Word Document Object from the *Clipboard* options (left hand side of ribbon).

3. This should give a graph with the same crisp axis/line/text formatting as the original chart in Excel 2007.

The alternative approach is to use Excel 2007 to print the entire graph (chart) as a single sheet, and then add this to the print-out from your word-processed document. However, the disadvantage with this approach is that you cannot produce a professional looking figure legend below your graph.

Choosing graphical symbols – plotted curves are usually drawn using a standard set of symbols: ●, ○, ■, □, ▲, △, ◆, ◇. By convention, paired symbols ('closed' and 'open') are often used to represent 'plus' (treatment) and 'minus' (control) treatments.

Adding error bars to Microsoft Excel graphs – you can do this as follows (for Excel 2007):

1. On your graph, right-click on one of the data points of the series to which you want to add error bars;

2. Select *Format Data Series* and use either the *Y Error Bars* tab (vertical error bars) or the *X Error Bars* tab (horizontal error bars):

   - select the type of error bar that you want under Display (e.g. *Both*);
   - select the method to be used to input the error values under *Error amount;* typically, you will want to select *Custom,* to input pre-calculated numerical values. Then, in the *Plus* and *Minus* boxes, either specify the range of cells in your worksheet where the error values are located, or enter the relevant numbers directly, separated by commas.

Data points

Each data point must be shown accurately, so that any reader can determine the exact values of x and y. The results of each treatment must be readily identifiable. A useful technique is to use a dot for each data point, surrounded by a hollow symbol for each treatment (see Fig. 60.1) or to use symbols only (Fig. 60.15), though the coordinates of each point are defined less accurately. Use the same symbol for the same entity if it occurs in several graphs and provide a key to all symbols.

Statistical measures

If you are plotting average values for several replicates and if you have the necessary statistical knowledge, you can calculate the standard error (p. 504), or the 95% confidence limits (p. 518) for each mean value and show these on your graph as a series of vertical bars (see Fig. 60.1). Make it clear in the legend whether the bars refer to standard errors or 95% confidence limits and quote the value of n (the number of replicates per data point). Another approach is to add a least significant difference bar to the graph.

Interpolation

Once you have plotted each point, you must decide whether to link them by straight lines or a smoothed curve. Each of these techniques conveys a different message to your reader. Joining the points by straight lines may seem the simplest option, but may give the impression that errors are very low or non-existent and that the relationship between the variables is complex. Joining points by straight lines is appropriate in certain graphs only, such as, for repeat measurements where measurement error can be assumed to be minimal (e.g. recording the temperature rise in an exothermic reaction, to emphasise any variation from one time point to the next). However, in most plotted curves the best straight line or curved line should be drawn (according to appropriate mathematical or statistical models, or by eye) to highlight the relationship between the variables – after all, your choice of a plotted curve implies that such a relationship exists. Don't worry if some of your points do not lie on the line: this is caused by errors of measurement and by chemical variation. Most curves drawn by eye should have an equal number of points lying on either side of the line. You may be guided by 95% confidence limits, in which case your curve should pass within these limits wherever possible.

Conveying the correct message – the golden rule is: 'always draw the simplest line that fits the data reasonably well and is chemically reasonable'.

Extrapolating plotted curves – try to avoid the need to extrapolate by better experimental design.

Drawing a histogram – each datum is represented by a column with an area proportional to the magnitude of y: in most cases, you should use columns of equal width, so that the height of each column is then directly proportional to y. Shading or stippling may be used to identify individual columns, according to your needs.

Using computers to produce graphs – never allow a computer program to dictate size, shape and other aspects of a graph: find out how to alter scales, labels, axes, etc. and make appropriate selections (see Box 60.2 for Microsoft Excel). Draw curves freehand if the program only has the capacity to join the individual points by straight lines.

Interpreting proportions and percentages – you will need to establish how the values have been calculated (see p. 89).

Curved lines can be drawn using a flexible curve, a set of French curves or freehand. In the latter case, turn your paper so that you can draw the curve in a single, sweeping stroke by a pivoting movement at the elbow (for larger curves) or wrist (for smaller ones). Do not try to force your hand to make complex, unnatural movements as the resulting line will not be smooth.

Extrapolation

Be wary of extrapolation beyond the upper or lower limit of your measured values. This is rarely justifiable and may lead to serious errors. Whenever extrapolation is used, a dotted line ensures that the reader is aware of the uncertainty involved. Any assumptions behind an extrapolated curve should also be stated clearly in your text.

The histogram

While a plotted curve assumes a continuous relationship between the variables by interpolating between individual data points, a histogram involves no such assumptions. Histograms are also used to represent frequency distributions (p. 477), where the y-axis shows the number of times a particular value of x was obtained (e.g. Fig. 60.10b). As in a plotted curve, the x-axis represents a continuous quantitative variable which can take any value within a given range (e.g. compound concentration), so the scale must be broken down into discrete classes and the scale marks on the x-axis should show either the mid-points (mid-values) of each class, or the boundaries between the classes.

The columns are contiguous (adjacent to each other) in a histogram, in contrast to a bar chart, where the columns are separate because the x-axis of a bar chart represents discrete values.

Interpreting graphs

The process of analysing a graph can be split into five phases:

1. **Consider the context.** Look at the graph in relation to the aims of the study in which it was reported. Why were the observations made? What hypothesis was the experiment set up to test? This information can usually be found in the Introduction or Results section of a report. Also relevant are the general methods used to obtain the results. This might be obvious from the figure title and legend, or from the Experimental section.

2. **Recognise the graph form and examine the axes.** First, what kind of graph is presented (e.g. histogram, plotted curve)? You should be able to recognise the main types summarised on page 473 and their uses. Next, what do the axes measure? You should check what quantity has been measured in each case and what units are used.

3. **Look closely at the scale of each axis.** What is the starting point and what is the highest value measured? For the x-axis, this will let you know the scope of the treatments or observations (e.g. whether they lasted for 5 min or 20 years; whether a concentration span was two-fold or 50-fold). For each axis, it is especially important to note whether the values start at zero; if not, then the differences between any treatments shown may be magnified by the scale chosen (see Box 60.3).

Box 60.3 How graphs can misrepresent and mislead

1. **The 'volume' or 'area' deception** – this is mainly found in histogram or bar chart presentations where the size of a symbol is used to represent the measured variable. For example, the amount of hazardous waste produced in different years might be represented on a chart by different sizes of a chemical drum, with the *y*-axis (height of drum) representing the amount of waste. However, if the symbol retains its *shape* for all heights as in Figure 60.11(a), its *volume* will increase as a cubic function of the height, rather than in direct proportion. To the casual observer, a twofold increase may look like an eightfold one, and so on. Strictly, the *height* of the symbol should be the measure used to represent the variable, with no change in symbol width, as in Fig. 60.11(b).

2. **Effects of a non-zero axis** – A non-zero axis acts to emphasise the differences between measures by reducing the range of values covered by the axis. For example, in Figure 60.12(a), it looks as if there are large differences in mass between males and females; but if the scale is adjusted to run from zero (Fig. 60.12(b)), then it can be seen that the differences are not large as a proportion of the overall mass. Always scrutinise the scale values carefully when interpreting any graph.

3. **Use of a relative rather than absolute scale** – this is similar to the above, in that data compared using relative scales (e.g. percentage or ratio) can give the wrong impression if the denominator is not the same in all cases. In Figure 60.13(a), the action of two are shown as equal in *relative* effect, both resulting in 50% relative response compared (say) to the respective controls. However, if reagent A is 50% of a control value of 200 and reagent B is 50% of a control value of 500, then the actual difference in *absolute* response would have been masked, as shown by Fig. 60.13(b).

4. **Effects of a non-linear scale** – when interpreting graphs with non-linear (e.g. logarithmic) scales, you may interpret any changes on an imagined linear scale. For example, the pH scale is logarithmic, and linear changes on this scale mean less in terms of absolute H^+ concentration at high (alkaline) pH than they do at low (acidic) pH. In Figure 60.14(a), the cell density in two media is compared on a logarithmic scale, while in Fig. 60.14(b), the same data are graphed on a linear scale. Note, also, that the log *y*-axis scale in Fig. 60.14(a) cannot be shown to zero, because there is no logarithm for 0.

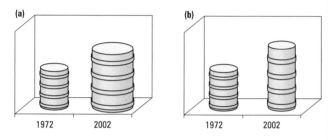

Fig. 60.11 Increase in pesticide use over a 30 year period.

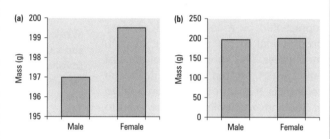

Fig. 60.12 Average mass of males and females in test group.

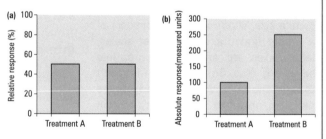

Fig. 60.13 Responses to reagents A and B.

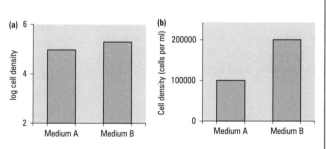

Fig. 60.14 Effect of different media on cell density.

5. **Unwarranted extrapolation** – a graph may be extrapolated to indicate what would happen if a trend continued, as in Figure 60.15(a). However, this can only be done under certain assumptions (e.g. that certain factors will remain constant or that relationships will hold under new conditions). There may be no guarantee that this will actually be the case. Figure 60.15(b) illustrates other possible outcomes if the experiment were to be repeated with higher values for the x-axis.

6. **Failure to account for data point error** – this misrepresentation involves curves that are overly complex in relation to the scatter in the underlying data. When interpreting graphs with complex curves, consider the errors involved in the data values. It is probably unlikely that the curve would pass through all the data points unless the errors were very small. Figure 60.16(a) illustrates a curve that appears to assume zero error and is thus overly complex, while Fig. 60.16(b) shows a curve that takes possible errors of the points into account.

7. **Failure to reject outlying points** – this is a special case of the previous example. There may be many reasons for outlying data, from genuine mistakes to statistical 'freaks'. If a curve is drawn through such points on a graph, it indicates that the point carries equal weight with the other points, when in fact, it should probably be ignored. To assess this, consider the accuracy of the measurement, the number and position of adjacent points, and any special factors that might be involved on a one-off basis. Figure 60.17(a) shows a curve where an outlier has perhaps been given undue weight when showing the presumed relationship. If there is good reason to think that the point should be ignored, then the curve shown in Fig. 60.17(b) would probably be more valid.

8. **Inappropriate fitted line** – here, the mathematical function chosen to represent a trend in the data might be inappropriate. A straight line might be fitted to the data, when a curve would be more correct, or *vice versa*. These cases can be difficult to assess. You need to consider the theoretical validity of the model used to generate the curve (this is not always stated clearly). For example, if a straight line is fitted to the points, the implicit underlying model states that one factor varies in direct relation to another, when the true situation may be more complex. In Figure 60.18(a), the relationship has been shown as a linear relationship, whereas an exponential relationship, as shown in Fig. 60.18(b), could be more correct.

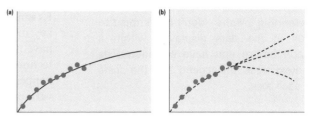

Fig. 60.15 Extrapolation of data under different assumptions.

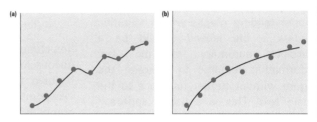

Fig. 60.16 Fitted curves under different assumptions of data error.

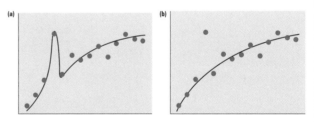

Fig. 60.17 Curves with and without outlier taken into account.

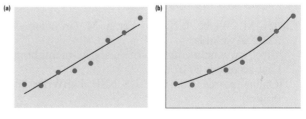

Fig. 60.18 Different mathematical model used to represent trends in data.

Examining graphs – don't be tempted to look at the data displayed within a graph before you have considered its context, read the legend and the scale of each axis.

Understanding graphs within scientific papers – the legend should be a succinct summary of the key information required to interpret the figure without further reference to the main text. This is a useful approach when 'skimming' a paper for relevant information.

4. **Examine the symbols and curves.** Information will be provided in the key or legend to allow you to determine what these refer to. If you have made your own photocopy of the figure, it may be appropriate to note this directly on it. You can now assess what appears to have happened. If, say, two conditions have been observed while a variable is altered, when exactly do they differ from each other; by how much; and for how long?

5. **Evaluate errors and statistics.** It is important to take account of variability in the data. For example, if mean values are presented, the underlying errors may be large, meaning that any difference between two treatments or observations at a given x-value could simply have arisen by chance. Thinking about the descriptive statistics used (Chapter 63) will allow you to determine whether apparent differences could be significant.

Sometimes graphs are used to mislead. This may be unwitting, as in an unconscious favouring of a 'pet' hypothesis of the author. Graphs may be used to 'sell' a product in the field of advertising or to favour a viewpoint as, perhaps, in politics. Experience in drawing and interpreting graphs will help you spot these flawed presentations, and understanding how graphs can be erroneously presented (Box 60.3) will help you avoid the same pitfalls.

Sources for further study

Billo, E.J. (2007) *Excel for Scientists and Engineers*. Wiley, Chichester.

Briscoe, M.H. (1996) *Preparing Scientific Illustrations: A Guide to Better Posters, Presentations and Publications*. Springer-Verlag, New York.

Carter, M., Wiebe, E.N. and Ferzli, M. *Graphing with Excel*. Available: http://www.ncsu.edu/labwrite/res/gt/gt-menu.html Last accessed: 20/07/09. [Online-tutorial from the US–NSF LabWrite 2000 Project]

Currell, G. and Dowman, T. (2009) *Essential Mathematics and Statistics for Science*, 2nd edn. Wiley, Chichester.

De Levie, R. (2001) *How to use Excel in Analytical Chemistry and in General Scientific Data Analysis*. Cambridge University Press, Cambridge.

Miller, J.N. and Miller, J.C. (2005) *Statistics and Chemometrics for Analytical Chemistry*, 5th edn. Prentice Hall, Harlow. [Gives detailed coverage of calibration methods and the validity of analytical measurements]

Monk, P. and Munro, L.J. (2010) *Maths for Chemists: A Chemist's Toolkit of Calculations*. Oxford University Press, Oxford.

Robbins, N.B. (2005) *Creating More Effective Graphs*. Wiley, New York.

Steiner, E. (2008) *The Chemistry Maths Book*, 2nd edn. Oxford University Press, Oxford.

Study exercises

60.1 Select appropriate graphical presentations. Choose an appropriate graphical form for each of the following examples:

(a) A titration curve showing the influence of 0.1 M NaOH on pH following the addition of 0.1 M HCl.

(b) The concentration of lead in blood from 100 children.

(c) The determination of selenium in bread flour.

(d) The sand, silt and clay content of a soil sample.

(e) A quality control chart for the paracetamol content of tablets.

60.2 Create a pie chart. Display the following information in the form of a pie chart.

Typical composition of a breakfast cereal.

Content	Typical value per 100 g
Protein	6 g
Carbohydrate	83 g
Fat	5 g
Fibre	4 g
Other	2 g

60.3 Create a frequency distribution histogram. The table below gives data for the fructose concentration in 100 samples of fruit juice. Plot a histogram showing the frequency distribution of the data. Write a brief description of the important features of the distribution.

Fructose content (g L^{-1}) in fruit juice

11.1	14.2	13.5	9.8	12.0	13.9	14.1	14.6	11.0	12.3
13.4	12.9	12.9	10.0	13.1	11.8	12.6	10.7	8.1	11.2
13.8	12.4	12.9	11.3	12.7	12.4	14.6	15.1	11.2	9.7
11.3	14.7	10.8	13.3	11.9	11.4	12.5	13.0	11.6	13.1
9.3	13.5	14.6	11.2	11.7	10.9	12.4	12.0	12.1	12.6
10.9	12.1	13.4	9.5	12.5	11.6	12.2	8.8	10.7	11.1
10.2	11.7	10.4	14.0	14.9	11.5	12.0	13.2	12.1	13.3
12.4	9.4	13.2	12.5	10.8	11.7	12.7	14.1	10.4	10.5
13.3	10.6	10.5	13.7	11.8	14.1	10.3	13.6	10.4	13.9
11.7	12.8	10.4	11.9	11.4	10.6	12.7	11.4	12.9	12.1

60.4 Find examples of misleading graphs. Create a portfolio of examples of misleading graphs taken from newspapers. For each graph, state what aspect is misleading (see Box 60.3) and, where possible, attempt to show the data correctly in a new graph.

A table is often the most appropriate way to present numerical data in a concise, accurate and structured form. Assignments and project reports should contain tables which have been designed to condense and display results in a meaningful way and to aid numerical comparison. The preparation of tables for recording primary data is discussed on page 210.

Decide whether you need a table, or whether a graph is more appropriate. Histograms and plotted curves can be used to give a visual impression of the relationships within your data (p. 473). On the other hand, a table gives you the opportunity to make detailed numerical comparisons.

> **KEY POINT** Always remember that the primary purpose of your table is to communicate information and allow appropriate comparison, not simply to put down the results on paper.

Alternatives to tables for presenting numerical data – if you have only a few numbers, consider simply presenting these within the text; an alternative approach is to show the data values on a bar chart (e.g. Fig. 60.5).

Preparation of tables

Title

Every table must have a brief descriptive title. If several tables are used, number them consecutively so they can be quoted in your text. The titles within a report should be compared with one another, making sure they are logical and consistent and that they describe accurately the numerical data contained within them.

Constructing titles – take care over titles as it is a common mistake in student practical reports to present tables without titles, or to misconstruct the title.

Structure

Display the components of each table in a way that will help the reader understand your data and grasp the significance of your results. Organise the columns so that each category of like numbers or attributes is listed vertically, while each horizontal row shows a different experimental treatment, organism, sampling site, etc. (as in Table 61.1). Where appropriate, put control values near the beginning of the table. Columns that need to be compared should be set out alongside each other. Use rulings to subdivide your table appropriately, but avoid cluttering it up with too many lines.

Saving space in tables – you may be able to omit a column of control data if your results can be expressed as percentages of the corresponding control values.

Headings and subheadings

These should identify each set of data and show the units of measurement, where necessary. Make sure that each column is wide enough for the headings and for the longest data value.

Table 61.1 Selected properties of elements in the Periodic Table

Element	Symbol	Atomic number	Relative atomic mass**	Atomic radius (pm)	Important oxidation states	Density $(g\,mL^{-1})$*	Compounds in ores
Aluminium	Al	13	26.98	143	+3	2.7	Al_2O_3
Cobalt	Co	27	58.93	125	+2, +3	8.7	$CoAsS$, $CoAs_2$, CoS
Iron	Fe	26	55.84	126	+2, +3	7.9	Fe_2O_3, Fe_3O_4, $FeCO_3$, FeS_2
Manganese	Mn	25	54.94	126	+2, +3, +4, +7	7.2	MnO_2, Mn_2O_3, Mn_3O_4, mixed oxides
Zinc	Zn	30	65.38	138	+2	7.1	ZnS, ZnO, $ZnCO_3$

* Determined at 28 °C.
** Relative to the atomic mass of ^{12}C (= 12).

Example Quote the radius of an atom as 0.126 nm or 126 pm, rather than 0.000 000 000 126 m or 0.126 × 10^{-9} m (or 126 × 10^{-12} m). However, some texts still use the angstrom, Å. An angstrom is equivalent to 10^{-10} m; hence the radius of an atom would be 1.26 Å in this example.

Saving further space in tables – in some instances a footnote can be used to replace a whole column of repetitive data.

Using spreadsheets and word processing packages – these can be used to prepare high quality versions of tables for project work (Box 61.2).

Numerical data

Within the table, do not quote values to more significant figures than necessary, as this will imply spurious accuracy (pp. 209, 491). By careful choice of appropriate units for each column you should aim to present numerical data within the range 0 to 1000. As with graphs, it is less ambiguous to use derived SI units, with the appropriate prefixes, in the headings of columns and rows, rather than quoting multiplying factors as powers of 10. Alternatively, include exponents in the main body of the table (see Table 26.1), to avoid any possible confusion regarding the use of negative powers of 10.

Other notations

Avoid using dashes in numerical tables, as their meaning is unclear; enter a zero reading as '0' and use 'NT' not tested or 'ND' if no data value was obtained, with a footnote to explain each abbreviation. Other footnotes, identified by asterisks, superscripts or other symbols in the table, may be used to provide relevant experimental detail (if not given in the text) and an explanation of column headings and individual results, where appropriate. Footnotes should be as condensed as possible. Table 61.1 provides examples.

Statistics

In tables where the dispersion of each data set is shown by an appropriate statistical parameter, you must state whether this is the (sample) standard deviation, the standard error (of the mean) or the 95% confidence limits and you must give the value of n (the number of replicates). Other descriptive statistics should be quoted with similar detail, and hypothesis-testing statistics should be quoted along with the value of P (the probability). Details of any test used should be given in the legend, or in a footnote.

Text

Sometimes a table can be a useful way of presenting textual information in a condensed form (see examples on p. 421).

When you have finished compiling your tabulated data, carefully double-check each numerical entry against the original information, to ensure that the final version of your table is free from transcriptional errors. Box 61.1 gives a checklist for the major elements of constructing a table.

Box 61.1 Checklist for preparing a table

Every table should have the following components:

1. **A title**, plus a reference number and date where necessary.

2. **Headings for each column and row**, with appropriate units of measurement.

3. **Data values**, quoted to the nearest significant figure and with statistical parameters, according to your requirements.

4. **Footnotes** to explain abbreviations, modifications and individual details.

5. **Rulings to emphasise groupings** and distinguish items from each other.

Box 61.2 How to use a word processor (Microsoft Word 2007) or a spreadsheet (Microsoft Excel 2007) to create a table for use in coursework reports and dissertations

Creating tables with Microsoft Word: word-processed tables are suitable for text-intensive or number-intensive tables, although in the second case entering data can be laborious. When working in this way, the natural way to proceed is to create the 'shell' of the table, add the data, then carry out final formatting on the table.

1. **Move the cursor to the desired position in your document.** This is where you expect the top left corner of your table to appear. Go to the *Table* command, then choose *Insert > Table*.

2. **Select the appropriate number of columns and rows.** Don't forget to add rows and columns for headings. As default, a full-width table will appear, with single rulings for all cell boundaries, with all columns of equal width and all rows of equal height.

   Example of a 4 × 3 table:

3. **Customise the columns.** By placing the cursor over the vertical rulings then 'dragging', you can adjust their width to suit your heading text entries, which should now be added.

Heading 1	Heading 2	Heading 3	Heading 4

4. **Work through the table adding the data.** Entries can be numbers or text.

Heading 1	Heading 2	Heading 3	Heading 4
xx	xx	xx	xx
xx	xx	xx	

5. **Make further adjustments to column and row widths to suit.** For example, if text fills several rows within a cell, consider increasing the column width and if a column contains only single or double digit numbers, consider shrinking its width. To combine cells, first highlight them, then use *Table > Merge Cells.* You may wish to reposition text within a cell using *Format > Paragraph > Spacing.*

Heading 1	Heading 2	Heading 3	Heading 4
xx	xx	xx	xx
	xx	xx	xx

6. **Remove selected borders to cells.** One way to do this is using the table borders options accessed from the *Table borders* button on the toolbar, so that your table looks like the examples shown in this chapter.

7. **Add a table title.** This should be positioned *above* the table (*cf* a figure title/legend p. 471), legend and footnotes.

Final version of the Table:

***Table xx.* A table of some data.**

Heading 1	Heading 2*	Heading 3	Heading 4
Aaa	xx	xx	xx
	xx	xx	xx

*An example of a footnote

Creating tables with Microsoft Excel: tables derived from spreadsheets are effective when you have lots of numerical data, especially when these are stored or created using the spreadsheet itself. When working in this way, you can design the table as part of an output or summary section of the spreadsheet, add explanatory headings, format, then possibly export to a word processor when complete.

1. **Design the output or summary section.** Plan this as if it were a table, including adding text headings within cells.

17				
18	Heading 1	Heading 2	Heading 3	Heading 4
19				
20				
21				
22				

2. **Insert appropriate formulae within cells to produce data.** If necessary, formulae should draw on the other parts of the spreadsheet.

17				
18	Heading 1	Heading 2	Heading 3	Heading 4
19	Aaa	=A1	=C3*5	=SDEV(A1:A12)
20	Bbb	=A2	=F45/G12	=SDEV(B1:B12)
21				
22				

3. **Format the cells.** This is important to control the number of decimal places presented (*Format > Cells > Number*).

4. **Adjust column width to suit.** You can do this *via* the column headings, by placing the cursor over the rulings between columns then 'dragging'.

17				
18	Heading 1	Heading 2	Heading 3	Heading 4
19	Aaa	=A1	=C3*5	=SDEV(A1:A12)
20	Bbb	=A2	=F45/G12	=SDEV(B1:B12)
21				
22				

5. **Add rulings as appropriate.** Use the borders menu on the toolbar as described above.

17				
18	Heading 1	Heading 2	Heading 3	Heading 4
19	Aaa	=A1	=C3*5	=SDEV(A1:A12)
20	Bbb	=A2	=F45/G12	=SDEV(B1:B12)
21				

6. **Add 'real' data values to the spreadsheet.** This should result in the summary values within the table being filled. Check that these are presented with the appropriate number of significant figures (p. 491).

7. **The table can now be copied and pasted to a Word document.** If you wish to link the spreadsheet and the word-processed document so that the latter is updated whenever changes are made to the spread sheet values, then click *Paste* on the *Formatting* toolbar, click *Paste Options* next to the data, and then select *Match Destination Table Style and Link to Excel* or *Keep Source Formatting and Link to Excel.*

Sources for further study

Billo, E.J. (2007) *Excel for Scientists and Engineers.* Wiley, Chichester.

Currell, G. and Dowman, T. (2009) *Essential Mathematics and Statistics for Science*, 2nd edn. Wiley, Chichester.

Kirkup, L. (1994) *Experimental Methods: An Introduction to the Analysis and Presentation of Data.* Wiley, New York.

Miller, J.N. and Miller, J.C. (2005) *Statistics and Chemometrics for Analytical Chemistry*, 5th edn. Prentice Hall, Harlow.

Monk, P. and Munro, L.J. (2010) *Maths for Chemists: A Chemist's Toolkit of Calculations*, Oxford University Press, Oxford.

Simmonds, D. and Reynolds, L. (1994) *Data Presentation and Visual Literacy in Medicine and Science.* Butterworth-Heinemann, London.

Steiner, E. (2008) *The Chemistry Maths Book*, 2nd edn. Oxford University Press, Oxford.

Study exercises

61.1 Redesign a table of data. Using the following example, redraft the table to improve layout and correct inconsistencies.

Concentrations of drug and metabolites found in a blood sample

Diazepam	0.2	mg/L^{-1}
Desmethyl diazepam	0.075	μg/mL^{-1}
Temazepam	0.1	mg/L^{-1}
Methadone	0.23	μg/mL^{-1}
Alcohol*	86	mg/100 mL^{-1}
Caffeine	–	–
Nicotine	–	–

* nicotine and caffeine were not quantified

61.2 Devise a text-based table. After reading through this chapter, and working from memory, draw up a table listing the principal components of a typical table in the first column, and brief comments on the major features of each component in the second column.

Advice on dealing with numerical procedures – see:

- *Box 23.1: preparing solutions (p. 156);*
- *Box 23.2: preparing solutions (p. 158);*
- *Box 25.1: molar concentrations (p. 187);*
- *Box 47.1: calibration curves (p. 328);*
- *Box 49.1: stock solutions (p 342);*
- *Box 49.2: calibration solutions (p. 343);*
- *Box 49.3: standard additions (p. 344);*
- *Box 49.5: dilution factor (p. 345);*
- *Box 52.1: calibration solutions (p. 372);*
- *Box 55.1: radioactivity (p. 423).*

Chemistry often requires a numerical or statistical approach. Not only is mathematical modelling an important aid to understanding, but computations are often needed to turn raw data into meaningful information or to compare them with other data sets. Moreover, calculations are part of laboratory routine, perhaps required for making up solutions of known concentration (see pp. 156, 158, 187) or for the calibration curves (see p. 328). In research, 'trial' calculations can reveal what input data are required and where errors in their measurement might be amplified in the final result (see p. 209).

> **KEY POINT** If you find numerical work difficult, practice at problem-solving is especially important.

Practising at problem-solving:

- demystifies the procedures involved, which are normally just the elementary mathematical operations of addition, subtraction, multiplication and division (Table 62.1);

- allows you to gain confidence so that you don't become confused when confronted with an unfamiliar or apparently complex form of problem;

- helps you recognise the various forms a problem can take as, for instance, in the different forms of titrations (Chapters 42–45).

Steps in tackling a numerical problem

The step-by-step approach outlined below may not be the fastest method of arriving at an answer, but most mistakes occur where steps are missing, combined or not made obvious, so a logical approach is often better. Error tracing is distinctly easier when all stages in a calculation are laid out.

Tracing errors in mathematical problems – this is always easier when all the stages in a calculation are laid out clearly.

Have the right tools ready

Scientific calculators (p. 140) greatly simplify the numerical part of problem solving. However, the seeming infallibility of the calculator may lead you to accept an absurd result which could have arisen because of faulty key-pressing or faulty logic. Make sure you know how to use all the features on your calculator: especially how the memory works; how to introduce a constant multiplier or divider; and how to obtain an exponent (note that the 'exp' button on most calculators gives you 10^x, not 1^x or y^x; so 1×10^6 would be entered as $\boxed{1}\ \boxed{\text{exp}}\ \boxed{6}$, *not* $\boxed{10}\ \boxed{\text{exp}}\ \boxed{6}$).

Using a computer spreadsheet for numerical problems – this may be very useful in repetitive work or for 'what if?' case studies (see Chapter 12).

Approach the problem thoughtfully

If the individual steps have been laid out on a worksheet, the 'tactics' will already have been decided. It is more difficult when you have to adopt a strategy on your own, especially if the problem is presented as a story and it isn't obvious which equations or rules need to be applied.

- Read the problem carefully as the text may give clues as to how it should be tackled. Be certain of what is required as an answer before starting.

Table 62.1 Sets of numbers and operations

Sets of numbers

Whole numbers:	0, 1, 2, 3, ...
Natural numbers:	1, 2, 3, ...
Integers:	... −3, −2, −1, 0, 1, 2, 3, ...
Real numbers:	integers and anything between (e.g. −5, 4.376, 3/16, π, $\sqrt{5}$)
Prime numbers:	subset of natural numbers divisible by 1 and themselves only (i.e. 2, 3, 5, 7, 11, 13, ...)
Rational numbers:	p/q where p (integer) and q (natural) have no common factor (e.g. 3/4)
Fractions:	p/q where p is an integer and q is natural (e.g. $-6/8$)
Irrational numbers:	real numbers with no exact value (e.g. π)
Infinity:	(symbol ∞) is larger than any number (technically not a number as it does not obey the laws of algebra)

Operations and symbols

Basic operators:	$+$, $-$, $\times$ and $\div$ will not need explanation; however, / may substitute for $\div$, $*$ may substitute for $\times$ or this operator may be omitted
Powers:	a^n, i.e. 'a to the power n', means a multiplied by itself n times (e.g. $a^2 = a \times a = $ 'a squared', $a^3 = a \times a \times a = $ 'a cubed'). n is said to be the index or exponent. Note $a^0 = 1$ and $a^1 = a$
Logarithms:	the common logarithm (log) of any number x is the power to which 10 would have to be raised to give x (i.e. the log of 100 is 2; $10^2 = 100$); the antilog of x is 10^x. Note that there is no log for 0, so take this into account when drawing log axes by breaking the axis. Natural or Napierian logarithms (ln) use the base e ($= 2.71828\ldots$) instead of 10
Reciprocals:	the reciprocal of a real number a is $1/a$ ($a \neq 0$)
Relational operators:	$a > b$ means 'a is greater (more positive) than b', $<$ means less than, $\leqslant$ means less-than-or-equal-to and $\geqslant$ means greater-than-or-equal-to
Proportionality:	$a \propto b$ means 'a is proportional to b' (i.e. $a = kb$, where k is a constant). If $a \propto 1/b$, a is inversely proportional to b ($a = k/b$)
Sums:	Σx_i is shorthand for the sum of all x values from $i = 0$ to $i = n$ (more correctly the range of the sum is specified under the symbol)
Moduli:	$|x|$ signifies modulus of x, i.e. its absolute value (e.g. $|4| = |-4| = 4$)
Factorials:	$x!$ signifies factorial x, the product of all integers from 1 to x (e.g. $3! = 6$). Note $0! = 1! = 1$

Table 62.2 Simple algebra – rules for manipulating

If $a = b + c$, then $b = a - c$ and $c = a - b$

If $a = b \times c$, then $b = a \div c$ and $c = a \div b$

If $a = b^c$, then $b = a^{1/c}$ and $c = \log a \div \log b$

$a^{1/n} = \sqrt[n]{a}$

$a^{-n} = 1 \div a^n$

$a^b \times a^c = a^{(b+c)}$ and $a^b \div a^c = a^{(b-c)}$

$(a^b)^c = a^{(b \times c)}$

$a \times b = $ antilog$(\log a + \log b)$

- Analyse what kind of problem it is, which effectively means deciding which equation(s) or approach will be applicable. If this is not obvious, consider the dimensions/units of the information available and think how they could be fitted to a relevant formula. In examinations, a favourite ploy of examiners is to present a problem such that the familiar form of an equation must be rearranged (see Table 62.2 and Box 62.1). Another is to make you use two or more equations in series. If you are unsure whether a recalled formula is correct, a dimensional analysis can help: write in all the units for the variables and make sure that they cancel out to give the expected answer.

- Check that you have, or can derive, all of the information required to use your chosen equation(s). It is unusual but not unknown for examiners to supply redundant information. So, if you decide not to use some of the information given, be sure why you do not require it.

- Decide on what format and units the answer should be presented in. This is sometimes suggested to you. If the problem requires many changes in the prefixes to units, it is a good idea to convert all data to base SI units (multiplied by a power of 10) at the outset.

- If a problem appears complex, break it down into component parts.

Box 62.1 Example of the use of the algebraic rules of Table 62.2

Problem: if $a = (b - c) \div (d + e^n)$, **find** e.

1. Multiply both sides by $(d + e^n)$; formula becomes: $a(d + e^n) = (b - c)$

2. Divide both sides by a; formula becomes: $d + e^n = \dfrac{b - c}{a}$

3. Subtract d from both sides; formula becomes: $e^n = \dfrac{b - c}{a} - d$

4. Raise each side to the power $1/n$; formula becomes: $e = \left\{\dfrac{b - c}{a} - d\right\}^{1/n}$

Presenting calculations in assessed work – always show the steps in your calculations, as most markers will only penalise a mistake once and part marks will be given if the remaining operations are performed correctly. This can only be done if those operations are visible.

Units – never write any answer without its unit(s) unless it is truly dimensionless.

Rounding off to a specific number of significant figures – do not round off numbers until you arrive at the final answer or you will introduce 'rounding' errors into the calculation.

Present your answer clearly

The way you present your answer obviously needs to fit the individual problem. The example shown in Box 62.1 has been chosen to illustrate several important points, but this format would not fit all situations. Guidelines for presenting an answer include:

(a) Make your assumptions explicit. Most mathematical models of chemical phenomena require that certain criteria are met before they can be legitimately applied (e.g. 'assuming the sample is homogeneous ...'), while some approaches involve approximations which should be clearly stated (e.g. 'to estimate the volume of a tube, it was approximated to a cylinder with radius x and height y ...').

(b) Explain your strategy for answering, perhaps giving the applicable formula or definitions which suit the approach to be taken. Give details of what the symbols mean (and their units) at this point.

(c) Rearrange the formula to the required form with the desired unknown on the left-hand side (see Table 62.2).

(d) Substitute the relevant values into the right-hand side of the formula, using the units and prefixes as given (it may be convenient to convert values to SI beforehand). Convert prefixes to appropriate powers of 10 as soon as possible.

(e) Convert to the desired units step by step, i.e. taking each variable in turn.

(f) When you have the answer in the desired units, rewrite the left-hand side and <u>underline the answer</u>, for emphasis. Make sure that the result is presented to an appropriate number of significant figures (see below).

Check your answer

Having written out your answer, you should check it methodically, answering the following questions:

● Is the answer realistic? You should be alerted to an error if a number is absurdly large or small. In repeated calculations, a result standing out from others in the same series should be double-checked.

- Do the units make sense and match up with the answer required? Don't, for example, present a volume in units of m^2.

- Do you get the same answer if you recalculate in a different way? If you have time, recalculate the answer using a different 'route', entering the numbers into your calculator in a different form and/or carrying out the operations in a different order.

Rounding: decimal places and significant figures

In many instances, the answer you produce as a result of a calculation will include more figures than is justified by the accuracy and precision of the original data. Sometimes you will be asked to produce an answer to a specified number of decimal places or significant figures, and other times you will be expected to decide for yourself what would be appropriate.

> **KEY POINT** Do not simply accept the numerical answer from a calculator or spreadsheet, without considering whether you need to modify this to give an appropriate number of significant figures or decimal places.

Rounding to n *decimal places*

This is relatively easy to do.

1. Look at the number to the right of the *n*th decimal place.

2. If this is less than 5, simply 'cut off' all numbers to the right of the *n*th decimal place to produce the answer (i.e. round down).

3. If the number is greater than 5, 'cut off' all numbers to the right of the *n*th decimal place and add one to the *n*th decimal place to produce the answer (i.e. round up).

4. If the number is 5, then look at further numbers to the right to determine whether to round up or not.

5. If the number is *exactly* 5 and there are no further numbers to the right, then round the *n*th digit to the nearest even number. *Note:* When considering a large number of calculations, this procedure will not affect the overall mean value. Some rounding systems do the opposite to this (i.e. round to the nearest odd number), while others always round up where the number is exactly 5 (which *will* affect the mean). Take advice from your tutor and stick to one system throughout a series of calculations.

Whenever you see any numbers quoted, you should assume that the last digit has been rounded. For example, in the number 22.4, the '.4' is assumed to be rounded and the calculated value may have been between 22.35 and 22.45.

Quoting to n *significant figures*

The number of significant figures indicates the degree of approximation in the number. For most cases, it is given by counting all the figures except zeros that occur at the beginning or end of the number. Zeros *within* the number are always counted as significant. The number of

> **Examples**
> - The number 4.123 correct to two decimal places is 4.12
> - The number 4.126 correct to two decimal places is 4.13
> - The number 4.1251 correct to two decimal places is 4.13
> - The number 4.1250 correct to two decimal places is 4.12
> - The number 4.1350 correct to two decimal places is 4.14
> - The number 99.99 correct to one decimal place is 100.0.

> **Examples**
> - The number of significant figures in 194 is three
> - The number of significant figures in 2305 is four
> - The number of significant figures in 0.003 482 is four
> - The number of significant figures in 210×10^8 is three (21×10^9 would be two).

> **Examples**
>
> - The number of significant figures in 3051.93 is six
> - To five significant figures, this number is 3051.9
> - To four significant figures, this number is 3052
> - To three significant figures, this number is 3050
> - To two significant figures, this number is 3100
> - To one significant figure, this number is 3000
>
> 3051.93 to the nearest 10 is 3050
> 3051.93 to the nearest 100 is 3100
>
> Note that in this last case you must include the zeros before the decimal point to indicate the scale of the number (even if the decimal point is not shown). For a number less than 1, the same would apply to the zeros before the decimal point. For example, 0.003 051 93 to three significant figures is 0.003 05. Alternatively, use scientific notation (in this case, 3.05×10^{-3}).

> **Examples**
>
> 1/8 as a percentage is $1 \div 8 \times 100 = 100 \div 8 = 12.5\%$
>
> 0.602 as a percentage is $0.602 \times 100 = 60.2\%$.

> **Examples**
>
> 190% as a decimal fraction is $190 \div 100 = 1.9$
>
> 5/2 as a percentage is $5 \div 2 \times 100 = 250\%$.

> **Example** A population falls from 4 million to 3.85 million. What is the percentage change? The decrease in numbers is $4 - 3.85 = -0.15$ million. The fractional decrease is $-0.15 \div 4 = -0.0375$ and we multiply by 100 to get the percentage change = minus 3.75%.

significant figures in a number like 200 is ambiguous and could be one, two or three; if you wish to specify clearly, then quote as e.g. 2×10^2 (one significant figure), 2.0×10^2 (two significant figures), etc. to avoid spurious accuracy. When quoting a number to a specified number of significant figures, use the same rules as for rounding to a specified number of decimal places, but do not forget to keep zeros before or after the decimal point. The same principle is used if you are asked to quote a number to the 'nearest 10', 'nearest 100', etc.

When deciding for yourself how many significant figures to use, adopt the following rules of thumb:

- Always round *after* you have done a calculation. Use *all* significant figures available in the measured data during a calculation.

- If adding or subtracting with measured data, then quote the answer to the number of decimal places in the data value with the least number of decimal places (e.g. $32.1 - 45.67 + 35.6201 = 22.1$, because 32.1 has one decimal place).

- If multiplying or dividing with measured data, keep as many significant figures as are in the number with the least number of significant places (e.g. $34\,901 \div 3445 \times 1.341\,034\,4 = 13.59$, because 3445 has four significant figures).

- For the purposes of significant figures, assume 'constants' (e.g. number of mm in a m) have an infinite number of significant figures.

Some reminders of basic mathematics

Errors in calculations sometimes appear because of faults in mathematics rather than computational errors. For reference purposes, Tables 62.1 and 62.2 give some basic mathematical principles that may be useful. Miller and Miller (2000) should be consulted for more advanced/specific needs.

Percentages and proportions

A percentage is just a fraction expressed in terms of hundredths, indicated by putting the percentage sign (%) after the number of hundredths. So 35% simply means 35 hundredths. To convert a fraction to a percentage, just multiply the fraction by 100. When the fraction is in decimal form, multiplying by 100 to obtain a percentage is easily achieved just by moving the decimal point two places to the right.

To convert a percentage to a fraction, just remember that, since a percentage is a fraction multiplied by 100, the fraction is the percentage divided by 100. For example: $42\% = 42/100 = 0.42$. In this example, since we are dealing with a decimal fraction, the division by 100 is just a matter of moving the decimal point two places to the left (42% could be written as 42.0%). Percentages greater than 100% represent fractions greater than 1. Percentages less than 1 may cause confusion. For example, 0.5% means half of one per cent (0.005) and must not be confused with 50% (which is the decimal fraction 0.5).

To find a percentage of a given number, just express the percentage as a decimal fraction and multiply the given number. For example: 35% of 500 is given by $0.35 \times 500 = 175$. To find the percentage change in a quantity, work out the difference (= value 'after' − value 'before'), and divide this difference by the original value to give the fractional change, then multiply by 100.

Exponents

> **Example** $2^3 = 2 \times 2 \times 2 = 8$.

Exponential notation is an alternative way of expressing numbers in the form a^n ('a to the power n'), where a is multiplied by itself n times. The number a is called the base and the number n the exponent (or power or index). The exponent need not be a whole number, and it can be negative if the number being expressed is less than 1. See Table 62.2 for other mathematical relationships involving exponents.

Scientific notation

> **Example** Avogadro's number, $\approx 602\,352\,000\,000\,000\,000\,000\,000$, is more conveniently expressed as $6.023\,52 \times 10^{23}$.

In scientific notation, also known as 'standard form', the base is 10 and the exponent a whole number. To express numbers that are not whole powers of 10, the form $c \times 10^n$ is used, where the coefficient c is normally between 1 and 10. Scientific notation is valuable when you are using very large numbers and wish to avoid suggesting spurious accuracy. Thus if you write 123 000, this may suggest that you know the number to ± 0.5, whereas 1.23×10^5 might give a truer indication of measurement accuracy (i.e. implied to be ± 500 in this case). Engineering notation is similar, but treats numbers as powers of 10 in groups of 3, i.e. $c \times 10^0$, 10^3, 10^6, 10^9, etc. This corresponds to the SI system of prefixes (p. 214).

A useful property of powers when expressed to the same base is that when multiplying two numbers together, you simply add the powers, while if dividing, you subtract the powers. Thus, suppose you counted 8 bacteria in a known value of a 10^{-7} dilution, there would be 8×10^7 in the same volume of undiluted solution; if you now dilute this 500-fold (5×10^2), then the number present in the same volume would be $8/5 \times 10^{(7-2)} = 1.6 \times 10^5 = 160\,000$.

Logarithms

> **Examples** The logarithm to the base 10 ($\log_{10}$) of 1000 is 3, since $10^3 = 1000$.
>
> The logarithm to the base e ($\log_e$ or ln) of 1000 is 6.907 755 (to six decimal places).

When a number is expressed as a logarithm, this refers to the power n that the base number a must be raised to give that number. Any base could be used, but the two most common are 10, when the power is referred to as $\log_{10}$ or simply log, and the constant e (2.718 282), used for mathematical convenience in certain situations, when the power is referred to as $\log_e$ or ln (natural logarithm). Note that (a) logs need not be whole numbers; (b) there is no log value for the number zero; and (c) $\log_{10} = 0$ for the number 1.

To obtain logs, you will need to use the log key on your calculator, or special log tables (now largely redundant). To convert back ('antilog') use

> **Examples** (use to check the correct use of your own calculator)
> 102 963 as a log (to base 10) = 5.012 681 (to six decimal places)
> $10^{5.012681} = 102\,962.96$
> (Note loss of accuracy due to loss of decimal places.) 102 963 as a natural logarithm (ln) = 11.542 125 (to six decimal places) thus $2.718\,282^{11.542125} = 102\,963$.

- the $\boxed{10^x}$ key, with $x = $ log value;

- the $\boxed{\text{inverse}}$ then the $\boxed{\log}$ key; or

- the $\boxed{y^x}$ key, with $y = 10$ and $x = $ log value.

If you have used log tables, you will find complementary antilogarithm tables to do this.

There are many uses of logarithms in chemistry, including pH $(= -\log[\mathrm{H^+}])$, where $[\mathrm{H^+}]$ is expressed in $\mathrm{mol\,L^{-1}}$ (see p. 198); rate constants in physical chemistry, where a plot ln (reactant) against time produces a straight line if the reaction is first order.

Linear functions and straight lines

One of the most straightforward and widely used relationships between two variables x and y is that represented by a straight-line graph, where the corresponding mathematical function is known as the equation of a straight line, where:

$$y = a + bx \qquad\qquad [62.3]$$

> **Example** Using eqn [62.3], the predicted value for y for a linear function where $a = 2$ and $b = 0.5$, where $x = 8$ is: $y = 2 + (0.5 \times 8) = 6$.

In this relationship, a represents the intercept of the line on the y (vertical) axis, i.e. where $x = 0$, and therefore $bx = 0$, while b is equivalent to the slope (gradient) of the line, i.e. the change in y for a change in x of 1. The constants a and b are sometimes given alternative symbols, but the mathematics remains unchanged, e.g. in the equivalent expression for the slope of a straight line, $y = mx + c$. Fig. 62.1 shows what happens when these two constants are changed, in terms of the resultant straight lines.

The two main applications of the straight-line relationship are:

1. **Function fitting.** Here, you determine the mathematical form of the function, i.e. you estimate the constants a and b from a data set for x and y, either by drawing a straight line by eye and then working out the slope and y intercept, or by using linear regression (p. 518) to obtain the most probable values for both constants. When putting a straight line of best fit by eye on a hand-drawn graph, note the following:

- Always use a *transparent* ruler, so you can see data points on either side of the line.

- For a data series where the points do not fit a perfect straight line, try to have an equal number of points on either side of the line, as in Figure 62.2(a), and try to minimise the average distance of these points from the line.

- Once you have drawn the line of best fit use this line, rather than your data values, in all subsequent procedures (e.g. in a calibration curve, Chapter 60).

- Tangents drawn to a curve give the slope (gradient) at a particular point, e.g. in a titration curve. These are best drawn by bringing your ruler up to the curve at the exact point where you wish to estimate the slope and then trying to make the two angles immediately on either side of this point approximately the same, by eye (Fig. 62.2(b)).

- Once you have drawn the straight line or tangent, choose two points reasonably far apart at either end of your line and then draw construction lines to represent the change in y and the

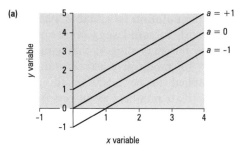

(a)

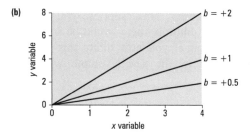

(b)

Fig. 62.1 Straight-line relationships $(y = a + bx)$, showing the effects of (a) changing the intercept at constant slope, and (b) changing the slope at constant intercept.

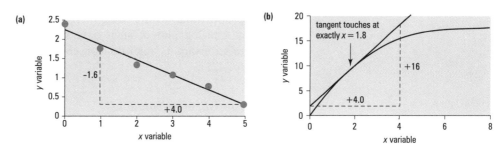

Fig. 62.2 Drawing straight lines. (a) Simple linear relationship, giving a straight line with an intercept of 2.3 and a slope of $-1.6 \div 4.0 = 0.4$. (b) Tangent drawn to a curve at $x = 1.8$, giving a slope of $16 \div 4 = 4$.

> **Example** Using eqn [62.4], the predicted value for x for a linear function where $a = 1.5$ and $b = 2.5$, where $y = -8.5$ is:
> $x = (-8.5 - 1.5) \div 2.5 = -4$.
> Using eqn [62.4] the predicted x intercept for a linear function where $a = 0.8$ and $b = 3.2$ is:
> $x = (0 - 0.8) \div 3.2 = -0.25$.

> **Example** A lab schedule states that 5 g of a compound with a relative molecular mass of 220 are dissolved in 400 ml of solvent. For writing up your Experimental section, you wish to express this as $mol\,L^{-1}$.
> 1. If there are 5 g in 400 mL, then there are $5 \div 400$ g in 1 mL.
> 2. Hence, 1000 mL will contain $5 \div 400 \times 1000$ g $= 12.5$ g.
> 3. 12.5 g $= 12.5 \div 220$ mol $= 0.0568$ mol, so [solution] $= 56.8\,mmol\,L^{-1}$ ($= 56.8\,mol\,m^{-3}$).

> **Example** For a geometric dilution series involving ten-fold dilution steps, calculation of concentrations is straightforward, e.g. two serial decimal dilutions ($= 100$-fold dilution) of a solution of NaCl of $250\,mmol\,L^{-1}$ will produce a dilute solution of $250 \div 100 = 2.5\,mmol\,L^{-1}$. Similarly, for an arithmetic dilution series, divide by the overall dilution to give the final concentration, e.g. a sixteen-fold dilution of a solution of NaCl of 200 mg mL^{-1} will produce a dilute solution of $200 \div 16 = 12.5$ mg mL^{-1}.

change in x between these two points: make sure that your construction lines are perpendicular to each other. Determine the slope as the change in y divided by the change in x (Fig. 62.2(b)).

2. **Prediction**. Where a and b are known, or have been estimated, you can re-arrange eqn [62.3] to predict any value of x for a specified value of y (e.g. in calibration curves, p. 327), as follows:

$$x = (y - a) \div b \qquad [62.4]$$

This equation can also be used to determine the intercept on the x (horizontal) axis, i.e. where $y = 0$.

Hints for some typical problems

Calculations involving proportions or ratios

The 'unitary method' is a useful way of approaching calculations involving proportions or ratios, such as those required when making up solutions from stocks (see also Chapter 22) or as a subsidiary part of longer calculations.

1. If given a value for a multiple, work out the corresponding value for a single item or unit.

2. Use this 'unitary value' to calculate the required new value.

Calculations involving series

Series (used in e.g. dilutions, see also p. 159) can be of three main forms:

1. Arithmetic, where the *difference* between two successive numbers in the series is a constant, e.g. 2, 4, 6, 8, 10, ...

2. Geometric, where the *ratio* between two successive numbers in the series is a constant, e.g. 1, 10, 100, 1000, 10 000, ...

3. Harmonic, where the values are reciprocals of successive whole numbers, e.g. $1, \frac{1}{2}, \frac{1}{3}, \frac{1}{4}, \ldots$

Note that the logs of the numbers in a geometric series will form an arithmetic series (e.g. 0, 1, 2, 3, 4, ... in the above case). Thus, if a quantity y varies with a quantity x such that the rate of change in y is proportional to the value of y (i.e. it varies in an exponential manner), a semi-log plot of such data will form a straight line. This form of relationship is relevant for chemical kinetics and radioactive decay (p. 421).

Statistical calculations

The need for long, complex calculations in statistics has largely been removed because of the widespread use of spreadsheets with statistical functions (Chapter 12) and specialised programs such as SPSS and Minitab. It is, however, important to understand the principles behind what you are trying to do (see Chapters 63 and 64) and interpret the program's output correctly, either using the 'help' function or a reference manual.

Text reference

Miller, J.N. and Miller, J.C. (2000) *Statistics and Chemometrics for Analytical Chemistry*, 4th edn. Prentice Hall, Harlow.

Sources for further study

Anon. *S.O.S. Mathematics.* Available: http://www.sosmath.com Last accessed: 01/04/07. [A basic Web-based guide with very wide coverage]

Anon. *Discover Maths.* Available: http://discovermaths.rsc.org/ Last accessed: 03/09/10. [A basic Web-based guide with examples]

Billo, E.J. (2007) *Excel for Scientists and Engineers.* Wiley, Chichester.

Currell, G. and Dowman, T. (2009) *Essential Mathematics and Statistics for Science*, 2nd edn. Wiley, Chichester.

Koehler, K.R. *College Physics for Students of Biology and Chemistry.* Available: http://www.rwc.uc.edu/koehler/biophys/text.html Last accessed: 01/04/07. [A 'hypertextbook' written for first-year undergraduates. Assumes that you have a working knowledge of algebra]

Lawler, G. (2006) *Understanding Maths. Basic Mathematics Explained.* Studymates, Abergele.

Miller, J.N. and Miller, J.C. (2005) *Statistics and Chemometrics for Analytical Chemistry*, 5th edn. Prentice Hall, Harlow.

Monk, P. and Munro, L.J. (2010) *Maths for Chemists: A Chemist's Toolkit of Calculations.* Oxford University Press, Oxford.

Steiner, E. (2008) *The Chemistry Maths Book*, 2nd edn. Oxford University Press, Oxford.

62.1 Rearrange a simple formula. The Beer–Lambert relationship (p. 333), is written in the form $A = \varepsilon l [C]$. Rearrange, in the form:

(a) $[C] =$; (b) $\varepsilon =$

62.2 Rearrange the following formulae:

(a) If $y = ax + b$, find b
(b) If $y = ax + b$, find x

62.3 Work with decimal places or significant figures. Give the following numbers to the accuracy indicated:

(a) 214.51 to three significant figures
(b) 107 029 to three significant figures
(c) 0.0450 to one significant figure
(d) 99.817 to two decimal places
(e) 99.897 to two decimal places
(f) 99.997 to two decimal places
(g) 6255 to the nearest 10
(h) 134 903 to the nearest ten thousand

State the following:

(i) the number of significant figures in 3400
(j) the number of significant figures in 3400.3
(k) the number of significant figures in 0.001 67
(l) the number of significant figures in 1.001 67
(m) the number of decimal places in 34.46
(n) the number of decimal places in 0.001 67

62.4 Practise working with linear functions (note also that Chapter 47 includes study exercises based on linear functions and plotting straight lines). Assuming a linear relationship between x and y, calculate the following (give your answers to three significant figures):

(a) x, where $y = 7.0$, $a = 4.5$ and $b = 0.02$;
(b) x, where $y = 15.2$, $a = -2.6$ and $b = -4.46$;
(c) y, where $x = 10.5$, $a = 0.2$ and $b = -0.63$;
(d) y, where $x = 4.5$, $a = -1.8$ and $b = 4.1$.

The purpose of most practical work is to observe and measure a particular characteristic of an atom, molecule or chemical system. However, it would be extremely rare if the same value was obtained every time the characteristic was measured, or with every experimental subject. More commonly, such measurements will show variability, due to measurement error, sampling variation and/or chemical variability (p. 209). Such variability can be displayed as a frequency distribution (e.g. Fig. 60.3), where the y-axis shows the number of times (frequency, f) each particular value of the measured (dependent) variable (Y) has been obtained. Descriptive (or summary) statistics quantify aspects of the frequency distribution of a sample. You can use them to condense a large data set, for presentation in figures or tables. An additional application of descriptive statistics is to provide estimates of the true values of the underlying frequency distribution of the population being sampled, allowing the significance and precision of the observations to be assessed (pp. 209, 504).

Summarising your results – original data belong only in your primary record, either in laboratory books or as computer records. You should produce summary tables to condense and describe original data.

> **KEY POINT** The appropriate descriptive statistics to choose will depend on both the type of data, i.e. whether quantitative, ranked or qualitative (see p. 207) and the nature of the underlying frequency distribution.

Initial steps – organising numbers and displaying distributions

In order to organise and summarise data, you should:

- **Display the data in graphical form** – this provides an immediate visual summary which is relatively easy to interpret.

- **Look for an overall pattern in the data** – avoid getting lost in the details at this stage.

- **Look for any striking exceptions to that pattern (outliers)** – they often point to special cases of particular interest or to errors in the data produced through mistakes during the acquisition, recording or copying of data.

- **Move from graphical interpretations to numerical summaries** and/or verbal descriptions including, where applicable, an explanatory hypothesis.

Colour	Tally	Total
Green	III	3
Blue	HHt III	8
Red	IIII	4
White	HHt HHt II	12
		= 27

Fig. 63.1 An example of a tally chart.

After collecting data, the first step is often to count how often each value occurs and to produce a frequency table. The frequency is simply the number of times a value occurs in the data set, and is, therefore, a count. The raw data could be acquired using a tally chart system to provide a simple frequency table to construct a tally chart (e.g. Fig. 63.1):

- enter only one tally at a time;

- if working from a data list, cross out each item on the list as you enter it onto the tally chart, to prevent double entries;

- check that all values are crossed out at the end and that the totals agree.

Producing a histogram – a *neatly* constructed tally chart doubles as a rough histogram or bar chart, with a horizontal layout of the 'columns' (Fig. 63.1).

Table 63.1 An example of a frequency table

Size class	Frequency	Relative frequency (%)
0–4.9	7	2.6
5–9.9	23	8.6
10–14.9	56	20.9
15–19.9	98	36.7
20–24.9	50	18.7
25–29.9	30	11.2
30–34.9	3	1.1
Total	267	99.8*

* $\neq$ 100 due to rounding error

stem	leaves
8	233
8	45555
8	77
8	888899
9	0000111111
9	2333333
9	44555555555
9	66677777
9	88888999
10	00

Fig. 63.2 A simple 'stem and leaf' plot of a data set. The 'stem' shows the common component of each number, while the 'leaves' show the individual components, e.g. the top line in this example represents the numbers 82, 83 and 83.

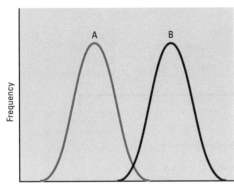

Fig. 63.3 Two distributions with different locations but the same dispersion. The data set labelled B could have been obtained by adding a constant to each datum in the data set labelled A.

Convert the data to a formal table when complete (e.g. Table 63.1). Because proportions are easier to compare than class totals, the table may contain a column to show the relative frequency of each class. Relative frequency can be expressed in decimal form (as a proportion of 1) or as a percentage (as a proportion of 100).

A visual display of a distribution of values is often useful for quantitative variables measured on an interval or ratio scale (p. 208). The distribution of a variable can be displayed by a frequency table for each value (Table 63.1) or, if the possible values are numerous, groups (classes) of values of the variable. Graphically, there are two main ways of viewing such data:

- histogram (see p. 477), or frequency distribution, can be used for large samples;

- stem and leaf plots (e.g. Fig. 63.2), often used for samples of less than 100: these retain the actual values and are faster to draw by hand. The main drawback is the limitation imposed by the choice of stem values since the class boundaries may obscure some features of the distribution.

Histograms allow you to look at the overall shape of a distribution and to observe any significant deviations from the idealised theoretical ones. Where necessary, you can use data transformations to investigate any departures from standard distribution patterns.

In many instances, the normal (Gaussian) distribution (Chapter 64) best describes the observed pattern for a quantitative variable, giving a symmetrical, bell-shaped frequency distribution (p. 500), for example, measurements of a quantitative continuous variable in a number of individuals (e.g. metal content of several soil samples), or replicate measurements of a particular characteristic (e.g. repeated measurements of the metal content of an individual soil sample). If you have no clear theoretical grounds for assuming what the underlying frequency distribution is like, graph one or more sample frequency distributions, ideally with a sample size >100.

Three important features of a frequency distribution that can be summarised by descriptive statistics are:

- the sample's location, i.e. its position along a given dimension representing the dependent (measured) variable (Fig. 63.3);

- the dispersion of the data, i.e. how spread out the values are (Fig. 63.4);

- the shape of the distribution, i.e. whether symmetrical, skewed, U-shaped (Fig. 63.5).

Measuring location

Here, the objective is to pinpoint the 'centre' of the frequency distribution, i.e. the value about which most of the data are grouped. The chief measures of location are the mean, median and mode. Fig. 63.6 shows how to choose among these for a given data set.

Mean

The mean (denoted $\bar{Y}$ and also referred to as the arithmetic mean) is the average value of the data. It is obtained from the sum of all the data

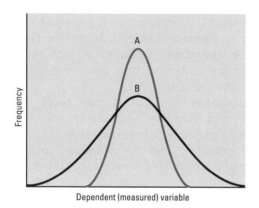

Fig. 63.4 Two distributions with different dispersions but the same location. The data set labelled A covers a relatively narrow range of values of the dependent (measured) variable while that labelled B covers a wider range.

Example Box 63.1 shows a set of data and the calculated values of the measures of location, dispersion and shape for which methods of calculation are outlined here. Check your understanding by calculating the statistics yourself and confirming that you arrive at the same answers.

Definitions

An outlier – any datum that has a value much smaller or bigger than most of the other data values.

Rank – the position of a data value when all the data are placed in order of ascending magnitude. If ties occur, an average rank of the tied variates is used. Thus, the rank of the datum 6 in the sequence 1,3,5,6,8,8,10 is 4; the rank of each datum with value 8 is 5.5.

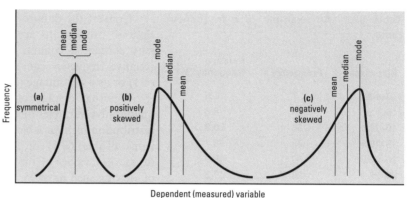

Fig. 63.5 Symmetrical and skewed frequency distributions, showing relative positions of mean, median and mode.

values divided by the number of observations (in symbolic terms, $\Sigma Y/n$). The mean is a good measure of the centre of symmetrical frequency distributions. It uses all of the numerical values of the sample and therefore incorporates all of the information content of the data. However, the value of a mean is greatly affected by the presence of extreme values (outliers). The arithmetic mean is a widely used statistic in chemistry, but there are situations when you should be careful about using it (see Box 63.2 for examples).

Median

The median is the mid-point of the observations when ranked in increasing order. For odd-sized samples, the median is the middle observation; for even-sized samples it is the mean of the middle pair of observations. Where data are grouped into classes, the median can only

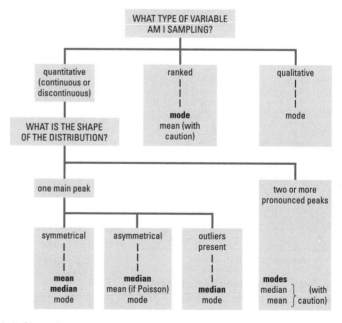

Fig. 63.6 Choosing a statistic for characterising a distribution's location. Statistics written in bold are the preferred option(s).

Box 63.1 Descriptive statistics for a sample of data – an example

Value (Y)	Frequency (f)	Cumulative frequency	fY	fY^2
1	0	0	0	0
2	1	1	2	4
3	2	3	6	18
4	3	6	12	48
5	8	14	40	200
6	5	19	30	180
7	2	21	14	98
8	0	21	0	0
Totals	$21 = \Sigma f\,(=n)$		$104 = \Sigma fY$	$548 = \Sigma fY^2$

In this example, for simplicity and ease of calculation, integer values of Y are used. In many practical exercises, where continuous variables are measured to several significant figures and where the number of data values is small, giving frequencies of 1 for most of the values of Y, it may be simpler to omit the column dealing with frequency and list all the individual values of Y and Y^2 in the appropriate columns. To gauge the underlying frequency distribution of such data sets, you would need to group individual data into broader classes (e.g. all values between 1.0 and 1.9, all values between 2.0 and 2.9, etc.) and then draw a histogram (p. 477). Calculation of certain statistics for data sets that have been grouped in this way (e.g. median, quartiles, extremes) can be tricky and a statistical text should be consulted.

Statistic	Value*	How calculated
Mean	4.95	$\Sigma fY/n$, i.e. 104/21
Median	5	Value of the $(n+1)/2$ variate, i.e. the value ranked $(21+1)/2 = 11$th (obtained from the cumulative frequency column)
Mode	5	The most common value (Y value with highest frequency)
Upper quartile	6	The upper quartile is between the 16th and 17th values, i.e. the value exceeded by 25% of the data values
Lower quartile	4	The lower quartile is between the 5th and 6th values, i.e. the value exceeded by 75% of the data values
Semi-interquartile range	1.0	Half the difference between the upper and lower quartiles, i.e. $(6-4)/2$
Upper extreme	7	Highest Y value in data set
Lower extreme	2	Lowest Y value in data set
Range	5	Difference between upper and lower extremes
Variance (s^2)	1.65	$s^2 = \dfrac{\Sigma fY^2 - (\Sigma fY)^2/n}{n-1}$ $= \dfrac{548 - (104)^2/21}{20}$
Standard deviation (s)	1.28	$\sqrt{s^2}$
Standard error (SE)	0.280	$s/\sqrt{n}$
95% confidence limits	4.36 – 5.54	$\bar{Y} \mp t_{0.05}[20] \times \text{SE}$, (where $t_{0.05}[20] = 2.09$, Table 64.2)
Coefficient of variation (cov)	25.9%	$100s/\bar{Y}$

*Rounded to three significant figures (see p. 491), except when it is an exact number.

be estimated. This is most simply done from a graph of the cumulative frequency distribution, but can also be worked out by assuming the data to be evenly spread within the class. The median may represent the location of the main body of data better than the mean when the distribution is asymmetric or when there are outliers in the sample.

Mode

The mode is the most common value in the sample. The mode is easily found from a tabulated frequency distribution as the most frequent value. If data have been grouped into classes then the term modal class is used for the class containing most values. The mode provides a rapidly and easily found estimate of sample location and is unaffected by outliers. However, the mode is affected by chance variation in the shape of a sample's distribution and it may lie distant from the obvious centre of the distribution.

The mean, median and mode have the same units as the variable under discussion. However, whether these statistics of location have the same or similar values for a given frequency distribution depends on the symmetry and shape of the distribution. If it is near-symmetrical with a single peak, all three will be very similar; if it is skewed or has more than one peak, their values will differ to a greater degree (see Fig. 63.5).

Measuring dispersion

Here, the objective is to quantify the spread of the data about the centre of the distribution. Figure 63.7 indicates how to decide which measure of dispersion to use.

Range

The range is the difference between the largest and smallest data values in the sample (the extremes) and has the same units as the measured variable. The range is easy to determine, but is greatly affected by outliers. Its value may also depend on sample size: in general, the larger

Describing the location of qualitative data – the mode is the only statistic that is suitable for this task. For example, 'the modal (most frequent) titre value was 20.7 mL'.

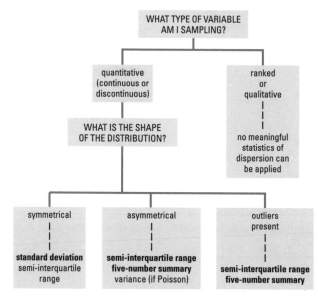

Fig. 63.7 Choosing a statistic for characterising a distribution's dispersion. Statistics written in bold are the preferred option(s). Note that you should match statistics describing dispersion with those you have used to describe location, i.e. standard deviation with mean, semi-interquartile range with median.

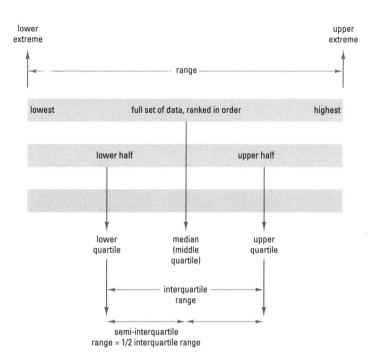

Fig. 63.8 Illustration of median, quartiles, range and semi-interquartile range.

Example In a sample of data with values 3, 7, 15, 8, 5, 10 and 4, the range is 12 (i.e. the difference between the highest value, 15, and the lowest value, 3).

this is, the greater will be the range. These features make the range a poor measure of dispersion for many practical purposes.

Semi-interquartile range

The semi-interquartile range is an appropriate measure of dispersion when a median is the appropriate statistic to describe location. For this, you need to determine the first and third quartiles, i.e. the medians for those data values ranked below and above the median of the whole data set (see Fig. 63.8). To calculate a semi-interquartile range for a data set:

1. Rank the observations in ascending order.

2. Find the values of the first and third quartiles.

3. Subtract the value of the first quartile from the value of the third.

4. Halve this number.

For data grouped in classes, the semi-interquartile range can only be estimated. Another disadvantage is that it takes no account of the shape of the distribution at its edges. This objection can be countered by using the so-called 'five number summary' of a data set, which consists of the three quartiles and the two extreme values; this can be presented on graphs as a box and whisker plot (see Fig. 63.9) and is particularly useful for summarising skewed frequency distributions. The corresponding 'six number summary' includes the sample's size.

Variance and standard deviation

For symmetrical frequency distributions, an ideal measure of dispersion would take into account each value's deviation from the mean and provide a measure of the average deviation from the mean. Two such statistics are the sample variance, which is the sum of squares $(\Sigma(Y - \bar{Y})^2)$ divided by $n - 1$ (where n is the sample size), and the sample standard deviation, which is the positive square root of the sample variance.

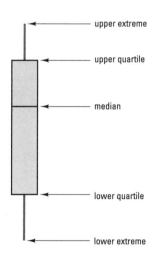

Fig. 63.9 A box and whisker plot, showing the 'five number summary' of a sample as it might be used on a graph.

The variance (s^2) has units which are the square of the original units, while the standard deviation (s, or SD) is expressed in the original units, one reason s is often preferred as a measure of dispersion. Calculating s or s^2 longhand is a tedious job and is best done with the help of a calculator or computer. If you don't have a calculator that calculates s for you, an alternative formula that simplifies calculations is:

$$s = +\sqrt{\frac{\Sigma Y^2 - (\Sigma Y)^2/n}{n-1}}$$ [63.1]

To calculate s using a calculator:

1. Obtain ΣY, square it, divide by n and store in memory.

2. Square Y values, obtain ΣY^2, subtract the memory value from this.

3. Divide this answer by $n - 1$.

4. Take the positive square root of this value.

Take care to retain significant figures, or errors in the final value of s will result. If continuous data have been grouped into classes, the class mid-values or their squares must be multiplied by the appropriate frequencies before summation (see example in Box 63.1). When data values are large, longhand calculations can be simplified by coding the data, e.g. by subtracting a constant from each datum, and decoding when the simplified calculations are complete.

Coefficient of variation

The coefficient of variation (CoV) is a dimensionless measure of variability relative to location which expresses the sample standard deviation, usually as a percentage of the sample mean, i.e.

$$\text{CoV} = 100s/\bar{Y}\,(\%)$$ [63.2]

This statistic is useful when comparing the relative dispersion of data sets with widely differing means, or where different units have been used for the same or similar quantities.

A useful application of the CoV is to compare different analytical methods or procedures, so that you can decide which involves the least proportional error – create a standard stock solution, then base your comparison on the results from several subsamples analysed by each method. You may find it useful to use the CoV to compare the precision of your own results with those of a manufacturer, e.g. for a pipettor (p. 148). The smaller the CoV, the more precise (repeatable) is the apparatus or technique (note: this does not mean that it is necessarily more *accurate*, see p. 209).

Measuring the precision of the sample mean as an estimate of the true value using the standard error

Most practical exercises are based on a limited number of individual data values (a sample) which are used to make inferences about the population from which they were drawn. For example, the haemoglobin content might be measured in blood samples from 100 adult females and used as an estimate of the adult female haemoglobin content, with the sample mean ($\bar{Y}$) and sample standard deviation (s) providing estimates of the true values of the underlying population mean (μ) and the

Using a calculator for statistics – make sure you understand how to enter individual data values and which keys will give the sample mean (usually shown as $\bar{X}$ or $\bar{x}$) and sample standard deviation (often shown as σ_{n-1}). In general, you should *not* use the population standard deviation (usually shown as σ_n).

Example Consider two methods of bioassay for a toxin in fresh water. For a given standard, Method A gives a mean result of $= 50$ 'response units' with $s = 8$, while Method B gives a mean result of $= 160$ 'response units' with $s = 18$. Which bioassay gives the more reproducible results? The answer can be found by calculating the CoV values, which are 16 and 11.25% respectively. Hence, Method B is the more precise ($\equiv$ reproducible), even though the absolute value of s is larger.

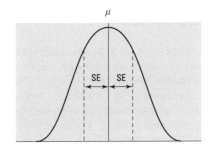

Fig. 63.10 Frequency distribution of sample means around the population mean (μ). Note that SE is equivalent to the standard deviation of the sample means, for sample size = n.

Example Summary statistics for the sample mean and standard error for the data shown in Box 63.1 would be quoted as 4.95 ± 0.280 ($n = 21$).

Calculating the extent of skew and kurtosis of a data set – use the SKEW and KURT functions in Microsoft Excel.

population standard deviation (σ). The reliability of the sample mean as an estimate of the true (population) mean can be assessed by calculating a statistic termed the standard error of the sample mean (often abbreviated to standard error or SE), from:

$$SE = s/\sqrt{n} \qquad [63.3]$$

Strictly, the standard error is an estimate of the dispersion of repeated sample means around the true (population) value: if several samples were taken, each with the same number of data values (n), then their means would cluster around the population mean (μ) with a standard deviation equal to SE, as shown in Figure 63.10. Therefore, the *smaller* the SE, the more reliable the sample mean is likely to be as an estimate of the true value, since the underlying frequency distribution would be more tightly clustered around μ. At a practical level, eqn [63.3] shows that SE is directly affected by the dispersion of individual data values within the sample, as represented by the sample standard deviation (s). Perhaps more importantly, SE is inversely related to the *square root* of the number of data values (n). Therefore, if you wanted to increase the precision of a sample mean by a factor of 2 (i.e. to reduce SE by half), you would have to increase n by a factor of 2^2 (i.e. fourfold).

Summary descriptive statistics for the sample mean are often quoted as $\bar{Y} \pm SE$ (n), with the SE being given to one significant figure more than the mean. You can use such information to carry out a *t*-test between two sample means (Box 64.1); the SE is also useful because it allows calculation of confidence limits for the sample mean (p. 518).

Describing the 'shape' of frequency distributions

Frequency distributions may differ in the following characteristics:

- number of peaks;
- skewness or asymmetry;
- kurtosis or pointedness.

The shape of a frequency distribution of a small sample is affected by chance variation and may not be a fair reflection of the underlying population frequency distribution: check this by comparing repeated samples from the same population or by increasing the sample size. If the original shape were due to random events, it should not appear consistently in repeated samples and should become less obvious as sample size increases.

Genuinely bimodal or polymodal distributions may result from the combination of two or more unimodal distributions, indicating that more than one underlying population is being sampled (Fig. 63.11). An example of a bimodal distribution is the height of adult humans (females and males combined).

A distribution is skewed if it is not symmetrical, a symptom being that the mean, median and mode are not equal (Fig. 63.5). Positive skewness is where the longer 'tail' of the distribution occurs for higher values of the measured variable; negative skewness where the longer tail occurs for lower values. Some chemical examples of characteristics distributed in a skewed fashion are pollutant levels in soil samples, insulin levels in human plasma and pesticide levels in agricultural products.

Box 63.2 Three examples where simple arithmetic means are inappropriate

1. **If means of samples are themselves meaned, an error can arise if the samples are of different size.** For example, the arithmetic mean of the means in the table shown below is 7, but this does not take account of the different 'reliabilities' of each mean due to their sample sizes. The correct weighted mean is obtained by multiplying each mean by its sample size (n) (a 'weight') and dividing the sum of these values by the total number of observations, i.e. in the case shown, $(24 + 49 + 8)/12 = 6.75$.

Mean	n
6	4
7	7
8	1

2. **When making a mean of ratios (e.g. percentages) for several groups of different sizes, the ratio for the combined total of all the groups is not the mean of the proportions for the individual groups.** For example, if 20 tablets from a batch of 50 are yellow, this implies 40% are yellow. If 60 tablets from a batch of 120 are yellow, this implies 50% are yellow. The mean percentage of yellow tablets $(50 + 40)/2 = 45\%$ is *not* the percentage of yellow tablets in the two groups combined, because there are $20 + 60 = 80$ yellow tablets in a total of 170 tablets $= 47.1\%$ approx.

3. **If the measurement scale is not linear, arithmetic means may give a false value.** For example, if three media had pH values 6, 7 and 8, the appropriate mean pH is not 7 because the pH scale is logarithmic. The definition of pH is $-\log_{10}[H^+]$, where $[H^+]$ is expressed in $mol\,L^{-1}$ ('molar'); therefore, to obtain the true mean, convert data into $[H^+]$ values (i.e. put them on a linear scale) by calculating $10^{(-pH\,value)}$ as shown. Now calculate the mean of these values and convert the answer back into pH units. Thus, the appropriate answer is pH 6.43 rather than 7. Note that a similar procedure is necessary when calculating statistics of dispersion in such cases, so you will find these almost certainly asymmetric about the mean.

pH value	$[H^+]$ ($mol\,L^{-1}$)
6	1×10^{-6}
7	1×10^{-7}
8	1×10^{-8}
mean	3.7×10^{-7}
$-\log_{10}$ mean	6.43

Mean values of log-transformed data are often termed geometric means – they are sometimes used in biochemistry, where log-transformed values for antibody concentrations in human blood serum are averaged and plotted, rather than using the raw data values. The use of geometric means in such circumstances serves to reduce the effects of outliers on the mean.

Kurtosis is the name given to the 'pointedness' of a frequency distribution. A platykurtic frequency distribution is one with a flattened peak, while a leptokurtic frequency distribution is one with a pointed peak (Fig. 63.12). While descriptive terms can be used, based on visual observation of the shape and direction of skew, the degree of skewness and kurtosis can be quantified and statistical tests

Fig. 63.11 Frequency distributions with different numbers of peaks. A unimodal distribution (a) may be symmetrical or asymmetrical. The dotted lines in (b) indicate how a bimodal distribution could arise from a combination of two underlying unimodal distributions. Note here how the term 'bimodal' is applied to any distribution with two major peaks – their frequencies do not have to be exactly the same.

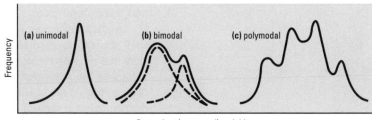

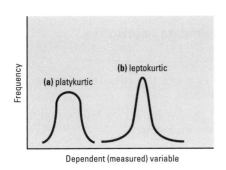

Fig. 63.12 Examples of the two types of kurtosis.

exist to test the 'significance' of observed values, but the calculations required are complex and best done with the aid of a computer.

Using computers to calculate descriptive statistics

There are many specialist statistical packages (e.g. SPSS) that can be used to simplify the process of calculation of statistics. Note that correct interpretation of the output requires an understanding of the terminology used and the underlying process of calculation, and this may best be obtained by working through one or more examples by hand before using these tools. Spreadsheets offer increasingly sophisticated statistical analysis functions, some examples of which are provided in Box 63.3 for Microsoft Excel.

Box 63.3 How to use a spreadsheet (Microsoft Excel 2007) to calculate descriptive statistics

Method 1: Using spreadsheet functions to generate the required statistics. Suppose you had obtained the following set of data, stored within an array (block of columns and rows) of cells (A2:L6) within a spreadsheet:

	A	B	C	D	E	F	G	H	I	J	K	L
1	My data set											
2	4	4	3	3	5	4	3	7	7	3	5	3
3	6	2	9	7	3	4	5	6	6	9	4	8
4	5	3	2	5	4	5	7	2	8	3	6	3
5	11	3	5	2	4	3	7	8	4	4	4	3
6	3	6	8	5	6	4	3	4	3	6	10	5

The following functions could be used to extract descriptive statistics from this data set:

Descriptive statistic	Example of use of function[a,b]	Result for the above data set
Sample size n	=COUNT((A2:L6)	60
Mean	=AVERAGE(A2:L6)[c]	4.9
Median	=MEDIAN(A2:L6)	4.0
Mode	=MODE(A2:L6)	3
Upper quartile	=QUARTILE(A2:L6,3)[d]	6.0
Lower quartile	=QUARTILE(A2:L6,1)	3.0
Semi-interquartile range	=QUARTILE(A2:L6,3)-QUARTILE(A2:L6,1)	3.0
Upper extreme	=QUARTILE(A2:L6,4) or =MAX(A2:L6)	11
Lower extreme	=QUARTILE(A2:L6,0) or =MIN(A2:L6)	2
Range	=MAX(A2:L6)- MIN(A2:L6)[e]	9.0
Variance	=VAR(A2:L6)	4.464
Standard deviation	=STDEV(A2:L6)	2.113
Standard error	=STDEV(A2:L6)/(SQRT(COUNT(A2:L6)))[f]	0.273
Coefficient of variation	=100*STDEV(A2:L6)/AVERAGE(A2:L6)	43.12%

Notes:

[a] Typically, in an appropriate cell, you would *Insert > Function >* COUNT, then select the input range and press return.

[b] Other descriptive statistics can be calculated – these mirror those shown in Box 63.1, but for this specific data set.

[c] There is no 'MEAN' function in Microsoft Excel.

[d] The first argument within the brackets relates to the array of data, the second relates to the quartile required (consult *Help* feature for further information).

[e] There is no direct 'RANGE' function in Microsoft Excel.

[f] There is no direct 'STANDARD ERROR' function in Microsoft Excel. The SQRT function returns a square root and the COUNT function determines the number of filled data cells in the array.

(continued)

Box 63.3 How to use a spreadsheet (Microsoft Excel 2007) to calculate descriptive statistics (continued)

Method 2: using the *Tools > Data Analysis* option. This can automatically generate a table of descriptive statistics for the data array selected, although the data must be presented as a single row or column. This option might need to be installed for your network or personal computer before it is available to you (in the latter case use the *Add Ins > Analysis ToolPak* option from the *Tools* menu – consult the *Help* feature for details). Having entered or rearranged your data into a row or column, the steps involved are as follows:

1. Select *Tools > Data Analysis*.

2. From the *Data Analysis box,* select *Descriptive Statistics.*

3. Input your data location into the *Input Range* (left click and hold down to highlight the column of data).

4. From the menu options, select *Summary Statistics* and *Confidence Level for Mean: 95%.*

5. When you click *OK,* you should get a new work-sheet, with descriptive statistics and confidence limits shown. Alternatively, at step 3, you can select an area of your current worksheet as a data output range (select an area away from any existing content as these cells would otherwise be overwritten by the descriptive statistics output table).

6. Change the format of the cells to show each number to an appropriate number of decimal places. You may also wish to make the columns wider so you can read their content.

7. For the data set shown above, the final output table should look as shown below:

Descriptive statistics for a data set

Column 1[a,b]	
Mean	4.9
Standard error	0.27
Median	4.0
Mode	3
Standard deviation	2.113
Sample variance	4.464
Kurtosis	0.22
Skewness	0.86
Range	9.00
Minimum	2.0
Maximum	11.0
Sum	294
Count	60
Confidence level (95.0%)	0.55

Notes:

[a] These descriptive statistics are specified (and are automatically presented in this order) – any others required can be generated using Method 1.

[b] A more descriptive heading can be added if desired – this is the default.

Text references and sources for further study

Anon. *Discover Maths.* Available: http://discovermaths.rsc.org/ Last accessed: 03/09/10. [A basic Web-based guide with examples]

Currell, G. and Dowman, T. (2009) *Essential Mathematics and Statistics for Science,* 2nd edn. Wiley, Chichester.

Dytham, C. (2003) *Choosing and Using Statistics: A Biologists' Guide,* 2nd edn. Blackwell, Oxford.

Miller, J.N. and Miller, J.C. (2000) *Statistics and Chemometrics for Analytical Chemistry,* 4th edn. Prentice Hall, Harlow.

Monk, P. and Munro, L.J. (2010) *Maths for Chemists: A Chemist's Toolkit of Calculations.* Oxford University Press, Oxford.

Schmuller, J. (2005) *Statistical Analysis with Excel for Dummies.* Wiley, Hoboken.

Steiner, E. (2008) *The Chemistry Maths Book,* 2nd edn. Oxford University Press, Oxford.

Taylor, J.K. and Cihon, C. (2004) *Statistical Techniques for Data Analysis,* 2nd edn. CRC Press, Boca Raton.

63.1 Practise calculating descriptive statistics. Using the data set given in Box 63.3 (p. 507), calculate the following statistics:

(a) range
(b) variance
(c) standard deviation
(d) coefficient of variation
(e) standard error.

Answers (b) to (e) should be given to three significant figures.

63.2 Calculate and interpret standard errors. Two samples, A and B, gave the following descriptive statistics (measured in the same units): Sample A, mean = 16.2, standard deviation = 12.7, number of data values = 12; Sample B, mean = 13.2, standard deviation 14.4, number of data values = 20. Which has the lower standard error in absolute terms and in proportion to the sample mean? (Express answers to three significant figures.)

63.3 Compute a mean value correctly. A researcher finds that the mean vitamin concentration in three replicate samples designated A, B and C is 3.0, 2.5 and 2.0 mg, respectively. He computes the mean vitamin concentration as 2.5 mg, but forgets that the sample sizes were 24, 37 and 6, respectively. What is the true mean vitamin concentration? (Answer to three significant figures.)

This chapter outlines the philosophy of hypothesis-testing statistics, indicates the steps to be taken when choosing a test, and discusses features and assumptions of some important tests. For details of the mechanics of tests, consult appropriate texts (e.g. Miller and Miller, 2000). Most tests are now available in statistical packages for computers (see p. 98) and many in spreadsheets (Chapter 12).

To carry out a statistical test:

1. Decide what it is you wish to test (create a null hypothesis and its alternative).

2. Determine whether your data fit a standard distribution pattern.

3. Select a test and apply it to your data.

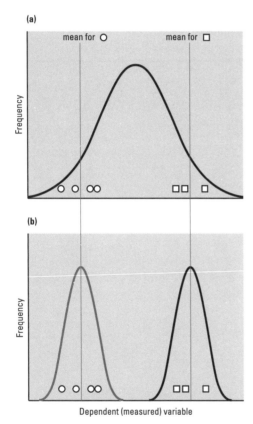

(a)

mean for ○   mean for □

Frequency

Dependent (measured) variable

Fig. 64.1 Two explanations for the difference between two means. In case (a) the two samples happen by chance to have come from opposite ends of the same frequency distribution, i.e. there is no true difference between the samples. In case (b) the two samples come from different frequency distributions, i.e. there is a true difference between the samples. In both cases, the means of the two samples are the same.

Setting up a null hypothesis

Hypothesis-testing statistics are used to compare the properties of samples either with other samples or with some theory about them. For instance, you may be interested in whether two samples can be regarded as having different means, whether the counts of an organism in different locations can be regarded as randomly distributed, or whether characteristic A of an organism is linearly related to characteristic B.

> **KEY POINT** You can't use statistics to *prove* any hypothesis, but they can be used to assess *how likely* it is to be wrong.

Statistical testing operates in what at first seems a rather perverse manner. Suppose you think a treatment has an effect. The theory you actually test is that it has no effect; the test tells you how improbable your data would be if this theory were true. This 'no effect' theory is the null hypothesis (NH). If your data are very improbable under the NH, then you may suppose it to be wrong, and this would support your original idea (the 'alternative hypothesis'). The concept can be illustrated by an example. Suppose two groups of subjects were treated in different ways, and you observed a difference in the mean value of the measured variable for the two groups. Can this be regarded as a 'true' difference? As Fig. 64.1 shows, it could have arisen in two ways:

● Because of the way the subjects were allocated to treatments, i.e. all the subjects liable to have high values might, by chance, have been assigned to one group and those with low values to the other (Fig. 64.1a).

● Because of a genuine effect of the treatments, i.e. each group came from a distinct frequency distribution (Fig. 64.1b).

A statistical test will indicate the probabilities of these options. The NH states that the two groups come from the same population (i.e. the treatment effects are negligible in the context of random variation). To test this, you calculate a test statistic from the data, and compare it with tabulated critical values giving the probability of obtaining the observed or a more extreme result by chance (see Boxes 64.1 and 64.2). This probability is sometimes called the significance of the test.

Note that you must take into account the degrees of freedom (d.f.) when looking up critical values of most test statistics. The d.f. is related to the size(s) of the samples studied; formulae for calculating it depend on the test being used. Chemists normally use two-tailed tests, i.e. we have no expectation beforehand that the treatment will have a positive or negative effect compared to the control (in a one-tailed test we expect one particular treatment to be bigger than the other). Be sure to use critical values for the correct type of test.

By convention, the critical probability for rejecting the NH is 5% (i.e. $P = 0.05$). This means we reject the NH if the observed result would have come up by chance a maximum of one time in twenty. If the modulus of the test statistic is less than or equal to the tabulated critical value for $P = 0.05$, then we accept the NH and the result is said to be 'not significant' (NS for short). If the modulus of the test statistic is greater than the tabulated value for $P = 0.05$, then we reject the NH in favour of the alternative hypothesis that the treatments had different effects and the result is 'statistically significant'.

Two types of error are possible when making a conclusion on the basis of a statistical test. The first occurs if you reject the NH when it is true and the second if you accept the NH when it is false. To limit the chance of the first type of error, choose a lower probability, e.g. $P = 0.01$, but note that the critical value of the test statistic increases when you do this and results in the probability of the second error increasing. The conventional significance levels given in statistical tables (usually 0.05, 0.01, 0.001) are arbitrary. Increasing use of statistical computer programs now allows the actual probability of obtaining the calculated value of the test statistic to be quoted (e.g. $P = 0.037$).

Note that if the NH is rejected, this does not tell you which of many alternative explanations are true. Also, it is important to distinguish between statistical significance and chemical relevance: identifying a statistically significant difference between two samples doesn't mean that this will carry any chemical importance.

Comparing data with parametric distributions

A parametric test is one that makes particular assumptions about the mathematical nature of the population distribution from which the samples were taken. If these assumptions are not true, then the test is obviously invalid, even though it might give the answer we expect. A non-parametric test does not assume that the data fit a particular pattern, but it may assume some things about the distributions. Used in appropriate circumstances, parametric tests are better able to distinguish between true but marginal differences between samples than their non-parametric equivalents (i.e. they have greater 'power').

The distribution pattern of a set of data values may be chemically relevant, but it is also of practical importance because it defines the type of statistical tests that can be used. The properties of the main distribution types found in chemistry are given below, with both rules-of-thumb and more rigorous tests for deciding whether data fit these distributions.

Definition

Modulus – the absolute value of a number, e.g. modulus $-3.385 = 3.385$.

Quoting significance – the convention for quoting significance levels in text, tables and figures is as follows:

$P > 0.05 =$ 'not significant' (or NS)

$P \leqslant 0.05 =$ 'significant' (or *)

$P \leqslant 0.01 =$ 'highly significant' (or **)

$P \leqslant 0.001 =$ 'very highly significant' (or ***)

Thus, you might refer to a difference in means as being 'highly significant $(P \leqslant 0.01)$'. For this reason, the word 'significant' in its everyday meaning of 'important' or 'notable' should be used with care in scientific writing.

Choosing between parametric and non-parametric tests – always plot your data graphically when determining whether they are suitable for parametric tests as this may save a lot of unnecessary effort later.

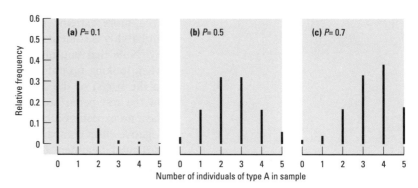

Fig. 64.2 Examples of binomial frequency distributions with different probabilities. The distributions show the expected frequency of obtaining n individuals of type A in a sample of 5. Here P is the probability of an individual being type A rather than type B.

Binomial distributions

These apply to samples of any size from populations when data values occur independently in only two mutually exclusive classes (e.g. type A or type B). They describe the probability of finding the different possible combinations of the attribute for a specified sample size k (e.g. out of 10 specimens, what is the chance of 8 being type A). If p is the probability of the attribute being of type A and q the probability of it being type B, then the expected mean sample number of type A is kp and the standard deviation is $\sqrt{kpq}$. Expected frequencies can be calculated using mathematical expressions (see Miller and Miller, 2000). Examples of the shapes of some binomial distributions are shown in Fig. 64.2. Note that they are symmetrical in shape for the special case $p = q = 0.5$ and the greater the disparity between p and q, the more skewed the distribution.

Chemical examples of data likely to be distributed in a binomial fashion occur when an observation or a set of trial results produce one of only two possible outcomes; for example, to determine the absence or presence of a pesticide in a soil sample or a drug in a pharmaceutical preparation. To establish whether a set of data is distributed in binomial fashion: calculate expected frequencies from probability values obtained from theory or observation, then test against observed frequencies using a χ^2-test or a G-test.

Poisson distributions

These apply to discrete characteristics which can assume low whole number values, such as counts of events occurring in area, volume or time. The events should be 'rare' in that the mean number observed should be a small proportion of the total that could possibly be found. Also, finding one count should not influence the probability of finding another. The shape of Poisson distributions is described by only one parameter, the mean number of events observed, and has the special characteristic that the variance is equal to the mean. The shape has a pronounced positive skewness at low mean counts, but becomes more and more symmetrical as the mean number of counts increases (Fig. 64.3).

A chemical example of characteristics distributed in a Poisson fashion is the number of radioactive disintegrations per unit time. One of the main uses for the Poisson distribution is to quantify errors in count

Quantifying skew – the Microsoft Excel SKEW function can be used to assess the extent of skewness in a data set.

Tendency towards the normal distribution – under certain conditions, binomial and Poisson distributions can be treated as normally distributed:

- where samples from a binomial distribution are large (i.e. > 15) and p and q are close to 0.5;
- for Poisson distributions, if the number of counts recorded in each outcome is greater than about 15.

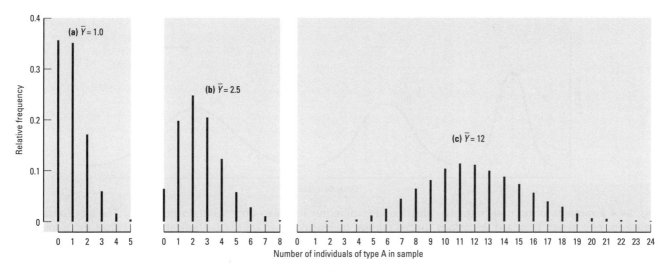

Fig. 64.3 Examples of Poisson frequency distributions differing in mean. The distributions are shown as line charts because the independent variable (events per sample) is discrete.

data such as estimates of the number of minor accidents in the chemical laboratory over the course of an academic year. To decide whether data are Poisson distributed:

- Use the rule of thumb that if the coefficient of dispersion ≈ 1, the distribution is likely to be Poisson.

- Calculate 'expected' frequencies from the equation for the Poisson distribution and compare with actual values using a χ^2-test or a G-test.

It is sometimes of interest to show that data are *not* distributed in a Poisson fashion. If $s^2/\bar{Y} > 1$, the data are 'clumped' and occur together more than would be expected by chance; if $s^2/\bar{Y} < 1$, the data are 'repulsed' and occur together less frequently than would be expected by chance.

Normal distributions (Gaussian distributions)

These occur when random events act to produce variability in a continuous characteristic (quantitative variable). This situation occurs frequently in biology, so normal distributions are very useful and much used. The bell-like shape of normal distributions is specified by the population mean and standard deviation (Fig. 64.4): it is symmetrical and configured such that 68.27% of the data will lie within ± 1 standard deviation of the mean, 95.45% within ± 2 standard deviations of the mean, and 99.73% within ± 3 standard deviations of the mean.

Some chemical examples of data likely to be distributed in a normal fashion are: pH of natural waters; and melting point of a solid compound. To check whether data come from a normal distribution, you can:

- Use the rule of thumb that the distribution should be symmetrical and that nearly all the data should fall within $\pm 3s$ of the mean and about two-thirds within $\pm 1s$ of the mean.

- Plot the distribution on normal probability graph paper. If the distribution is normal, the data will tend to follow a straight line

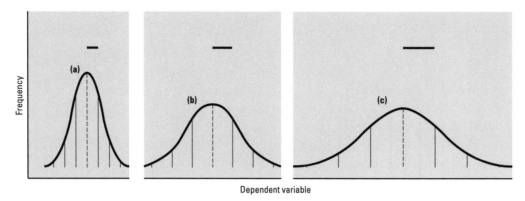

Fig. 64.4 Examples of normal frequency distributions differing in mean and standard deviation. The horizontal bars represent population standard deviations for the curves, increasing from (a) to (c). Vertical dashed lines are population means, while vertical solid lines show positions of values ±1, 2 and 3 standard deviations from the means.

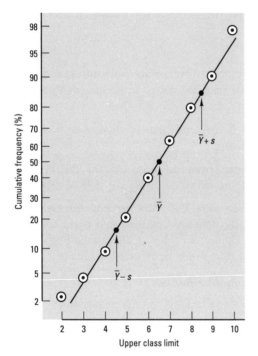

Fig. 64.5 Example of a normal probability plot. The plotted points are from a small data set where the mean $\bar{Y} = 6.93$ and the standard deviation $s = 1.895$. Note that values corresponding to 0% and 100% cumulative frequency cannot be used. The straight line is that predicted for a normal distribution with $\bar{Y} = 6.93$ and $s = 1.895$. This is plotted by calculating the expected positions of points for $\bar{Y} \pm s$. Since 68.3% of the distribution falls within these bounds, the relevant points on the cumulative frequency scale are $50 \pm 34.15\%$; thus this line was drawn using the points (4.495, 15.85) and (8.285, 84.15) as indicated on the plot.

(see Fig. 64.5). Deviations from linearity reveal skewness and/or kurtosis (see p. 506), the significance of which can be tested statistically (see Miller and Miller, 2000).

- Use a suitable statistical computer program to generate predicted normal curves from the $\bar{Y}$ and s values of your sample(s). These can be compared visually with the actual distribution of data and can be used to give 'expected' values for a χ^2-test or a G-test.

The wide availability of tests based on the normal distribution and their relative simplicity means you may wish to transform your data to make them more like a normal distribution. Table 64.1 provides transformations that can be applied. The transformed data should be tested for normality as described above before proceeding – don't forget that you may need to check that transformed variances are homogeneous for certain tests (see below).

A very important theorem in statistics, the Central Limit Theorem, states that as sample size increases, the distribution of a series of means from any frequency distribution will become normally distributed. This fact can be used to devise an experimental or sampling strategy that ensures that data are normally distributed, i.e. using means of samples as if they were primary data.

Table 64.1 Suggested transformations altering different types of frequency distribution to the normal type. To use, modify data by the formula shown; then examine effects with the tests described on pp. 511–514.

Type of data; distribution suspected	Suggested transformation(s)
Proportions (including percentages); binomial	arcsine $\sqrt{x}$ (also called the angular transformation)
Scores; Poisson	$\sqrt{x}$ or $\sqrt{(x + 1/2)}$ if zero values present
Measurements; negatively skewed	x^2, x^3, x^4, etc. (in order of increasing strength)
Measurements; positively skewed	$1/\sqrt{x}$, $\sqrt{x}$, $\ln x$, $1/x$ (in order of increasing strength)

Choosing a suitable statistical test

Comparing location (e.g. means)

If you can assume that your data are normally distributed, the main test for comparing two means from independent samples is Student's *t*-test (see Boxes 64.1 and 64.2, and Table 64.2). This assumes that the variances of the data sets are homogeneous. Tests based on the *t*-distribution are also available for comparing means of paired data or for comparing a sample mean with a chosen value.

When comparing means of two or more samples, analysis of variance (ANOVA) is a very useful technique. This method also assumes data are normally distributed and that the variances of the samples are homogeneous. The samples must also be independent (e.g. not subsamples). The test statistic calculated is denoted F and it has two different degrees of freedom related to the number of means tested and the pooled number of replicates per mean. The nested types of ANOVA are useful for letting you know the relative importance of different sources of variability in your data. Two-way and multi-way ANOVAs are useful for studying interactions between treatments.

For data satisfying the ANOVA requirements, the least significant difference (LSD) is useful for making planned comparisons among several means (see Miller and Miller, 2000). Any two means that differ by more than the LSD will be significantly different. The LSD is useful for showing on graphs.

Definition

Homogeneous variance – uniform (but not necessarily identical) variance of the dependent variable across the range of the independent variable. The term homoscedastic is also used in this sense. The opposite of homogeneous is heterogeneous (= heteroscedastic).

Understanding 'degrees of freedom' – this depends on the number of values in the data set analysed, and the method of calculation depends on the statistical test being used. It relates to the number of observations that are free to vary before the remaining quantities for a data set can be determined.

Table 64.2 Critical values of Student's *t* statistic (for two-tailed tests). Reject the null hypothesis at probability P if your calculated *t* value equals or exceeds the value shown for the appropriate degrees of freedom $= (n_1 - 1) + (n_2 - 1)$

Degrees of freedom	Critical values for $P = 0.05$	Critical values for $P = 0.01$	Critical values for $P = 0.001$
1	12.71	63.66	636.62
2	4.30	9.92	31.60
3	3.18	5.84	12.94
4	2.78	4.60	8.61
5	2.57	4.03	6.86
6	2.45	3.71	5.96
7	2.36	3.50	5.40
8	2.31	3.36	5.04
9	2.26	3.25	4.78
10	2.23	3.17	4.59
12	2.18	3.06	4.32
14	2.14	2.98	4.14
16	2.12	2.92	4.02
20	2.09	2.85	3.85
25	2.06	2.79	3.72
30	2.04	2.75	3.65
40	2.02	2.70	3.55
60	2.00	2.66	3.46
120	1.98	2.62	3.37
∞	1.96	2.58	3.29

Box 64.1 How to carry out a *t*-test

The *t*-test was devised by a statistician who used the pen-name 'Student', so you may see it referred to as Student's *t*-test. It is used when you wish to decide whether two samples come from the same population or from different ones (Fig. 64.1). The samples might have been obtained by observation, or by applying two different treatments to an originally homogeneous population (Chapter 29).

The null hypothesis (NH) is that the two groups can be represented as samples from the same overlying population (Fig. 64.1(a)). If, as a result of the test, you accept this hypothesis, you can say that there is no significant difference between the group means.

The alternative hypothesis is that the two groups come from different populations (Fig. 64.1(b)). By rejecting the NH as a result of the test, you can accept the alternative hypothesis and say that there is a significant difference between the sample means, or, if an experiment were carried out, that the two treatments affected the samples differently.

How can you decide between these two hypotheses? On the basis of certain assumptions (see below), and some relatively simple calculations, you can work out the probability that the samples came from the same population. If this probability is very low, then you can reasonably reject the NH in favour of the alternative hypothesis, and if it is high, you will accept the NH.

To find out the probability that the observed difference between sample means arose by chance, you must first calculate a '*t* value' for the two samples in question. Some computer programs (e.g. Minitab) provide this probability as part of the output, otherwise you can look up statistical tables (e.g. Table 64.2). These tables show 'critical values' – the borders between probability levels. If your value of *t* equals or exceeds the critical value for probability *P*, you can reject the NH at this probability ('level of significance').

Note that:

- for a given difference in the means of the two samples, the value of *t* will get larger the smaller the scatter within each data set; and

- for a given scatter of the data, the value of *t* will get larger the greater the difference between the means.

So, at what probability should you reject the NH? Normally, the threshold is arbitrarily set at 5% – you quite often see descriptions like 'the sample means were significantly different ($P < 0.05$)'. At this 'significance level' there is still up to a 5% chance of the *t* value arising by chance, so about 1 in 20 times, on average, the conclusion will be wrong. If *P* turns out to be lower, then this kind of error is much less likely.

Tabulated probability levels are generally given for 5%, 1% and 0.1% significance levels (see Table 64.2). Note that this table is designed for 'two-tailed' tests, i.e. where the treatment or sampling strategy could have resulted in either an increase or a decrease in the measured values.

These are the most likely situations you will deal with in chemistry.

Examine Table 64.2 and note the following:

- The larger the size of the samples (i.e. the greater the 'degrees of freedom') the smaller *t* needs to be to exceed the critical value at a given significance level.

- The lower the probability the greater *t* needs to be to exceed the critical value.

The mechanics of the test

A calculator that can work out means and standard deviations is helpful.

1. **Work out the sample means $\bar{Y}_1$ and $\bar{Y}_2$ and calculate the difference between them.**

2. **Work out the sample standard deviations s_1 and s_2.** (NB if your calculator offers a choice, choose the '$n - 1$' option for calculating s – see p. 504).

3. **Work out the sample standard errors $SE_1 = s_1/\sqrt{n_1}$ and $SE_2 = s_2/\sqrt{n_2}$; now square each, add the squares together, then take the positive square root of this** (n_1 and n_2 are the respective sample sizes, which may, or may not, be equal).

4. **Calculate *t* from the formula:**

$$t = \frac{\bar{Y}_1 - \bar{Y}_2}{\sqrt{((SE_1)^2) + (SE_2)^2)}} \qquad [64.1]$$

The value of *t* can be negative or positive, depending on the values of the means; this does not matter and you should compare the modulus (absolute value) of *t* with the values in tables.

5. **Work out the degrees of freedom = $(n_1 - 1) + (n_2 - 1)$.**

6. **Compare the *t* value with the appropriate critical value (see e.g. Table 64.2) and decide on the significance of your finding (see p. 511).**

Box 64.2 provides a worked example – use this to check that you understand the above procedures.

Assumptions that must be met before using the test

The most important assumptions are:

- The two samples are independent and randomly drawn (or if not, drawn in a way that does not create bias). The test assumes that the samples are quite large.

- The underlying distribution of each sample is normal. This can be tested with a special statistical test, but a rule of thumb is that a frequency distribution of the data should be (a) symmetrical about the mean and (b) nearly all of the data should be within 3 standard deviations of the mean and about two-thirds within 1 standard deviation of the mean (see p. 515).

- The two samples should have uniform variances. This again can be tested (by an *F*-test), but may be obvious from inspection of the two standard deviations.

Box 64.2 Worked example of a *t*-test

Suppose the following data were obtained in an experiment (the units are not relevant):

Control: 6.6, 5.5, 6.8, 5.8, 6.1, 5.9

Treatment: 6.3, 7.2, 6.5, 7.1, 7.5, 7.3

Using the steps outlined in Box 64.1, the following values are obtained (denoting control with subscript 1, treatment with subscript 2):

1. $\bar{Y}_1 = 6.1167$; $\bar{Y}_2 = 6.9833$: difference between means $= \bar{Y}_1 - \bar{Y}_2 = -0.8666$

2. $s_1 = 0.49565$; $s_2 = 0.47504$

3. $SE_1 = 0.49565/2.44949 = 0.202348$

   $SE_2 = 0.47504/2.44949 = 0.193934$

4. $t = \dfrac{-0.8666}{\sqrt{(0.202348^2 + 0.193934^2)}} = \dfrac{-0.8666}{0.280277} = -3.09$

5. d.f. $= (5 + 5) = 10$

6. Looking at Table 64.2, we see that the modulus of this t value exceeds the tabulated value for $P = 0.05$ at 10 degrees of freedom ($= 2.23$). We therefore reject the NH, and conclude that the means are different at the 5% level of significance. If the modulus of t had been $\leqslant 2.23$, we would have accepted the NH. If modulus of t had been > 3.17, we could have concluded that the means are different at the 1% level of significance.

Checking the assumptions of a test – always acquaint yourself with the assumptions of a test. If necessary, test them before using the test.

The chief non-parametric tests for comparing the locations of two samples are the Mann–Whitney U-test and the Kolmogorov–Smirnov test. The former assumes that the frequency distributions of the samples are similar, whereas the latter makes no such assumption. In both cases the sample's size must be $\geqslant 4$ and for the Kolmogorov–Smirnov test the samples must have equal sizes. In the Kolmogorov–Smirnov test, significant differences found with the test could be due to differences in location or shape of the distribution, or both.

Suitable non-parametric comparisons of location for paired data (sample size $\geqslant 6$) include Wilcoxon's signed rank test, which is used for quantitative data and assumes that the distributions have similar shape. Dixon and Mood's sign test can be used for paired data scores where one variable is recorded as 'greater than' or 'better than' the other.

Non-parametric comparisons of location for three or more samples include the Kruskal–Wallis H-test. Here, the number of samples is without limit and they can be unequal in size, but again the underlying distributions are assumed to be similar. The Friedman S-test operates with a maximum of five samples and data must conform to a randomised block design. The underlying distributions of the samples are assumed to be similar.

Comparing dispersions (e.g. variances)

If you wish to compare the variances of two sets of data that are normally distributed, use the F-test. For comparing more than two samples, it may be sufficient to use the F_{max}-test, on the highest and lowest variances. The Scheffé–Box (log-ANOVA) test is recommended for testing the significance of differences between several variances. Non-parametric tests exist but are not widely available: you may need to transform the data and use a test based on the normal distribution.

Determining whether frequency observations fit theoretical expectation

The χ^2-test is useful for tests of 'goodness of fit' e.g. comparing observed frequency distributions with some theoretical function. One limitation is that simple formulae for calculating χ^2 assume that no expected number is less than 5. The *G*-test (*2I* test) is used in similar circumstances.

Comparing proportion data

When comparing proportions between two small groups (e.g. whether 3/10 is significantly different from 5/10), you can use probability tables such as those of Finney *et al.* (1963) or calculate probabilities from formulae; however, this can be tedious for large sample sizes. Certain proportions can be transformed so that their distribution becomes normal.

Placing confidence limits on an estimate of a population parameter

On many occasions, a sample statistic is used to provide an estimate of a population parameter, and it is often useful to indicate the reliability of such an estimate. This can be done by putting confidence limits on the sample statistic, i.e. by specifying an interval around the statistic within which you are confident that the true value (the population parameter) is likely to fall, at a specified level of probability. The most common application is to place confidence limits on the mean of a sample taken from a population of normally distributed data values. In practice, you determine a confidence factor for a particular level of probability which is added to and subtracted from the sample mean ($\overline{Y}$) to give the upper confidence limit and lower confidence limit respectively. These are calculated as:

$$\overline{Y} + (t_{P[n-1]} \times \text{SE}) \text{ for the upper limit and}$$
$$\overline{Y} - (t_{P[n-1]} \times \text{SE}) \text{ for the lower limit} \qquad [64.2]$$

where $t_{P[n-1]}$ is the tabulated critical value of Student's *t*-statistic for a two-tailed test with $n - 1$ degrees of freedom at a specified probability level (*P*) and SE is the standard error of the sample mean (p. 504). The 95% confidence limits (i.e. $P = 0.05$) tells you that on average, 95 times out of 100, the interval between the upper and lower limits will contain the true (population) value. Confidence limits are often shown as 'error bars' for individual sample means plotted in graphical form. Fig. 64.6 illustrates how this is applied to plotted curves and histograms (note that this can be carried out for data series within a Microsoft Excel graph (chart) using the *Format data series* and *Y error bars* commands).

Confidence limits for statistics other than the mean – consult an advanced statistical text (e.g. Miller and Miller, 2000) if you wish to indicate the reliability of estimates of e.g. population variances.

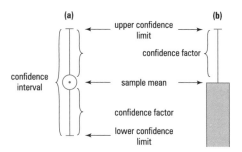

Fig. 64.6 Graphical representation of confidence limits as 'error bars' for (a) a sample mean in a plotted curve, where both upper and lower limits are shown; and (b) a sample mean in a histogram, where, by convention, only the upper value is shown. For data that are assumed to be symmetrically distributed, such representations are often used in preference to the 'box and whisker' plot shown on p. 503. Note that SE is an alternative way of representing sample imprecision/error (e.g. Fig. 60.1). See p. 478 for how to add error bars to Microsoft Excel graphs.

Correlation and regression

These methods are used when testing the relationship between data values for two variables. Correlation is used to measure the extent to which changes in the two sets of data values occur together in a linear manner. If one variable can be assumed to be dependent upon the other (i.e. a change in *X* causes a particular change in *Y*), then regression techniques can be used to provide a mathematical description of the underlying relationship between the variables, e.g. to find a line of best fit for a data series. If there is no *a priori* reason to assume dependency, then correlation methods alone are appropriate.

A correlation coefficient measures the strength of the linear relationship between two variables, but does not describe the

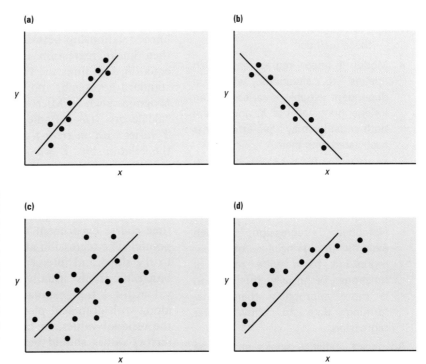

Fig. 64.7 Examples of correlation. The linear regression line is shown. In (a) and (b), the correlation between x and y is good: for (a) there is a positive correlation and the correlation coefficient, r, would be close to 1; for (b) there is a negative correlation and the correlation coefficient would be close to -1. In (c) there is a weak positive correlation and r would be close to 0. In (d) the correlation coefficient may be quite large, but the choice of linear regression is clearly inappropriate.

relationship. The coefficient is expressed as a number between -1 and $+1$: a positive coefficient indicates a direct relationship, where the two variables change in the same direction, while a negative coefficient indicates an inverse relationship, where one variable decreases as the other increases (Fig. 64.7). The nearer the coefficient is to -1 or $+1$, the stronger the linear relationship between the variables, i.e. the less 'scatter' there would be about a straight line of best fit (note that this does *not* imply that one variable is dependent upon the other). A coefficient of 0 implies that the two variables show no linear association and therefore the closer the correlation coefficient is to zero, the weaker the linear relationship. The importance of graphing data is shown by the case illustrated in Fig. 64.7(d).

Pearson's product moment correlation coefficient (r) is the most commonly used statistic for testing correlations. The test is valid only if both variables are normally distributed. Statistical tests can be used to decide whether the correlation is significant, e.g. using a one-sample t-test to see whether r is significantly different from zero, based on the following equation:

$$t = r \div \sqrt{[(1 - r^2) \div (n - 2)]} \qquad [64.3]$$

at $n - 2$ degrees of freedom, where n is the number of paired observations. If one or both variables are not normally distributed, then you should calculate an alternative non-parametric coeffcient, e.g. Spearman's coefficient of rank correlation (r_S) or Kendall's coefficient of rank correlation (τ). These require the two sets of data to be ranked separately, and the calculation can be complex if there are tied (equal) ranks. Spearman's coefficient is said to be better if there is any uncertainty about the reliability of closely ranked data values.

Using more advanced types of regression – these include:

- Model II linear regression, which applies to situations where a dependent variable Y varies with an independent variable X, and where both variables may have error terms associated with them.

- Multiple regression, which applies when there is a relationship between a dependent variable and two or more independent variables.

- Non-linear regression, which extends the principles of linear regression to a wide range of functions. Technically, this method is more appropriate than transforming data to allow linear regression.

Advanced statistics books should be consulted for details of these methods, which also may be offered by some statistical computer programs.

Example If a regression analysis gives a value for r^2 of 0.75 (i.e. $r = 0.84$), then 75% of the variance in Y can be explained by the trend line, with $1 - r^2 = 0.25$ (25%) remaining as unexplained (residual) variation.

If underlying theory or empirical graphical analysis indicates a linear relationship between a dependent and an independent variable, then linear regression can be used to estimate the mathematical equation that links the two variables. Model I linear regression is the standard approach, and is available within general-purpose software programs such as Microsoft Excel (Box 64.3), and on some scientific calculators. It is suitable for experiments where a dependent variable Y varies with an *error-free* independent variable X in accordance with the relationship $Y = a + bX + e_Y$, where e_Y represents the residual (error) variability in the Y variable. For example, this relationship might apply in a laboratory procedure where you have carefully controlled the independent variable and the X values can be assumed to have zero error (e.g. in a calibration curve, see Chapter 47, or in a time course experiment where measurements are made at exact time points). The regression analysis gives estimates for a and b (equivalent to the slope and intercept of the line of best fit, p. 494): computer-based programs usually provide additional features, e.g. residual values for Y (e_Y), estimated errors for a and b, predicted values of Y along with graphical plots of the line of best fit (the trend line) and the residual values. In order for the model to be valid, the residual (error) values should be normally distributed around the trend line and their variance should be uniform (homogeneous), i.e. there should be a similar scatter of data points around the trend line along the x-axis (independent variable).

If the relationship is not linear, try a transformation. For example, this is commonly done in analysis of enzyme kinetics. However, you should be aware that the transformation of data to give a straight line can lead to errors when carrying out linear regression analysis: take care to ensure that (a) the assumptions listed in the previous paragraph are valid for the transformed data set, and (b) the data points are evenly distributed throughout the range of the independent variable. If these criteria cannot be met, non-linear regression may be a better approach, but for this you will require a suitable computer program, e.g. GraphPad Prism.

The strength of the relationship between Y and X in model I linear regression is best estimated by the coefficient of determination (r^2 or R^2), which is equivalent to the square of the Pearson correlation coefficient. The coefficient of determination varies between 0 and +1 and provides a measure of the goodness of fit of the Y data to the regression line: the closer the value is to 1, the better the fit. In effect, r^2 represents the fraction of the variance in Y that can be accounted for by the regression equation. Conversely, if you subtract this value from 1, you will obtain the residual (error) component, i.e. the fraction of the variance in Y that cannot be explained by the line of best fit. Multiplying the values by 100 allows you to express these fractions in percentage terms.

Using computers to calculate hypothesis-testing statistics

As with the calculation of descriptive statistics (p. 498), specialist statistical packages such as **SPSS** and **MINITAB** can be used to simplify the calculation of hypothesis-testing statistics. The correct use of the software and interpretation of the output requires an understanding of relevant terminology and of the fundamental principles governing the test,

Presented below are three examples of the use of Microsoft Excel to investigate hypotheses about specific data sets. In each case, there is a brief description of the problem; a table showing the data analysed; an outline of the Excel commands used to carry out the analysis; and an annotated table of results from the spreadsheet (you can use the same data to check your ability to carry out the procedures).

Example 1: a *t*-test. As part of a project, a student applied a chemical treatment to a series of flasks containing fungal cultures with nutrient solution. An otherwise similar set of control flasks received no chemical treatment. After 3 weeks' growth, the student measured the wet mass of the filtered cultures:

Wet mass of samples (g)

Replicate	1	2	3	4	5	6	7	8	Mean	Variance
Treated with ZH52	2.342	2.256	2.521	2.523	2.943	2.481	2.601	2.449	2.515	0.042
Control	2.658	2.791	2.731	2.402	3.041	2.668	2.823	2.509	2.703	0.038

The student proposed the null hypothesis that there was no difference between the two means and tested this using a *t*-test, and had evidence from other studies that the fungal masses of replicate flasks were normally distributed. The student had also established, by calculation, that the assumption that the populations had homogeneous variances was likely to be valid. Using the *Tools > Data Analysis > t-Test: Two-Sample Assuming Equal Variance* option, with *Hypothesized Mean Difference* = 0 and *Alpha* (= *P*) = 0.05, and adjusting the number of significant figures displayed, the following table was obtained:

t-Test: two-sample assuming equal variances

	Variable 1	Variable 2
Mean	2.515	2.703
Variance	0.042	0.038
Observations	8	8
Pooled variance	0.040	
Hypothesised mean difference	0	
df	14	
t Stat	−1.881	
$P(T \leq t)$ one-tail	0.040	
t Critical one-tail	1.761	
$P(T \leq t)$ two-tail	0.081	
t Critical two-tail	2.145	

The value of *t* obtained was −1.881 (row 7 '*t* Stat') and the probability of obtaining this value for a two-tailed test (row 10) was 0.081 (or 8.1%), so the student was able to accept the null hypothesis and conclude that ZH52 had no significant effect on fungal growth in these circumstances.

Example 2: an ANOVA test. An analytical biochemist made six replicate measurements of four different batches (A–D) of alcohol dehydrogenase, obtaining the following data:

Alcohol dehydrogenase activity (U L^{-1})

Batch \ replicate	1	2	3	4	5	6	Mean	Variance
A	0.562	0.541	0.576	0.545	0.542	0.551	0.552833	0.000189
B	0.531	0.557	0.537	0.521	0.559	0.538	0.540500	0.000221
C	0.572	0.568	0.551	0.549	0.564	0.559	0.560500	0.000085
D	0.532	0.548	0.541	0.538	0.547	0.536	0.540333	0.000039

The analytical biochemist wanted to know whether the observed differences were statistically significant, so he carried out an ANOVA test, assuming the samples were normally distributed and the variances in the three populations were homogeneous. Using the *Tools > Data Analysis > Anova: Single Factor* option, with *Alpha* (= *P*) = 0.05, and adjusting the number of significant figures displayed, the following table was obtained:

ANOVA: single factor

SUMMARY

Groups	Count	Sum	Average	Variance
A	6	3.317	0.552833	0.000189
B	6	3.243	0.5405	0.000221
C	6	3.363	0.5605	8.51E-05
D	6	3.242	0.540333	3.95E-05

ANOVA

Source of variation	SS	df	MS	F	P-value	F crit
Between groups	0.001761	3	0.000587	4.397856	0.015669	3.098391
Within groups	0.002669	20	0.000133			
Total	0.00443	23				

The *F* value calculated was 4.397856. This comfortably exceeds the stated critical value (F_{crit}) of 3.098391 and the probability of obtaining this result by chance (*P*-value) was calculated as 0.015669 (1.57% to three significant figures), hence the analytical biochemist was able to reject the null hypothesis and conclude that there was a significant difference in average enzyme activity between the four batches, since $P < 0.05$. Such a finding might lead onto an investigation into why there was batch variation, e.g. had they been stored differently?

Example 3: testing the significance of a correlation. A researcher wanted to know whether there was any correlation between the levels of tar and nicotine in cigarettes. The researcher made measurements of both

(continued)

Box 64.3 (continued)

consitituents for 10 different brands and obtained the following results:

Tar and nicotine content (mg g^{-1}) of cigarettes

Brand	Tar	Nicotine
1	12.6	0.92
2	8.5	0.58
3	15.7	1.14
4	32.5	2.16
5	14.5	1.03
6	3.1	0.17
7	18.9	1.32
8	7.7	0.98
9	10.7	1.13
10	6.2	0.55

The researcher assumed that both variables were normally distributed and used the Microsoft Excel function *PEARSON (array1, array 2)* to obtain a value of +0.950 260 385 for the Pearson's product moment correlation coefficient r, specifying the tar content data as array1 and the nicotine content data as array2 (the Excel *CORREL* function can also be used to carry out the same task). The researcher then used a spreadsheet to calculate the t statistic (p. 516) for this r value, using the formula for eqn [64.3]. The calculated value of t was 8.6296, with 8 degrees of freedom. The critical value from tables (e.g. Table 64.2) at $P = 0.001$ is 5.04, so the researcher concluded that there was a very highly significant positive correlation between the two constituents.

which is probably best obtained by working through one or more examples by hand before using these tools (e.g. Box 64.2). Spreadsheets offer increasingly sophisticated statistical analysis functions, three examples of which are provided in Box 64.3.

Text references and sources for further study

Anon. *Discover Maths*.
Available: http://discovermaths.rsc.org/
Last accessed: 03/09/10.
[A basic web-based guide with examples]

Finney, D.J., Latscha, R., Bennett, B.M. and Hsu, P. (1963) *Tables for Testing Significance in a 2 × 2 Table*. Cambridge University Press, Cambridge.

Leardi, R. (2009) Experimental design in chemistry: A tutorial. *Analytica Chimica Acta*, **652**, 161–172.

Miller, J.N. and Miller, J.C. (2000) *Statistics and Chemometrics for Analytical Chemistry*, 4th edn. Prentice Hall, Harlow.

Monk, P. and Munro, L.J. (2010) *Maths for Chemists: A Chemist's Toolkit of Calculations*. Oxford University Press, Oxford.

Schmuller, J. (2005) *Statistical Analysis with Excel for Dummies*. Wiley, Hoboken.

Steiner, E. (2008) *The Chemistry Maths Book*, 2nd edn. Oxford University Press, Oxford.

Taylor, J.K. and Cihon, C. (2004) *Statistical Techniques for Data Analysis*, 2nd edn. CRC Press, Boca Raton.

Study exercises

64.1 Calculate 95% confidence limits. What are the 95% confidence limits of a sample with a mean = 24.7, standard deviation = 6.8 and number of data values = 16? (Express your answer to three significant figures.)

64.2 Practise using a *t*-test. A chemistry student measures the paracetamol concentration (mg g^{-1}) in tablets by two different analytical methods. Seven tablets from different batches were analysed to see whether the results obtained by the two methods differed. Carry out a *t*-test on the data and draw appropriate conclusions.

Paracetamol concentration (mg g^{-1})

Method 1	7.5	8.1	7.6	6.2	7.5	7.8	8.9
Method 2	5.6	7.5	8.2	6.7	3.5	6.5	5.9

64.3 Interpret the output from Microsoft Excel linear regression analysis. The following output represents a regression analysis for an experiment measuring the uptake of an amino acid by a cell suspension (in $pmol\,cell^{-1}$) against time (in minutes). Based on this output, what is the form and strength of the underlying linear relationship? (Express the coefficients to three significant figures.)

Output from Excel spreadsheet linear regression analysis

Summary output

Regression statistics

Multiple R	0.985 335 951
R square	0.970 886 937
Adjusted R square	0.963 608 672
Standard error	2.133 876 419
Observations	6

ANOVA

	df	SS	MS	F	Significance F
Regression	1	607.406 285 7	607.4063	133.3954	0.000 320 975
Residual	4	18.213 714 29	4.553 429		
Total	5	625.62			

	Coefficients	Standard error	t Stat	P-value
Intercept	1.171 428 571	1.544 386 367	0.758 507	0.490 383
X variable 1	2.945 714 286	0.255 047 014	11.549 69	0.000 321

Drawing the structure of a chemical compound is probably one of the first basic requirements of any chemist. It requires knowledge of the chemical composition of the structure to be drawn, an understanding of the type of bonding, and frequently a mental visualisation of the arrangement of atoms (or ions). Once this has been assimilated it is not uncommon to draw a representation of the structure on paper. What is often lacking is the realisation that the molecule should be represented in three dimensions. To some extent it is possible to represent a three-dimensional chemical structure on a piece of paper. Fig. 65.1 shows the structure of methane, CH_4, where standard symbols e.g. the hatched line, are used to imply a direction of the bond, and one that is different to, for example, the solid line. This simple notation is commonly used to give a molecule the perception of three-dimensionality.

In co-ordination chemistry, a different approach is used; for example, in the structure for hexaamminecobaltate complex, $[Co(NH_3)_6]^{3+}$, there are several alternative approaches. The simplest way to express this structure is shown in Fig. 65.2.

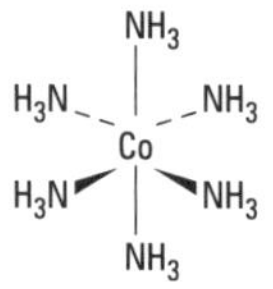

The general points to remember are as follows:

- Always draw chemical structures in ink (pencil fades with time).

- Always ensure that the chemical structure is drawn large enough, so that no ambiguity is possible.

- If drawing by hand, ensure that each atom is clearly identified. This may require the use of coloured pens.

- Try to keep the structure as simple as possible, highlighting only the key features.

- Any text should appear in a clear script (by hand or word processed).

- When possible, it is advisable to use computer software packages to generate chemical structures.

- Make sure no confusion is possible between different letters of the alphabet representing elements in the Periodic Table.

- If necessary, show the number of electrons (pairs or individual electrons) clearly. Remember, a . (full stop) may be mistaken for a mark in the paper.

- It may be necessary to indicate the structural formula of a molecule, e.g. in isomerism.

Selected examples of drawing chemical structures

Organic structures

Organic molecules vary from the simplest structures containing a few atoms to the most complex molecules comprising hundreds (see Chapter 67). Chemists have devised many methods of unambiguously communicating structures which illustrate the features under discussion. Most organic chemistry is based on the reactions of functional groups, e.g. alcohol, ester, acid, amine, etc., with the carbon skeleton making no

Fig. 65.1 Methane.

Fig. 65.2 Structure of hexaammine-cobaltate.

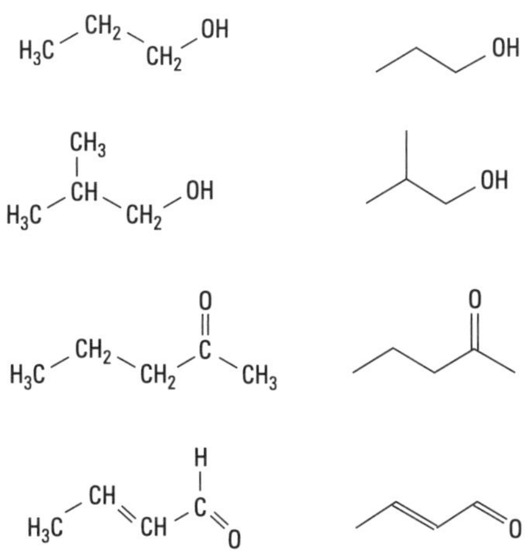

Table 65.1 Common abbreviations for the carbon skeleton

Abbreviation	Carbon skeleton	Formula
Me	Methyl	CH_3-
Et	Ethyl	CH_3CH_2-
Pr	Propyl	$CH_3CH_2CH_2-$
Pr^i	Iso-propyl	$(CH_3)_2CH-$
Bu	Butyl	$CH_3CH_2CH_2CH_2-$
Bu^i	Iso-butyl	$(CH_3)_2CHCH_2-$
Bu^t	Tert-butyl	$(CH_3)_3C-$
Ph	Phenyl	C_6H_5-
Ac	Acetyl (ethanoyl)	CH_3CO-
Ts	p-Toluenesulphonyl (tosyl)	$CH_3C_6H_5SO_2-$

Fig. 65.3a Examples of bond-line formulae.

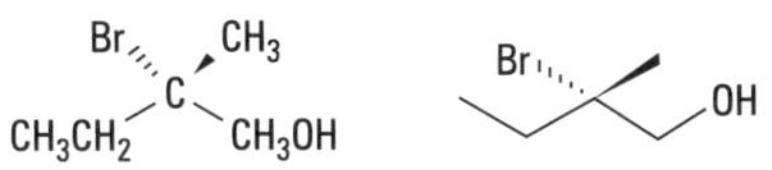

Fig. 65.3b Stereochemical representation using bond-line formulae.

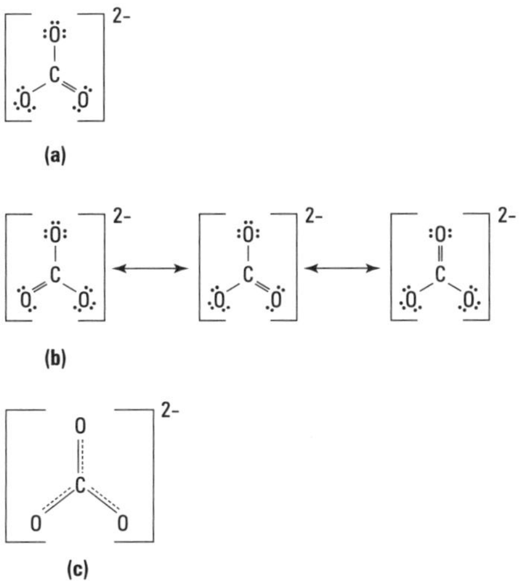

Fig. 65.4 Lewis diagrams for CO_3^{2-}.

contribution to the chemistry. This has led to the development of two common methods of depicting organic structures: (a) abbreviated formulae and (b) bond–line structures, which avoid the complexity and irrelevance of writing out all the C−H and C−C bonds in a structural formula.

(a) **Abbreviated formulae** The carbon skeleton, usually a saturated hydrocarbon chain or mono-substituted benzene ring, is depicted by a two-letter combination as shown in Table 65.1. All other functional groups are shown normally.

Simple illustrative examples of this system are: bromomethane (MeBr), 2-propanol (Pr^iOH), 2-chloro-2-methylpropane (Bu^tCl), nitrobenzene ($PhNO_2$) and *N*-phenylethanamide (PhNHAc).

(b) **Bond-line formulae** This is one of the most common systems in use today and is compatible with computer-based structure drawing programs. The carbon skeleton is represented by a series of lines showing the bonds between the saturated carbon atoms but the hydrogen atoms and their bonds to carbon are not shown. All other atoms and multiple bonds are shown. These ideas are illustrated by the following examples (Fig. 65.3(a)) and stereochemistry can be shown by the usual 'wedge' bonds (Fig. 65.3(b)).

Lewis structures

When drawing Lewis structures it is important to show the position and number of electrons. For example, the Lewis structure for CO_3^{2-} is shown in Fig. 65.4(a). Note the position of the double bond. Also, both carbon and oxygen obey the octet rule, i.e. the number of electrons around each atom adds up to eight (a single bond is composed of two electrons, a double bond of four electrons). Lewis structures sometimes give rise to canonical forms. The three possible canonical forms for CO_3^{2-} are shown in Fig. 65.4(b). It is noted that as the position of the double bond moves the number of lone pairs of electrons changes. In reality, experimental evidence indicates that the C–O bond in carbonate is composed of neither single nor double bonds but is intermediate in bond length and strength. A more appropriate method of representing this structure is by delocalisation of bonding electrons (Fig. 65.4(c)).

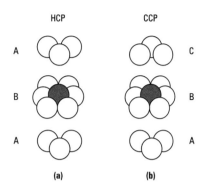

Fig. 65.5 Close-packing arrangement for (a) hexagonal close packing (ABABA etc.) and (b) cubic close packing (ABCABCA etc.).

Ionic structures

In solid-state chemistry it is often necessary to draw a 'unit cell'. The most commonly found are the hexagonal close-packed (HCP) crystal structure and cubic close-packed (CCP) crystal structure. In the HCP structure atoms are arranged in an ABABA repeating pattern, while in the CCP structure the arrangement is an ABCABCA pattern. In both cases it is difficult to represent the structures without resorting to the drawing of circles. Fig. 65.5 shows the close-packing arrangement for both the HCP and CCP crystal structures. In the HCP structure the first and third layers of atoms are orientated in the same direction (directly above one another) while in the CCP structure, the first and third layers do not coincide, i.e. no atom in the third layer is directly above an atom in the first layer.

It is usually not recommended to attempt drawing ionic structures of greater complexity without resorting to a specialised computer-based drawing package.

> **KEY POINT** It is often important when drawing chemical structures to impart some structural identity.

Atomic orbitals

You may need to draw a visualisation of atomic orbitals, usually the s, p and d orbitals. This can be simplified by the use of Cartesian co-ordinates which allow a three-dimensional representation on paper. This is neither easy to replicate or often necessary. A simplified approach is, for example, to replace the spherical s orbital with a circle (Fig. 65.6). Similarly, the three p orbitals can be represented in two dimensions by the use of correct labelling of the axes (Fig. 65.6). Finally, the same approach can be replicated on the five d orbitals (Fig. 65.6). It is worthwhile remembering that the d_{xy}, d_{xz} and d_{yz} orbitals do not reside on the axes (x, y or z), but in the plane of their respective axes. In addition, the $d_{x^2-y^2}$ orbital occupies the x- and y-axes and the d_{z^2} orbital occupies the z-axis.

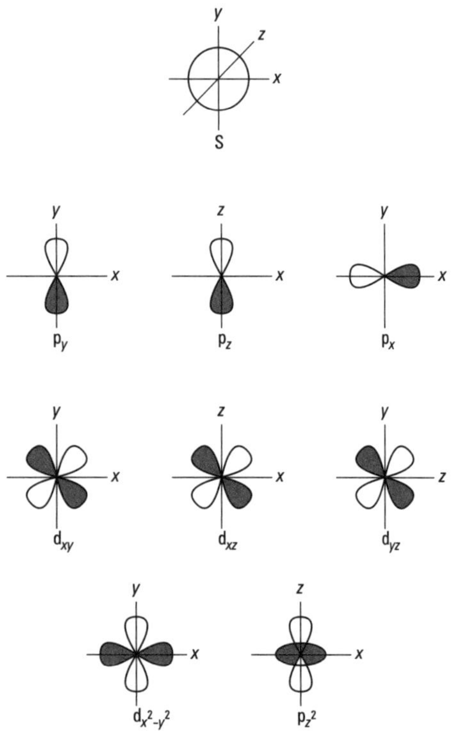

Electronic configuration

It is often difficult to recollect the order of filling of the electronic structures of atoms of different elements. Fig. 65.7 shows the usual order of filling of the orbitals of an atom according to the Aufbau principle (lowest energy first). However, a simple mnemonic exists to facilitate the correct order for each element in the Periodic Table (Fig. 65.8). In order to use the mnemonic all you need to remember is that:

- s orbitals can have up to $2\,e^-$
- p orbitals can have up to $6\,e^-$
- d orbitals can have up to $10\,e^-$
- f orbitals can have up to $14\,e^-$.

Fig. 65.6 Atomic orbitals.

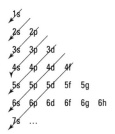

Fig. 65.8 Mnemonic for electronic configuration determination based on the Aufbau principle.

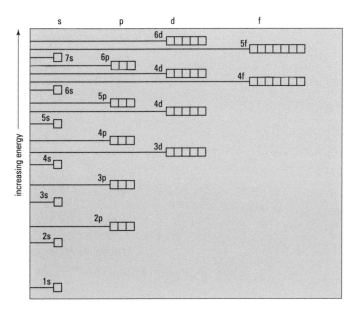

Fig. 65.7 Electronic configuration.

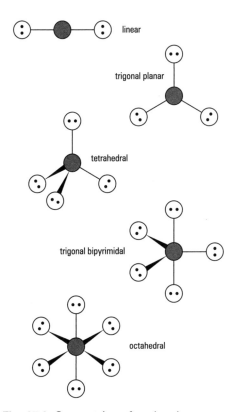

Fig. 65.9 Geometries of molecules.

Then, it is simply a case of addition. In general terms, the order of electron filling is as follows (simply translating the mnemonic into an order):

1s 2s 2p 3s 3p 4s 3d 4p 5s 4d 5p 6s 4f 5d 6p 7s ...

For example, the atomic number of calcium is 20 (corresponding to 20 electrons). Therefore the electronic configuration is:

$$1s^2 \ 2s^2 \ 2p^6 \ 3s^2 \ 3p^6 \ 4s^2$$

Valence shell electron pair repulsion (VSEPR) theory

This is used to predict the shape of molecules. In order to be able to predict the geometry (or shape) of a molecule several simple steps are required. For example, consider the case of $\underline{Br}F_3$. In this case we have indicated by underlining that the central atom is bromine. The first step is to determine the number of valence electrons for bromine; this is done by establishing the electron configuration for bromine, i.e. $1s^2 \ 2s^2 \ 2p^6 \ 3s^2 \ 3p^6 \ 4s^2 \ 3d^{10} \ 4p^5$. We can determine that the number of outer electrons is seven (from $4s^2$ and $4p^5$). We then determine how many atoms are attached to the central bromine atom – the answer is three. By simple addition we have $7 + 3 = 10$ electrons. We know that two electrons are required per bond; therefore we have enough electrons for five bonds. Then, it is simply the case to determine a geometry that allows for five bonds to be at the maximum distance from each other. Commonly, five different arrangements of atoms are found: linear, trigonal planar, tetrahedral, trigonal bipyramidal and octahedral. These arrangements are shown in Fig. 65.9. We can therefore see that the geometry of BrF_3 is trigonal bipyramidal. VSEPR also works for anions and cations using the same procedure. For a cation, a positively charged species, simply deduct one electron from the total; similarly for an anion, a negatively charged species, add one electron to the total. In all cases the total number of electrons obtained will be an even number.

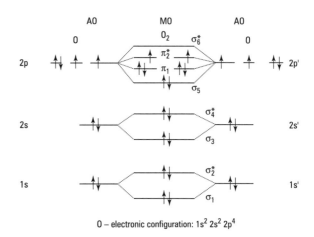

0 – electronic configuration: $1s^2\ 2s^2\ 2p^4$

Fig. 65.10 Molecular orbital diagram for oxygen.

Molecular orbital diagrams

Molecular orbital diagrams (see Fig. 65.10) are required in the study of chemical bonding. For a diatomic molecule these consist of two atomic orbitals (AOs) and two molecular orbitals (MOs). In the case of the two MOs, one is the bonding MO and the other the anti-bonding MO. An asterisk (*) is used to represent an anti-bonding MO. Bonding MOs (of lower energy) are always occupied first. Two types of MO are shown, σ and π, using oxygen, O_2, as an example. The first task is to determine the electronic configuration for each oxygen atom, i.e. $1s^2\ 2s^2\ 2p^4$. An outline of the MO diagram is constructed such that one AO is located on the left-hand side of the page and the other on the right-hand side (the use of $'$ indicates that a different AO is represented) with the MOs positioned in the centre (bonding MOs in the lowest position). You then have an MO diagram composed of three different energy levels corresponding to the 1s, 2s and 2p orbitals. Then, by simply adding the correct number of electrons into the two AOs first, total up the number of electrons. Electrons are then placed into the MO in the following sequence: lowest available position first; and then, individual electrons prior to pairing of electrons. The completed diagram is shown in Fig. 65.10 where all solid lines (in both the AO and MO positions) represent places where up to two electrons can be paired up (dashed lines simply indicate association with a particular AO). Arrows ($\uparrow\downarrow$) indicate that the electrons are spinning (paired electrons have opposite spins). The numbering of bonding and anti-bonding MOs is merely for numerical sequencing and has no other significance. It is also worth noting that O_2 has unpaired electrons in the anti-bonding MO, i.e. π_2*.

Sources for further study

Anon. (2009) *ChemDraw 12.0*. CambridgeSoft Corp., Cambridge, USA. Available: http://www. cambridgesoft.com/ Last accessed 05/03/10. [Commercial structure drawing program: free trial download available.]

Anon. (2009) *ChemSketch 12.0*. Available: http://www. acdlabs.com/download/chemsk Last accessed 05/03/10. [Free download for personal and academic use.]

Anon. (2009) *Symyx Draw*. Available: http://symyx.com/downloads Last accessed 05/03/10. [Free download for personal and academic use.]

Study exercises

65.1 Convert the following abbreviated formulae to structural formulae:

(a) BuOH

(b) $PhCH_2Br$

(c) Pr^iNH_2

(d) AcOEt

(e) TsCl

65.2 Convert the following structural formulae to bond-line formulae:

(a) $CH_3CH_2CH(OH)CH_3$

(b) $(CH_3)_3Cl$

(c) $(CH_3CH_2)_2C=O$

(d) $CH_3COCH_2COOCH_2CH_3$

(e)

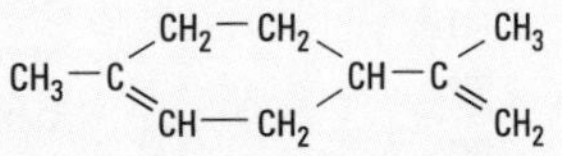

65.3 Using VSEPR theory, predict the shapes of the following molecules:

(a) $AlCl_3$

(b) H_2O

(c) BeF_2

(d) SF_6

(e) IF_5

Chemometrics has been defined as the chemical discipline that uses mathematical and statistical methods to design or select optimal measurement procedures and experiments and to provide maximum chemical information by analysing chemical data (Kowalski, 1978). It can assist with (i) the planning of experiments, and (ii) the manipulation and interpretation of large data sets. Some aspects of chemometrics can be done using an appropriate spreadsheet but the majority of applications require the use of dedicated software. The fundamental principles of most of the processes involved in chemometrics are those of statistics. You are therefore advised to become familiar with the material in Chapters 63 and 64 before proceeding.

When carrying out any experimental work, e.g. an undergraduate practical, you should always read the entire practical script before starting the experimentation. This is important as it allows you to plan each step of the process and to organise space and time to perform the experiment. This initial planning is further complicated in project work and research projects when, often, there is no laboratory script to follow. In these situations, you finally come down to planning the initial experiments after background research (e.g. reading the appropriate scientific literature on the subject area to be investigated), purchasing/ obtaining the appropriate chemicals/reagents, etc. (see also Box 29.1). It is at this stage that chemometrics can be of some assistance. Assuming that you are able to identify the dependent variables in the experiment, then you can apply 'experimental design' which allows you to gain the maximum amount of knowledge about the system you are investigating from a limited number of experiments.

Once the experimental work has been completed you then need to consider how to interpret the results, i.e. how to maximise the chemical information inherent in the data. Initial attempts are often centred around plotting the data, to visualise trends and to allow conclusions to be drawn. The simplest form of data visualisation is simply to tabulate the results (Chapter 61). As an example, if a class of students has determined the melting point of naphthalene, it is a relatively simple matter to tabulate the data (see Table 66.1). One possibility for the data is then to calculate the mean and standard deviation. Another approach would be to plot the data as a histogram, as in Fig. 66.1, so we are then able to make a visual interpretation of the quality of this univariate (one-variable) data.

However, what if we had more than one variable to consider? In other words, we have multivariate data. For example, what if we want to identify trends in the properties of a range of organic molecules? The variables we might want to consider could be: melting point, boiling point, M_r, solubility in a solvent and vapour pressure. We can, of course, tabulate the data, as before, but this does not allow us to consider any trends in the data. To do this we need to be able to plot the data. However, once we exceed three variables (which we need to be able to plot in three dimensions) it becomes impossible to produce a straightforward plot. It is in this context that chemometrics offers a solution, reducing the dimensionality to a smaller number of dimensions

Table 66.1 Melting points for naphthalene

Student	m.pt. (°C)
A	79
B	81
C	80
D	77
E	80
F	80
G	79
H	76
I	81
J	80
K	79
L	78
M	82
N	81

Mean melting point of naphthalene is 79.5 °C.

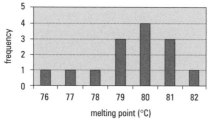

Fig. 66.1 Histogram: melting point of naphthalene.

Useful sources of information

Journals:

Annual Review of Physical Chemistry
Chemical Physics
Chemical Physics Letters
International Journal of Quantum
Chemistry
Journal of Chemical Physics
Journal of Computational Chemistry
Journal of Molecular Structure/
Theochem
Journal of Physical Chemistry
Reviews in Computational Chemistry
Theoretica Chimica Acta

and hence the ability to display multivariate data. The most important technique in this context is called principal component analysis (PCA).

The following discussion highlights only the basic principles. For more detailed information you are advised to consult the literature and dedicated chemometric software packages. It should always be borne in mind, however, that the choice of which variables to optimise should be selected (i) by someone with prior knowledge of the system under investigation, or (ii) after performing preliminary experiments to determine which are the most important variables.

Experimental design

There are two main multivariate optimisation strategies: those based on sequential designs and those based on simultaneous designs.

Sequential design

Sequential optimisation is based on the one-at-a-time approach. The major limitation of this approach is that it assumes that no interaction effects occur between the variables. Unfortunately this is not always the case. A sequential design strategy involves carrying out a few experiments at a time and using the results of those experiments to determine the next experiment to be done. The best known of the sequential design approaches is called the simplex method. A simplex is essentially a geometric figure having a number of vertices equal to one more than the number of variables. For example, if we have two variables, the simplex is a triangle, three variables a tetrahedron, and so on.

Let us consider the case of two variables, x_1 and x_2. An algorithm describes the initial simplex to be performed (Fig. 66.2). By performing experiments 1–3, described by the initial simplex, and recording their responses, the next set of experiments can be described. If we obtain the lowest response for experiment 2, it can therefore be assumed that a higher response would be obtained in the opposite direction. By reflecting point 2, we can obtain point 4. By performing the experiment described by point 4 we obtain its response, thereby perpetuating the simplex.

Four rules can be described for a simplex design:

1. A new simplex is formed by rejecting the point with the lowest response and replacing it with its mirror image across the line defined by the two remaining points.

2. If the new point in the simplex has the lowest response, return to the preceding simplex and create the new simplex by using instead the point with the second-lowest response.

3. If a point is retained in three consecutive simplexes, then it can be assumed that an optimum has been reached. (Note: it may be that this optimum is not the true optimum, but that the simplex has been trapped at a false optimum. In this situation, it is necessary to start the simplex again, or use a modified simplex in which the step size is not fixed but variable, see Fig. 66.3.)

4. If a point is suggested by the simplex algorithm that is beyond the limit of the variables, i.e. it is beyond the safe working limits of an instrument, then the point is rejected and an artificially low response is assigned to it, and the simplex is continued with rules 1–3.

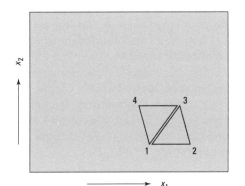

Fig. 66.2 Simplex optimisation.

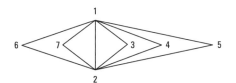

Fig. 66.3 Step-size simplex.

Box 66.1 Example of a two-level factorial design

The recovery of phenols by liquid–liquid extraction, from 1 litre of river water, and subsequent analysis by high-performance liquid chromatography is to be optimised. It has been determined that the following are critical to achieving an optimum extraction: the volume of extraction solvent, the mass of salt added and the pH of the water sample. Therefore, a 2^3 design is required. The experimental levels are: volume of extraction solvent (5 and 50 mL); mass of salt added (0.0 and 1.0 g); and pH (4 and 7). The coded values for the experiment are shown in Table 66.2. The +1 values represent the higher value, e.g. pH 7, while −1 represents the lower value, e.g. pH 4. The number of experiments can be reduced if a fractional factorial design is used. For example, in this situation the fractional factorial design would become $2^{3-1} = 4$ experiments. In this situation the experiments labelled with an asterisk in Table 66.2 would be done.

Simultaneous design

In a simultaneous approach the relationship between variables and results is studied as follows: carry out an appropriate design, apply a mathematical model to the design, and then apply a response surface method to the data. Appropriate designs might be based on factorial designs (full or fractional) or a central composite design. Response surface methods frequently rely on visualisation of the data for interpretation.

Factorial design

In general terms, consider the case of two variables at two levels, e.g. a high value and a low value. This is termed a two-level design or a (full) 2^k factorial design, where k is the number of variables. Therefore we have $2^2 = 4$ experiments to be done. Often the values of the variables are coded; this is done for convenience purposes only. In this example, high and low values will be coded as (+) and (−). Alternatively, it might be the case that the number of variables is three. In this situation we would have a 2^3 factorial design, requiring eight experiments. An example of a two-level factorial design is shown in Box 66.1.

Table 66.2 Two-level factorial design

Experiment	Volume of solvent	salt	pH	Result
1	−1	−1	−1	Y_1
2*	+1	−1	−1	Y_2
3	+1	+1	−1	Y_3
4*	−1	+1	−1	Y_4
5*	−1	−1	+1	Y_5
6	+1	−1	+1	Y_6
7	+1	+1	+1	Y_7
8*	−1	+1	+1	Y_8

The limitation of the two-level factorial design approach is that no estimation of curvature can be determined. In order to take this into account the use of designs with at least three levels is required. Three-level designs are therefore often known as response surface designs. Probably

Table 66.3 Central composite design for three variables

Experiment	Variable 1	Variable 2	Variable 3	Result
Factorial design, 2^3				
1	−1	−1	−1	Y_1
2	+1	−1	−1	Y_2
3	+1	+1	−1	Y_3
4	−1	+1	−1	Y_4
5	−1	−1	+1	Y_5
6	+1	−1	+1	Y_6
7	+1	+1	+1	Y_7
8	−1	+1	+1	Y_8
Star design, $2k$				
9	−α	0	0	Y_9
10	+α	0	0	Y_{10}
11	0	−α	0	Y_{11}
12	0	+α	0	Y_{12}
13	0	0	−α	Y_{13}
14	0	0	+α	Y_{14}
Centre points				
15	0	0	0	Y_{15}
16	0	0	0	Y_{16}

the most important design in this context is the central composite design (CCD). Central composite designs consist of a full (or fractional) factorial design onto which is superimposed a star design. The number of experiments to be done (R) can be worked out as follows:

$$R = 2^k + 2k + n_0 \qquad [66.1]$$

where k is the number of variables, and n_0 is the number of experiments in the centre of the design.

For a design with three variables we would require $[2^3 + (2 \times 3) + 1]$ = 15 experiments. In order to obtain repeatability information it is necessary to run an experiment several times. This is done by performing the centre point experiment twice. The total number of experiments would therefore be 16. The list of experiments is shown in Table 66.3 while Fig. 66.4 shows a diagrammatic representation of the CCD. The CCD is composed of a 3^k factorial design superimposed with a star design ($+α$, $−α$). In order to minimise systematic error (bias) it is necessary to randomise the experimental run order. This is shown in Table 66.4.

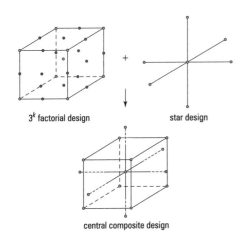

3^k factorial design   star design

central composite design

Fig. 66.4 Central composite design.

Response surface methodology

Response surface methodology allows the relationship between the responses and variables to be quantified, using a mathematical model, and to be visualised. Thus the equation for a straight-line graph can be written as:

$$y = mx + c \qquad [66.2]$$

where m is a constant and c is the intercept. This describes the relationship between a single variable (x) and its response (y). Using the previous example, with three variables (x_1, x_2 and x_3) it is possible to extend this mathematical model.

Table 66.4 A typical randomised CCD

Original experiment (from Table 66.3)	(New) Experiment run order	Variable 1	Variable 2	Variable 3	Result
8	1	−1	+1	+1	Y_1
3	2	+1	+1	−1	Y_2
14	3	0	0	+α	Y_3
6	4	+1	−1	+1	Y_4
12	5	0	+α	0	Y_5
13	6	0	0	−α	Y_6
4	7	−1	+1	−1	Y_7
1	8	−1	−1	−1	Y_8
7	9	1	1	1	Y_9
15	10	0	0	0	Y_{10}
10	11	+α	0	0	Y_{11}
16	12	0	0	0	Y_{12}
9	13	−α	0	0	Y_{13}
2	14	+1	−1	−1	Y_{14}
5	15	−1	−1	+1	Y_{15}
11	16	0	−α	0	Y_{16}

First of all we can consider how each of the variables influences the response (y) in a linear manner. However, the relationship between y and x_1, x_2 and x_3 may not be linear, so it is necessary to consider the possibility of curvature. This is done in terms of a quadratic variable, i.e. a squared dependence (x_1^2, x_2^2 and x_3^2). Finally, it is also important to consider the effects of possible interactions between the variables, $x_1 \rightarrow x_2 \rightarrow x_3$, i.e. $x_1 x_2$, $x_1 x_3$ and $x_2 x_3$. The overall general equation can therefore be written as:

$$Y = b_0 + b_1 x_1 + b_2 x_2 + b_3 x_3 + b_4 x_1^2 + b_5 x_2^2 + b_6 x_3^2 + b_7 x_1 x_2 +$$

$$b_8 x_1 x_3 + b_9 x_2 x_3 \qquad [66.3]$$

where b_0 is the intercept parameter and $b_1 - b_9$ are the regression coefficients for linear, quadratic and interaction effects.

This equation can be analysed using multiple linear regression and tested for statistical significance at, for example, the 95% confidence interval (see p. 518). In addition, the response can be explored by plotting a three-dimensional graph. Unfortunately, in the above example, three variables are present. This immediately constrains what it is possible to plot on the graph (one of the axes must be the response). One way to select the two variables to plot is by considering their statistical significance and then selecting two variables which are significant at the 95% confidence interval. An alternative approach might be simply to plot the two variables you might wish to discuss in your experimental report. A typical response surface is shown in Fig. 66.5. It can be seen that the 'time' variable has a maximum at 8–12 min while the 'temperature' variable has a maximum at 160–180 °C. Further experiments might be carried out at these two maxima to determine the repeatability of the approach. However, it is necessary to plot all variables consecutively to identify all maxima.

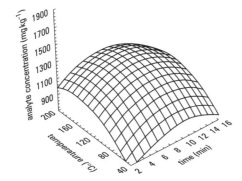

Fig. 66.5 Example of a response surface.

In general, it is important to consider the following issues when carrying out an experimental design:

- Carry out repeat measurements for a particular combination of variables, to determine the repeatability of the approach.

- To remove systematic error (bias), you should randomise the order in which experiments are done (p. 209).

- It is important to eliminate intervariable effects (confounding), i.e. the situation where one variable is interrelated to another.

- Often, the large number of experiments to be carried out makes it impossible to run all of them on the same day. If this happens run your experiments in discrete groups or 'blocks'.

Principal component analysis

The use of modern automated instrumentation allows the acquisition of large amounts of chemical data. As well as simply tabulating the data, other forms of 'analysis' are required to interrogate the chemical information contained within the data. One such approach, enabling the simplification of large data sets by reducing the number of independent variables, is principal component analysis (PCA). The basis of this approach is:

- To reduce the number of original independent variables into new axes, so-called 'principal components', PCs, each of which can be estimated unambiguously. The data contained in these new PCs, and which are expressed as 'scores', are uncorrelated with each other.

- To express, in a few PCs, the amount of variation in the data.

- To have each new PC express a decreasing amount of variation.

An example of the application of PCA is shown in Box 66.2.

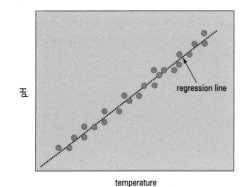

Fig. 66.6 Determination of principal component 1.

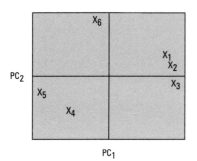

Fig. 66.7 Principal component analysis.

Box 66.2 Example of principal component analysis

Consider a chemical reaction where reactants, X and Y, produce product Z. The yield of Z is dependent upon the temperature of the reaction and its pH. And suppose that the reaction has been carried out by a class of students, providing a large amount of data. By plotting temperature against pH (Fig. 66.6), we can identify a single new variable, PC_1, which obviously contains aspects of pH and temperature, i.e.

$$PC_1 = a(\text{temperature}) + b(\text{pH}) \qquad [66.4]$$

PC_1 can then be used to replace the original two variables. In addition, the direction of PC_1 indicates where the greatest variation in the data lies. The other information that can be obtained is the scatter of the data on either side of the regression line. This is due to random variation rather than a trend. In this example therefore it is not possible to extract any further PCs.

In eqn [66.4], the coefficients a and b indicate the relative importance of the two variables to PC_1, and are called factor loadings. In general, therefore, the plotting of factor loadings between any two PCs can provide useful information as to the relationship of variables to the PCs. Fig. 66.7 shows such a plot. It is seen that variables 1–3 contribute strongly (positively) and variable 5 (negatively) to PC_1. Variable 6 contributes strongly to PC_2, whereas variable 4 contributes significantly to both PCs.

Sources for further study

Beebe, K.R., Pell, R.J. and Seasholz, M.B. (1998) *Chemometrics: A Practical Guide*. Wiley, Chichester.

Brereton, R.G. (2003) *Chemometrics: Data Analysis for the Laboratory and Chemical Plant*. Wiley, Chichester.

Brereton, R.G. (2007) *Applied Chemometrics for Scientists*. Wiley, Chichester.

Brereton, R.G. (2009) *Chemometrics for Pattern Recognition*. Wiley, Chichester.

Miller, J.N. and Miller, J.C. (2005) *Statistics and Chemometrics for Analytical Chemistry*, 5th edn.

Prentice Hall, Harlow.
[Gives detailed coverage of calibration methods and the validity of analytical measurements.]

Otto, M. (2007) *Chemometrics: Statistics and Computer Application in Analytical Chemistry*, 2nd edn. Wiley, Chichester.

Steiner, E. (2008) *The Chemistry Maths Book*, 2nd edn. Oxford University Press, Oxford.

Varmuza, K. and Filzmoser, P. (2009) *Introduction to Multivariate Statistical Analysis in Chemometrics*. CRC Press, Boca Raton.

Study exercises

66.1 Search the scientific literature and find a journal article in which a factorial design or central composite design has been used to optimise a set of variables. Consider how they selected the boundaries of their chosen variables.

66.2 Search the scientific literature and find a journal article in which a principal component analysis has been used to interrogate data and identify patterns within the data. Consider how the visualisation of data using PCA may be beneficial.

66.3 Consider how to might use either optimisation or pattern recognition techniques in your work, e.g. research project.

A chemist is normally visualised as someone in a white laboratory coat performing an experiment. However, some chemists never actually go into a 'wet chemical' laboratory but utilise computers to perform experiments.

Why do chemistry on computers?

- Safety: invariably all laboratory experiments carry some risk, associated with the chemicals or apparatus to be used. It is usual to perform a COSHH assessment (p. 142) prior to experimental work. Computational chemistry allows the user to carry out work on 'dangerous' chemicals with no risk!

- Cost: apart from the financial outlay on a computer and associated peripherals together with the appropriate software, no further costs are involved, unlike the experimental laboratory where most chemicals require disposal after use.

- Understanding: computational chemistry has the ability to provide a basis for understanding chemical principles.

Although chemistry has always been primarily about experiments in the laboratory, it is also true that molecular models and calculations have been essential parts of the chemist's toolkit for a very long time. The pioneering computational chemists often had little more than home-made molecular models and their knowledge of maths and chemistry to help them to understand the link between basic physical laws and the properties of different molecules. Although there were some spectacular early successes, such as the first insights into the structures of DNA (Watson and Crick) and proteins (Pauling and Ramachandran), computational chemistry as a whole was held back by the sheer complexity of molecules. However, the twentieth century saw two great advances that have transformed the power of computational chemistry to solve real world problems. The first was the development of quantum mechanics, which provided the essential mathematical framework for accurate prediction of the behaviour of molecules. The second was the development of cheap and fast computers, which have provided the essential number-crunching power needed for almost all modern computational chemistry.

Today, many chemists do all their research at the computer, and computational chemistry has become an essential part of many undergraduate courses. The field has grown to include a number of overlapping areas. Although the names of the different branches are often used quite loosely and interchangeably we can identify a number of sub-disciplines within computational chemistry.

Quantum mechanics

Now almost 100 years old, quantum mechanics is a mathematical description of molecules on their own terms; where the rules of the universe appear shockingly different to those of the everyday world that we are used to. In its early days, only geniuses like Schrödinger and Dirac could make use of quantum mechanics, because of its sheer difficulty. However, many years of development have produced computer programs that do almost all of the hard work, allowing even novices to 'borrow' the knowledge and skill of the writers of the program. There are

---

Computational chemistry uses commercially available software to enhance chemical knowledge.

Definitions

An **ab initio method** is a quantum-mechanical approach which attempts to calculate, from first principles, solutions to the Schrödinger wave equation.

Molecular mechanics describes a system in which the energy depends only on the nuclei present.

Quantum mechanics describes a molecular system in which both electrons and nuclei are involved.

A **semi-empirical method** is a type of quantum-mechanical theory that incorporates information derived from experimental data.

a number of different types of quantum calculations. Probably the most widely used method at the moment is density functional theory, or DFT. This is a general purpose quantum method that can be used to calculate the properties of almost any molecule, which provides the best compromise between speed and accuracy for many applications. Other important flavours of quantum mechanics include Hartree–Fock (HF), which is similar to DFT but a bit more limited in scope, and semi-empirical methods, which are much faster than DFT and HF, but also much more limited in their versatility and power. Quite a few quantum chemistry programs are now available; most of them are commercial products, and their power and 'user-friendliness' are quite variable. Most of these programs have been developed over several decades, and are capable of several different types of calculation, including DFT, HF and semi-empirical. The main commercial quantum chemistry packages used by researchers include **Amsterdam Density Functional (ADF), Gaussian, Spartan** and **Turbomole**. These have broadly similar capabilities and performance, although each has its own special strengths. Such programs also vary in their degree of 'user-friendliness'. For example, not all of them have built-in graphical user interfaces (known as a GUI); in the case of Gaussian, for example, the GUI comes as an optional extra called **GaussView**. Several non-commercial graphics programs such as **Moldraw** and **Molden** can be used with one or more of these quantum chemistry programs. Also worthy of mention here is **Hyperchem**; although not as powerful as Gaussian or ADF, Hyperchem is more user-friendly, and as it can perform a range of quantum calculations it is often preferred for teaching purposes.

Molecular mechanics

The main limitation of quantum mechanics is the size of the calculations. Calculations on typical molecules might take several days to run on a desktop computer, while larger molecules such as small proteins need a supercomputer. Therefore, many types of molecule are still beyond the practical reach of routine quantum calculations, and we need a faster method in order to be able to model these systems. Molecular mechanics provides a much simpler treatment of chemical bonds, which is very much faster and so can look at much bigger molecules. The penalty is that molecular mechanics fails when we are interested in properties of molecules that depend on their quantum nature; for example, chemical reactions. However, molecular mechanics is very useful when we are interested in the structures of molecules, or how the energy changes with conformation. This area is often called molecular modelling, and it relies heavily on graphical interfaces to allow the user to build and edit molecules. As with quantum mechanics, many different molecular mechanics programs are available. Some of these are used extensively in industry, particularly by drug companies, and so tend to be quite expensive (tens of thousands of pounds!). Examples of these commercial packages include **Discovery Studio** by Accelrys and **Sybyl** by Tripos. Also worth mentioning here is **Hyperchem**, which again provides a good introduction to the area at much lower cost. Many academics use **Gromacs**, which is a powerful molecular mechanics program available as open source software, and **DeepView**, which is a protein homology modelling program, freely available from the Swiss Institute of Bioinformatics.

What can calculations tell us?

In principle, quantum calculations can tell you almost anything you might wish to know about a molecule. In practice, of course, some properties are much easier to calculate than others. The three main properties which are routinely calculated are:

- *Molecular geometries.* This is the most widely calculated property. Geometries can be obtained by both quantum and molecular mechanics. For many small molecules, the calculated geometry can often be as good as an experimental geometry (e.g. an X-ray crystal structure). However, an important consideration for all but the simplest of cases is that molecules are not rigid, but flexible; in particular, some of the bonds can show rotation. In this case, the molecule may have more than one stable geometry. The problem is then to find the most realistic model. The structure with the lowest possible energy is called the **global minimum** and other stable structures are called **local minima**. As modellers, we would like to find the global minimum; but as the molecule grows in size and complexity, it becomes increasingly more difficult to find the one global minimum in a large set of possible local minima. It is worth remembering that molecules in solution do not sit rigidly in their global minimum structures. Instead, the structure of each individual molecule continually cycles through all of the allowed conformations, spending most time around the global minimum. This type of process can be modelled through a special type of calculation called **molecular dynamics (MD)**. MD simulates how the structure of a molecule changing over time. Since MD simulations require a lot of computer time, they are usually run using molecular mechanics rather than quantum mechanics. (See Fig. 67.1 for an illustrative example.)

- *Energies.* Here again, both quantum and molecular mechanics can be used to provide the energies of molecules. However, in this case molecular mechanics calculations are more limited; one can only compare energies for the same molecule in different geometries. For example, if you are interested in the energies of different isomers with the same chemical formula, you have to use a quantum method. Nevertheless, molecular mechanics energies can be very useful, for example, in the molecular dynamics simulations mentioned above. Using quantum calculations, we can also access energy-dependent properties of molecules, such as redox potentials, pK_a values, reaction energies, etc.

- *Spectra.* Using reasonably powerful quantum methods, it is possible to calculate many different spectroscopic properties. The most common types of spectroscopic calculation are UV/visible, IR and NMR; all of these can be calculated with reasonable accuracy for many types of molecule. Many other more exotic types of spectrum have been calculated by specialists in the field, for example, photoelectron, microwave and EPR, to name but a few.

It is worth mentioning that there are many more specialist types of modelling in use for different purposes. To give a few examples, protein **homology modelling** is a very useful way of building 3D models for proteins, based on known experimental structures. **Q**uantitative **S**tructure **A**ctivity **R**elationships (QSAR) is an important tool in drug development,

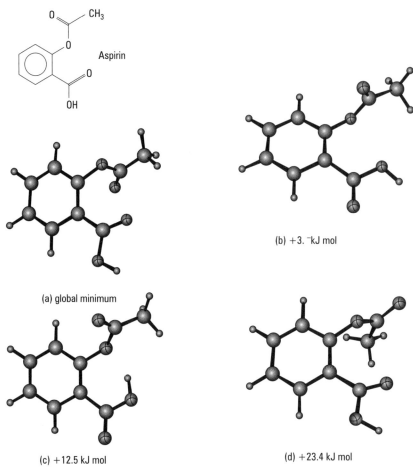

Fig. 67.1 Four minimum energy structures for the aspirin molecule. The geometries were calculated using DFT and the energies are for the gas phase. Structure (**a**) has the lowest energy and is therefore referred to as the global minimum. Structure (**b**) has a slightly higher energy, while structures (**c**) and (**d**) show progressively higher energies. Structure (**b**) corresponds to the experimental solid state structure, as determined by X-ray crystallography; the small energy difference between structures (**a**) and (**b**) could reflect the differences between the solid and gas phases as much as inaccuracies in the calculations. A solution of aspirin would contain all four isomers, in proportions related to their relative energies.

where the structures of known drug molecules are used to develop models that allow the prediction of new biologically active compounds. Chemical engineers routinely use simulation programs to model the behaviour of chemical reactions under different industrial processing conditions.

The computational laboratory

Like all laboratory classes it is important to go prepared so that you will get the most out of your time in the laboratory. This might include background reading, making an outline of the experimental procedure, a sketch (or photocopy) of the chemical structure of all molecules to be worked on, and a plan of how you will draw each molecule – obviously the more complex molecules may require more thought than a simple molecule. Once there, it is important to:

- Get a comfortable chair – you may be sitting in it for quite a while. Make yourself feel at ease and relax.

- Plan your work – a considerable amount of time in the laboratory will be spent constructing models, setting up calculations and evaluating results. It is therefore important to maximise your time on the computer by planning in advance.

- Make sure that enough computer running time is available – some processes can be lengthy.

- Follow all instructions carefully – remember that a computer carries out your instructions.

- Examine all results carefully – do not accept everything the computer prints out/displays. Question the results yourself – do they make sense? If not recheck your initial data entry.

- Save all your results for rechecking by yourself at a later date or for assessment by your tutor.

Computer software

A typical software package used to perform computational chemistry should be able to:

- Build and display molecules.

- Optimise the structure of molecules.

- Investigate the reactivity of molecules.

- Generate and view orbitals and electronic plots.

- Evaluate chemical pathways and mechanisms.

- Study the dynamic behaviour of molecules.

It is inappropriate to describe any particular software system. Nevertheless, all software is usually accompanied by a user manual or a 'help' file to make the use of commercial software packages user-friendly.

Text references

Watson, J.D. and Crick, F.C.H. (1953) *Nature*, **171**, 737.

Pauling, L., Corey, R.B. and Branson, H.R. (1951) *Proc. Natl. Acad. Sci. USA*, **31**, 205.

Ramachandran, G.N., Ramakrishnan, C. and Sasisekharan, V. (1963) *J. Mol. Biol.*, **7**, 95.

Sources for further study

Bachrach, S.M. (2007) *Computational Organic Chemistry*. John Wylie & Sons Ltd, Chichester.

Filszar, S. (2008) *Atomic Charges, Bond Properties and Molecular Energies*. John Wylie & Sons Ltd, Chichester.

Guha, R. and Bender, A. (eds) (2010) *Computational Approaches in Cheminformatics and Bioinformatics*. John Wylie & Sons Ltd, Chichester.

Hayward, D.O. (2002) *Quantum Mechanics for Chemists*. Royal Society of Chemistry, Cambridge.

Heine, T., Joswig, J.-O. and Gelessus, A. (2009) *Computational Chemistry Workbook: Learning Through Examples*. John Wylie & Sons Ltd, Chichester.

Hinchcliffe, A. (2008) *Molecular Modelling for Beginners*, 2nd edn. John Wylie & Sons Ltd, Chichester.

Jensen, F. (2006) *Introduction to Computational Chemistry*. 2nd edn. John Wylie & Sons Ltd, Chichester.

Leach, A.R. (2001) *Molecular Modelling: Principles and Applications*, 2nd edn. Pearson Education Ltd, Prentice Hall, Harlow.

Leszczynski, J. and Shukla, M. (eds) (2010) *Practical Aspects of Computational Chemistry*. Springer Publishing Co., New York.

Lewars, E. (2003) *Computational Chemistry: Introduction to the Theory and Applications of Molecular and Quantum Mechanics*. Kluwer Academic Publishers Group, The Netherlands.

Puzyn, T., Leszczynski, J. and Cronin, M.T.D. (2009) *Recent Advances in QSAR Studies: Methods and Applications*. Springer Publishing Co., New York.

Young, D.C. (2001) *Computational Chemistry: A Practical Guide for Applying Techniques to Real World Problems*. John Wylie & Sons Ltd, Chichester.

Study exercise

67.1 Figure 67.2 shows the energy of the chlorine molecule as a function of the Cl–Cl distance. The solid curve and points were calculated by DFT, and the dotted curve and open points were calculated by molecular mechanics (MM). The DFT curve reaches a minimum at 2.05 Å, and the MM curve reaches a minimum at 1.98 Å. The experimental Cl_2 bond length is 1.99 Å.

- Why are the curves very different when the Cl–Cl distance is greater than ~2.1 Å, and which one is correct?

- Why does the energy increase very rapidly as the Cl–Cl distance drops below 2 Å?

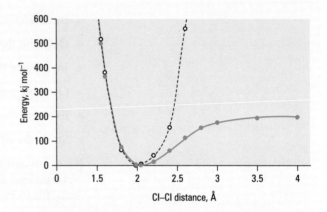

Fig. 67.2 Plot of energy against inter-atomic distance for the Cl_2 molecule.

Answers to study exercises

We have attempted to provide an 'answer' to all of the study exercises. Where the question is open-ended and no 'correct' answer can be given, we have provided a *Tip* which should either help with your general approach, indicating which resources are worth consulting, or provide a pointer to relevant material within the book. Where a non-numerical question has a 'correct' answer, we have provided a model text-based answer. If a calculation is involved, we have shown the steps involved and have indicated the **correct answer underlined in bold**.

1 The importance of transferable skills

1.1 *Tips:* Where you feel confident about skills you have learned at school, take care to consider whether they might need to be upgraded for university/college use. When thinking about opportunities for developing skills, remember that these may occur outside university, perhaps in work or social contexts.

1.2 *Tip:* Possible keywords/phrases for a Web search include: chemistry skills, C&IT skills, numeracy skills, study skills, time management.

1.3 *Tip:* You could create a grid to record your thoughts, with column headings 'University'; 'Work' and 'Social' and rows for 'Short term', 'Medium term' and 'Long term'. Short term and medium term could refer to your time at university, while long term could refer to after graduation.

2 Managing your time

2.1 *Tips:* Model your spreadsheet on Fig. 2.1. It isn't too difficult to fill in details at the end of each day either directly into the spreadsheet or on a printed version. You will need to collect information for at least a week and possibly longer before you see patterns emerging.

2.2 *Tips:* It is important to include both social and study-related activities on your lists. Short-term lists deal with issues of the day or week; medium-term for the term or semester and longer-term for one year onwards. Relate each of these lists to appropriate goals you may have over these timescales.

2.3 *Tips:* This task could be related to (a) your self-analysis of transferable skills (Chapter 1), or (b) to some large task such as carrying out a final-year project. In the latter case, for example, there are small jobs that can be done as you proceed with the larger task, such as writing parts of the Introduction or compiling a list of references, and these will reduce time pressure towards the end of the task.

3 Working with others

3.1 *Tips:* Think about your contributions to past group activities while doing this exercise, and, if necessary, get feedback from friends and colleagues. You may feel that you fit into more than one 'natural' role: this is quite often the case.

3.2 *Tip:* This exercise might best be associated with a specific teamwork activity, but this need not be restricted to study – group contributions with clubs, societies or in employment are equally valid. Strategies for improvement will depend on your identified weaknesses. For example, if you felt too shy to contribute effectively, you might want to practise public speaking (see Chapter 15) or attend an assertiveness workshop.

3.3 *Tip:* Columns 4 and 5 of Table 3.1 are relevant, particularly if you are able to identify a 'natural' role or roles for yourself in group situations (as in exercise 3.1). Can you relate your strengths and weaknesses to specific events that have occurred during teamwork, and might you handle the situation differently in future?

4 Taking notes from lectures and texts

4.1 *Tips:* If you are used to using a particular note-taking method that seems to work well, you may feel reluctant to experiment. Try out the new method by taking notes at a seminar, tutorial or meeting where it will not matter so much if the technique does not work well at the first attempt.

4.2 *Tip:* Make a list of any missing notes or handouts and ask a colleague if you can work from their notes to fill in these gaps.

4.3 *Tip:* To compare methods, test your recall some time afterwards. Take a blank sheet of paper and see what you can write about each topic.

5 Learning and revising

5.1 *Tips:* When constructing your revision timetable, remember the following important points:

- Break large topics into 'bite-sized' units.
- Mix up hard or less interesting topics with those you enjoy revising (don't ignore them).
- Keep an appropriate balance between work and relaxation.
- Offer yourself rewards if work targets are completed.

5.2 *Tips:* You may wish to keep one of the past papers (preferably a recent one) aside to use in a mock exam. Remember that learning objectives can be just as important as exam papers in helping you to revise.

5.3 *Tips:* Read through the list of active revision tips on pp. 28–29 and decide which might work best for you. Carry out a trial of the method with one of your topics where the material has seemed difficult to learn. Experiment until you arrive at a solution that works, remembering (a) that different techniques might work best in different subjects and (b) a little variety might make the revision process more interesting.

Answers to study exercises

6 Curriculum options, assessments and exams

6.1 *Tip:* Some questions to ask yourself about past exam performances... Did you prepare well enough? Did you run out of time during the exam? Did you spend too long on a particular question or section, and have to rush another? Were your answers direct and at the appropriate depth? Did you misinterpret any questions, or miss out part of any answers? Were your writing skills, including planning, up to the standard required?

6.2 *Tip:* When revising, try to find a topic you find hard to understand and see whether your colleague has approached it in the same way as you. If not, you may be able to learn from this.

6.3 *Tip:* Discuss your tactics with a colleague sitting the same exam. What topics do you agree are likely to come up?

7 Preparing your curriculum vitae

7.1 *Tip:* This exercise might be attempted with a friend you can trust to give you a frank opinion. Remember that your personal qualities can be developed in both curricular and extra-curricular activities.

7.2 *Tip:* Working with a friend or group from your class, compare notes on how you have organised your CVs and then modify your own CV, taking on board good ideas from your peers. Create a physical file for your revised CV and add handwritten notes, updating it as and when required.

7.3 *Tip:* Use the 'Prospects' website noted in the sources for further study to gain ideas before your appointment with the careers service. The library or careers resource centre may have useful information, often accessible *via* the Web.

8 Finding and citing published information

8.1 (a) The Dewey Decimal Classification system; the US Library of Congress system; or other, as appropriate.
(b) *Nature*: Dewey: 505.0942; Library of Congress: Q1.N3; (or other, as appropriate). Note: the 'Per' or 'per' that may precede these numbers refers to the fact that this is a periodical, rather than a book.
(c) *Tip:* Answer as appropriate – this will depend on the layout of your particular library.
(d) (i) 'A structure for deoxyribose nucleic acid'; (ii) 'C_{60}: Buckminsterfullerene'.

8.2 *Tips:* The main point here is that methods of writing down references are diverse. You should also find that the details recorded are the same, although they may be in a different order or font style. You must pay attention to the *precise* instructions given for your course, to ensure that you get this right when writing up a project report or dissertation.

8.3 *Tips:* Three possible sites are:
(a) SI Units: http://physics.nist.gov/cuu/Units/index.html (last accessed 01/03/10).
(b) Diels–Alder reaction: http://www.chempensoftware.com/reactions/RXNl70.htm (last accessed 01/03/10) is a starting point.
(c) melting point determination: for example, http://www.wpi.edu/Academics/Depts/Chemistry/Courses/General/meltingpoint.html (last accessed 01/03/10).

8.4 *Tips:* When writing a handwritten essay, the variant of the Vancouver method in which references are listed in the order cited might be the most convenient to use, because you could write down all the references cited on a separate sheet as you wrote out the essay. However, if you felt that it was important for the reader to see the author(s) and publication dates of the papers, then the Harvard method might be more appropriate – however, you would need to wait until the essay was fully written before organising the literature cited section in author and date order. In a word processed review, you might prefer the Vancouver method as this might allow the text to flow more smoothly without being interrupted by lists of author names and dates. On the other hand, the Harvard system is easier to use as you write with a word processor, because you can simply 'slot' each new reference into the correct place in the list. In an academic journal, it might be assumed that the readership would want to know the authors and dates of the references cited, so the Harvard system would probably be the most appropriate. In contrast, the journal *Nature* uses the Vancouver system in order to present important new scientific advances to a wide audience. *Nature* readers want to be able to assimilate each paper's findings rapidly without getting distracted by citation details.

9 Evaluating information

9.1 (a) P; (b) P; (c) P; (d) S; (e) P; (f) P; (g) P; (h) P; (i) S; (j) P; (where P = primary, S = secondary). Where journals contain both original papers and reviews, we have classed them as primary.

9.2 *Tip:* Discuss with a friend one of the topics. If one of you takes a 'for' stance and the other an 'against' stance, see how many points each of you can make. Remember to try to back up your view with scientific facts.

9.3 *Tip:* Use Box 60.3 as a source to indicate ways in which graphs may be used to misrepresent information. You may find this exercise easier to accomplish with printed graphs. Those on television may not be shown for long enough to allow you to carry out a detailed analysis. Nevertheless, they represent a rich source of material to criticise!

10 Using online resources

10.1 (a) Linus C. Pauling (1901–1994) is famous for winning two undivided Nobel Prizes; the first for Chemistry in 1954 and the second for Peace in 1962. In winning the Nobel Prize for Chemistry he was cited 'for his research into the nature of the chemical bond and its application to the elucidation of the structure of complex substances'. http://nobelprize.org/nobel_prizes/chemistry/laureates/1954/index.html (last accessed 01/03/10).
(b) Dichloromethane (CH_2Cl_2) is also known as methylene chloride. http://www.environment-agency.gov.uk/business/topics/pollution/l 92.aspx (last accessed 01/03/10).
(c) The postal address of the London headquarters of the Royal Society of Chemistry is: Royal Society of Chemistry, Burlington House, Piccadilly, London

W1J 0BA. http://www.rsc.org/AboutUs/contacts/ (last accessed 01/03/10).

10.2 *Tips:* Note the number of hits found for each search engine. Make a note or printout of the top 10 sites located by each search engine. Compare these site listings to reveal the quality of data obtained. Repeat this exercise for meta-search engines. Make lists of the component search engines used by the main meta-search engines to help you devise a strategy for the best coverage of the Internet.

10.3 *Tips:* Within the bookmark editor for your browser, create folders for each of your study courses and then create sub-folders for each module that you are doing. Now use some searches to put relevant bookmarks in each folder. Don't forget to include a folder for transferable skills sites; there are a lot of supportive sites available that are worth visiting.

11 Bioinformatics – Internet resources

11.1 Visit WebElements (http://www.webelements.com/) and identify the following properties of chromium:
(a) melting point (K) is 2180 K or 1907 °C
(b) electronegativity (Pauling) is 1.66
(c) atomic weight is 51.9961
(d) ground state electron configuration is $[Ar].3d^5.4s^1$
(e) atomic number is 24.

11.2 *Tips:*
(a) The latest articles obviously change on a frequent basis. However, it is worth having a look at what is happening in these dedicated electronic chemistry journals.
(b) The Royal Society of Chemistry and American Chemical Society are both professional bodies that work across international boundaries promoting chemistry; both are also major publication houses and have dedicated areas for members. IUPAC is recognised worldwide as the authority on chemical nomenclature, terminology, standardised methods for measurement, atomic weights and other critically evaluated data.
(c) Identify which of the websites listed in Table 11.3 may be useful for you. By gaining some familiarity with each website and bookmarking them on your PC, you will be able to use them in the future, as required.

11.3 By using your login password, obtainable from your own Institution's library, you will gain access to a vast resource of journal material available in html and pdf format from your PC. Your effectiveness in using these searchable databases does require some prior knowledge, so please consult with your librarian for specific guidance.

12 Using spreadsheets

12.1 See the figure below. *Tips:* Depending on the precise method you use, you may need to provide the *Name*, *Values* and *Category Labels* for the *Chart Wizard* or adjust those assumed. When creating the graph, select the 'as new sheet' option when prompted for a *Chart Location*. For printing in black and white, select black and white

hatching/shading options after click-selecting chart segments. Ensure the segments of the chart are labelled (i.e. not the default legend option) using the *Chart/Chart Options* menu.

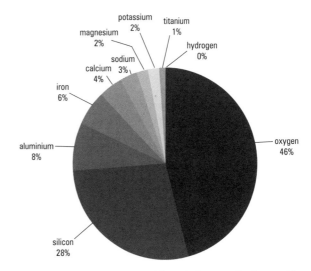

Relative percentage composition of elements in the earth's crust.

12.2 See the figure below. *Tips:* When setting up the spreadsheet, create appropriate formulae in new columns for the transformed data; graph using the '*XY (Scatter)*' option in the Microsoft Excel *Chart Wizard* to make sure the data are correctly spaced on the *x*-axis. Plot time on the *x*-axis and the transformed cell count data on the *y*-axis. You will need to create a separate graph to examine the effects of each transformation, because the *y*-axis scales will be different. Select the *Line None* option for the relevant (log transformed) series on the *Data Series* menu, then use the *Add Trendline* option (linear model) within the *Chart* menu to add a linear regression line (note: this can also be done using the *Regression* command in the *Data Analysis* option on the *Tools* menu, but the procedures required are much more complex). Adjust the chart output to suit, e.g. by changing gridlines, background and legends, before copying and pasting to the MS Word document.

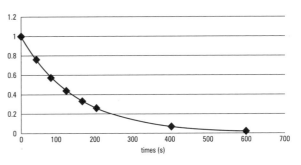

Decomposition of N_2O_5.

12.3 *Tips:* Take care when entering the date data in the spreadsheet. You may need to specify the format of the cells for the date column (*Format* menu, *Cells* option). Highlight all parts of the spreadsheet table including column headers, then use the *Data* menu, *AZ↓ Sort* option to rearrange data. You do not need to fill in all the response boxes and can select 'none' if a box contains criteria from a previous sort.

13 Word processors, databases and other packages

13.1 *Tips:*
(a) Ensure list components are in separate paragraphs; highlight list; from the *Table* menu select *AZ↓ Sort* function; ensure options are set to *paragraphs*, *text*, *ascending*.
(b) From the *Edit* menu, select *Replace* option, then fill in the relevant boxes.
(c) From *Edit* menu, select *Replace* option, then fill in the relevant boxes; select *More ▾* then *Format, Font, Italic*.
(d) From the *View* menu, select *Header and Footer* and use the small on-screen menu to add text and numbering as desired. Formatting commands (e.g. centre) will work in the header and footer boxes. As an alternative for adding page numbers, this can be done from the *Insert* menu, *Page Numbers . . .* option.
(e) Margins can be adjusted from *File* menu, *Page Setup*, *Margins* option.
(f) Select paragraphed text, then use the *Format* menu, *Bullets and Numbering* option, using *Customize* if the option you desire is not displayed within the panel.
(g) Type 'alternative' within a Word page. Ensure cursor is within word (or highlight word); from *Tools* menu select *Language, Thesaurus* options. Perhaps 'option' might be a useful synonym?
(h) From *Tools* menu, select *Spelling and Grammar* to start a spell check. Take care if the checker queries UK spellings (it may be set to accept US spellings). Note: this is *not* a substitute for reading your document – the spell checker will miss typing errors like 'form' instead of 'from'.
(i) For whole document, triple click in left margin to select all, then use *Tools* menu, *Word Count* option. For selected text, highlight (select) the part you wish to count, then carry out same instructions.
(j) While in first document, use *File* menu, *Open* option to open another. You can switch between them using the *Window* menu, where you will see all open documents listed. Note: remember to save changes to all documents when closing down your editing session.

13.2 *Tips:* Although there are several ways to modify tables, you may find it useful to try the following commands (think carefully about their order).
- *Table, Insert Table*
- *Table, Merge Cells*
- *Table, Distribute Columns Evenly*
- *Tables and borders*, modify borders commands (various)

Consult Box 61.2 or use the *Help* feature if you run into problems.

13.3 *Tips:* You might start your search on the networked 'desktop' and icons visible to you when you log on. Use 'help' menus and 'wizards' to investigate how to use the programs, or consult any manuals available in the computer suite.

14 Organising a poster display

14.1 *Tip:* Use Figure 14.1 and the subheadings of Chapter 14 as a starting point for assessing the pros and cons of your designs.

14.2 Ten-point checklist – what makes a good poster presentation?
- ☐ *Title* – is this concise, specific and interesting?
- ☐ *Author(s)* – does the poster show details of the names and addresses of all contributors?
- ☐ *Structure* – is the overall structure clear to the observer, with good use of subheadings?
- ☐ *Flow* – is the layout of the poster clear, in terms of how the audience is expected to 'read' each section?
- ☐ *Content* – does the presentation have a clear introduction, main message and conclusion?
- ☐ *Text* – does the poster contain an appropriate amount of written material in a 'readable' font?
- ☐ *Graphics* – does the poster make good use of diagrams, figures and images?
- ☐ *Size and scale* – does the poster make effective use of the space available?
- ☐ *Colour* – does the presentation use colour effectively?
- ☐ *Conclusion* – is the 'take-home message' clear to the observer?

14.3 *Tip:* you might use the 10-point checklist given above, or your own version from exercise 14.2 to assess selected posters by giving a mark out of 10 for each item in the list. In a group exercise, you can see how your 'scores' compare with those of other students, and discuss items where scores are different.

15 Giving a spoken presentation

15.1 Ten-point checklist – what makes a good spoken presentation?
- ☐ *Introduction* – does the speaker explain the structure and rationale of the topic at the outset?
- ☐ *Audience* – is the material presented at an appropriate level?
- ☐ *Content* – does the presentation cover the topic effectively?
- ☐ *Speed and structure* – are the main elements of the presentation presented clearly, and at an appropriate pace?
- ☐ *Voice* – is the presentation delivered in an engaging, active vocal style?
- ☐ *Audio-visual aids* – does the speaker make good use of visual images (e.g. graphs, photographs, etc.)?

☐ *Image* – does the presenter make good use of body language?

☐ *Notes* – does the speaker use notes to structure the talk, rather than reading from a written text?

☐ *Conclusion* – is a clear 'take-home message' delivered in the final stages of the presentation?

☐ *Questions* – does the presenter deal with questions effectively?

15.2 *Tips:* You could try marking speakers out of 10 for each of the points listed in exercise 15.1 (either using the checklist provided above or your own version), or you could simply prepare a list of the good and bad points of the presentations you have evaluated.

15.3 *Tips:* When evaluating your own performance: (i) remember that most of us are overcritical when viewing ourselves on video, tending to focus on relatively minor points, e.g. facial expression, rather than broader aspects, e.g. clarity of delivery and content; (ii) when giving a talk to a group of fellow students you might ask them to use all or part of the checklist from exercise 15.1 as a way of providing feedback.

16 General aspects of scientific writing

16.1 *Tips:* When brainstorming, think of all aspects of the topic that could be relevant (even if you could not give precise details at this stage). When you meet together, discuss which of your combined ideas would be most important in crafting an answer and what order you might place them in.

16.2 *Tip:* Try to apply what you have learned in the next assignment you write – ask a tutor for specific feedback if you are unsure about whether your technique has improved.

16.3 *Tips:* Use the spelling list to help you when writing and make a conscious effort to memorise the spelling each time you use it. The act of writing the vocabulary list will assist you to memorise new words and their meanings. If you have trouble learning definitions, e.g. terms in chemistry, you could extend these ideas to create a personal glossary of terms and acronyms.

17 Writing essays

17.1 *Tip:* Can you determine what lies behind each question? Some question titles are quite direct, but others ask for information in a more subtle way. Use your imagination to think beyond the immediate question, linking to learning objectives or to other relevant material covered in lectures.

17.2 *Tips:* Compare your ideas with those of a partner, or ask tutors or lecturers what they think of your efforts. A useful adjunct to this exercise is to write the first sentence of your answer to avoid writer's block (p. 122).

17.3 *Tips:* Note that each of the stages (b)–(d) requires a separate 'review' – it is difficult, if not impossible to make a good job of all aspects in a single 'pass' through the text. Ideally, you would reprint the essay between reviews, having made corrections.

18 Reporting practical and project work

18.1 *Tips:* To assimilate the required style for Experimental, you may find it appropriate to read some research papers from the journal section of your library. Note particularly that Experimental is a description of 'what was done', not a set of instructions.

18.2 *Tips:* Again, you may find it appropriate to read some research papers from the journal section of your library to assimilate the normal style for describing research results.

18.3 *Tips:* Abstracts are difficult to write: try to include a synopsis of all the main sections of the paper, including its aims, methods, key results and conclusions. Ignore the word length restriction until you have noted the main points, then try to reduce (or, less likely, expand) your effort to match the requirement.

19 Writing literature surveys and reviews

19.1 Five differences between reviews and papers are:
1. Reviews deal with material in general terms taking an overview, whereas papers tend to look at a focused, single aspect of a topic.
2. The subdivisions are generally not the same – papers usually follow the IERaD format (p. 126), while reviews are structured according to the major components of the topic.
3. There is little or no reference to original data in reviews.
4. There is little *detail* of methods in reviews.
5. They tend to use different reference citation systems, with Harvard (p. 50) most commonly used in papers and Vancouver (p. 50) used in reviews.

19.2 *Tip:* It should be possible to do the second part of study exercise 19.2 online at your library – you may need to enlist the help of library staff if unsure of how to do this.

19.3 *Tip:* Obviously, the Abstract and Conclusions sections will provide information about the key points addressed. It might be helpful to use a highlighter on a photocopied version of the review to note important statements within the main body of the review.

20 Your approach to practical work.

20.1 Possible reasons why practical work might be of value in a university course include:
- practicals reinforce lecture material, in agreement with the adage: 'I hear and I forget, I see and I remember, I do and I understand';
- practical procedures provide students with an opportunity to develop their manual skills and laboratory competences;
- investigative procedures and problem-solving practical exercises enable students to improve their skills in experimental design and application of scientific method;
- practicals enable students to develop their abilities to observe and measure chemical systems, and to record the outcome;

- the results of practical procedures give students an opportunity to develop skills in reporting and presenting 'experiments' in a written format.

20.2 *Tip:* Possible items for aqueous recrystallisation: Bunsen burner, tripod and gauze; two 250 mL conical flasks; anti-bumping granules or boiling stick or glass rod; small watch glass, clock glass; stemless filter funnel: fluted filter paper; charcoal, two-dp balance; spatula; Büchner flask and funnel; rubber collar; filter paper; ice/water bath; water suction pump; drying oven.

20.3 (a) **40**;

(b) 44.266 66, expressed to 4 significant figures = **44.27**;

(c) 0.019 531 25, expressed to 3 significant figures = **0.0195**;

(d) $\underline{\mathbf{1.6 \times 10^5}}$;

(e) 0.0313, expressed to 3 decimal places = **0.031**.

21   Health and Safety

21.1 (a) p. 142;

(b) Fig. 21.1 (p. 142);

(c) Fig. 21.3 (p. 144);

(d) Fig. 21.3 (p. 144).

21.2 *Tip:* The locations of each item will vary, according to the layout of your chosen laboratory. You should ask someone in charge (e.g. lecturer technician, demonstrator or laboratory manager) if you are unable to find any of the items listed.

21.3 *Tip:* Use either your department's chemical hazard information system or an appropriate reference text (e.g. Merck Index or Bretherick) or the online MSDS available.

(a) Ethanol is highly flammable, with a b.pt. 78 °C. Eye protection must be worn. Use in fume cupboard with no naked flames. Water bath or spark proof electric mantle as heat source and reflux apparatus (pp. 173, 174) to prevent loss of solvent during heating.

(b) Sodium oxalate is highly poisonous. Eye protection and gloves must be worn for all operations involving oxalates. Dispose of residual solutions and gloves appropriately, and wash all glassware thoroughly with water.

(c) Sodium hydroxide is highly corrosive, poisonous and an irritant. Protective gloves and safety glasses must be worn when making solutions using solid NaOH. Contact with moisture generates considerable heat so it should always be added in small amounts to a large volume of water.

22   Working with liquids

22.1 (a) Use measuring cylinders (e.g. measure out 700 mL of ethanol using a 1000 mL measuring cylinder and measure out 300 mL of water using a 500 mL measuring cylinder: mix together in a large conical flask or beaker with a capacity of > 1000 mL).

(b) Use a pipette (25.00 mL) with three valve pipette filler. (Fig. 22.2). Using the procedure described in Chapter 41 (p. 302) to transfer conc HCl

(25.00 mL) to water (100 mL by measuring cylinder) in a beaker (250 mL). Stir with a glass rode to ensure complete mixing.

(c) Use a pipettor set to deliver 10 μL to transfer the propanone into the volumetric flask containing distilled water (~20 mL). This prevents loss of propanone by evaporation. Make up to the mark with distilled water using a Pasteur pipette for the final adjustment. Stopper the flask and invert at least eight times to ensure complete mixing.

(d) Use a pipette (25.00 mL) to transfer the NaOH solution to a conical flask (250 mL) and deliver the H_2SO_4 solution from a burette. (See Chapter 41.)

22.2 *Tip:* Box 22.1 (p. 149) gives stepwise details of how to use a pipettor.

23   Basic laboratory procedures I

23.1 *Tip:* Box 23.1 and Box 23.2 give advice on preparing solutions:

(a) volume = 0.25 L: use eqn [23.1] 0.05 = amount (mol) ÷ 0.25, thus amount (mol) = 0.05 × 0.25 = 0.0125 mol; M_r for NaCl = 58.44 g mol^{-1}; convert mol to g by multiplying = 58.44 × 0.0125 = **0.7305 g**.

(b) volume = 0.1 L: use eqn [23.1] 0.02 = amount (mol) ÷ 0.1, thus amount (mol) = 0.02 × 0.1 = 0.002 mol; M_r for KIO_3 = 214.00 g mol^{-1}; convert mol to g by multiplying = 214.00 × 0.002 = **0.4280 g**.

(c) volume = 0.05 L: use eqn [23.1] 0.05 = amount (mol) ÷ 0.05, thus amount (mol) = 0.05 × 0.05 = 0.0025 mol; M_r for $Na_2S_2O_3.5H_2O$ = 248.18 g mol^{-1}; convert mol to g by multiplying = 248.18 × 0.0025 = **0.6205 g**.

(d) volume = 0.25 L: use eqn [23.1] 0.1 = amount (mol) ÷ 0.25, thus amount (mol) = 0.1 × 0.25 = 0.025 mol; M_r for $CuSO_4.5H_2O$ = 249.60 g mol^{-1}; convert mol to g by multiplying = 249.60 × 0.025 = **6.2400 g**.

(e) Note each molecule contains two potassium ions, therefore you need half the number of moles of K_2SO_4 i.e. 0.025 mol; volume = 0.1 L: use eqn. [23.1] 0.025 = amount (mol) ÷ 0.1, thus amount (mol) = 0.025 × 0.1 = 0.0025 mol; M_r for K_2SO_4 = 172.47 g mol^{-1}; convert mol to g by multiplying = 172.47 × 0.0025 = **4.3118 g**.

23.2 *Tip:* For all these calculations you can use $[C_1]V_1 = [C_2]V_2$ as outlined in Box 23.2.

(a) 0.4 × 1.0 = $[C_2]$ × 10; therefore $[C_2]$ = **0.04 M**;

(b) 0.1 × V_1 = 0.02 × 500; therefore V_1 = **100.00 mL**;

(c) $[C_1]$ × 10.00 = 0.001 × 250; therefore $[C_1]$ = **0.025 M**;

(d) 0.02 × 5.00 = 0.001 × V_2; therefore V_2 = **100.00 mL**.

24   Basic laboratory procedures II

24.1 (a) Either (i) conical flask or beaker, stemmed funnel and fluted filter paper or (ii) Büchner flask and funnel, rubber collar, filter paper, water vacuum pump.

(b) Büchner flask and funnel, rubber collar, filter paper, water vacuum pump.

(c) Conical flask, stemless funnel and fluted filter paper, hot plate (to keep filtrate and funnel and filter paper hot to prevent crystallisation.

(d) Hot plate or Bunsen burner, tripod and gauze, conical flask, watch glass (to prevent rapid evaporation of water, anti-bumping precautions.

(e) Reflux set up (p. 265), oil bath or hot plate, anti-bumping precautions.

(f) Ice–$CaCl_2.6H_2O$ bath (see Table 24.2), plastic bowl or beaker, clamp and stand, thermometer.

25   Principles of solution chemistry

25.1   *Tip:* Box 23.2 and Box 24.1 give useful procedures and example calculations for molar concentrations;

(a) 1000 mL of 1.0 M NaCl $= 1.0$ mol L^{-1} thus need 1 mol; M_r NaCl $= 58.44$ g mol^{-1} – weigh out **58.4400 g**.

(b) 1000 mL of 0.2004 M $KMnO_4 = \overline{0.2004}$ mol L^{-1} thus need 0.2004/4 mol $= 0.0501$ mol; M_r for $KMnO_4 = 158.04$ g mol^{-1} – weight out $158.04 \times 0.0501 =$ **7.9178 g**.

(c) 5% of $400 = 20$; weigh out **20.0000** g of NaOH and dissolve in 400 mL of water.

(d) 10% of $300 = 30$; weigh out **30.0000** g of KNO_3 and dissolve in 270 g (270 mL since density $= 1$ g mL^{-1}) of water.

25.2   *Tip:* Make stepwise changes and always show your working out in any written report or assessment in calculations involving the interconversion of concentrations.

(a) $4 \div 40$ (convert g L^{-1} to mol L^{-1}) $=$ **0.1000 mol L^{-1}**.

(b) 0.1×294.19 (convert mol L^{-1} to g L^{-1}) $=$ **29.4190 g L^{-1}**.

(c) 5×10 (convert % to mL of ethanol in 1000 mL $= 50$ mL; $50 \times 0\,7892$ (convert mL to g) $= 39.4600$ g; $39.4600 \div 46$ (convert g to mol) $=$ **0.8578 mol L^{-1}**.

(d) $150 \div 1000$ (convert mmol to mol) $= 0.1500$ mol L^{-1}: 0.1500×180 (convert mol to g) $= 27.0000$ g L^{-1} $=$ **27.0000%**.

25.3   *Tip:* Box 25.4 and Box 25.5 give procedures for balancing redox equations.

(a) Identify the partial equations for reduction and oxidation using oxidation numbers:

$$Cr_2O_7^{2-} \rightarrow Cr^{3+} \text{ and } Fe^{2+} \rightarrow Fe^{3+}$$

Balance the central element, balance oxygen by adding water and balance hydrogen by adding H^+

$$14\,H^+ + Cr_2O_7^{2-} \rightarrow 2Cr^{3+} + 7H_2O$$
$$Fe^{2+} \rightarrow Fe^{3+}$$

Balance the charge on each side of the equations by adding electrons and then balance the electrons, since number of electrons gained equals number of electrons lost:

$$6\varepsilon + 14H^+ + Cr_2O_7^{2-} \rightarrow 2Cr^{3+} + 7H_2O$$
$$6Fe^{2+} \rightarrow 6Fe^{3+} + 6\varepsilon$$

Add the partial ionic equations to give the overall balanced ionic equation

$$\underline{14H^+ + 6Fe^{2+} + Cr_2O_7^{2-} \rightarrow 2Cr^{3+} + 6Fe^{3+} + 7H_2O}$$

(b) Identify the partial equations for reduction and oxidation using oxidation numbers:

$$S_2O_3^{2-} \rightarrow S_4O_6^{2-} \text{ and } I_2 \rightarrow I^-$$

Balance the central element, balance oxygen by adding water and balance hydrogen by adding H^+

$$2S_2O_3^{2-} \rightarrow S_4O_6^{2-}$$
$$I_2 \rightarrow 2I^-$$

Balance the charge on each side of the equations by adding electrons and then balance the electrons since number of electrons gained equals number of electrons lost:

$$2S_2O_3^{2-} \rightarrow S_4O_6^{2-} + 2\varepsilon$$
$$2\varepsilon + I_2 \rightarrow 2I^-$$

Add the partial ionic equations to give the overall balanced ionic equation

$$\underline{2S_2O_3^{2-} + I_2 \rightarrow S_4O_6^{2-} + 2I^-}$$

(c) Identify the partial equations for reduction and oxidation using oxidation numbers:

$$IO_3^- \rightarrow I_2 \text{ and } I^- \rightarrow I_2$$

Balance the central element, balance oxygen by adding water and balance hydrogen by adding H^+

$$12H^+ + 2IO_3^- \rightarrow I_2 + 6H_2O$$
$$2I^- \rightarrow I_2$$

Balance the charge on each side of the equations by adding electrons and then balance the electrons since number of electrons gained equals number of electrons lost:

$$10\varepsilon + 12H^+ + 2IO_3^- \rightarrow I_2 + 6H_2O$$
$$10I^- \rightarrow 5I_2 + 10\varepsilon$$

Add the partial ionic equations to give the overall balanced ionic equation

$$10I^- + 12H^+ + 2IO_3^- \rightarrow 6I_2 + 6H_2O$$

Divide by 2

$$\underline{5I^- + 6H^+ + IO_3^- \rightarrow 3I_2 + 3H_2O}$$

(d) Identify the partial equations for reduction and oxidation using oxidation numbers:

$$(COOH)_2 \rightarrow CO_2 \text{ and } MnO_4^- \rightarrow Mn^{2+}$$

Balance the central element, balance oxygen by adding water and balance hydrogen by adding H^+

$$(COOH)_2 \rightarrow 2CO_2 + 2H^+$$
$$8H^+ + MnO_4^- \rightarrow Mn^{2+} + 4H_2O$$

Balance the charge on each side of the equations by adding electrons and then balance the electrons since number of electrons gained equals number of electrons lost:

$$5(COOH)_2 \rightarrow 10CO_2 + 10H^+ + 10\varepsilon$$
$$10\varepsilon + 16H^+ + 2MnO_4^- \rightarrow 2Mn^{2+} + 8H_2O$$

Add the partial ionic equations to give the overall balanced ionic equation

$$\underline{5(COOH)_2 + 6H^+ + 2MnO_4^-}$$
$$\rightarrow 2Mn^{2+} + 10CO_2 + 8H_2O$$

26 pH and buffer solutions

26.1 *Tip:* Use eqn [26.5] to interconvert between pH and $[H^+]$.
(a) $7.4 = -\log_{10}[H^+]$, therefore $[H^+] = \mathbf{3.98 \times 10^{-8}\,mol\,L^{-1}}$.
(b) $4.1 = -\log_{10}[H^+]$, therefore $[H^+] = \mathbf{7.94 \times 10^{-5}\,mol\,L^{-1}}$.
(c) $pH = -\log_{10}[2 \times 10^{-5}]$, therefore $\mathbf{pH = 4.70}$.
(d) $pH = -\log_{10}[2 \times 10^{-12.5}]$, therefore $\mathbf{pH = 12.50}$.

26.2 *Tip:* Rearrange eqn [26.7] to give $\log_{10}[A^-]/[HA] = pH - pK_a$
(a) $\log_{10}[A^-]/[HA] = 3.8 - 4.8 = -1$, so $\mathbf{[A^-]/[HA] = 0.1}$ (1 to 10).
(b) $\log_{10}[A^-]/[HA] = 9.5 - 9.2 = 0.3$ so $\mathbf{[A^-]/[HA] = 1.995}$ (approximately 2 to 1).
(c) $\log_{10}[A^-]/[HA] = 8.1 - 7.5 = 0.6$ so $\mathbf{[A^-]/[HA] = 3.98}$ (approximately 4 to 1).

27 Making and recording measurements

27.1 (a) quantitative, discontinuous, ratio
(b) quantitative, continuous, ratio
(c) qualitative, discontinuous, nominal
(d) quantitative, discontinuous, ratio
(e) qualitative, discontinuous, nominal
(f) qualitative, discontinuous, ordinal

27.2 The results indicate that balance A has a bias of $+0.05\,g$ across the weighing range, while balance B has a consistent bias of about $+0.04\%$. Both balances are precise, but not accurate.

27.3 *Tip:* Use a spreadsheet to lay out the table once you have decided what it needs to contain and what statistics you might wish to calculate. You can use spreadsheet functions to help you calculate some of the statistics.

28 SI units and their use

28.1 *Tip:* Box 28.2 gives procedures for interconversion of units.
(a) Rearrange the equation and add units:

$$R = \frac{PV}{nT} = \frac{kg\,m^{-1}s^{-2} \times m^3}{mol \times K} = kg\,m^2\,s^{-2}mol^{-1}K^{-1}$$
$$= \mathbf{J\,mol^{-1}\,K^{-1}}$$

(b) Rearrange the equation and add units:

$$\varepsilon = \frac{A}{c \times l} = \frac{1}{mol\,L^{-1} \times cm} = mol^{-1}L \times (10^{-2}\,m)^{-1}$$
$$= mol^{-1} \times 10^{-3}m^3 \times 10^2m^{-1} = \mathbf{mol^{-1}10^{-1}m^2}$$

(c) Square the equation and rearrange:

$$k = v^2 \times \mu \times 4\pi^2 = s^{-2} \times kg = \mathbf{kg\,s^{-2}}$$

29 Scientific method and design of experiments

29.1 A possible answer (one of many) is given in the figure:

W	Z	Y	X
X	W	Z	Y
Y	X	W	Z
Z	Y	X	W

Z	W	X	Y
W	Z	Y	X
Y	X	W	Z
X	Y	Z	W

W	Y	X	Z
Y	Z	W	X
Z	X	Y	W
X	W	Z	Y

A possible layout of treatments in the glasshouse experiment.

The Latin square design ensures that treatments appear with equal probability in each row and column; hence, if there are gradients of potentially confounding variables, such as temperature and light in this case, their effects are spread evenly among treatments.

29.2 *Tip:* For Microsoft Excel, try the formula $= INT(5*(RAND())+1)$.

30 Project work

30.1 *Tips:*
- Divide the time available for your project into relevant parts concerned with different aspects of your work (note some of these could run in parallel such as experimentation and research for your Introduction).
- A Gantt chart might be an appropriate way of presenting this (see, e.g., http://associate.comk/gantt).
- Set yourself realistic target dates for completion of each section.
- Identify important 'sticking points' (e.g. time taken for delivery of chemicals and other supplies) and work round there (e.g. by doing library work).
- Make sure you allow some flexibility (say 10%) to allow for slippage or unforeseen problems).

30.2 *Tip:* Even if you prefer to write up your work on paper first, create appropriate computer files soon afterwards. Devise a simple and logical system for naming the files.

30.3 *Tip:* Remember that a word processor or a spreadsheet may have sufficient functions for your database needs for storing reference details (see p. 98).

31 Melting points

31.1 (1) The product is impure and needs to be purified by recrystallisation.
(2) The compound is NOT N-phenylethanamide.
(3) The thermometer used should be calibrated.

31.2 (1) The compound is NOT benzoic acid.

(2) You have heated the sample too rapidly and overshot the actual m.pt.

(3) The thermometer used should have been calibrated.

31.3 Your product IS 4-nitroaniline, since the mixed melting point is undepressed.

32 Recrystallisation

32.1 Your list should include the following: hot water bath or hot plate, two conical flasks, boiling sticks/glass rods/anti-bumping granules, watch glass, decolorising charcoal, stemless filter funnel, fluted filter paper, ice-water bath, Büchner funnel and flask, filter paper to fit, water vacuum system, two clock glasses, drying oven, balance (2 dp).

33 Solvent extraction

33.1 (1) Clamp on stem of funnel – unless the funnel is absolutely vertical, the mass of the liquid will cause the funnel to tip sideways and the stem may snap.

(2) The tap is open.

(3) There is no 'safety' beaker.

(4) There is no stemmed funnel to aid in filling the separatory funnel. Liquid will evaporate from the joint, resulting in a poor fit of the stopper and hence spillage when the separatory funnel is inverted.

34 Distillation

34.1 *Tip:* Remember that this is only an **approximate** estimation:

(a) 760 to 190 is equivalent to $2 \times 10 = 20$ °C, therefore **b.pt. $\approx$ 320 °C.**

(b) 760 to 100 is equivalent to $3 \times 10 = 30$ °C, therefore **b.pt. $\approx$ 310 °C.**

(c) 760 to 20 is equivalent to $5 \times 10 = 50$ °C, therefore **b.pt. $\approx$ 290 °C.**

(d) 760 to 1.0 is equivalent to $9 \times 10 = 90$ °C, therefore **b.pt. $\approx$ 250 °C.**

(e) 760 to 0.1 is equivalent to $12 \times 10 = 120$°C, therefore **b.pt. $\approx$ 220 °C.**

34.2 (a) 275 °C

(b) 260 °C

(c) 222 °C

(d) 135 °C

(e) 110 °C.

35 Reflux

35.1 Hazard Assessment: cyclohexene – b.pt. = 58.8 °C, flammable, harmful by absorption (skin and lungs), use in fume cupboard; bromine – b.pt. = 83 °C, extremely harmful. Corrosive and toxic liquid and vapour, wear gloves and use in fume cupboard; (*E*)-1,2 dibromocyclohexane – b.pt. = 145°C at 100 mm Hg, flammable, harmful by absorption (skin and lungs), use in fume cupboard. Apparatus required is illustrated in Fig 35.6(a). Requires use of pressure equalising dropping funnel to prevent escape of bromine vapour during addition.

36 Evaporation

36.1 (a) Because of small volume and boiling point considerations can use open flask on water bath.

(b) Large volume implies use of a 'rovap'.

(c) Very small volume implies use of gas 'blow-down' with little or no heating.

37 Inert atmosphere methods

37.1 (a) Ethoxyethane: test for peroxides using acidified 10% (w/v) aqueous potassium iodide. If positive, shake the ethoxyethane with 1/5 volume 5% (w/v) aqueous sodium bisulphite until test for peroxides is negative. Separate the ethoxyethane. Dry by standing over anhydrous $MgSO_4$ overnight, filter, and stand over sodium wire for two days (do not seal the flask/bottle since H_2 is evolved. Decant the ethoxyethane through a fluted filter system and distil (b.pt. 35 °C) in clean, dry apparatus. Do not distil to dryness.

(b) Tetrahydrofuran (THF): test for peroxides using acidified 10% (w/v) aqueous potassium iodide. If positive, shake the THF with 1/5 volume 5% (w/v) aqueous sodium bisulphite until test for peroxides is negative. Dry by standing over KOH pellets overnight, decant off the THF and then reflux the THF over sodium and a little benzophenone until a deep purple colour of sodium benzophenone ketyl develops. Distil (b.pt. 64–66 °C) THF from the sodium benzophenone ketyl and metallic sodium. Do not distil to dryness. If only a small volume of THF is required, it can be dried by passing it through a column of Activity 1 alumina.

(c) Hexane: Dry by standing over anhydrous $MgSO_4$ overnight, filter off the $MgSO_4$ and distil (b.pt. 67–71 °C), rejecting the fore-run, which contains water. Hexane is poisonous.

38 Combinatorial chemistry

38.1 $20 \times 20 \times 20 = 8000$.

38.2 $(12 \times 5 \times 8)/96 = 5$ plates.

39 Qualitative techniques for inorganic chemistry

39.1 Tap water contains a selection of inorganic ions which will give 'false–positive' results and therefore an incorrect analysis.

39.2 The first test indicates the presence of carbonate (CO_3^{2-}) or bicarbonate (HCO_3^-) ions. The second test indicates the presence of barium (Ba^{2+}) or copper (Cu^{2+}) ions. Copper and barium bicarbonates do not exist as solids and copper carbonate only as the basic carbonate $CuCO_3.Cu(OH)_2$ in which the OH group is not detected by the tests. The unknown solid could be $CuCO_3.Cu(OH)_2$ or $BaCO_3$, but since the former is blue and the latter is white an easy distinction can be made.

40 Gravimetry

40.1 *Tip:* Work in moles and then convert to grams. For % (w/w) need g of NaCl in 100 g of sea water. Assume the density of sea water is 1.00 g mL^{-1}

1 mol of AgCl ≡ 1 mol of NaCl
0.8329 ≡ 0.8329/143.32 mol = 0.005812 mol of AgCl

Therefore 10.00 mL of seawater contains 0.005812 mol of NaCl

$$0.005812 \text{ mol of NaCl} = 58.5 \times 0.005812$$
$$= 0.3400 \text{ g of NaCl}$$

Therefore 100 mL ≡ 100 g of sea water contain 3.4000 g of NaCl = **3.4% (w/w)**

40.2 Tap water contains Cl$^-$ ions which will nullify the determination.

41 Procedures in volumetric analysis

41.1 i. First the equation

$$Na_2CO_3 + H_2SO_4 \rightarrow Na_2SO_4 + H_2O + CO_2$$

1 mol H_2SO_4 reacts with 1 mol Na_2CO_3
We know the concentration and volume of the H_2SO_4 and the volume of Na_2CO_3 solution. We need to find the number of moles of Na_2CO_3 in 1.0 L = 1000 mL.

1000 mL of 1.0 M H_2SO_4 ≡ 1.0 mol of Na_2CO_3
1000 mL of 0.1 M H_2SO_4 ≡ 1.0 × 0.1 mol of Na_2CO_3

$$1.00 \text{ mL of 0.1 M } H_2SO_4 \equiv \frac{1.0 \times 0.1}{1000} \text{ mol}$$
of Na_2CO_3

$$26.00 \text{ mL of 0.1 M } H_2SO_4 \equiv \frac{1.0 \times 0.1 \times 26.00}{1000} \text{ mol}$$
of Na_2CO_3 = 0.0026 mol Na_2CO_3

Therefore 25.00 mL of Na_2CO_3 solution contain 0.0026 mol of Na_2CO_3

Therefore 1000 mL of Na_2CO_3 solution contain
$$\frac{0.0026 \times 1000}{25.00} = \textbf{0.1040 mol L}^{-1} \textbf{ Na}_2\textbf{CO}_3$$

ii. First the equation

$$2NaOH + H_2SO_4 \rightarrow Na_2SO_4 + 2H_2O$$

1 mol H_2SO_4 reacts with 2 mol NaOH

1000 mL of 1.0 M H_2SO_4 ≡ 2.0 mol of NaOH
1000 mL of 0.05 M H_2SO_4 ≡ 2.0 × 0.05 mol of NaOH

1.00 mL of 0.05 M H_2SO_4
$$\equiv \frac{2.0 \times 0.05}{1000} \text{ mol of NaOH}$$
24.00 mL of 0.05 M H_2SO_4
$$\equiv \frac{2.0 \times 0.05 \times 24.00}{1000} \text{ mol of NaOH}$$
$$= 0.0024 \text{ mol NaOH}$$

Therefore 25.00 mL of NaOH solution contain 0.0024 mol of NaOH

Therefore 1000 mL of NaOH solution contain
$$\frac{0.0024 \times 1000}{25.00} = \textbf{0.0960 mol L}^{-1} \textbf{ NaOH}$$

41.2 12 drops = 1.00 mL, therefore 1 drop = 0.08333 mL; therefore 8 drops = 0.6667 mL; therefore total titre = 25.20 + 0.6667 = **25.87 mL**.

42 Acid-base titrations

$$2HCl_{aq} + Na_2CO_3.xH_2O_{aq} \rightarrow 2NaCl_{aq} + CO_{2g}$$
$$+ (x + 2)H_2O_{aq}$$

2 mol of HCl ≡ 1 mol of $Na_2CO_3.xH_2O$
2 × 1000 mL of HCl (1.0 M) ≡ 1 mol of $Na_2CO_3.xH_2O$
2 × 1000 mL of HCl (0.1 M) ≡ 0.1 × 1 mol of
$$Na_2CO_3.xH_2O$$

$$25.4 \text{ mL of HCl (0.1 M)} \equiv \frac{25.4 \times 0.1 \times 1}{2 \times 1000} \text{ mol of}$$
$$Na_2CO_3.xH_2O$$
$$\equiv 0.00127 \text{ mol of } Na_2CO_3.xH_2O$$

Therefore 25.00 mL of $Na_2CO_3.xH_2O$ contains 0.00127 mol of $Na_2CO_3.xH_2O$
Therefore 250.00 mL of $Na_2CO_3.xH_2O$ contains 0.0127 mol of $Na_2CO_3.xH_2O$
Therefore 0.0127 mol of $Na_2CO_3.xH_2O$ = 3.6284 g of $Na_2CO_3.xH_2O$

Therefore 1.0 mol of $Na_2CO_3.xH_2O = \dfrac{3.6284 \times 1\text{ g}}{0.0127\text{mol}}$ of
$$Na_2CO_3.xH_2O$$
$$= 285.7 \text{ g mol}^{-1}$$
$$= M_r$$

$Na_2CO_3.xH_2O = 46 + 12 + 48 + (x \times 18) = 285.7$
Therefore $18x = 285.7 - 106$
Therefore $x = 9.983$. But x must be a whole number
Therefore formula is **Na$_2$CO$_3$.10H$_2$O**

43 Complexometric titrations

43.1 *Tip:* Do not be flustered by the apparent complexity of the procedure and remember the following points:
- EDTA reacts with metal ions in a 1:1 ratio.
- The first titration gives the total metal (Mg^{2+} and Ca^{2+}) ion concentration/amount in 25.00 mL of diluted urine solution.
- The second titration is known as a 'back titration' in which the amount of Ca^{2+} ion is measured by adding a known excess of EDTA and then titrating the excess EDTA with a metal ion solution, in this case Mg^{2+}. This tells us how much Ca^{2+} there is in 50.00 mL of diluted urine solution and you now know how much Ca^{2+} there is in 25.00 mL of solution.
- You can now calculate the amount of Mg^{2+} in 25.00 mL of solution.

Look at the second titration first: the $MgCl_2$ reacts with the EDTA left over from reaction with the Ca^{2+}. Since the

EDTA and $MgCl_2$ solutions are the same concentration (0.0500 M) then 1.0 mL of EDTA ≡ 1.0 mL of $MgCl_2$ solution:

Therefore 25 − 10 mL ≡ 15.00 mL of EDTA solution must have reacted with the Ca^{2+} solution.

1000 mL of 1.0 M EDTA solution ≡ 1 mol of Ca^{2+}
1000 mL of 0.0500 M EDTA solution
$$≡ 0.0500 \text{ mol of } Ca^{2+}$$

15 mL of 0.0500 M EDTA solution
$$≡ \frac{15 \times 0.0500}{1000} \text{ mol of } Ca^{2+}$$
$$= 0.00075 \text{ mol of } Ca^{2+}$$

Therefore 50.00 mL of diluted urine solution contains 0.00075 mol of Ca^{2+}

Therefore 25.00 mL of diluted urine solution contains $0.00075/2 = 0.000375$ mols of Ca^{2+}

Now look at the first titration

1000 mL of 1.0 M EDTA solution
$$≡ 1 \text{ mol of metal ions}$$
1000 mL of 0.0500 M EDTA solution
$$≡ 0.0500 \text{ mol of metal ions}$$
24.00 mL of 0.0500 M EDTA solution
$$≡ \frac{24 \times 0.0500}{1000} = 0.0012 \text{ mol of metal ions}$$

But from the second titration above, there are 0.000375 mol of Ca^{2+} ions in 25.00 mL of diluted urine solution. Therefore there must be

$$0.0012 − 0.000375 = 0.000825 \text{ mol of } Mg^{2+} \text{ ions}$$
in 25.00 mL of diluted solution.

In 2000 mL of diluted urine solution there must be

$$\frac{0.000375 \times 2000}{25.00} = 0.03 \text{ mol of } Ca^{2+} \text{ ions}$$

and in 2000 mL of diluted urine solution there must be

$$\frac{0.000825 \times 2000}{25.00} = 0.066 \text{ mol of } Mg^{2+} \text{ ions}$$

Amount of Mg^{2+} in diluted urine solution = 0.066 × 24.312 × 1000 = **1605 mg**

Amount of Ca^{2+} in diluted urine solution = 0.03 × 40.08 × 1000 = **1202 mg**

44 Redox titrations

44.1 Using the principles outlined in Chapter 25, identify the partial ionic equations and balance the full redox equation

$$2H_2O_2 \rightarrow 2H_2O + O_2$$
$$MnO_4^- \rightarrow Mn^{2+}$$
$$2\,MnO_4^- + 2H_2O_2 + 6H^+ \rightarrow 2\,Mn^{2+} + 8H_2O + 5O_2$$

Therefore

2 moles of $KMnO_4$ ≡ 5 moles of H_2O_2
2 × 1000 mL of 1.0 M $KMnO_4$ ≡ 5 moles of H_2O_2
2 × 1000 mL of 0.02 M $KMnO_4$ ≡ 0.02 × 5 moles of H_2O_2
1.0 mL of 0.02 M $KMnO_4$ ≡ $\dfrac{0.02 \times 5}{2 \times 1000}$ moles of H_2O_2
48.0 mL of 0.02 M $KMnO_4$ ≡ $\dfrac{48 \times 0.02 \times 5}{2 \times 1000}$ moles of H_2O_2
$$≡ 0.0024 \text{ moles of } H_2O_2$$

Therefore 25.00 mL of diluted solution contain 0.0024 moles of H_2O_2

Therefore 250.00 mL of diluted solution contain 0.024 moles of H_2O_2

Therefore 25.00 mL of 10-volume H_2O_2 contain 0.024 moles of H_2O_2

Therefore 1000 mL of 10-volume H_2O_2 contain 0.96 moles of H_2O_2

Concentration of 10-volume H_2O_2 is 0.96 × 34 g L^{-1}
$$= 32.64 \text{ g L}^{-1} = \mathbf{3.264\ \%}$$

45 Precipitation titrations

45.1 The equation:

$$AgNO_{3(aq)} + NaCl_{(aq)} \rightarrow AgCl_{(s)} + NaNO_{3(aq)}$$

Thus 1.0 mol of $AgNO_3$ ≡ 1.0 mol of NaCl

1000 mL of 1.0 M $AgNO_3$ ≡ 58.5 g of NaCl
1000 mL of 0.1 M $AgNO_3$ ≡ 0.1 × 58.5 g of NaCl

1.0 mL of 0.1 M $AgNO_3$ ≡ $\dfrac{0.1 \times 58.5}{1000}$ g of NaCl

10.3 mL of 0.1 M $AgNO_3$ ≡ $\dfrac{10.3 \times 0.1 \times 58.5}{1000}$ g of NaCl
$$= 0.06025 \text{ g of NaCl}$$

Therefore 25.00 mL of 'potassium nitrate' solution contains 0.06025 g of NaCl

Therefore 250.00 mL of 'potassium nitrate' solution contains 0.6025 g of NaCl

% (w/w) NaCl in the 'potassium nitrate' is

$$\frac{0.6205 \times 100}{4.0124} = 15.4646\% = \mathbf{15.5\%}$$

46 Fundamental principles of quantitative chemical analysis

46.1 (a) Accuracy – the closeness of a measurement to the true value.

(b) Precision – the closeness of measurements to each other.

(c) Quality control – measures in place to ensure that the results generated meet your laboratory's standards.

(d) Quality assurance – measures in place to monitor and document the performance of a test procedure

(e) Replicate – a repeat measurement

(f) Detection limit – the minimum concentration of an analyte that can be detected at a particular confidence level.

46.2 As a discussion point with colleagues you may find that UKAS accreditation could either be a positive attribute or a negative one. Some points to consider are:
- Would your work always want to adhere to standard operating procedures?
- Would you always use certified reference materials in your work?
- How would you establish and maintain quality assurance procedures?
- Is your recording of results in your lab note book always up-to-date? It would need to be for UKAS accreditation.

46.3 The responses to these specific questions require some specific instrumental analytical technique knowledge. You might need to refer to Chapters 48–55 inclusive for some guidance.

(a) The main physical forms encountered are likely to be solid or liquids (though gaseous samples might also need to be considered). In general most instrumental analytical techniques require samples to be in liquid (aqueous or organic solvent) form; on that basis some sample preparation is normally required to convert a sample into a suitable form.

(b) Determination of the linear calibration range for a particular instrumental analytical technique is necessary to obtain accurate and precise data. The linearity of your calibration graph is very strongly influenced by your manipulative and manual dexterity skills in preparing standard solutions.

(c) Most techniques have some interferences issues that you need to be aware of; sometimes as part of avoidance is better than cure or the required for additional sample preparation regimes to minimise potential interferents.

(d) A range of approaches are available and are discussed in Chapters 49–50 and 52 specifically.

47 Calibration and quantitative analysis

47.1 **Determine unknowns from a calibration curve produced in Excel.**

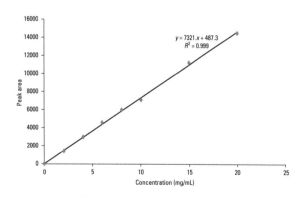

(a) 1.13 mg L^{-1}; (b) 3.14 mg L^{-1}; (c) 5.19 mg L^{-1}.

47.2 *Tip:* Check that you understand the general requirements for good graph drawing, detailed in Chapter 60.

(a) The title of the figure ('calibration graph') does not give sufficient information to enable the reader to understand the content.

(b) No details are given as to the nature of each set of data values – are these curves for two separate substances?

(c) The *x*-axis has a poor choice of units – it would be better to use µg, then all of the values would be 1000 times smaller.

(d) The *x*-axis runs beyond the highest value (8 µg), wasting around 20% of the horizontal space.

(e) The scale marks (tic marks) on the *x*-axis are missing.

(f) The *x*-axis has no zero shown.

(g) The *y*-axis has too many numbers, and too many minor scale marks – it is probably better to have a tic mark every 0.1 absorbance unit. (Note that absorbance (*A*) is a dimensionless term, so no units are required – this is *not* an error.)

(h) The data values represented by the square symbols show a reasonable fit to the lower linear trend line, but the data values represented by the round symbols do not – the latter set of data shows a clear curvilinear relationship and therefore a linear trend line is not appropriate.

47.3 *Tip:* Based on your responses to 47.1 and 47.2 you should be able to create a properly labelled calibration graph using linear regression.

48 Basic spectroscopy

48.1 *Tip:* Box 48.1 gives stepwise instructions for using a spectrophotometer – check that you have covered all of the major points. However, the exact details will vary from instrument to instrument.

48.2 *Tip:* Substitute values into eqn [48.3] and solve for [*C*] (margin examples are given on p. 335).

(a) Note that you must convert the path length from mm to cm beforehand: $0.57 = 20 \times 0.5 \times [C] = 0.057\,\text{g L}^{-1} = 57.0\,\mu\text{g mL}^{-1}$

(b) First calculate the concentration, using eqn [48.3]: $0.31 = 20 \times 1 \times [C] = 0.0155\,\text{g L}^{-1}$. Next, express the concentration in the required units: 0.0155×10^9 (convert to ng) $\div 10^6$ (convert to µL) $= 15.5\,\text{ng mL}^{-1}$. Then, calculate the amount in 50 µL: $15.5 \times 50 = 775\,\text{ng}$.

48.3 First determine the concentration of *p*-nitrophenol, in mol L^{-1}. Thus $8.8\,\mu\text{g mL}^{-1} \div 10^6$ (convert to g mL^{-1}) $\times 10^3$ (convert to g L^{-1}) $\div 291.27$ (convert to mol L^{-1}) $= 0.000\,030\,212\,5\,\text{mol L}^{-1}$. Next, substitute values into eqn [48.3] and solve for ε: $0.535 = e \times 1 \times 0.000\,030\,212\,5$, so $\varepsilon = 17707.902\,36 = 17\,700\,\text{L mol}^{-1}\text{cm}^{-1}$. Note that you should use the full numerical value until the final stage, to avoid introducing 'rounding' errors.

49   Atomic spectroscopy

49.1 The calibration graph is shown below. The test solution has a K^+ concentration of $0.32\,\text{mmol L}^{-1}$. This is equivalent to $0.32 \div 1000 \times 25 = 0.008$ mmol in 25 mL (the test sample volume). Next, divide by the weight of sample used in grams: $0.008 \div 0.482 = 0.016\ 598$ mmol $(\text{g sample})^{-1} = 16.6\ \mu\text{mol} (\text{g sample})^{-1}$.

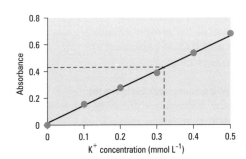

Calibration curve for a series of standards, assayed for K^+ and based on the data in the table in Study exercise 49.1.

49.2 See the graph below – note that this calibration line is approximately linear up to $\sim 4.0\ \mu\text{g mL}^{-1}$ but it becomes increasingly curved above this point. Water sample (a) contains Zn at $1.70\ \mu\text{g mL}^{-1}$; water sample (b) contains Zn at $3.5 \times 20 = 70.0\ \mu\text{g mL}^{-1}$; water sample (c) contains Zn at $8.3 \times 5 = 41.5\ \mu\text{g mL}^{-1}$ (note that the graph curves at higher concentrations, making the estimate for water sample (c) less reliable than the other two – a better approach might have been to dilute this sample further and reassay).

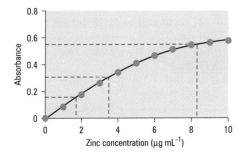

50   X-ray fluorescence spectroscopy

50.1 *Tips:* Write down the key points on how XRF works; consider whether a jury would understand the science of your explanation; prepare, practise and rehearse answers with your colleagues.

50.2 Interferences include:

(a) Spectral – occur from sources other than the analyte you wish to measure.

(b) Environmental – occur from lighter elements and can be avoided by purging the instrument with an inert gas or creating a vacuum by the removal of air.

(c) Matrix – any element can absorb or scatter the fluorescence of the element, but can be corrected mathematically by alpha corrections.

50.3 *Tips:* When you are writing your protocol, consider whether someone else could pick it up and follow your instructions to achieve the same result. Use Box 50.2 as a guide but you will have to consider how you could 'dry' the soil sample first.

51   Chromatography – toxic principles

51.1 (a) Capacity factor for each compound using

$$k' = \frac{t_R - t_M}{t_M}$$

quinaldine $= 4.9$ and nicotine 5.2.

(b) Resolution using the following equation:

$$R_s = \frac{2[t_{RB} - t_{RA}]}{WA + WB} \text{ is calculated as follows}$$

$$R_s = \frac{2[6.2 - 5.9]}{0.16 + 0.18}$$

$$R_s = \frac{0.60}{0.34}$$

$$R_s = 1.76$$

(c) Average number of plates in the column using

$$N = 16\left(\frac{t_R}{w_b}\right)^2 \text{ or } N = 5.54\left(\frac{t_R}{w_{1/2}}\right)^2$$

For quinaldine:

$$N = 16\left(\frac{5.9}{0.16}\right)^2 \text{ or } N = 5.54\left(\frac{5.9}{0.08}\right)^2$$

$$N = 16(36.9)^2 \text{ or } N = 5.54(73.8)^2$$

$$N = 21\,786 \text{ or } N = 30\,173$$

For nicotine:

$$N = 16\left(\frac{6.2}{0.18}\right)^2 \text{ or } N = 5.54\left(\frac{6.2}{0.09}\right)^2$$

$$N = 16(34.4)^2 \text{ or } N = 5.54(68.9)^2$$

$$N = 18\,934 \text{ or } N = 26\,300$$

51.2 **Test your knowledge of chromatographic theory**

(a) Dead time (t_o) = amount of time the component spends in mobile phase, essentially the dead volume of the column. (Determined by injection of methane in GC.)

(b) Retention time (t_R) = time taken for a component to elute from the column. Measured from point of injection.

(c) Capacity factor = retention number $k' = \dfrac{t_R - t_M}{t_M}$ (where t_M is the dead time).

(d) Separation factor α = tells us where peaks elute relative to each other: $\alpha = \dfrac{k'_2}{k'_1}$

(e) Column efficiency N is a measure of peak narrowness: $N = 5.54\,(t_r/w_{0.5})^2$

51.3 Calculate the resolution and efficiency of two compounds

(a) The resolution factor for the two peaks.

$$R_s = t_{r2} - t_{r1}/0.5\,(w_1 + w_2)$$

$$\frac{\text{Compound X}}{\text{Compound Y}} = \frac{20.63 - 18.40}{0.5(1.11 + 1.21)}$$

$$= \frac{2.23}{1.16} = 1.92 = R_s$$

(b) The efficiency of each peak.

$$N = 16(t_r/w_b)^2$$

Using the above equation:

Compound X $= 16\,(18.4/1.11)^2 = 4397$
Compound Y $= 16\,(20.63/1.21)^2 = 4651$

52 Gas and liquid chromatography

52.1 *Tip:* Use eqn 52.4 to determine R_f values based on the measured distances travelled by each component, relative to the solvent front.

Using eqn 52.4, the corresponding R_F values are:
pigment A $= 63 \div 114 = \textbf{0.553}$;
pigment B $= 76 \div 114 = \textbf{0.667}$;
pigment C $= 86 \div 114 = \textbf{0.754}$.

52.2 (a) Flame ionisation detector.
(b) Thermal conductivity detector.
(c) Electron capture detector.
(d) Diode array detector.

52.3 Electrochemical detectors, then fluorescence detectors, then UV/visible detectors. Many molecules, either intrinsically or after reaction with a colour reagent, can be detected by UV/visible spectroscopy. However, fewer molecules show native fluorescence or the electrical properties necessary for electrochemical detection, making UV/visible detection the most versatile approach.

53 Electrophoresis

53.1 *Tip:* The dissociation of two important amino acids is shown below:

Glutamate: R-COOH $\rightleftharpoons$ R-COO$^-$ + H$^+$
  low pH   neutral/high pH
Lysine: R-NH$_3^+$ $\rightleftharpoons$ R-NH$_2$ + H$^+$
  low/neutral pH   high pH

Note that the charge on a given amino acid side chain at a given pH will depend on the dissociation constant or pK_a, (see p. 202) of the ionisable group.

53.2 In PAGE any diffusion of sample proteins that occurs reduces resolution, so it is best to start with as narrow a sample zone as possible. For most protein separations, the buffer pH is chosen so that the proteins are negatively charged and will migrate from the cathodic end to the anodic end of the gel. In IEF, the separation is carried out on a pH gradient – because proteins will all migrate to their pI values irrespective of the starting point, the position of sample application is not important. The only exception would be if any of the proteins to be separated were unstable at extreme pH values, in which case it would be best to avoid application at either end of the pH gradient (e.g. pH 3.0 and pH 10.0). Once a given protein has reached the position corresponding to its pI, it will remain in a narrow band because any diffusion away from the pI will result in the protein acquiring a net charge and being focused back to its pI.

54 Electroanalytical techniques

54.1 These assumptions are given on p. 415. The electrical potential measured at an ISE can be approximate to ion concentration assuming (i) the ion is in dilute solution (since the relationship is based on activity, Eqn 54.3); (ii) the ionic strength of the calibration standards matches that of the test sample and (iii) there is no substantial binding of the ion to sample components (e.g. to proteins or nucleic acids).

54.2 The two functional components of a biosensor are (i) an immobilised enzyme (the biocatalyst) and (ii) a transducer, to convert the biochemical signal into the electrical signal that can be measured. A representative example (there are many others) would be the Biotrace luminescence-based system for monitoring microbial ATP in food, using luciferase (see: http://www.biotrace.com).

54.3 (a) $0.285 \div 1000 \times 4$ (to calculate mmol in 4 mL) $\times 1000$ (to convert from mmol to μmol) $= \textbf{1.14 } \mu\textbf{mol}$.
(b) $0.273 \div 1000 \times 20$ (to calculate mmol in 20 mL) $\times 1000$ (to convert from mmol to μmol) $= \textbf{5.46 } \mu\textbf{mol}$.
(c) 0.317 (estimated as the mid-point between the values at 14 and 16 °C) $\div 1000 \times 10$ (to calculate mmol in 10 mL) $\times 1000$ (to convert from mmol to μmol) $= \textbf{3.17 } \mu\textbf{mol}$.
(d) $6.75 \div 1000 \times 250$ (to calculate mg in 250 mL) $= 1.6875 = \textbf{1.69 mg}$.
(e) 4.73 (estimated as the mid-point between the values at 24 and 26 °C) $\div 1000 \times 200$ (to calculate mL in 200 mL) $= 0.946$ mL.

55 Radioactive isotopes and their uses

55.1 Assume a ^{14}C half-life of 5715 years (Table 55.2). Using eqn [55.1], $e^x = 0.5725$, and so $x = \ln(0.5725) = -0.5578$. If $-0.5578 = -0.693(t/5715)$, then $t = (-0.5578/-0.693) \times 5715 = 4600$. **The rat visited about 4600 years ago.**

55.2 (a) **1200 Bq**.
(b) **4.44×10^7 d.p.m.**
(c) **1.20 μCi**.
(d) **30.0 Bq g^{-1}**.
(e) **28.0 pmol**.

55.3 (a) The solution contains $250 \times 10^{-6} \times 5$ mol $= 1.25 \times 10^{-3}$ mol. The specific activity is therefore $55 \times 10^6/1.25 \times 10^{-3}$ Bq mol^{-1} $= \textbf{4.4} \times \textbf{10}^{\textbf{10}}$ **Bq mol**$^{-1}$.

(b) $79.2 \times 10^5/4.4 \times 10^{10} = 1.8 \times 10^{-4}$ mol per 2 h per 10^7 cells is equivalent to **2.5 fmol s^{-1} cell^{-1}**.

Therefore 25.00 mL of 'potassium nitrate' solution contains 0.06025 g of NaCl

Therefore 250.00 mL of 'potassium nitrate' solution contains 0.6025 g of NaCl

% (w/w) NaCl in the 'potassium nitrate' is $\dfrac{0.6205 \times 100}{4.0124} = 15.4646\% = \underline{\textbf{15.5\%}}$

56 Infrared spectroscopy

(A) Lots of sharp peaks – aromatic; sharp peak at 2200 cm^{-1} C$\equiv$N; ***benzonitrile***

(B) Large peak at 1720 cm^{-1} C=O; large peaks at 1250 cm^{-1} and 1100 cm^{-1} C–O; ***ethyl ethanoate.***

(C) Large broad peak at 3400 cm^{-1} O–H; ***1-octanol***

(D) No functional group peaks, only $\leq$ 3000 cm^{-1} and 1460 cm^{-1}/1375 cm^{-1} CH$_3$/CH$_2$ stretches and bends; ***heptane***

57 Nuclear magnetic resonance spectroscopy

57.1 (i) Three types: CH$_3$ (triplet), CH$_2$ (sextet), CH$_2$ (triplet).

(ii) Two types: 2 $\times$ CH$_3$ (doublet), CH (septet).

(iii) Three types: CH$_3$ (doublet), CH (quintet), CH (doublet).

(iv) Molecule is symmetrical, therefore three types: 2 $\times$ CH$_3$ (triplet), 2 $\times$ CH$_2$ (quartet), 2 $\times$ CH$_2$ (singlet).

(v) Molecule is unsymmetrical, therefore six types: CH$_3$ (triplet), CH$_2$ (quartet), CH$_2$ (triplet), CH$_2$ (triplet), CH$_2$ (quartet), CH$_3$ (triplet).

57.2 (i) Two types: 3 $\times$ CH$_3$ (quartet), C (singlet).

(ii) Two types: 2 $\times$ CH$_3$ (quartet), 2 $\times$ CH$_2$ (triplet).

(iii) Five types: CH$_3$ (quartet), CH (doublet), 2 $\times$ C=O (singlet), 2 $\times$ CH$_2$ (triplet), 2 $\times$ CH$_3$ (quartet).

(iv) Two types: CH$_3$ (quartet), C (singlet).

(v) Five types: *para*- CH (doublet), 2 $\times$ *meta*-CH (doublet), 2 $\times$ *ortho*-CH (doublet).

(vi) C (singlet), CH$_3$ (quartet).

57.3 The CH$_2$ group has a phenyl substituent ($\sigma = 1.83$) and a –C(=O)OR ($\sigma = 1.46$) so the estimated chemical shift is: $\delta = 0.23 + 1.83 + 1.46 = \textbf{3.52 ppm}$. (The experimental value in CDCl$_3$ is 3.57 ppm: so good agreement.)

57.4 The CH group has 2 $\times$ OEt groups ($\sigma = 1.14$) and one CH$_3$ group ($\sigma = 2.50$) so the estimated chemical shift is $\delta = 2.50 + 1.14 + 1.14 + 0 = \textbf{4.78 ppm}$. (The experimental value is 4.72.)

57.5 Ha: has Ph in gem position ($\sigma_{gem} = 1.35$) and CO$_2$H in cis position ($\sigma_{cis} = 1.35$). The estimated chemical shift $\delta = 5.25 + 1.35 + 1.35 = \textbf{7.95 ppm}$. Hb: has Ph in cis position ($\sigma_{cis} = 0.37$) and CO$_2$H in gem position ($\sigma_{gem} = 1.00$). The estimated chemical shift $\delta = 5.25 + 0.37 + 1.00 = \textbf{6.62 ppm}$. (The experimental ones are 7.78 and 6.44 ppm respectively.)

57.6 H$_a$: has –NO$_2$ in *ortho* position ($\sigma_{ortho} = 0.95$) and –OH in *meta* position ($\sigma_{meta} = -0.12$). Estimated chemical shift $\delta = 7.27 + 0.95 - 0.12 = \textbf{8.10 ppm}$. H$_b$: has –NO$_2$ in *meta* position ($\sigma_{meta} = 0.26$) and –OH in *para* position ($\sigma_{para} = -0.45$). Estimated chemical shift $\delta = 7.27 + 0.26 - 0.45 = \textbf{7.08 ppm}$. H$_c$: has –NO$_2$ in *para* position ($\sigma_{para} = 0.38$) and –OH in *meta* position ($\sigma_{meta} = -0.12$). Estimated chemical shift $\delta = 7.27 + 0.38 - 0.12 = \textbf{7.53 ppm}$. H$_d$: has –NO$_2$ in *meta* position ($\sigma_{meta} = 0.26$) and –OH in *ortho* position ($\sigma_{ortho} = -0.56$). Estimated chemical shift $\delta = 7.27 + 0.26 - 0.56 = \textbf{6.97 ppm}$.

57.7 Ha has NH$_2$ in *ortho* position ($\sigma_{ortho} = -0.75$), Br in the *meta* position ($\sigma_{meta} = -0.13$) and NO$_2$ in the *meta* position ($\sigma_{meta} = 0.17$). Estimated chemical shift $\delta = 7.27 + 0.17 - 0.75 - 0.13 = \textbf{6.56 ppm}$. Hb has NO$_2$ in *ortho* position ($\sigma_{ortho} = 0.95$), NH$_2$ in the *meta* position ($\sigma_{meta} = -0.24$) and Br in the *para* position ($\sigma_{para} = -0.03$). Estimated chemical shift $\delta = 7.27 + 0.95 - 0.24 - 0.03 = \textbf{7.95 ppm}$. Hc has NO$_2$ in *ortho* position ($\sigma_{ortho} = 0.95$), Br in the *ortho* position ($\sigma_{ortho} = 0.22$) and NH$_2$ in the *meta* position ($\sigma_{meta} = -0.24$). Estimated chemical shift $\delta = 7.27 + 0.95 + 0.22 - 0.24 = \textbf{8.22 ppm}$. (Very good agreement with spectrum.)

58 Mass spectrometry

58.1 CH$_3$CH$_2$COOCH$_2$CH$_2$CH$_3$; α-cleavages: (M $-$ OCH$_2$CH$_2$CH$_3$) = (M $-$ 59) = m/z = 67, (M $-$ CH$_3$CH$_2$) = (M $-$ 29) = m/z = 97; β-cleavage: (M $-$ CH$_2$=CHCH$_3$) = (M $-$ 42) = m/z 84. CH$_3$CH$_2$CH$_2$COOCH$_2$CH$_3$: α-cleavages: (M $-$ CH$_3$CH$_2$CH$_2$) = (M $-$ 43) = m/z = 83, (M $-$ OCH$_2$CH$_3$) = (M $-$ 45) = m/z = 81; β-cleavages: (M $-$ CH$_2$=CH$_2$) = (M $-$ 28) = m/z = 98, (M $-$ CH$_2$=CH$_2$) = (M $-$ 28) = m/z = 98.

59 Thermal analysis

59.1 The M_r of CuSO$_4$.5H$_2$O is 249.6

First decomposition: $\dfrac{249.6 \times 14.4}{100} = 35.9$ (corresponds to 2H$_2$O)

Second decomposition: $\dfrac{249.6 \times 14.8}{100} = 36.9$ (corresponds to 2H$_2$O)

Third decomposition: $\dfrac{249.6 \times 6.9}{100} = 17.9$ (corresponds to H$_2$O)

Therefore final residue is 100 $-$ 36.1 = 63.9%
Therefore final residue is 249.6 $\times$ 63.9 = 159.49 = CuSO$_4$ (159.6)
The thermal decomposition of CuSO$_4$.5H$_2$O involves relatively easy loss of four molecules of water (ligand water) and then one molecule of tightly bound water which is associated with the SO$_4^{2-}$ anion.

60 Using graphs

60.1 (a) Three-dimensional graph
(b) Pie chart
(c) Scatter diagram with an added trend line
(d) Plotted curve

60.2

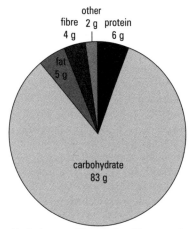

Typical composition of a breakfast cereal

60.3 *Tip:* First decide on the class boundaries and number of classes – in this case, the values range from 8.1 to 15.1. The subdivisions shown in the table below provide eight classes, which gives a frequency distribution with a reasonable number of classes to aggregate the data sufficiently, but also provide enough detail to indicate the overall shape of the distribution. Note that Excel also has a useful histogram function, but you will need to learn how to set the class boundaries (termed 'bin values') to make effective use of this function (see Box 60.2).

A histogram for these data is shown in the figure opposite. Your brief description should include something about the location, dispersion and shape of the distribution (see Chapter 63), for example: 'The modal class of the distribution is $12.0-12.9 \, \mathrm{g \, L^{-1}}$, with a range of $7.0 \, \mathrm{g \, L^{-1}}$ $(15.5-8.5 \, \mathrm{g \, L^{-1}})$. The data show a slight negative skew, with 28 values in the three classes above the mode and 46 in the four classes below it'.

Data of table in study exercise 60.3
presented as a frequency distribution

Class	Frequency
8.0–8.9	2
9.0–9.9	5
10.0–10.9	17
11.0–11.9	22
12.0–12.9	26
13.0–13.9	17
14.0–14.9	10
15.0–15.9	1

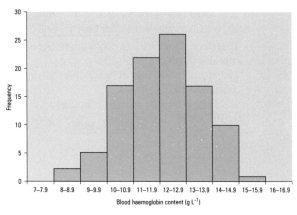

Frequency distribution of data of table in study exercise 60.3.

60.4 *Tip:* The Sunday newspaper supplements often analyse news stories with the aid of graphs, and might be a good source for material, as their articles are often slanted towards a particular viewpoint, and you may find that the graphical presentation has been chosen to support this.

61 Presenting data in tables

61.1 Concentrations of drug and metabolites found in a blood sample ($\mathrm{mg \, L^{-1}}$); alcohol expressed in mg per $100 \, \mathrm{mL^{-1}}$.

Methadone	0.23
Diazepam	0.2
Desmethyl diazepam	0.075
Temazepam	0.1
Nicotine	NQ
Caffeine	NQ
Alcohol	86

NQ = positive result, but not qualified

61.2 *Tip:* Box 61.1 gives the key aspects. The following table gives one possible layout.

The principal components of a typical table

Component	Comment
Title	Concise, self-contained description of table contents, with numbering where appropriate
Column/row headings	Identifies the content of each column and row, showing units of measurement, where appropriate
Data values	Quoted to an appropriate number of significant figures/decimal places
Footnotes	All abbreviations and other individual details must be explained
Rulings	Used to emphasise any groupings within the table, and to separate individual items

62   Hints for solving numerical problems

62.1   (a) $[C] = A/\varepsilon l$
    (b) $\varepsilon = A/[C]l$

62.2   (a) Subtract ax from both sides and then swap sides, so: $\boldsymbol{b = y - ax}$

(b) 1. Subtract b from both sides and then swap sides, so: $ax = y - b$
    2. Divide both sides by a, so: $\boldsymbol{x = (y - b)/a}$

(c) Raise each side to the power $\frac{1}{3}$, then swap sides, so: $\boldsymbol{y = x^{1/3}}$

(d) 1. Take logs of both sides, so: $\log x = \log(3^y)$
    2. Noting $\log(3^y) = y \log 3$, substitute on right-hand side, so $\log x = y \log 3$
    3. Divide both sides by $\log 3$, then swap sides, so: $\boldsymbol{y = \log x / \log 3}$

(e) 1. Divide both sides by $1 - y$, so: $z^p + 3 = x/(1 - y)$
    2. Subtract 3 from both sides, so: $z^p = x/(1 - y) - 3$
    3. Raise both sides to the power $1/p$, so: $\boldsymbol{z = ((x \div (1 - y)) - 3)^{1/p}}$

(f) 1. Multiply both sides by pq, so: $zpq = (y - z)^{1/n}$
    2. Raise each side to the power n, so: $zpq^n = (y - z)$
    3. Take logs of both sides, so: $n\log(zpq) = \log(y - z)$
    4. Hence $\boldsymbol{n = (\log(zpq)) \div (\log(y - z))}$

62.3   (a) **215**
    (b) **107 000**
    (c) **0.04**
    (d) **99.82**
    (e) **99.90**
    (f) **100.00**
    (g) **6260**
    (h) **130 000**
    (i) **2 3 or 4, depending on circumstances (see p. 491)**
    (j) **5**
    (k) **3**
    (l) **6**
    (m) **2**
    (n) **5**

62.4   (a) **17.14%**
    (b) **7.55%**
    (c) **14.01**
    (d) $100 \times (75.02 - 55.23) \div 55.23 = 35.831\,975 = \boldsymbol{35.83\%}$

63   Descriptive statistics

63.1   (a) **Range = 9**
    (b) **Variance = 4.46**
    (c) **Standard deviation = 2.11**
    (d) **Coefficient of variation = 43.1%**   (CoV $= 100 \times 2.113/4.9$)
    (e) **Standard error = 0.273**

63.2   *Tip:* Substitute values into eqn [63.3] to calculate the SE of each sample.
For sample A: $12.7 \div 3.464\,101\,615 = 3.666\,174\,209 = \boldsymbol{3.67}$.
For sample B: $14.4 \div 4.472\,135\,955 = 3.219\,937\,888 = \boldsymbol{3.22}$.
Thus, in absolute terms, sample B has the lower standard error (note that the higher standard deviation of sample B is more than offset by the increased number of data values).

To calculate the proportional standard error, divide the SE by the mean, as follows:
For sample A: $3.666\,174\,209 \div 16.2 = 0.226\,307\,05 = \boldsymbol{0.226}$.
For sample B: $3.219\,937\,888 \div 13.2 = 0.243\,934\,688 = \boldsymbol{0.244}$.
Thus, in proportion to the mean, sample A has the lower standard error.

63.3   Vitamin concentration data (recalculated)

Replicate sample	Mean vitamin concentration (mg)	Sample number	Mean size × sample size
A	3.0	24	72.0
B	2.5	37	92.5
C	2.0	6	12.0
Total		67	176.5

True mean $= 176.5/67 = \boldsymbol{2.63\,mg}$

64   Choosing and using statistical tests

64.1   *Tip:* First calculate the standard error using eqn [63.3], as $6.8 \div 4 = 1.7$. Then, substitute values into eqn [64.2] to calculate the 95% confidence limits (note that you also need the value for $t_{0.05[15]} = 2.131$). The upper limit is calculated as: $24.7 + (2.131 \times 1.7) = 28.3227 = \boldsymbol{28.3}$. The lower limit is calculated as $24.7 - (2.131 \times 1.7) = 21.0773 = \boldsymbol{21.1}$.

64.2   *Tip:* The calculated $t = \boldsymbol{2.136}$ with 12 degrees of freedom; the critical value at $P = 5\%$ is 2.18 (Table 64.2); hence you would accept the null hypothesis that the samples came from the same population and hence conclude that the different analytical methods had no significant effect.

64.3   *Tip:* Amino acid uptake will be the dependent (y) variable and time the independent (x) variable. From the Excel output, the coefficients are: intercept $= \boldsymbol{1.17}$ (to 3 significant figures) and slope (labelled as 'X variable 1') $= \boldsymbol{2.95}$ (to 3 significant figures), so the linear relationship has the following form: $y = 1.17 + 2.95x$. The strength of the relationship is measured by the coefficient of determination, termed 'R squared' in the Excel output. In this case, a value of $\boldsymbol{0.971}$ (to 3 significant figures) shows that there is a very strong fit of the y data to the trend line.

65   Drawing chemical structures

65.1   (a) $CH_3CH_2CH_2CH_2OH$ (b)   (c) CH_3CHCH_3 with NH_2

(d)   (e)

65.2

(a) (b) (c) (d)

(e)

65.3 (a) Three bonding pairs, no lone pars, therefore trigonal planar.
(b) Two bonding pairs, two lone pairs, therefore tetrahedral based.
(c) Two bonding pairs therefore linear.
(d) Six bonding pairs, therefore octahedral.
(e) Five bonding pairs and one lone pair, therefore octahedral based.

66 Chemometrics

66.1 *Tip:* Use the information provided in Chapter 8 to identify a scientific paper that has used either a factorial or central composite design. The boundaries of their chosen variables may have been determined by some preliminary experiments or because of practical limitations, e.g. it was not possible to operate under the conditions.

66.2 *Tip:* Use the information provided in Chapter 8 to identify a scientific paper that has used a principal component analysis (PCA). The visualisation of large data sets to identify trends can be effectively done using PCA.

66.3 *Tip:* Discuss with other students or your project supervisor how you might use optimisation approaches to assist with identify best operating conditions, e.g. designing a new organic synthesis and wanting to determine the optimum conditions for yield or to maximise the signal output from an instrumental analytical technique. Also how might you use PCA to visualise a large data set.

67 Computational chemistry

67.1 The two methods both give equilibrium bond distances close to the experimental value. However, the molecular mechanics calculations fail at distances beyond $\sim$2.1 Å, because they predict that as the Cl_2 molecule is pulled apart, the energy again increases very rapidly (like a very strong spring being stretched). In fact, as the atoms are pulled apart, the Cl–Cl bond starts to break, so the energy tails off to the value for two isolated chlorine atoms. The DFT method models this reasonably accurately; the curve levels off to give a bond dissociation energy of 200 kJ mol^{-1}, compared to the experimental value of 243 kJ mol^{-1}. As the two chlorine atoms are brought closer than the equilibrium distance, the energy increases very rapidly due to the electrostatic repulsion between the two positively charged nuclei.

Index

Index

MOLECULAR MODEL SET FOR ORGANIC CHEMISTRY

ISBN: 9780132019866

This kit enables users to build virtually all simple molecules encountered in organic chemistry.

- Includes space-filling models that simulate the true shape of saturated compounds
- Provides open models that form realistic single, double, and triple bonds – even strained rings
- Allows smooth rotation of the bonds to make conformational analysis easy
- Includes a Instruction Book – with photos, diagrams, and concise discussions of chemical principles

The set includes:

28 Hydrogen (white)

14 Carbon (black)

8 Oxygen (red)

4 Nitrogen (blue)

8 Chlorine (green)

2 Bromine (orange)

2 Iodine (purple)

40 Single Bond, Space-filling Models (white)

40 Single Bond, Open Models (short grey)

12 Double and Triple Bonds, Open Models (long grey)

For further information and to view other Chemistry titles from Pearson Education, please visit:
www.pearsoned.co.uk/chemistry